Checklist for Revising Paragraphs

- Can a reader understand and follow my ideas?
- Is the topic sentence clear?
- Have I fully supported the topic sentence with details and facts?
- Does the paragraph have unity? Does every sentence relate to the main idea?
- Does the paragraph have coherence? Does it follow a logical order and guide the reader from point to point?
- Have I varied the length and type of my sentences?
- Is my language exact, concise, and fresh?
- Have I proofread carefully for grammatical and spelling errors?

Checklist for Revising Essays

- Is the thesis statement clear?
- Does the body of the essay fully support the thesis statement?
- Does the essay have unity? Does every paragraph relate to the thesis statement?
- Does the essay have coherence? Do the paragraphs follow a logical order?
- Are the topic sentences clear?
- Does each paragraph provide good details and well-chosen examples?
- Does the essay conclude, not just leave off?

From *Evergreen: A Guide to Writing*, Tenth Edition
by Susan Fawcett

If found, please return to:

Name: _____

Phone: (_____) _____

Personal Error Patterns Chart			
Error Type & Symbol	Specific Error	Correction	Rule or Reminder

Proofreading Strategies

Many writers have found that the proofreading strategies described below help them see their own writing with a fresh eye. You will learn more strategies throughout *Evergreen*. Try a number of methods and see which ones work best for you.

Proofreading Strategy: Allow enough time to proofread.

Many students don't proofread at all, or they skim their paper for grammatical errors two minutes before class. This just doesn't work. Set aside enough time to proofread slowly and carefully, searching for errors and especially hunting for your personal error patterns.

Proofreading Strategy: Work from a paper copy.

People who proofread on computers tend to miss more errors. If you write on a computer, do not proofread on the monitor. Instead, print a copy of your paper, perhaps enlarging the type to 14 point. Switching to a paper copy seems to help the brain see more clearly.

Proofreading Strategy: Read your words aloud.

Reading silently makes it easier to skip over small errors or mentally fill in missing details, whereas listening closely is a great way to hear mistakes. Listen and follow along on your printed copy, marking errors as you hear them.

a. Read your paper aloud to *yourself*. Be sure to read *exactly* what's on the page, and read with enthusiasm.

b. Ask a *friend* or *writing tutor* to read your paper out loud to you. Tell the reader you just want to hear your words and that you don't want any other suggestions right now.

Proofreading Strategy: Read "bottoms up," from the end to the beginning.

One way to fool the brain into taking a fresh look at something you've written is to proofread the last sentence first. Read slowly, word by word. Then read the second-to-last sentence, and so on, all the way back to the first sentence.

Proofreading Strategy: Isolate your sentences.

If you write on a computer, spotting errors is often easier if you reformat so that each sentence appears isolated, on its own line. Double space between sentences. This visual change can help the brain focus clearly on one sentence at a time.

Proofreading Strategy: Check for one error at a time.

If you make many mistakes, proofread separately all the way through your paper for each error pattern. Although this process takes time, you will catch many more errors this way and make real progress. You will begin to eliminate some errors altogether as you learn about fixing each error and as you get better at spotting and correcting it. You will learn more recommended proofreading strategies in upcoming chapters.

Evergreen
A Guide to Writing with Readings

TENTH EDITION

Susan Fawcett

WADSWORTH
CENGAGE Learning

Australia • Brazil • Japan • Korea • Mexico • Singapore • Spain • United Kingdom • United States

Evergreen: A Guide to Writing with Readings
Tenth Edition
Susan Fawcett

Publisher: Monica Eckman

Director of Developmental Studies: Annie Todd

Senior Development Editor: Leslie Taggart

Freelance Development Editor: Stephanie Carpenter

Assistant Editor: Elizabeth Rice

Editorial Assistant: Matthew Conte

Media Editor: Christian Biagetti

Brand Manager: Lydia LeStar

Marketing Communications Manager: Linda Yip Beckstrom

Senior Content Project Manager: Aimee Chevrette Bear

Art Director: Faith Brosnan

Print Buyer: Betsy Donaghey

Rights Acquisition Specialist: Alexandra Ricciardi

VP, Director, Advanced and Elective Products Program: Alison Zetterquist

Editorial Coordinator, Advanced and Elective Products Program: Jean Woy

Production Service: Lachina Publishing Services

Text Designer: Lachina Publishing Services

Cover Designer: LMA/Leonard Massiglia

Cover Image: Zen Shui/Superstock

Compositor: Lachina Publishing Services

For product information and technology assistance, contact us at
Cengage Learning Customer & Sales Support, 1-800-354-9706
For permission to use material from this text or product,
submit all requests online at **www.cengage.com/permissions**.

Further permissions questions can be emailed to
permissionrequest@cengage.com.

Library of Congress Control Number: 2012951252

ISBN-13: 978-1-285-17483-9

ISBN-10: 1-285-17483-6

Wadsworth
20 Channel Center Street
Boston, MA 02210
USA

Cengage Learning is a leading provider of customized learning solutions with office locations around the globe, including Singapore, the United Kingdom, Australia, Mexico, Brazil and Japan. Locate your local office at **international.cengage.com/region**

Cengage Learning products are represented in Canada by Nelson Education, Ltd.

Cengage Learning products are represented in high schools by Holt McDougal, a division of Houghton Mifflin Harcourt.

For your course and learning solutions, visit **www.cengage.com**.

For online supplements and other instructional support, please visit **www.cengagebrain.com**.

* "Advanced Placement" and "AP" are registered trademarks of the College Board, which is not involved in the production of, and does not endorse, this product.

Printed in the United States of America
1 2 3 4 5 6 7   16 15 14 13 12

Contents

Preface

"*Evergreen* works." Again and again, I hear this comment from instructors and students alike, and I consider it the greatest possible compliment. Based on my experience teaching and directing the writing lab at Bronx Community College, City University of New York, *Evergreen* is designed for students who need to improve the writing skills necessary for success in college and in most careers. The text's clear, paced lessons, inspiring student and professional models, high-interest practices and assignments, and provocative reading selections have guided over two million students through the process of writing effectively, from prewriting to final draft. This book was written for students diverse in language background, age, ethnicity, and dominant learning style. I am proud that *Evergreen with Readings* has won juried awards for excellence and has remained, from its first edition, the most widely used developmental writing text in the United States. My goal in revising *Evergreen* is always to ensure that it serves the changing needs of instructors and their students.

As I weighed reviewers' suggestions for this important Tenth Edition, two strong themes emerged. First, instructors wanted students to be able to recognize and correct their own grammatical errors, both in English class and beyond. In addition, more instructors than ever wanted to help their students think critically and better meet the written challenges of college coursework and the workplace. Some felt pressure to transition more quickly from personal narrative—which is easier for students—to academic or third-person writing and reading. These vital concerns inspired the two most important changes in this edition: 1) its unique proofreading and error-correction method that helps students take more responsibility for their grammatical mistakes and 2) its intensified coverage of critical thinking and academic writing.

In addition, five new professional essays stress persuasion and exposition. I've added a number of fresh visual images, with more opportunities for critical viewing, and, as ever, replaced many models and practices with current, high-interest subjects intended to hold students' attention as they learn.

Special Features of *Evergreen with Readings*, Tenth Edition

New Method for Personal Error Tracking

Unique new proofreading and error-tracking tools frame and permeate Units 6 and 7, the grammar and spelling units, helping students take responsibility for error correction:

- A new chapter 25, "Proofreading to Correct Your Personal Error Patterns," teaches students how to recognize, scan for, and correct their own errors. It also introduces six basic proofreading strategies.

- Every subsequent grammar and spelling chapter introduces a specific proofreading strategy targeting predictable errors.

- A removable Personal Error Patterns Chart helps students track and eradicate their mistakes.

Expanded Critical-Thinking Coverage

Evergreen has been the leader in integrating critical thinking with writing instruction, but this edition has even more critical-thinking opportunities woven throughout the text. The expanded coverage includes a *Teamwork* feature for critical thinking or critical viewing in each rhetorical pattern chapter (see Chapters 5–13 and 16–17), numerous thinking practices throughout, and Teaching Tips with critical-thinking suggestions for that lesson. Students are challenged to analyze, evaluate, infer, and apply writing concepts to real-life problems or visual images.

New More Academic Models and Assignments

Each of nine essay patterns in Chapters 16 and 17 is illustrated by one student essay in the first-person and another in the third person. Enriched instruction on subject, audience, and purpose now stresses the choice between writing about oneself or about impersonal material, and some textbook excerpts now serve as models. Reinforcing this emphasis, four of the five new reading selections are expository or persuasive, not personal narratives.

Five Provocative New Reading Selections

Five fresh essays by eminent authors enrich Unit 8: Martin Lindstrom on supermarkets' hidden sales tactics, Ellen Goodman on the woes of multitasking, Jhumpa Lahiri on an immigrant's "two lives," Malcolm Gladwell on practice as the key to all success, and Maya Szalavitz on the rise in bullying and alarming loss of empathy among young people. All were selected to provoke vigorous discussion and good writing. Instructor and student favorites from the last edition have been kept, for a new total of 19. A rich thematic index of the readings has been added, in addition to the rhetorical index.

35 New High-Interest Models and Practices.

Engaging models and content-based practice sets are vital to *Evergreen*'s effectiveness—motivating students to read on and promoting cultural literacy. New subjects include the negative effects of Facebook, AIDS researcher David Ho, educational uses of video games, Native American rock musicians, San Francisco's bold Zero-Waste plan, dogs that smell cancer, the invention of Gatorade, "showboat" athletes, Words with Friends, a soldier's desert combat experience, viral videos, and the careers of reporter Lisa Ling, Salman Khan of the Khan Academy, and environmentalist Erica Fernandez.

New 120 Visual Images

Evergreen's popular critical-viewing program, which grew out of the author's brain-based learning research, features 70 large photos, paintings, graphics, ads, and cartoons and 50 smaller margin images—many accompanied by critical-thinking questions or group tasks. These images help visual learners and others grasp key writing concepts, evaluate visual material, and connect more deeply with the course. The flow of instruction and images is supported by *Evergreen*'s clear and purposeful design.

Coverage of Every Common Core Standard for Developmental Writing

Colleges using the national K-12 Common Core standards as a guide to what students need to know will see that *Evergreen* thoroughly covers all bases, with its rich emphasis on critical thinking, academic and third-person writing, and deep commitment to preparing students for college and workplace challenges.

I have kept or enhanced features that have made *Evergreen* so successful:

- Clear, step by step coverage of paragraph and essay writing, with many engaging practices, writing assignments, and critical thinking activities

- Superior essay coverage, with two inspiring student models and a colorful graphic organizer for each essay pattern

- Varied, thought-provoking writing assignments

- Collaborative Writers' Workshops that feature revision of student writing

- ESL coverage integrated throughout

Flexible Organization

Evergreen's full range of materials and flexible modular organization adapt easily to almost any course design and to a wide range of student needs. Because each chapter and unit is self-contained, chapters can be taught in any order, and the text works well for laboratory work, self-teaching, and tutorials.

Unit 1 provides an overview of the writing process and introduces five prewriting techniques. Unit 2 guides students step by step through the paragraph-writing process, while Unit 3 teaches students the rhetorical modes most often required in college writing (illustration, narration, description, process, definition, comparison/contrast, classification, cause/effect, and persuasion). Unit 4 devotes six chapters to essay writing: writing essays; applying the modes taught in Unit 3 to essays; crafting an introduction, conclusion, and title that stress the main idea; summarizing and quoting from sources; strengthening an essay with research; and answering essay examination questions. Unit 5 teaches students to revise for consistency, sentence variety, and language awareness. A new chapter on proofreading and error correction launches Unit 6, which thoroughly covers grammar and students' major problem areas. Unit 7 reviews spelling and homonyms. Unit 8, now with a rich thematic index, features 19 richly varied reading selections by top authors like Leonard Pitts, Jr., Sandra Cisneros, Wang Ping, Ian Frazier, Ellen Goodman, Andrew Sullivan, Ana Veciana-Suarez, Brent Staples, Malcolm Gladwell, and Jhumpa Lahiri. Headnotes, vocabulary glosses, critical thinking questions, and writing assignments accompany each piece. An ESL appendix gives additional support to ESL and ELL students, and a bank of memorable short quotations concludes *Evergreen with Readings*.

Extensive New Online Teaching Program

Evergreen's strong new technology package provides an array of tools and resources:

For Students

aplia™

- *Aplia for Evergreen* is a student supplement that provides developmental writing students with clear, succinct, and engaging writing instruction and practice to help students master basic writing and grammar skills. *Aplia for Evergreen* features ongoing individualized practice, immediate feedback, and grades that can be automatically uploaded, so instructors can see where students are having difficulty (allowing for personalized assistance.) To learn more, visit **http://www.aplia.com/developmentalenglish**.

- *Evergreen e-Book*, a standalone digital version of the text, includes media segments such as author-recorded audio introductions to each chapter as well as live links to websites.

- *Write Experience* is the first solution in higher education to offer you the opportunity to improve your written and critical thinking skills with instant automated feedback. Write Experience provides real-time guidance, in your native language, as you write. After submitting your assignment, Write Experience evaluates your written assignment and provides immediate feedback on your writing while it's fresh in your mind. Write Experience not only scores your writing instantly and accurately, it provides detailed revision goals and detailed feedback on your writing to help you improve. Better Writing. Better Outcomes. Write Experience.

- *CourseMate for Evergreen.* If an instructor chooses this package, students can log in to access a wealth of resources. CourseMate features are designed to enhance the student's classroom experience with opportunities for further practice and additional resources to support students in academic and professional pursuits. These features include:

  - *Practice Quizzes* for every chapter that review key concepts and provide students with immediate feedback, so they know what they need to review.

  - *Flashcards* for additional vocabulary practice.

  - *Additional Writing Assignments* provide more thought-provoking suggestions for paragraphs and essays.

  - *Web Links* take students to every Exploring Online site recommended in the text.

  - *Test Your Visual IQ* exercises help students learn to read and analyze visual images, from advertisements to works of art.

  - *Plagiarism Prevention Site* provides examples of both intentional and unintentional plagiarism, with instructions on how to appropriately provide source information.

  - *Career and Job Search Resources* include guidance on writing a résumé and useful links to career preference tests and career information.

  - *ESL Resources* provide focused practice on common ESL problems and how to correct them, and links to helpful sites with vocabulary flashcards for each chapter in the text, quizzes, exercises, and games.

  - *Look-Alikes/Sound-Alikes* downloadable practice sets for every pair or group of words in this chapter allow instructors to individualize instruction for students with persistent error patterns.

Students can also purchase an access card separately at CengageBrain.com.

For Instructors

■ *Write Experience* is a technology product that allows you to assess written communication skills without adding to your workload. Instructors in all areas have told us it's important that students can write effectively in order to communicate and think critically. Through an exclusive partnership with a technology company, Cengage Learning's Write Experience allows you to do just that! This new product utilizes artificial intelligence to not only score student writing instantly and accurately, but also provide students with detailed revision goals and feedback on their writing to help them improve. Write Experience is the first product designed and created specifically for the higher education market through an exclusive agreement with McCann Associates, and powered by e-Write IntelliMetric Within™. IntelliMetric is the gold standard for automated scoring of writing and is used to score the Graduate Management Admissions Test® (GMAT®) analytical writing assessment. Better Writing. Better Outcomes. Write Experience. Visit www.cengage.com/writeexperience to learn more.

■ **Thoroughly Updated and Reorganized** *Evergreen Test Bank and Instructor's Manual* **for the 10ᵗʰ edition.** The *Evergreen Test Bank*, authored by Ann Marie McNeely of Western Piedmont Community College and Susan Fawcett, provides diagnostic, mastery, unit, and chapter tests for every chapter in the book—with 88 all new or updated items. The Test Bank is available in print, online, or in ExamView® format. The revised Instructor's Manual includes the author's teaching suggestions for every chapter and reading, sample syllabi, and more. Also included is the *Evergreen Instructor's Guide to Teaching ESL Students* written by Dr. Donald L. Weasenforth and updated by Catherine Mazur Jefferies, which provides extensive assistance in teaching classes that include ELL or Generation 1.5 students, including a Language Transfer Chart that shows common errors in each main language group.

■ **ExamView® Test Bank**, which allows instructors to create, deliver, and customize print and online tests.

■ **Instructor Companion Site**, a password-protected website, provides a downloadable version of the *Evergreen Test Bank and Instructor's Manual*, Creative Classroom Links to teaching strategies and tested classroom activities; resources for preventing plagiarism; customizable rubrics for every paragraph and essay type; and chapter-specific *PowerPoint* slides for classroom use.

Acknowledgments

Thanks to the many instructors who provided feedback for this edition of *Evergreen*:

Martha Bugher, Ivy Tech Community College

Kylie Carrithers, Indiana State University

Joanna Cattanach, Mountain View College

Deborah Chaffin, Norco College

Malkiel Choseed, Onondaga Community College

Karen Cole, Miami University Hamilton

Karen Castellucci Cox, City College of San Francisco

Roger Craik, Kent State University Ashtabula Campus

Paula Davis, Northland Community and Technical College

Patricia Dungan, Austin Community College

Judith Gonzales, Ohlone College

Phyllis Gowdy, Tidewater Community College

Harold Halbert, Montgomery County Community College

Judy Haberman, Phoenix College

L. Allison Harrell, Guilford Technical Community College

Catherine Higdon, Tarrant County College Northwest

Elizabeth Huergo, Montgomery College

Deborah Keeler, Miami Dade College

Richard Kuss, Century College

Eric Lane, Valencia College

Michelle Livote, Santa Ana College

Brian Longacre, Asheville-Buncombe Technical Community College

Jane Marlowe, Clinton Community College

Rachel McDermott, Palm Beach State College

Judy McKenzie, Lane Community College

Ann Marie McNeely, Western Piedmont Community College

Amy Nawrocki, University of Bridgeport

Mary Ann Nestmann, Jefferson Community & Technical College

Kristen Nichols, Coastline Community College

Michael O'Connor, Onondaga Community College

Ellen Olmstead, Montgomery College

Robin Ouzts, Thomas University

Catherine Pressimone Beckowski, Cabrini College

Josh Pryor, Saddleback College

Carmen Subryan, Howard University

Holly Susi, Community College of Rhode Island

Caryl Terrell-Bamiro, Chandler-Gilbert Community College

Jonathan Wise, A-B Technical Community College

Karen Taghi Zoghi, Miami Dade College

Michelle Van de Sande, Arapahoe Community College

I am indebted to the team at Cengage Learning whose market research, hard work, and vision helped make *Evergreen* Tenth Edition the best book of its kind in the country: in particular, the discerning and delightful Annie Todd, Director of Developmental Studies; the talented Stephanie Carpenter, my Development Editor and colleague extraordinaire; Assistant Editor Beth Rice, who kept *Evergreen*'s revised supplements on track and on time; Aimee Bear, Content Project Manager; Christian Biagetti, Media Editor and Lydia LeStar, *Evergreen*'s Brand Manager. Heartfelt thanks to Marcy Kagan, my photo editor and friend, whose artist's eye and sensibility made *Evergreen*'s superior visual program even better. In the hands of Whitney Thompson and Lachina Publishing Services, the flow from manuscript to printed book seemed almost easy.

Ann Marie Radaskiewicz, Dean of Developmental Education Western Piedmont Community College, contributed her many talents to research, writing, and troubleshooting throughout the revision process. I am grateful to Patricia Bandiga Dungan at Austin Community College-Rio Grande for sharing her ideas about targeted proofreading strategies; her insights have influenced my approach to error correction. ESL expert Emmy Smith Ready proofread the manuscript, keeping the new edition error-free even as she mastered the role of new mother. Nationally recognized ESL expert Don Weasonforth of the Collin County Community College District provided our practical and nuanced guide to more effectively teaching ESL students in our *Evergreen* classes. English colleagues around the country shared teaching strategies, fine student writing, and opinions on issues in higher education, including Karen Castellucci Cox of the City College of San Francisco; Marta Magellan, Deborah Keeler, and Ivonne Lamazares of Miami Dade College, Kendall Campus; Frederick de Naples and Andrew Rowan of Bronx Community College, CUNY; and Jennifer Bubb of Illinois Valley Community College.

My abiding inspiration is our students, whose hard work, aspirations, and fortitude in the face of sometimes unthinkable obstacles drive my life's goal of helping them learn and thrive. To those special friends and family who stay steadfast in dark as well as bright times, my love and gratitude: Maggie Smith, Colleen Huff, Bryan Hoffman, Trisha Nelson, Elaine Unkeless, Laraine Flemming, my beloved brother David Fawcett, his partner Eddie Brown—my other cherished brother, and fiction writer and English professor Richard Donovan, my dear husband. This beautiful 10th Anniversary Edition of *Evergreen* is dedicated to my mother, the watercolorist Harriet Fawcett, who passed away in 2010. The cover and interior design pay tribute to her gifts and her example of lifelong creativity.

Susan Fawcett
October 2012

Evergreen

A Guide to Writing with Readings

Unit 1

Getting Started

CHAPTER 1

Exploring the Writing Process

A: The Writing Process

B: Subject, Audience, and Purpose

Did you know that the ability to write well characterizes the most successful college students and employees—in fields from education to medicine to computer science? Skim the job postings in career fields that interest you and notice how many stress "excellent writing and communication skills." Furthermore, reading and writing enrich our daily lives; in surveys, adults always rate reading, writing, and speaking well as the most important life skills a person can possess.

The goal of this book is to help you become a more skilled, powerful, and confident writer. You will see that writing is not a magic ability only a few are born with, but a life skill that can be learned. The first chapter presents a brief overview of the writing process, explored in greater depth throughout the book. Now I invite you to decide to excel in this course. Let *Evergreen* be your guide, and enjoy the journey.

A. The Writing Process

Many people have the mistaken idea that good writers simply sit down and write out a perfect letter, paragraph, or essay from start to finish. In fact, writing is a **process** consisting of a number of steps:

The Writing Process

1 Prewriting

- Thinking about possible subjects
- Freely jotting ideas on paper or computer
- Narrowing the subject and writing your main idea in one sentence
- Deciding which ideas to include
- Arranging ideas in a plan or outline

Writing { Writing the first draft

Revising { Rethinking, rearranging, and revising as necessary
Writing one or more new drafts
Proofreading for grammar and spelling errors

Not all writers perform all the steps in this order, but most **prewrite**, **write**, and **revise**. Actually, writing can be a messy process of thinking, writing, reading what has been written, and rewriting. Sometimes steps overlap or need to be repeated. The important thing is that writing the first draft is just one stage in the process. "I love being a writer," jokes Peter De Vries. "What I can't stand is the paperwork."

Good writers take time at the beginning to **prewrite**—to think, jot ideas, and plan the paper—because they know it will save time and prevent frustration later. Once they write the first draft, they let it "cool off." Then they read it again with a fresh, critical eye and **revise**—crossing out, adding, and rewriting for more clarity and punch. Good writers are like sculptors, shaping and reworking their material into something more meaningful. Finally, they **proofread** for grammar and spelling errors so that their writing seems to say, "I am proud to put my name on this work." As you practice writing, you will discover your own most effective writing process.

PRACTICE 1

Think of something that you wrote recently—and of which you felt proud—for college, work, or your personal life. Now on paper or with classmates, discuss the *process* you followed in writing it. Did you do any *planning* or *prewriting*—or did you just sit down and start writing? How much time did you spend rewriting and *revising* your work? What one change in your writing process do you think would most improve your writing? Taking more time to prewrite? Taking more time to revise? Improving your grammar and spelling?

PRACTICE 2

Bring in several newspaper help-wanted sections. In a group with four or five classmates, study the ads in career fields that interest you. How many fields require writing and communication skills? Which job ad requiring these skills most surprised you or your group? Be prepared to present your findings to the class. If your class has Internet access, visit *Monster.com* or other job-search websites and perform the same exercise.

EXPLORING ONLINE

http://www.google.com

Search "Writing: A Ticket to Work… or a Ticket Out" and read the summary.
This survey of business leaders finds that good writing is the key to career
success. What two facts or comments do you find most striking?

B. Subject, Audience, and Purpose

Early in the prewriting phase, writers should give some thought to their **subject**, **audience**, and **purpose**.

In college courses, you may be assigned a broad **subject** by your instructor. First, make sure you understand the assignment. Then focus on one aspect of the subject that intrigues you. Whenever possible, choose something that you know and care about: life in Cleveland, working with learning-disabled children, repairing motorcycles, overcoming shyness, watching a friend struggle with drug addiction, playing soccer. You may not realize how many subjects you do know about.

To find or focus your subject, ask yourself:

- What special experience or expertise do I have?

- What inspires, angers, or motivates me? What do I love to do?

- What story in the news affected me recently?

- What campus, job, or community problem do I have ideas about solving?

Your answers will suggest good subjects to write about. Keep a list of all your best ideas.

How you approach your subject will depend on your **audience**—your readers. Are you writing for your professor, classmates, boss, closest friend, youngsters in the community, or the editor of a newspaper?

To focus on your audience, ask yourself:

- For whom am I writing? Who will read this?

- How much do they know about the subject? Are they beginners or experts?

- Will they likely agree or disagree with my ideas?

- Will my readers expect a composition about my *personal experience* or about more *formal, factual material*?

Keeping your audience in mind helps you know what information to include and what to leave out. For example, if you are writing about women's college basketball for readers who think that hoops are big earrings, you will approach your subject in a basic way, perhaps discussing the explosion of interest in women's teams. But an audience of sports lovers will already know about this; for them, you would write in more depth, perhaps comparing the techniques of two point guards. Often in college courses like history as well as in the workplace, you will be expected to write about factual subjects—not yourself, your feelings, or your experiences.

Finally, keeping your **purpose** in mind will help you write more effectively. Do you want to explain something to your readers, persuade them that a certain view is correct, entertain them, tell a good story, or some combination of these?

PRACTICE 3

List five subjects that you might like to write about. Consider your audience and purpose: For whom are you writing? What do you want them to know about your subject? Notice how the audience and purpose will help shape your paper. For ideas, reread the boxed questions on the previous page.

		Subject	Audience	Purpose
EXAMPLE	1.	my recipe for seafood gumbo	inexperienced cooks	to show how easy it is to make seafood gumbo
	2.	_____	_____	_____
	3.	_____	_____	_____
	4.	_____	_____	_____
	5.	_____	_____	_____

PRACTICE 4

Jot ideas for the following two assignments, by yourself or in a group with four or five classmates. Notice how your ideas and details differ depending on the audience and purpose.

1. You have been asked to write a description of your college for local high school students. Your purpose is to explain what advantages the college offers its students. What kinds of information should you include? What will your audience want to know? What information should you leave out?

2. You have been asked to write a description of your college for the governor of your state. Your purpose is to persuade him or her to spend more money to improve your college. What information should you include? What will your audience want to know? What information should you leave out?

PRACTICE 5

In a group with three or four classmates, read these sentences from real job-application letters and résumés, published in *Fortune* magazine. Each writer's *subject* was his or her job qualifications; the *audience* was an employer, and the *purpose* was to get a job. How did each person undercut his or her own purpose? What writing advice would you give each of these job seekers?

1. I have lurnt Word and computer spreasheet programs.

2. Please don't misconstrue my 14 jobs as "job-hopping." I have never quit a job.

3. I procrastinate, especially when the task is unpleasant.

4. Let's meet, so you can "ooh" and "aah" over my experience.

5. It is best for employers that I not work with people.

6. Reason for leaving my last job: maturity leave.

7. As indicted, I have over five years of analyzing investments.

8. References: none. I have left a path of destruction behind me.

 **PRACTICE 6**   **TEAMWORK: CRITICAL VIEWING AND WRITING**

Study the public service advertisement below and then answer these questions: What *subject* is the ad addressing? Who is the target *audience*? What is the intended *purpose*? In your view, how successful is this ad in achieving its purpose?

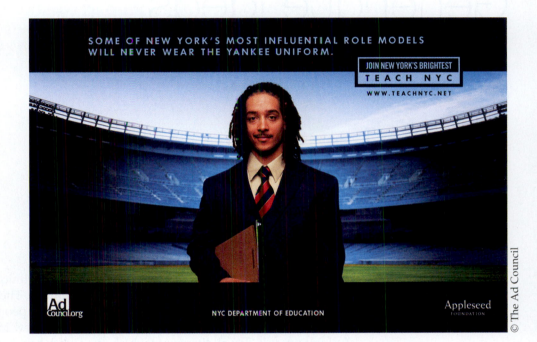

EXPLORING ONLINE

Throughout this book, Exploring Online features will suggest ways to use the Internet to improve your writing and grammar. A number of online writing labs—called OWLs—based at colleges around the country offer excellent additional practice or review in areas where you might need extra help. Here are three good sites to explore:

http://owl.english.purdue.edu/owl/

Purdue University's OWL

http://grammar.ccc.commnet.edu/grammar/

Capital Community College's OWL

CourseMate for *Evergreen*

Visit *Evergreen CourseMate* for more practices and quizzes, videos to accompany the readings, career and job-search resources, ESL help, and live links for every website in the book.

CHAPTER 2

Prewriting to Generate Ideas

A: Freewriting

B: Brainstorming

C: Clustering

D: Asking Questions

E: Keeping a Journal

This chapter presents five effective prewriting techniques that will help you get your ideas onto paper (or onto the computer). These techniques can help you overcome the "blank-page jitters" that many people face when they first sit down to write. You can also use them to generate new ideas at any point in the writing process. Try all five to see which ones work best for you.

In addition, if you write on a computer, try prewriting in different ways: on paper and on computer. Some writers feel they produce better work if they prewrite by hand and only later transfer their best ideas onto the computer. Every writer has personal preferences, so don't be afraid to experiment.

A. Freewriting

Freewriting is an excellent method that many writers use to warm up and to generate ideas. These are the guidelines: for five, ten, or fifteen minutes, write rapidly, without stopping, about anything that comes into your head. If you feel stuck, just repeat or rhyme the last word you wrote, but *don't stop writing*. And don't worry about grammar, logic, complete sentences, or grades.

The point of freewriting is to write so quickly that ideas can flow without comments from your inner critic. The *inner critic* is the voice inside that says, every time you have an idea, "That's dumb; that's no good; cross that out." Freewriting helps you tell this voice, "Thank you for your opinion. Once I have lots of ideas and words on paper, I'll invite you back for comment."

After you freewrite, read what you have written, underlining or marking any parts you like.

Freewriting is a powerful tool for helping you turn thoughts and feelings into words, especially when you are unsure about what you want to say. Sometimes freewriting produces only nonsense; often, however, it can help you zoom in on possible topics, interests, and worthwhile writing you can use later. Focused freewriting can help you find subjects to write about.

Focused Freewriting

In **focused freewriting**, you simply try to focus your thoughts on one subject as you freewrite. The subject might be one assigned by your instructor, one you choose, or one you have discovered in unfocused freewriting. The goal of most writing is a polished, organized piece of writing; focused freewriting can help you generate ideas or narrow a topic to one aspect that interests you.

Here is one student's focused freewriting on the topic of *someone who strongly influenced you*:

> Mr. Martin, the reason I'm interested in science. Wiry, five-foot-four-inch, hyperactive guy. A darting bird in the classroom, a circling teacher-bird, now jabbing at the knee bone of a skeleton, now banging on the jar with the brain in it. Like my brain used to feel, pickled, before I took his class. I always liked science but everything else was too hard. I almost dropped out of school, discouraged, but Martin was fun, crazy, made me think. Encouragement was his thing. Whacking his pencil against the plastic model of an eyeball in his office, he would bellow at me, "Taking too many courses! Working too many hours in that restaurant! Living everyone else's life but your own!" Gradually, I slowed down, got myself focused. Saw him last at graduation, where he thwacked my diploma with his pencil, shouting, "Keep up the good work! Live your own life! Follow your dreams!"

● This student later used this focused freewriting—its vivid details about Mr. Martin and his influence—as the basis for an effective paper. Underline any words or lines that you find especially striking or appealing. Be prepared to explain why you like what you underlined.

PRACTICE 1

Do a three-minute focused freewriting on three of these topics:

job	body piercing
friendship	parent (or child)
news	tests

Underline as usual. Did you surprise yourself by having so much to say about any one topic? Perhaps you would like to write more about that topic.

PRACTICE 2

1. Read over your earlier freewritings and notice your underlinings. Would you like to write more about any underlined words or ideas? Write two or three such words or ideas here:

   Sample answers: _____

   Sometimes I feel closer to my children than to my parents. _____

   I'm often most content on a rainy day. _____

2. Now choose one word or idea. Focus your thoughts on it and do a ten-minute focused freewriting. Try to stick to the topic as you write but don't worry too much about keeping on track; just keep writing.

B. Brainstorming

Another prewriting technique that may work for you is **brainstorming** or freely jotting down ideas about a topic. As in freewriting, the purpose is to generate lots of ideas so you have something to work with and choose from. Write everything that comes to you about a topic—words and phrases, ideas, details, examples.

After you have brainstormed, read over your list, underlining interesting or exciting ideas you might develop further. As with freewriting, many writers brainstorm on a general subject, underline, and then brainstorm again as they focus on one aspect of that subject.

Here is one student's brainstorm list on the topic of *managing your time*:

> time, who has it?
> classes, getting to campus
> work 20 hours a week, plus time for Marina
> always tired
> hey Alicia, I don't feel like a Superwoman
> help? I don't ask
> studying falls to last place
> why be in college if I don't study?
> if only I had 10 hrs a week outside class to read, write
> get help where?
> library has study places, ask my counselor
> trade child care time with Flo?
> take 5 minutes every morning to read my spiritual books
> start the day fresh
> maybe I can plan my time to find time

With brainstorming, this writer generated many ideas and started to move toward a more focused topic: *By planning ahead, I am learning to find time for what matters.* With a narrowed topic, brainstorming once more can help the writer generate details and reasons to support the idea.

PRACTICE 3

Choose one of the following topics that interests you and write it at the top of your paper or computer screen. Then brainstorm. Write anything that comes into your head about the topic. Just let ideas pour out fast!

1. a place I want to go back to
2. my goals in this course
3. my best/worst job
4. qualities that will help me succeed
5. dealing with difficult people
6. an unforgettable person from work, school, or family life

Once you fill a page with your list, read it over, marking the most interesting ideas. Draw arrows or highlight and move text on your screen to connect related ideas. Is there one idea that might be the subject of a paper?

C. Clustering

Some writers use still another method—called **clustering** or **mapping**—to get their ideas on paper. To begin clustering, simply write an idea or a topic, usually one word, in the center of a piece of paper. Then let your mind make associations, and write these associations branching out from the center.

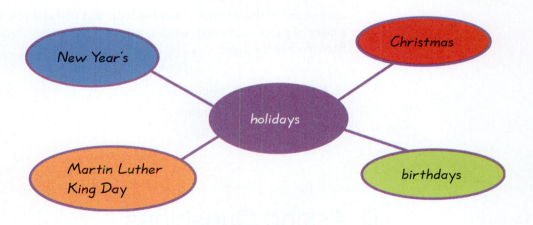

When one idea suggests other ideas, details, and examples, write these around it in a "cluster." After you finish, pick the cluster that most interests you. You may wish to freewrite for more ideas.

PRACTICE 4

Choose one of these topics or another topic that interests you. Write it in the center of a piece of paper and then try clustering. Keep writing down associations until you have filled most of the page.

1. heroes
2. holidays
3. food
4. inspiration
5. a dream
6. movies

D. Asking Questions

Many writers get ideas about a subject by asking questions and trying to answer them. This section describes two ways of doing this.

The Reporter's Six Questions

Newspaper reporters often answer six basic questions at the beginning of an article: **Who? What? Where? When? Why? How?** Here is the way one student used these questions to explore the general subject of *sports* assigned by his instructor:

Who?	Players, basketball and football players, coaches, fans. Violence— I'm tired of that subject. Loyal crazy screaming fans—Giants fans.
What?	Excitement. Stadium on the day of a game. Tailgate parties. Cookouts. Incredible spreads—Italian families with peppers, stuff to spread on sandwiches. All-day partying. Radios, TVs, grills, Giants caps.
Where?	Giants Stadium parking lot. People gather in certain areas—meet me in 10-B. Stadiums all over the country, same thing. People party on tailgates, in cars, on cars, plastic chairs, blankets.
When?	People arrive early morning—cook breakfast, lunch. After the game, many stay on in parking lot, talking, drinking beer. Year after year they come back.
Why?	Big social occasion, emotional outlet.
How?	They come early to get space. Some stadiums now rent parking spaces. Some families pass on season tickets in their wills!

Notice the way this writer uses the questions to focus his ideas about tailgate parties at Giants Stadium. He has already come up with many interesting details for a good paper.

Ask Your Own Questions

If the reporter's six questions seem too confining, just ask the questions *you* want answered about a subject. Let each answer suggest the next question.

Here is how one student responded to the subject *a career that interests you* (she chose nursing):

What do I know about nursing? I know that hospitals never seem to have enough nurses, so many jobs must be available. Nurses work hard, but their work seems interesting, exciting. The pay is good. Nurses also help people, which is important to me.

What would I like to know? What kind of education and training do nurses need? Is it better to work in a hospital, clinic, doctor's office, school, nursing home? I think nurses specialize in certain areas, like ER medicine or pediatrics. I'd like to know how they pick and how they get specialized training.

Where can I get more information? A friend of my mom's is a nurse in the intensive care unit at Mt. Sinai. I could interview her. I could speak with the career counselor on campus. Kendra told me to check out a great U.S. government website on careers, **http://stats.bls.gov/oco/**.

What would I like to focus on? Well, I'd like to know more about the real-life experience of being a nurse and the specific knowledge and skills nurses need. What are the rewards and drawbacks of a nursing career?

What is my angle or point? I want to give readers (and myself!) a sense of what it means to be a good nurse and how to prepare for a successful career. I think readers would be interested in practical tips about the education, choices, and what to do to become a nurse.

Who is my audience? I would like to write for people who might be considering nursing as a career.

PRACTICE 5

Answer the reporter's six questions on one of the following topics or on a topic of your own choice.

1. career goals
2. sports
3. stress among students

4. music
5. family get-togethers
6. neighbors/neighborhood

PRACTICE 6

Ask and answer at least five questions of your own about one of the topics in Practice 5. Use these questions if you wish: What do I know about this subject? What would I like to know? Where can I find answers to my questions? What would I like to focus on? What is my point of view about this subject? Who is my audience?

E. Keeping a Journal

Keeping a journal is an excellent way to practice your writing skills and discover ideas for further writing. Your journal is mostly for you—a private place where you record your experiences and your inner life; it is the place where, as one writer says, "I discover what I really think by writing it down."

You can keep a journal in a notebook or on a computer. If you prefer handwriting, get yourself an attractive notebook with 8½-by-11-inch paper. If you prefer to work on a computer, just open a "Journal" and keep your journal there. Then every morning or night, or several times a week, write for at least fifteen minutes in this journal. Don't just record the day's events. ("I went to the store. It rained. I came home.") Instead, write in detail about what most angered, moved, or amused you that day.

Write about what you really care about—motorcycles, loneliness, building websites, working in a doughnut shop, family relationships, grades, ending or starting a relationship. You may be surprised by how much you know. Write, think, and write some more. Your journal is private, so don't worry about grammar or correctness. Instead, aim to capture your truth so exactly that someone reading your words might experience it too.

You might also carry a little 3-by-5-inch pad with you during the day for "fast sketches," jotting down things that catch your attention: a man playing drums in the street; a baby wearing a bib that reads *Spit Happens*; a compliment you receive at work; something your child just learned to do.

Every journal is unique—and usually private—but here is a sample journal entry to suggest possibilities. The student links a quotation he has just learned to a disturbing "lesson of love":

Apr. 11. Two weeks ago, our professor mentioned a famous quote: "It is better to have loved and lost than never to have loved at all." The words had no particular meaning for me. How wrong I was. Last Sunday I received some very distressing news that will change my life from now on.

My wife has asked me why I never notified any family members except my mother of the birth of our children. My reply has been an argument or an angry stare. Our daughter Angelica is now two months shy of her second birthday, and we were also blessed with the birth of a son, who is five months old. I don't know whether it was maturity or my conscience, but last Sunday I decided it was time to let past grievances be forgotten. Nothing on this green earth would shelter me from what I was to hear that day.

I went to my father's address, knocked on his door, but got no response. Nervous but excited, I knocked again. Silence. On leaving the building, I bumped into his neighbor and asked for the possible whereabouts of my father. I couldn't brace myself for the cold shock of hearing from him that my father had died. I was angry as well as saddened, for my father was a quiet and gentle man whose love of women, liquor, and good times exceeded the love of his son.

Yes, it would have been better to have loved my father as he was than never to have gotten the opportunity to love such a man. A lesson of love truly woke me up to the need to hold dearly the ones you care for and overcome unnecessary grudges. "I love you, Pop, and may you rest in peace. Que Dios te guíe."

—Anthony Falu, Student

The uses of a journal are limited only by your imagination. Here are some ideas:

- Write down your goals and dreams; then brainstorm steps you can take to make them reality. (Notice negative thoughts—"I can't do that. That will never work." Focus on positive thoughts—"Of course I can! If X can do it, so can I.")

- Write about a problem you are having and creative ways in which you might solve it.

- Analyze yourself as a student. What are your strengths and weaknesses? What can you do to build on the strengths and overcome the weaknesses?

- What college course do you most enjoy? Why?

- Who believes in you? Who seems not to believe in you?

- If you could spend time with one famous person, living or dead, who would it be? Why?

- List five things you would love to do if they didn't seem so crazy.

- If you could change one thing about yourself, what would it be? What might you do to change it?

● Use your journal as a place to think about material that you have read in a textbook, newspaper, magazine, or online.

● What news story most upset you or made you laugh out loud in the past month? Why?

● Write down facts that impress you—the average American child watches 200,000 acts of violence before graduating from high school! Analyzing that one fact could produce a good paper.

● Read through the Quotation Bank at the end of this book, and copy your five favorite quotations into your journal.

This student likes to write in the "crowded coziness" of a diner. Many writers have a favorite place that helps them concentrate. What is yours?

David Grossman / Alamy

PRACTICE 7   **TEAMWORK: CRITICAL VIEWING AND WRITING**

Many people have a favorite writing spot, a place where they can think, write, and perhaps feel inspired. Some writers, like the student pictured, need "privacy in public." Others crave solitude, quiet, or a glimpse of nature. In a group with several classmates, discuss the place where each of you writes best. What qualities draw you to this spot? Now journal about the discussion. What did you learn about yourself or others?

PRACTICE 8

Get a notebook or set up your computer journal. Write for at least fifteen minutes three times a week.

   At the end of each week, reread what you have written or typed. Underline sections or ideas you like and put a check mark next to subjects you might like to write more about.

PRACTICE 9

Choose one passage in your journal that you would like to rewrite and let others read. Mark the parts you like best. Now rewrite and polish the passage so you would be proud to show it to someone else.

EXPLORING ONLINE

http://www.powa.org/
Under "Invent," click "Choosing Your Subject" for practical advice about finding a subject *you* want to write about.

http://grammar.ccc.commnet.edu/grammar/composition/brainstorm_freewrite.htm
Tips and timed practice on using freewriting to get started

CourseMate for *Evergreen*
Visit *Evergreen CourseMate* for more practices and quizzes, videos to accompany the readings, career and job-search resources, ESL help, and live links to every Exploring Online in the book.

Writers' Workshop

Using One or Two of Your Five Senses, Describe a Place

Readers of a finished paper can easily forget that they are reading the *end result* of someone else's writing process. The writer has already thought about audience and purpose, zoomed in on a subject, and prewritten to get ideas.

Here is one student's response to the following assignment: *Using one or two of the five senses—smell, hearing, taste, touch, or sight—describe a special place.* In your class or group, read the paper, aloud if possible. As you read, underline words or lines that strike you as especially well written or powerful.

Sounds and Smells of Home

At my grandmother's house in Puerto Rico, I woke to a hundred sounds and smells of happiness. As a child on vacation, I was called from my sleep by birds chirping in the trees. I kept my eyes closed and smiled to remember where I was. Then the distant lawnmowers started up, bringing smell of cut grass. At the break of dawn, my grandma would sing, "Bésame mucho como si fuera la última vez," which means "kiss me a lot as though it is for the last time." She sang those words like a record that keeps repeating the same thing. The kitchen cabinets creaked open and closed, and I would hear the old, outdated radio tuning to her favorite talk show. A man's smooth radio voice spoke fast Spanish, like the rhythm of a different world. Clanking and pulling signaled that utensils were being laid out for breakfast. The cracking of the first egg, the sizzle of frying bacon, and the smell of fresh bread made me salivate. Time to get up. With heavy footsteps, my uncles came in, and their chair legs screeched against the tile floor. My grandmother's gardenia perfume embraced me as she kissed my forehead. This Christmas Eve, my dear grandma succumbed to cancer. I am grown, married, and have a son. But to this day, I can hear and smell those long-ago days when gave me so much.

—Awilda Scarpetta, Student

1. How effective is Ms. Scarpetta's paper?

    _____ Good topic for a college audience?   _____ Clear main idea?

    _____ Rich supporting details?   _____ Logical organization?

2. Does the first sentence make you want to read on? Why or why not?

3. Which of the five senses does the writer emphasize? What words show this?

4. Discuss your underlinings with the group or class. Try to explain why a particular word or sentence is effective. For instance, the sentence "The cracking of the first egg, the sizzle of frying bacon, and the smell of fresh bread made me salivate" contains precise words and details of sound and scent.

5. Would you suggest that the writer make any changes or improvements? If so, what?

6. Last, proofread for grammar, spelling, and omitted words. Do you spot any error patterns (the same type of error made two or more times) that this student should watch out for?

> Of her prewriting process, Awilda Scarpetta writes: "I decided to write about my grandmother's house in Puerto Rico because I thought my classmates (my audience) would find that more interesting than the local neighborhood. This paper also taught me the importance of brainstorming. I filled two whole pages with my brainstorming list, and then it was easy to pick the best details."

 ## GROUP WORK

Imagine that you have been given this assignment: *Using just one or two of the five senses, describe a special place.* Your audience will be your college writing class. Working as a group, plan a paper and prewrite. First, choose a place that your group will describe; if it is a place on campus, your instructor might even want you to go there. Second, decide whether you will emphasize sound, smell, taste, touch, or sight. Choose someone to write down the group's ideas, and then brainstorm. List as many sounds (or smells, etc.) as your group can think of. Fill at least one page. Now read back the list and put a check next to the best details; does your group agree or disagree about which ones are best?

You are well on your way to an excellent paper. Each group member can now complete the assignment, based on the list. If necessary, prewrite again for more details.

WRITING AND REVISING IDEAS

1. Using one or two of your five senses, describe a place. You might use a first sentence like this:

   At _____, I experienced a hundred _____ of _____ .
         (place)   (sounds, smells, etc.)   (an emotion)

2. List any interesting experiences or hobbies you know about that might interest your classmates and instructor (an intriguing job, time in another country, and so on). Choose one of these and prewrite; use the prewriting method of your choice and fill at least a page with ideas.

Unit 2

Discovering the Paragraph

The Process of Writing Paragraphs

This chapter will guide you step by step from examining basic paragraphs to writing them. The paragraph makes a good learning model because it is short yet contains many of the elements found in longer compositions. Therefore, you easily can transfer the skills you gain by writing paragraphs to longer essays, reports, and letters.

In this chapter, you will first look at finished paragraphs and then move through the process of writing paragraphs of your own.

A. Defining and Looking at the Paragraph

A **paragraph** is a group of related sentences that develops one main idea. Although there is no definite length for a paragraph, it is often from five to twelve sentences long. A paragraph usually occurs with other paragraphs in a longer piece of writing—an essay, an article, or a letter, for example. Before studying longer compositions, however, we will look at single paragraphs.

A paragraph looks like this on the page:

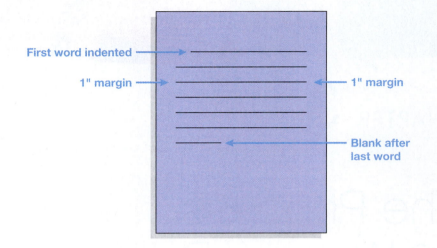

First word indented

1" margin

1" margin

Blank after
last word

- Clearly **indent** the first word of every paragraph about 1 inch (five spaces on the computer).

- Extend every line of a paragraph as close to the right-hand margin as possible.

- However, if the last word of the paragraph comes before the end of the line, leave the rest of the line blank.

Topic Sentence and Body

Most paragraphs contain one main idea to which all the sentences relate.

The **topic sentence** states this main idea.

The **body** of the paragraph develops and supports this main idea with particular facts, details, and examples:

> I allow the spiders the run of the house. I figure that any predator that hopes to make a living on whatever smaller creatures might blunder into a four-inch-square bit of space in the corner of the bathroom where the tub meets the floor needs every bit of my support. They catch flies and even field crickets in those webs. Large spiders in barns have been known to trap, wrap, and suck hummingbirds, but there's no danger of that here. I tolerate the webs, only occasionally sweeping away the very dirtiest of them after the spider itself has scrambled to safety. I'm always leaving a bath towel draped over the tub so that the big, haired spiders, who are constantly getting trapped by the tub's smooth sides, can use its rough surface as an exit ramp. Inside the house the spiders have only given me one mild surprise. I washed some dishes and set them to dry over a plastic drainer. Then I wanted a cup of coffee, so I picked from the drainer my mug, which was still warm from the hot rinse water, and across the rim of the mug, strand after strand, was a spider web.
>
> —Annie Dillard, *Pilgrim at Tinker Creek*

- The first sentence of Dillard's paragraph is the **topic sentence**. It states the main idea of the paragraph: that *the spiders are allowed the run of the house.*

- The rest of the paragraph, the **body**, fully explains and supports this statement. The writer first gives a reason for her attitude toward spiders and then gives particular examples of her tolerance of spiders.

The topic sentence is more *general* than the other sentences in the paragraph. The other sentences in the paragraph provide specific information relating to the topic sentence. Because the topic sentence tells what the entire paragraph is about, *it is usually the first sentence,* as in the example. Sometimes the topic sentence occurs elsewhere in the paragraph, for instance, as the sentence after an introduction or as the last sentence. Some paragraphs contain only an implied topic sentence but no stated topic sentence at all.

As you develop your writing skills, however, it is a good idea to write paragraphs that *begin* with the topic sentence. Once you have mastered this pattern, you can try variations.

PRACTICE 1

Find and underline the **topic sentence** in each of the following paragraphs. Look for the sentence that states the **main idea** of the entire paragraph. Be careful: the topic sentence is not always the first sentence.

Paragraph 1

In the mid-1980s, 340,000 people in the United States owned cell phones. Today, that number is well over 380 million. Worldwide, five billion people have gone wireless, and most of them have no idea that inside the sleek, plastic exterior of every cell phone sits a package of electronics laden with hazardous substances called persistent, bioaccumulative and toxic chemicals (PBTs). When cell users toss their phones into the trash, PBTs like lead, arsenic, and cadmium leak into the land, air, and water, eventually entering the tissues of animals and humans. Every year, 150 million cell phones—complete with batteries and chargers—are pitched into the garbage instead of being recycled or safely disposed of. As the popularity of cellular phones soars, growing numbers of cell users are creating growing piles of toxic trash.

—Adapted from Rene Ebersole,
"Recycle Cell Phones, Reduce Toxic Trash," *National Wildlife*

Cell phones can be recycled safely at plants like this one in Hilliard, Ohio, but Americans still throw 3 million tons of electronics into the trash each year.

© Richard Barnes/OTTO

Paragraph 2

The summer picnic gave ladies a chance to show off their baking hands. On the barbecue pit, chickens and spareribs sputtered in their own fat and in a sauce whose recipe was guarded in the family like a scandalous affair. However, every true baking artist could reveal her prize to the delight and criticism of the town. Orange sponge cakes and dark brown mounds dripping Hershey's chocolate stood layer to layer with ice-white coconuts and light brown caramels. Pound cakes sagged with their buttery weight and small children could no more resist licking the icings than their mothers could avoid slapping the sticky fingers.

—Maya Angelou, *I Know Why the Caged Bird Sings*

Paragraph 3

Eating sugar can be worse than eating nothing. Refined sugar provides only empty calories. It contributes none of the protein, fat, vitamins, or minerals needed for its own metabolism in the body, so these nutrients must be obtained elsewhere. Sugar tends to replace nourishing food in the diet. It is a thief that robs us of nutrients. A dietary emphasis on sugar can deplete the body of nutrients. If adequate nutrients are not supplied by the diet—and they tend not to be in a sugar-rich diet—they must be leached from other body tissues before sugar can be metabolized. For this reason, a U.S. Senate committee labeled sugar as an "antinutrient."

—Janice Fillip, "The Sweet Thief," *Medical Self-Care*

PRACTICE 2

Each group of sentences below could be unscrambled and written as a paragraph. Circle the letter of the **topic sentence** in each group of sentences. Remember: the topic sentence should state the main idea of the entire paragraph and should be general enough to include all the ideas in the body.

EXAMPLE

   a. Next, a social phobia is an intense fear of a social or performance situation, like standing in a checkout line.

   b. Agoraphobia, the third type, is a morbid terror of public places.

   (c.) Phobias, the most common anxiety disorder, can be divided into three types.

   d. A specific phobia, the first type, is an irrational fear of a specific thing, like spiders, dogs, elevators, or needles.

(Sentence c includes the ideas in all the other sentences.)

1. a. The United States military uses video games like America's Army to recruit and train soldiers for combat.

   b. Studies show that surgeons who improve their eye-hand coordination by playing video games perform difficult procedures faster and make 37 percent fewer mistakes.

   c. More and more elementary schools employ the Wii gaming console to improve comprehension in math, geography, and science.

   d. Video games are being used as creative learning tools in many settings.

2. a. Invited to join the space program, she trained as an astronaut and flew on the space shuttle *Endeavor* in 1992.

    b. The young Dr. Jemison headed to West Africa, where she worked in the Peace Corps for two years.

    c. Though a childhood teacher urged her to be a nurse, Mae Jemison knew she wanted to be a scientist and doctor.

    d. After eight years at NASA, she became a professor at Dartmouth College and started a company to help poor countries use solar energy.

    e. The life of Dr. Mae Jemison, the first African American female astronaut, is characterized by daring achievements and a strong desire to give back.

    f. A fine student, Jemison entered Stanford University at sixteen and later earned her M.D. degree from Cornell in 1981.

3. a. The left side of the human brain controls spoken and written language.

    b. The right side, on the other hand, seems to control artistic, musical, and spatial skills.

    c. Emotion is also thought to be controlled by the right hemisphere.

    d. The human brain has two distinct halves, or hemispheres, and in most people, each one controls different functions.

    e. Logical reasoning and mathematics are left-brain skills.

    f. Interestingly, the left brain controls the right hand, and vice versa.

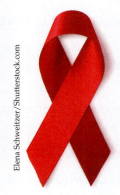

4. a. Although David Ho was born in Taiwan to poor parents, they named him Da-I, or "great one," revealing their high expectations.

    b. When he arrived in the United States at age twelve and was teased about speaking no English, he focused on mathematics, developing a fierce work ethic.

    c. With a medical degree from Harvard, Ho worked in a large Los Angeles hospital, where he saw many of the world's first AIDS cases.

    d. A gift for math and science, plus luck and hard work, helped Dr. David Ho become one of the world's greatest AIDS researchers.

    e. As a young boy, Ho created a math and science laboratory in the family garage.

    f. In 1996, David Ho invented the cocktail of antiretroviral drugs that has since saved millions of lives around the world.

5. a. People who don't know basic algebra can be more easily fooled by dishonest manipulation of numbers.

    b. Because studying algebra has so many benefits, every college student should be required to pass an algebra course.

    c. Learning algebra helps build problem-solving skills and reasoning skills.

    d. According to the U.S. Secretary of Education, Americans must know algebra in order to compete with well-educated citizens from other nations in this global economy.

    e. An understanding of algebra is required in a surprising range of professions, from architect to banker to photographer.

6. a. Albert Einstein, whose scientific genius awed the world, did not speak until he was four and could not read until he was nine.

    b. Inventor Thomas Edison had such severe problems reading, writing, and spelling that he was called "defective from birth," taken out of school, and taught at home.

    c. Many famous people have suffered from learning disabilities.

    d. Film actress Keira Knightley suffers from dyslexia, yet she has mastered many complex roles and been nominated for Golden Globe and Academy Awards.

7. a. Male and female insects are attracted to each other by visual, auditory, and chemical means.

    b. Through its chirping call, the male cricket attracts a mate and drives other males out of its territory.

    c. Butterflies attract by sight, and their brightly colored wings play an important role in courtship.

    d. Some female insects, flies among them, release chemicals called *pheromones* that attract males of the species.

8. a. Believe it or not, the first contact lens was drawn by Leonardo da Vinci in 1508.

    b. However, not until 1877 was the first thick glass contact actually made by a Swiss doctor.

    c. The journey of contact lenses from an idea to a comfortable, safe reality took nearly five hundred years.

    d. In 1948, smaller, more comfortable plastic lenses were introduced to enthusiastic American eyeglass wearers.

    e. These early glass lenses were enormous, covering the whites of the eyes.

    f. Today, contact lens wearers can choose ultra-thin, colored, or even disposable lenses.

B. Narrowing the Topic and Writing the Topic Sentence

A writer can arrive at the goal—a finished paragraph—in several ways. However, before writing a paragraph, most writers go through a process that includes these important steps:

1. Narrowing the topic

2. Writing the topic sentence

3. Generating ideas for the body

4. Selecting and dropping ideas

5. Arranging ideas in a plan or an outline

The rest of this chapter will explain these steps and guide you through the process of writing basic paragraphs.

Narrowing the Topic

As a student, you may be assigned broad writing topics by your instructor—success, cheating in schools, a description of a person. Your instructor is giving you the chance to cut the topic down to size and choose one aspect of the topic *that interests you*.

Suppose, for example, that your instructor gives this assignment: *Write a paragraph describing a person you know.* The challenge is to pick someone you would *like* to write about, someone who interests you and also would probably interest your readers.

Thinking about your *audience* and *purpose* may help you narrow the topic. In this case, your audience probably will be your instructor and classmates; your purpose is to inform or perhaps to entertain them by describing a person you want to write about.

Many writers find it useful at this point—on paper or on the computer—to brainstorm, freewrite, or ask themselves questions: "What person do I love or hate or admire? Is there a family member I would enjoy writing about? Who is the funniest, most unusual, or most talented person I know?"

Let's suppose you choose Pete, an unusual person and one about whom you have something to say. But Pete is still too broad a subject for one paragraph; you could probably write pages and pages about him. To narrow the topic further, you might ask yourself, "What is unusual about him? What might interest others?" Pete's room is the messiest place you have ever seen; in fact, Pete's whole life is sloppy, and you decide that you could write a good paragraph about that. You have now narrowed the topic to just one of Pete's qualities: *his sloppiness.*

You might visualize the process like this:

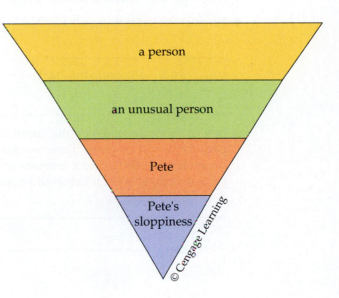

Writing the Topic Sentence

The next important step is to state your topic clearly *in sentence form*. Writing the topic sentence helps you further narrow your topic by forcing you to make a statement about it. The simplest possible topic sentence about Pete might read *Pete is sloppy*, but you might wish to strengthen it by saying, for instance, *Pete's sloppiness is a terrible habit*.

Writing a good topic sentence is an important step toward an effective paragraph because the topic sentence controls the direction and scope of the body. A topic sentence should have a clear *controlling idea* and should be a *complete sentence*.

You can think of the topic sentence as having two parts, a **topic** and a **controlling idea**. The controlling idea states the writer's point of view or attitude about the topic.

---

                    topic   controlling idea

TOPIC SENTENCE: Pete's sloppiness is a terrible habit.

The controlling idea helps you focus on just one aspect or point. Here are three possible topic sentences about the topic *a memorable job*:

1. My job in the complaint department taught me how to calm down angry people.
2. Two years in the complaint department persuaded me to become an assistant manager.
3. Working in the complaint department persuaded me to become a veterinarian.

● These topic sentences all explore the same topic—working in a complaint department—but each controlling idea is different. The controlling idea in 1 is *taught me how to calm down angry people*.

● What is the controlling idea in 2?

_____

What is the controlling idea in 3?

_____

● Notice the way in which the controlling idea lets the reader know what the paragraph will be about. There are many possible topic sentences for any topic, depending on the writer's interests and point of view. If you were assigned the topic *a memorable job*, what would your topic sentence be?

_____

_____

PRACTICE 3

Read each topic sentence below. Circle the topic and underline the controlling idea.

1. A low-fat diet provides many health benefits.

2. *Animal Planet* is both entertaining and educational.

3. Our football coach works to build players' self-esteem.

4. This campus offers many peaceful places where students can relax.

5. My cousin's truck looks like something out of *Star Wars*.

As a rule, the more specific and limited your topic and controlling idea, the better the paragraph; in other words, your topic sentence should not be so broad that it cannot be developed in one paragraph. Which of these topic sentences do you think will produce the best paragraphs?

4. Five wet, bug-filled days at Camp Nirvana made me a fan of the great indoors.
5. This town has problems.
6. Road rage is on the rise for three reasons.

● Topic sentences 4 and 6 are both specific enough to write a good paragraph about. In each, the topic sentence is carefully worded to suggest clearly what ideas will follow. From topic sentence 4, what do you expect the paragraph to include?

_____

● What do you expect paragraph 6 to include?

_____

● Topic sentence 5, on the other hand, is so broad that a paragraph could include almost anything. Just what problems does the town have? Strained relations between police and the community? Litter in public parks? Termites? The writer needs to rewrite the controlling idea, focusing on just one problem for an effective paragraph.

The topic sentence also must be a **complete sentence**. It must contain a subject and a verb, and express a complete thought.* Do not confuse a topic with a topic sentence. For instance, *a celebrity I would like to meet* cannot be a topic sentence because it is not a sentence; however, it could be a title† because topics and titles need not be complete sentences. One possible topic sentence might read, *A celebrity I would like to meet is writer Julia Alvarez.*

Do not write *This paragraph will be about . . .* or *In this paper I will write about. . . .* Instead, craft your topic sentence carefully to focus the topic and let your reader know what the paragraph will contain. Make every word count.

_____

* For practice in correcting fragments, see Chapter 28, "Avoiding Sentence Errors," Part B.

† For practice in writing titles, see Chapter 15, "The Introduction, the Conclusion, and the Title," Part C.

PRACTICE 4

Put a check beside each topic sentence that is focused enough to allow you to write a good paragraph. If a topic sentence is too broad, narrow the topic according to your own interests and write a new topic sentence with a clear controlling idea.

EXAMPLES __✔__ Keeping a journal can improve a student's writing.

Rewrite: _____

_____ This paper will be about my family.

Rewrite: _My brother Mark has a unique sense of humor._ _____

1. _____ Eugene's hot temper causes problems at work.

   Rewrite: _____

   _____

2. _____ This paragraph will discuss my two closest friends.

   Rewrite: _____

   _____

3. _____ Learning a foreign language has several benefits.

   Rewrite: _____

   _____

4. _____ Child abuse is something to think about.

   Rewrite: _____

   _____

5. _____ Company officials should not read employees' e-mail.

   Rewrite: _____

   _____

PRACTICE 5

Here is a list of broad topics. Choose three that interest you from this list or from your own list in Chapter 1, page 6. Narrow each topic, choose your controlling idea, and write a topic sentence focused enough to write a good paragraph about. Make sure that each topic sentence has a clear controlling idea and is a complete sentence.

overcoming fears   insider's tour of your community

popular music   balancing work and play

| credit cards | a person you like or dislike |
| an act of cowardice or courage | a time when you were (or were not) in control |

1. Narrowed topic: _____

   Controlling idea: _____

   Topic sentence: _____

   _____

2. Narrowed topic: _____

   Controlling idea: _____

   Topic sentence: _____

   _____

3. Narrowed topic: _____

   Controlling idea: _____

   Topic sentence: _____

   _____

PRACTICE 6

Many writers adjust the topic sentence after they have finished drafting the paragraph. In a group of three or four classmates, study the body of each of these paragraphs to find the main, or controlling, idea. Then, working together, write the most exact and interesting topic sentence you can for each paragraph.

Paragraph 1

_____

_____

A pet parrot recently saved his owner's life. Harry Becker was watching TV in his living room when he suddenly slumped over with a heart attack. The parrot screamed loudly until Mr. Becker's wife awoke and called 911. In another reported case of animal rescue, a family cat saved six-week-old Stacey Rogers. When the cat heard the baby gasping for breath in her crib, it ran howling to alert the baby's mother, who called paramedics. Even more surprising was an event reported in newspapers around the world. In 1996 in a Chicago zoo, a female gorilla rushed to save a three-year-old boy who fell accidentally into the gorilla enclosure. Still carrying her own baby on her back, the 150-pound gorilla gently picked up the unconscious child and carried him to the cage door to be rescued. Such stories reveal a mysterious and sometimes profound bond between animals and humans.

Paragraph 2

_____

_____

blinkblink/Shutterstock.com

The first advantage of smartphones is mobile Internet access. Gone are the days of having to return to the home or office computer in order to browse the Web. Instead, no matter where smartphone users are, they can quickly look up a weather forecast, the meaning of a word, or the best Thai restaurant in walking distance. Another major advantage is the ability to receive and send e-mails anywhere, anytime. The business benefits of this feature alone have prompted many companies to equip their employees with smartphones. Third, tools like a calendar, address book, international alarm clock, and GPS help smartphone users stay organized and efficient. Finally, thousands of downloadable apps can tailor a smartphone to each individual's needs. These apps range from music, video, and entertainment downloads to study tools and apps on parenting, car repair, diabetes, or stargazing.

C. Generating Ideas for the Body

One good way to generate ideas for the body of a paragraph is **brainstorming**—freely jotting on paper or the computer anything that relates to your topic sentence: facts, details, examples, little stories. This step might take just a few minutes, but it is one of the most important elements of the writing process. Brainstorming can provide you with specific ideas to support your topic sentence. Later you can choose from these ideas as you compose your paragraph.

Here, for example, is a possible brainstorm list for the topic sentence *Pete's sloppiness is a terrible habit*:

1. His apartment is full of dirty clothes, books, candy wrappers

2. His favorite candy—M&Ms

3. He is often a latecomer or a no-show

4. He jots time-and-place information for dates and appointments on scraps of paper that are soon forgotten

5. Stacks of old newspapers sit on chair seats

6. Socks are on the lampshades

7. Papers for classes are wrinkled and carelessly scrawled

8. I met Pete for the first time in math class

9. His sister is just the opposite, very neat

10. Always late for classes, out of breath

11. He is one messy person

12. Papers are stained with coffee or M&Ms

Instead of brainstorming, some writers freewrite or ask themselves questions to generate ideas for their paragraphs. Some like to perform this step on paper, whereas others use a computer. Do what works best for you. The key is to write down lots of ideas during prewriting. If you need more practice in any of these methods, reread Chapter 2, "Prewriting to Generate Ideas."

PRACTICE 7

Now choose the topic from Practice 5 that most interests you. Write your narrowed topic, controlling idea, and topic sentence here.

Narrowed topic: _____

Controlling idea: _____

Topic sentence: _____

_____

Next, brainstorm. On paper or on the computer, write anything that comes to you about your topic sentence. Just let your ideas pour out. Try to fill at least one page.

D. Selecting and Dropping Ideas

Next, simply read over what you have written, **selecting** those ideas that relate to and support the topic sentence and **dropping** those that do not. That is, keep the facts, examples, or little stories that provide specific information about your topic sentence. Drop ideas that just **repeat** the topic sentence but that add nothing new to the paragraph.

If you are not sure which ideas to select or drop, underline the **key word(s)** of the topic sentence, the ones that indicate the real point of your paragraph. Then make sure that the ideas that you select are related to those key words.

Here again is the brainstorm list for the topic sentence *Pete's sloppiness is a terrible habit*. The key word in the topic sentence is *sloppiness*. Which ideas would you keep? Why? Which would you drop? Why?

1. His apartment is full of dirty clothes, books, candy wrappers

2. His favorite candy—M&Ms

3. He is often a latecomer or a no-show

4. He jots time-and-place information for dates and appointments on scraps of paper that are soon forgotten

5. Stacks of old newspapers sit on chair seats

6. Socks are on the lampshades

7. Papers for classes are wrinkled and carelessly scrawled

8. I met Pete for the first time in math class

9. His sister is just the opposite, very neat

10. Always late for classes, out of breath

11. He is one messy person

12. Papers are stained with coffee or M&Ms

You probably dropped ideas 2, 8, and 9 because they do not relate to the topic—Pete's sloppiness. You should also have dropped idea 11 because it merely repeats the topic sentence.

Read through your own brainstorm list from Practice 7. Select the ideas that relate to your topic sentence and drop those that do not. In addition, drop any ideas that just repeat your topic sentence. Be prepared to explain why you drop or keep each idea.

E. Arranging Ideas in a Plan or an Outline

After you have selected the ideas you wish to include in your paragraph, you can begin to make a **plan** or an **outline**. A plan briefly lists and arranges the ideas you wish to present in your paragraph. An outline does the same thing a bit more formally, but in an outline, letters or numbers indicate the main groupings of ideas.

First, group together ideas that have something in common, that are related or alike in some way. Then order your ideas by choosing which one you want to present first, which one second, and so on.

Below is a plan for a paragraph about Pete's sloppiness:

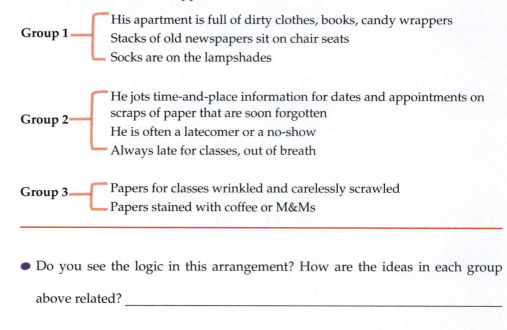

TOPIC SENTENCE: Pete's sloppiness is a terrible habit.

Group 1
- His apartment is full of dirty clothes, books, candy wrappers
- Stacks of old newspapers sit on chair seats
- Socks are on the lampshades

Group 2
- He jots time-and-place information for dates and appointments on scraps of paper that are soon forgotten
- He is often a latecomer or a no-show
- Always late for classes, out of breath

Group 3
- Papers for classes wrinkled and carelessly scrawled
- Papers stained with coffee or M&Ms

● Do you see the logic in this arrangement? How are the ideas in each group

above related? _____

_____

_____

● Does it make sense to discuss Pete's apartment first, his lateness second, and his written work third? Why? _____

_____

_____

● Once you have finished arranging ideas, you should have a clear **plan** from which to write your paragraph.*

PRACTICE 9

On paper or on the computer, arrange the ideas from your brainstorm list according to some plan or outline. First, group together related ideas; then decide which ideas will come first, which second, and so on.

Keep in mind that there is more than one way to group ideas. Think about what you want to say; then group ideas according to what your point is.

F. Writing and Revising the Paragraph

Writing the First Draft

The first draft should contain all the ideas you have decided to use in the order you have chosen in your plan. Be sure to start with your topic sentence. Try to write the best, most interesting, or most amusing paragraph you can, but avoid getting stuck on any one word, sentence, or idea. If you are unsure about something, put a check in the margin and come back to it later. Writing on every other line or double-spacing if you write on the computer will leave room for later corrections.

Once you have included all the ideas from your plan, think about adding a concluding sentence that summarizes your main point or adds a final idea. Not all paragraphs need concluding sentences. For example, if you are telling a story, the paragraph can end when the story does. Write a concluding sentence only if it will help to bring your thoughts to an end for your reader.

If possible, once you have finished the first draft, set the paper aside for several hours or several days.

PRACTICE 10

Write a first draft of the paragraph you have been working on.

Revising

Revising means rethinking and rewriting your first draft and then making whatever changes, additions, or corrections are necessary to improve the paragraph. You may cross out and rewrite words or entire sentences. You may add, drop, or rearrange details.

_____

* For more work on order, see Chapter 4, "Achieving Coherence," Part A.

As you revise, keep the *reader* in mind. Ask yourself these questions:

- Is my topic sentence clear?
- Can a reader understand and follow my ideas?
- Does the paragraph follow a logical order and guide the reader from point to point?
- Will the paragraph keep the reader interested?

In addition, check your paragraph for adequate support and unity, characteristics that we'll consider in the following pages.

Revising for Support

As you revise, make sure your paragraph contains excellent **support**—that is, specific facts, details, and examples that fully explain your topic sentence.

Be careful, too, that you have not simply repeated ideas—especially the topic sentence. Even if they are in different words, repeated ideas only make the reader suspect that your paragraph is padded and that you do not have enough facts and details to support your main idea properly.

Which of the following paragraphs contains the most convincing support?

Paragraph 1

(1) By making study time a priority every week, I raised my grade-point average from 2.4 to 3.3 in one year. (2) I have a really busy life, so I never studied enough. (3) When my average went down, I knew I had to do something. (4) I made myself study more often. (5) Because I made study time more important, my average went from C to B. (6) I also picked prime times to study, and this made a difference. (7) So sticking to my schedule definitely paid off.

Paragraph 2

(1) By making study time a priority every week, I raised my grade-point average from 2.4 to 3.3 in one year. (2) I work fifteen hours a week at the Gap while taking four courses a semester, so finding study time is hard. (3) I used to grab fifteen minutes here or twenty there, usually during breaks at work, on the subway to and from school, or right before bedtime. (4) When my average slipped to a C, I knew I had to take action and make my college education count. (5) I decided to make a real commitment to regular, high-quality study time. (6) I scheduled a two-hour study block at least four days a week, either at the library with a classmate from 12 to 2 p.m. or at home from 7 to 9 p.m. (7) It was really tough to resist the temptation to go out with friends, gab on the phone, or relax in front of the TV, but I scheduled my study times like appointments I had to keep. (8) As a result, I studied not only regularly but also for longer periods of time. (9) By increasing my study time this way, I began to understand the material much better. (10) In addition, I studied at times when I was more alert—not 10 or 11 p.m., when I was too tired to concentrate. (11) Soon I was earning more As and Bs, so sticking to my schedule definitely paid off.

- *Paragraph 1* contains general statements but little specific information to support the topic sentence.

- *Paragraph 1* also contains needless repetition. What is the number of the sentence or sentences that just repeat the topic sentence? _____

- *Paragraph 2*, however, supports the topic sentence with specific details and examples: *fifteen hours at the Gap, four courses, two-hour study block four days a week, library with a classmate from 12 to 2 p.m.* What other specific support does it give?

_____

_____

_____

_____

PRACTICE 11

Check the following paragraphs for adequate support. As you read each one, decide which places need more or better support—specific facts, details, and examples. Then rewrite the paragraphs, inventing facts and details whenever necessary and dropping repetitious words and sentences.

Paragraph 1

(1) My uncle can always be counted on when the family faces hardship. (2) Last year, when my mother was very ill, he was there, ready to help in every way. (3) He never has to be called twice. (4) When my father became seriously depressed, my uncle's caring made a difference. (5) Everyone respects him for his willingness to be a real "family man." (6) He is always there for us.

Paragraph 2

(1) Lending money to a friend can have negative consequences. (2) For example, Ashley, a student at Tornado Community College, agreed to lend $200 to her best friend, Jan. (3) This was a bad decision even though Ashley meant well. (4) The results of this loan were surprising and negative for Ashley, for Jan, and for the friendship. (5) Both women felt bad about it but in different ways. (6) Yes, lending money to a friend can have very negative consequences, like anger and hurt.

Paragraph 3

(1) Many television talk shows don't really present a discussion of ideas. (2) Some people who appear on these shows don't know what they are talking about; they just like to sound off about something. (3) I don't like these shows at all. (4) Guests shout their opinions out loud but never give any proof for what they say. (5) Guests sometimes expose their most intimate personal and family problems before millions of viewers—I feel embarrassed. (6) I have even heard hosts insult their guests and guests insult them back. (7) Why do people watch this junk? (8) You never learn anything from these dumb shows.

Revising for Unity

It is sometimes easy, in the process of writing, to drift away from the topic under discussion. Guard against doing so by checking your paragraph for **unity**; that is, make sure the topic sentence, every sentence in the body, and the concluding sentence all relate to one main idea.*

This paragraph lacks unity:

> (1) A popular rival to the Barbie doll is provoking protests from angry parents. (2) Designed for four- to eight-year-olds and marketed with the slogan "a passion for fashion," the multi-ethnic Bratz dolls wear heavy makeup, sultry facial expressions, and skimpy outfits. (3) The "hooker chic" style of these dolls concerns many parents, who worry that such toys expose their daughters to adult sexuality too soon. (4) Boys are harmed too, they claim, because the dolls encourage them to see girls as sex objects in little tops and glittery mini-skirts. (5) Parents who buy Bratz dolls might think, "Hey, it's just a toy," but many child psychologists say that Bratz dolls send the wrong message and can negatively impact a developing girl's identity and values. (6) Many video games and music videos show damaging images of women. (7) Because Bratz accessories include items like a "party plane," drinks that look like cocktails, and jewelry with slivers of real diamond, critics maintain that these dolls glorify a lifestyle of partying and materialism while undermining the importance of education and achievement.

Some parents claim that Bratz dolls expose children to adult sexuality too soon. What do you think?

● What is the number of the topic sentence in this paragraph?

_____

● Which sentence in the paragraph does not clearly relate to the topic sentence?

_____

This paragraph also lacks unity:

> (1) Quitting smoking was very difficult for me. (2) When I was thirteen, my friend Janice and I took up smoking because we thought it would make us look cool. (3) We practiced smoking in front of a mirror, striking poses with our cigarettes. (4) Even though we often were seized with violent fits of coughing, we thought we seemed grown up and sophisticated. (5) Gradually, I began to smoke not just to appear worldly but also to calm myself when I felt stressed. (6) I smoked to give myself confidence on dates and to feel less anxious before taking tests at school. (7) Reading, talking on the phone, and driving all became reasons to light up. (8) Soon, I was smoking all the time.

● Here the topic sentence itself, sentence 1, does not relate to the rest of the paragraph. The main idea in sentence 1, that quitting smoking was difficult, is not developed by the other sentences. Since the rest of the paragraph *is* unified, a more appropriate topic sentence might read, *As a teenager, I developed the bad habit of smoking.*

_____

* For more work on revising, see Chapter 24, "Putting Your Revision Skills to Work."

PRACTICE 12

Check the following paragraphs for unity. If a paragraph has unity, write *U* in the blank. If not, write the number of the sentence that does not belong in the paragraph.

Paragraph 1

_____ (1) During the sweltering Miami summer of 1965, a worried football coach helped create the world's most popular sports drink. (2) The coach asked University of Florida scientist Tom Cade why so many players got sick in the heat, losing up to 18 pounds in one game. (3) Cade knew the athletes were losing vital water and minerals, so he mixed salt and potassium into a balancing drink. (4) After players spit out the first, foul-tasting samples, Cade's wife suggested adding lemon juice and sweetener. (5) The rest is history. (6) Sipping the new beverage, the Florida Gators stopped wilting and roared into a winning streak. (7) The new drink was named in their honor. (8) Other Florida teams are the Hurricanes and the Seminoles. (9) Today 8 million bottles of Gatorade are consumed daily.

Paragraph 2

_____ (1) Technology enables people like the famous physicist Dr. Stephen Hawking to continue working despite serious physical disabilities. (2) For more than 45 years, Dr. Hawking has lived with Lou Gehrig's disease, which attacks the muscles, but his brilliant mind works perfectly. (3) He can no longer walk, speak, or feed himself. (4) Nevertheless, a high-tech wheelchair with computer attachments allows him to continue his research and stay in touch with friends and colleagues around the world. (5) His computer is hooked up full-time to the Internet. (6) To speak, he chooses words displayed on the computer screen, and then an electronic voice machine pronounces each word. (7) A pressure-sensitive joystick even lets Dr. Hawking make his way through traffic. (8) In his home, infrared remote controls operate doors, lights, and his personal entertainment center. (9) He has three children with his first wife, Jane, and one grandchild. (10) Dr. Hawking continues to search for new ways to overcome his problems through technology.

Paragraph 3

_____ (1) Across the country, thousands of college students and others are attending or performing poetry at "poetry slams." (2) A poetry slam is a competitive event in which participants perform one original poem before an audience. (3) With words, rhymes, and dramatic skill as their only tools, these fast-talking bards have just three minutes to win over the audience. (4) After each performance, judges selected from the audience give a numerical score, usually from 1 to 10. (5) Gymnastics competitions are judged using a similar ten-point scoring system. (6) Although most slammers would love to win first prize, they say that poetry slams also allow them to express their deepest thoughts, boost self-esteem, hone their English skills, and connect with a community of people who "speak from the heart." (7) Poetry slams are gaining popularity as schools, arts organizations, and groups of young writers start poetry clubs or sponsor contests. (8) Now, as online videos of the winning performances reveal the power of poetry slams, the excitement has spread worldwide.

EXPLORING ONLINE

To listen to winning poets, go to **http://www.youtube.com** and search "national poetry slam winners." Would you like to attend or perform at a poetry slam? Why or why not? What do you think is the reason so many people attend slams?

Revising with Peer Feedback

Sometimes you may wish to show or read your first draft to a respected friend, asking questions like these:

Peer Feedback Sheet

To _____   From _____   Date _____

1. What I like about this piece of writing is _____

   _____

2. Your main point seems to be _____

   _____

3. These particular words or lines struck me as powerful:

   Words or lines   I like them because

   _____   _____

   _____   _____

   _____   _____

4. Some things aren't clear to me. These lines or parts could be improved (meaning not clear, supporting points missing, order seems mixed up, writing not lively):

   Lines or parts   Need improving because

   _____   _____

   _____   _____

   _____   _____

5. The one change you could make that would make the biggest improvement

   in this piece of writing is _____

   _____

   _____

● Ask this person to give you an honest response, *not* to rewrite your work. You might want to ask your own specific questions or to modify the Peer Feedback Sheet.

Writing the Final Draft

When you are satisfied with your revisions, recopy your paper or print a fresh copy. If you are writing in class, the second draft will usually be the last one. Be sure to include all your corrections, writing neatly and legibly.

The first draft of the paragraph about Pete, showing the writer's changes, and the revised, final draft follow. Compare them.

First Draft with Revisions

Pete's sloppiness is a terrible habit. He lives by him-

carpeted

self in a <u>small</u> apartment with dirty clothes, books, and

Add details to show his sloppiness!

how small?—better word needed

candy wrappers. Stacks of papers cover the chair seats.

bake

Socks ~~are~~ on the lampshades. When Pete makes a date or

an appointment, he may jot down the time and place on a

tucked into a pocket and

scrap of paper that is soon forgotten, or—more likely—he

As a result,

doesn't jot down the information at all. Pete often arrives

Show consequences

late, or he completely forgets to appear. His grades have

because

suffered, too, few instructors will put up with a student

Add more details—better support

who arrives out of breath and whose <u>messy</u> papers arrive

punctuated with coffee stains and melted M&Ms.

(late of course) ~~with stains on them~~. Pete's sloppiness

This repeats t.s. Better conclusion needed.

<u>really is a terrible habit.</u>

Final Draft

Pete's sloppiness is a terrible habit. He lives by himself in a one-room apartment carpeted with dirty clothes, books, and crumpled candy wrappers. Stacks of papers cover the chair seats. Socks bake on the lampshades. When Pete makes a date or an appointment, he may jot down the time and place on a scrap of paper that is soon tucked into a pocket and forgotten, or—more likely—he doesn't jot down the information at all. As a result, Pete often arrives late, or he completely forgets to appear. His grades have suffered, too, because few instructors will put up with a student who arrives out of breath ten minutes after the class has begun and whose wrinkled, carelessly scrawled papers arrive (late, of course) punctuated with coffee stains and melted M&Ms. The less Pete controls his sloppiness, the more it seems to control him.

- Note that the paragraph contains good support—specific facts, details, and examples that explain the topic sentence.

- Note that the paragraph has unity—every idea relates to the topic sentence.

- Note that the final sentence provides a brief conclusion, so that the paragraph *feels finished*.

Proofreading

Whether you write by hand or on the computer, be sure to **proofread** your final draft carefully for grammar and spelling errors. Pointing to each word as you read it will help you catch errors or words you might have left out, especially small words like *to*, *the*, or *a*. If you are unsure of the spelling of a word, consult a dictionary and run spell checker if you work on a computer.* Make neat corrections in pen or print a corrected copy of your paper. Chapter 39, "Putting Your Proofreading Skills to Work," and all of Units 6 and 7 in this book are devoted to improving your proofreading skills.

PRACTICE 13

Now read the first draft of your paragraph with a critical eye. Revise and rewrite it, checking especially for a clear topic sentence, strong support, and unity.

PRACTICE 14

Exchange *revised* paragraphs with a classmate. Ask specific questions or use the Peer Feedback Sheet displayed earlier.

When you *give* feedback, try to be as honest and specific as possible; saying a paper is "good," "nice," or "bad" doesn't really help the writer. When you *receive* feedback, think over your classmate's responses; do they ring true?

Now *revise* a second time, with the aim of writing a fine paragraph. Proofread carefully for grammar errors, spelling errors, and omitted words.

WRITING ASSIGNMENTS

The assignments that follow will give you practice in writing basic paragraphs. In each, aim for (1) a topic sentence with a clear controlling idea and (2) a body that fully supports and develops the topic sentence.

Remember to **narrow the topic, write the topic sentence, freewrite** or **brainstorm**, and **select** and **arrange ideas** in a plan or an outline before you write. Rethink and **revise** as necessary before composing the final version of the paragraph. As you work, refer to the checklist at the end of this chapter.

Paragraph 1

Discuss an important day in your life

Think back to a day when you learned something important. In the topic sentence, tell what you learned. Freewrite or brainstorm to gather ideas. Then

---

* For tips and cautions on using a computer spell checker, see Chapter 39, Part B.

describe the lesson in detail, including only the most important steps or events in the learning process. Conclude with an insight.

Paragraph 2

Describe your ideal job

Decide on the job for which you are best suited and, in your topic sentence, tell what this job is. Then describe the qualities of this job that make it ideal. Include information about the pay, benefits, intangible rewards, working conditions, and duties this perfect job would offer you. Explain how each quality you describe matches your needs and desires. Revise your work, checking for support and unity.

Paragraph 3

Interview a classmate about an achievement

Write about a time when your classmate achieved something important, like winning an award for a musical performance, getting an A in a difficult course, or helping a friend through a hard time. To gather interesting facts and details, ask your classmate questions like these and take notes: *Is there one accomplishment of which you are very proud? Why was this achievement so important?* Keep asking questions until you feel you can give the reader a vivid sense of your classmate's triumph. In your first sentence, state the person's achievement—for instance, *Being accepted into the honors program improved Gabe's self-esteem.* Then explain specifically why the achievement was so meaningful.

Paragraph 4

Tell a story of justice or injustice

Think about someone you know or heard about in news reports who did or did *not* get what he or she deserved. For example, you may have an athletic family member whose years of practice and hard work were rewarded with a college scholarship. On the other hand, you might have read about a person who spent time in prison for a crime he or she did not commit, thus losing precious years before being released. Make sure that you state your main idea and point of view clearly in a topic sentence. Then, use vivid supporting details to tell this person's story.

Paragraph 5

Discuss a quotation

Look through the quotations in the Quotation Bank before the indexes in this book. Pick a quotation you strongly agree or disagree with. In your topic sentence, state how you feel about the quotation. Then explain why you feel the way you do, giving examples from your own experience to support or contradict the quotation. Make sure your reader knows exactly how you feel.

Paragraph 6

Give advice to busy working parents

Help busy working parents by giving them some advice that will make their lives easier. You might explain how to prepare quick and easy meals, how to know a good day care when you see one, how to reduce morning chaos, or how to control your anger when a child misbehaves. Use humor if you wish. State your controlling idea in the topic sentence and support this idea fully with details, explanations, and examples.

Checklist

The Process of Writing Basic Paragraphs

Refer to this checklist as you write a basic paragraph.

- [ ] 1. Narrow the topic in light of your audience and purpose.
- [ ] 2. Write a topic sentence that has a clear controlling idea and is a complete sentence. If you have trouble, freewrite or brainstorm first; then narrow the topic and write the topic sentence.
- [ ] 3. Freewrite or brainstorm, generating facts, details, and examples to develop your topic sentence.
- [ ] 4. Select and drop ideas for the body of the paragraph.
- [ ] 5. Arrange ideas in a plan or an outline, deciding which ideas will come first, which will come second, and so forth.
- [ ] 6. Write the best first draft you can.
- [ ] 7. Conclude. Don't just leave the paragraph hanging.
- [ ] 8. Revise as necessary, checking your paragraph for support and unity.
- [ ] 9. Proofread for grammar and spelling errors.

EXPLORING ONLINE

http://owl.english.purdue.edu/owl/resource/606/01/

Quick review of paragraph writing

http://owl.english.purdue.edu/owl/resource/561/01

Good proofreading strategies to improve your writing and your grade

CourseMate for *Evergreen*

Visit *Evergreen* CourseMate for more practices and quizzes, videos to accompany the readings, career and job-search resources, ESL help, and live links to every Exploring Online in the book.

CHAPTER **4**

Achieving Coherence

A: Coherence Through Order

B: Coherence Through Related Sentences

Every composition should have **coherence**. A paragraph *coheres*—holds together—when the sentences are arranged in a clear, logical *order* and when the sentences are *related* like links in a chain.

A. Coherence Through Order

An orderly presentation of ideas within the paragraph is easier to follow and more pleasant to read than a jumble. *After* jotting down ideas but *before* writing the paragraph, the writer should decide which ideas to discuss first, which second, which third, and so on, according to a logical order.

There are many possible orders, depending on the subject and the writer's purpose. This section will explain three basic ways of ordering ideas: **time order, space order**, and **order of importance**.

Time Order

One of the most common methods of ordering sentences in a paragraph is through **time**, or **chronological, order**, which moves from present to past or from past to present. Most stories, histories, and instructions follow the logical order of time.* The following paragraph employs time order:

(1) I love to talk, but I never thought twice about listening. (2) So when my College Skills instructor said that becoming an active listener improves academic performance, I thought, "Whatever." (3) Now I believe that working on my listening skills has raised my GPA. (4) *First*, I arrive in the classroom early and pick a seat near the front of the room; that way, windows, latecomers, and jokers won't distract me. (5) *Then* I take out my paper, pen, and textbook. I like to converse with my classmates during these moments, but I have learned to

---

* For work on narrative paragraphs, see Chapter 6, "Narration," and for work on process paragraphs, see Chapter 8, "Process."

politely end these conversations as soon as the instructor comes in. (6) *Next*, I stop slouching, sit up in my chair, and look straight at the instructor. (7) Doing this signals my brain that it's time to learn. (8) *As class proceeds*, I participate and keep my mind focused on the lesson. (9) If the instructor lectures, I take notes. (10) If the instructor leads a discussion, I think about what is being said, answer questions, and contribute my comments. (11) *Finally*, I resist the urge to have side conversations, text, make calls, or do homework during class. (12) Becoming an active listener takes some effort, especially if, like me, you have to break bad habits, but you'll be amazed at how much more you'll remember.

—Tony Aguera, Student

- The steps or actions in this paragraph are clearly arranged in the order of time. They are presented as they happen, *chronologically*.

- Throughout the paragraph, key words like *first, then, next, as class proceeds*, and *finally* emphasize time order and guide the reader from action to action.

Careful use of time order helps prevent confusing writing like this: *Oops, I forgot to mention that before the instructor comes in, I arrange my paper, pen, and book.*

Occasionally, when the sentences in a paragraph follow a very clear time order, the topic sentence is only implied, not stated directly, as in this example:

(1) In 1905, a poor washerwoman with a homemade hair product started a business—with $1.50! (2) In just five years, Madame C. J. Walker established offices and manufacturing centers in Denver, Pittsburgh, and Indianapolis. (3) The Madame C. J. Walker Manufacturing Company specialized in hair supplies, but Madame Walker specialized in independence for herself and for others. (4) Although she was not formally educated, she developed an international sales force, teaching her African American agents the most sophisticated business skills. (5) Eight years after starting her business, Madame Walker was the first African American woman to become a self-made millionaire. (6) In addition, she drew thousands of former farm and domestic workers into the business world. (7) One of her most original ideas was to establish "Walker Clubs," and she awarded cash prizes to the clubs with the most educational and philanthropic projects in their African American communities. (8) When she died in 1919, Madame Walker left two-thirds of her fortune to schools and charities. (9) Another of her contributions also lived on. (10) After her death, many of her former employees used their experience to start businesses throughout the United States and the Caribbean.

- Time order gives coherence to this paragraph. Sentence 1 tells us about the beginning of Madame Walker's career as a businessperson. However, it does not express the main idea of the entire paragraph.

- What is the implied topic sentence or main idea developed by the paragraph?

_____

_____

_____

- The implied topic sentence or main idea of the paragraph might read, *With nothing but natural business ability and vision, Madame C. J. Walker achieved history-making success for herself and others.*

- Because the writer arranges the paragraph in chronological order, the reader can easily follow the order of events in Madame Walker's life. What words and phrases indicate time order? Underline them and list them here:

_____

_____

_____

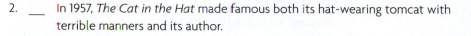

PRACTICE 1

Arrange each set of sentences in logical time order, numbering the sentences 1, 2, 3, and so on, as if you were preparing to write a paragraph. Underline any words and phrases, like *first, next,* and *in 1692,* that give time clues.

1. ___ First, lie on your back with your knees comfortably bent.

   ___ Next, put your hands at your sides or fold them over your chest.

   ___ Finally, focus on your abs and do your crunches slowly, three sets of ten each.

   ___ Lift your torso until the shoulder blades leave the floor, and then slowly roll back down.

   ___ The perfect crunch should be done slowly and deliberately, working the whole abdominal wall.

2. ___ In 1957, *The Cat in the Hat* made famous both its hat-wearing tomcat with terrible manners and its author.

   ___ Before he died in 1991, Dr. Seuss inspired millions to love language with such creations as the Grinch, Nerds, Wockets, Bar-ba-loots, bunches of Hunches, and fox in sox.

   ___ *Green Eggs and Ham* came out in 1960 and told a memorable story, using only fifty-five different words.

   ___ In his long career, Theodor Geisel, better known as Dr. Seuss, wrote forty-six wildly imaginative children's books, now read all over the world.

   ___ His first book was rejected by 28 publishers, who found it "too strange for children."

   ___ In 1937, when it finally was published, readers loved the rhythmic march of tongue-twisting, invented words and the wacky characters.

3. ___ The official cleanup has ended, but residents and scientists say that the extent of damage from the worst oil spill in United States history is not yet known.

___ On April 20, 2010, an explosion rocked the offshore oil-rig *Deepwater Horizon*, setting off a massive effort to stop leaking oil from polluting the Gulf of Mexico.

___ For the next four months, scientists tried in vain to close the well and stop the destruction of fish, birds, plants, and a way of life on the Gulf Coast.

___ By September 19, experts finally sealed the oil well with a cement plug.

___ Two days after the explosion, the damaged rig sank five thousand feet underwater, making it much more difficult to reach the gushing pipe.

WRITING ASSIGNMENT 1

Use **time order** to give coherence to a paragraph. Choose one of the following two topics. Compose a topic sentence, freewrite or brainstorm to generate ideas, and then arrange your ideas *chronologically*. You may wish to use transitional words and phrases like these to guide the reader from point to point:*

first, second	before	soon	suddenly
then	during	when	moments later
next	after	while	finally

Paragraph 1

Narrate the first hour of your average day
Start with getting up in the morning and continue to describe what you do for that first hour. Record your activities, your conversations, if any, and possibly your moods as you go through this hour of the morning. As you revise, make sure that events clearly follow time order.

Paragraph 2

Record an unforgettable event
Choose a moment in sports or in some other activity that you vividly remember, either as a participant or as a spectator. In the topic sentence, tell in a general way what happened. (*It was the most exciting touchdown I have ever seen*, or *Ninety embarrassing seconds marked the end of my brief surfing career.*) Then record the experience, arranging details in time order.

Space Order

Another useful way to arrange ideas in writing is through **space order**—describing a person, a thing, or a place from top to bottom, from left to right, from foreground to background, and so on. Space order is often used in descriptive writing because it moves from detail to detail like a movie camera's eye:†

---

* For a more complete list of transitional expressions, see page 63.

† For more work on space order, see Chapter 7, "Description."

2. Describe the security measures protecting the original Declaration of Independence.

   _____

   ___ room's perimeter ringed with security cameras and motion sensors

   ___ two armed guards standing next to the bronze and marble shrine

   ___ the National Archives building in Washington, D.C.

   ___ parchment of document touched only by decay-preventing helium gas

   ___ bulletproof glass case

3. Describe a city scene. _____

   ___ dented trash cans in the alley

   ___ a bird riding the wind in blue sky

   ___ rusty metal fire escape zigzagging up from the ground

   ___ laundry flapping on a line near the eighth floor

   ___ glimpse of an old rooftop water tower

WRITING ASSIGNMENT 2

Use **space order** to give coherence to one of the following paragraphs. Compose a topic sentence, freewrite or brainstorm for more details, and then arrange them in space order. Use transitional words and phrases like these if you wish:*

on the left	above	next to
on the right	below	behind
in the middle	beside	farther out

Paragraph 1

Describe a memorable face
Describe the face of someone you know well, perhaps a friend, family member, or person you admire. Study the actual face of the person or visualize it vividly as you jot down the five or six most important or striking details. Then, before writing your paragraph, arrange these details according to space order—moving from left to right or from top to bottom.

Paragraph 2

Describe a possession
Choose one material object that you hold dear. As you examine or visualize it, brainstorm at least ten details that capture its essence. Now draft a topic sentence and choose your best details. Use space order to weave these details into sentences.

_____

* For a more complete list of transitional expressions, see page 63.

Order of Importance

Ideas in a paragraph can also be arranged in the **order of importance**. You may start with the most important idea and end with the least, or you may begin with the least important idea and build to a climax with the most important one.

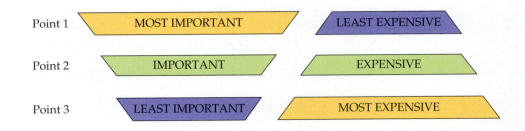

Point 1   MOST IMPORTANT   LEAST EXPENSIVE

Point 2   IMPORTANT   EXPENSIVE

Point 3   LEAST IMPORTANT   MOST EXPENSIVE

If you wish to persuade your reader with arguments or examples, beginning with the most important points impresses the reader with the force of your ideas and persuades him or her to continue reading.* On essay examinations and in business correspondence, be especially careful to begin with the most important idea. In those situations, the reader definitely wants your important points first.

Read the following paragraph and note the order of ideas:

(1) Louis Pasteur is revered as a great scientist for his three major discoveries. (2) Most important, this Frenchman created vaccines that have saved millions of human and animal lives. (3) The vaccines grew out of his discovery that weakened forms of a disease could help the person or animal build up antibodies that would prevent the disease. (4) The vaccines used today to protect children from serious illnesses owe their existence to Pasteur's work. (5) Almost as important was Pasteur's brilliant idea that tiny living beings, not chemical reactions, spoiled beverages. (6) He developed a process, pasteurization, that keeps milk, wine, vinegar, and beer from spoiling. (7) Finally, Pasteur found ways to stop a silkworm disease that threatened to ruin France's profitable silk industry. (8) Many medical researchers regard him as "the father of modern medicine."

● The ideas in this paragraph are explained in the **order of importance**, from the *most important to the least important*:

What was Pasteur's most important discovery? _____

_____

What was his next most important discovery? _____

_____

What was his least important one? _____

_____

● Note how the words *most important, almost as important,* and *finally* guide the reader from one idea to another.

———
* See Chapter 5, "Illustration," and Chapter 13, "Persuasion."

Sometimes, if you wish to add drama and surprise to your paragraphs, you may want to begin with the least important idea and build toward a climax by saving the most important idea for last. This kind of order can help counter the tendency of some writers to state the most important idea first and then let the rest of the paragraph dwindle away.

Read the following paragraph and note the order of ideas:

(1) Called a genius by some and a publicity seeker by others, Salvador Dali was one of the best-known painters of the twentieth century. (2) Dali was a *surrealist*—that is, he painted scenes in bizarre or *surreal* ways, trying to express inner realities and shake up the viewer. (3) Recently, shows of his work at major museums have created new Dali admirers, who give at least three reasons for his lasting importance. (4) First, Dali was a larger-than-life creative force—an artist, sculptor, writer, filmmaker, adviser to fashion designers, and international party animal. (5) Even more important, his work strongly influenced younger painters like Andy Warhol, whose brightly colored portraits of Marilyn Monroe and Campbell's Soup cans are known worldwide. (6) But the premiere reason for Dali's importance is that his dreamlike paintings and surreal combinations of images changed people's idea of art. (7) His canvases, like *The Persistence of Memory*, capture unconscious states. Dali continues to inspire, anger, and amuse viewers from the grave, which no doubt would please him.

- The reasons for Dali's importance that develop this paragraph are discussed in the **order of importance**: *from the least to the most important.*
- The fact that Dali influenced younger painters is more important than his range of talents. However, the fact that his work changed the world's idea of art is the most important of all.
- Transitional words like *first, even more important*, and *premiere reason* help the reader follow clearly from one reason to the next.

The Persistence of Memory by Salvador Dali

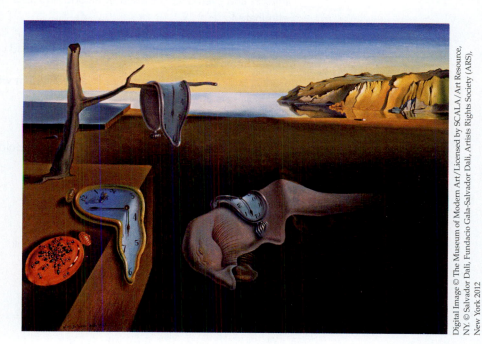

EXPLORING ONLINE

http://www.virtualdali.com/

On this enjoyable site, you can learn more about Dali and view many of his works. Choose one painting; write three things about it that command your attention, arrange them in order of importance, and write a paragraph.

PRACTICE 4

Arrange the ideas that develop each topic sentence in their **order of importance**, numbering them *1, 2, 3,* and so on. *Begin with the most important* (or largest, most severe, most surprising) and continue to the *least* important. Or reverse the order if you think that the paragraph would be more dramatic by beginning with the *least* important ideas and building toward a climax, with the most important last.

1. Cynthia Lopez's first year of college brought many unexpected expenses.

   ___ Her English professor wanted her to own a college dictionary.

   ___ All those papers to write made a $500 laptop computer a necessity.

   ___ She had to spend $235 for textbooks.

   ___ Her solid geometry class required various colored pencils and felt-tip pens.

2. Alcoholic beverages should not be sold at sporting events.

   ___ Injuries and even deaths caused by alcohol-induced crowd violence would be eliminated.

   ___ Fans could save money by buying soft drinks instead of beer.

   ___ Games and matches would be much more pleasant without the yelling, swearing, and rudeness often caused by alcohol.

3. The apartment needed work before the new tenants could move in.

   ___ The handles on the kitchen cabinets were loose.

   ___ Every room needed plastering and painting.

   ___ Grime marred the appearance of the bathroom sink.

   ___ Two closet doors hung off the hinges.

WRITING ASSIGNMENT 3

Use **order of importance** to give coherence to one of the paragraphs that follow. Use transitional words and phrases like these to guide the reader along:*

first	even more	another
next	last	least of all
above all	especially	most of all

Paragraph 1

Describe a day in which everything went right (or wrong)
Freewrite or brainstorm to generate ideas. Choose three or four of the day's best (or worst) events and write a paragraph in which you present them in order of importance—either from the most to the least important, or from the least to the most important.

Paragraph 2

Persuade someone to attend your college
Choose a person you know—a friend, relative, or co-worker—and write a paragraph to convince that person to enroll in classes at your college. Write your topic sentence and generate ideas; choose three to five reasons to use to convince your reader. Arrange these reasons according to their order of importance—either from the most to the least important or from the least to the most important.

B. Coherence Through Related Sentences

In addition to arranging ideas in a logical order, the writer can ensure paragraph coherence by linking one sentence to the next. This section will present four basic ways to link sentences: **repetition of important words, substitution of pronouns, substitution of synonyms,** and **transitional expressions**.

Repetition of Important Words and Pronouns

Link sentences within a paragraph by *repeating important words and ideas*:

> (1) An Amber Alert is a notice to the general public that a child has been kidnapped. (2) This notification system was named after Amber Hagerman, a nine-year-old girl abducted from her neighborhood and found murdered a few days later. (3) The term *Amber Alert* is also an acronym for "America's Missing Broadcast Emergency Response." (4) The goal of an Amber Alert is to collect and spread information about the abduction with utmost speed, thus increasing the chances of finding the child alive. (5) First, police confirm that a child is missing and race to collect descriptive details about the child, the suspected abductor, and the suspect's vehicle. (6) Then broadcasts on television, radio, the Internet, and electronic highway signs spread these details and urge people to report any sightings or clues immediately. (7) To date, the program has saved 540 young lives.

* For a more complete list of transitional expressions, see page 63.

- What important words are repeated in this paragraph?

- The words *Amber Alert* appear three times, in sentences 1, 3, and 4. The word *child* appears four times, in sentences 1, 4, and 5. The word *abducted* appears in sentence 2, *abduction* in sentence 4, and *abductor* in sentence 5.

- Repetition of these key words helps the reader follow from sentence to sentence as these terms are defined or the relationships between them are explained.

Although repetition of important words can be effective, it can also become boring if overused.* To avoid *unnecessary* repetition, substitute *pronouns* for words already mentioned in the paragraph, as this author does:

(1) Paul Revere's ride to warn of a British attack is the stuff of legend, yet few have heard of Sybil Ludington. (2) This courageous sixteen-year-old and *her* horse Star also rode through the night, saving thousands of lives. (3) Early one evening in April, 1777, *her* father, Colonel Ludington, was warned by a messenger that Danbury, Connecticut, was burning and the British were pushing inland to attack. (4) When the messenger said *he* was too exhausted to ride on, the teenager volunteered, riding 40 miles at breakneck speed through Putnam County, New York, and rousing 400 militiamen from *their* beds.

- The use of pronouns in this paragraph avoids unnecessary repetition. The pronoun *her* in sentences 2 and 3 refers to the antecedent *this courageous sixteen-year-old*.

- In sentence 4, the pronouns *he* and *their* give further coherence to the paragraph by referring to what antecedents? _____ and _____

Use pronoun substitution together with the repetition of important words for a smooth presentation of ideas.

PRACTICE 5

What important words are repeated in the following paragraph? Underline them. Circle any pronouns that replace them. Notice the varied pattern of repetitions and pronoun replacements.

I have always considered my father a very intelligent person. His intelligence is not

the type usually tested in schools; perhaps he would have done well on such tests,

but the fact is that he never finished high school. Rather, my father's intelligence is his

ability to solve problems creatively as they arise. Once when I was very young, we were

_____

* For practice in eliminating wordiness (repetition of unimportant words), see Chapter 23, "Revising for Language Awareness," Part B.

† For more work on pronouns and antecedents, see Chapter 33, "Pronouns," Parts A, B, and C.

driving through the desert at night when the oil line broke. My father improvised a light,

squeezed under the car, found the break, and managed to whittle a connection to join the

two severed pieces of tubing; then he added more oil and drove us over a hundred miles

to the nearest town. Such intelligent solutions to unforeseen problems were typical of

him. In fact, my father's brand of brains—accurate insight, followed by creative action—is

the kind of intelligence that I admire and most aspire to.

WRITING ASSIGNMENT 4

Paragraph 1

Explain success
How do you measure *success*? By the money you make, the number or quality of friends you have? Freewrite or brainstorm for ideas. Then answer this question in a thoughtful paragraph. Give the paragraph coherence by repeating important words and using pronouns.

Paragraph 2

Discuss a public figure
Choose a public figure whom you admire—from the arts, politics, media, or sports—and write a paragraph discussing *one quality* that makes that person special. Name the person in your topic sentence. Vary repetition of the person's name with pronouns to give the paragraph coherence.

Synonyms and Substitutions

When you do not wish to repeat a word or use a pronoun, give coherence to your paragraph with a **synonym** or **substitution**. **Synonyms** are two or more words that mean nearly the same thing. For instance, if you do not wish to repeat the word *car*, you might use the synonym *automobile* or *vehicle*. If you are describing a *sky* and have already used the word *bright*, try the synonym *radiant*.

Or instead of a synonym, **substitute** other words that describe the subject. If you are writing about Albert Pujols, for example, refer to him as *this powerful slugger* or *this versatile athlete*. Such substitutions provide a change from constant repetition of a person's name or a single pronoun.*

Use synonyms and substitutions together with repetition and pronouns to give coherence to your writing:

(1) *The main building of Ellis Island* in New York Harbor reopened as a museum in 1990. (2) Millions of people visit *the huge brick and limestone structure* every year. (3) From 1892 to 1954, *this famous immigrant station* was the first stop for millions of newcomers to American shores. (4) In fact, the ancestors of nearly 40 percent of American citizens passed through *this building*. (5) Abandoned

* For more work on exact language, see Chapter 23, "Revising for Language Awareness," Part A.

in 1954, *it* deteriorated so badly that snow and rain fell on its floor. (6) Today visitors can follow the path of immigrants from a ferryboat, through the great arched doorway, into the room where the weary travelers left their baggage, up the stairway where doctors kept watch, and into the registry room. (7) Here questions were asked that determined if each immigrant could stay in the United States. (8) *This magnificent monument to the American people* contains exhibits that help individuals search for their own relatives' names and that tell the whole immigration history of the United States.

- This paragraph effectively mixes repetition, pronouns, and substitutions. The important word *building* is stated in sentence 1 and repeated in sentence 4.

- Sentence 5 substitutes the pronoun *it*.

- In sentence 2, *the huge brick and limestone structure* is substituted for *building*, and a second substitution, *this famous immigrant station*, occurs in sentence 3. Sentence 8 refers to the building as *this magnificent monument to the American people* and concludes the paragraph.

EXPLORING ONLINE

http://www.ellisisland.org/genealogy/ellis_island.asp

This site has links to Ellis Island immigration stories and records; however, your name or a family story might be fine writing topics, wherever you are from.

To find synonyms, check a **dictionary**. For instance, the entry for *smart* might list *clever, witty, intelligent*. An even better source of synonyms is the **thesaurus**, a book of synonyms. For example, if you are describing a city street and cannot think of other words meaning "noisy," look in the thesaurus. The number of choices will amaze you.

PRACTICE 6

Read each paragraph carefully. Then write on the lines any synonyms and substitutions that the writer has used to replace the word(s) in italics.

Paragraph 1

Quick thinking and creativity led fitness instructor Alberto Perez to invent *a popular workout routine* called Zumba. When Perez forgot the cassette tapes for his aerobics class in Cali, Colombia, he grabbed a few Latin music tapes from his car and taught the class some dance moves. This was the birth of Zumba, local slang for "fast moving." The rapid-fire exercise regimen combines steps from samba, salsa, and tango with aerobics and belly dance. Zumba quickly spread around the globe, offering an enjoyable way to lose weight or get in shape. The fitness craze, with its slogan "Ditch the workout, join the party," has even sparked a clothing line and video games.

A popular workout routine is also referred to as _____ and

_____.

Paragraph 2

   Lori Arviso Alvord, M.D., spent her childhood playing on the red mesas of a New Mexico Indian reservation. Later, while training to become the first Navajo woman surgeon, she encountered a very different world, the sterilized steel-and-chrome environment of the modern hospital. There, as she broke her culture's taboos against touching the dead and removing parts of the body, she felt disconnected from her Native American heritage. Yet even as the skilled doctor used the latest medical technology to repair injuries and remove tumors, she felt that something important was missing. Returning to her roots to search for answers, she realized that scientific medicine alone cannot restore the harmony among body, mind, and spirit the Navajos call "walking in beauty." This pioneering healer resolved to integrate her culture's ancient healing traditions with high-tech procedures. Her skill with a scalpel begins a patient's healing process, but her blend of healing ceremonies and the involvement of families and neighbors restores the balance of good health.

Lori Arviso Alvord, M.D., is also referred to as _____,

_____, and _____.

Dr. Lori Alvord, surgeon, associate dean, and author, is featured in this ad for the American Indian College Fund. Why does the ad ask, "Have you ever seen a real Indian?"

HAVE YOU EVER SEEN A REAL INDIAN?

AMERICAN INDIAN COLLEGE FUND ◊
EDUCATION IS STRENGTH

Courtesy of American Indian College Fund

PRACTICE 7

Give coherence to the following paragraphs by thinking of appropriate synonyms or substitutions for the words in italics. Then write them in the blanks.

Paragraph 1

J.K. Rowling was not always a multi-millionaire. In fact, before the success of her first book, *Harry Potter and the Sorcerer's Stone*, the *best-selling author* endured many hardships. She began writing when her mother was in the final stages of multiple sclerosis. Discovering a gift for writing, the _____ used her grief to deepen her narrative about a boy wizard. After the birth of her daughter, Rowling quit her teaching job to write full time, living on public assistance. When the manuscript was finished, she sent it to twelve different publishers. Unable to foresee the global appeal of Harry Potter, all twelve rejected it. Finally, after a glowing review from the eight-year-old daughter of a publishing company executive, the _____ could at last share her imaginative tales with readers. By the time her last book was released in 2007, the franchise had made over fifteen billion dollars. In just over a decade, J.K. Rowling went from being a struggling mother to a _____.

Paragraph 2

Although *sodas* are hugely popular, experts say that drinking them can have harmful health effects. These _____ are full of high-fructose corn syrup, which contributes to diabetes and high blood pressure. Because they contain sugar but no vitamins, minerals, fiber, or nutrients of any kind, they also contribute to obesity. Surprisingly, diet _____ are not the answer; for reasons that experts don't entirely understand, they actually seem to make many people gain weight. Other research shows that the phosphorus in _____ promotes bone loss, and the acid hastens tooth decay. For all these reasons, many schools have banned or restricted the sale of _____ to children, who too often reach for a pop-top can instead of a healthier choice like milk, juice, or water. As more schools put limits on what children can drink, the soda companies are busy marketing "vitamin water" and fruit juice to keep up with the trend.

WRITING ASSIGNMENT 5

As you do the following assignments, try to achieve paragraph coherence by using repetition, pronouns, synonyms, and substitutions.

Paragraph 1

Discuss your favorite form of relaxation

Write about what you like to do when you have free time. Do you like to get together with friends? Do you like to go to a movie or to some sporting event? Or do you prefer to spend your time alone, perhaps listening to music, reading, or going fishing? Whatever your favorite free-time activity, name it in your topic sentence. Be sure to tell what makes your activity *relaxing*. Then give your paragraph coherence by using pronouns and synonyms such as *take it easy*, *unwind*, and *feel free*.

Paragraph 2

Describe your ideal mate

Decide on three or four crucial qualities that your ideal husband, wife, or friend would possess, and write a paragraph describing this extraordinary person. Use repetition, pronouns, and word substitutions to give coherence to the paragraph. For example, *My ideal husband … he … my companion.*

Transitional Expressions

Skill in using transitional expressions is vital to coherent writing. **Transitional expressions** are words and phrases that point out the exact relation between one idea and another, one sentence and another. Words like *therefore, however, for example,* and *finally* are signals that guide the reader from sentence to sentence. Without them, even orderly and well-written paragraphs can be confusing and hard to follow.

The transitional expressions in this paragraph are italicized:

> (1) Zoos in the past often contributed to the disappearance of animal populations. (2) Animals were cheap, and getting a new gorilla, tiger, or elephant was easier than providing the special diet and shelter needed to keep captive animals alive. (3) *Recently, however,* zoo directors have realized that if zoos themselves are to continue, they must help save many species now facing extinction. (4) *As a result,* some zoos have redefined themselves as places where endangered animals can be protected and even revived. (5) The San Diego Zoo and the National Zoo, in Washington, D.C., *for example,* have both successfully bred giant pandas, a rapidly disappearing species. (6) The births of such endangered-species babies make international news, and the public can follow the babies' progress on zoo websites and "animal cams." (7) If zoos continue such work, perhaps they can, like Noah's ark, save some of Earth's wonderful creatures from extinction.

- Each transitional expression in the previous paragraph links, in a precise way, the sentence in which it appears to the sentence before. The paragraph begins by explaining the destructive policies of zoos in the past.

- In sentence 3, two transitional expressions of contrast—*recently* (as opposed to the past) and *however*—introduce the idea that zoo policies have *changed*.

- The phrase *as a result* makes clear that sentence 4 is a *consequence* of events described in the previous sentence(s).

- In sentence 5, *for example* tells us that the National Zoo is *one particular illustration* of the previous general statement, and the San Diego Zoo is another.

Zoos in China and the United States are breeding pandas like this healthy six-month-old, thus helping to save this endangered species.

© AP Images / Eugene Hoshiko

EXPLORING ONLINE

On Google or another search engine, type the words, "endangered species, zoos."
Take notes on writing ideas, and bookmark websites that intrigue you.

As you write, use various transitional expressions, together with the other linking devices, to connect one sentence to the next. Well-chosen transitional words also help stress the purpose and order of the paragraph.

Particular groups of transitional expressions are further explained and demonstrated in each chapter of Unit 3. However, here is a combined partial list for handy reference as you write:

Transitional Expressions at a Glance

Purpose	Transitional Expressions
to add	also, as well, besides, beyond that, first (second, third, last, and so on), for one thing, furthermore, in addition, moreover, next, then, what is more
to compare	also, as well, equally, in the same way, likewise, similarly
to contrast	be that as it may, however, in contrast, nevertheless, on the contrary, on the other hand
to concede (a point)	certainly, granted that, of course, no doubt, to be sure
to emphasize	above all, especially, indeed, in fact, in particular, most important, surely
to illustrate	as a case in point, as an illustration, for example, for instance, in particular, one such, yet another
to place	above, below, beside, beyond, farther, here, inside, nearby, next to, on the far side, opposite, outside, to the east (south, and so on)
to qualify	perhaps, maybe
to give a reason or cause	as, because, for, since
to show a result or effect	and so, as a consequence, as a result, because of this, consequently, for this reason, hence, so, therefore, thus
to summarize	all in all, finally, in brief, in other words, lastly, on the whole, to conclude, to sum up
to place in time	after a while, afterward, at last, at present, briefly, currently, eventually, finally, first (second, and so on), gradually, immediately, in the future, later, meanwhile, next, now, recently, soon, suddenly, then

PRACTICE 8

Carefully determine the exact relationship between the sentences in each pair below. Then choose a transitional expression from the list that clearly expresses this relationship and write it in the blank. Pay attention to punctuation and capitalize the first word of every sentence.*

1. No one inquired about the money found in the lobby. _____, it was given

   to charity.

2. First, cut off the outer, fibrous husk of the coconut. _____, poke a hole

   through one of the dark "eyes" and sip the milk through a straw.

3. The English Department office is on the fifth floor. _____ to it is a small

   reading room.

---

* For practice using conjunctions to join ideas, see Chapter 27, "Coordination and Subordination."

4. Some mountains under the sea soar almost as high as those on land. One underwater mountain in the Pacific, _____, is only 500 feet shorter than Mount Everest.

5. All citizens should vote. Many do not, _____.

6. Mrs. Dalworth enjoys shopping in out-of-the-way thrift shops. _____, she loves bargaining with the vendors at outdoor flea markets.

7. In 1887, Native Americans owned nearly 138 million acres of land. By 1932, _____, 90 million of those acres were owned by whites.

8. Kansas corn towered over the fence. _____ the fence, a red tractor stood baking in the sun.

9. Most street crime occurs between 2 and 5 a.m. _____, do not go out alone during those hours.

10. Dr. Leff took great pride in his work at the clinic. _____, his long hours often left him exhausted.

11. George Washington Carver developed hundreds of uses for a single agricultural product, the peanut. _____, he created peanut butter, peanut cooking oil, and printing ink from this legume.

12. We waited in our seats for over an hour. _____ the lights dimmed, and the Fabulous String Band bounded on stage.

PRACTICE 9

Add **transitional expressions** to this essay to guide the reader smoothly from sentence to sentence. To do so, consider the relationship between sentences (shown in parentheses). Then write the transitional word or phrase that best expresses this relationship.

Oldest Child, Youngest Child—Does It Matter?

A number of studies show that birth order—whether a person is the first-born, middle, or last-born child in the family—can affect both personality and career choice. _____, first-borns carry the weight of their parents' expectations
(illustration)

and _____ are urged to be responsible and set a good example for their
(time)

younger siblings. _____ , they may develop leadership skills and a strong
(result)

motivation to achieve. Many eldest children _____ become leaders. High
(time)

percentages of U.S. presidents and CEOs, _____ , are first-borns.
(illustration)

Middle children, _____ , get less attention and applause in childhood.
(contrast)

_____ , they tend to become flexible and good at resolving conflicts.
(result)

_____ , some middle children become rebellious or creative as they make
(addition)

their place in the world. _____ , many choose careers as entrepreneurs,
(time)

negotiators, or businesspeople. _____ , later-born or last-born children,
(addition)

in order to compete with their older siblings, may become rule-breakers or family

clowns. Professionally, babies of the family tend to become musicians, adventurers,

and comedians. _____ , there are countless exceptions to these general
(conceding a point)

trends; _____ it is interesting to ponder the evidence that our birth order
(contrast)

_____ helps shape who we are.
(emphasis)

PRACTICE 10 — TEAMWORK: CRITICAL THINKING AND WRITING

In small groups, discuss what you learned about birth order and personality in
Practice 9. What is your place in the family? Do the typical traits apply to you? Take
notes for later writing while you describe the classic first-born, middle-born, or youngest
child; then apply these traits to yourself or someone you know well who fills that birth
spot. Is the portrait accurate? To learn more, visit **http://www.parents.com/baby/
development/social/birth-order-and-personality/**.

PRACTICE 11 — REVIEW

Most paragraphs achieve coherence through a variety of linking devices: repetition, pronouns,
substitutions, and transitional expressions. Read the following paragraphs with care, noting
the kinds of linking devices used by each writer. Answer the questions after each paragraph.

Paragraph 1

(1) The film *Super Size Me* explores the effects of America's fast food diet. (2) Director
Morgan Spurlock stars in this hilarious but shocking documentary, eating nothing but
fast food from McDonald's for thirty days. (3) Doctors assess his physical condition
before, during, and after the diet, which has such negative effects on his health that
they urge him to quit early. (4) Woven into this plot is crucial information about the fast
food industry, school lunch programs, and obesity. (5) This brilliant work is one to see.

—Jun Harada, *crazy4film.com*

1. What important words are repeated in sentences 1, 2, and 4? _____

2. In sentences 2 and 5, "the film *Super Size Me*" is referred to as _____

_____ and _____

Paragraph 2

(1) In the annals of great escapes, the flight by seventeen-year-old Lester Moreno Perez from Cuba to the United States surely must rank as one of the most imaginative. (2) At 8:30 on the night of Thursday, March 1, Lester crept along the beach in Varadero, a resort town on the north coast of Cuba. (3) Working quickly, he launched his sailboard—a surfboard equipped with a movable sail—into the shark-haunted waters off the Straits of Florida. (4) At first guided by the stars and later by the hazy glow from electric lights in towns beyond the horizon, Lester sailed with twenty-knot winds toward the Florida Keys, ninety miles away. (5) All night he balanced on the small board, steering through black waters. (6) Just past daybreak on Friday, Lester was sighted thirty miles south of Key West by the Korean crew of the freighter *Tina D.* (7) The boom on his tiny craft was broken. (8) The astonished sailors pulled him aboard, fed him chicken and rice, and finally radioed the U.S. Coast Guard.

—Adapted from Sam Moses, "A New Dawn," *Sports Illustrated,* April 23, 1990. Used with permission.

1. Underline the transitional expressions in this paragraph.

2. What *order* of ideas does the paragraph employ? _____

Cuban rafters attempting to reach the United States. What would you risk to live in freedom?

PRACTICE 12   **TEAMWORK: CRITICAL VIEWING AND WRITING**

In small groups, study the photograph of Cuban rafters trying to reach the United States (page 66). What do you think would drive them to risk their lives on such a flimsy, homemade raft in shark-filled seas? Are they running from or to something? Would anything make you take such a risk? What? What or whom would you bring with you?

Paragraph 3

   (1) *Phishing* is the term for tricking computer users into revealing sensitive information such as credit card or social security numbers. (2) A person who goes phishing first sets up a seemingly official website and e-mail address to pose as a legitimate individual or business. (3) Next, the phisher casts the bait. (4) He or she e-mails unsuspecting individuals, either threatening account suspension if a request for information is ignored or perhaps promising a funny or racy video. (5) When an unfortunate recipient takes the bait and sends back the information, the phisher can reel it in and use it to commit fraud or identity theft. (6) In recent years, social networking sites have become targets for phishing scams. (7) For example, a con artist might create a site that looks exactly like Facebook. (8) When victims log onto the dummy site, they unwittingly give their usernames, passwords, personal information, and entire address books to the waiting thief.

1. What important words are repeated in this paragraph? _____

2. What synonyms and pronouns are used for "a person who goes phishing"? _____

   _____

3. What transitional expressions are used in sentences 3 and 7? _____

EXPLORING ONLINE

http://www.powa.org/

For advice on ordering your ideas in the most powerful way, go to "Arrange" and click "Arranging and Ordering."

http://www.powa.org/

For work on transitional expressions, go to "Arrange" and click "Showing the Links."

CourseMate for *Evergreen*
www.cengage.com/devenglish/Fawcett/evergreen9e

Visit *Evergreen* CourseMate for more practices and quizzes,
videos to accompany the readings, career and job-search resources,
ESL help, and live links to every Exploring Online in the book.

Writers' Workshop

Discuss the Pressures of Living in Two Worlds

In this unit, you learned that most good paragraphs have a clear topic sentence, convincing support, and an order that makes sense. In your group or class, read this student's paragraph, aloud if possible. Underline any parts you find especially well written. Put a check next to anything that could be improved.

Young Immigrant Translators

This paper will discuss children as translators. When immigrant children become translators for their parents, this can change the normal relationship between parent and child. Many immigrant parents do not have the time or opportunity to develop their English skills, even though they know that speaking English is the most important part of surviving in the United States. When they need to understand or speak English, they often ask their school-age children for help. The children must act like little adults, helping their parents with all kinds of problems. They end up taking time away from school and their friends because they are responsible for everything related to English. For example, they might have to answer the phone, fill out forms, pay bills, or shop for groceries. Even in more serious situations, like medical or financial problems, the children might have to translate for the doctor or accountant. Eventually, some children can start to resent their parents for relying on them so much. Instead of turning to their parents for help with homework or personal worries, they might turn instead to friends or teachers who understand the culture better. Although most immigrant children know their parents love them and want a better life for them, the role reversal of being child translators can make them become adults too soon.

—Mandy Li, Student

1. How effective is this paragraph?

   _____ Clear topic sentence?   _____ Good supporting details?

   _____ Logical organization?   _____ Effective conclusion?

2. Which sentence, if any, is the topic sentence? Is sentence 1 as good as the rest of the paragraph? If not, what revision advice would you give the writer?

3. Does this student provide adequate support for her main idea? Why or why not?

4. Discuss your underlinings with the group or class. Which parts or ideas in this essay did you find most powerful? As specifically as you can, explain why. For example, the list of possible tasks a child translator must handle vividly supports the main idea of the paragraph.

5. Do you agree with Ms. Li that children being asked to translate for their parents makes children grow up too soon? Have you experienced or witnessed other situations in which children must become adults too soon? What are those situations?

6. Do you see any error patterns (one error made two or more times) that this student needs to watch out for?

 **GROUP WORK**

In your group or class, make a plan or outline of Ms. Li's paragraph. How many points does she use to support her topic sentence? How can a writer know whether a paragraph has good support or needs better support? List three ways. Did this paragraph make you think? How would you rate the ideas in this paragraph? Extremely interesting? Interesting? Not very interesting? Be prepared to explain your rating to the full class.

WRITING AND REVISING IDEAS

1. Discuss the ways in which you or someone you know has had to live in two different cultures or "worlds."

2. What is the most important tool for surviving in the United States, in your view?

Unit 3

Developing the Paragraph

CHAPTER **5**

Illustration

To **illustrate** is to explain a general statement by means of one or more specific examples.

Illustration makes what we say more vivid and more exact. Someone might say, "My math professor is always finding crazy ways to get our attention. Just yesterday, for example, he wore a high silk hat to class." The first sentence is a general statement about this professor's unusual ways of getting attention. The second sentence, however, gives a specific example of something he did that *clearly shows* what the writer means.

Writers often use illustration to develop a paragraph. They explain a general topic sentence with one, two, three, or more specific examples. Detailed and well-chosen examples add interest, liveliness, and power to your writing.

Topic Sentence

Here is the topic sentence of a paragraph that is later developed by examples:

> Great athletes do not reach the top by talent alone but by pushing themselves to the limit and beyond.

- The writer begins an illustration paragraph with a topic sentence that makes a general statement.
- This generalization may be obvious to the writer, but if he or she wishes to convince the reader, some specific examples would be helpful.

Paragraph and Plan

Here is the entire paragraph:

> Great athletes do not reach the top by talent alone but by pushing themselves to the limit and beyond. For instance, basketball superstar Lebron James keeps striving to improve. Branded the next Michael Jordan in high school and drafted

71

by the Cleveland Cavaliers, he propelled the Cavaliers to three NBA playoffs, led the Miami Heat to the NBA Championship in 2012, and later that year, won his second gold medal on a U.S. Olympic team. Even off-season, James perfects his agility, strength, and health routines, recently adding squats on a vibrating platform to activate more muscles. Another example is record-breaking swimmer Dara Torres. After winning nine medals at four Olympic Games and becoming a mother at age 39, Torres kept building power and speed with brutal daily workouts: 90 minutes each of swimming and strength training, plus two hours of stretching. At 41, the oldest female swimmer ever to compete in the Olympics, Dara scored three more silver medals. Few players in any sport, however, can match the work ethic of NFL quarterback Drew Brees, who suffered a nearly career-ending shoulder injury. During months of grueling rehabilitation, "Cool Brees" had to re-learn how to throw a football. When the New Orleans Saints took a chance by signing him, Brees trained harder, always the last off the practice field. Between seasons, he built strength, flexibility, and focus with three-hour workouts that ended when the coach threw playing cards in the air one at a time as Brees caught them one-handed. In 2010, four years after surgery, Brees led the Saints to a Super Bowl victory. Like many top athletes, he turned talent into greatness through sheer hard work.

● How many examples does the writer use to develop the topic sentence?

_____

● Who are they?

_____

41-year-old Dara Torres wins a 50-meter freestyle heat at the Olympic Games.

Before completing this illustration paragraph, the writer probably made an **outline** like this:

TOPIC SENTENCE: Great athletes do not reach the top by talent alone but by pushing themselves to the limit and beyond.

Example 1:   Lebron James
    —branded next Michael Jordan, drafted by Cavaliers
    —brought Cavs to the three NBA playoffs and Miami Heat to 2012 Championship
    —won gold medals on two U.S. Olympic teams
    —off-season, perfects agility, strength, and health routines
    —does squats on a vibrating platform

Example 2:   Dara Torres
    —won nine medals at four Olympic Games
    —brutal daily workouts: 90 minutes swimming, 90 minutes strength, two hours stretching

Example 3:   Drew Brees
    —gifted NFL quarterback with severe shoulder injury
    —months of rehab, relearned throwing a football
    —last one on the field after practice
    —between-season: strength, flexibility, focus, playing cards
    —led Saints to 2010 Super Bowl win

CONCLUSION: Like many top athletes, he turned talent into greatness through sheer hard work.

● Note that each example clearly relates to and supports the topic sentence.

Instead of using three or four examples to support the topic sentence, the writer may prefer instead to discuss one single example:

Dreams alone are not enough when it comes to creating the future. As professional life coach Diana Robinson says, "A dream is a goal without legs." And without legs, that goal is going nowhere. Making dreams come true requires planning and hard work. Gloria Gonzalez is an example. She chose the fashion design curriculum because she liked clothes, and people always admired her style. As she continues through college, however, she will need to master the nuts and bolts of the fashion business. Her abilities will be tested. Can she create under pressure, spot trends, meet tight deadlines, and work her way up? Perhaps she will learn that even brilliant fashion designer Yves Saint Laurent got his first big break, designing for Christian Dior, only after winning a major international design competition. Breaking into the fashion industry is challenging, but that doesn't mean Gloria should abandon her dream. Instead, she must find a reality-based path to help her turn that dream into goals.

—Adapted from Constance Staley, *Focus on College Success*

● What is the general statement?

_____

● What specific example does the writer give to support the general statement?

_____

The single example may also be a **narrative**,* a _story_ that illustrates the topic sentence:

> Aggressive drivers not only are stressed out and dangerous, but often they save no time getting where they want to go. Recently I was driving south from Oakland to San Jose. Traffic was heavy but moving. I noticed an extremely aggressive driver jumping lanes, speeding up, and slowing down. Clearly, he was in a hurry. For the most part, I remained in one lane for the entire forty-mile journey. I was listening to a new audiotape and daydreaming. I enjoyed the trip because driving gives me a chance to be alone. As I was exiting off the freeway, the aggressive driver crowded up behind me and raced on by. Without realizing it, I had arrived in San Jose ahead of him. All his weaving, rapid acceleration, and putting families at risk had earned him nothing except perhaps some high blood pressure and a great deal of wear and tear on his vehicle.
>
> —Adapted from Richard Carlson, _Don't Sweat the Small Stuff_

● What general statement does the aggressive driver story illustrate?

_____

_____

● Note that this narrative follows time order.†

Transitional Expressions

The simplest way to tell your reader that an example is going to follow is to say so: "_For instance_, Lebron James …" or "Gloria Gonzalez _is an example_." This partial list should help you vary your use of **transitional expressions** that introduce an illustration:

Transitional Expressions for Illustration	
for instance	another instance of
for example	another example of
an illustration of this	another illustration of
a case in point is	here are a few examples (illustrations, instances)
to illustrate	

● Be careful not to use more than two or three of these transitional expressions in a single paragraph.‡

---

* For more on narrative, see Chapter 6, "Narration," and Chapter 16, "Types of Essays," Part B.

† For more work on time order, see Chapter 4, "Achieving Coherence," Part A.

‡ For complete essays developed by illustration, see Chapter 16, Part A.

PRACTICE 1

Read each of the following paragraphs of illustration. Underline each topic sentence. Note in the margin how many examples are provided to illustrate each general statement.

Paragraph 1

Random acts of kindness are those little sweet or grand lovely things we do for no reason except that, momentarily, the best of our humanity has sprung…into full bloom. When you spontaneously give an old woman the bouquet of red carnations you had meant to take home to your own dinner table, when you give your lunch to the guitar-playing beggar who makes music at the corner between your two subway stops, when you anonymously put coins in someone else's parking meter because you see the red "Expired" medallion signaling to a meter maid—you are doing not what life requires of you, but what the best of your human soul invites you to do.

—Daphne Rose Kingma, *Random Acts of Kindness*

Paragraph 2

There are many quirky variations to lightning. A "bolt from the blue" occurs when a long horizontal flash suddenly turns toward the earth, many miles from the storm. "St. Elmo's Fire," often seen by sailors and mountain climbers, is a pale blue or green light caused by weak electrical discharges that cling to trees, airplanes, and ships' masts. "Pearl lightning" occurs when flashes are broken into segments. "Ball lightning" can be from an inch to several feet in diameter. Pearls and balls are often mistaken for flying saucers or UFOs, and many scientists believe they are only optical illusions.

—Reed McManus, *Sierra* magazine

PRACTICE 2

Each example in a paragraph of illustration must clearly relate to and support the general statement. Each general statement in this practice is followed by several examples. Circle the letter of any example that does *not* clearly illustrate the generalization. Be prepared to explain your choices.

EXAMPLE   The museum contains many fascinating examples of African art.

  a. It houses a fine collection of Ashanti fertility dolls.

  b. Drums and shamans' costumes are displayed on the second floor.

  (c.) The museum building was once the home of Frederick Douglass.
  (The fact that the building was once the home of Frederick Douglass is *not an example* of African art.)

1. The International Space Station is designed for efficient use of limited space.

  a. Food has been dehydrated so it can be stored in tiny packages.

  b. Dozens of tiny laboratories for science experiments are tucked in custom-made racks, compartments, and drawers.

  c. Daily life in the space station can be observed by 90 percent of the world's population.

  d. Each little closet-sized "bedroom" holds just one person in a sleeping bag.

2. Today's global companies sometimes find that their product names and slogans can translate into embarrassing bloopers.

   a. Pepsi's slogan "Come alive with the Pepsi Generation" didn't work in Taiwan, where it meant "Pepsi will bring your ancestors back from the dead."

   b. When General Motors introduced its Chevy Nova in South America, company officials didn't realize that *no va* in Spanish means "it won't go."

   c. In Chinese, the Kentucky Fried Chicken slogan "finger-lickin' good" means "eat your fingers off."

   d. Nike runs the same ad campaign in several countries, changing the ad slightly to fit each culture.

3. Many life-enhancing products that we take for granted were invented by women.

   a. Josephine Cochran invented the dishwasher in 1893, declaring that if no one else would build a machine to perform this boring task, she would do it herself.

   b. In 1966, chemist Stephanie Louise Kwoleck patented Kevlar, a fabric five times stronger than steel, now used in bulletproof vests and other important products.

   c. Lonnie Johnson got the idea for the famous Super Soaker squirtgun after the homemade nozzle on his sink sprayed water across the room.

4. Nature has provided us with many powerful medicines.

   a. Aspirin comes from willow bark, penicillin from fungus, and the cancer drug Taxol from the Pacific yew tree.

   b. Drugs that lower cholesterol and blood pressure are helping people with heart disease lead longer, healthier lives.

   c. A newly discovered compound from a New Zealand deep-sea sponge, called Halichondrin B, has been eliminating tumors in laboratory tests.

   d. Prialt, a drug that blocks pain signals in the human spinal cord, comes from the venom of the deadly cone snail of the Indian and Pacific Oceans.

5. Single parents must cope with a variety of stresses that couples do not.

   a. With just one paycheck instead of two, even single parents who receive child support can find themselves struggling to pay the monthly bills.

   b. Because single parents have no partner to share errands and household chores, they may have little time for stress-relieving recreation.

   c. Assigning household chores is a way to help children learn good habits.

   d. Stressful emotions like guilt can plague single parents, who wonder how their children will be affected by growing up without a full-time mom or dad.

6. Since a series of tragic accidents in 2000 and 2001 killed several drivers, the National Association of Stock Car Racing (NASCAR) has taken steps to make the sport safe.

   a. All new race car seats wrap around the driver's rib cage and shoulders, providing better support during a crash.

New safety measures have prevented deaths from NASCAR crashes like this one at Daytona Beach, 2012.

b. The fastest NASCAR track is the one in Talladega, Alabama, where the average race speed is 188 miles per hour.

c. All drivers are now required to wear the head and neck support (HANS) device, a collar that prevents the head from snapping forward or sideways during a wreck.

d. NASCAR tracks now have softer walls and barriers that better absorb the impact of cars at high speeds.

7. A number of Native American musicians influenced popular music although most are not well known.

   a. Shawnee guitarist Link Wray invented the reverberating power chord, the signature sound of Led Zeppelin and The Who.

   b. Buffy St. Marie, a Cree Indian, wrote and introduced a new genre of songs protesting the plight of modern Native Americans.

   c. George Harrison, the famous Beatles guitarist, introduced the sitar, a stringed instrument from India, into pop music.

   d. Jesse Ed Davis, of Kiowa, Creek, and Seminole ancestry, was a fretboard innovator and guitarist for Jackson Browne, Willie Nelson, and Eric Clapton.

8. Many meaningful gifts can be created for little cost or even for free.

   a. A hand-drawn book of coupons redeemable for services like "one home-cooked meal," "one car wash," or "an evening of babysitting" costs only time, not money.

   b. For the low price of supplies, handmade gifts like a crocheted scarf, a collection of favorite photos or recipes, or a quilt often become treasured heirlooms.

   c. Go shopping in your own house and gather unopened, unused items—such as soaps, lotions, or candles—to "regift" in gift baskets.

   d. A notebook computer makes a great gift for a student or an adult on the go.

PRACTICE 3

The secret of good illustration lies in well-chosen, well-written examples. Think of one example that illustrates each of the following general statements. Write out the example in sentence form (one to three sentences) as clearly and exactly as possible.

1. A few contemporary singers work hard to send a positive message.

   Example _____

   _____

   _____

2. In a number of ways, this college makes it easy for working students to attend classes.

   Example _____

   _____

   _____

3. Believing in yourself is 90 percent of success.

   Example _____

   _____

   _____

4. Many teenagers believe they must have expensive designer clothing.

   Example _____

   _____

   _____

5. Growing up in a large family can teach the value of compromise.

   Example _____

   _____

   _____

6. A number of shiny classic cars cruised up and down Ocean Drive.

   Example _____

   _____

   _____

7. Children say surprising things.

   Example _____

   _____

   _____

8. Sadly, rudeness seems more and more common in America.

   Example _____

   _____

   _____

PRACTICE 4   TEAMWORK: CRITICAL THINKING AND WRITING

Illustrate Random Acts of Kindness

The phrase "random acts of kindness" refers to kind acts whose recipients are often perfect strangers. In a group with four or five classmates, read about random acts of kindness (Practice 1, paragraph 1, page 75). Now think of one good example of a real-life random act of kindness, performed by you or someone else—either at college or work, or in everyday life. Share and discuss these examples with your group. Which examples are the most striking or moving? Why?

Write up your example in one paragraph. Begin with a clear topic sentence and present the act of kindness as movingly as you can. Refer to the checklist, and ask your group mates for feedback.

EXPLORING ONLINE

http://www.randomactsofkindness.org/

On this site, you can find kindness ideas and look for writing topics in the Resources section. Under "Stories," click "Share Your Story" to submit your group's best writing for online publication.

Checklist

The Process of Writing an Illustration Paragraph

Refer to this checklist of steps as you write an illustration paragraph of your own.

☐ 1. Narrow the topic in light of your audience and purpose.

☐ 2. Compose a topic sentence that can honestly and easily be supported by examples.

☐ 3. Freewrite or brainstorm to find six to eight examples that support the topic sentence. If you wish to use only one example or a narrative, sketch out your idea. (You may want to freewrite or brainstorm before you narrow the topic.)

☐ 4. Select only the best two to four examples and drop any examples that do not relate to or support the topic sentence.

☐ 5. Make a plan or an outline for your paragraph, numbering the examples in the order in which you will present them.

6. Write a draft of your illustration paragraph, using transitional expressions to show that an example or examples will follow.

7. Revise as necessary, checking for support, unity, logic, and coherence.

8. Proofread for errors in grammar, punctuation, sentence structure, spelling, and mechanics.

Suggested Topic Sentences for Illustration Paragraphs

1. Even the busiest people can incorporate more exercise into their daily routines.

2. Most people have special places where they go to relax or find inspiration.

3. In my family, certain traditions (beliefs or activities) are very important.

4. In my chosen profession, I will have to write several kinds of different documents.

5. Misfortunes can sometimes teach valuable lessons.

6. College students face a number of pressures.

7. Unfortunately, cheating at college (or stealing at work) is more common than most people realize.

8. A true friend is someone who sees and encourages the best in us.

9. Sexual harassment is a fact of life for some employees.

10. Some lucky people love their jobs.

11. Certain fellow students (or co-workers) inspire me to do my best.

12. Eating disorders harm people in many ways.

13. A sense of humor can make difficult times easier to bear.

14. Choose a quotation from the Quotation Bank at the end of this book. First, state whether you think this saying is true; then use an example from your own or others' experience to support your view.

15. Writer's Choice: _____

EXPLORING ONLINE

http://www.google.com

Search the words "une.edu, paragraph types illustration" for a visual review of illustration writing and sample illustration paragraphs from the University of New England.

http://writesite.cuny.edu/projects/keywords/example/hand2.html

Online practice: brainstorming examples for your paragraph

CourseMate for *Evergreen*

Visit *Evergreen* CourseMate for more practices and quizzes, videos to accompany the readings, career and job-search resources, ESL help, and live links to every Exploring Online in the book.

CHAPTER 6

Narration

To **narrate** is to tell a story that explains what happened, when it happened, and who was involved.

A news report may be a narrative telling how a man was rescued from icy flood waters or how a brave whistle blower risked her career and perhaps her life to expose an employer's harmful practices. When you read a bedtime story to a child, you are reading a narrative. In a college paper on campus drug use, telling the story of a friend who takes ecstasy would help bring that subject to life. In an e-mail or letter, you might entertain a friend by narrating your failed attempts to windsurf during a seaside vacation.

We tell stories to teach a lesson, illustrate an idea, or make someone laugh, cry, or get involved. No matter what your narrative is about, every narrative should have a clear **point**: It should reveal what you want your reader to learn or take away from the story.

Topic Sentence

Here is the topic sentence of a **narrative** paragraph:

> The crash of a Brinks truck on a Miami overpass still raises disturbing questions.

- The writer begins a narrative paragraph with a topic sentence that tells or sets up the point of the narrative.
- What is the point of this narrative? _____

_____

_____

81

Paragraph and Plan

Here is the entire paragraph:

> The crash of a Brinks truck on a Miami overpass still raises disturbing questions. January 8, 1997, was just another crowded, rude, and crazy day in Miami traffic until an armored Brinks truck flipped and broke open, sending nearly a million dollars in cash swirling over the highway. Hundreds of motorists screeched to a stop, grabbing whatever money they could. People in nearby houses raced outside, shouting and scooping up bills. When it was over, a tiny handful of people returned some money. Firefighter Manny Rodriguez turned in a huge bale of bills worth $330,000, and one teenager returned some quarters. However, nearly half a million dollars was missing—stolen by everyday people like you and me. In the following days, some rationalized the mass theft as a kind of Robin Hood action because the truck had crashed in a poor area of town. Most people claimed to be shocked. Now we are all left with hard questions: *Why did a few people "do the right thing"? Why did the majority do the "wrong thing"? What causes people to act virtuously, even if no one is watching? What would you or I have done?*

- The body of a narrative paragraph is developed according to time, or chronological, order.* That is, the writer explains the narrative—the entire incident—as a series of small events or actions in the order in which they occurred. By keeping to strict chronological order, the writer helps the reader follow the story more easily and avoids interrupting the narrative with, *But I forgot to mention that before this happened....*

- What smaller events make up this paragraph? _____

  _____

  _____

  _____

- What strong verbs or details help the writing come alive? _____

  _____

  _____

  _____

- The writer ends the paragraph with some "hard questions." Do these questions

  express the point of the story? _____

  _____

———

*For more work on time, see Chapter 4, "Achieving Coherence," Part A.

Before writing this narrative paragraph, the writer may have brainstormed or freewritten to gather ideas, and then he may have made an **outline** like this:

TOPIC SENTENCE: The crash of a Brinks truck on a Miami overpass still raises disturbing questions.

Event 1: Brinks truck flips, spilling cash on the highway.
Event 2: Hundreds of motorists stop, grab money.
Event 3: People race out of houses, grabbing money.
Event 4: Later, firefighter Rodriguez returns $330,000.
Event 5: Just a few others give anything back; half million is gone.
Event 6: Days after, some call it "Robin Hood" action.
Event 7: Some say they are shocked.

CONCLUSION: Now we are all left with hard questions. (Some questions are listed.)

- Note that all of the events occur in chronological order.
- The conclusion provides a strong and thought-provoking ending.
- Finally, the specific details of certain events (like events 2 and 4) make the narrative more vivid.

Transitional Expressions

Because narrative paragraphs tell a story in **chronological** or **time order**, transitional expressions that indicate time can be useful.*

Transitional Expressions for Narratives		
afterward	finally	next
after that	first	now
currently	later	soon
eventually	meanwhile	then

PRACTICE 1

Read the following narrative paragraph carefully and answer the questions:

The Cherokee people tell the story of a young boy who has been badly wronged by someone he considered a friend. The boy, hurt and furious, tells his grandfather about the incident. His grandfather nods and replies, "At times, I too have felt hatred for those who do great harm and seem to feel no sorrow about it. But hate wears a person down and does not hurt the enemy. It is like taking poison and wishing the enemy would die. I have struggled with these feelings

---

*For complete essays developed by narration, see Chapter 16, "Types of Essays," Part B.

many times. It is as if two wolves live inside me; they live inside you, too. One wolf is good. He is peaceful, generous, compassionate, and wise. He lives in harmony with all those around him and does not easily take offense. He fights only when it is right to do so. But the other wolf lives in me as well—and in you. He is full of anger, envy, self pity, and pain. The smallest thing infuriates him. He cannot think clearly because his anger is so great, yet that anger changes nothing. Sometimes, it is hard to live with two wolves inside me, for both of them struggle to dominate my spirit.

The boy looked intently into his grandfather's eyes and asked, "Which wolf wins, Grandfather?" The grandfather smiled and said quietly, "The one I feed."

1. What is the point of the narrative? _____

_____

2. What events make up this narrative? _____

_____

_____

_____

3. Do you relate to this story? In what way?_____

_____

_____

PRACTICE 2

Here are three plans for narrative paragraphs. The events in the plans are not in correct chronological order. The plans also contain events that do not belong in each story. Number the events in the proper time sequence and cross out any irrelevant ones.

1. A combination of talent and hard work has propelled Alicia Keys to musical stardom.

_____ In 1988, seven-year-old Alicia dazzled her first piano teacher by mastering both classical and jazz pieces.

_____ By 2005, her distinctive voice and blending of soul, jazz, hip-hop, and classical styles had won a huge fan base and four more Grammies.

_____ As a teenager in the "Hell's Kitchen" section of New York City, she wrote her first songs and blossomed as a pianist.

_____ Every year since 1959, the Grammy, the Academy Award of music, has been given to musicians of outstanding achievement.

_____ At age twenty, she released *Songs in A Minor*, the debut album that scored five Grammy awards in 2002, including Best New Artist and Song of the Year for her hit single "Fallin'."

Alicia Keys in concert

2. In a treasured letter home from the Civil War, my great great-grandfather William, then sixteen, describes an evening of surprising calm.

_____ Suddenly, one of William's buddies spotted Confederate soldiers watching from the opposite bank.

_____ The Civil War lasted from 1861 to 1865.

_____ Yanks and Rebs swam, whooped, and even shared cigarettes together before returning to their camps.

_____ William did not know what signal was given, but instead of shooting, both armies suddenly stripped to their underwear and splashed into the water.

_____ The next morning, these young men continued the slaughter.

_____ After a day of bloody fighting in July 1863, William and his Union company were settling down on a wooded hill above a pond.

3. The ancient Greek story of Sisyphus depicts the terrible frustration of work that is never done.

_____ Every time Sisyphus neared the top of the hill, the massive boulder rolled back down, forcing him to start all over again.

_____ Sisyphus was a brutal king who murdered, stole, and fooled the gods by cheating death for years.

_____ When Sisyphus finally did die, the Greek god Zeus sought the worst possible punishment.

_____ Zeus condemned Sisyphus to roll a huge stone up a steep hill—forever.

Why does this artist call his cartoon "The Myth of Sisyphus"? What is he saying about the U.S. debt? For clues, read item 3, beginning on page 85.

_____ According to Greek mythology, Zeus once turned himself into a swan.

_____ Thus, the story goes, for all eternity, Sisyphus has pointlessly pushed, sweated, and worked, forever deprived of the satisfaction of completing his task.

PRACTICE 3

TEAMWORK: CRITICAL THINKING AND WRITING

Read the story of Sisyphus in Practice 2, item 3. Did you ever have a job, relationship, or situation that made *you* feel like Sisyphus? What was it about the experience that made you feel you kept doing the same thing without getting anywhere? Share your experience with the group.

PRACTICE 4

Here are topic sentences for three narrative paragraphs. Make a plan for each paragraph, placing the events of the narrative in the proper time sequence.

1. When I had trouble with _____ , help came from an unexpected source.

   _____

   _____

   _____

   _____

   _____

2. The accident (or performance) lasted only a few moments, but I will never forget it.

_____

_____

_____

_____

_____

3. _____ was the craziest day I've ever experienced on the job.
    (day and date)

_____

_____

_____

_____

_____

PRACTICE 5   TEAMWORK: CRITICAL THINKING AND WRITING

Narrate an Experience of Stereotyping

Good narratives have a *point*; they bring to life a moral, lesson, or idea. In a group with four or five classmates, read this narrative passage about "The Latina Stereotype" by Judith Ortiz Cofer and then discuss and answer the questions.

> My first public poetry reading took place at a restaurant where a luncheon was being held before the event. I was nervous and excited as I walked in with a notebook in hand. An older woman motioned me to her table, and thinking (foolish me) that she wanted me to autograph a copy of my newly published slender volume of verse, I went over. She ordered a cup of coffee from me, assuming that I was the waitress. (Easy enough to mistake my poems for menus, I suppose.) I know it wasn't an intentional act of cruelty. Yet of all the good things that happened later, I remember that scene most clearly, because it reminded me of what I had to overcome before anyone would take me seriously.

● What is the point of this story? Exactly what *stereotype* did the writer encounter? What did the woman assume about her and why?

● Have you ever been stereotyped? That is, has anyone ever treated you a certain way based only on your age, clothing, race, gender, major, accent, piercings or other decoration, or even things you are carrying, like books or a beeper? Share a story with the group. What stereotype was imposed on you, and how did you react? Now narrate vividly in writing your experience of stereotyping. You might wish to place your topic sentence, stating the meaning or point, last. Refer to the checklist, and ask your group mates for feedback.

EXPLORING ONLINE

http://www.tolerance.org/

Explore this interesting site about increasing tolerance. Take notes on any ideas for further writing.

Checklist

The Process of Writing a Narrative Paragraph

Refer to this checklist of steps as you write a narrative paragraph of your own.

☐ 1. Narrow the topic in light of your audience and purpose.

☐ 2. Compose a topic sentence that tells the point of the story.

☐ 3. Freewrite or brainstorm for all of the events and details that might be part of the story. (You may want to freewrite or brainstorm before you narrow the topic.)

☐ 4. Select the important events and details; drop any that do not clearly relate to the point in your topic sentence.

☐ 5. Make a plan or an outline for the paragraph, numbering the events in the correct time (chronological) sequence.

☐ 6. Write a draft of your narrative paragraph, using transitional expressions to indicate time sequence.

☐ 7. Revise as necessary, checking for support, unity, logic, and coherence.

☐ 8. Proofread for errors in grammar, punctuation, sentence structure, spelling, and mechanics.

Suggested Topics for Narrative Paragraphs

1. Your best (or worst) job interview

2. A risk that paid off

3. An important family story or a story someone told you

4. A turning point (personal, academic, or professional)

5. An episode in a courtroom, ER, or other interesting place

6. How you developed a career skill (in customer service, computers, attitude, and so on)

7. A breakthrough (emotional, physical, or spiritual)

8. An experience in a new country (city, school, or job)

9. An incident that provoked an intense emotion (such as rage, grief, pride, or joy)

10. A triumphant (or embarrassing) moment

11. The first time you encountered a role model or important friend

12. A serious choice or decision

13. An encounter with prejudice

14. Interview a person you admire and tell, in short form, his or her story

15. Writer's choice: _____

EXPLORING ONLINE

http://grammar.ccc.commnet.edu/grammar/composition/narrative.htm
Review the elements of a good narrative, and read some fine examples.

www.healingstory.org
Do you think that stories can heal? Explore this website and decide for yourself. Click "Treasure Chest."

CourseMate for *Evergreen*
Visit *Evergreen* CourseMate for more practices and quizzes, videos to accompany the readings, career and job-search resources, ESL help, and live links to every Exploring Online in the book.

CHAPTER 7

Description

To **describe** something—a person, a place, or an object—is to capture it in words so others can imagine it or see it in their mind's eye.

The best way for a writer to help the reader get a clear impression is to use language that appeals to the senses: sight, sound, smell, taste, and touch. For it is through the senses that human beings experience the physical world around them, and it is through the senses that the world is most vividly described.

Imagine, for instance, that you have just gone boating on a lake at sunset. You may not have taken a photograph, yet your friends and family can receive an accurate picture of what you have experienced if you *describe* the pink sky reflected in smooth water, the creak of the wooden boat, the soothing drip of water from the oars, the occasional splash of a large bass jumping, the faint fish smells, the cool and darkening air. Writing down what your senses experience will teach you to see, hear, smell, taste, and touch more acutely than ever before.

Description is useful in English class, the sciences, psychology—anywhere that keen observation is important.

Topic Sentence

Here is the topic sentence of a descriptive paragraph:

> On November 27, 1922, when archaeologist Howard Carter unsealed the door to the ancient Egyptian tomb of King Tut, he stared in amazement at the fantastic objects heaped all around him.

- The writer begins a descriptive paragraph by pointing out what will be described. What will be described in this paragraph?

_____

- The writer can also give a general impression of this scene, object, or person. What overall impression of the tomb does the writer provide?

_____

_____

Paragraph and Plan

Here is the entire paragraph:

> On November 27, 1922, when archaeologist Howard Carter unsealed the door to the ancient Egyptian tomb of King Tut, he stared in amazement at the fantastic objects heaped all around him. On his left lay the wrecks of at least four golden chariots. Against the wall on his right sat a gorgeous chest brightly painted with hunting and battle scenes. Across from him was a gilded throne with cat-shaped legs, arms like winged serpents, and a back showing King Tut and his queen. Behind the throne rose a tall couch decorated with animal faces that were half hippopotamus and half crocodile. The couch was loaded with more treasures. To the right of the couch, two life-sized statues faced each other like guards. They were black, wore gold skirts and sandals, and had cobras carved on their foreheads. Between them was a second sealed doorway. Carter's heart beat loudly. Would the mummy of King Tut lie beyond it?

- The overall impression given by the topic sentence is that the tomb's many objects were amazing. List three specific details that support this impression.

  _____

  _____

  _____

- Note the importance of words that indicate richness and unusual decoration in helping the reader visualize the scene.* List as many of these words as you can:

  _____

  _____

  _____

- This paragraph, like many descriptive paragraphs, is organized according to space order.† The author uses transitional expressions that show where things are. Underline the transitional expressions that indicate place or position.

Before composing this descriptive paragraph, the writer probably brainstormed and freewrote to gather ideas and then made an **outline** like this:

---

* For more work on vivid language, see Chapter 23, "Revising for Language Awareness."
† For more work on space order and other kinds of order, see Chapter 4, "Achieving Coherence," Part A.

TOPIC SENTENCE: On November 27, 1922, when archaeologist Howard Carter unsealed the door to the ancient Egyptian tomb of King Tut, he stared in amazement at the fantastic objects heaped all around him.

1. **To the left:**	chariots
	—wrecked
	—golden
2. **To the right:**	a gorgeous chest
	—brightly painted with hunting and battle scenes
3. **Across the room:**	a throne
	—gilded
	—cat-shaped legs
	—arms like winged serpents
4. **Behind the throne:**	a couch
	—decorated with faces that were half hippopotamus and half crocodile
5. **To the right of the couch:**	two life-sized statues
	—black
	—gold skirts and sandals
	—cobras carved on foreheads
6. **Between the two statues:**	a second sealed doorway

CONCLUSION: expectation that King Tut's mummy was beyond the second door

● Note how each detail supports the topic sentence.

Egyptian officials in King Tut's tomb prepare the boy king's mummy for placement in a climate-controlled glass box.

Transitional Expressions

Since space order is often used in description, **transitional expressions** indicating place or position can be useful:

<table>
<tr><td colspan="2" align="center">Transitional Expressions Indicating Place</td></tr>
<tr><td>next to, near</td><td>on top, beneath</td></tr>
<tr><td>close, far</td><td>toward, away</td></tr>
<tr><td>up, down, between</td><td>left, right, center</td></tr>
<tr><td>above, below</td><td>front, back, middle</td></tr>
</table>

Of course, other kinds of order are possible. For example, a description of a person might have two parts: details of physical appearance and details of behavior.*

PRACTICE 1

Read the following paragraph carefully and answer the questions.

The woman who met us had an imposing beauty. She was tall and large-boned. Her face was strongly molded, with high cheekbones and skin the color of mahogany. She greeted us politely but did not smile and seemed to hold her head very high, an effect exaggerated by the abundant black hair slicked up and rolled on the top of her head. Her clothing was simple, a black sweater and skirt, and I remember thinking that dressed in showier garments, this woman would have seemed overwhelming.

1. What overall impression does the writer give of the woman? _____

_____

_____

2. What specific details support this general impression? _____

_____

_____

_____

_____

3. What kind of order does the writer use? _____

_____

* For complete essays developed by description, see Chapter 16, Part C.

It is important that the details in a descriptive paragraph support the overall impression given in the topic sentence. In each of the following plans, one detail has nothing to do with the topic sentence; it is merely a bit of irrelevant information. Find the irrelevant detail and circle its letter.

1. In the video of yesterday's dramatic win, soccer star Leo Messi looks triumphant.
   a. mouth grinning broadly
   b. arms raised high above his head
   c. first began playing soccer at age five
   d. both index fingers pointing into the air
   e. head flung back, looking at the sky

2. Magda's sewing shop is crammed with the items of her trade.
   a. racks of clothing awaiting alterations
   b. thread, thimbles, and tailor's chalk scattered on the work table
   c. dress forms for all shapes and sizes in one corner
   d. large mug half full of coffee on the window sill
   e. sewing machine in front of the window

3. The Calle Ocho Festival, named after S.W. 8th Street in Little Havana, is a giant Latino street party.
   a. as far as the eye can see on S.W. 8th Street, thousands of people stroll, eat, and dance
   b. on the left, vendors sell hot pork sandwiches, *pasteles* (spiced meat pies), and fried sweets dusted with powdered sugar
   c. up close, the press of bare-limbed people, blaring music, and rich smells
   d. during the 1980s, Dominican merengue music hit the dance clubs of New York
   e. on the right, two of many bands play mambo or merengue music

4. In the photograph from 1877, Chief Joseph looks sad and dignified.
   a. long hair pulled back, touched with gray
   b. dark eyes gaze off to one side, as if seeing a bleak future
   c. strong mouth frowns at the corners
   d. ceremonial shell necklaces cover his chest
   e. Nez Percé tribe once occupied much of the Pacific Northwest

5. Many people are taking personal steps to curb global warming.
   a. hybrid cars in high demand
   b. increasing popularity of public transportation and carpools

    c. recycling a priority in many households

    d. use of special bulbs for energy-saving light

    e. glaciers melting at fast rates

PRACTICE 3

Here are three topic sentences for descriptive paragraphs. Give five specific details that would support the overall impression given in each topic sentence. Appeal to as many of the senses as possible. Be careful not to list irrelevant bits of information.

EXAMPLE   Stopped in time by the photographer, my mother appears confident.

Details:

    a. *her hair swept up in a sophisticated pompadour*

    b. *a determined look in her young eyes*

    c. *wide, self-assured smile*

    d. *her chin held high*

    e. *well-padded shoulders*

(These five details support *confident* in the topic sentence.)

1. This was clearly a music (sports, or computer) lover's room.

    a. _____

    b. _____

    c. _____

    d. _____

    e. _____

2. The buildings on that street look sad and run-down.

    a. _____

    b. _____

    c. _____

    d. _____

    e. _____

3. The beach on a hot summer day presented a constant show.

    a. _____

    b. _____

c. _____

d. _____

e. _____

PRACTICE 4

Pick the description you like best from Practice 3. Prewrite for more details if you wish. Choose a logical order in which to present the best details, make a plan or an outline, and then write an excellent descriptive paragraph.

PRACTICE 5

TEAMWORK: CRITICAL VIEWING AND WRITING

Describe a Painting

In a group with four or five classmates, study the painting below. Your task is to write one paragraph describing this painting so that someone who has never seen it can visualize it. As a group, craft a good topic sentence that gives an overall impression of the scene. Your topic sentence might take this form:

"George Tooker's 1950 painting, *Subway*, shows (or captures) *the subway as a frightening*

place, prison-like environment. "

Have one person take notes as you brainstorm important details, using rich language to capture the scene. Now decide the best order in which to present your details—right to left, center to sides, or some other. Use transitional expressions to guide the reader's eye from detail to detail. Revise the writing to make it as exact and fresh as possible. Be prepared to read your work to the full class.

Subway by George Tooker. 1950

George Tooker, 1920-2011, The Subway, 1950. Egg Tempera on composition board, 18⅛ x 36⅛ in. (46 x 91.8 cm). Whitney Museum of American Art, New York: purchase, with funds from the Juliana Force Purchase Award #50.23 © Estate of George Tooker. Photo courtesy of the Whitney Museum of American Art.

EXPLORING ONLINE

http://www.artic.edu/

Art Institute of Chicago: find a work of art that intrigues you and describe it.

http://www.moma.org/

Museum of Modern Art: find a work of art that captures you and write about it.

Checklist

The Process of Writing a Descriptive Paragraph

Refer to this checklist of steps as you write a descriptive paragraph of your own.

- [ ] 1. Narrow the topic in light of your audience and purpose.

- [ ] 2. Compose a topic sentence that clearly points to what you will describe or gives an overall impression of the person, object, or scene.

- [ ] 3. Freewrite or brainstorm to find as many specific details as you can to capture your subject in words. Remember to appeal to your readers' senses. (You may want to freewrite or brainstorm before you narrow the topic.)

- [ ] 4. Select the best details and drop any irrelevant ones.

- [ ] 5. Make a plan or an outline for the paragraph, numbering the details in the order in which you will present them.

- [ ] 6. Write a draft of your descriptive paragraph, using transitional expressions wherever they might be helpful.

- [ ] 7. Revise as necessary, checking for support, unity, logic, and coherence.

- [ ] 8. Proofread for errors in grammar, punctuation, sentence structure, spelling, and mechanics.

Suggested Topics for Descriptive Paragraphs

1. An unusual man or woman: for example, an athlete, an entertainer, someone with amazing hair or clothing, or a teacher you won't forget

2. A food, object, or scene from another country

3. A workspace or place on campus that needs improvement (to be safer, more useful, more attractive)

4. A painting, sculpture, or other work of art

5. A scene of poverty or despair

6. Someone or something you found yourself staring at

7. A workspace or environment that would motivate employees to work

8. A scene of peace (or of conflict)

9. A room that reveals something about its owner

10. A tool or machine you use at work

11. A shop that sells only one type of item: cell phones, Western boots, flowers, car parts, cooking items

12. An interesting person you have met on campus

13. A crowded place: dance club, library, fast-food restaurant, town square, or theater lobby

14. A fascinating or frightening outdoor scene

15. Writer's choice: _____

EXPLORING ONLINE

http://leo.stcloudstate.edu/acadwrite/descriptive.html
Good tips for improving your description writing, with sample paragraphs

http://grammar.about.com/od/developingparagraphs/a/descparhub.htm
In-depth tutorial for writing a descriptive paragraph, with professional samples

CourseMate for *Evergreen*
Visit *Evergreen* CourseMate for more practices and quizzes, videos
to accompany the readings, career and job-search resources,
ESL help, and live links to every Exploring Online in the book.

CHAPTER 8

Process

wo kinds of **process paragraphs** will be explained in this chapter: the how-to paragraph and the explanation paragraph.

The **how-to paragraph** gives the reader directions on how he or she can do something: how to install a software program, how to get to the airport, or how to make tasty barbecued ribs. The goals of such directions are the installed software, the arrival at the airport, or the great barbecued ribs. In other words, the reader should be able to do something after reading the paragraph.

The **explanation paragraph**, on the other hand, tells the reader how a particular event occurred or how something works. For example, an explanation paragraph might explain how an internal combustion engine works or how palm trees reproduce. After reading an explanation paragraph, the reader is not expected to be able to do anything, just to understand how it happened or how it works.

Process writing is useful in history, business, the sciences, psychology, and many other areas.

Topic Sentence

Here is the topic sentence of a **how-to paragraph**:

> Careful preparation before an interview is the key to getting the job you want.

- The writer begins a how-to paragraph with a topic sentence that clearly states the goal of the process—what the reader should be able to do.

- What should the reader be able to do after he or she has read the paragraph following this topic sentence?

_____

_____

Paragraph and Plan

Here is the entire paragraph:

"Luck is preparation meeting opportunity," it has been said, and this is true for a job interview. Careful preparation before an interview is the key to getting the job you want. The first step is to learn all you can about the employer. Read about the company in its brochures or in newspaper and magazine articles. A reference librarian can point you to the best sources of company information. You can also find company websites and other useful material on the Internet. Second, as you read, think about the ways your talents match the company's goals. Third, put yourself in the interviewer's place, and make a list of questions that he or she will probably ask. Employers want to know about your experience, training, and special skills, like foreign languages. Remember, every employer looks for a capable and enthusiastic team player who will help the firm succeed. Fourth, rehearse your answers to the questions out loud. Practice with a friend or a tape recorder until your responses sound well prepared and confident. Finally, select and prepare a professional-looking interview outfit well in advance to avoid the last-minute panic of a torn hem or stained shirt. When a job candidate has made the effort to prepare, the interviewer is much more likely to be impressed.

- The topic sentence is the second sentence. In the first sentence, the writer has used a quotation to open the paragraph and spark the reader's interest.

- The body of the how-to paragraph is developed according to time, or chronological, order.* That is, the writer gives directions in the order in which the reader is to complete them. Keeping to a strict chronological order avoids the necessity of saying, *By the way, I forgot to tell you . . .* , or *Whoops, a previous step should have been to. . . .*

- How many steps are there in this how-to paragraph and what are they? _____

  _____

  _____

  _____

Before writing this how-to paragraph, the writer probably brainstormed or freewrote to gather ideas and then made an **outline** like this:

TOPIC SENTENCE: Careful preparation before an interview is the key to getting the job you want.

Step 1: Learn about the employer

—read company brochures, papers, magazines

—reference librarian can help

—check company website

---

* For more work on order, see Chapter 4, "Achieving Coherence," Part A.

Step 2:   Think how your talents match company goals

Step 3:   List interviewer questions

        —think about experience, training, special skills

        —employers want capable team players

Step 4:   Rehearse your answers out loud

        —practice with friend or tape recorder

Step 5:   Select your interview outfit

        —avoid last-minute panic

        —avoid torn hem, stained shirt

CONCLUSION: Interviewer more likely to be impressed

● Note that each step clearly relates to the goal stated in the topic sentence.

The second kind of process paragraph, the **explanation paragraph**, tells how something works, how it happens, or how it came to be:

> Many experts believe that recovery from addiction, whether to alcohol or other drugs, has four main stages. The first stage begins when the user finally admits that he or she has a substance abuse problem and wants to quit. At this point, most people seek help from groups like Alcoholics Anonymous or treatment programs because few addicts can "get clean" by themselves. The next stage is withdrawal, when the addict stops using the substance. Withdrawal can be a painful physical and emotional experience, but luckily, it does not last long. After withdrawal comes the most challenging stage—making positive changes in one's life. Recovering addicts have to learn new ways of spending their time, finding pleasure and relaxation, caring for their bodies, and relating to spouses, lovers, family, and friends. The fourth and final stage is staying off drugs. This open-ended part of the process often calls for ongoing support or therapy. For people once defeated by addiction, the rewards of self-esteem and a new life are well worth the effort.

● What process does the writer explain in this paragraph? _____

_____

● How many stages or steps are explained in this paragraph? _____

● What are they? _____

_____

_____

● Make a plan of the paragraph in your notebook.

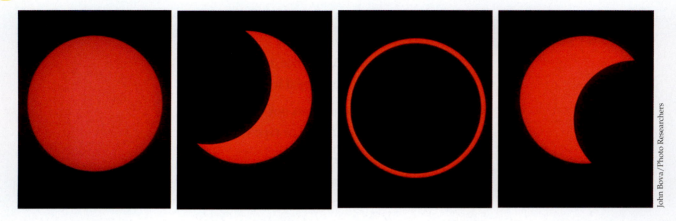

Just as these photos show each stage of a solar eclipse—as the moon passes between the sun and Earth—so your process paragraphs should clearly describe each step or stage for the reader. Before you write, try to visualize the process as if it were a series of photographs.

Transitional Expressions

Since process paragraphs rely on **chronological order**, or **time sequence**, words and expressions that locate the steps of the process in time are extremely helpful.

Transitional Expressions for Process

Beginning a Process	*Continuing a Process*		*Ending a Process*
first	afterward	then	finally
initially	after that	second	last
the first stage	later	third	the final step
the first step	meanwhile	the second stage	
	next	the next step	

PRACTICE 1

Read the following how-to paragraph carefully and answer the questions.

If someone nearby collapses and does not respond to shouting or shaking, performing the three steps of cardiopulmonary resuscitation, or CPR, could determine whether that person lives or dies. The first step is to call for help by dialing 911. If you are not certified to deliver CPR, keep the emergency dispatcher on the line to talk you through the next two steps until paramedics arrive. The second step, performing chest compressions, should occur if the victim remains unresponsive and has stopped breathing or is breathing abnormally. With one hand over your other hand, push down two inches with the heel of your hand on the center of the victim's chest. Compress the chest hard and fast thirty times. Then perform the third step, blowing air into the victim's mouth. Tilt his or her head back and lift the chin. Pinch the victim's nose closed, cover his or her mouth with your mouth, and blow until you see the chest rise. Provide two breaths, each one second long. Continue alternating 30 pumps with two breaths until help arrives. Remember that time is the enemy of someone who is not breathing. By following these steps to keep precious oxygen and blood moving through the victim's body, you may save a life.

—Eleanor Steiger, Student

1. What should you be able to do after reading this paragraph? _____

   _____

   _____

2. Are any "materials" necessary for this process? _____

   _____

3. How many steps are there in this paragraph? List them.

   _____

   _____

4. What order does the writer employ? _____

PRACTICE 2

Here are five plans for process paragraphs. The steps for the plans are not in the correct chronological order. The plans also contain irrelevant details that are not part of the process. Number the steps in the proper time sequence and cross out any irrelevant details.

1. The process of taking digital fingerprints, which requires specialized scanning equipment, consists of several simple steps.

   _____ The computer converts these finger scans into digital data patterns, mapping points on the patterns.

   _____ One by one, the subject places his or her fingers on the optical or silicon scanner surface for a few seconds while the computer scans.

   _____ The technician begins by cleaning the subject's fingers with alcohol to remove any dirt or sweat.

   _____ For years, the only fingerprints were made by rolling the fingers in wet ink and pressing the fingers onto a card.

   _____ At the technician's command, the computer can compare this subject's fingerprint patterns to millions of patterns in the national database and identify possible matches.

2. Stress, which is your body's response to physical or mental pressures, occurs in three stages.

    _____ In the resistance stage, your body works hard to resist or handle the threat, but you may become more vulnerable to other stressors, like flu or colds.

    _____ If the stress continues for too long, your body uses up its defenses and enters the exhaustion stage.

    _____ Trying to balance college courses, parenthood, and work is sure to cause stress.

    _____ During the alarm stage (also called *fight or flight*), your body first reacts to a threat by releasing hormones that increase your heart rate and blood pressure, create muscle tension, and supply quick energy.

3. Chewing gum is made entirely by machine.

    _____ Then the warm mass is pressed into thin ribbons by pairs of rollers.

    _____ First, the gum base is melted and pumped through a high-speed spinner that throws out all impurities.

    _____ The gum base makes the gum chewy.

    _____ Huge machines mix the purified gum with sugar, corn syrup, and flavoring, such as spearmint, peppermint, or cinnamon.

    _____ Finally, machines wrap the sticks individually and then package them.

    _____ Knives attached to the last rollers cut the ribbons into sticks.

4. Many psychologists claim that marriage is a dynamic process consisting of several phases.

    _____ Sooner or later, romance gives way to disappointment as both partners really see each other's faults.

    _____ Idealization is the first phase, when two people fall romantically in love, each thinking the other is perfect.

    _____ The last phase occurs as the couple face their late years as a twosome once again.

    _____ The third phase is sometimes called the productivity period, when two people work at parenting and career development.

    _____ Men and women may have different expectations in a marriage.

    _____ As the children leave home and careers mature, couples may enter a stage when they rethink their lives and goals.

5. Helping to save rare stranded sea turtles, our service learning project, was a rewarding series of steps.

_____ Inside, we rubbed Vaseline on each turtle's shell and put saline in its eyes; the sickest turtles needed IV fluids.

_____ We gently loaded each tired giant in the front seat of a pickup truck and hurried back to the sanctuary.

_____ In the fall, when temperatures dropped, we volunteers at the Wellfleet Wildlife Sanctuary raced to the beaches to find any giant sea turtles that had not swum south.

_____ Two volunteers so loved working with endangered turtles that they are now pursuing careers in marine biology.

_____ Within 12 hours, we drove our patients to the aquarium in Boston, to spend the winter and get well before their release in warm Florida seas.

PRACTICE 3

Here are topic sentences for three process paragraphs. Make a plan for each paragraph, listing in proper time sequence all the steps that would be necessary to complete the process. Now choose one plan and write an excellent process paragraph.

1. Although I'm still not the life of the party, I took these steps to overcome my shyness at parties.

   _____

   _____

   _____

   _____

   _____

   _____

2. Good kids turning bad: it is a process occurring all over the country.

   _____

   _____

   _____

   _____

_____

_____

3. _____ is/was a very complicated (or simple) process.

_____

_____

_____

_____

_____

_____

PRACTICE 4   **TEAMWORK: CRITICAL THINKING AND WRITING**

Explain the Process of Intoxication

In a group with four or five classmates, study and discuss these percentages that show rising blood alcohol content (BAC), a measure of intoxication. Now plan and write a paragraph that describes what happens as BAC rises. Your purpose is to inform your audience—nursing students—about this process. Write a topic sentence that gives an overview; in the body, include three or four percentages if you wish. In your concluding sentence or sentences, you might wish to emphasize the dangerous human meaning of these numbers. Be prepared to read your paragraph to the full class.

BAC	Effect
0.03%	relaxation, mood change
0.05%	decrease in motor skills; legal driving limit in New York
0.07%	legal driving limit in sixteen states
0.09%	delayed reaction time, decreased muscle control, slurred speech
0.15%	blurred vision, unsteadiness, impaired coordination
0.18%	difficulty staying awake
0.30%	semi-stupor
0.50%	coma and risk of death

Now assume your purpose is to write another paragraph convincing high school students not to binge drink. Would BAC percentages help persuade your audience, or would you take another approach? What might that approach be?

EXPLORING ONLINE

http://www.collegedrinkingprevention.gov/

Under "Stats & Summaries," click "Snapshot of Drinking Consequences" for facts on alcohol's link to violence and other harmful behaviors. Under "NIAAA College Materials," click "A Call to Action" for facts on drinking as a "college culture."

Checklist

The Process of Writing a Process Paragraph

Refer to this checklist of steps as you write a process paragraph of your own.

☐ 1. Narrow the topic in light of your audience and purpose.

☐ 2. Compose a topic sentence that clearly states the goal or end result of the process you wish to describe.

☐ 3. Freewrite or brainstorm to generate steps that might be part of the process. (You may want to freewrite or brainstorm before you narrow the topic.)

☐ 4. Drop any irrelevant information or steps that are not really necessary for your explanation of the process.

☐ 5. Make an outline or a plan for your paragraph, numbering the steps in the correct time (chronological) sequence.

☐ 6. Write a draft of your process paragraph, using transitional expressions to indicate time (chronological) sequence.

☐ 7. Revise as necessary, checking for support, unity, logic, and coherence.

☐ 8. Proofread for errors in grammar, punctuation, sentence structure, spelling, and mechanics.

Suggested Topics for Process Paragraphs

1. How to get information about a company you want to work for

2. How to prepare your favorite dish

3. How to relax or meditate

4. How to establish credit (or improve your credit score)

5. How to land an interesting job

6. How an important discovery was made

7. How to find information in the library's electronic card catalog (or reference book section)

8. How to be a true friend

9. How to get the most out of a doctor visit

10. How to get fired, ruin a love affair, or alienate your in-laws (humorous)

11. How to break an unhealthy habit

12. A process you learned at work or school (how to handcuff a suspect, how to take blood pressure, how to make a customer feel welcome, how a lithograph is made, and so forth)

13. How to motivate someone to_____

14. How to shop on a budget for a computer, phone, or television

15. Writer's choice:_____

EXPLORING ONLINE

http://www.ehow.com/how_1323_make-peanut-butter.html
Do you think you can make a scrumptious peanut butter and jelly sandwich? Follow the clear instructions in this video.

http://www.ehow.com/
Learn how to do all sorts of things; categories include careers, health, cars, legal, games, and more.

CourseMate for *Evergreen*
Visit the *Evergreen* CourseMate for more practices and quizzes, videos to accompany the readings, career and job-search resources, ESL help, and live links to every Exploring Online in the book.

CHAPTER 9

Definition

A: Single-Sentence Definitions

B: The Definition Paragraph

To **define** is to explain clearly what a word or term means.
As you write, you will sometimes find it necessary to explain words or terms that you suspect your reader may not know. For example, *net profit* is the profit remaining after all deductions have been taken; a *bonsai* is a dwarfed, ornamentally shaped tree. Such terms can often be defined in just a few carefully chosen words. However, other terms—like *courage, racism*, or *a good marriage*—are more difficult to define. They will test your ability to explain them clearly so that your reader knows exactly what you mean when you use them in your writing. They may require an entire paragraph for a complete and thorough definition.

In this chapter, you will learn to write one-sentence definitions and then whole paragraphs of definition. The skill of defining clearly will be useful in such courses as psychology, business, the sciences, history, and English.

A. Single-Sentence Definitions

There are many ways to define a word or term. Three basic ways are **definition by synonym, definition by class**, and **definition by negation**.

Definition by Synonym

The simplest way to define a term is to supply a **synonym**, a word that means the same thing. A good synonym definition always uses an easier and more familiar word than the one being defined.

1. *Gregarious* means *sociable.*
2. *To procrastinate* means *to postpone needlessly.*
3. A *wraith* is a *ghost* or *phantom.*
4. *Adroitly* means *skillfully.*

109

Although you may not have known the words *gregarious, procrastination, wraith,* and *adroitly* before, the synonym definitions make it very clear what they mean.

A synonym should usually be the same part of speech as the word being defined, so it could be used as a substitute. *Gregarious* and *sociable* are both adjectives; *to procrastinate* and *to postpone* are verb forms; *wraith, ghost,* and *phantom* are nouns; *adroitly* and *skillfully* are adverbs.

5. Quarterback Peyton Manning *adroitly* moved his team up the field.
6. Quarterback Peyton Manning *skillfully* moved his team up the field.

- In this sentence *skillfully* can be substituted for *adroitly*.

Unfortunately, it is not always possible to come up with a good synonym definition.

Definition by Class

The **class** definition is the one most often required in college and formal writing—in examinations, papers, and reports.

The class definition has two parts. First, the writer places the word to be defined into the larger **category**, or **class**, to which it belongs.

7. *Lemonade* is a *drink* …
8. An *orphan* is a *child* …
9. A *dictatorship* is a *form of government* …

Second, the writer provides the **distinguishing characteristics** or **details** that make this person, object, or idea *different* from all others in that category. What the reader wants to know is what *kind* of drink is lemonade? What *specific* type of child is an orphan? What *particular* form of government is a dictatorship?

10. *Lemonade* is a drink *made of lemons, sugar, and water.*
11. An *orphan* is a child *without living parents.*
12. A *dictatorship* is a form of government *in which one person has absolute control over his or her subjects.*

Here is a class definition of the substance pictured: *Plumpy'nut is a peanut-based food paste that has helped reverse malnutrition and starvation during famines.*

Think of class definitions as if they were in chart form:

Word	Category or Class	Distinguishing Facts or Details
lemonade	drink	made of lemons, sugar, and water
orphan	child	without living parents
dictatorship	form of government	one person has absolute control over his or her subjects

When you write a class definition, be careful not to place the word or term in too broad or vague a category. For instance, saying that lemonade is a *food* or that an orphan is a *person* will make your job of zeroing in on a distinguishing detail more difficult.

Besides making the category or class as limited as possible, be sure to make your distinguishing facts as specific and exact as you can. Saying that lemonade is a drink *made with water* or that an orphan is a child *who has lost family members* is not specific enough to give your reader an accurate definition.

Definition by Negation

A definition by **negation** means that the writer first says what something is not, and then says what it is.

13. A *good parent* does not just feed and clothe a child but loves, accepts, and supports that child for who he or she is.
14. *College* is not just a place to have a good time but a place to grow intellectually and emotionally.
15. *Liberty* does not mean having the right to do whatever you please but carries the obligation to respect the rights of others.

Definitions by negation are extremely helpful when you think that the reader has a preconceived idea about the word you wish to define. You say that *it is not* what the reader thought, but that *it is* something else entirely.

PRACTICE 1

Write a one-sentence definition by **synonym** for each of the following terms. Remember, the synonym should be more familiar than the term being defined.

1. *irate*: _____

2. *elude*: _____

3. *pragmatic*: _____

4. *fiasco*: _____

5. *elated*: _____

PRACTICE 2

Here are five **class** definitions. Circle the category and underline the distinguishing characteristics in each. You may find it helpful to make a chart.

1. A *haiku* is a Japanese poem that has seventeen syllables.
2. *Plagiarism* is stealing writing or ideas that are not one's own.
3. A *homer* is a referee who unconsciously favors the home team.
4. An *ophthalmologist* is a doctor who specializes in diseases of the eye.
5. The *tango* is a ballroom dance that originated in Latin America and is in 2/4 or 4/4 time.

PRACTICE 3

Define the following words by **class definition**. You may find it helpful to use this form:

"A _____ is a _____
          (noun)   (class or category)

that _____."
               (distinguishing characteristic)

1. *hamburger*: _____

_____

_____

2. *bikini*: _____

_____

_____

3. *snob*: _____

_____

_____

4. *mentor*: _____

_____

_____

5. *adolescence*: _____

_____

_____

PRACTICE 4

Write a one-sentence definition by **negation** for each of the following terms. First say what each term is not; then say what it is.

1. *hero*: _____

_____

_____

2. *final exam*: _____

_____

_____

3. *self-esteem*: _____

_____

_____

4. *intelligence*: _____

_____

_____

5. *freedom of speech*: _____

_____

_____

B. The Definition Paragraph

Sometimes a single-sentence definition may not be enough to define a word or term adequately. In such cases, the writer may need an entire paragraph in which he or she develops the definition by means of examples, descriptions, comparisons, contrasts, and so forth.

Topic Sentence

The topic sentence of a definition paragraph is often one of the single-sentence definitions discussed in Part A: definition by synonym, definition by class, definition by negation.

Here is the topic sentence of a definition paragraph:

> A *flashbulb memory* can be defined as a vivid, long-lasting memory that is formed at the moment a person learns of a highly emotional event.

- What kind of definition does the topic sentence use? _____

- To what larger category or class does a *flashbulb memory* belong? _____

  _____

- What are the distinguishing details about a *flashbulb memory* that make it

  different from other kinds of memories? _____

  _____

Paragraph and Plan

Here is the entire paragraph:

> A *flashbulb memory* can be defined as a vivid and long-lasting memory formed at the moment a person experiences a highly emotional event. It is as though a mental flashbulb pops, preserving the moment in great detail. Although flashbulb memories can be personal, they often are triggered by public events. For example, many older Americans recall exactly what they were doing when they learned that Pearl Harbor was bombed in 1941. Time froze as people crowded around their radios to find out what would happen next. Many more people recall in detail the shocking moment on November 11, 1963, when they heard that President John F. Kennedy had been assassinated. Considered the most widely shared flashbulb memory of our time, the image of Kennedy's death is burned into the minds of people the world over. More recently, the terrorist attack on the World Trade Center became a flashbulb memory for millions. Whether they heard the terrible news on their morning commute or were awakened by a panicked voice on the phone telling them to turn on the television, research into memory suggests that they will never forget that day. As these examples show, flashbulb memories mark some of our most permanent and haunting experiences, moments that were scored into our hearts.

- One effective way for a writer to develop the body of a definition paragraph is to provide examples.*

- What three examples does this writer give to develop the definition in the topic

  sentence? _____

  _____

- By repeating the word being defined—or a form of it—in the context of the definition paragraph, the writer helps the reader understand the definition better: "Although *flashbulb memories* can be personal …," "Considered the most widely shared *flashbulb memory* of our time …," "… on the World Trade Center became a *flashbulb memory* for millions."

- Before writing the paragraph, the writer probably brainstormed or freewrote to gather ideas and then made an **outline** like this:

TOPIC SENTENCE: A flashbulb memory is a vivid and long-lasting memory formed at the moment a person experiences a highly emotional event.

Example 1:   Pearl Harbor
—older Americans recall what they were doing in 1941
—people crowded around radios

Example 2:   J. F. Kennedy's assassination
—most widely shared flashbulb memory of our time
—image of Kennedy's death burned into minds all over the world

Example 3:   World Trade Center attack
—more recent flashbulb memory for millions
—whether on morning commute or phone, will never forget

CONCLUSION: Flashbulb memories mark our most permanent and haunting experiences.

- Note that each example in the body of the paragraph clearly relates to the definition in the topic sentence.

Although examples are an excellent way to develop a definition paragraph, other methods of development are also possible. For instance, you might compare and contrast† *love* and *lust, assertiveness* and *aggressiveness,* or *the leader* and *the follower.* You could also combine definition and persuasion.‡ Such a paragraph might begin, *College is a dating service* or *Alcoholism is not a moral weakness but a disease.* The rest of the paragraph would have to persuade readers that this definition is valid.

There are no transitional expressions used specifically for definition paragraphs. Sometimes phrases like *can be defined as* or *can be considered* or *means that* can help alert the reader that a definition paragraph will follow.§

---

* For more work on examples, see Chapter 5, "Illustration."

† For more work on contrast, see Chapter 10, "Comparison and Contrast."

‡ For more work on persuasion, see Chapter 13, "Persuasion."

§ For entire essays developed by definition, see Chapter 16, Part E.

PRACTICE 5

Read the following paragraph carefully and then answer the questions.

A feminist is *not* a man-hater, a masculine woman, a demanding shrew, or someone who dislikes housewives. A feminist is simply a woman or man who believes that women should enjoy the same rights, privileges, opportunities, and pay as men. Because society has deprived women of many equal rights, feminists have fought for equality. For instance, Susan B. Anthony, a famous nineteenth-century feminist, worked to get women the right to vote. Today, feminists want women to receive equal pay for equal work. They support a woman's right to pursue her goals and dreams, whether she wants to be an astronaut, athlete, banker, or full-time homemaker. On the home front, feminists believe that two partners who work should equally share the housework and child care. Because the term is often misunderstood, some people don't call themselves feminists even though they share feminist values. But courageous feminists of both sexes continue to speak out for equality.

1. The definition here spans two sentences. What kind of definition does the writer use in sentence 1? _____

2. What kind of definition appears in sentence 2? _____

3. The paragraph is developed by describing some key beliefs of feminists. What are these? _____

    _____

    _____

4. Which point is supported by an example? _____

    _____

5. Make a plan or an outline of the paragraph.

    _____

    _____

    _____

    _____

    _____

    _____

    _____

    _____

PRACTICE 6

Read the following paragraphs and answer the questions.

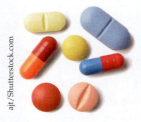

ajt/Shutterstock.com

A *placebo* is a fake medical treatment. Prescribed as if it were the real thing, a placebo is used to test new drugs. One group of patients takes the real drug while the other takes a placebo, maybe a simple sugar pill. The results show how many people are truly helped by a new medication and how many feel better just because they *think* they've been treated.

Here it gets interesting. Many people who receive fake treatments do improve; they experience the mysterious *placebo effect*. The placebo effect is symptom relief that is caused by receiving a fake treatment. In one famous study, arthritis patients in Texas who thought they had knee surgeries reported the same improvement in pain and mobility as patients who had real surgeries! Apparently, if the patient believes in the treatment, the healing power of the mind might do the rest.

—Dan Robinson, *PsychologyWatch.com*

1. What two terms or concepts are defined? _____

_____

2. What kind of definition is used for *placebo*? _____

3. What kind of definition is used for *placebo effect*? _____

4. Into what larger category does the writer place *placebo effect*? _____

5. What defining characteristic completes the definition? _____

_____

6. What example does the author give to illustrate the *placebo effect*? _____

_____

PRACTICE 7

Here are some topic sentences for definition paragraphs. Choose one that interests you and make a plan for a paragraph, using whatever method of development seems appropriate.

1. An optimist is someone who usually expects the best from life and from people.

2. Prejudice means prejudging people on the basis of race, creed, age, or sex—not on their merits as individuals.

3. A wealthy person does not necessarily have money and possessions, but he or she might possess inner wealth—a loving heart and a creative mind.

4. Registration is a ritual torture that students must go through before they can attend their classes.

5. Bravery and bravado are very different character traits.

PRACTICE 8 **TEAMWORK: CRITICAL THINKING AND WRITING**

Define a Team Player

Whether or not we play sports, most of us know what it means to be a *team player* on a basketball or soccer team. But these days, many employers also want to hire "team players." What, exactly, are they looking for? What qualities does a team player bring to the job?

In a group with four or five classmates, discuss the meaning of *team player*, listing all the qualities that you think a team player has. List at least eight qualities. Now craft a topic sentence of definition; have a group member write it down, using the form, "A team player is a(n) _____ who _____." Choose the three or four most important qualities and write a paragraph defining *team player*. Use examples or details to bring your paragraph to life. Be prepared to share your paragraph with the full class.

EXPLORING ONLINE

http://www.studententerprise.ie/are-you-a-team-player.html

At the bottom of the page, click "Are you a team player Quiz." Take the quiz and write about your results.

Checklist

The Process of Writing a Definition Paragraph

Refer to this checklist of steps as you write a definition paragraph of your own.

☐ 1. Narrow the topic in light of your audience and purpose.

☐ 2. Compose a topic sentence that uses one of the three basic methods of definition discussed in this chapter: synonym, class, or negation.

☐ 3. Decide on the method of paragraph development that is best suited to what you want to say.

☐ 4. Freewrite or brainstorm to generate ideas that may be useful in your definition paragraph. (You may want to freewrite or brainstorm before you narrow the topic.)

☐ 5. Select the best ideas and drop any ideas that do not clearly relate to the definition in your topic sentence.

☐ 6. Make a plan or an outline for your paragraph, numbering the ideas in the order in which you will present them.

☐ 7. Write a draft of your definition paragraph, using transitional expressions wherever they might be helpful.

☐ 8. Revise as necessary, checking for support, unity, logic, and coherence.

☐ 9. Proofread for errors in grammar, punctuation, sentence structure, spelling, and mechanics.

Suggested Topics for Definition Paragraphs

1. The gossip (or life of the party, Internet addict, co-worker from hell)
2. Professionalism
3. Self-esteem
4. A term from your field of study (like *green building, concussion, Oedipus complex, Harlem Renaissance, Pacific garbage patch, Baroque*)
5. A term from popular culture (*Spanglish, sampling* in music, *whistle-blower, Twitter, avatar*)
6. Unemployed (or uninsured)
7. Family
8. A disability, such as dyslexia, autism, or ADHD
9. A military term or symbol, such as the Purple Heart medal
10. A slang term you or your friends use
11. Urban legend (see **http://www.snopes.com**)
12. Plagiarism
13. A racist (terrorist, artist, sexist, activist, or other *-ist*)
14. The video-game (or fashion, football, racing car or other) fanatic
15. Writer's choice: _____

EXPLORING ONLINE

http://www.quintcareers.com/jobseeker_glossary.html
Check out this job seeker's glossary of career terms and words.

http://grammar.ccc.commnet.edu/grammar/composition/definition.htm
Read advice about writing longer definitions and one student's essay defining *Yankee*.

CourseMate for *Evergreen*
Visit *Evergreen* CourseMate for more practices and quizzes, videos
to accompany the readings, career and job-search resources,
ESL help, and live links to every Exploring Online in the book.

CHAPTER 10

Comparison and Contrast

A: The Contrast Paragraph and the Comparison Paragraph

B: The Comparison and Contrast Paragraph

To **contrast** two persons, places, or things is to examine the ways in which they are different. To **compare** them is to examine the ways in which they are similar.

Contrast and comparison are useful skills in daily life, work, and college. When you shop, you often compare and contrast. For instance, you might compare and contrast two dishwashers to get the better value. In fact, the magazine *Consumer Reports* was created to help consumers compare and contrast different product brands.

Your employer might ask you to compare and contrast two computers, two telephone services, or two shipping crates. Your job is to gather information about the similarities and differences to help your employer choose one over the other. In nearly every college course, you will be expected to compare and contrast—two generals, two types of storm systems, two minerals, or two painters of the same school.

A. The Contrast Paragraph and the Comparison Paragraph

Topic Sentence

Here is the topic sentence of a **contrast** paragraph:

> Although soul and hip hop both spring from African American roots, they are very different musical expressions.

● The writer begins a contrast paragraph with a topic sentence that clearly states what two persons, things, or ideas will be contrasted.

● What two things will be contrasted?

_____

● What word or words in the topic sentence make it clear that the writer will contrast soul and hip hop?

_____

Paragraph and Plan

Here is the entire paragraph:

> Although soul and hip hop both spring from African American roots, they are very different musical expressions. Soul music borrows from gospel and rhythm and blues. The singer's voice, backed up by live instruments, soars with emotion, with soul. This music captures the optimism of its time—the civil rights movement of the 1960s and hope for social change. There are two types of soul— the smooth Detroit style of the Supremes, Stevie Wonder, and The Temptations and the more gritty, gospel-driven Memphis style of Otis Redding and Booker T and the MGs. Soul music is upbeat and often joyful; its subjects are love and affirmation of the human condition. On the other hand, hip hop (or rap) draws on hard rock, funk, and techno. The rapper chants rhymes against a driving instrumental background that may be prerecorded. Rap grew out of the New York ghettos in the late 1970s and the 1980s, when crack and guns flooded "the hood" and many dreams seemed broken. Of the rival East and West Coast rappers, New Yorkers include Grandmaster Flash, LL Cool J, and the murdered Biggie Smalls, while Los Angeles rappers include Ice Cube and the murdered Tupac Shakur. The subjects of hip hop are racism, crime, and poverty. Both soul and hip hop claim to "tell it like it is." Hip hop's answer to the soulful Four Tops is the Furious Four. What's in a name? Perhaps the way the listener experiences reality.
>
> —Maurice Bosco, Student

● The writer first provides information about (A) soul music and then gives contrasting parallel information about (B) hip hop.

● What information about (A) soul does the writer provide in the first half of the

paragraph? _____

_____

_____

● What contrasting parallel information does the writer provide about (B) hip

hop in the second half of the paragraph? _____

_____

_____

● Why do you think the writer chose to present the points of contrast in this order?

_____

_____

_____

● Note that the last four sentences provide a thoughtful conclusion. What final

point does the writer make? _____

_____

Before composing the paragraph, the writer probably brainstormed or freewrote to gather ideas and then made an **outline** like this:

TOPIC SENTENCE: Although soul and hip hop both spring from African American roots, they are very different musical expressions.

Points of Contrast	A. Soul	B. Hip Hop
1. influences	gospel, R&B	hard rock, funk, techno
2. sound	soaring voice, live instruments	chanted rhymes; instrumentals may be prerecorded
3. time period	1960s, civil rights, hope for change	1970s–1980s, crack, guns
4. types	Detroit, Memphis	New York, Los Angeles
5. subjects	love, affirmation	racism, crime, poverty

Organized in this manner, the plan for this contrast paragraph helps the writer make sure that the paragraph will be complete. That is, if the historical period of soul is discussed, that of hip hop must also be discussed, and so on, for every point of contrast.

Here is another way to write the same paragraph:

Although soul and hip hop both spring from African American roots, they are very different musical expressions. Soul music borrows from gospel and rhythm and blues, whereas hip hop (or rap) draws on hard rock, funk, and techno. The soul singer's voice, backed up by live instruments, soars with emotion, with soul; however, the rapper chants rhymes against a driving instrumental background that may be prerecorded. Soul music captures the optimism of its time—the civil rights movement of the 1960s and hope for social change. On the other hand, hip hop grew out of the New York ghettos in the late 1970s and the 1980s, when crack and guns flooded "the hood" and many dreams seemed broken. There are two types of soul—the smooth Detroit style of the Supremes, Stevie Wonder, and The

Temptations and the more gritty, gospel-driven Memphis style of Otis Redding and Booker T and the MGs. Of the rival East and West Coast rappers, New Yorkers include Grandmaster Flash, LL Cool J, and the murdered Biggie Smalls, while Los Angeles rappers include Ice Cube and the murdered Tupac Shakur. Whereas soul music's subjects are love and affirmation of the human condition, the subjects of hip hop are racism, crime, and poverty. Both soul and hip hop claim to "tell it like it is." Hip hop's answer to the soulful Four Tops is the Furious Four. What's in a name? Perhaps the way the listener experiences reality.

● Instead of giving all the information about soul music and then going on to hip hop, this paragraph moves back and forth between soul and hip hop, dealing with *each point of contrast separately.*

Use either one of these **two patterns** when writing a contrast or a comparison paragraph:

1. Present all the information about **A** and then provide parallel information about **B**:

<table>
<tr><td>**First all A :** Point 1
Point 2
Point 3</td><td>**Then all B :** Point 1
Point 2
Point 3</td></tr>
</table>

● This pattern is good for paragraphs and for short compositions. The reader can easily remember what was said about A by the time he or she gets to B.

2. Move back and forth between **A** and **B**. Present one point about **A** and then go to the parallel point about **B**. Then move to the next point and do the same:

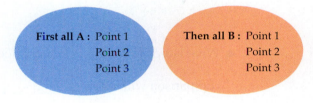

First A, Point 1   **Then B,** Point 1

First A, Point 2   **Then B,** Point 2

First A, Point 3   **Then B,** Point 3

● The second pattern is better for longer papers, where it may be hard for the reader to remember what the writer said about A by the time he or she gets to B a few paragraphs later. By going back and forth, the writer makes it easier for the reader to keep the contrasts or comparisons in mind.

What you have learned so far about planning a contrast paragraph holds true for a comparison paragraph as well. Just remember that *contrast stresses differences* whereas *comparison stresses similarities.*

Here is a **comparison** paragraph:

> In my family, personality traits are said to skip generations, so that might explain why my grandfather and I have so much in common. My grandfather arrived in the United States at sixteen, a penniless young man from Italy looking for a new life and ready to earn it. He quickly apprenticed himself to a shoe cobbler and never stopped working until he retired fifty-three years later. Similarly, when I was fourteen, I asked permission to apply for my first job as a bank teller. My parents smiled and said, "She's just like Grandpa." Though everyone else in my family spends money the minute it reaches their hands, my habit of saving every penny does not seem strange to them. My grandfather also was careful with money, building his own shoe repair business out of nothing. He loved to work in his large vegetable garden and brought bags of carrots and tomatoes to our house on Saturday mornings. Like him, I enjoy the feeling of dirt on my fingers and the surprise of seedlings sprouting overnight. Though I raise zinnias instead of zucchinis, I know where I inherited a passion to make things grow. Only in opportunities, we differed. Although my grandfather's education ended with third grade, I am fortunate to attend college—and hope that education will be my legacy to the generations that come after me.
>
> —Angela De Renzi, Student

- What words in the topic sentence does the writer use to indicate that a comparison will follow? _____

  _____

- In what ways are the writer and her grandfather similar? _____

  _____

  _____

- What transitional words stress the similarities? _____

- What pattern of presentation does the writer use? _____

  _____

- What one point of *contrast* serves as a strong punch line for the paragraph?

  _____

  _____

- Make a plan or an outline of this comparison paragraph.

Transitional Expressions

Transitional expressions in contrast paragraphs stress *opposition* and *difference*:

Transitional Expressions for Contrast	
conversely	nevertheless
however	on the contrary
in contrast	on the one hand
in opposition	on the other hand
although, even though, whereas, while*	but, yet†

Transitional expressions in comparison paragraphs stress *similarities*:

Transitional Expressions for Comparison	
also	in a similar way
as well	in the same way
equally	likewise
in addition	similarly

As you write, avoid using just one or two of these transitional expressions. Learn new ones from the list and practice them in your paragraphs.‡

PRACTICE 1

Read the following paragraph carefully and answer the questions.

Certain personality traits, like whether a person is more reactive or proactive, can predict success or its opposite. In his book *The Seven Habits of Highly Effective People*, Steven Covey writes that reactive people tend to sit back and wait for life or circumstances to bring them opportunities. They react instead of act. When good things happen, they are happy, but when bad things happen, they feel like victims. Reactive people often say things like, "There's nothing I can do," "I can't because . . . ," and "If only." In the short term, reactive people might feel comfortable playing it safe, holding back, and avoiding challenges; in the long term, though, they are often left dreaming. On the other hand, proactive people know that they

---

* For more work on subordinating conjunctions like *although* and *while*, see Chapter 27, Part B.

† For more work on coordinating conjunctions like *but* and *yet*, see Chapter 27, Part A.

‡ For entire essays developed by comparison or contrast, see Chapter 17, Part A.

have the power to choose their responses to whatever life brings. They act instead of react: if things aren't going their way, they take action to help create the outcome they desire. Proactive people can be recognized by their tendency to say things like "Let's consider the alternatives," "I prefer," "We can," and "I will." In the short term, proactive people might face the discomfort of failing because they take on challenges, set goals, and work toward them. But in the long term, Covey says, proactive people are the ones who achieve their dreams.

1. Can you tell from the topic sentence whether a contrast or comparison will follow? _____
    _____

2. What two personality types are being contrasted? _____

3. What information does the writer provide about reactive people? _____
    _____

4. What parallel information does the writer provide about proactive people? _____
    _____
    _____

5. What pattern does the writer of this paragraph use to present the contrasts? _____
    _____

6. What transitional expression does the writer use to stress the shift from A to B? _____
    _____

PRACTICE 2

This paragraph is hard to follow because it lacks transitional words and expressions that emphasize contrast. Revise the paragraph, adding transitional words of contrast. Strive for variety.

American restaurant portions have increased dramatically between 1985 and the present, a trend that worries many nutritionists. The small food servings of twenty years ago were healthy, according to the U.S. Food and Drug Administration (FDA). Modern portions have dangerously ballooned. For example, in 1985, a blueberry muffin weighed just 1.5 ounces. Today's typical muffin is a whopping 5 ounces. Compared with portions in 1985, today's supersized foods pack excess calories. For instance, a turkey sandwich once provided 320 calories. Now it delivers 820 calories, nearly half the fuel a male should consume in one day. The smaller food portions of years past contained reasonable amounts of dietary fat. Today's portions often ooze with fat. In 1985, a typical fast-food hamburger delivered 15 fat grams. Today's burger contains 34 artery-clogging grams—even before the consumer adds extra sauce. Huge portions do give us more for our money: more calories, more fat, more obesity, more heart disease. Don't be a victim of portion distortion.

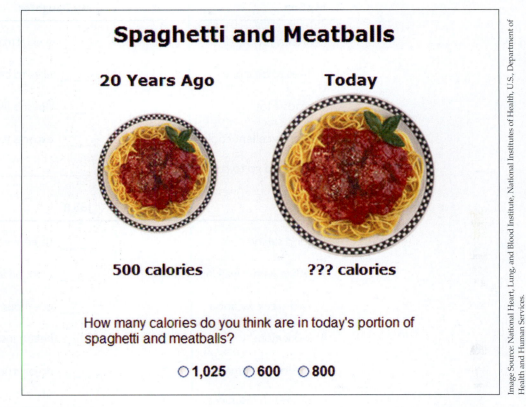

A picture is worth a thousand words at the U.S. government's "Portion Distortion" website, which contrasts typical food portions 20 years ago and now.

EXPLORING ONLINE

http://hp2010.nhlbihin.net/portion/

Learn more about "portion distortion" and maintaining a healthy weight; take notes on facts or ideas for further writing.

PRACTICE 3

Below are three plans for contrast paragraphs. The points of contrast in the second column do not follow the same order as the points in the first column. In addition, one detail is missing. First, number the points in the second column to match those in the first. Then fill in the missing detail.

1. **Shopping at a Supermarket**	**Shopping at a Local Grocery**
1. carries all brands	_____ personal service
2. lower prices	_____ closed on Sundays

3. open seven days a week	_____ prices often higher
4. little personal service	_____ _____
5. no credit	_____ credit available for steady customers

2. My Son   **My Daughter**

1. fifteen years old	_____ good at making minor household repairs
2. likes to be alone	_____ likes to be with friends
3. reads a lot	_____ doesn't like to read
4. is an excellent cook	_____ expects to attend a technical college
5. wants to go to culinary school	_____ _____

3. Job A   **Job B**

1. good salary	_____ three-week vacation
2. office within walking distance	_____ work on a team with others
3. two-week vacation	_____ one-hour bus ride to office
4. work alone	_____ health insurance
5. lots of overtime	_____ no overtime
6. no health insurance	_____ _____

PRACTICE 4

Here are three topics for either contrast or comparison paragraphs. Compose two topic sentences for each topic, one for a possible contrast paragraph and one for a possible comparison paragraph.

            Topic   **Topic Sentences**

EXAMPLE Two members of my family   A. *My brother and sister have different attitudes toward exercise.*

                                            B. *My parents are alike in that they're easygoing.*

           1. Two friends or coworkers   A. _____

                                              _____

                                              _____

B. _____
_____
_____

2. You as a child and you as
   an adult

A. _____
_____
_____

B. _____
_____
_____

3. Two vacations

A. _____
_____
_____

B. _____
_____
_____

PRACTICE 5

Here are four topic sentences for comparison or contrast paragraphs. For each topic sentence, think of one supporting point of comparison or contrast and explain that point in one or two sentences.

1. When it comes to movies (TV shows, books, entertainment), Demetrios and Arlene have totally different tastes.

_____
_____

2. My mother and I have few personality traits in common.

_____
_____

3. Although there are obvious differences, the two neighborhoods (blocks, houses) have much in common.

_____
_____

4. Paying taxes is like having a tooth pulled.*

_____

_____

PRACTICE 6   **TEAMWORK: CRITICAL THINKING AND WRITING**

Contrast Toys for Boys and Toys for Girls

Retail stores and websites frequently recommend toys for children, often dividing their gift ideas into two groups: "toys for boys" and "toys for girls." These were the top-selling toys in 2010, according to the National Retail Federation.

Top Toys for Boys	**Top Toys for Girls**
1. Video Games	1. Barbie
2. LEGO	2. Dolls (generic)
3. Cars (generic)	3. Dora the Explorer
4. Disney Toy Story	4. Video Games
5. Hot Wheels	5. Disney Princess
6. Transformers	6. Zhu Zhu Pets
7. Xbox 360	7. American Girl
8. Fisher-Price Toys	8. Fisher-Price Toys
9. Iron Man	9. Disney Hannah Montana
10. (tie) Nintendo Wii and trucks (generic)	10. Bratz

Make sure every group member knows what these toys are. Then, based on the lists, discuss what contrasting messages are being sent about what boys and girls supposedly like to do. Do these lists put unfair limits on children of either sex? Now plan and write a comparison or contrast paragraph based on your discussion.

EXPLORING ONLINE

http://www.google.com

Or visit your favorite search engine; search "toys, gender roles" and see what information you find.

_____

* For more work on this kind of comparison, see Chapter 23, "Revising for Language Awareness," Part D.

Checklist

The Process of Writing a Comparison or Contrast Paragraph

Refer to this checklist of steps as you write a comparison or contrast paragraph of your own.

- ☐ 1. Narrow the topic in light of your audience and purpose.
- ☐ 2. Compose a topic sentence that clearly states that a comparison or a contrast will follow.
- ☐ 3. Freewrite or brainstorm to generate as many points of comparison or contrast as you can think of. (You may want to freewrite or brainstorm before you narrow the topic.)
- ☐ 4. Choose the points you will use, and drop any details that are not really part of the comparison or the contrast.
- ☐ 5. List parallel points of comparison or of contrast for both A and B.
- ☐ 6. Make a plan or an outline, numbering all the points of comparison or contrast in the order in which you will present them in the paragraph.
- ☐ 7. Write a draft of your comparison or contrast paragraph, using transitional expressions that stress either differences or similarities.
- ☐ 8. Revise as necessary, checking for support, unity, logic, and coherence.
- ☐ 9. Proofread for errors in grammar, punctuation, sentence structure, spelling, and mechanics.

Suggested Topics for Comparison or Contrast Paragraphs

1. Compare or contrast two attitudes toward money (the spendthrift and the miser) or partnership (the confirmed single and the committed partner).
2. Compare or contrast two ways of dealing with anger, loss, grief, or disappointment.
3. Compare or contrast a job you hated and a job you loved.
4. Compare or contrast two consumer items of the same type (cars, computers, phones).
5. Compare or contrast the way something is done in the United States and the way it is done in another country (or the ways something is done in two different states).
6. Compare or contrast two high schools or colleges you have attended (perhaps one in the United States and one in another country).
7. Compare or contrast two athletes in the same sport (or two entertainers, politicians, professors).

8. Compare or contrast your expectations of a person, place, or situation and the reality.

9. Compare or contrast two career fields you are considering.

10. Writer's choice: _____

B. The Comparison and Contrast Paragraph

Sometimes you will be asked to write a paragraph that both compares and contrasts, one that stresses both similarities and differences.

Here is a comparison and contrast paragraph:

> Although contemporary fans would find the game played by the Knickerbockers—the first organized baseball club—similar to modern baseball, they would also note some startling differences. In 1845, as now, the four bases of the playing field were set in a diamond shape, ninety feet from one another. Nine players took the field. The object of the game was to score points by hitting a pitched ball and running around the bases. The teams changed sides after three outs. However, the earlier game was also different. The umpire sat at a table along the third base line instead of standing behind home plate. Unlike the modern game, the players wore no gloves. Rather than firing the ball over the plate at ninety miles an hour, the pitcher gently tossed it underhand to the batter. Since there were no balls and strikes, the batter could wait for the pitch he wanted. The game ended not when nine innings were completed but when one team scored twenty-one runs, which were called "aces."

● How are the Knickerbockers' game and modern baseball similar?

_____

_____

_____

● How are these two versions of the game different? _____

_____

_____

_____

_____

_____

● What transitional words and expressions in the paragraph emphasize similarities and differences? _____

_____

_____

Before composing this comparison and contrast paragraph, the writer probably brainstormed or freewrote to gather ideas and then made an **outline** like this:

TOPIC SENTENCE: Although contemporary fans would find the game played by the Knickerbockers—the first organized baseball club—similar to modern baseball, they would also note some startling differences.

Comparisons	Knickerbockers	Modern Game
Point 1	four bases, ninety feet apart, in diamond shape	
Point 2	nine players	
Point 3	scoring points	
Point 4	three outs	

Contrasts		
Point 1	umpire sat at third base line	umpire at home plate
Point 2	no gloves	gloves
Point 3	pitcher gently tossed ball	pitcher fires ball at plate
Point 4	no balls and strikes	balls and strikes
Point 5	twenty-one "aces" to win, no innings	most runs to win, nine innings

---

● A plan or outline such as this makes it easier for the writer to organize a great deal of material.
● The writer begins by listing all the points of comparison—how the Knickerbockers' game and modern baseball are similar. Then the writer lists all the points of contrast—how they are different.

PRACTICE 7

Here is a somewhat longer comparison and contrast (two paragraphs). Read it carefully and answer the questions.

Most people don't connect Dr. Gregory House, the brilliant medical detective on the television show *House*, with Sherlock Holmes, the legendary crime-solver invented by writer Sir Arthur Conan Doyle in 1887. The differences are obvious. House is a medical doctor confronting people's illnesses while Holmes is a detective who tracks murderers and jewel thieves. House stars in a TV drama created by David Shore, but Holmes stars in Doyle's four novels and fifty-six short stories. House is a 21st-century American man, whereas Holmes is a British character of the last century, with his quaint pipe and old-fashioned plaid cap.

Yet despite these differences, the two sleuths share startling similarities. Both solve mysteries by their brilliant powers of deduction. Both are extremely arrogant, alienating people around them, and both are lazy until a good case rivets their attention. House is notoriously addicted to pain-killers, supposedly to help him cope with a wounded leg; similarly, the fictional Holmes is addicted to cocaine. Dr. Greg House's only true friend is his colleague Dr. Wilson, just as Sherlock Holmes's only friend is his assistant, Dr. Watson. Each of these troubled loners turns to music. House plays the guitar, and Holmes, a violin. "House" is another word for "home," which sounds like Holmes. One TV episode showed House's address as 221B, with the street name covered. Sherlock Holmes fictional address is 221B Baker Street. For those doubters who still say all this is just coincidence, *House* creator David Shore admitted in a 2005 interview that the brilliant and complex Sherlock Holmes inspired him to create Dr. Gregory House.

1. What two persons or things does this writer compare and contrast? _____

   _____

2. What words indicate that both contrast and comparison will follow? _____

   _____

3. How are Dr. House and Sherlock Holmes different? _____

   _____

TV's Dr. House and Sherlock Holmes have more in common than inquiring minds.

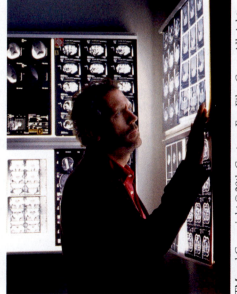

4. How are Dr. House and Sherlock Holmes similar? _____

_____

5. On a sheet of paper, make a plan or outline for these paragraphs.

Working Through the Comparison and Contrast Paragraph

You can work through the comparison and contrast paragraph in the same way that you do a comparison paragraph or a contrast paragraph. Follow the steps in the earlier checklist, but make certain that your paragraph shows both similarities and differences.

Suggested Topics for Comparison and Contrast Paragraphs

1. Compare and contrast two different places you've lived.

2. Compare and contrast the requirements of two jobs or careers.

3. Compare and contrast weddings, parties, or funerals in two different cultures.

4. Compare and contrast two albums, videos, or websites on similar subjects.

5. Compare and contrast your life now and your life five years ago.

6. Compare and contrast two singers, bands, or artists.

7. Compare and contrast shopping at two different discount stores (or another type).

8. Compare and contrast two popular television programs of the same type (newscasts, talk shows, situation comedies, and so on).

9. Compare and contrast two attitudes toward one subject (firearms, immigration, and so on).

10. Writer's choice: _____

EXPLORING ONLINE

http://web.uvic.ca/wguide/Pages/ParDevCC.html

Review of the comparison/contrast paragraph, with examples

http://muskingum.edu/~cal/database/general/organization.html#Comparison

Print these graphic outlines to help plan your paragraph.

CourseMate for *Evergreen*

Visit *Evergreen* CourseMate for more practices and quizzes, videos to accompany the readings, career and job-search resources, ESL help, and live links to every Exploring Online in the book.

CHAPTER 11

Classification

To **classify** is to gather into types, kinds, or categories according to a single basis of division.

Mailroom personnel, for example, might separate incoming mail into four piles: orders, bills, payments, and inquiries. Once the mail has been divided in this manner—according to which department should receive each pile—it can be efficiently delivered.

The same information can be classified in more than one way. The Census Bureau collects a variety of data about the people living in the United States. One way to classify the data is by age group—the number of people under eighteen, between eighteen and fifty-five, over fifty-five, and over seventy. Such information might be useful in developing programs for college-bound youth or for the elderly. Other ways of dividing the population are by geographic location, occupation, family size, level of education, and so on.

Whether you classify rocks by their origin for a geology course or children by their stages of growth for a psychology course, you will be organizing large groups into smaller, more manageable units that can be explained to your reader.

Topic Sentence

Here is the topic sentence for a classification paragraph:

> Gym-goers can be classified according to their priorities at the gym as sweaty fanatics, fashionistas, busybodies, or fit normals.

- The writer begins a classification paragraph with a topic sentence that clearly states what group of people or things will be classified.

- What group of people will be classified? _____

- Into how many categories will they be divided? What are the categories?

  _____

  _____

Paragraph and Plan

Here is the entire paragraph:

> Gym-goers can be classified according to their priorities at the gym as sweaty fanatics, fashionistas, busybodies, and fit normals. Sweaty fanatics take gym-going to the extreme. They hog the machines, drip sweat everywhere, and barely look up if someone falls off the treadmill beside them. Occasionally, they will stare at the mirror, admiring the muscle group they are working on. The fashionistas also admire their own reflections, but they barely break a sweat. For them, the gym is just another excuse to buy clothes. They wear perfectly matched workout clothes with color-coordinated sport watches and gym shoes. The third group, the busybodies, can't stop talking. Whether it's making idle chitchat or correcting another exerciser's form on a machine, they seem unable to shut up. Not even headphones and one-word answers can stop the busybodies from babbling. Luckily, the fit normals keep things from getting too far out of control. They come to the gym to work out, stay healthy, and go home, but they remember that basic good manners apply in every setting.
>
> —Laurie Zamot, Student

- On what basis does the writer classify gym-goers? _____
  _____

- What information does the writer provide about the first type, sweaty fanatics?
  _____
  _____

- What information does the writer provide about the second type, fashionistas?
  _____
  _____

- What information does the writer provide about the third type, busybodies?
  _____
  _____

- What information does the writer provide about the fourth type, the fit normals?
  _____
  _____

● Why do you think the writer discusses fit normals last? _____

_____

_____

Before composing the paragraph, the writer probably brainstormed or freewrote to gather ideas and then made an **outline** like this:

TOPIC SENTENCE: Gym-goers can be classified according to their priorities at the gym as sweaty fanatics, fashionistas, busybodies, or fit normals.

Type 1: Sweaty fanatics
—hog machines; drip sweat
—barely look if someone falls
—stare in mirror, admiring muscles

Type 2: Fashionistas
—admire themselves but don't sweat
—excuse to buy clothes
—matched workout clothes
—coordinating sport watches and gym shoes

Type 3: Busybodies
—can't stop talking, advising
—headphones, short answers don't work

Type 4: Fit normals
—keep things from going out of control
—work out, go home
—remember good manners even in gym

● Note that the body of the paragraph discusses all four types of gym-goers mentioned in the topic sentence and does not add any new ones.

This classification paragraph sticks to a single method of classification: *the priorities of gym-goers at the gym.* If the paragraph had also discussed a fourth category—*left-handed gym-goers*—the initial basis of classification would fall apart because *left-handedness* has nothing to do with *the priorities of different gym-goers.*

The topic sentence of a classification paragraph usually has two parts: the *topic* and the *basis of classification.* The basis of classification is the controlling idea: it *controls* how the writer will approach the topic. Stating it in writing will help keep the paragraph on track.

There is no set rule about which category to present first, second, or last in a classification paragraph. However, the paragraph should follow some kind of **logical sequence** from the most to least outrageous, least to most expensive, from the largest to the smallest category, and so on.*†

Transitional Expressions

Transitional expressions in classification paragraphs stress divisions and categories:

Transitional Expressions for Classification	
can be divided	the first type
can be classified	the second kind
can be categorized	the last category

PRACTICE 1

Read the following paragraph carefully and answer the questions.

In his classic discussion of friendship, the Greek philosopher Aristotle divided friends into three categories, based on the reason for the friendship. *Friendships of utility* are those in which two people are drawn together for mutual benefit. For example, two nurse's aides may develop a friendship through helping each other on the job, or two classmates may become friends because they study together. In this type of friendship, the connection frequently is broken when the situation changes, when one person takes another job or the class ends. In the second type, *friendships of pleasure*, two people find it pleasurable to spend time together. Two passionate lovers fall into this category. Other examples are young people who hang out for fun, golf buddies, or hiking pals. When the pleasure fades, these friends may part ways. Either of these two types, however, can evolve into the more lasting third type, *friendships of the good*, or true friendships. These relationships are based on mutual admiration for the other's values and overall goodness, which creates a desire to interact and offer assistance. Lifelong friendships formed in childhood and friendships that endure despite separations, hardship, or changes in personal circumstances are true friendships. Aristotle's categories might explain why some people consider themselves lucky if they count just one true friend in a lifetime.

1. How many categories are there, and what are they? _____

_____

_____

* For more work on order, see Chapter 4, "Achieving Coherence," Part A.

† For complete essays developed by classification, see Chapter 17, Part B.

2. On what basis does the writer classify friendships? _____

_____

3. Make a plan of the paragraph on a separate sheet of paper.

PRACTICE 2

Each group of things or persons in this practice has been divided according to a single basis of classification. However, one item in each group does not belong—it does not fit that single basis of classification.

Read each group of items carefully; then circle the letter of the one item that does *not* belong. Next write the single basis of classification that includes the rest of the group.

EXAMPLE   Shirts

    a. cotton

    b. suede

    (c.) short-sleeved

    d. polyester

       material they are made of _____

1. Shoes

    a. flat heels

    b. 2-inch heels

    c. patent leather heels

    d. 3-inch heels

    _____

2. Dates

    a. very good-looking

    b. sometimes pay

    c. always pay

    d. expect me to pay

    _____

3. Students

    a. moderately hard-working

    b. very hard-working

    c. goof-offs

    d. talkative in class

    _____

4. Contact lenses

    a. soft

    b. green

    c. brown

    d. lavender

    _____

5. Milk

   a. two percent fat

   b. whole

   c. chocolate

   d. one percent fat

_____

6. Drivers

   a. obey the speed limit

   b. teenage drivers

   c. speeders

   d. creepers

_____

PRACTICE 3

Any group of persons, things, or ideas can be classified in more than one way, depending on the basis of classification. For instance, students in your class can be classified on the basis of height (short, average, tall) or on the basis of class participation (often participate, sometimes participate, never participate). Both of these groupings are valid classifications of the same group of people.

Think of two ways in which each of the following groups could be classified.

Group	Basis of Classification
EXAMPLE Bosses	(A) _how demanding they are_
	(B) _how generous they are_
1. Members of my family	(A) _____
	(B) _____
2. Hurricanes	(A) _____
	(B) _____
3. Fans of a certain sport	(A) _____
	(B) _____
4. Vacations	(A) _____
	(B) _____
5. Fitness magazines	(A) _____
	(B) _____

PRACTICE 4

Listed below are three groups of people or things. Decide on a single basis of classification for each group and the categories that would develop from your basis of classification. Finally, write a topic sentence for each of your classifications.

	Group	Basis of Classification	Categories
EXAMPLE	Professors at Pell College	*methods of*	*lectures*
		instruction	*class discussions*
			both
			_____

TOPIC SENTENCE: *Professors at Pell College can be classified according to their methods of instruction: those who lecture, those who encourage class discussions, and those who do both.*

_____

Group	Basis of Classification	Categories
1. Car owners	_____	_____
	_____	_____
		_____
		_____

TOPIC SENTENCE: _____

_____

_____

Group	Basis of Classification	Categories
2. Credit-card users	_____	_____
	_____	_____
		_____
		_____

TOPIC SENTENCE: _____

_____

_____

3. Ways of reacting   _____   _____

    to a crisis   _____   _____

    _____

    _____

TOPIC SENTENCE: _____

_____

_____

PRACTICE 5

Now choose the classification in Practice 4 that most interests you and make a plan or outline for a paragraph on a separate sheet of paper. As you work, make sure that you have listed all possible categories for your basis of classification. Remember, every car owner or credit-card user should fit into one of your categories. Finally, write your paragraph, describing each category briefly and perhaps giving an example of each.

PRACTICE 6

TEAMWORK: CRITICAL THINKING AND WRITING

Classify Students on Campus

In a group with four or five classmates, discuss some interesting ways in which you might classify the students at your college. List at least five possible ways. You might focus on students in just one place—like the computer lab, swimming pool, coffee stand, library, or an exam room during finals week. Then come up with one basis of classification, either serious or humorous. For example, you could classify swimmers according to their level of expertise or splashing, students during finals week according to their fashion statements, or students standing in line for coffee according to their degree of impatience.

Now choose the most interesting basis of classification. Name three or four categories that cover the group, and write a paragraph classifying your fellow students. You might wish to enrich your categories with details and examples. Be prepared to read your paragraph to the full class.

Checklist

The Process of Writing a Classification Paragraph

Refer to this checklist of steps as you write a classification paragraph.

☐ 1. Narrow the topic in light of your audience and purpose. Think in terms of a group of people or things that can be classified easily into types or categories.

☐ 2. Decide on a single basis of classification. This basis will depend on what information you wish to give your audience.

☐ 3. Compose a topic sentence that clearly shows what you are dividing into categories or types. If you wish, your topic sentence can state the basis on which you are making the classification and the types that will be discussed in the paragraph.

☐ 4. List the categories into which the group is being classified. Be sure that your categories cover all the possibilities. Do not add any new categories that are not logically part of your original basis of classification.

☐ 5. Freewrite, cluster, or brainstorm to generate information, details, and examples for each of the categories. (You may want to prewrite before you narrow the topic.)

☐ 6. Select the best details and examples, and drop those that are not relevant to your classification.

☐ 7. Make a plan or an outline for your paragraph, numbering the categories in the order in which you will present them.

☐ 8. Write a draft of your classification paragraph, using transitional expressions wherever they may be helpful.

☐ 9. Revise as necessary, checking for support, unity, logic, and coherence.

☐ 10. Proofread for errors in grammar, punctuation, sentence structure, spelling, and mechanics.

Suggested Topics for Classification Paragraphs

1. Ways that people manage their finances (organize or make decisions)
2. Co-workers at your job
3. Problems facing college freshmen or someone new to a job
4. Clothing in your closet
5. Types of viral videos on YouTube
6. College instructors
7. Dancers at a party or club
8. Ways that students prepare for exams
9. Shoppers

10. Performers of one kind of music

11. Marriages or partnerships

12. Financial aid sources for college

13. Styles of jeans

14. Colleges in your city or area

15. Writer's choice: _____

EXPLORING ONLINE

http://www.filmratings.com

Click "Ratings" for movie classifications.

http://sln.fi.edu/tfi/units/life/classify/classify.html

Amazing introduction to the classification of plants and animals

CourseMate for *Evergreen*

Visit *Evergreen* CourseMate for more practices and quizzes, videos
to accompany the readings, career and job-search resources,
ESL help, and live links to every Exploring Online in the book.

CHAPTER 12

Cause and Effect

The ability to think through **causes and effects** is a key to success in many college courses, jobs, and everyday situations. Daily we puzzle over the **causes** of, or reasons for, events: What caused one brother to drop out of school and another to succeed brilliantly? What causes Jenine's asthma attacks? Why did the stock market plunge 300 points?

Effects are the *results* of a cause or causes. Does playing violent computer games affect a child's behavior? What are the effects of being a twin, keeping a secret, or winning the lottery?

Most events worth examining have complex, not simple, causes and effects. That is, they may have several causes and several effects. Certainly, in many fields, questions of cause and effect challenge even the experts: *What will be the long-term effects of the breakup of the former Soviet Union? What causes the HIV virus to disappear from the blood of some infected babies?* (This one answer could help save millions of lives.)

Topic Sentence

Here is the topic statement of a cause and effect paragraph; the writer has chosen to break the information into two sentences.

> What killed off the dinosaurs—and 70 percent of life on earth—65 million years ago? According to recent research, this massive destruction had three causes.

● The writer begins a cause and effect paragraph by clearly stating the subject and indicating whether causes or effects will be discussed. What is the subject of this paragraph? Will causes or effects be the focus?

_____

_____

● The writer states the topic in two sentences rather than one. Is this effective? Why or why not? (A single sentence might read, "According to recent research, the massive destruction of dinosaurs and other creatures 65 million years ago had three causes.")

_____

_____

● Words like *causes*, *reasons*, and *factors* are useful to show causes. Words like *effects*, *results*, and *consequences* are useful to show effects.

Paragraph and Plan

Here is the entire paragraph:

What killed off the dinosaurs—and 70 percent of life on Earth—65 million years ago? According to recent research, this massive destruction had three causes. Dr. Peter Ward of the University of Washington reports that the first cause was simple "background extinction." This is the normal disappearance of some animals and plants that goes on all the time. Second, a drop in sea level during this period slowly destroyed about 25 percent more of the world's species. Last and most dramatic, a comet as big as Manhattan smashed into the earth near Mexico's Yucatan Peninsula, literally shaking the world. The huge buried crater left by this comet was found in 1991. Now Dr. Ward has proved that ash and a rare metal from that fiery crash fell around the globe. This means that the impact, fires, smoke, and ash quickly wiped out the dinosaurs and much of life on earth. This great "die-off" cleared the way for mammals to dominate Earth.

● How many causes does this writer give for the destruction of the dinosaurs and

other species? What are they?_____

_____

● Did the writer make up these ideas? If not, who or what is the source of the

information?_____

_____

● What transitional words introduce each of the three causes? _____

_____

● What kind of order is used in this paragraph?*_____

_____

_____

* For more work on order, see Chapter 4, "Achieving Coherence," Part A.

Before writing the paragraph, the writer probably jotted an outline or plan like this:

TOPIC SENTENCE: According to recent research, this massive destruction had three causes.

        —write a catchy introductory sentence?

        —mention time, 65 million years ago

Cause 1:   "background extinction"

        —normal disappearance of animals and plants

        —give credit to Dr. Ward

Cause 2:   drop in sea level

        —25 percent more species destroyed

Cause 3:   giant comet hit earth

        —big as Manhattan

        —crater found in 1991 near Yucatan Peninsula

        —now Ward proves ash and rare metal circled globe

        —this comet destroyed dinosaurs and others

CONCLUSION: "die-off" cleared way for mammals—OR tie to current news and films about comet danger

---

Other paragraphs examine *effects*, not causes. Either they try to predict future effects of something happening now, or they analyze past effects of something that happened earlier, as does this paragraph:

> For Christy Haubegger, the lack of Latina role models had life-changing consequences. As a Mexican American girl adopted by Anglo parents, Christy found no reflection of herself in teen magazines or books. One result of seeing mostly blonde, blue-eyed models was an increase in her adolescent insecurities. A more damaging effect was Christy's confusion as she wondered what career to pursue; there were no Hispanic role models in schoolbooks to suggest possible futures for this excellent student. Even at Stanford Law School, Christy and her friends missed the inspiration and encouragement of professional Latina role models. At Stanford, Christy began to see this problem as an opportunity. She decided to start a national magazine that would showcase talented and successful Latinas. The 27-year-old made a detailed business plan and, incredibly, won the financial backing of the CEO of *Essence* magazine. In 1996, the first issue of *Latina* hit the newstands—the very positive consequence of an old loneliness.

- Underline the topic sentence in this paragraph.
- For Ms. Haubegger, the lack of Latina role models caused "life-changing consequences." What effects are discussed? _____

_____

● What order does the writer follow? _____

_____

● Notice that the paragraph first discusses negative effects and then a positive one.

Before you write about causes or effects, do some mental detective work. First, search out the three most important causes or effects. For example, if you are trying to understand the causes of a friend's skiing accident, you might consider the snow conditions that day, whether he took unnecessary risks, and whether he had been drinking.

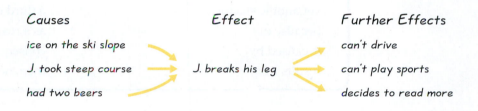

Causes	Effect	Further Effects
ice on the ski slope		can't drive
J. took steep course	J. breaks his leg	can't play sports
had two beers		decides to read more

In exploring the effects of something, consider both short-term and long-term effects and both negative and positive effects. (Although Jay could *not* do many things, perhaps he took advantage of his recovery time to read more or to learn a new computer program.)

Artist Joe Mariscal calls this large ceramic work "Cause and Effect." Why do you think he chose this title? What is the cause, and what is the effect? What statement is the artist making?

© Joe Mariscal

Problems to Avoid in Cause and Effect Writing

1. **Do not oversimplify.** Avoid the trap of naming one cause for a complex problem: *Why did they divorce? Because she is a hothead.* Or, *The reason that reading scores have fallen in the school is television.* Searching for the three most important causes or effects is a good way to avoid oversimplifying.

2. **Do not confuse time order with causation.** If your eye starts watering seconds after the doorbell rings, you cannot assume that the doorbell made your eye water. Were you peeling onions? Is it allergy season? Do you need to wet your contact lenses?

3. **Do not confuse causes and effects.** This sounds obvious, but separating causes and effects can be tricky. (Is Rita's positive attitude the cause of her success in sales or the result of it?)

Transitional Expressions

These transitional expressions are helpful in cause and effect paragraphs, which often imply order of importance or time order:*

<table>
<tr><td colspan="2" align="center">**Transitional Expressions**</td></tr>
<tr><td>*To Show Causes*</td><td>*To Show Effects*</td></tr>
<tr><td>the first cause (second, third)</td><td>one important effect</td></tr>
<tr><td>the first reason (second, third)</td><td>another result</td></tr>
<tr><td>yet another factor</td><td>a third outcome</td></tr>
<tr><td>because of</td><td>as a result</td></tr>
<tr><td>is caused by</td><td>consequently</td></tr>
<tr><td>results from</td><td>then, next, therefore, thus</td></tr>
</table>

PRACTICE 1

Read this paragraph and answer the questions.

Type 2 diabetes is a damaging blood sugar disease that often can be prevented, but new cases in the United States have doubled in just ten years. To protect themselves and their families from type 2 diabetes, all Americans, especially parents, should understand its possible causes. The most important cause is obesity. The more fatty tissue a person has, the more his or her cells have trouble controlling blood sugar. Not surprisingly, as the numbers of overweight Americans increase, so do cases of type 2 diabetes. Second, inactivity feeds this disease. Inactive people gain more weight, but exercise doesn't just keep off pounds; it also turns blood sugar into energy and helps the cells control blood sugar. Third, a poor diet with lots of fried and fatty foods brings on type 2 diabetes, especially in people with a fourth cause, family history. Anyone with diabetes in the family or from certain racial backgrounds (for example, Hispanics, blacks, and Asians) has a higher risk. People can't change their genes, but they can fight type 2 diabetes by losing weight, exercising, and saying no to fatty foods.

—Itan Harjo, student

1. Underline the topic sentence. Does this paragraph discuss the causes or effects of

   type 2 diabetes? _____

2. How many causes does this writer discuss? Which ones are controllable, and which

   are not? _____

   _____

3. On a separate sheet of paper, make a plan of this paragraph.

---

* To read essays of cause and effect, see Chapter 17, Part C.

PRACTICE 2

To practice separating cause from effect, write the cause and the effect contained in each item below.

EXAMPLE   Fewer people are attending concerts at the Boxcar Theater because ticket prices have nearly doubled.

Cause: *ticket prices nearly doubled*

Effect: *fewer people attending concerts*

1. A thunderstorm was approaching, so we moved our picnic into the van.

Cause: _____

Effect: _____

2. Seeing my father suffer because he could not read motivated me to excel in school.

Cause: _____

Effect: _____

3. One study showed that laughter extended the lives of cancer patients.

Cause: _____

Effect: _____

4. Americans are having fewer children and doing so later in life. Some experts believe this is why they are spending more money every year on their pets.

Cause: _____

Effect: _____

5. Many doctors urged that trampolines be banned because of an "epidemic" of injuries to children playing on them.

Cause: _____

Effect: _____

6. I bought this glow-in-the-dark fish lamp for one reason only: it was on sale.

Cause: _____

Effect: _____

7. As more people spend time surfing the Internet, television viewing is declining for the first time in fifty years.

Cause: _____

Effect: _____

8. For years, Charboro cigarettes outsold all competitors as a result of added ammonia. This ammonia gave smokers' brains an extra "kick."

Cause: _____

First Effect: _____

Second Effect: _____

PRACTICE 3

List three causes *or* three effects to support each topic sentence below. First, read the topic sentence to see whether causes or effects are called for. Then think, jot, and list your three best ideas.

1. The huge success of Barbie (or some other toy, game, or product) has a number of causes.

   _____

   _____

   _____

2. There are several reasons why AIDS continues to spread among teenagers, despite widespread knowledge about the deadly nature of the disease.

   _____

   _____

   _____

3. Reading books by authors of many nationalities, instead of just American and English authors, has many positive (or negative) effects on American students.

   _____

   _____

   _____

PRACTICE 4

Now choose one topic from Practice 3 that interests you and write a paragraph of cause or effect on notebook paper. Before you write a draft, think and make a plan. Have you chosen the three most important causes or effects and decided on an effective order in which to present them? As you write, use transitional expressions to help the reader follow your ideas.

PRACTICE 5   **TEAMWORK: CRITICAL THINKING AND WRITING**

Analyze Possible Reasons Why Teenagers Drop Out of High School

In a group with four or five classmates, read these statistics aloud. Then follow the directions.

1. Every year in the United States, more than 1.2 million high school students drop out. That's one student every 26 seconds—7,000 a day.

2. Recent dropouts will earn $200,000 less in their lifetimes than high school graduates and over $800,000 less than college graduates.

3. In the U.S., dropouts commit about 75 percent of the crimes.

—"11 Facts about Dropping Out," *www.DoSomething.org*

What do you think are the causes or reasons why so many American teens drop out of high school? Choose a member to jot the group's ideas; then discuss and brainstorm possible causes of this disturbing trend. List your strongest three causes in the order of importance. How would you try to persuade a teenage relative to stay in school?

Checklist

The Process of Writing a Cause and Effect Paragraph

Refer to this checklist of steps as you write a paragraph.

☐ 1. Narrow the topic in light of your audience and purpose. Think of a subject that can be analyzed for clear causes or effects.

☐ 2. Decide whether you will emphasize causes or effects. What information would be most interesting to your audience?

☐ 3. Compose a topic sentence that states the subject and indicates whether causes or effects will be discussed.

☐ 4. Now freewrite, brainstorm, or cluster to find at least three possible causes or effects. Do your mental detective work. At this stage, think of all possible causes; think of short- and long-term effects, as well as positive and negative effects.

☐ 5. Select the best causes or effects with which to develop your paragraph. Drop those that are not relevant.

☐ 6. Make a plan or an outline for your paragraph, numbering the causes or effects in the order in which you will present them.

☐ 7. Write a first draft of your cause and effect paragraph, explaining each point fully so that your reader understands just how X caused Y. Use transitional expressions to emphasize these relationships.

☐ 8. Revise as necessary, checking for good support, unity, logic, and coherence. Does your paragraph have an interesting opening sentence?

☐ 9. Proofread for errors in grammar, punctuation, sentence structure, spelling, and mechanics. Especially watch for your personal error patterns.

Suggested Topics for Cause and Effect Paragraphs

1. Reasons why someone made an important decision

2. Causes of dropping out of school (or attending college)

3. Reasons for doing volunteer work

4. Causes of a marriage or divorce (friendship or end of friendship)

5. Reasons why a child dislikes school

6. Causes of an act of courage or cowardice

7. Causes or effects of membership in a group (choir, band, sports team, church, or gang)

8. Effects of high blood pressure, alcoholism, diabetes, or some other illness

9. Effects of a certain event (like the death of a loved one, a medical diagnosis, or a move to a new place)

10. Effects of losing one's job

11. Effects of living in a particular place (such as a repressive country or home or a place that is rural, urban, poor, rich, ethnically diverse)

12. Effects (positive or negative) of a habit or practice, such as meditation or overeating

13. Effects of a superstition or prejudice

14. Effects of e-mail, a computer, cell phone, or other technology on a person's life

15. Writer's choice: _____

EXPLORING ONLINE

http://www2.elc.polyu.edu.hk/cill/exercises/cause&effect.htm

Review of vocabulary and grammar needed to describe causes and effects

http://www.shsu.edu/~txcae/Powerpoints/prepostest/causeeffect2.html

Test yourself! Quiz on the words showing cause and effect

http://dmc122011.delmar.edu/swc/handouts/Composition_Website/Cause.htm

Helpful advice and review for writing cause and effect papers

CourseMate for *Evergreen*

Visit *Evergreen* CourseMate for more practices and quizzes, videos to accompany the readings, career and job-search resources, ESL help, and live links to every Exploring Online in the book.

CHAPTER 13

Persuasion

To **persuade** is to convince someone that a particular opinion or point of view is the correct one.

Any time you argue with a friend, you are each trying to persuade or convince the other that your opinion is the right one. Commercials and advertisements are another form of persuasion. Advertisers attempt to convince the audience that the product they sell—whether jeans, a soft drink, or an automobile—is the best one to purchase.

You will often have to persuade in writing. For instance, if you want a raise, you will have to write a persuasive memo to convince your employer that you deserve one. You will have to back up, or support, your request with proof, listing important projects you have completed, noting new responsibilities you have taken upon yourself, or showing how you have increased sales.

Once you learn how to persuade logically and rationally, you will be less likely to accept the false, misleading, and emotional arguments that you hear and read every day. Persuasion is vital in daily life, in nearly all college courses, and in most careers.

Topic Sentence

Here is the topic sentence of a **persuasive** paragraph:

> Passengers should refuse to ride in any vehicle driven by someone who has been drinking.

- The writer begins a persuasive paragraph by stating clearly what he or she is arguing for or against. What will this persuasive paragraph argue against?

  _____

  _____

- Words like *should, ought*, and *must* (and the negatives *should not, ought not*, and *must not*) are especially effective in the topic sentence of a persuasive paragraph.

Paragraph and Plan

Here is the entire paragraph:

Passengers should refuse to ride in any vehicle driven by someone who has been drinking. First and most important, such a refusal could save lives. The National Council on Alcoholism reports that drunk driving causes 25,000 deaths and 50 percent of all traffic accidents each year. Not only the drivers but the passengers who agree to travel with them are responsible. Second, riders might tell themselves that some people drive well even after a few drinks, but this is just not true. Dr. Burton Belloc of the local Alcoholism Treatment Center explains that even one drink can lengthen the reflex time and weaken the judgment needed for safe driving. Other riders might feel foolish to ruin a social occasion or inconvenience themselves or others by speaking up, but risking their lives is even more foolish. Finally, by refusing to ride with a drinker, one passenger could influence other passengers or the driver. Marie Furillo, a student at Central High School, is an example. When three friends who had obviously been drinking offered her a ride home from school, she refused, despite the driver's teasing. Hearing Marie's refusal, two of her friends got out of the car. Until the laws are changed and a vast re-education takes place, the bloodshed on American highways will probably continue. But there is one thing people can do: they can refuse to risk their lives for the sake of a party.

● The first reason in the argument **predicts the consequence**. If passengers refuse to ride with drinkers, what will the consequence be?

_____

● The writer also supports this reason with **facts**. What are the facts?

_____

● The second reason in the argument is really an **answer to the opposition**. That is, the writer anticipates the critics. What point is the writer answering?

_____

● The writer supports this reason by **referring to an authority**. That is, the writer gives the opinion of someone who can provide unbiased and valuable information about the subject. Who is the authority and what does this person say?

_____

● The third reason in the argument is that risking your life is foolish. This reason is really another **answer to the opposition**. What point is the writer answering?

_____

_____

● The final reason in the argument is that one passenger could influence others. What **example** does the writer supply to back up this reason?

_____

_____

● Persuasive paragraphs either can begin with the most important reason and then continue with less important ones, or they can begin with the least important reasons, saving the most important for last.* This paragraph begins with what the author considers *most* important. How can you tell?

_____

Before composing this persuasive paragraph, the writer probably brainstormed or freewrote to gather ideas and then made an **outline** like this:

TOPIC SENTENCE: Passengers should refuse to ride in any vehicle driven by someone who has been drinking.

Reason 1:   Refusal could save lives (**predicting a consequence**).
             —statistics on deaths and accidents (**facts**)
             —passengers are equally responsible
Reason 2:   Riders might say some drinkers drive well—not true (**answering the opposition**).
             —Dr. Belloc's explanation (**referring to authority**)
Reason 3:   Others might feel foolish speaking up, but risking lives is more foolish (**answering the opposition**).
Reason 4:   One rider might influence other passengers.
             —Marie Furillo (**example**)

CONCLUSION: Bloodshed will probably continue, but people can refuse to risk their lives.

● Note how each reason clearly supports the topic sentence.

Transitional Expressions

The following transitional expressions are helpful in persuasive paragraphs:

Transitional Expressions for Persuasion		
Give Reasons	*Answer the Opposition*	*Draw Conclusions*
another, next	granted that	consequently
first (second, third)	of course	hence
importantly	on the other hand	therefore
last, finally	some may say	thus

---
* For work on order of importance, see Chapter 4, "Achieving Coherence," Part A.

Methods of Persuasion

The drinking-and-driving example showed the basic kinds of support used in persuasive paragraphs: **facts, referring to an authority, examples, predicting the consequences**, and **answering the opposition**. Although you will rarely use all of them in one paragraph, you should be familiar with them all. Here are some more details:

1. **Facts: Facts** are simply statements of *what is*. They should appeal to the reader's mind, not just to the emotions. The source of your facts should be clear to the reader. If you wish to prove that children's eyesight should be checked every year by a doctor, you might look for supporting facts in appropriate books and magazines, or you might ask your eye doctor for information. Your paper might say, "Many people suffer serious visual impairment later in life because they received insufficient or inadequate eye care when they were children, according to an article in *Better Vision*."*

   Avoid the vague "everyone knows that" or "it is common knowledge that" or "they all say." Such statements will make your reader justifiably suspicious of your "facts."

2. **Referring to an authority:** An **authority** is an expert, someone who can be relied on to give unbiased facts and information. If you wish to convince your readers that asthma is a far more serious illness than most people realize, you might speak with an emergency-room physician about the numbers of patients treated for asthma attacks, or you might quote experts from the literature of national organizations like the Asthma and Allergy Foundation of America or the American Lung Association. These are all excellent and knowledgeable authorities whose opinions on medical matters would be considered valid and unbiased.

   Avoid appealing to "authorities" who are interesting or glamorous but who are not experts. A basketball player certainly knows about sports, but probably knows little about cameras or cookware.

3. **Examples:** An **example** should clearly relate to the argument and should be typical enough to support it.† If you wish to convince your reader that high schools should provide more funds than they do for women's sports, you might say, "Jefferson High School, for instance, has received inquiries from sixty female students who would be willing to join a women's basketball or softball team if the school could provide the uniforms, the space, and a coach."

   Avoid examples that are not typical enough to support your general statement. That your friend was once bitten by a dog does not adequately prove that all dogs are dangerous pets.

4. **Predicting the consequence: Predicting the consequence** helps the reader visualize what will occur if *something does or does not happen*. To convince your readers that a college education should be free to all qualified students, you might say, "If bright but economically deprived students cannot attend college because they cannot afford it, our society will be robbed of their talents."

---

* For more work on summarizing and quoting outside sources, see Chapter 19, "Strengthening an Essay with Research."

† For more work on examples, see Chapter 5, "Illustration."

Avoid exaggerating the consequence. For instance, telling the reader, "If you don't eat fresh fruit every day, you will never be truly healthy," exaggerates the consequences of not eating fresh fruit and makes the reader understandably suspicious.

5. **Answering the opposition: Answering possible critics** shows that you are aware of the opposition's argument and are able to respond to it. If you wish to convince your readers that your candidate is the best on the ballot, you might say, "Some have criticized him for running a low-key campaign, but he feels that the issues and his stand on them should speak for themselves."

Avoid calling the opposition "fools" or "crooks." Attack their ideas, not their character.

Building Blocks of Effective Persuasive Writing

Topic: Every college student should complete an internship in his or her field of study.

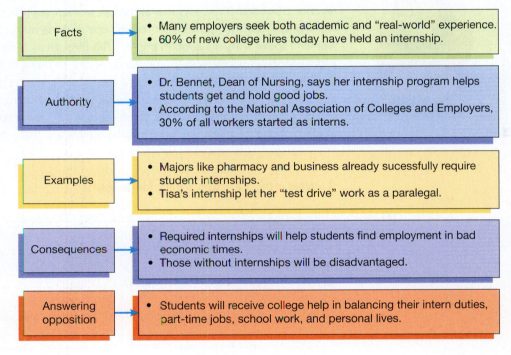

Facts	• Many employers seek both academic and "real-world" experience. • 60% of new college hires today have held an internship.
Authority	• Dr. Bennet, Dean of Nursing, says her internship program helps students get and hold good jobs. • According to the National Association of Colleges and Employers, 30% of all workers started as interns.
Examples	• Majors like pharmacy and business already sucessfully require student internships. • Tisa's internship let her "test drive" work as a paralegal.
Consequences	• Required internships will help students find employment in bad economic times. • Those without internships will be disadvantaged.
Answering opposition	• Students will receive college help in balancing their intern duties, part-time jobs, school work, and personal lives.

Considering the Audience

In addition to providing adequate proof for your argument, pay special attention to the **audience** as you write persuasively. In general, we assume that our audience is much like us—reasonable people who wish to learn the truth. But because argument can evoke strong feelings, directing your persuasive paper toward a particular audience can be helpful. Consider just *what kind of evidence* this audience would respond to. For instance, if you were attempting to persuade parents to volunteer their time to establish a local Scout troop, you might explain to them the various ways in which their children would benefit from the troop. In other words, show these parents how the troop is important to *them*. You might also say that you realize how much time they already spend on family matters and how little spare time they have. By doing so, you let them know that you understand their resistance to the argument and that you are sympathetic to their doubts. When you take your audience into consideration, you will make your persuasive paragraph more convincing.*†

PRACTICE 1

Read the following persuasive paragraph carefully and answer the questions.

American women should stop buying so-called women's magazines because these publications lower their self-esteem. First of all, publications like *Glamour* and *Cosmo* appeal to women's insecurities and make millions doing it. Topics like "Ten Days to Sexier Cleavage" and "How to Attract Mr. Right" lure women to buy 7 million copies a month, reports Claire Ito in *The Tulsa Chronicle*, May 4, 2009. The message: women need to be improved. Second, although many people—especially magazine publishers—claim these periodicals build self-esteem, they really do the opposite. One expert in readers' reactions, Deborah Then, says that almost all women, regardless of age or education, feel worse about themselves after reading one of these magazines. Alice, one of the women I spoke with, is a good example: "I flip through pictures of world-class beauties and six-foot-tall skinny women, comparing myself to them. In more ways than one, I come up short." Finally, if women spent the money and time these magazines take on more self-loving activities—studying new subjects, developing mental or physical fitness, setting goals and daring to achieve them—they would really build self-worth. Sisters, seek wisdom, create what you envision, and above all, know that you can.

—Rochelle Revard, Student

1. What is this paragraph arguing for or against? _____

   _____

2. What audience is the writer addressing? _____

3. Which reason is supported by facts? _____

   What are the facts, and where did the writer get them? _____

   _____

   _____

4. Which reason answers the opposition? _____

5. Which reason is supported by an example? _____

   What is the example? _____

   _____

———

* For more work on audience, see Chapter 1, "Exploring the Writing Process," Part B.

† For complete essays developed by persuasion, see Chapter 17, Part D.

6. Which reason appeals to an authority? _____

   Who is the authority? _____

   _____

PRACTICE 2

Read the following paragraph carefully and answer the questions.

This state should offer free parenting classes, taught by experts, to anyone who wishes to become a parent. First and most important, such parenting classes could save children's lives. Every year, over 2 million American children are hurt, maimed, or killed by their own parents, according to the National Physicians Association. Some of these tragedies could be prevented by showing parents how to recognize and deal with their frustration and anger. Next, good parenting skills do not come naturally, but must be learned. Dr. Phillip Graham, chairman of England's National Children's Bureau, says that most parents have "no good role models" and simply parent the way they were parented. The courses would not only improve parenting skills but might also identify people at high risk of abusing their children. Third, critics might argue that the state has no business getting involved in parenting, which is a private responsibility. However, the state already makes decisions about who is a fit parent—in the courts, child-protection services, and adoption agencies—but often this is too late for the well-being of the child. Finally, if we do nothing, the hidden epidemic of child abuse and neglect will continue. We train our children's teachers, doctors, day-care workers, and bus drivers. We must also educate parents.

1. What is this paragraph arguing for or against? _____

   _____

   _____

2. Which reason appeals to an authority for support? _____

   Who is the authority? _____

3. Which reason answers the opposition? _____

4. Which reason includes facts? What is the source of these facts? _____

   _____

   _____

5. What consequence does the writer predict if parenting classes are not offered? _____

   _____

6. Does this writer convince you that parenting classes might make a difference? If you were writing a persuasion paragraph to oppose or support this writer, what would your topic sentence be?

_____

_____

_____

PRACTICE 3

So far you have learned five basic methods of persuasion: **facts, referring to an authority, examples, predicting the consequence**, and **answering the opposition**. Ten topic sentences for persuasive paragraphs follow. Write one reason in support of each topic sentence, using the method of persuasion indicated.

Facts

1. A stop sign should be placed at the busy intersection of Hoover and Palm streets.

   Reason: _____

   _____

   _____

2. People should not get married until they are at least twenty-five years old.

   Reason: _____

   _____

   _____

Referring to an Authority

(If you cannot think of an authority offhand, name the kind of person who would be an authority on the subject.)

3. These new Sluggo bats will definitely raise your batting average.

   Reason: _____

   _____

   _____

4. Most people should get at least one hour of vigorous exercise three times a week.

   Reason: _____

   _____

Examples

5. Pets should be allowed in children's hospital rooms because they speed healing.

   Reason: _____

   _____

   _____

   _____

6. Mace and pepper spray should be legalized because they can prevent crime without causing permanent injury.

   Reason: _____

   _____

   _____

   _____

Predicting the Consequence

7. Companies should (should not) be allowed to conduct random drug testing on employees.

   Reason: _____

   _____

   _____

   _____

8. The federal government should (should not) prohibit the sale of handguns through the mail.

   Reason: _____

   _____

   _____

   _____

Answering the Opposition

(State the opposition's point of view and then refute it.)

9. This college should (should not) drop its required-attendance policy.

   Reason: _____

   _____

   _____

   _____

10. Teenagers should (should not) be required to get their parents' permission before being allowed to have an abortion.

Reason: _____

_____

_____

_____

PRACTICE 4

Each of the following sentences tells what you are trying to persuade someone to do. Beneath each sentence are four reasons that attempt to convince the reader that he or she should take this particular course of action. Circle the letter of the reason that *seems irrelevant, illogical,* or *untrue.*

1. If you wanted to persuade someone to do holiday shopping earlier, you might say that

   a. shopping earlier saves time.

   b. more gifts will be in stock.

   c. stores will not be overly crowded.

   d. Usher shops early.

2. If you wanted to persuade someone to buy a particular brand of cereal, you might say that it

   a. is inexpensive.

   b. contains vitamins and minerals.

   c. comes in an attractive box.

   d. makes a hearty breakfast.

3. If you wanted to persuade someone to move to your town, you might say that

   a. two new companies have made jobs available.

   b. by moving to this town, he or she will become the happiest person in the world.

   c. there is a wide selection of housing.

   d. the area is lovely and still unpolluted.

4. If you wanted to persuade someone to vote for a particular candidate, you might say that she

   a. has always kept her promises to the voters.

   b. has lived in the district for thirty years.

   c. has substantial knowledge of the issues.

   d. dresses very fashionably.

5. If you wanted to persuade someone to learn to read and speak a foreign language, you might say that

   a. knowledge of a foreign language can be helpful in the business world.

   b. he or she may want to travel in the country where the language is spoken.

   c. Enrique Iglesias sings in two languages.

   d. being able to read great literature in the original is a rewarding experience.

6. If you wanted to persuade someone to quit smoking, you might say that

   a. smoking is a major cause of lung cancer.

   b. smoking stains teeth and softens gums.

   c. ashtrays are often hard to find.

   d. this bad habit has become increasingly expensive.

PRACTICE 5

As you write persuasive paragraphs, make sure that your reasons can withstand close examination. Here are some examples of *invalid* arguments. Read them carefully. Decide which method of persuasion is being used and explain why you think the argument is invalid. Refer to the list on pages 158–159.

1. Men make terrible drivers. That one just cut right in front of me without looking.

   Method of persuasion: _____

   Invalid because _____

   _____

2. Many people have become vegetarians during the past ten or fifteen years, but such people have lettuce for brains.

   Method of persuasion: _____

   Invalid because _____

   _____

3. Candy does not really harm children's teeth. Tests made by scientists at the Gooey Candy Company have proved that candy does not cause tooth decay.

   Method of persuasion: _____

   Invalid because _____

   _____

4. Stealing pens and pads from the office is perfectly all right. Everyone does it.

   Method of persuasion: _____

   Invalid because _____

   _____

5. We don't want _____ in our neighborhood. We had a

   _____ family once, and they made a lot of noise.

   Method of persuasion: _____

   Invalid because _____

   _____

6. If our city doesn't build more playgrounds, a crime wave will destroy our homes and businesses.

   Method of persuasion: _____

   Invalid because _____

   _____

7. Studying has nothing to do with grades. My brother never studies and still gets As all the time.

   Method of persuasion: _____

   Invalid because _____

   _____

8. Women bosses work their employees too hard. I had one once, and she never let me rest for a moment.

   Method of persuasion: _____

   Invalid because _____

   _____

9. The Big Deal Supermarket has the lowest prices in town. This must be true because the manager said on the radio last week, "We have the lowest prices in town."

   Method of persuasion: _____

   Invalid because _____

   _____

10. If little girls are allowed to play with cars and trucks, they will grow up wanting to be men.

   Method of persuasion: _____

   Invalid because _____

   _____

PRACTICE 6   **TEAMWORK: CRITICAL VIEWING AND WRITING**

Persuade Through Humor

Advertisements bombard us every day—through TV, newspapers, magazines, billboards, store windows, and the labels on people's clothing and possessions. The billions of dollars that Americans spend on brand-name products tell us that ads are very persuasive, usually making their argument with a strong visual image and a few catchy words. To expose the great power of advertising, a group called Adbusters creates stylish spoof ads for real products. The goal is to expose the truth that real-life ads often hide. In a group of four or five classmates, study the ad below and then answer the questions.

What hugely popular product is being "busted" by this Adbusters spoof? What is the persuasive message of this ad? Working together, write down the ad's "topic sentence" and argument. How effective is Adbuster's ad? Does it successfully answer the "opposition"—that is, McDonald's worldwide campaign to convince us to buy more Big Macs?

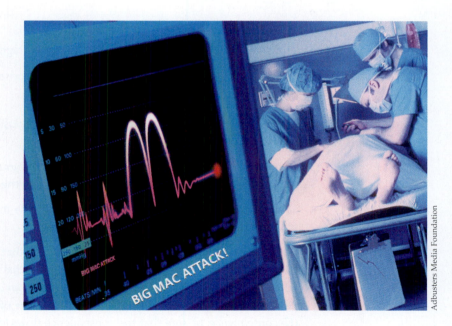

Adbusters Media Foundation

EXPLORING ONLINE

http://www.adbusters.org/spoofads

Study other Adbuster spoof ads, especially those for fashion, alcohol, and tobacco. Pick the funniest and write about its persuasive message. For help creating your own print ad, go to
https://www.adbusters.org/spoofads/printad
In your group, create a persuasive ad, perhaps using the slogan,
"Got _____?"

WRITING ASSIGNMENT

To help you take a stand for a persuasive paragraph of your own, try the following exercises on notebook paper:

1. List five things you would like to see changed at your college.

2. List five things you would like to see changed in your home *or* at your job.

3. List five things that annoy you or make you angry. What can be done about them?

4. Imagine yourself giving a speech on national television. What message would you like to convey?

From your lists, pick one topic you would like to write a persuasive paragraph about and write the topic sentence here:

_____

_____

Now make a plan or an outline for a paragraph on a separate sheet of paper. Use at least two of the five methods of persuasion. Arrange your reasons in a logical order, and write the most persuasive paragraph you can.

Checklist

The Process of Writing a Persuasive Paragraph

Refer to this checklist of steps as you write a persuasive paragraph of your own.

☐ 1. Narrow the topic in light of your audience and purpose. What do you wish to persuade your reader to believe or do?

☐ 2. Compose a topic sentence that clearly states your position for or against. Use *should, ought, must*, or their negatives.

☐ 3. Freewrite or brainstorm to generate all the reasons you can think of. (You may want to freewrite or brainstorm before you narrow the topic.)

☐ 4. Select the best three or four reasons and drop those that do not relate to your topic sentence.

☐ 5. If you use *facts*, be sure that they are accurate and that the sources of your facts are clear. If you use an *example*, be sure that it is a valid one and adequately supports your argument. If you *refer to an authority*, be sure that he or she is really an authority and *not biased*. If one of your reasons *predicts the consequence*, be sure that the consequence flows logically from your statement. If one of your reasons *answers the opposition*, be sure to state the opposition's point of view fairly and refute it adequately.

☐ 6. Make a plan or an outline for the paragraph, numbering the reasons in the order in which you will present them.

☐ 7. Write a draft of your persuasive paragraph, using transitional expressions wherever they may be helpful.

8. Revise as necessary, checking for support, unity, logic, and coherence.

9. Proofread for errors in grammar, punctuation, sentence structure, spelling, and mechanics.

Suggested Topic Sentences for Persuasive Paragraphs

A list of possible topic sentences for persuasive paragraphs follows. Pick one statement and decide whether you agree or disagree with it. Modify the topic sentence accordingly. Then write a persuasive paragraph that supports your view, explaining and illustrating from your own experience, your observations of others, or your reading.

1. Companies should not be allowed to read their employees' e-mail.

2. Occasional arguments are good for friendship.

3. A required course at this college should be _____ (Great American Success Stories, Survey of World Art, How to Manage Money, or another).

4. The families of AIDS patients are the hidden victims of AIDS.

5. Condom machines should be permitted on campus.

6. The death penalty should (or should not) be used to punish certain crimes.

7. Expensive weddings are an obscene waste of money.

8. Gay people should be allowed to marry.

9. Smoking marijuana should be legal for adults over the age of 21.

10. Drunk drivers who cause accidents with fatalities should be charged with murder.

11. _____ is the most _____ (hilarious, educational, mindless, racist) show on television.

12. To improve academic achievement, this town should create same-sex high schools (all boys, all girls).

13. No one under the age of 21 should be allowed to have body piercing (tattoos, cosmetic surgery, or other).

14. _____ (writer, singer, or actor) has a message that more people need to hear.

15. Writer's choice: _____

EXPLORING ONLINE

http://www.readwritethink.org/materials/persuasion_map/

This online persuasion map helps you create your argument.

http://www.tesoltasks.com/ArgVocab.htm

Practice using the vocabulary of argument.

CourseMate for *Evergreen*

Visit *Evergreen* CourseMate for more practices and quizzes, videos to accompany the readings, career and job-search resources, ESL help, and live links to every Exploring Online in the book.

Writers' Workshop

Give Advice to College Writers

When you are assigned a writing task, take a few minutes to think about the different types of paragraphs you have studied in this unit. Could a certain type of paragraph help you present your ideas more forcefully? You might ask yourself, "Would a paragraph developed by examples work well for this topic? How about a paragraph of cause and effect?"

When he received the assignment "Give advice to other college writers," this student not only made use of one paragraph pattern he had learned, but he added something of his own—humor. In your class or group, read his work, aloud if possible, underlining any lines that you find especially funny or effective.

English Students, Listen Up!

You may think that years of school have taught you how to put off writing a paper; however, true procrastination is an art form, and certain steps must be followed to achieve the status of Master Procrastinator. The first step is to come up with a good reason to put off writing the paper. Reasons prevent others from hassling you about your procrastination. A reason should not be confused with an excuse. An excuse would be, "I am too tired." A reason would be, "It is important that I rest in order to do the best possible job." The second step is to come up with a worthwhile task to do before starting the paper. If you put off writing your paper by watching *Gossip Girl*. You will feel guilty. On the other hand, if you put off writing your paper by helping your child do his or her homework or by doing three weeks' worth of laundry or by organizing your sock drawer, there will be no guilt. After completing your worthwhile task. You will be hungry. In order to have the energy necessary to write the paper, you will need to eat something. The true artist can make this third step last even longer by either cooking a meal or going out for food. It is important not to risk your energy level by simply eating a bowl of cereal or a ketchup sandwich. After you eat, the fourth step is to prepare the space in which you will write the paper. This includes cleaning all the surfaces, sharpening pencils. And making sure the lighting is exactly right. You may think that after this fourth step is completed, you will have no choice but to start your paper, but you do if you have done the other steps correctly. It is now too late in the day to start your paper. The fifth step is, of course, to go to bed and start over with step one in the morning.

—Thomas Capra, Student

1. How effective is this paragraph?

   ___Clear topic sentence?   ___ Good supporting details?

   ___ Logical organization?   ___ Effective conclusion?

2. What type of paragraph development does Capra use here? How do you know? Does the topic sentence indicate what kind of paragraph will follow?

3. One step in the process of becoming a Master Procrastinator contains a *contrast*. Which step? What two things are contrasted?

4. Discuss your underlinings with the group or class. Tell what parts of the paragraph you like best, explaining as specifically as possible why. For example, the mention of a ketchup sandwich in step three adds an extra dash of humor.

5. Although this writer is having fun, procrastination is a serious problem for some people. Do you think Capra is writing from experience? Why or why not?

6. This otherwise excellent writer makes the same grammar error three times. Can you spot and correct the error pattern that he needs to avoid?

GROUP WORK

In your group or class, make a chart like the one below, listing all the types of paragraph development that you have studied. Now suppose that you have been assigned the topic *procrastination*. Discuss how different paragraphs could be developed on the subject of procrastination, each one using a different paragraph pattern. For instance, you could *illustrate* procrastination by discussing examples of procrastinators you have known. Fill in the chart with one idea per paragraph type. Then share your group's ideas with the whole class.

Topic: Procrastination

Method of Development:	A Paragraph Could
Illustration	
Narration	
Description	
Process	
Definition	
Comparison and contrast	
Classification	
Cause and effect	
Persuasion	

WRITING AND REVISING IDEAS

1. Give humorous advice on how to get fired, how to fail a course, how to get robbed, or how to embarrass yourself for years to come by posting stupid pictures on the Internet.

2. Discuss procrastination, using one kind of paragraph development that you studied this term.

Unit 4

Writing the Essay

CHAPTER 14

The Process of Writing an Essay

A: Looking at the Essay

B: Writing the Thesis Statement

C: Generating Ideas for the Body

D: Organizing Ideas into an Outline

E: Ordering and Linking Paragraphs in the Essay

F: Writing and Revising Essays

Although writing effective paragraphs will help you complete short-answer exams and brief writing assignments, much of the time—in college and in the business world—you will be required to write essays and reports several paragraphs long. Essays are longer and contain more ideas than the single paragraphs you have practiced so far, but they require many of the same skills that paragraphs do.

This chapter will help you apply the skills of paragraph writing to the writing of short essays. It will guide you from a look at the essay and its parts through planning and writing essays of your own.

A. Looking at the Essay

An **essay** is a group of paragraphs about one subject. In many ways, an essay is like a paragraph in longer, fuller form. Both have an introduction, a body, and a conclusion. Both explain one main, or controlling, idea with details, facts, and examples. An essay is not just a padded paragraph, however. An essay is longer because it contains more ideas.

The paragraphs in an essay are part of a larger whole, so each one has a special purpose.

● The **introductory paragraph*** opens the essay and tries to catch the reader's interest. It usually contains a **thesis statement**, one sentence that states the main idea of the entire essay.

● The **body** of an essay consists of one, two, three, or more paragraphs, each one making a different point about the main idea.

● The **conclusion**† brings the essay to a close. It might be a sentence or a paragraph long.

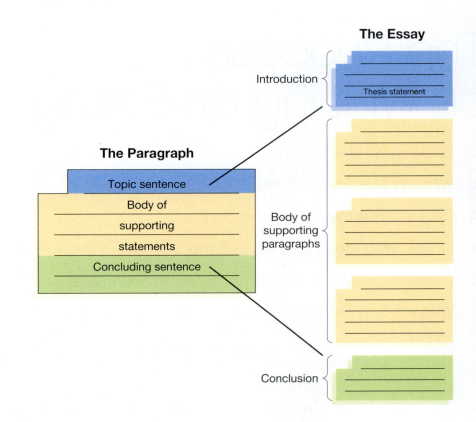

Here is a student essay:

SUNLIGHT

Introduction

(1) An old proverb says, "He who brings sunlight into the lives of others cannot keep it from himself." Students who volunteer through the Center for Community Service often experience this wisdom firsthand. By giving their time and talents to the local community, these students not only enrich the lives of others, but they receive many surprising benefits for themselves.

Thesis statement

Topic sentence introducing point 1

(2) Most important, volunteering can bring a sense of empowerment, a knowledge that we can make a difference. This is significant because many students feel passive and hopeless about "the way things are." My first volunteer assignment was working with a group of troubled teenagers. Together we transformed a dismal vacant lot into a thriving business. The three-acre lot in the South Bronx, surrounded by abandoned buildings, was full of junk and heaps of wood. One teenager kicked a piece of wood and said, "Why don't we chop this up and sell it?" We surprised him by taking his idea seriously. We helped these young men, some of whom already had rap sheets, to chop up the

Details, facts, examples supporting point 1

———
* For more work on introductions, see Chapter 15, "The Introduction, the Conclusion, and the Title."

† For more work on conclusions, see Chapter 15, "The Introduction, the Conclusion, and the Title."

Volunteers clean an oil-covered pelican after the BP oil spill in the Gulf of Mexico.

wood, bundle it, contact restaurants with wood-burning ovens, and make deliveries. The restaurants, most of them very elegant, were happy to get cheap firewood, and the teenagers were thrilled to be treated like businesspeople. Most rewarding for me was seeing the changes in Raymond, "Mr. Apathy," as he took on a leading role in our project.

Topic sentence introducing point 2

(3) Second, the volunteer often gains a deeper understanding of others. Another student, Shirley Miranda, worked with SHARE, a food cooperative that distributes bulk food once a month to its members. SHARE does not give food as charity; rather, each person does a job like unloading trucks at 5 A.M. on delivery day or packing boxes in exchange for healthy, inexpensive food. For Shirley, SHARE was a lesson in human relationships. Reflecting on her service, she wrote: "I learned that people may sometimes need guidance with dignity rather than total dependency on others. I saw that true teamwork is based on people's similarities, not their differences." SHARE so impressed Shirley that she worked in the program through her graduation.

Details, facts, examples supporting point 2

Topic sentence introducing point 3

(4) Finally, volunteering can be a way to "try on" a work environment. Sam Mukarji, an engineering student, volunteers on Saturdays as a docent, or guide, at the Museum of Science and Industry, which he describes as "my favorite place on the planet." Sam admires the creative uses of science in this museum, such as the virtual-reality experience of piloting an airplane. When many visitors asked Sam how the exhibit was put together, he suggested that the museum include signs explaining the technology. His idea was accepted, and he was asked to help implement it. Struggling to explain the exhibit in a clear way taught Sam how important writing skills are, even for an engineering major. Now he is paying closer attention to his English assignments and has discovered that working in a science museum would be his "dream job."

Details, facts, examples supporting point 3

Conclusion

(5) Stories like these are not unusual at the Center for Community Service. Whenever the volunteers meet there, we always seem to end up talking about the positive ways in which volunteering has changed our lives. The Center is in a cinder-block basement without a single window, but it is filled with sunlight.

- The last sentence in the introduction is the **thesis statement**. Just as a topic sentence sets forth the main idea of a paragraph, so the thesis statement sets forth the main idea of the whole essay. It must be *general enough to include the topic sentence of every paragraph in the body*.

- Underline the topic sentence of each supporting paragraph. Each topic sentence introduces one *benefit* that volunteers receive.

- Note that the thesis and topic sentences of paragraphs 2, 3, and 4 make a rough **outline** of the entire essay:

1. **INTRODUCTION** and **thesis statement:**	By giving their time and talents to the local community, these students not only enrich the lives of others, but they receive many surprising benefits for themselves.
2. **Topic sentence:**	Most important, volunteering can bring a sense of empowerment, a knowledge that we can make a difference.
3. **Topic sentence:**	Second, the volunteer often gains a deeper understanding of others.
4. **Topic sentence:**	Finally, volunteering can be a way to "try on" a work environment.
5. **CONCLUSION**	

- Note that every topic sentence supports the thesis statement. Every paragraph in the body discusses in detail one *benefit* that students receive from volunteering. Each paragraph also provides an *example* to explain that benefit.

- The last paragraph **concludes** the essay by mentioning sunlight, a reference to the proverb in paragraph 1.

PRACTICE 1

Read this student essay carefully and then answer the questions.

BOTTLE WATCHING

(1) Every time I see a beer bottle, I feel grateful. This reaction has nothing to do with beer. The sight reminds me of the year I spent inspecting bottles at a brewery. That was the most boring and painful job I've ever had, but it motivated me to change my life.

(2) My job consisted of sitting on a stool and watching empty bottles pass by. A glaring light behind the conveyor belt helped me to spot cracked bottles or bottles with something extra—a dead grasshopper, for example, or a mouse foot. I was supposed to grab such bottles with my hooked cane and break them before they went into the washer. For eight or nine hours a day that was all I did. I got dizzy and sore in the eyes. I longed to fall asleep. I prayed that the conveyor would break down so the bottles would stop.

(3) After a while, to put some excitement into the job, I began inventing little games. I would count the number of minutes that passed before a broken bottle would come by, and I would compete against my own past record. Or I would see how many broken bottles I could spot in one minute. Once, I organized a contest for all the bottle watchers with a prize for the best dead insect or animal found in a bottle—anything to break the monotony of the job.

(4) After six months at the brewery, I began to think hard about my goals for the future. Did I want to spend the rest of my life looking in beer bottles? I realized that I wanted a job I could believe in. I wanted to use my mind for better things than planning contests for bleary-eyed bottle watchers. I knew I had to hand in my hook and go back to school.

(5) Today I feel grateful to that terrible job because it motivated me to attend college.

—Pat Barnum, Student

1. Which sentence in the introductory paragraph is the thesis statement? _____

   _____

2. Did Mr. Barnum's introduction catch and hold your interest? Why or why not? _____

   _____

3. Underline the topic sentences in paragraphs 2, 3, and 4.

4. What is the controlling idea of paragraph 2? _____

5. What is the controlling idea of paragraph 3? What examples support this idea? _____

   _____

   _____

6. What do you like best about this essay? What, if anything, would you change?

   _____

B. Writing the Thesis Statement

The steps in the essay-writing process are the same as those in the paragraph-writing process: **narrow the topic, write the thesis statement, generate ideas for the body, organize ideas in an outline, draft, and revise.** However, in essay writing, planning on paper, prewriting, and outlining are especially important because an essay is longer than a paragraph and more difficult to organize.

Narrowing the Topic

The essay writer usually starts with a broad subject and then narrows it to a manageable size. An essay is longer than a paragraph and gives the writer more room to develop ideas; nevertheless, the best essays, like the best paragraphs, are often quite specific. For example, if you are assigned a 400-word essay titled "A Trip I Won't Forget," a description of your recent trip to Florida would be too broad a subject. You would need to *narrow* the topic to just one aspect of the trip. Many writers list possible narrowed subjects on paper or on computer:

1. huge job of packing, more tiring than the trip
2. how to pack for a trip with children without exhausting yourself
3. Disney World, more fun for adults than for children
4. our afternoon of deep-sea fishing: highlight of the trip
5. terrible weather upsetting many of my sightseeing plans

Any one of these topics is narrow enough and specific enough to be the subject of a short essay. If you had written this list, you would now consider each narrowed topic and perhaps freewrite or brainstorm possible ways to support it. Keeping your audience and purpose in mind may also help you narrow your topic. Your audience here might be your instructor and classmates; your purpose might be to inform (by giving tips about packing) or to entertain (by narrating a funny or a dramatic incident). Having considered your topic, audience, and purpose, you would then choose the topic that you could best develop into a good essay.

If you have difficulty with this step, reread Chapter 2, "Prewriting to Generate Ideas."

Writing the Thesis Statement

The **thesis statement**—like the topic sentence in a paragraph—further focuses the narrowed subject because it must clearly state, in sentence form, the writer's **controlling idea**—the main point, opinion, or angle that the rest of the essay will support and discuss.

Narrowed subject:	My job at the brewery
Controlling idea:	So bad it changed my life
Thesis statement:	That was the most boring and painful job I've ever had, but it motivated me to change my life.

- This thesis statement has a clear controlling idea. From it, we expect the essay to discuss specific ways in which this job was boring and painful and how it motivated a change.

The thesis statement and its controlling idea should be as **specific** as possible. By writing a specific thesis statement, you focus the subject and give yourself and your readers a clear idea of what will follow. Here are three ways to make a vague thesis statement more specific:

1. As a general rule, replace vague words with more exact words* and replace vague ideas with more exact information:

Vague thesis statement:	My recent trip to Florida was really bad.
Revised thesis statement:	My recent trip to Florida was disappointing because the weather upset my sightseeing plans.

- The first thesis statement above lacks a clear controlling idea. The inexact words *really bad* do not say specifically enough *why* the trip was bad or *what* the rest of the essay might discuss.

- The second thesis statement is more specific. The words *really bad* are replaced by the more exact word *disappointing*. In addition, the writer has added more complete information about why the trip was disappointing. From this thesis statement, it is clear that the essay will discuss how the weather upset the writer's plans.

2. **Sometimes you can make the thesis statement more specific by stating the natural divisions of the subject.** If a subject naturally has two, three, or four divisions, stating these in the thesis can set up an outline for your entire essay:

Vague thesis statement:	The movie *Southern Smoke* seemed phony.
Revised thesis statement:	The costumes, the dialogue, and the plot of the movie *Southern Smoke* all seemed phony.

- The first thesis statement above gives little specific direction to the writer or the reader.

- The second thesis statement, however, actually sets up a plan for the whole essay. The writer has divided the subject into three parts—the costumes, the dialogue, and the plot—and he or she will probably devote one paragraph to discussing the phoniness of each one, following the order in the thesis statement.

3. **Avoid a heavy-handed thesis statement that announces, "Now I will write about…" or "This essay will discuss.…"** Don't state the obvious. Instead, craft a specific thesis statement that will capture the reader's interest and control what the rest of your essay will be about. Make every word count.

———

* For more practice in choosing exact language, see Chapter 23, "Revising for Language Awareness," Part A.

PRACTICE 2

Revise each vague thesis statement, making it more specific. Remember, a good thesis statement should have a clear controlling idea and indicate what the rest of the essay will be about.

EXAMPLE Watching TV news programs has its good points.

Watching news programs on TV can make one a more

informed and responsible citizen.

1. A visit to the emergency room can be interesting.

   _____

   _____

2. I will write about my job, which is very cool.

   _____

   _____

3. Professors should teach better.

   _____

   _____

4. There are many unusual people in my family.

   _____

   _____

5. School uniforms are a good idea.

   _____

   _____

PRACTICE 3

Eight possible essay topics follow. Pick three that interest you. For each one, **narrow** the topic, choose your **controlling idea**, and then compose a specific **thesis statement**.

a volunteer experience	handling anger (or other emotion)
when parents work	a story or issue in the news now
an addictive habit	a problem on campus or at work
the value of pets	advantages or disadvantages of Internet research

EXAMPLE   Subject: _handling anger_

Narrowed subject: _my angry adolescence_

Controlling idea: _channeling adolescent anger into art_

Thesis statement: _In a photography workshop for "at-risk" teenagers, I learned_
that anger can be channeled positively into art.

1. Subject: _____

   Narrowed subject: _____

   Controlling idea: _____

   Thesis statement: _____

2. Subject: _____

   Narrowed subject: _____

   Controlling idea: _____

   Thesis statement: _____

3. Subject: _____

   Narrowed subject: _____

   Controlling idea: _____

   Thesis statement: _____

C. Generating Ideas for the Body

The thesis statement sets forth the main idea of the entire essay, but it is the **body** of the essay that must fully support and discuss that thesis statement. In composing the thesis statement, the writer should already have given some thought to what the body will contain. Now he or she uses one or more prewriting methods—_brainstorming, freewriting, clustering_, or _asking questions_—to generate ideas for the body.

To get enough material to flesh out an essay, many writers brainstorm or freewrite on paper or on the computer screen—jotting down any ideas that develop the thesis statement, including main ideas, specific details, and examples, all jumbled together. Only after creating a long list do they go back over it, drop any ideas that do not support the thesis statement, and then group ideas that might go together in body paragraphs.

Suppose, for instance, that you have written this thesis statement: _Although people often react to stress in harmful ways, there are many positive ways to handle stress._ By brainstorming and then dropping ideas that do not relate, you might eventually produce a list like this:

work out

dig weeds or rake leaves

call a friend

talking out problems relieves stress

jogging

many sports ease tension

go to the beach

take a walk

taking breaks, long or short, relieves stress

talk to a shrink if the problem is really bad

escape into a hobby—photography, bird watching

go to a movie

talk to a counselor at the college

talk to a minister, priest, rabbi, etc.

many people harm themselves trying to relieve stress

they overeat or smoke

drinking too much, other addictions

do vigorous household chores—scrub a floor, beat the rugs, pound pillows

doing something physical relieves stress

some diseases are caused by stress

take a nap

some people blow up to help tension, but this hurts their relationships

Now read over the list, looking for groups of ideas that could become paragraphs. You might want to use colored highlighters to mark related ideas. Some ideas might become topic sentences; others might be used to support a topic sentence. How many possible paragraphs can you find in this list?

PRACTICE 4

Choose one of the thesis statements you wrote on page 181 and generate ideas to develop an essay. Using your favorite prewriting method, try to fill at least a page. If you get stuck, reread the thesis statement to focus your thoughts or switch to another prewriting method.

D. Organizing Ideas into an Outline

Many writers make an **outline** before they write an essay. Because an essay is longer, more complex, and harder to control than a paragraph, an outline, even a rough one, helps the writer stay on track and saves time later. The outline should include the following:

1. Two to four main ideas to support the thesis statement

2. Two to four topic sentences stating these ideas

3. A plan for each paragraph in the body (developed in any of the ways explained earlier in this book)

4. A logical order in which to present paragraphs

Different writers create such outlines in different ways. Some writers examine their brainstorming or other prewriting, looking for paragraph groups. Others write their topic sentences first and then generate ideas to support these topic sentences.

Reread prewriting and find paragraph groups. In Part C, you read one student's brainstorm list developing the thesis statement, *Although people often react to stress in harmful ways, there are many positive ways to handle stress*. Here is one possible way to group those ideas:

1. many people harm themselves trying to relieve stress
   they overeat or smoke
   drinking too much, other addictions
   some diseases are caused by stress
   some people blow up to help tension, but this hurts their relationships

2. work out
   dig weeds or rake leaves
   jogging
   many sports ease tension
   take a walk
   do vigorous household chores—scrub a floor, beat the rugs, pound pillows
   doing something physical relieves stress

3. call a friend
   talking out problems relieves stress
   talk to a shrink if the problem is really bad
   talk to a counselor at the college
   talk to a minister, priest, rabbi, etc.

4. go to the beach
   taking breaks, long or short, relieves stress
   escape into a hobby—photography, bird watching
   go to a movie
   take a nap

● What is the main idea of each group? Each group contains a possible topic sentence that expresses its main idea. Underline these topic sentences.

Here is the completed outline from which the student wrote her essay:

1. **INTRODUCTION and thesis statement:**   Although people often react to stress in harmful ways, there are many positive ways to handle stress.

2. **Topic sentence:**   Many people actually harm themselves trying to relieve stress.
   —overeat, smoke, or drink too much
   —get stress-induced diseases
   —blow up at others

3. **Topic sentence:**   For some people, doing something physical is a positive way to relieve stress.

—walk or jog

—work out

—vigorous household chores

—dig weeds or rake leaves

4. **Topic sentence:**   Taking breaks, long or short, is another positive way to relieve stress.

—take a nap

—escape into a hobby

—go to a movie, to the beach

5. **Topic sentence:**   Discussing one's problems can relieve stress and sometimes resolve the cause of it.

—call a friend

—talk to a minister, etc.

—talk to a counselor at the college

—talk to a therapist if necessary

CONCLUSION: Stress is a fact of life, but we can learn positive responses to be happier and more productive.

● Note that this writer now has a well-organized outline from which to write her paper.

● She has chosen a new order for the four supporting paragraphs. Does this order make sense? Explain.

     Write topic sentences and then plan paragraphs. Sometimes a writer can compose topic sentences directly from the thesis statement without extensive jotting first. This is especially true if the thesis statement itself shows how the body will be divided or organized. Such a thesis statement makes the work of planning paragraphs easy because the writer has already broken down the subject into supporting ideas or parts:

> Thesis statement: Because the student cafeteria has many problems, the college should hire a new administrator to see that it is properly managed in the future.

● This thesis statement contains two main ideas: (1) that the cafeteria has many problems and (2) that a new administrator should be hired. The first idea states the problem and the second offers a solution.

From this thesis statement, a writer could logically plan a two-paragraph body, with one paragraph explaining each idea in detail. He or she might compose two topic sentences as follows:

> **Thesis statement:** Because the student cafeteria has many problems, the college should hire a new administrator to see that it is properly managed in the future.
>
> **Topic sentence:** Foremost among the cafeteria's problems are unappetizing food, slow service, and high prices.
>
> **Topic sentence:** A new administrator could do much to improve these terrible conditions.

These topic sentences might need to be revised later, but they will serve as guides while the writer further develops each paragraph.

The writer might develop the first paragraph in the body by giving **examples***
of the unappetizing foods, slow service, and high prices.

He or she could develop the second paragraph through **process**,† by describing the **steps** that the new administrator could take to solve the cafeteria's problems. This planning will create a clear **outline** from which to write the essay.

PRACTICE 5

Complete this outline as if you were planning the essay. First, state in sentence form each problem that will develop the topic sentence: unappetizing food, slow service, and high prices. Then develop each with details and examples.

1. **INTRODUCTION and thesis statement:**   Because the student cafeteria has many problems, the college should hire a new administrator to see that it is properly managed in the future.

2. **Topic sentence:**   Foremost among the cafeteria's problems are unappetizing food, slow service, and high prices.

Problem 1: _____

_____

_____

_____

Problem 2: _____

_____

_____

_____

---

* For more work on developing paragraphs with examples, see Chapter 5, "Illustration."

† For more work on developing paragraphs by process, see Chapter 8, "Process."

Problem 3: _____

_____

_____

_____

3. **Topic sentence:**   A new administrator could do much to improve these terrible conditions.

Step 1. Set minimum quality standards

—personally oversee purchase of healthful food

—set and enforce rules about how long food can be left out

—set cooking times for hot meals

Step 2. Reorganize service lines

—study which lines are busiest at different times of the day

—shift cooks and cashiers to those lines

—create a separate beverage line

Step 3. Lower prices

—better food and faster service would attract more student customers

—cafeteria could then lower prices

4. **CONCLUSION**

PRACTICE 6

Write from two to four topic sentences to support each of the thesis statements that follow. (First you may wish to brainstorm or freewrite on paper or on the computer.) Make sure that every topic sentence really supports the thesis statement and that every one could be developed into a good paragraph. Then arrange your topic sentences in a rough outline in the space provided.

EXAMPLE Before you buy a computer, do these three things.

Topic sentence: *Decide how much you can spend, and determine your price range.*

_____

Topic sentence: *Examine the models that are within your price range.*

_____

Topic sentence: *Shop around; all computer dealers are not created equal.*

_____

1. I vividly recall the sights, smells, and tastes of _____

   _____

   Topic sentence: _____

   _____

   Topic sentence: _____

   _____

   Topic sentence: _____

   _____

   Topic sentence: _____

   _____

2. Living alone has both advantages and disadvantages.

   Topic sentence: _____

   _____

   Topic sentence: _____

   _____

   Topic sentence: _____

   _____

   Topic sentence: _____

   _____

3. Doing well at a job interview requires careful planning.

   Topic sentence: _____

   _____

   Topic sentence: _____

   _____

   Topic sentence: _____

   _____

   Topic sentence: _____

   _____

PRACTICE 7

Now choose *one* thesis statement you have written, or write one now. Generate ideas for the body and organize them in an outline for an essay of your own. (For ideas, reread the thesis statements you wrote for Practice 3, pages 180–181.) Your outline should include your thesis statement; two to three topic sentences; and supporting details, facts, and examples. Prewrite every time you need ideas; revise the thesis statement and the topic sentences until they are sharp and clear.

E. Ordering and Linking Paragraphs in the Essay

An essay, like a paragraph, should have **coherence**. That is, the paragraphs in an essay should be arranged in a clear, logical order and should follow one another like links in a chain.

Ordering Paragraphs

It is important that the paragraphs in your outline, and later in your essay, follow a **logical order**. The rule for writers is this: Use your common sense and plan ahead. Do *not* leave the order of your paragraphs to chance.

The types of order often used in single paragraphs—**time order, space order, and order of importance***—can sometimes be used to arrange paragraphs within an essay. Essays about subjects that can be broken into stages or steps, with each step discussed in one paragraph, should be arranged according to *time. Space order* is used occasionally in descriptive essays. A writer who wishes to save the most important or convincing paragraph for last would use *order of importance*. Or he or she might wish to reverse this order and put the most important paragraph first.

Very often, however, the writer simply arranges paragraphs in whatever order makes sense in the particular essay. Suppose, for example, that you have written the thesis statement, *Electric cars, which are now being developed by many vehicle manufacturers, have strong advantages and disadvantages*, and you plan four paragraphs with these topic sentences:

The high price tag and cost of parts for electric cars make them unaffordable for many Americans.

Electric cars will generate less pollution-per-mile than cars with gasoline engines even though they get their power from fossil fuel-burning electric plants.

Because electric cars must be plugged in and charged about six hours for every 50–100 miles driven, they will be impractical for those who drive long distances.

Electric cars will help to reduce America's dependence on foreign oil sources and thus improve our national security.

The writer lists four points about electric cars. Points two and four both state advantages of electric cars; therefore, it makes sense to order the paragraphs so that those two advantages are grouped together. Points one and three state two disadvantages—high cost and limits of operation—so these two points should be grouped together. The thesis statement refers to *advantages and disadvantages*, so it

---

* For more work on time order, space order, and order of importance, see Chapter 4, "Achieving Coherence," Part A.

would make sense to discuss the advantages first. A logical order of paragraphs, then, might be the following:

1. **INTRODUCTION** and **thesis statement:**	Electric cars, which are now being developed by many vehicle manufacturers, have strong advantages and disadvantages.
2. **Topic sentence:**	Electric cars will generate less pollution-per-mile than cars with gasoline engines even though they get their power from fossil fuel-burning electric plants.
3. **Topic sentence:**	Electric cars will help to reduce America's dependence on foreign oil sources and thus improve our national security.
4. **Topic sentence:**	The high price tag and cost of parts for electric cars make them unaffordable for many Americans.
5. **Topic sentence:**	Because electric cars must be plugged in and charged about six hours for every 50–100 miles driven, they will be impractical for those who drive long distances.

6. **CONCLUSION**

Finally, if your thesis statement is divided into two, three, or four parts, the paragraphs in the body should follow the order in the thesis; otherwise, the reader will be confused. Assume, for instance, that you are planning three paragraphs to develop the thesis statement, *Using an online database for the first time can be overwhelming, exciting, and educational.*

Paragraph 2 should discuss _____

Paragraph 3 should discuss _____

Paragraph 4 should discuss _____

PRACTICE 8

Plans for three essays follow, each containing a thesis statement and several topic sentences in scrambled order. Number the topic sentences in each group according to *an order that makes sense*. Be prepared to explain your choices.

1. **Thesis statement**:		An immigrant who wishes to become a U.S. citizen must complete a three-stage naturalization process.
Topic sentences:	_____	After submitting an application, the would-be citizen interviews with an immigration officer and takes tests on the English language and American civics.

_____ An immigrant who meets general requirements for minimum length of residency and good moral character begins by filling out Form N-400, the Application for Naturalization.

_____ Applicants who perform well in the interview and on the tests take the Oath of Allegiance to the United States in a moving group ceremony, thus becoming American citizens.

2. **Thesis statement:** To meet the demands of a growing computer industry and aging population, the fastest growing job markets through 2018 will be in the information technology and medical fields.

Topic sentences: _____ A second group of medical jobs will exist in private homes, where health-care aides will be needed to tend the elderly.

_____ Skilled computer software engineers, systems designers, and database administrators will find many job opportunities from which to choose.

_____ In hospitals and doctors' offices, the need for medical assistants, pharmacy technicians, and dental hygienists will grow rapidly.

3. **Thesis statement:** The practice of tai chi can improve one's concentration, health, and peace of mind.

Topic sentences: _____ In several ways, tai chi boosts physical health.

_____ Peace of mind increases gradually as one becomes less reactive.

_____ Concentrating on the movements of tai chi in practice promotes better concentration in other areas of life.

PRACTICE 9

Now, go over the essay outline that you developed in Practice 7 and reconsider which paragraphs should come first, which second, and so forth. Does time order, space order, or order of importance seem appropriate to your subject? Number your paragraphs accordingly.

Linking Paragraphs

Just as the sentences within a paragraph should flow smoothly, so the paragraphs within an essay should be clearly **linked** one to the next. As you write your essay, do not make illogical jumps from one paragraph to another. Instead, guide your reader. Link the first sentence of each new paragraph to the thesis statement or to the paragraph before. Here are four ways to link paragraphs:

1. Repeat key words or ideas from the thesis statement.
2. Refer to words or ideas from the preceding paragraph.
3. Use transitional expressions.
4. Use transitional sentences.

1. Repeat key words or ideas from the thesis statement.* The topic sentences in the following essay plan repeat key words and ideas from the thesis statement.

> Thesis statement: Spending time in nature can promote inner peace and a new point of view.
>
> Topic sentence: A stroll in the woods or a picnic by the sea often brings feelings of inner peace and well-being.
>
> Topic sentence: Natural places can even give us a new point of view by putting our problems in perspective.

- In the first topic sentence, the words *feelings of inner peace* repeat, in slightly altered form, words from the thesis statement. The words *a stroll in the woods or a picnic by the sea* refer to the idea of *spending time in nature*.
- Which words in the second topic sentence repeat key words or ideas from the thesis statement?

_____

2. Refer to words or ideas from the preceding paragraph. Link the first sentence of a new paragraph to the paragraph before, especially by referring to words or ideas near the end of the paragraph. Note how the two paragraphs are linked in the following passage:

> (1) The Great Depression was the worst economic collapse of modern times, lasting ten years. It began with the stock market crash of 1929. By 1932, one quarter of all Americans were unemployed. Manufacturing areas fared even worse. In Chicago, for instance, 40 percent of those seeking jobs could not find them. During one year, 80 percent of workers in Toledo, Ohio were unemployed.
>
> (2) Workers who did hold onto their jobs gladly took pay cuts. From 1929 to 1933, pay for manufacturing work fell from $25 to $17 a week. Farmers slashed prices, selling five bushels of wheat to buy one pair of shoes. By the winter of 1932–1933, farmers who couldn't sell their corn were burning it to heat their homes.
>
> —adapted from Joseph R. Conlin,
> *The American Past: A Survey of American History*, 9th Edition

- What words and groups of words in paragraph 2 clearly refer to paragraph 1?

_____

3. Use transitional expressions.† Transitional expressions—words like *for example, therefore,* and *later on*—are used within a paragraph to show the

_____

* For more work on repetition of key words, see Chapter 4, "Achieving Coherence," Part B. See also "Synonyms and Substitutions" in the same section.

† For a complete list of transitional expressions, see Chapter 4, "Achieving Coherence," Part B. See also the chapters in Unit 3 for ways to use transitional expressions in each paragraph and essay pattern.

relationship between sentences. Transitional expressions can also be used within an essay to show the relationships between paragraphs:

> (1) The house where I grew up was worn out and run-down. The yard was mostly mud, rock hard for nine months of the year but wet and swampy for the other three. Our nearest neighbors were forty miles away, so it got pretty lonely. Inside, the house was shabby. The living room furniture was covered in stiff, nubby material that had lost its color over the years and become a dirty brown. Upstairs in my bedroom, the wooden floor sagged a little farther west every year.
>
> (2) *Nevertheless,* I love the place for what it taught me. There I learned to thrive in solitude. During the hours I spent alone, when school was over and the chores were done, I learned to play the guitar and sing. Wandering in the fields around the house or poking under stones in the creek bed, I grew to love the natural world. Most of all, I learned to see and to appreciate small wonders.

- The first paragraph describes some of the negative details about the writer's early home. The second paragraph *contrasts* the writer's attitude, which is positive. The transitional expression *nevertheless* eases the reader from one paragraph to the next by pointing out the exact relationship between the paragraphs.

- Transitional expressions can also highlight the *order* in which paragraphs are arranged.* Three paragraphs arranged in time order might begin: *First...*, *Next...*, *Finally....* Three paragraphs arranged in order of importance might begin: *First...*, *More important...*, *Most important....* Use transitional expressions alone or together with other linking devices.

4. Use transitional sentences. From time to time, you may need to write an entire sentence of transition to link one paragraph to the next, as shown in this passage:

> (1) Zainab Salbi lived through the ravages of war in her native Iraq. She experienced the violence committed against women under Saddam Hussein. After escaping to the United States, she worried about other women. In the 1990s, upset by stories of women in concentration camps in the former Yugoslavia, she and her husband Amjad Atallah decided to make a difference by volunteering. Unfortunately, they could find no organization dedicated to helping women affected by war.
>
> (2) *This setback did not stop the couple, however.* Salbi and Atallah resolved to start their own group dedicated to helping women hurt physically and psychologically by war. The young couple spent their honeymoon connecting American female sponsors with female victims of the war in Bosnia and Herzegovina. They returned from the trip and started Women to Women International, which has since helped over 150,000 women in countries like Nigeria, Colombia, and Afghanistan, distributing over forty million dollars in aid. Salbi has become a champion of women's rights and published books about women's war experiences. "Women who survive war are strong and courageous," she says. "They just need some support to deal with the aftermath of conflict."

---

* For more work on transitional expressions of time, space, and importance, see Chapter 4, "Achieving Coherence," Part A.

● In paragraph 1, Salbi and Atallah focus on a goal but lack the tools to achieve it. In paragraph 2, they achieve their goal. The topic sentence of paragraph 2 is the second sentence: *Salbi and Atallah resolved to start their own group dedicated to helping women hurt physically and psychologically by war.*

● The first sentence of paragraph 2 is actually a **sentence of transition** that eases the reader from a challenge to success. (Note that it includes a transitional expression of contrast, *however*.)

Use all four methods of linking paragraphs as you write your essays.

PRACTICE 10

Read the essay that follows, noting the paragraph-to-paragraph *links*. Then answer the questions.

SKIN DEEP

(1) What do Johnny Depp, Lady Randolph Churchill, Whoopi Goldberg, and Charles Manson all have in common? Perhaps you guessed tattoos: body decorations made by piercing the skin and inserting colored pigments. In fact, tattoos have a long and nearly worldwide history, ranging from full-body art to a single heart, from tribal custom to pop-culture fad.

(2) The earliest known tattoo was found on the mummy of an Egyptian priestess dating back to 2200 BC. Tattoos were also used in the ancient world to decorate Japanese noblemen, mark Greek spies, and hide expressions of fear on Maori tribesmen in New Zealand. Full-body tattooing was practiced for centuries in the South Seas; in fact, the word *tattoo* comes from the Tahitian word *tattaw*. In medieval times, small tattoos were common in Europe. For instance, in 1066, after the famous Battle of Hastings, the only way that the body of the Anglo Saxon King Harold could be identified was by the word *Edith* tattooed over his heart.

(3) For the next 600 years, however, Europeans lost interest in tattoos. Then, in the 1700s, explorers and sailors rekindled public excitement. Captain Cook, returning from

A tattoo artist at work

© Atlantide Phototravel/Corbis

a trip to Tahiti in 1761, described the wonders of tattoos. Cook enthusiastically paraded a heavily tattooed Tahitian prince named Omai through England's finest drawing rooms. People were intrigued by the colorful flowers, snakes, and geographical maps covering Omai's body. Although large tattoos were too much for the British, the idea of a pretty little bee or royal crest on the shoulder was very appealing. Tattooing remained popular with Europe's royalty and upper classes through the nineteenth century. The Prince of Wales, the Duke of York, Tsar Nicholas of Russia, and Winston Churchill's mother all had tattoos.

(4) When tattooing first reached America, on the other hand, its image was definitely not refined. American soldiers and sailors, feeling lonely and patriotic during World War II, visited tattoo parlors in South Pacific ports and came home with *Mother* or *Death Before Dishonor* inked into their arms. Soon motorcyclists started getting tattoos as part of their rebellious, macho image. The process was painful, with a high risk of infection, so the more elaborate a cyclist's bloody dagger or skull and crossbones, the better.

(5) Tattooing did not remain an outlaw rite of passage for long. Safer and less painful methods developed in the 1970s and 1980s brought tattooing into the American mainstream, especially among the young. Designs ranged from one butterfly to black-and-white patterns like Native American textiles to flowing, multicolored, stained-glass designs. With the media documenting the tattoos of the rich and famous, tattooing became a full-blown fad by the 1990s. Now the one-time symbols of daring have become so common that many rebels are having their tattoos removed. About one-third of all the work performed by tattoo artists in the United States is "erasing" unwanted tattoos.

1. What transitional expressions does this writer use to link paragraphs? (Find at least two.)

   _____

   _____

2. How does the writer link paragraphs 1 and 2? _____

   _____

3. How does the writer link paragraphs 4 and 5? _____

   _____

F. Writing and Revising Essays

Writing the First Draft

Now you should have a clear plan or outline from which to write your first draft. This plan should include your thesis statement, two to four topic sentences that support it, details and facts to develop each paragraph, and a logical order. Write on every other line to leave room for later corrections, including all your ideas and paragraphs in the order you have chosen to present them. Explain your ideas fully, but avoid getting stuck on a particular word or sentence. When you have finished the draft, set it aside, if possible, for several hours or several days.

PRACTICE 11

Write a first draft of the essay you have been working on in Practices 7 and 9.

Revising and Proofreading

Revising is perhaps the most important step in the essay-writing process. Revising an essay involves the same principles as revising a paragraph.* Read your first draft slowly and carefully to yourself—aloud if possible. Imagine you are a reader who has never seen the paper before. As you read, underline trouble spots, draw arrows, and write in the margins, if necessary, to straighten out problems.

Here are some questions to keep in mind as you revise:

1. Is my thesis statement clear?
2. Does the body of the essay fully support my thesis statement?
3. Does the essay have unity; does every paragraph relate to the thesis statement?
4. Does the essay have coherence; do the paragraphs follow a logical order?
5. Are my topic sentences clear?
6. Does each paragraph provide good details, well-chosen examples, and so on?
7. Is the language exact, concise, and fresh?
8. Are my sentences varied in length and type?
9. Does the essay conclude, not just leave off?

If possible, ask a **peer reviewer**—a trusted classmate or friend—to read your paper and give you feedback. Of course, this person should not rewrite or correct the essay but should simply tell you which parts are clear and which parts are confusing.

To guide your peer reviewer, you might ask him or her to use the Peer Feedback Sheet on page 40 or to answer these questions in writing:

1. What do you like about this piece of writing?
2. What seems to be the main point?
3. Which parts could be improved (unclear sentences, supporting points missing, order mixed up, writing not lively, and so forth)? Please be specific.
4. What one change would most improve this essay?

Proofreading and Writing the Final Draft

Next, carefully **proofread** the draft for grammar and spelling. Check especially for those errors you often make: verb errors, comma splices, and so forth.† If you are unsure about the spelling of a word, check a dictionary or use the spell checker on your computer.

---

* For more work on revising, see Chapter 3, "The Process of Writing Paragraphs," Part F, and Chapter 24, "Putting Your Revision Skills to Work."

† For practice proofreading for individual errors, see chapters in Unit 6; for mixed-error proofreading, see Chapter 39, "Putting Your Proofreading Skills to Work."

Finally, neatly recopy your essay or print out a final copy on 8 ½-by-11-inch paper. Write on one side only. When you finish, proofread the final copy.

The following sample essay by a student shows his first draft, the revisions he made, and the revised draft. Each revision has been numbered and explained to give you a clear idea of the thinking process involved.

First Draft

PORTRAIT OF A BIKE FANATIC

(1) I first realized how serious Diane was when I joined her on a long trip one Sunday afternoon. Her bike looked new, so I asked her if it was. When she told me she had bought it three years ago, I asked her how she kept it looking so good. She showed me how she took good care of it.

(2) Diane had just about every kind of equipment I've ever seen. She put on her white crash helmet and attached a tiny rearview mirror on it—the kind the dentist uses to check out the backs of your teeth. She put a warning light on her left leg. She carried a whole bag full of tools. When I looked into it, I couldn't believe how much stuff was in there (wrenches, inner tubes, etc.)—tools to meet every emergency. I was tempted to see if it had a false bottom.

(3) I had no idea she was such a bike nut. We rode thirty miles and I was exhausted. Her equipment was something else, but useful because she had a flat and was able to fix it, saving our trip.

(4) She doesn't look like a bike fanatic, just a normal person. You'd never guess that her bike has more than 10,000 miles on it.

(5) As we rode, Diane told me about her travels throughout the Northeast (Cape Cod, Vermont, Penn., New York). Riding to work saved her money, kept her in shape. Her goal for the next summer was a cross-country tour over the Rockies!.

(6) Our trip was no big deal to her but to me it was something. I might consider biking to work because it keeps you in shape. But basically I'm lazy. I drive a car or take the bus. I do like to walk though.

Revisions

PORTRAIT OF A BIKE FANATIC

① Add intro and thesis

② about bicycling   ③ thirty-mile

I first realized how serious Diane was when I joined her on a ~~long~~ trip one Sunday afternoon. Her bike looked new, so I asked her if it was. When she told me she had bought it three years ago, I asked her how she kept it looking so good. ~~She showed me how she took good care of it~~.   ④ Describe in detail

⑤ For example, Diane had just about every kind of equipment I've ever seen. She put on her white crash helmet and attached a tiny rearview mirror on it—the

⑥ examine   ⑦ strapped

⑧ Mention trip location

kind the dentist uses to ~~check out~~ the backs of your teeth. She ~~put~~ a warning light ~~on~~ her leg.   to   just below the knee

> She carried a whole bag full of tools. When I looked into it,
> I couldn't believe how much stuff was in there (wrenches, inner tubes,
> etc.)—tools to meet every emergency. I was tempted to see if it had a
> false bottom.

⑨ *New ¶ on tools, flat tire*

⑩ ~~I had no idea she was such a bike nut. We rode thirty miles and I was exhausted.~~ Her equipment was something else, but useful because she had a flat and was able to fix it, saving our trip.

⑪ *Combine into one ¶ on tools*

⑫ *Move to intro?*

She doesn't look like a bike fanatic, just a normal person. You'd never guess that her bike has more than 10,000 miles on it.

⑬ *Describe in detail. Make interesting!*

As we rode, Diane told me about her travels throughout the Northeast (Cape Cod, Vermont, Penn., New York). Riding to work saved her money, kept her in shape. Her goal for the next summer was a cross-country tour over the Rockies!

⑭ *Help Mother Earth!*

⑮ *Better conclusion needed*

Our trip was no big deal to her, but to me it was something. ~~I might consider biking to work because it keeps you in shape. But basically I'm lazy. I drive a car or take the bus. I do like to walk though.~~

⑯ *Drop. Irrelevant*

Reasons for Revisions

1. No thesis statement. Add catchy introduction. (introduction and thesis statement)

2. Add *bicycling*. What she is serious *about* is not clear. (exact language)

3. Tell *how* long! (exact language)

4. Expand this; more details needed. (support, exact language)

5. Add transition. (transitional expression)

6. Wrong tone for college essay. (exact language)

7. Find more active verb; be more specific. (exact language)

8. Conclude paragraph; add details to show time order. (order)

9. This section is weak. Add one paragraph on tools. Tell story of flat tire? (paragraphs, support)

10. Drop! Repeats thesis. Not really a paragraph. (unity, paragraphs)

11. Put this in tools paragraph. Order is mixed up. (order)

12. Put this in introduction? (order)

13. Add details; make this interesting! (support, exact language)

14. Add the point that biking helps the environment.

15. Write a better conclusion. (conclusion)

16. Drop! Essay is about Diane and biking, not my bad exercise habits. (unity)

Final Draft

PORTRAIT OF A BIKE FANATIC

(1) You'd never guess that the powder-blue ten-speed Raleigh had more than 10,000 miles on it. And you'd never guess that the tiny woman with the swept-back hair and the suntanned forearms had ridden those miles over the last two years, making trips through eleven states. But Diane is a bicycle fanatic.

(2) I first realized how serious Diane was about bicycling when I joined her on a thirty-mile trip one Sunday afternoon. Her bike looked new, so I asked her if it was. When she told me she had bought it three years ago, I asked her how she kept it looking so good. From her saddlebag she took the soft cloth that she wiped the bike down with after every long ride and the plastic drop cloth that she put over it every time she parked it outdoors overnight.

(3) Diane had just about every kind of bike equipment I've ever seen. For example, she put on her white crash helmet and attached a tiny rearview mirror to it—the kind the dentist uses to examine the backs of your teeth. She strapped a warning light to her left leg, just below the knee. Then we set off on our trip, starting at Walden Pond in Concord and planning to go to the Wayside Inn in Sudbury and back again before the sun set.

(4) We were still in Concord when Diane signaled me to stop. "I think I have a flat," she said. I cursed under my breath. I was sure that would mean the end of our trip; we'd have to walk her bike back to the car and she'd have to take it to the shop the next day. But she reached into her saddlebag again, and out came a wrench and a new tube. Before I knew it, she took the rear wheel off the bike, installed the new tube, and put the wheel back on. I began to wonder what else was in that saddlebag. When I asked, she showed me two sets of wrenches, another spare inner tube, two brake pads, a can of lubricating oil, two screwdrivers, a roll of reflective tape, extra bulbs for her headlight and taillight, and an extra chain. She had so much in the bag, I was tempted to see if it had a false bottom. Diane is one of those bicyclists who has tools to meet any emergency and knows how to use them.

(5) As we rode along, Diane told me about her travels throughout the Northeast. She had taken her bike on summer vacations on Cape Cod and fall foliage tours in Vermont. She had ridden all over Pennsylvania and upstate New York, covering as much as seventy miles in a single day. She also rode to and from work every day, which she said saved money, kept her in shape, and made a small contribution to the environment. Her goal for the next summer, she said, was a cross-country tour. "All the way?" I asked. "What about the Rockies?" "I know," she said. "What a challenge!"

(6) Our trip took a little less than three hours, but I'm sure Diane was slowing down to let me keep up with her. When we got back to the parked car, I was breathing hard and had worked up quite a sweat. Diane was already there waiting for me, looking as if she did this every day—which she does. For Diane, riding a bike is as easy and natural as walking is for most people. Look out, Rockies.

PRACTICE 12

Now, carefully read over the first draft of your essay from Practice 11 and **revise** it, referring to the checklist of questions on page 195. You might wish to ask a peer reviewer for feedback before you revise. Ask specific questions or use the Peer Feedback Sheet on page 40. Take your time and write the best essay you can. Once you are satisfied, **proofread** your essay for grammar and spelling errors. Neatly write the final draft or print a final copy.

WRITING ASSIGNMENTS

The assignments that follow will give you practice in writing essays. In each, concentrate on writing a clear thesis statement and a full, well-organized body. Because introductions and conclusions are not discussed until Chapter 15, you may wish to begin your essay with the thesis statement and conclude as simply as possible.

Before you write, make sure you have the specific *audience* to whom you are writing and your *purpose* clearly in mind. Then make an outline that includes:

- a clear thesis statement
- two to four topic sentences that support the thesis statement
- details, facts, and examples to develop each paragraph
- a logical order of paragraphs

1. Do you socialize mostly with members of your own ethnic or racial group? Why? Should you broaden your circle of friends to include more diverse people? Write an essay that either explores in detail the advantages or disadvantages of a diverse social life or the ways that you could go about making this change happen. Begin by writing a clear thesis statement and making a plan for a well-organized essay.

2. Interview a classmate (or, if you do this assignment at home, someone with an unusual skill). As you talk to the person, look for a thesis: ask questions, take notes. What stands out about the person? Is there an overall impression or idea that can structure your essay? Do you notice an overall quality, skill, or goal that seems to characterize this person? Formulate a thesis statement that points out this quality or trait, organize your ideas, and write.

3. Write to a judge or probation officer explaining why a friend or family member deserves a second chance. Your friend or relative has gotten in trouble with the law (anything from a speeding ticket to armed robbery), and your goal is to convince the judge or officer to act with leniency. In your letter, briefly explain the crime or offense. Then set forth two to three solid reasons why you believe this person deserves a break. You could discuss stresses that contributed to the offense, as well as positive traits, a desire to change, or circumstances that predict a brighter future.

4. What are the most important qualities of a committed relationship? What factors help keep such a relationship positive and alive? Would it be shared interests, trust, humor, or nurturing each other's growth? Your audience is anyone who wants a devoted relationship. Jot your ideas, and perhaps ask happy couples for advice. Then write an essay that explains three key qualities of committed partnership. Support your points with details, examples, and perhaps a quote.

5. Some college students cheat on their papers and exams; some people cheat on the job. Why do people cheat? What are the advantages and disadvantages of cheating? Does cheating pay off? Does it achieve the

end that the cheater desires? Focus on cheating at college or at work, and choose one main idea to write about. You might wish to use examples to support your thesis. Plan your essay carefully on paper before you write it.

6. Write a letter to an elected official, newspaper editor, school principal, college president, or other authority figure about an issue or incident that concerns you. Begin by crafting a thesis statement that mentions both the problem and at least one possible solution. Support your thesis first by clearly describing the problem, using specific details from your observations or experience. Then, carefully explain each of your proposed solutions, anticipating and answering all of the reader's potential questions.

Checklist

The Process of Writing an Essay

- [ ] 1. Narrow the topic in light of your audience and purpose. Be sure you can discuss this topic fully in a short essay.

- [ ] 2. Write a clear thesis statement. If you have trouble, freewrite or brainstorm first; then narrow the topic and write the thesis statement.

- [ ] 3. Freewrite or brainstorm, generating facts, details, and examples to support your thesis statement.

- [ ] 4. Plan or outline your essay, choosing from two to four main ideas to support the thesis statement.

- [ ] 5. Write a topic sentence that expresses each main idea.

- [ ] 6. Decide on a logical order in which to present the paragraphs.

- [ ] 7. Plan the body of each paragraph, using all you learned about paragraph development in Unit 2 of this book.

- [ ] 8. Write the first draft of your essay.

- [ ] 9. Revise as necessary, checking your essay for support, unity, and coherence. Refer to the list of revision questions on page 195.

- [ ] 10. Proofread carefully for grammar, punctuation, sentence structure, spelling, and mechanics.

Suggested Topics for Essays

1. The career for which I am best suited

2. Tips for balancing work, school, and home

3. How to do something that will improve your life (get better organized, learn a new language)

4. Why many Americans don't _____ (save money for the future, give their all at work, value education, read poetry)

5. A valuable discipline or practice (lifting weights, rock climbing, bicycling, or other)

6. The best (or worst) teacher I ever had

7. A story of courage

8. A lesson in diversity, race, or difference

9. The joys of homework (or housework or some other supposedly unpleasant task)

10. How to resolve a disagreement peacefully

11. A film, book, or magazine

12. The best gift I ever gave (or received)

13. Three ways that a certain type of ads (for cigarettes, cereal, or toys, for example) "hook" children

14. Should courts require a one-year "cooling-off" period before a divorce?

15. Writer's choice:_____

EXPLORING ONLINE

http://www.powa.org

Click "Explain" for a good review of the college essay-writing process. Topics include "Subject to Thesis," "Stating Your Thesis," "Supporting Your Thesis," "Developing Your Paragraphs," and more.

http://www.gallaudet.edu/TIP/English_Works/ Writing/Pre-Writing_Writing_and_Revising.html

Review the steps of the writing process. If organizing is a problem for you, review the "Outlining" section.

http://www.google.com

Search "Purdue OWL, proofreading" for good revising and proofreading techniques to sharpen your awareness and raise your grade.

CourseMate for *Evergreen*

Visit *Evergreen* CourseMate for more practices and quizzes, videos to accompany the readings, career and job-search resources, ESL help, and live links to every Exploring Online in the book.

CHAPTER 15

The Introduction, the Conclusion, and the Title

A: The Introduction

B: The Conclusion

C: The Title

A catchy title and introduction are important parts of an essay. Both attract the reader's attention and make him or her want to read on. The conclusion of an essay performs a different job, leaving the reader with something to think about or with a sense of why the topic matters. Most writers polish these three elements *after* they have planned and written the essay though, sometimes, a great title or the idea for a good introduction might occur to them earlier. This chapter will teach you how to write memorable introductions, conclusions, and titles.

A. The Introduction

An **introduction** has two functions in an essay. First, it contains the **thesis statement** and, therefore, tells the reader what central idea will be developed in the rest of the paper. Since the reader should be able to spot the thesis statement easily, it should be given a prominent place—for example, the first or the last sentence in the introduction. Second, the introduction has to interest the reader enough that he or she will want to continue reading the paper.

Sometimes the process of writing the essay will help clarify your ideas about how best to introduce it. So once you have completed your essay, you may wish to revise and rewrite the introduction, making sure that it clearly introduces the essay's main idea.

There is no best way to introduce an essay, but you should certainly avoid beginning your work with "I'm going to discuss" or "This paper is about." You needn't tell the reader you are about to begin; just begin!

Here are six basic methods for beginning your composition effectively. In each example, the thesis statement is italicized.

1. Begin with a single-sentence thesis statement. A single-sentence thesis statement can be effective because it quickly and forcefully states the main idea of the essay:

> *Time management should be a required course at this college.*

- Note how quickly and clearly a one-sentence thesis statement can inform the reader about what will follow in the rest of the essay.

2. Begin with a general idea and then narrow to a specific thesis statement. The general idea gives the reader background information or sets the scene. Then the topic narrows to one specific idea—the thesis statement. The effect is like a funnel, from broad to narrow.

> I spent most of my adolescent years surrounded by policemen, social workers, and counselors. I have been arrested, detained, and interrogated more times than I can remember. I wasn't a drug or criminal offender. *I was a teenage runaway.*
>
> —Emelyn Cruz Lat, "Emancipated," *Mother Jones*

- What general idea precedes the thesis statement and then leads the reader to focus on the specific main point of the essay?

_____

- The rest of the essay will focus on the experiences of a teenage runaway.

3. Begin with an illustration or anecdote (a brief narrative). A brief illustration or anecdote in the introduction of an essay makes the thesis statement more concrete and vivid, a good technique for catching the reader's interest.

> The other day I was watching a Reebok commercial. It was about a young male who, after purchasing a pair of sneakers, was walking down the street to a smooth jazz tune. As this "pretty boy" walked in his new pair of sneakers, he drew the attention of all in his path, especially the females. For a second I was envious of this "dude." I've been purchasing sneakers for over eighteen years, and I haven't had one girl look at me the way they did him during his thirty-second stroll down some dark and filthy sidewalk. As I watched this ad and others like it, I started to analyze the ads' underlying message. *I wondered why the majority of sneaker ads are geared to inner-city youth, especially ads for brand-name sneakers.*
>
> —Saladin Brown, Student, "The Illusion of Ads"

● Mr. Brown's thesis poses a question that his essay will try to answer.

● What example does the writer provide to make the thesis statement more concrete?

_____

● The rest of the essay will discuss the reasons why athletic shoe advertisers seem to target inner-city males.

4. Begin with a surprising fact or idea. A surprising fact or idea arouses the reader's curiosity about how you will support this initial startling statement.

© Terekhov Igor/Shutterstock.com

> *Millions of law-abiding Americans are physically addicted to caffeine—and most of them don't even know it.* Caffeine is a powerful central nervous system stimulant with substantial addiction potential. When deprived of their caffeine, addicts often experience severe withdrawal symptoms, which may include a throbbing headache, disorientation, constipation, nausea, sluggishness, depression, and irritability. As with other addictive drugs, heavy users develop a tolerance and require higher doses to obtain the expected effect.
>
> —Tom Ferguson and Joe Graedon, "Caffeine," *Medical Self-Care*

● Why are the facts in this introduction likely to startle or surprise the reader?

_____

● The rest of the essay will discuss caffeine addiction in depth.

5. Begin with a contradiction. In this type of introduction, your thesis statement contradicts what many or most people believe. In other words, your essay will contrast your opinion with the widely held view.

> When I became an Emergency Medical Technician (EMT), I was excited by the opportunity to assist others and save lives. Like most people, I didn't think of an EMT job as dangerous. After all, EMTs arrive *after* the accident or crime has occurred, so the riskiest part of our work would seem to be the high-speed ambulance ride to or from the scene. I never expected to encounter a situation that put my life and my partner's life in danger when we answered someone's call for help. *But one night a year ago, responding to a 911 call to aid a gunshot victim, we found ourselves in a situation that soon turned deadly dangerous.*
>
> —Marlena Torres Ballard, Student

● The writer first describes her excitement at becoming an EMT. What widely held view of this job does she set forth?

_____

● How does she then contradict this idea?

_____

_____

● The rest of the essay will tell the story of her frightening experience.

6. Begin with a direct quotation. A direct quotation is likely to catch your reader's attention and to show that you have explored what others have to say about the subject. You can then proceed to agree or to disagree with the direct quotation.

> "All glory comes from daring to begin," according to an old saying. The last two-and-a-half-year chapter of my life shows just how true this saying is. It started when I got laid off from my job at the furniture manufacturing plant in Morganton, North Carolina. I had worked there for ten years after high school and assumed I always would. The chapter ended with me wearing a light blue cap and gown, walking across the stage to receive my college degree in dental assisting as my family and friends cheered me on. *By daring to find a new path and stay on it through the hardships, I have changed my life for the better.*
>
> —Sam Chaich, Student

● Does the writer agree or disagree with the quotation?

_____

● Based on this introduction, what will the rest of the essay discuss?

_____

Of course, definitions, comparisons, or any of the other kinds of devices you have already studied can also make good introductions. Just make sure that the reader knows exactly which sentence is your thesis statement.

WRITING ASSIGNMENT 1

Here are five statements. Pick three that you would like to write about and compose an introduction for each one. Use any of the methods for beginning compositions discussed in this chapter thus far.

1. _____ is a wonderful vacation destination.

2. Marriage is the death of romance.

3. Serious illness—our own or someone else's—sometimes can bring surprising blessings.

4. Studying with someone else can pay off in better grades.

5. Space exploration is (not) worth the money.

B. The Conclusion

A conclusion signals the end of the essay and leaves the reader with a final thought. As with the introduction, you may wish to revise and rewrite the conclusion once you have completed your essay. Be certain your conclusion flows logically from the body of the essay.

Like introductions, conclusions can take many forms, and the right one for your essay depends on how you wish to complete your paper—with what thought you wish to leave the reader. However, never conclude your paper with "As I said in the beginning," and try to avoid the overused "In conclusion" or "In summary." Don't end by saying you are going to end; just end!

Here are three ways to conclude an essay.

1. End with a call to action. The call to action says that in view of the facts and ideas presented in this essay, the reader should *do something*.

> Single-gender schools work. As we have seen, boys-only and girls-only middle and high schools help steer young people toward academic achievement and higher self-esteem. Showing off for the opposite sex, dating too early, and, especially in the case of girls, failing to raise their hands for fear of outshining the boys, are problems avoided altogether in single-gender environments. Parents and concerned citizens must contact their representatives and school boards to demand the option of single-gender schools. We owe it to our children to fight for the schools that truly serve them.

● What does the writer want the reader to do?

_____

_____

2. End with a final point. Make a point that discusses one or more consequences of the ideas or experiences in your essay. Some writers also summarize their main ideas, but if you do this, be sure to add a new point or thought; don't just repeat what you have already said.

> My days struggling with anorexia taught me many lessons that I would not trade for the world. They taught me the joys of simple things like eating lunch and sharing gossip with a group of teenage girls. Through my struggles, I learned to be a better friend and gained an understanding of what true character is. I hold no grudges against those who so desperately tried to help me by watching my plate and urging me to eat. In fact, I owe them a great debt. But I deeply appreciate the people who helped me to see that there is more to life— and more to me—than having an eating disorder.
>
> —Student, name withheld

● With what final point does this student end her essay?

_____

3. End with a question. By ending with a question, you leave the reader with a final problem that you wish him or her to think about.

Yes, it is embarrassing to speak with our children about sex. We will feel awkward not knowing what to say, stymied as they resist the discussion. However, knowing the pressures that kids today face, the terrible examples bombarding them from popular culture, and the real threat of diseases, can we afford not to?

—Amelia Garcia, Student, "Talking to Kids about Sex"

● What problem does the writer's final question point to?

WRITING ASSIGNMENT 2

Review two or three essays that you have written recently. Do the conclusions bring the essays clearly to an end? Are those conclusions interesting? How could they be improved? Using one of the three strategies taught in this section, write a new conclusion for one of the essays.

C. The Title

If you are writing just one paragraph, chances are that you will not need to give it a title, but if you are writing a multiparagraph essay, a title is definitely in order.

The title is centered on the page above the body of the composition and separated from it by several blank lines (about 1 inch of space), as shown here.

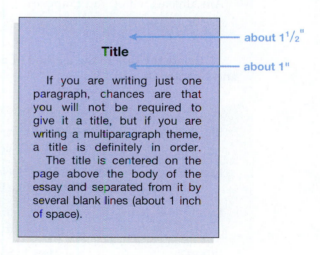

Title

If you are writing just one paragraph, chances are that you will not be required to give it a title, but if you are writing a multiparagraph theme, a title is definitely in order.

The title is centered on the page above the body of the essay and separated from it by several blank lines (about 1 inch of space).

about 1$\frac{1}{2}$"

about 1"

● Do *not* put quotation marks around the title of your own paper.

● Do *not* underline or italicize the title of your own paper.

● Remember, unlike the topic sentence, the title is not part of the first paragraph; in fact, it is usually only four to five words long and is rarely an entire sentence.

A good title has two functions: to suggest the subject of the essay and to spark the reader's interest. Although the title is the first part of your essay the reader sees, the most effective titles are usually written *after* the essay has been completed.

To create a title, reread your essay, paying special attention to the **thesis statement** and the **conclusion**. Try to come up with a few words that express the main point of your paper.

Here are some basic kinds of titles.

1. The most common title used in college writing is the no-nonsense descriptive title. In this title, stress key words and ideas developed in the essay:

> Anger in the Work of Jamaica Kincaid
> Advantages and Disadvantages of Buying on Credit

2. Two-part titles are also effective. Write one or two words stating the general subject, and then add several words that narrow the topic:

> Rumi: Poet and Mystic
> Legal Gambling: Pro and Con

3. Write the title as a rhetorical question. Then answer the question in your essay:

> What Can Be Done About the High Price of Higher Education?
> Are Athletes Setting Bad Examples?

4. Relate the title to the method of development used in the essay (see Unit 3 and Chapters 16 and 17):

Illustration:	Democracy in Action
	Three Roles I Play
Narration:	The Development of Jazz
	Edwidge Danticat: The Making of a Storyteller
Description:	Portrait of a Scientist
	A Waterfront Scene
Process:	How to Start a Book Group
	How to Get in Shape Fast
Definition:	What It Means to Be Unemployed
	A Definition of Respect
Comparison:	Two Country Stars Who Crossed Over
	Unconventional Dads: Homer Simpson and Tony Soprano

Contrast:	Pleasures and Problems of Owning a Home
	Montreal: City of Contrasts
Classification:	Three Types of Soap Operas
	What Kind of E-Mail User Are You?
Cause and Effect:	What Causes Whales to Beach Themselves?
	The Effects of Divorce on Children
Persuasion:	Internet Pornography Should Be Banned
	The Need for Metal Detectors in Our Schools

Use this list the next time you title a paper.*

WRITING ASSIGNMENT 3

Review two or three essays that you have written recently. Are the titles clear and interesting? Applying what you've learned in this chapter, write a better title for at least one paper.

EXPLORING ONLINE

http://www.powa.org

Click "Explain" and scroll to "Introductions and Conclusions." Read more about beginning and ending your essays effectively.

http://grammar.ccc.commnet.edu/grammar/

Under "Essay and Research Paper Level," scroll to "Structural Considerations" and click "Beginnings" for lively sample introductions, plus tips for the writer.

CourseMate for *Evergreen*

Visit *Evergreen* CourseMate for more practices and quizzes, videos to accompany the readings, career and job-search resources, ESL help, and live links to every Exploring Online in the book.

---

* For more on how to capitalize in titles, see Chapter 38, "Mechanics," Part B.

CHAPTER 16

Types of Essays, Part 1

A: The Illustration Essay

B: The Narrative Essay

C: The Descriptive Essay

D: The Process Essay

E: The Definition Essay

Because an essay is like an expanded paragraph, the methods for developing and organizing a paragraph that you learned in Unit 3—illustration, process, and so forth—can also be used to develop an entire essay. Chapters 16 and 17 will show you how.

A. The Illustration Essay

The **illustration** essay is one of the most frequently used in college writing and in business. For papers and exams in history, health, psychology, English, and other subjects, you often will be asked to develop a main point with examples. In careers as varied as engineering, nursing, and advertising, you will author reports that include examples of advantages of one computer system, patients' symptoms and behavior, or successful product launches. In a letter of job application, you might wish to give examples of achievements that demonstrate your special skills.

Here is an illustration essay:

GIRL HEROES IN THE HOUSE

Introduction

(1) Although a visitor might not notice, the small apartment I share with my daughters is very crowded. We live with a group of fantastic characters who fill my young daughters' imaginations and therefore our daily lives. Mostly female, they reveal a world beyond Cinderella and Barbie. These role models are teaching my girls to take pride in their heritage, their intelligence, and their unique talents.

Thesis statement

Topic sentence introducing example 1

(2) A good example is *Dora the Explorer,* a spunky preschool adventurer with an international fan club. My third grader, who once knew every Dora song by heart, has since moved on, but her little sister now calls Dora her best friend. As a mother, I have good reasons to admire Dora. She is bilingual like our family, and while she is Mexican and we are Guatemalan, Dora gives my lovely brown daughters a reason to like themselves even if they don't look like Barbie. Dora plunges into the unknown day after day, armed with little more than a talking backpack and a belief that she can overcome any obstacle. The world outside can be an unsavory place for a four-year-old, so I am thankful for the pleasures Dora uncovers on her journeys and the dignity she brings to our heritage.

Facts & details developing example 1

Topic sentence introducing example 2

(3) A new role model in our home is Hermione, the brainy heroine in J.K. Rowling's *Harry Potter* books. She is my older daughter's current obsession, and I confess that I am hooked on her too. Like most parents, I was thrilled when my cartoon-addicted third-grader wanted to read a chapter book, so every night we sit together absorbing the adventures of Harry and his best friends Ron and Hermione. We take turns reading pages, getting lost in the Hogwarts School of Witchcraft and Wizardry. I love that Hermione is neither graceful nor gorgeous and often comes across as a know-it-all. But experience reveals her as a brilliant young woman and a deeply loyal friend. Just two books into the series and Hermione has saved Harry more than once. I hope that my daughter internalizes the message that really cool girls value intelligence and loyalty more than superficial traits.

Facts & details developing example 2

Topic sentence introducing example 3

(4) With the "tween" years fast approaching, I suppose Hannah Montana will soon arrive in our home. While part of me dreads my girls' transition into rock music, boys, and fashion, there are worse role models than a perky high schooler who lives an average teenager's life by day and performs as a famous pop artist at night. The wild success of the *Hannah Montana* television show and merchandise shows the power this secret rock star has over little girls. Hannah solves everyday problems with a silly humor that girls love. She also offers a fantasy that preteens can escape into when their bodies begin to change and their social lives get complicated. Hannah's message is positive: pursue your talents, whatever they are.

Facts & details developing example 3

Conclusion

(5) The girl heroes in our home will keep changing as fast as my daughters do. I wonder if someday they will see me—raising them, working, going to college, pursuing my dreams—as a hero too. But for now, I am happy to share my home with a Latina adventurer, a smart witch-in-training, and a lively singer in lip gloss. They are helping me teach my daughters to embrace their lucky lives as modern girls.

—Irma Batres, Student

- The **thesis statement** in an illustration essay states the writer's central point—a general statement that the rest of the essay will develop with examples. Underline or highlight the thesis statement.

- How many **examples** does the writer use to develop the thesis statement? What are they?

_____

- Underline the topic sentence of each paragraph.

- What words connect each topic sentence to the introduction and thesis statement?

_____

● Notice that the thesis statement and topic sentences setting forth the three main examples create an **outline** for this essay. The writer no doubt made an outline well developed with specifics before she wrote the first draft.

PRACTICE 1

Read this student's illustration essay and answer the questions.

OTC: ONLY TAKE CARE!

(1) Many people take over-the-counter (OTC) medications for headaches, colds, and such. Over 100,000 OTC medications are for sale in stores, a number that surprised me even though I am pursuing my Pharmacy Technician certification. Most consumers think that OTC drugs are harmless because no prescription is needed, but, in fact, they can be hazardous to your health.

(2) Aspirin, for instance, is so common that people think it cannot hurt them. Every day, 43 million people take aspirin for pain, swelling or fever; some take it on their doctors' orders to prevent a heart attack or stroke. An excellent drug if used correctly, aspirin can cause bleeding in the organs or even a brain bleed. Coated aspirin helps protect from stomach bleeding, but only your doctor can say whether the dangers are worth the risks. Many people don't know that those on blood thinners like warfarin should never take aspirin or that aspirin can cause serious brain, liver, and other damage in children and teens who have fevers; this condition is called Reyes Syndrome. A widespread myth among teenagers that mixing Coca Cola with aspirin "gets you high" is not true; however, it can cause bleeding.

(3) A second illustration is cold medications. The decongestants in many of these can dangerously raise blood pressure in people who take blood pressure medications and in those on certain antidepressants. People with irregular heartbeats can be "set off" by the stimulants in these drugs. A serious new problem with cold medications is addiction to a chemical found in over 100 of them, called Dextromethorphan (DXM). More and more young people are abusing cold medications for the DXM high. Overdoses and deaths have been reported.

(4) Sleep aids are yet another example of problematic OTCs. Not being able to fall or stay asleep is a nerve-wracking problem for many people, but instead of studying their own habits to try and solve the problem naturally, often they just pop a pill. Most sleep aids contain antihistamines, which can cause not only drowsiness but also side effects during the day like sleepiness or headaches. Sleeping pills can become addictive, and people who use them should never drink alcohol. Studies differ as to whether these medications even work.

(5) These are just three examples of OTC medications and their possible side effects. Easy access to these drugs means that mistakes and abuse are common. As a consumer, it's up to you to protect your body and your health. Always read the Drug Facts label on everything you take. Ask your doctor or pharmacist about both your OTC and prescription medications to make sure there are no interactions among them.

—Bradley K. Knight, Student

1. Underline or highlight the **thesis statement**. What main examples does this student use to support the thesis and develop the essay?

2. Now, underline or highlight the **topic sentences**. Label the parts of this essay by writing these labels in the left margin opposite the correct part:

IN Introduction   E1 Example 1 and details
C   Conclusion   E2 Example 2 and details
                   E3 Example 3 and details

3. What transitional expressions of illustration help introduce each example?

_____

4. The writer mentions in the introduction that he is pursuing a certain certification. Is this sentence relevant to the paper, or should it be dropped?

_____

5. Mr. Knight drew on his curriculum to find a topic for his illustration essay. Have you learned material in your own courses that might interest your classmates? Can this material be presented through examples?

_____

PRACTICE 2   TEAMWORK: CRITICAL VIEWING AND WRITING

Often a writer will notice specific examples first, see a pattern, and then come up with a generalization—a thesis statement or topic sentence. In a group with four or five classmates, examine these photographs of houses designed by the great American architect Frank Lloyd Wright (1867–1959). Can your group make any *general statements* about Wright's houses, based just on these *examples*? Write down your generalizations.

Frank Lloyd Wright's Fallingwater, Mill Run, PA

Art Resource, NY. © 2012 Frank Lloyd Wright Foundation, Scottsdale, AZ/Artists Rights Society (ARS), NY

The Robie House, Chicago, IL
© Rick Gerharter/Lonely Planet Images

The Massaro House, Mahopac, NY
© David Allee

Planning and Writing the Illustration Essay

Before writing an illustration essay, you may wish to reread Chapter 5, "Illustration." As you pick a topic and plan the essay, make sure your thesis statement can be richly developed by examples. Prewrite to generate as many examples as possible, so you can choose the best two, three, or four. As you revise, make sure you have fully discussed each example, including all necessary details and facts.

The rest of the section will guide you as you write an illustration essay.

PRACTICE 3

1. Choose a topic from the list below or one your instructor has assigned. Make sure you can develop it well with examples. Determine your audience and purpose. Then brainstorm, cluster, or freewrite to get as many examples as possible. Choose the best ones. You're on your way.

   1. Role models (positive or negative)
   2. Failure as an effective teacher
   3. Qualities (or skills) that many employers look for
   4. TV shows that send a violent (hopeful, or other) message
   5. Everyday action steps to protect the environment
   6. Three people in the news who exemplify honesty or commitment to principles
   7. The skills, values, or traits that would make your friend a good store manager (police officer, cartoonist, and so forth)
   8. Musicians or artists of a particular type (R&B, tropical Latin, surrealist, French impressionist, and so on) or three works by the same artist
   9. Experiences that shaped your attitudes toward education (or family or work)
   10. Unusual places to go on dates (or to study, de-stress, get married, and so on)
   11. Writer's choice: _____

2. Many students find using a graphic organizer helpful as they plan an essay. In your notebook, draw a blank 8-by-11-inch organizer like the one below or use the illustration essay organizer on the CourseMate for *Evergreen*. In it, create an outline for your essay. The information you write in each box will become a paragraph.

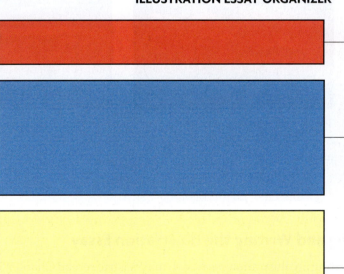

ILLUSTRATION ESSAY ORGANIZER

Title — Jot ideas for a title that clearly states the subject or refers to it in an interesting way.

Paragraph 1: Introduction & thesis statement — In box one, write a thesis statement that identifies your subject and point of view (" . . . but in fact, OTC drugs can be harmful to your health."). You also might refer to the examples to come. Jot ideas for an introduction that will grab the reader's attention or show the relevance of your topic.

Paragraph 2: Example 1 & detailed explanation — In box two, write a topic sentence introducing the first example. Brainstorm details and specifics to explain this example in one body paragraph. Use transitional expressions of illustration.

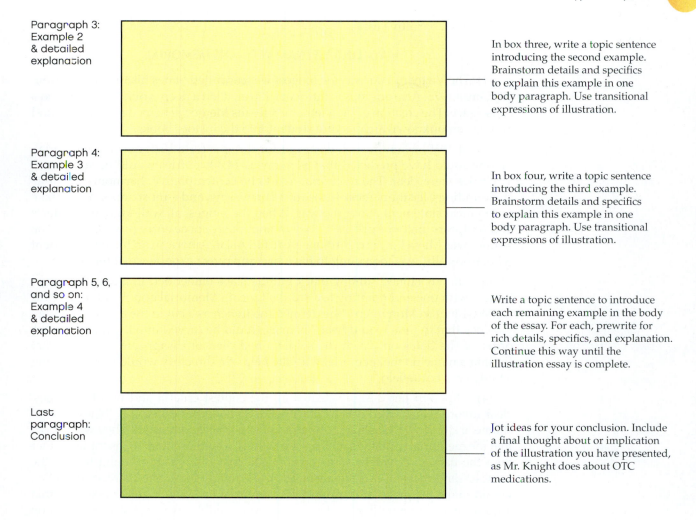

Paragraph 3:
Example 2
& detailed
explanation

In box three, write a topic sentence introducing the second example. Brainstorm details and specifics to explain this example in one body paragraph. Use transitional expressions of illustration.

Paragraph 4:
Example 3
& detailed
explanation

In box four, write a topic sentence introducing the third example. Brainstorm details and specifics to explain this example in one body paragraph. Use transitional expressions of illustration.

Paragraph 5, 6,
and so on:
Example 4
& detailed
explanation

Write a topic sentence to introduce each remaining example in the body of the essay. For each, prewrite for rich details, specifics, and explanation. Continue this way until the illustration essay is complete.

Last
paragraph:
Conclusion

Jot ideas for your conclusion. Include a final thought about or implication of the illustration you have presented, as Mr. Knight does about OTC medications.

PRACTICE 4

Now, referring to your plan, write the best first draft you can. Aim for clarity as you help the reader develop an understanding of each category in your illustration. Check your paragraphing, and use *transitional expressions** to guide the reader from example to example.

Let your draft cool for an hour or a day; then reread it as if you were a helpful, eagle-eyed stranger. Now revise and rewrite, emphasizing clarity and completeness, and keeping your reader in mind. Is each paragraph developed fully? Do transitions make the flow of ideas clear? Proofread for spelling, grammar, and sentence errors.

B. The Narrative Essay

The urge to tell stories and listen to them is as old as human beings, so it's not surprising that the **narrative** essay is used frequently in college writing. For instance, in a history course, you might be assigned a paper on the major battles in World War I or be given an essay examination question about the struggle of women to gain the right to vote. An English teacher might ask you to write a composition retelling a meaningful incident or personal experience. In police work, nursing, and social work, your ability to organize facts and details in clear chronological, or time, order—to tell a story well—will be a crucial factor in the effectiveness of your writing.

———
* For a list of transitional expressions of illustration, see page 74.

Here is a narrative essay:

MAYA LIN'S VIETNAM VETERANS MEMORIAL

(1) The Vietnam War was the longest war in United States history, lasting from 1965 until 1975. Also our most controversial war, it left a deep wound in the nation's conscience. The creation of the Vietnam Veterans Memorial helped heal this wound and put an unknown architecture student into the history books.

(2) In 1980, when the call went out for designs for a Vietnam war memorial, no one could have predicted that as many as 14,000 entries would be submitted. The rules were clear. The memorial had to be contemplative, harmonize with its surroundings, list the names of those dead or missing, and—most important—make no political statement about the war. When the judges, all well-known architects and sculptors, met in April 1981, they unanimously chose entry number 1026. The winner was Maya Lin, a twenty-one-year-old Asian American architecture student who, ironically, was too young to have had any direct experience of the war.

(3) Lin envisioned shining black granite slabs embedded in a long V-shaped trench, with one end pointing toward the Lincoln Memorial and the other toward the Washington Monument. She defined the trench as a cut in the earth, "an initial violence that in time would heal." Names would be carved into the granite in the order of the dates on which the soldiers had died or disappeared. Lin felt that finding a name on the memorial with the help of a directory would be like finding a body on a battlefield.

(4) Although her design satisfied all the contest criteria and was the judges' clear favorite, it aroused much controversy. Some critics called it a "black gash of shame and sorrow," labeling it unpatriotic, unheroic, and morbid. They were upset that the memorial contained no flags, no statues of soldiers, and no inscription other than the names. Privately, some complained that Lin was too young to win the contest—and that she was female besides. She fought back. She claimed that a flag would make the green area around the memorial look like a golf course and that a traditional statue on her modern structure would be like a mustache drawn on someone else's portrait. At last, a compromise was reached: A flag and a statue were added to the memorial, and the critics withdrew their complaints. On Veterans Day, November 11, 1982, the Vietnam Veterans Memorial was finally dedicated.

(5) Since then, the memorial has become the most popular site in Washington, D.C. Some visit to see the monument and pay tribute to those who died in the war. Others come to locate and touch the names of loved ones. As they stand before the wall, they also learn the names of those who served and died with their relatives and friends. When the rain falls, all the names seem to disappear. Visitors often leave memorials of their own—flowers, notes to the departed, bits of old uniforms. A place of national mourning and of love, Maya Lin's monument has helped heal the wounds of the Vietnam War.

● The thesis statement of a narrative essay usually gives the point of the essay. Underline or highlight the thesis statement of this essay.

● Paragraphs 2, 4, and 5 of this essay tell in chronological order the incidents of the narrative.

● What are the incidents?

_____

● What is the main idea of paragraph 3?

_____

● Paragraph 1 provides background information that helps the reader understand the narrative. What background material is given in this paragraph?

_____

Visitors to the Vietnam Memorial, 2011. What story does this picture tell? (See Practice 5)

PRACTICE 5

TEAMWORK: CRITICAL VIEWING AND WRITING

In a group with four or five classmates, study this photograph of recent visitors to the Vietnam Memorial. Look closely at the two men shown, the hand on one man's back, the wall and its reflections. What do you guess is the expression on the face of the man leaning into the wall? Why is he here? Who or what is the subject of this photograph? Write a paragraph in which you discuss the story that this picture tells.

PRACTICE 6

Read this student's narrative essay and answer the questions.

MY BLACK DOG

(1) I arrived at this college excited about changing my life. I was no longer the immature young man who thought education was boring. Through a neighbor in the field, I had become interested in studying to be a nuclear medicine technologist. My neighbor works in a cardiologist's office, interacts with patients, and does all the stress

testing. He helped me pick a program, and I enrolled. But soon after starting school, I began to feel overwhelmed, upset, and irritated much of the time; I had no idea that this was the Black Dog.

(2) The fact is I could barely keep up with all the assignments, tests, and papers in five challenging classes. Further, this was an unfamiliar environment where math skills and brains ruled, not smart (make that stupid) remarks. I worried about failing but was embarrassed to talk to anyone—not my neighbor, not even my wife. One day she told me I was turning into a mean guy.

(3) In the student lounge, I happened to see a pamphlet published by the health service. It was mostly a list of questions, such as "Are you irritable, anxious, withdrawn?" "Do you often feel fatigued or low in energy?" "Do you experience extreme sadness or angry outbursts?" I was surprised to find myself answering "yes" to most of the questions. The pamphlet was on male depression. Like many guys, the last thing I wanted to do was face this and talk about it. In my mind, depression was not manly. Reading that ten percent of college students are depressed and a third of freshmen feel overwhelmed helped a little.

(4) That night, I told my wife what was going on and decided to see a counselor. Amazingly, counseling at the college is free to students. I never loved talking about my insecurities, but it did help, especially problem solving with someone impartial. The counselor, Ron, encouraged me to use other campus resources, get a tutor, and improve the way I manage time. Ron, who knew that I like history, told me that the great leader Winston Churchill fought depression, which he called "the Black Dog." Before long, I felt more like the master of my Black Dog instead of the victim. I am still always rushing, but I don't feel so overwhelmed. My anger is gone, and my grades have climbed from Cs and Ds to As and Bs.

(5) It's impressive that the college has these programs, and I urge anyone who's feeling depressed to reach out, discuss it, and get help. No one should suffer alone because depression grows more vicious in isolation.

—Paul Frey, Student

1. Instead of a thesis statement that tells the point of the story, Mr. Frey writes, "But soon after starting school, I began to feel overwhelmed, upset, and irritated much of the time; I had no idea that this was the Black Dog." Why do you think he does not define "Black Dog" in the first paragraph?

   _____

   _____

2. Underline the topic sentences of paragraphs 2, 3, and 4. What main incidents make up the story?

   _____

   _____

3. What is the point of this narrative? Is it effective that the writer does not reveal the point until paragraphs 3 and 4?

_____

_____

4. The introduction, the incidents of the story, and the conclusion together form an outline for the narrative essay. Before sitting down to write, this student made such an outline to guide him as he wrote.

Planning and Writing the Narrative Essay

Before writing a narrative essay, you may wish to reread Chapter 6, "Narration." Pick a story idea that interests *you*—one with a point—and plan before you write. Your thesis statement will probably state the story's point. Supply any necessary background information. If your story consists of just a few major events, you may wish to devote one body paragraph to each one; if it has many small events, consider describing several events per paragraph. Follow chronological, or time, order. As you prewrite, search for exciting, precise details and words, just as you would if you were entertaining friends with a good story over lunch.

The rest of this section will guide you as you write a narrative essay.

PRACTICE 7

1. Choose a topic from the list below or one your instructor has assigned. Take your time deciding. Think of a story you want to tell—one with a point. Who is your audience? To whom will you tell your story?

   1. A favorite family story or a story from your ethnic tradition
   2. An immigrant's journey
   3. The story behind a key scientific discovery or invention
   4. How you chose your major or career path
   5. Someone's battle with a serious illness
   6. An important historical event
   7. The plot line of a movie or TV show you would like to produce
   8. The story of someone who inspires you (based on an interview you conduct)
   9. Learning a new language (or other subject or skill)
   10. An unforgettable incident you witnessed
   11. Writer's choice:_____

2. Many students find using a graphic organizer helpful as they plan an essay. In your notebook, draw a blank 8-by-11-inch organizer like the one that follows or use the narrative essay organizer on the *Evergreen* CourseMate. Use it to make an outline for your essay. The information you write in each box will become a paragraph.

NARRATIVE ESSAY ORGANIZER

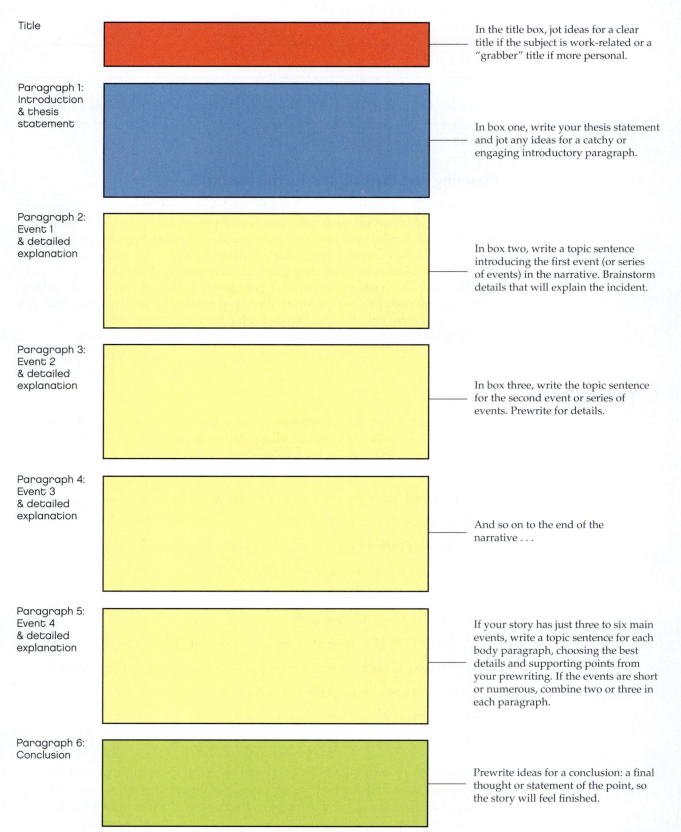

Title

In the title box, jot ideas for a clear title if the subject is work-related or a "grabber" title if more personal.

Paragraph 1:
Introduction
& thesis
statement

In box one, write your thesis statement and jot any ideas for a catchy or engaging introductory paragraph.

Paragraph 2:
Event 1
& detailed
explanation

In box two, write a topic sentence introducing the first event (or series of events) in the narrative. Brainstorm details that will explain the incident.

Paragraph 3:
Event 2
& detailed
explanation

In box three, write the topic sentence for the second event or series of events. Prewrite for details.

Paragraph 4:
Event 3
& detailed
explanation

And so on to the end of the narrative . . .

Paragraph 5:
Event 4
& detailed
explanation

If your story has just three to six main events, write a topic sentence for each body paragraph, choosing the best details and supporting points from your prewriting. If the events are short or numerous, combine two or three in each paragraph.

Paragraph 6:
Conclusion

Prewrite ideas for a conclusion: a final thought or statement of the point, so the story will feel finished.

PRACTICE 8

Follow your plan and write the best first draft you can. Make sure to include all the key events, and aim for a smooth flow that will keep the reader interested. Conveying the meaning or point of the story and keeping it moving are the keys to good narration. As you write, inspire yourself by thinking of great storytellers you know or have heard. Use transitional expressions of time to help the reader follow.* Conclude with a final point or idea that follows from the story you have just narrated. Does your title capture the essence of the tale and make people want to read on?

Let your draft cool for an hour or a day; then reread it as if you were a helpful stranger. Now revise and rewrite, avoiding wordiness and keeping your reader in mind. Proofread for spelling, grammar, and sentence errors.

C. The Descriptive Essay

Although paragraphs of **description** are more common than whole essays, you will sometimes need to write a descriptive essay. In science labs, you may need to describe accurately cells under a microscope or a certain kind of rock. In business, you may need to describe a product, a piece of equipment, or the behavior of consumers in a test group. In social work, medicine, and psychology, case notes require precise description. No doubt you already use your descriptive powers in personal e-mails and letters. As this chapter will show, descriptive and narrative writing often overlap.

Here is one student's descriptive essay:

THE DAY OF THE DEAD

(1) One of the most important holidays in Mexico is the Day of the Dead, *El Día de los Muertos*. Surprisingly, this holiday is anything but depressing. In the weeks before, Mexicans excitedly prepare to welcome the souls of the dead, who come back each year to visit the living. From October 31 through November 2 this year, I attended this fiesta with my roommate Manuel. By sharing Day of the Dead activities in his family's home, in

Skeleton in finery for Mexico's Day of the Dead. Like a photograph, a good description creates a vivid picture.

© Peter Hirth/laif/Redux

---

* For a list of transitional expressions of time, see page 83.

the marketplace, and in a cemetery, I have observed that Mexicans, unlike other North Americans, accept and celebrate death as a part of life.

(2) For this holiday, the home altar, or *ofrenda*, lovingly celebrates the dead. In the Lopez home, a trail of marigold petals and the rich smell of incense led us from the front door to the altar. The bright orange marigold blooms, the flowers of the dead, also trimmed a card table overflowing with everything the dead would need to take up their lives again. For Manuel's Uncle Angel there was a fragrant bowl of *mole*,* a glass of tequila, cigars, playing cards, and two Miles Davis jazz CDs. For Manuel's cousin Lucia, who died at eighteen months, there was a worn stuffed puppy, a coral blanket, and a bowl of the rice pudding she loved. Heavy black and yellow beeswax candles threw a soft glow on photos of Angel and Lucia. It was as if the dead had never left and would always have a place of honor.

(3) While death is given an honored place in the home, it is celebrated with humor and mockery in the marketplace. Here the skeleton, or *calavera*, rules. Shops sell sugar skulls, humorous bone figures, and even skeletons made of flowers. At the candy store, Manuel's niece picked out a white chocolate skull decorated with blue icing and magenta sequins in the eye sockets. In many bakeries, skull-and-crossbones designs decorated the delicious "bread of the dead." Most impressive were the stalls filled with *calacas*, handmade wooden skeletons, some no bigger than my thumb. The shelves showed a lively afterlife where skeleton musicians played in a band, skeleton writers tapped bony fingers on tiny typewriters, and teenage skeletons hoisted boom boxes on their matchstick-sized shoulder bones.

(4) On the evening of November first, reverence and fun combined in an all-night vigil at the cemetery. On a path outside the cemetery gate, rows of vendors sold soft drinks and cotton candy as if it were a sporting event. Men drank a strong fermented cactus beverage called *pulque* and played cards at picnic tables. The loud music of a mariachi band serenaded the dead, who would come back to eat the food laid out for them on the graves. Old grandmothers wearing hand-woven shawls mourned and wept while children chased each other around the pink- and blue-painted graves. Nobody scolded the children. Life and death did not seem so separate.

(5) While I have always felt fearful in cemeteries at home, there I felt excited and hopeful. When a soft breeze made the rows of candles flicker, I wondered if the souls of the children, the *angelitos*, had come back, laughing and giggling. Or was it the real children I heard laughing? I really didn't know. But I felt more alive than ever, waiting for the dead to arrive in a dusty cemetery in Mexico.

—Jason Eady, Student

- The **thesis statement** of a descriptive essay says what will be described and often gives an overall impression of it or tells how the writer will approach the subject. Underline or highlight the thesis statement in the introductory paragraph.

- Each paragraph in the body of this essay describes one scene or aspect of the topic. How many scenes or aspects are described, and what are they?

_____

_____

_____

* mole: A spicy Mexican sauce made of onions, chiles, and chocolate.

- What kind of order does the writer follow in organizing paragraph 2?

  _____

- Paragraph 5 completes and **concludes** the essay. How effective is this student's conclusion?

  _____

  _____

PRACTICE 9

Read this student's descriptive essay and answer the questions.

TORNADO

(1) Tornados are one of the most terrifying natural events that occur, destroying homes and ending lives every year. On April 29th, 1995, a calm, muggy night, I learned this firsthand. Joey, a buddy I grew up with, agreed to travel across state with me so we could visit a friend in Lubbock, Texas. Joey and I were admiring the blue bonnets, which went on for miles like little blue birds flying close to the ground. The warm breeze brushed the tips of the blue bonnets and allowed them to dance under the clear blue sky. In the distance, however, we could see darkness.

(2) As we drove, thunderclouds continued to rumble in, like an ocean tide rolling closer and closer to the beach front, and within minutes the entire landscape was calm and dark. It looked like a total eclipse of the sun, and the blue bonnets were now completely still and somber. The rain began to trickle down out of the sky. The sound of the rain as it hit our car was like that of pins dropping on a metal surface. The intensity of the rain increased as we ventured farther into the eye of the storm.

(3) As we approached an overpass, we noticed a parking lot of cars underneath. By now, the rain had created a wall of water, which surrounded our car. We decided to pull over and sprint to the underpass to join the other frightened observers. What Joey and I were unaware of was that a tornado was already on the ground frantically spinning towards our position. The whirling "finger of God" was approaching us.

(4) The sound surrounding us was outrageous, like a steam locomotive roaring, whining, and whistling with an awful high-pitched roar. The rain had almost stopped, but the wind was nearly blowing us off the ground as we huddled together under the overpass. We could hear the screeching of car tires as they started sliding across the rain-soaked pavement. Electrical explosions lit up the darkened sky as the tornado ripped over power lines, snapping them as if they were toothpicks. Screams erupted from the crowd as the tornado crossed directly over us, smashing large objects into the overpass pavement but leaving us untouched.

(5) Shortly thereafter the sky was bright again, revealing only shattered pieces of fence posts and telephone poles. Everyone unraveled from the huddle that had protected them moments earlier. The sun started poking holes in the dark rumbling sky; the wind and rain had ceased, leaving it morbidly calm. The sun burned away every trace of darkness. It was amazing to look back and see a mile-long trail of destruction surrounded by homes and

fences that were totally untouched. I remember thinking how amazing this moment was, and how grateful I was to be alive.

—Wesley Duke, Student

1. This writer's thesis statement is actually two sentences. Underline or highlight them.

2. Every paragraph in this essay describes one scene or aspect of the topic. How many scenes or aspects are described, and what are they?

   _____

   _____

3. This essay combines excellent, specific description with narration. What order does the writer use?

   _____

4. Which of the five senses does Mr. Duke emphasize in paragraph 4? Give some examples.

   _____

5. The thesis statement, the scenes or phases in the description, and the conclusion together form an **outline** for the descriptive essay. Before sitting down to write, Mr. Duke made a detailed outline to guide his writing process.

PRACTICE 10   TEAMWORK: CRITICAL VIEWING AND WRITING

In a group with four or five classmates, study this diagram showing the body position recommended for desk workers and students. This position avoids eyestrain, back and neck injury, and hand or wrist injury. In your group, convert the information shown here into the outline for a memo or short essay. Your audience is office workers and students; your purpose is to *describe* healthy workstation posture.

First, jot details that describe each important part of the diagram. Select the most important points to include and arrange them according to space order in an outline. If you have time, draft a clear essay or memo. Be prepared to share your work with the class.

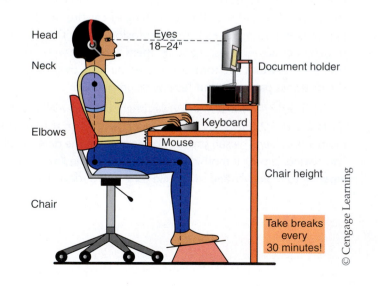

Planning and Writing the Descriptive Essay

Before writing a descriptive essay, you may wish to reread Chapter 7, "Description." Use your senses—sight, smell, hearing, taste, and touch—as you plan and prewrite ideas. Pay special attention to organizing your details and observations; space order is often the best choice, but time order might work for your subject. As you revise, aim for rich details and exact language; these are what make good descriptions come alive.

The rest of the section will guide you as you write a descriptive essay.

PRACTICE 11

1. Choose a topic from the list below or one your instructor has assigned. Take your time deciding. Think of a subject that will make a good description, perhaps an important scene or experience that you can still see in your mind's eye. Who is your audience?

    1. The rituals and decorations of a holiday you know well
    2. A place that people don't want to see, such as a public dump, a prison, or a very poor neighborhood
    3. The scene of a historic event or battle as you imagine it
    4. A lively public place, such as a campus hang-out, a fitness center, or a dance club
    5. A tourist attraction or a place of natural beauty
    6. Your present or future workplace, including setting, people, and action
    7. A computer, vehicle, or piece of equipment from your job
    8. Your family portrait
    9. The settings and costumes of a movie you admire
    10. A scene you will never forget
    11. Writer's choice: _____

2. Many students find using a graphic organizer helpful as they plan an essay. In your notebook, draw a blank 8-by-11-inch organizer like the one below or use the descriptive essay organizer on the *Evergreen* CourseMate. Use it to create an outline for your essay. The information you write in each box will become a paragraph.

DESCRIPTIVE ESSAY ORGANIZER

Title

In the title box, write a clear, engaging title.

Paragraph 1: Introduction & thesis statement

In box one, write a thesis statement that tells what will be described and conveys an overall impression. Jot ideas for an engaging introductory paragraph.

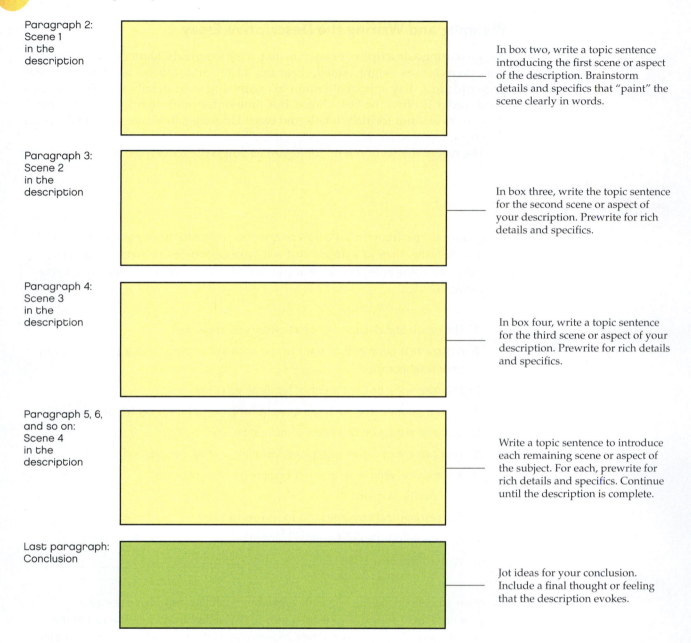

Paragraph 2:
Scene 1
in the
description

In box two, write a topic sentence
introducing the first scene or aspect
of the description. Brainstorm
details and specifics that "paint" the
scene clearly in words.

Paragraph 3:
Scene 2
in the
description

In box three, write the topic sentence
for the second scene or aspect of
your description. Prewrite for rich
details and specifics.

Paragraph 4:
Scene 3
in the
description

In box four, write a topic sentence
for the third scene or aspect of your
description. Prewrite for rich details
and specifics.

Paragraph 5, 6,
and so on:
Scene 4
in the
description

Write a topic sentence to introduce
each remaining scene or aspect of
the subject. For each, prewrite for
rich details and specifics. Continue
until the description is complete.

Last paragraph:
Conclusion

Jot ideas for your conclusion.
Include a final thought or feeling
that the description evokes.

PRACTICE 12

Now referring to your plan, write the best first draft you can. Mentally see, hear, and smell
the subject. Your *words* are your camera, paints, or graphic design program, so don't settle
for the first words that occur to you. Follow the order of space or time, whichever you
have selected, and be sure to use transitional expressions of space* or time† to guide the
reader along. For inspiration, you might reread the conclusion of "Day of the Dead" before
you conclude your paper.

Let your draft cool for an hour or a day; then reread it as if you were a helpful stranger.
Now revise and rewrite, emphasizing exact language, avoiding wordiness, and keeping
your reader in mind. Is each paragraph developed fully? Do transitions make the flow of
ideas clear? Proofread for spelling, grammar, and sentence errors.

———

* For a list of transitional expressions of space order, see page 93.

† For a list of transitional expressions of time, see page 83.

D. The Process Essay

The **process** essay is frequently used in college and business. Process essays either explain *how to do something* or describe *how something works* (or *how something happened*). In psychology, you might describe the stages of a child's moral development. In history, you might explain how a battle was won or lost, while in business, you might set forth the steps of an advertising campaign. In medicine, science, and technology, you must understand and perform numerous biological and technical processes.

Here is one student's process essay:

HOW TO PREPARE FOR A FINAL EXAM

(1) At the end of my first semester at college, I postponed thinking about final examinations, desperately crammed the night before, drank enough coffee to keep the city of Cincinnati awake, and then got Cs and Ds. I have since realized that the students who got As on their finals weren't just lucky; they knew how to *prepare*. There are many different ways to prepare for a final examination, and each individual must perfect his or her own style, but over the years, I have developed a method that works for me.

(2) First, when your professor announces the date, time, and place of the final—usually at least two weeks before—ask questions and take careful notes on the answers. What chapters will be covered? What kinds of questions will the test contain? What materials and topics are most important? The information you gather will help you study more effectively.

(3) Next, survey all the textbook chapters the test will cover, using a highlighter or colored pen to mark important ideas and sections to be studied later. Many textbooks emphasize key ideas with boldface titles or headlines; others are written so that key ideas appear in the topic sentences at the beginning of each paragraph. Pay attention to these guides as you read.

(4) Third, survey your class notes in the same fashion, marking important ideas. If your notes are messy or disorganized, you might want to rewrite them for easy reference later.

(5) Fourth, decide approximately how many hours you will need to study. Get a calendar and clearly mark off the hours each week that you will devote to in-depth studying. If possible, set aside specific times: Thursday from 1 to 2 P.M., Friday from 6 to 8 P.M., and so on. If you have trouble committing yourself, schedule study time with a friend, but pick someone as serious as you are about getting good grades.

(6) Fifth, begin studying systematically, choosing a quiet place free from distractions in which to work—the library, a dorm room, whatever helps you concentrate. One of my friends can study only in his attic; another, in her car. As you review the textbook and your notes, ask yourself questions based on your reading. From class discussions, try to spot the professor's priorities and to guess what questions might appear on the exam. Be creative; one friend of mine puts important study material on cassette tapes, which he plays walking to and from school.

(7) Finally, at least three days before the exam, start reviewing. At the least opportunity, refer to your notes, even if you are not prepared to digest all the material. Use the moments when you are drinking your orange juice or riding the bus; just looking at the material can promote learning. By the night before the exam, you should know everything you want to know—and allow for a good night's sleep!

(8) By following these simple procedures, you may find, as I do, that you are the most prepared person in the exam room, confident that you studied thoroughly enough to do well on the exam.

—Mark Reyes, Student

- The **thesis statement** in a process essay tells the reader what process the rest of the essay will describe. Underline or highlight the thesis statement.

- What **process** does this essay discuss? _____

- How many **steps or stages** make up this process? What are they?

  _____

  _____

- What kind of **order** does the writer use to organize his essay?

  _____

- Before writing his first draft, Mr. Reyes made a clear **outline**. An outline is even more important in essay writing than paragraph writing because it keeps the writer organized and on track.

- Underline or highlight the topic sentences of Mr. Reyes' body paragraphs. In your notebook, make an outline of Mr. Reyes' essay.

PRACTICE 13

Read this student's process essay and answer the questions.

THE MIRACLE OF BIRTH

(1) A woman is pregnant for approximately nine months. Within that time are three stages or trimesters, "tri" meaning three. Many women have said they loved being pregnant, but I like to refer to the trimesters as the puking stage, the fat stage, and the always-have-to-pee stage.

(2) In the first trimester, the baby is developing its nervous system and other important little body parts; while all of this is happening inside, the mom-to-be is usually puking her guts up. The fun doesn't stop there, however. Hormone levels skyrocket, and all of a sudden, mom-to-be is crying over the slightest thing, such as a McDonald's commercial that she finds unbearably sweet.

(3) The second trimester is often slightly gentler on one's stomach, perhaps because that stomach has doubled in size, along with mom's butt and thighs. The baby is growing fast now, and the vital organs are developing. The baby is beginning to do somersaults, and suddenly there is a new stabbing sensation, almost as if baby is using mom's ribs for gymnastic rings. Comfort is now a thing of the past.

(4) In the third trimester, baby is happily gaining about half a pound a week, but for the mother, the last stage of pregnancy never goes by fast enough. As all the intricate fine-tunings of development are happening on baby's major organs, hair, and skin, for some odd reason, sleep for mom is completely out of the question. Perhaps the lack of sleep is due to the up-and-coming gymnast in her stomach or the five hundred trips to the bathroom that mom must make in one night. The many sleepless nights may also be attributed to her anticipation of bladder control or actually having a waist again.

(5) Pregnancy is a wonderful experience as long as puking, gaining forty to sixty pounds, and stumbling in and out of bed do not bother the mom-to-be. To me, pregnancy was a bummer, but like the old saying goes, "no pain, no gain." The end definitely justifies the means, and now that I am almost back to normal functioning with a beautiful, crying baby, the fun really starts.

—Heather Artley, Student

1. Underline or highlight this writer's thesis statement. What process does her essay

   discuss? _____

2. How many stages or steps make up this process? What are they?

   _____

3. Underline or highlight the topic sentences in paragraphs 2, 3, and 4. What order does

   the writer employ? _____

4. Is her tone serious or light? What words or phrases tell you this?

   _____

   _____

PRACTICE 14   TEAMWORK: CRITICAL VIEWING AND WRITING

In a group with four or five classmates, study this diagram showing that heart disease is actually a *process*. Read about the four stages.

Heart disease is a process affecting 16,800,000 Americans.

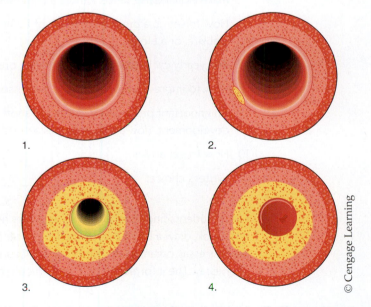

© Cengage Learning

Stage 1. Normal arteries are healthy and open. Stage 2. Cholesterol begins to be deposited in a damaged or inflamed artery wall. Stage 3. Cholesterol continues to build up, narrowing the artery. Stage 4. The artery becomes so clogged that a blood clot can block it, causing heart attack or stroke.

Do you know anyone who is likely in the process of developing heart disease? How would you go about learning more about this process and how to stop or reverse it? Come up with least two trustworthy sources of information on heart disease. Be prepared to share your thoughts.

Planning and Writing the Process Essay

Before writing a process essay, you may wish to reread Chapter 8, "Process." Choose a process topic that you know something about. What expertise, experience, or humorous attempt might you wish to share? If your process requires any equipment or ingredients (a recipe, for instance), list them in the first paragraph. As you plan the essay, jot down all the necessary steps or stages and arrange them logically, probably in time order. Then prewrite to gather details and examples about each step or stage.

The rest of this section will guide you as you write a process essay.

PRACTICE 15

1. Choose a topic from the list below or one your instructor has assigned. Take your time as you pick a process to describe that interests *you*. Who is your audience? That is, for whom are you explaining this process?

   1. A process that will help new students at your college learn how to register (how to drop or add courses, how to meet people on campus, how to apply for financial aid, and so on)

   2. How to get action on a community problem

   3. How to begin tracing your family's genealogy

   4. How to teach a child a skill or value

   5. How to perform a procedure at your workplace (help an elderly person dress, make Hollandaise sauce, handle a crime scene, and so on)

   6. How to set up a program or piece of technology (such as a cell phone, e-mail, a website, or a blog)

   7. The yearly cycle of a crop (corn, wheat, oranges, cocoa, and so on)

   8. How to impress the boss (in-laws, professor, person you are dating)

   9. An important process you learned in another course (stages of human moral development, how a lake becomes a meadow, and so on)

   10. How to get an A in _____

   11. Writer's choice: _____

2. Many students find using a graphic organizer helpful as they plan an essay. In your notebook, draw a blank 8-by-11-inch organizer like the one that follows or use the process essay organizer on the *Evergreen* CourseMate. Use it to create an outline for your essay. The information you write in each box will become a paragraph.

PROCESS ESSAY ORGANIZER

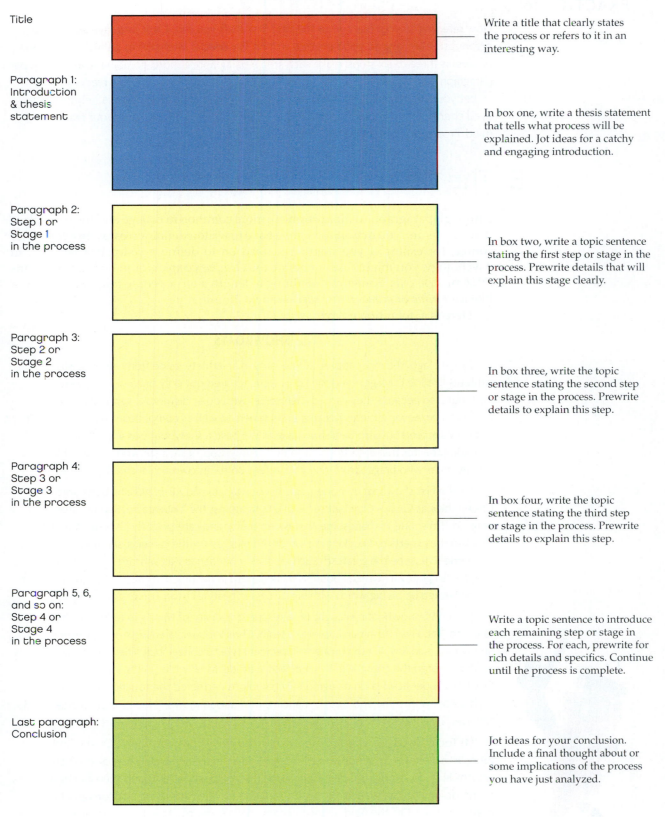

Title — Write a title that clearly states the process or refers to it in an interesting way.

Paragraph 1: Introduction & thesis statement — In box one, write a thesis statement that tells what process will be explained. Jot ideas for a catchy and engaging introduction.

Paragraph 2: Step 1 or Stage 1 in the process — In box two, write a topic sentence stating the first step or stage in the process. Prewrite details that will explain this stage clearly.

Paragraph 3: Step 2 or Stage 2 in the process — In box three, write the topic sentence stating the second step or stage in the process. Prewrite details to explain this step.

Paragraph 4: Step 3 or Stage 3 in the process — In box four, write the topic sentence stating the third step or stage in the process. Prewrite details to explain this step.

Paragraph 5, 6, and so on: Step 4 or Stage 4 in the process — Write a topic sentence to introduce each remaining step or stage in the process. For each, prewrite for rich details and specifics. Continue until the process is complete.

Last paragraph: Conclusion — Jot ideas for your conclusion. Include a final thought about or some implications of the process you have just analyzed.

Now referring to your plan, write the best first draft you can. Clear language and logical organization are keys to good process writing. Pay special attention to paragraphing; if the process is three to six steps, make each step a paragraph; if more, combine several steps per paragraph. Remember to use transitional expressions of time to help the reader follow.*

Let your draft cool for an hour or a day; then reread it as if you were a helpful, eagle-eyed stranger. Now revise and rewrite, avoiding wordiness and keeping your reader in mind. Proofread for spelling, grammar, and sentence errors.

E. The Definition Essay

Although paragraphs of **definition** are more common in college and the workplace than essays are, you may at some time have to write a definition essay. In a computer course, for example, you might be called on to define a *network* or *database*. In psychology, you might need to define the *Oedipus complex*, or in biology, the terms *DNA* or *stem cells*. Sometimes defining at length a term people think they know—like *work ethic* or *acquaintance rape*—can be illuminating.

Here is a definition essay:

SHOWBOATS

(1) Years ago, the most appreciated quality in an athlete, aside from success, was dignity. Athletes like Joe DiMaggio and Joe Louis were admired not only because they were the best, but also because they carried themselves with quiet dignity. As sports got linked to television, however, athletes became entertainers as well as competitors. A player should not only succeed but also be a showboat. In the past, a showboat was a riverboat with a floating theater that entertained people at every stop. Now, a showboat is an athlete, usually male, who brags, struts, and calls attention to his own achievements.

(2) The first showboat in modern sports was Muhammad Ali. In 1964, he burst onto the boxing stage as Cassius Clay. Before his title fight against the "unbeatable" Sonny Liston, Clay bragged, "I'm young, I'm handsome, I'm fast, I'm pretty, and can't possibly be beat." After he shocked the experts by knocking out Liston, Ali mugged for the cameras, shouting, "I shook up the world! I must be the greatest!" Such loud self-confidence was unheard-of before Ali. As he won more fights, Ali rhymed about his skills, danced in the ring, and trash talked to opponents. But he backed up his big words with big successes, beating Liston, Foreman, and Frazier.

(3) In 1991, showboating caught on after the University of Michigan recruited the talented "Fab Five" freshman basketball team. Chris Webber, Jalen Rose, Juwan Howard, Jimmy King, and Ray Jackson brought showboat style to college ball. They wore baggy shorts and dominated the court with in-your-face attitude. Meanwhile, in the NFL, two Dallas Cowboys Super Bowl (as in paragraph 4) champions perfected the touchdown celebration. High-stepping into the end zone or dancing after a touchdown, "Neon Deion" Sanders and Michael "The Playmaker" Irvin made sure that people noticed when they scored.

(4) Today, two NFL wide receivers define the new showboat. Terrell Owens and Chad Johnson have taken touchdown celebrations to an extreme level. A few of their on-field actions include removing a cellphone from the goalpost padding and then calling a sports agent, doing the Riverdance, proposing to a cheerleader, and using popcorn and pom-poms as props. Off the field, Johnson changed his name to Ochocinco, his jersey number, and both men starred in reality TV shows. They are champion showboats, but neither has won a Super Bowl.

---

* For a list of transitional expressions for process, see page 102.

(5) With their bragging, bold style, and creative celebrations, showboats bring some welcome fun to serious sports. However, if an athlete focuses too much on getting his video clip on *Sports Highlights* or Twitter, it could interfere with winning the game. Maybe the trend has gone too far.

—Mitch Borsano, Student

- The **thesis statement** of a definition essay tells the reader what term will be defined and usually defines it briefly as well. Underline or highlight the thesis statement in this essay.
- Underline or highlight the **topic sentences** in paragraphs 2, 3, and 4. How do these three paragraphs develop the thesis statement?

  _____

  _____

- What order does the writer follow in paragraphs 2, 3, and 4?

  _____

- Is Mr. Borsano's conclusion effective or not? Has showboating gone too far?

  _____

- Review the parts of this well-organized essay. You can see that the introduction and thesis statement; three body paragraphs, each explaining examples of "showboats"; and the conclusion form a clear **outline** of the essay. This student made just such an outline before he sat down to write.

PRACTICE 17

Now read another student's definition essay and answer the questions.

MORE THAN JUST GOOD

(1) I lean against our mango tree, waiting. The taxi is twenty minutes late, something only Americans like me would notice here in Costa Rica. I hear the roar of an engine that needs maintenance. A small gray Toyota speeds past and returns a few moments later, horn blasting. The driver sticks his head out the window and says, "Hello my friend, we go?" While I squeeze into the passenger seat, he says, "I no see you, *lo siento*. But *pura vida* man, where you going?" We seem to hit every pothole, and my body is jostled like a child playing with an old doll. Yet despite being late to meet my parents, despite the car having no air conditioning, and despite the driver's choice to blast salsa music loud enough for the entire neighborhood to throw a party, everything is indeed *pura vida*.

(2) The Spanish phrase *pura vida* is not just a Costa Rican slogan printed on t-shirts, and it does not merely mean "pure life." No other Latin American could tell you what it means beyond "something that *Ticos* (Costa Ricans) say." American culture lacks a similar idea. Often foreigners try to add *pura vida* to their pocket-dictionary vocabularies, but *pura vida* isn't planned. To experience *pura vida*, one must squeeze the best out of every experience—even bad lemons are used to make sweet *limonada*.

(3) *Pura vida* exists in the little things that make Costa Rica precious to the locals who have given so much to their country. *Pura vida* is the flavor of chilero sauce that spices up the rice and bean dish of *gallo pinto* that sits on their plates three meals a day. It is the plantain slices fried up to sweeten their palates when the rice and beans are finished. *Pura vida* is children and adults playing soccer together in

the abandoned dirt field next door. They yell, "Oooooopaaa!" in unison when their only soccer ball is accidentally kicked into traffic. *Pura vida* is the sweet ocean air that blows in from the Pacific coast, rolls up the western mountains, and seeps throughout the central valley.

(4) While traveling the coast, I stop at a roadside spot that advertises rice, beans, and meat. I am greeted warmly by a waiter who wants to practice his English. "Hey man, you American?" he asks loudly, "You come to Costa Rica?" making sure that everyone can hear him. I nod, and when I tell him that I actually live here, he smiles and replies, "*pura vida.*"

(5) This is the simple life, the pure life where you work hard to feed the family you love. Costa Rica is built on communities, friendship, and a willingness to help each other. When Ticos say *pura vida*, it's not just that life is good now. Life has always been good, and, if it's up to them, always will be.

—Anders Nelson, Student

1. In this essay, paragraph 1 introduces the term to be defined, but the thesis statement occurs in paragraph 2. Underline or highlight it.

2. How does the writer develop the definition of *pura vida* in paragraphs 3 and 4?

   _____

   _____

3. Mr. Nelson uses careful description to help readers see and experience his subject. What descriptive details did you find especially powerful and effective?

   _____

   _____

4. Let this student's work inspire you. Can you think of a term from your home town, neighborhood, or native country that might lend itself to an essay of definition? Write ideas here. Ask some classmates if they would like to read more about the term.

   _____

PRACTICE 18   **TEAMWORK: CRITICAL VIEWING AND WRITING**

In a group with several classmates, look closely at this poster, which is called *The Illiterate*. The picture seems to compare someone who cannot read and write with a blindfolded man walking off a cliff. What does the picture say about being illiterate? Does it accurately *define* illiteracy? Do you know anyone who is illiterate? If you were writing an essay called *The Illiterate*, how would you explain the term?

The Illiterate by Aleksei
Radakov

Hoover Institution Archives, Stanford University

Planning and Writing the Definition Essay

Before writing a definition essay, you should reread Chapter 9, "Definition."
Review the three types of definitions: by *synonym*, *class*, or *negation*. Take your time
choosing a word or term that truly interests you—a word from your job, a college
course, or your own experience. Prewrite for ideas to explain your definition.
Consider using two or three examples to develop the term, one paragraph per
example, the way the first student writer does above. If you use some short
examples like the second student, you might group them in one paragraph.

The rest of the section will guide you as you write a definition essay.

1. Choose a topic from the list below or one your instructor has assigned. You might
   wish to define a term from an important college course, your job, or your culture.
   Decide who your audience is and what type of definition you will use.

   1. A special term from sports, technology, business, art, or psychology

   2. An environmental term (*global warming*, *endangered species*, *recycling*,
      deforestation, and so on)

   3. A friend

   4. Poverty

5. Immigrant

6. Maturity

7. A disease or medical condition, such as diabetes, autism, depression, or alcoholism

8. A slang term in current use

9. A term from another language or culture (*salsa, joie de vivre, manga, machismo,* and so on)

10. Twitter (use humor if you like)

11. Writer's choice: _____

2. Many students find using a graphic organizer helpful as they plan an essay. In your notebook, draw a blank 8-by-11-inch organizer like the one below or use the definition essay organizer on the *Evergreen* CourseMate. Use it to create an outline for your essay. The information you write in each box will become a paragraph.

DEFINITION ESSAY ORGANIZER

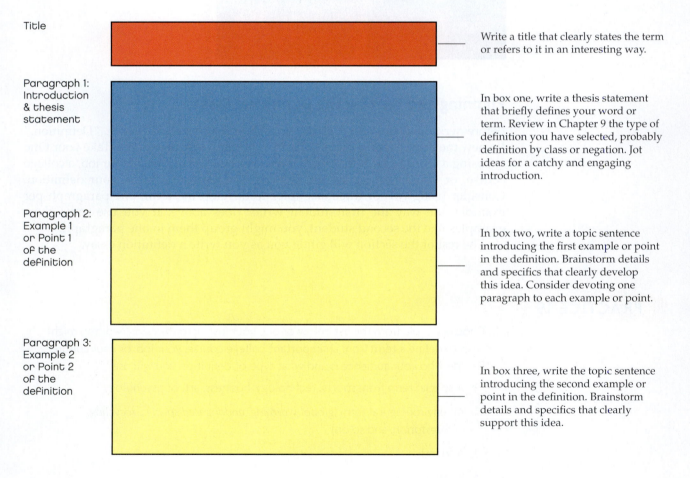

Title — Write a title that clearly states the term or refers to it in an interesting way.

Paragraph 1: Introduction & thesis statement — In box one, write a thesis statement that briefly defines your word or term. Review in Chapter 9 the type of definition you have selected, probably definition by class or negation. Jot ideas for a catchy and engaging introduction.

Paragraph 2: Example 1 or Point 1 of the definition — In box two, write a topic sentence introducing the first example or point in the definition. Brainstorm details and specifics that clearly develop this idea. Consider devoting one paragraph to each example or point.

Paragraph 3: Example 2 or Point 2 of the definition — In box three, write the topic sentence introducing the second example or point in the definition. Brainstorm details and specifics that clearly support this idea.

Paragraph 4:
Example 3
or Point 3
of the definition

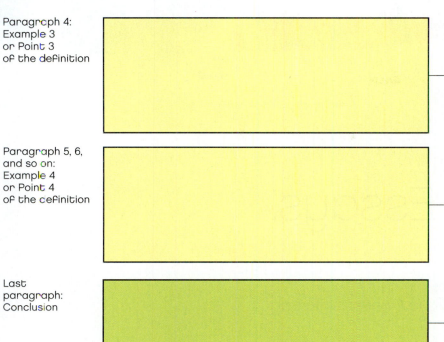

In box four, write the topic sentence introducing the third example or point in the definition. Brainstorm details and specifics that clearly support this idea.

Paragraph 5, 6,
and so on:
Example 4
or Point 4
of the definition

Write a topic sentence to introduce each remaining example or point in the definition. For each, prewrite for rich details and specifics. Continue until the definition is complete.

Last
paragraph:
Conclusion

Jot ideas for your conclusion. Include a final thought about or some implications of the definition you have developed.

PRACTICE 20

Now referring to your plan, write the best first draft you can. Aim for clarity as you help the reader develop an understanding of this word or term. Check your paragraphing, and use *transitional expressions** to guide the reader from point to point.

Let your draft cool for an hour or a day; then reread it as if you were a helpful, eagle-eyed stranger. Now revise and rewrite, emphasizing exact language, avoiding wordiness, and keeping your reader in mind. Is each paragraph developed fully? Do transitions make the flow of ideas clear? Proofread for spelling, grammar, and sentence errors.

EXPLORING ONLINE

http://grammar.ccc.commnet.edu/grammar/composition/narrative.htm

Interesting tips on writing narratives and descriptions, with professional examples

http://grammar.ccc.commnet.edu/grammar/composition/definition.htm

Excellent advice on crafting a valuable essay of definition, with professional examples

CourseMate for *Evergreen*

Visit *Evergreen* CourseMate for more practices and quizzes, videos to accompany the readings, career and job-search resources, ESL help, and live links to every Exploring Online in the book.

---

* For a list of transitional expressions, see page 63.

CHAPTER 17

Types of Essays, Part 2

A: The Comparison and the Contrast Essay

B: The Classification Essay

C: The Cause and Effect Essay

D: The Persuasive Essay

This chapter will show you how to apply four more methods of paragraph development that you learned in Unit 3 to the essay. Because an essay is like an expanded paragraph, the same methods you would use to prewrite, organize, and write a paragraph of comparision and contrast, for instance, can also be used to develop an entire essay. The rest of the chapter will show you how.

A. The Comparison and the Contrast Essay

Essays of **comparison** or **contrast** are frequently called for in college courses. In an English or a drama class, you might be asked to contrast two of Shakespeare's villains—perhaps Iago and Claudius. In psychology, you might have to contrast the training of the clinical psychologist and that of the psychiatrist, or in history, to compare ancient Greek and Roman religions.

Does the following essay compare or contrast?

E-NOTES FROM AN ONLINE LEARNER

Introduction

Thesis statement

(1) This year I attended my first U.S. history class at midnight, clad in my dancing cow pajamas and fluffy slippers. No, I was not taking part in some bizarre campus ritual. I am enrolled in two courses in the University of Houston's Distance Education Program. Although I took classes on campus at the same college last year, my experiences in the traditional classroom and in the virtual classroom have been vastly different.

Topic sentence introducing point 1

(2) Attending online courses has proved more convenient for me than traveling to regular classes each day. Because I live over an hour away from campus, I was often stalled in traffic when my 8 A.M. psychology lecture was beginning. Then I spent the last half hour of my afternoon English class praying that the discussion—however lively and interesting—would not go past 4 P.M. and make me late to pick up my son at day care. In contrast, my online classes are always convenient to attend because I set my own schedule. Lectures for my history survey course are posted to the class website, so I can log on whenever I want to read new material or review. My writing seminar is "asynchronous." This means that students and instructors communicate at their convenience on an electronic bulletin board. I can e-mail my questions, file homework, and respond to other students' work at night or on weekends without leaving home.

Topic sentence introducing point 2

(3) Though some students miss the human energy of a real classroom, the online format actually encourages me to participate more in discussions. As a shy woman who is older than many of my peers, I used to hide in the back row to avoid having to speak. I only answered questions when called upon. On the other hand, writing online, I am more confident. I have time to think about what I want to say, and I know people are not judging me by anything except my ideas. Even though bulletin board discussions can be painfully slow and disjointed compared to the back-and-forth of a great classroom discussion, I like the equality in a virtual classroom. Surprisingly, there I feel freer to be the real me.

Topic sentence introducing point 3

(4) The biggest difference in moving from a regular classroom to a virtual one, in my view, is learning to be self-motivated. Attending classes on campus, I was motivated by the personal involvement of my instructors. I also caught that group adrenaline rush, seeing other students hunched over their notebooks in a lecture hall or coffee shop. While my online courses still require written papers each week and tests turned in on time, now no instructor is prodding me to get busy. Instead, only the soft bubbling noise of my aquarium screen saver reminds me to tap the keyboard and dive into my coursework. Fortunately, I am self-motivated and focused. As a returning student with a job and a child, I have to be. Honestly, however, I have already seen some classmates post homework assignments later and later until they drop off the screen entirely.

Conclusion

(5) Overall, my experience with online classes has been more positive than my experience on campus, but online learning is not for everyone. So far I find online classes convenient, welcoming for self-expression, and well-suited to my particular personality, which is organized, shy, and prone to bouts of midnight energy. In fact, it's 12:14 A.M. now as I input the final draft of this essay assignment. My son is asleep in the next room and my cat, Miss Fleason, is nuzzling my hot pink fluffy slippers.

—Brenda Wilson, Student

- The **thesis statement** of a comparison or contrast essay tells what two persons or things will be compared or contrasted. Underline or highlight the thesis statement.

- Will this essay **compare** or **contrast** the two kinds of classrooms? What word or words in the thesis indicate this?

_____

- Does the writer discuss all points about A and then all points about B, or skip back and forth between A and B?

_____

● The pattern of supporting points in this essay might be shown like this:

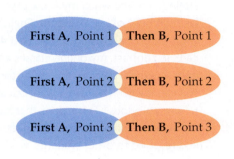

First A, Point 1 — Then B, Point 1

First A, Point 2 — Then B, Point 2

First A, Point 3 — Then B, Point 3

● Notice how the thesis statement, topic sentences, and supporting details form a clear **outline** of the essay.

PRACTICE 1

Now read this student's essay and answer the questions.

BAREBACK BRONC RIDING VERSUS BULL RIDING

(1) There are many different events in the sport of rodeo. Two of the best-known, bareback bronc riding and bull riding, might seem quite similar to the casual onlooker. Although they are both rough stock (bucking) events, they differ in the equipment required, riding technique, animal size, and bucking style.

(2) Bareback bronc riding requires a lot of equipment for a safe and successful ride. The bareback rigging is probably most important. It is a combination of wood and leather, molded into a suitcase-type handle for the rider to wedge his hand in while wearing a thick leather glove. Another important piece of equipment is the neck roll, a thick pad attached to the back of the neck with long straps to prevent whiplash or fractures during the ride and dismount. Bareback riders are also required to wear straight-shanked, free-spinning spurs with rounded rowels (or wheels) to keep from cutting the horse. A vest and chaps are optional safety features for the legs and torso.

(3) Bareback bronc riding also entails a very unnatural technique. In this event, the rider positions himself almost completely reclined on the horse, with his head near the flanks and his feet at the shoulders. Once the gate is opened, the rider is required to "mark out" the horse. This means that the rider must reach up with his legs and mash his spurs into the horse's neck before the first buck is made. The rider is then judged on his spurring ability, which is done by pulling his feet in an upward motion and into an almost spread-eagle position.

(4) Size and bucking style of a bronc differ as well. An average bucking horse weighs between 1200 and 1500 pounds and is approximately five and one-half feet tall at the top of the shoulder. These horses are extremely quick and generally buck straight down the arena.

(5) In contrast to bareback bronc riding, bull riding does not require a rigging. Instead, a woven grass rope and a thin leather glove are used. The protective vest is a requirement in this event due to the rather aggressive nature of the bulls. No neck roll is needed in this event because there is little strain on the neck. The spurs in bull riding have fixed rowels with sharp ends, and the shanks are angled inward at a forty-five degree angle to make gripping easy. Helmets and face masks are optional safety features for this event.

(6) Unlike bronc riding, bull riding technique is fairly natural. The rider sits in the upright position, straddling the bull just behind the shoulders. There is no mark out requirement in bull riding, and spurring is just a scoring bonus. Usually only the most experienced riders practice spurring.

(7) Bulls differ from horses in both weight and bucking style. Bulls are heavier, with an average weight between 1500 and 2100 pounds, and they stand approximately five feet tall at the top of the shoulders. Although they buck fairly slowly, they are very powerful and very aggressive. Unlike broncs, bulls seldom buck straight down the arena; instead they often fade from side to side, spin, and twist.

(8) In short, there are many differences between bareback bronc riding and bull riding. The primary elements that set these events apart are the variations in equipment, riding technique, size, and bucking style. Both events, however, thrill rodeo fans and riders.

—Matt Bodson, Student

1. Underline or highlight the thesis statement and topic sentences in this essay. Does this writer compare or contrast bronc and bull riding? What words tell you this?

_____

2. Does this writer follow the *all A, then all B* pattern or the *AB, AB, AB* pattern? If you aren't sure, label each part of the essay in the left margin. Use the terms below listed in scrambled order. A is bronc riding; B is bull riding.

B, point 2	**B, points 3 and 4**	**C = Conclusion**	**A, point 1**
A, point 2	**IN = Introduction**	**A, points 3 and 4**	**B, point 1**

_____

3. Do you think Mr. Bodson picked a subject that he knows a lot about? What aspects of the essay give you this impression?

_____

4. If this writer asked you for peer feedback, what would you say? What do you like most about this essay? Do you have any suggestions for improvement?

_____

PRACTICE 2   TEAMWORK: CRITICAL VIEWING AND WRITING

Comparing and contrasting two things requires concentration and focus. A few moments of thought are not enough to perceive all the similarities or differences. In fields like science, nursing, and medicine, close observation is key—for instance, spotting changes in a patient's appearance from day to day. In a group with several classmates, imagine you are scientists who must describe the differences between the poisonous butterfly on page 242 and a nonpoisonous copycat. Have someone take notes as your group describes at least five similarities and five differences.

INSECT MIMICS

A *mimic* is a copycat or look-alike. **Batesian mimics** are nonpoisonous insects that have evolved in color and shape to look like poisonous ones. This increases their chances of survival because their enemies have learned not to eat the poisonous ones.

Left: poisonous butterfly, *Danaus formosa*; Right: nonpoisonous mimic, *Papilio rex*

Planning and Writing the Comparison and Contrast Essay

Before writing your essay, you may wish to reread Chapter 10, "Comparison and Contrast." Outlining is especially important in comparison and contrast. As you plan, make a chart of all your points of comparison or contrast to make sure you give balanced coverage. Decide which pattern will better present your ideas: *AB, AB, AB,* or *all A, then all B.* Be sure to use transitional expressions* to help the reader follow.

The rest of the section will guide you as you write a comparison and contrast essay.

PRACTICE 3

1. Choose a topic from the list below or one your instructor has assigned. Bear in mind that the most interesting essays usually compare two things that are different or contrast two things that are similar. Otherwise, you run the risk of saying the obvious ("Cats and dogs are two different animals"). Visualize the audience for whom you are writing.

   1. Your mother's or father's childhood and your own

   2. Two cultural attitudes about one subject

   3. A neighborhood store and a chain store (bookstore, restaurant, music store, and so on)

   4. Two politicians, entertainers, athletes, public figures, artists, or historical figures

   5. Your expectations about parenthood (a job, or college) versus the realities

   6. Two different social networking websites (like Facebook and MySpace)

   7. A traditional doctor and an alternative healer

   8. Two views on a controversial issue

   9. A book and a movie based on that book

   10. Two job or career options you are considering

   11. Writer's choice: _____

* For a list of transitional expressions of comparison and contrast, see page 125.

2. Many students find using a graphic organizer helpful as they plan an essay. In your notebook, draw a blank 8-by-11-inch organizer like the one below or use the comparison and contrast essay organizer on the *Evergreen* CourseMate. Use it to create an outline for your essay. The information you write in each box will become a paragraph.

COMPARISON AND CONTRAST ESSAY ORGANIZER

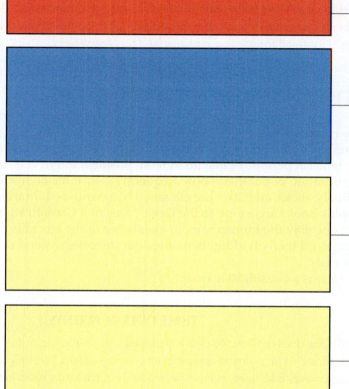

Title — Write a title that states the two persons or things you will compare or contrast.

Paragraph 1: Introduction & thesis statement — In box one, write a thesis statement that clearly states the two persons or things and whether your essay will compare or contrast them. Jot ideas for an engaging or informative introduction.

Paragraph 2: Point 1 of comparison or contrast — In box two, write a topic sentence introducing your first point of comparison or contrast. You should have decided by now whether to arrange your points in *AB, AB, AB* order or *all A, then all B*. Brainstorm details and specifics that clearly develop the topic sentence.

Paragraph 3: Point 2 of comparison or contrast — In box three, following your plan, write a topic sentence introducing the second point of comparison or contrast. Brainstorm details and specifics that clearly support this idea.

Paragraph 4: Point 3 of comparison or contrast — In box four, following your plan, write a topic sentence introducing the third point of comparison or contrast. Brainstorm details and specifics that clearly support this idea.

Paragraph 5, 6, and so on: Point 4 of comparison or contrast — Write a topic sentence to introduce each remaining point of comparison or contrast. For each, prewrite for rich details and specifics. Continue until the essay is complete.

Last paragraph: Conclusion — Jot ideas for your conclusion. Include a final thought about or some implications of the comparison or contrast you have just developed.

PRACTICE 4

Once your plan is finalized, write the best first draft you can. Refer to your plan to make sure you have included every point of comparison or contrast. If any section seems weak, prewrite for more details and revise. Organization is very important in a comparison or contrast essay, so use *transitional expressions** to highlight the order and guide the reader from point to point.

Let your draft cool for an hour or a day; then reread it as if you were a helpful, eagle-eyed stranger. Now revise and rewrite, emphasizing completeness, clear organization, and exact language. Is each point developed fully? Do transitions make the flow of ideas clear? Proofread for spelling, grammar, and sentence errors.

B. The Classification Essay

The **classification** essay is useful in college and business. In music, for example, you might have to classify Mozart's compositions according to the musical periods of his life. A retail business might classify items in stock according to popularity—how frequently they must be restocked. All plants, animals, rocks, and stars are classified by scientists. Libraries classify and display books according to the Dewey Decimal Classification System. It seems that one way the human mind makes sense of the world is by grouping similar things and then dividing them into subcategories; a good classification does just that.

Here is a classification essay:

THREE TYPES OF PARENTS

(1) One does not have to pass a qualifying examination to enter the state of parenthood. In fact, almost anyone can become a parent. Precisely because the group called *parents* is so large, many different kinds of parenting exist. In terms of how strict parents are with their children, however, there are three basic types: autocratic, permissive, and democratic.

(2) Autocratic parents think their word is the law, and when they say jump, everyone had better do it quickly. These parents assume that they alone know what is best for their children and that the kids will learn discipline and respect for authority from regimentation. What they do not even consider is that they may not know best and that rules untempered with mercy can breed rebellion and contempt for authority. The autocratic parent whose child comes home one hour late from a date because a major accident tied up traffic for miles will allow that child no opportunity to explain his or her reasons for being late. The child is immediately grounded, his or her allowance suspended. Parents of this type probably have good intentions, wanting their children to grow up "right," but they approach the task as if the family were in boot camp.

(3) At the other extreme, permissive parents set few or no rules for their children and offer little guidance. Frequently, these parents are too busy to take time with the children and tend to leave the child rearing to TV, the computer, school, and chance. Since parents of this type set few rules for their children, it would be nearly impossible for their child to come home late. They allow their children to come and go as they please, either because they don't care what their youngsters do or because they think

---

* For a list of transitional expressions of comparison and contrast, see page 125.

children need to learn to make their own rules. Permissive parents may not understand that all young people need guidance because when they mature, they will have to abide by society's rules. Not being taught to respect order early in life causes some children of permissive parents to resent the regulations everyone must obey.

(4) Democratic parents, the third type, are not as strict as autocrats and not as lenient as permissives. They are willing to discuss rules and punishments with their children and to listen to the other side of an argument. A democratic parent whose child comes in an hour late from a date will listen to the explanation about the major wreck that tied up traffic for miles. Since this is such an easily verifiable story, the democratic parent would suspend any punishment in this case when he or she hears the news or sees the morning paper. In general, democratic parents lay down fewer rules than their autocratic counterparts because they realize that children must learn some life lessons on their own. Democratic parents prefer to work in the role of advisors, always available when their children need help.

(5) Too few people with children are democratic parents, the most effective of the three types. Both too much authority and too little can breed disrespect and resentment. A good parent should offer boundaries and advice, trying neither to rule nor disregard his or her children completely.

—Sallie Duhling

- The **thesis statement** in a classification essay tells the reader what group will be classified and on what basis. Underline or highlight the thesis.

- Into how many categories are parents divided? What are they?

  _____

- On what **basis** are these categories examined?

  _____

- Can you see the logic of this writer's **order** of paragraphs? That is, why are autocratics discussed first, permissives second, and democratic parents last?

  _____

  _____

- Note that the thesis statement, topic sentences setting forth the three categories, and the conclusion create an **outline** for this essay. The writer made such an outline before she wrote the first draft.

PRACTICE 5

Although the classification essay is usually serious, the pattern can make a good humorous essay, as this student's paper shows. Read it and answer the questions.

THE POTATO SCALE

(1) For years, television has been the great American pastime. Nearly every household has at least one TV, which means that people are spending time watching it, unless, of course, they bought it to serve as a plant stand. Television viewers can be grouped in

many ways—by the type of shows they watch (but there is no accounting for taste) or by hours per week of watching (but that seems unfair since a working, twelve-hour-a-week viewer could conceivably become a fifty-hour-a-week viewer if he or she were out of a job). So I have developed the Potato Scale. The four major categories of the Potato Scale rank TV viewers on a combination of leisure time spent watching, intensity of watching, and the desire to watch versus the desire to engage in other activities.

(2) First, we have the True Couch Potatoes. They are diehard viewers who, when home, will be found in front of their televisions. They no longer eat in the dining room, and if you visit them, the television stays on. *TV Guide* is their Bible. They will plan other activities and chores around their viewing time, always hoping to accomplish these tasks in front of the tube. If a presidential address is on every channel but one, and they dislike the president, they will tune into that one channel, be it *Bugs Bunny* reruns or Polynesian barge cooking. These potatoes would never consider turning off the box.

(3) The second group consists of the Pseudo Couch Potatoes. These are scheduled potatoes. They have outside interests and actually eat at the table, but for a certain period of time (let's say from seven to eleven in the evening), they will take on the characteristics of True Couch Potatoes. Another difference between True and Pseudo Potatoes deserves note. The True Potato must be forced by someone else to shut off the television and do something different; however, if the Pseudo Potato has flipped through all the channels and found only garbage, he or she still has the capacity to think of other things to do.

(4) Third, we have the Selective Potatoes. These more discriminating potatoes enjoy many activities, and TV is just one of them. They might have a few shows they enjoy watching regularly, but missing one episode is not a world-class crisis. After all, the show will be on next week. They don't live by *TV Guide*, but use it to check for interesting specials. If they find themselves staring at an awful movie or show, they will gladly, and without a second thought, turn it off.

(5) The fourth group consists of Last Resort Potatoes. These people actually prefer reading, going to the theater, playing pickup basketball, walking in the woods, and many other activities to watching television. Only after they have exhausted all other possibilities or are dog tired or shivering with the flu, will they click on the tube. These potatoes are either excessively choosy or almost indifferent to what's on, hoping it will bore them to sleep.

(6) These are the principal categories of the Potato Scale, from the truly vegetable to the usually human. What type of potato are you?

—Helen Petruzzelli, Student

1. Underline or highlight the thesis statement and the topic sentences. Note that they form a clear outline of this well-organized classification essay.

2. The entire essay classifies people on the basis of their television viewing habits. Into how many categories are the TV viewers divided? What are they?

   _____

   _____

3. Does the writer's order make sense? What is the logic in presenting True Couch Potatoes first, Pseudo Couch Potatoes second, Selective Couch Potatoes third, and Last Resort Couch Potatoes fourth?

   _____

4. How successful is Ms. Petruzzelli's essay? Does it inspire you with any ideas for a humorous essay of your own?

PRACTICE 6

TEAMWORK: CRITICAL VIEWING AND WRITING

In a group with four or five classmates, examine this food pyramid. It shows what doctors believe to be the healthiest proportion of foods to eat in an ideal daily diet. How is *classification* used in the pyramid? How many food *classes* or *groups* are shown here? Label each food group in the white space; use nouns to keep your labels parallel. How do your group's personal eating habits compare to the ideal? Be prepared to share your findings.

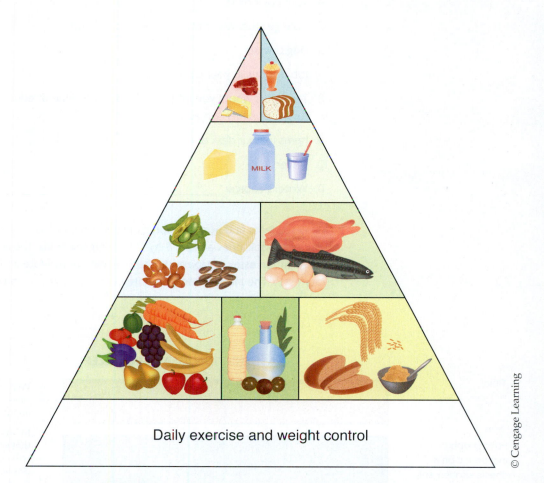

Daily exercise and weight control

Planning and Writing the Classification Essay

Before writing a classification essay, you might reread Chapter 11, "Classification." Choose a topic that lends itself to this pattern, and then make sure your *basis of classification* includes every member of the group. For instance, *all* TV viewers fall somewhere on the Potato Scale (from those who watch TV nearly all the time to those who almost never watch). As you plan your essay, make sure your categories follow a logical order. As you write, use transitional phrases like "The first type . . ." and "The second category . . ." to help the reader follow.*

The rest of the section will guide you as you write a classification essay.

---

* For a list of transitional expressions of classification, see page 139.

PRACTICE 7

1. Choose a topic from the list below or one your instructor has assigned, and then "try on" different bases of classification until you find one that inspires you. (For instance, you could discuss members of your family on the basis of how they spend their leisure time . . . or how good they are at home repairs . . . or how they handle stress.) Be clear on your audience and purpose for this paper.

   1. Members of your family

   2. People studying in the library

   3. Your monthly expenses

   4. Your coworkers

   5. College students' attitudes toward plagiarism

   6. Dog owners

   7. Job options in your career field

   8. Teenagers whom you interview (about the value of education, hope about the future, or other subject)

   9. Items in your desk drawer, handbag, or car trunk

   10. Drivers

   11. Writer's choice: _____

2. Many students find using a graphic organizer helpful as they plan an essay. In your notebook, draw a blank 8-by-11-inch organizer like the one below or use the classification essay organizer on the *Evergreen* CourseMate and, in it, create a plan for your essay. The information you write in each box will become a paragraph.

CLASSIFICATION ESSAY ORGANIZER

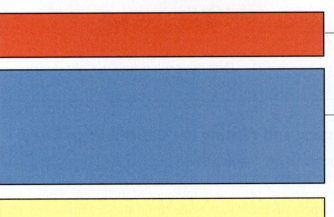

Title — Write a title that clearly states the classification subject or refers to it in an interesting way.

Paragraph 1: Introduction & thesis statement — In box one, write a thesis statement that sets forth the group you will classify and the basis of the classification; you also might name your categories (three or four is a good number). Jot ideas for an introductory paragraph that will convey to the reader the value or point of your classification.

Paragraph 2: Category 1 of the classification — In box two, write a topic sentence introducing the first category. Brainstorm details, specifics, and perhaps an example or two to explain the category in one body paragraph. Use transitional expressions to guide the reader along.

Paragraph 3:
Category 2 of
the classification

In box three, write a topic sentence
introducing the second category.
Brainstorm details, specifics, and
an example or two to explain the
category.

Paragraph 4:
Category 3 of
the classification

In box four, write a topic sentence
introducing the third category.
Brainstorm details, specifics, and
an example or two to explain the
category.

Paragraph 5, 6,
and so on:
Category 4 of
the classification

Write a topic sentence to introduce
each remaining category of the
classification. For each, prewrite for
rich details, specifics, and examples.
Continue this way until the
classification is complete.

Last paragraph:
Conclusion

Jot ideas for your conclusion.
Include a final thought about
or some implications of the
classification you have presented.

PRACTICE 8

Now, referring to your plan, write the best first draft you can. Aim for clarity as you help
the reader develop an understanding of each category in your classification. Check your
paragraphing, and use *transitional expressions** to guide the reader from category to
category.

Let your draft cool for an hour or a day; then reread it as if you were a helpful, eagle-
eyed stranger. Now revise and rewrite, emphasizing clarity, completeness, and keeping
your reader in mind. Is each paragraph developed fully? Do transitions make the flow of
ideas clear? Proofread for spelling, grammar, and sentence errors.

C. The Cause and Effect Essay

Essays of **cause and effect** are among the most important kinds of essays to master
because knowing how to analyze the causes and consequences of events will help
you succeed in college, at work, and in your personal life. What *caused* a historic
battle, an increase of homelessness, or a friendship breaking apart? How will a
certain child be *affected* by owning a computer, spending time at Sunshine Day
Care, or being teased because he loves to dance? In business, the success of every
company and product relies on a grasp of cause and effect in the marketplace.

---

* For a list of transitional expressions of classification, see page 139.

Why does this brand of smartphone outsell all others? What causes employees to want to work hard? How will the Internet affect business in 2030?

Here is an essay of cause and effect. As you will see, this writer's eventual understanding of causes and effects may have saved her life.

WHY I STAYED AND STAYED

(1) It has been proven that about 1.8 million women are battered each year, making battery the single largest cause of injury to women in the United States. Domestic violence can be physical, emotional, verbal, financial, or sexual abuse from a partner you live with. I suffered from most of these abuses for almost ten years. I have had black eyes, busted lips, bruises, and scars on my face. He had affairs with other women, yet he claimed that he loved me. People ask, "Why did you wait so long to leave him?" I stayed for many reasons.

(2) First, I was born in a country that is male-dominated. Many of my people accept violence against women as a part of life. I grew up seeing hundreds of women staying in violent relationships for the sake of their children. They wanted their children to grow up with a father at home. Relatives convinced these women to try to make their marriages work. This was all I knew.

(3) Another reason I stayed was that I was afraid to make changes in my life. I had been with him so long that I thought I had nowhere to go. I depended on him to provide me and my child with food and shelter. How could I manage on my own? Of course, the longer I believed these things, the more my self-confidence withered.

(4) Finally, I stayed because I was isolated. I felt ashamed to talk about the problem, believing it was somehow my fault. Fear was isolating, too. Living in a violent home is very frightening. Like many women, I was afraid to say anything to anyone, thinking he would get upset. If I just kept quiet, maybe he wouldn't hurt me. But nothing I did made any difference.

(5) When I finally realized that the abuse was not going to stop, I decided to do something about it. I was finally ready to end my pain. I began to talk to people and learn about ways to get help.

(6) On April 24th of this year, I fought back. When he punched me in the eye, I called 911. Thank God for changes in the way domestic violence cases are now being handled. The police responded quickly. He was arrested and taken to jail, where he waited for two days to go to court. The next day, I went to the courthouse to press charges. I spoke to the district attorney in charge, asking for an order of protection. This order forbids him from having any verbal or physical contact with me.

(7) It is very hard to see someone you love being taken away in handcuffs, but I had to put my safety and my child's well-being first. Although he is now out of jail, I feel safe with my order of protection; however, I understand that court orders sometimes do not stop abusers. These are very difficult days for me, but I pray that time will heal my wounds. I cry often, which helps my pain. But an innocent life depends on me for guidance, and I cannot let her down.

(8) Every case is different, and you know your partner better than anyone, but help is out there if you reach for it. Most cities have a twenty-four-hour hotline. There is help at this college at the PASS Center and the Department of Student Development. You can go to a shelter, to a friend, to your family. These people will not fail you. You too can break the chain.

—Student, name withheld by request

● The **thesis statement** of a cause and effect essay identifies the subject and tells whether causes or effects will be emphasized. Underline or highlight the thesis statement in this essay. Does it emphasize causes or effects?

- How many **causes** does the writer discuss, and what are they?

  _____

- Although some essays discuss either causes or effects, this one does both. Paragraph 5 marks a turning point, her decision to take action. What positive effects of this new decision does she discuss? Are there any negative effects?

  _____

  _____

  _____

- Before she wrote this essay, the writer probably made a **plan** or **outline** like this:

  Introduction and thesis statement
  Reasons for staying with abusive partner — upbringing / fear of change / isolation
  Decision to leave
  Effects of decision to leave abuser — reached out for help / fought back (911, order of protection) / acted for daughter / sadness, guilt
  Advice for women in the same situation

- What order does this essay follow?

  _____

- Do you think paragraph 8 makes an effective **conclusion**?

  _____

PRACTICE 9

Now read another student's cause and effect essay and answer the questions.

UNFRIENDING FACEBOOK

(1) Facebook is the most popular social networking site in the world. Over half its 800 million users log in every day, uploading millions of photos, chatting with friends, and playing games. College students today have been "Facebooking" since high school. It is fun, but Facebook can have negative effects on a person's life like wasting time, hurting relationships, and even keeping a person from getting a good job.

(2) One of the most obvious effects of Facebook is that it wastes time. My college friends say that just reading and responding to posts takes an hour or more daily, but many jump on Facebook every chance they get. That's time they don't have to study history, write papers, or exercise. Then there are Facebook games. Farmville players manage pretend farms and harvest a friend's pretend crops while he takes a real exam. Gardens of Time, where friends team up to find hidden objects, logged more than 5 billion sessions in 2011. It's nice to relax, but that's a LOT of time spent on Facebook.

(3) A less obvious negative effect of Facebooking is the cost to friendships. Facebook encourages social networking, so it seems like it would strengthen relationships, but the opposite is true. People talk about "friending" each other, but that doesn't mean they have become actual friends. Having the most Facebook friends is a sort of contest among college students. One of my classmates brags about his 370 online friends, but he has met only about 30 of them in person. In addition, Facebook has been blamed for many romantic breakups. It is humiliating for lovers to broadcast their fights online or to read that one's significant other has changed his relationship status to "single." Facebook may

be an easy way to update a list of people, but it will never replace personal sharing over coffee, the warmth of a phone call, or a loving, intimate relationship.

(4) A serious consequence of Facebook is revealing too much information, which can hurt a person professionally. Many students don't understand that some things should be kept private. When my friend Joi applied for an accounting internship, she never thought the interviewer would look her up online. On her Facebook page, Joi had photos of herself drinking at a party (she was underage) and complaints on her wall about "boring" classes and her supervisor at work, an "annoying ass." She hadn't set the privacy settings on her account, so these pictures and comments were the image she was broadcasting to the world. Yes, she lost the internship.

(5) Most people are not going to unfriend Facebook any time soon, but they can avoid its harmful effects. My roommate sets a timer when she gets on Facebook in the evening; when the timer goes off, so does her page. Another friend uses Facebook to keep up with her relatives in China, but for her friends and classmates here, she calls and texts instead. After losing a great internship, Joi opened a second Facebook account. The first one is now private, seen only by a few friends. Her second page is public and squeaky clean; Joi calls it her online résumé. These strategies can keep Facebook fun, not a time-wasting habit that might cause harm.

—Celia Menezes, Student

1. Underline or highlight the thesis statement and the topic sentences in paragraphs 2, 3, and 4.

2. Does the writer discuss causes or effects? What are they?

   _____

3. What technique for the conclusion is used for this essay?

   _____

TEAMWORK: CRITICAL VIEWING AND WRITING

In a group with four or five classmates, study the famous painting below by Pablo Picasso, called *Guernica*. The painting depicts the bombing of the town of Guernica, Spain, in 1937,

but it is widely thought to be a brilliant depiction of the effects of war. What are these effects? Picasso usually used vivid colors. Why do you think he created this painting without color, in black, white and gray?

Planning and Writing the Cause and Effect Essay

Before writing an essay of cause and effect, reread Chapter 12, "Cause and Effect," especially the section called "Problems to Avoid in Cause and Effect Writing." Choose a subject that lends itself to an analysis of causes or effects. Think on paper or computer screen, listing many possible causes and effects; then choose the best three or four. Don't forget to consider short- and long-term effects, as well as positive and negative effects. Decide on a logical order—probably time order or order of importance—and use transitional expressions to introduce your points.*

The rest of the section will guide you as you write a cause and effect essay.

PRACTICE 11

1. Choose a topic from the list below or one your instructor has assigned. Make sure your topic lends itself to cause and effect analysis. This list and the one in Chapter 12 will give you ideas. Write a clear thesis statement that identifies your subject and indicates whether causes or effects will be emphasized. Then prewrite a number of possible causes or effects, so you can choose the most important ones to develop your essay. Decide on a logical order in which to present them.

   1. What are the reasons why you are attending college?

   2. What are the reasons for the popularity of a certain product, musical group, or game?

   3. What caused you to do something you are (or are not) proud of?

   4. Analyze the main causes of a problem in society (like child abuse, homelessness among military veterans, or teen pregnancy).

   5. What causes a hurricane, tornado, or other natural disaster?

   6. Discuss the effects of video game addiction.

   7. What are the effects of shyness on someone's life (or pride, rage, curiosity or the lack of it)?

   8. Write a letter urging a young person not to make a bad choice with serious negative consequences (such as joining a gang or dropping out of school).

   9. What are the effects of a new experience (a trip, military service, living in another country, dorm life)?

   10. What are the effects of a divorce, death, or other loss?

   11. Writer's choice: _____

2. Many students find using a graphic organizer helpful as they plan an essay. In your notebook, draw a blank 8-by-11-inch organizer like the one that follows or use the cause and effect essay organizer on the *Evergreen* CourseMate; in it, create a plan for your essay. The information you write in each box will become a paragraph.

———

* For a list of transitional expressions for cause and effect, see page 150.

CAUSE AND EFFECT ESSAY ORGANIZER

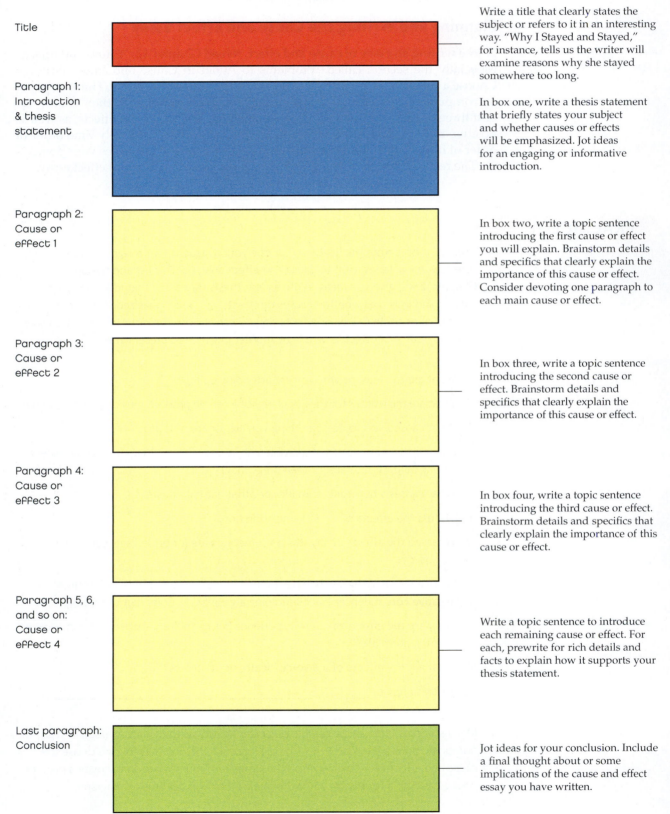

Title

Write a title that clearly states the subject or refers to it in an interesting way. "Why I Stayed and Stayed," for instance, tells us the writer will examine reasons why she stayed somewhere too long.

Paragraph 1: Introduction & thesis statement

In box one, write a thesis statement that briefly states your subject and whether causes or effects will be emphasized. Jot ideas for an engaging or informative introduction.

Paragraph 2: Cause or effect 1

In box two, write a topic sentence introducing the first cause or effect you will explain. Brainstorm details and specifics that clearly explain the importance of this cause or effect. Consider devoting one paragraph to each main cause or effect.

Paragraph 3: Cause or effect 2

In box three, write a topic sentence introducing the second cause or effect. Brainstorm details and specifics that clearly explain the importance of this cause or effect.

Paragraph 4: Cause or effect 3

In box four, write a topic sentence introducing the third cause or effect. Brainstorm details and specifics that clearly explain the importance of this cause or effect.

Paragraph 5, 6, and so on: Cause or effect 4

Write a topic sentence to introduce each remaining cause or effect. For each, prewrite for rich details and facts to explain how it supports your thesis statement.

Last paragraph: Conclusion

Jot ideas for your conclusion. Include a final thought about or some implications of the cause and effect essay you have written.

PRACTICE 12

Now referring to your plan, write the best first draft you can. Make sure that that each cause and/or effect you discuss is clear to you and the reader. Is the order logical? Tie each cause or effect into your thesis statement and main idea. Use *transitional expressions** to help the reader follow what happened.

Let your draft cool for an hour or a day; then reread it as if you were a helpful, eagle-eyed stranger. Now revise and rewrite, emphasizing clarity and a thoughtful explanation of causes or effects. Is each paragraph developed fully? Do transitions make the flow of ideas clear? Proofread for spelling, grammar, and sentence errors.

D. The Persuasive Essay

Persuasive essays are the essay type most frequently called for in college, business, and daily life. That is, you will often be asked to take a stand on an issue—censorship on the Internet, whether a company should invest in on-site child care, or whether a new super-store will help or hurt your community— and then try to persuade others to agree with you. Examination questions asking you to "agree or disagree" are really asking you to take a position and make a persuasive case for that position—for example, "The election of President Barack Obama signals an end to racism in the United States. Agree or disagree."

Here is a persuasive essay:

STOPPING YOUTH VIOLENCE: AN INSIDE JOB

(1) Every year, over 1 million twelve- to nineteen-year-olds are murdered, robbed, assaulted, or bullied—many by their peers—and teenagers are more than twice as likely as adults to become the victims of violence, according to the Children's Defense Fund. Although the problem is far too complex for any one solution, teaching young people conflict-resolution skills—that is, nonviolent techniques for resolving disputes—seems to help. To reduce youth violence, conflict-resolution skills should be taught to all children before they reach middle school.

(2) First and most important, young people need to learn nonviolent ways of dealing with conflict. In a dangerous society where guns are readily available, many youngsters feel they have no choice but to respond to an insult or an argument with violence. If they have grown up seeing family members and neighbors react to stress with verbal or physical violence, they may not know that other choices exist. Robert Steinback, a former *Miami Herald* columnist who worked with at-risk youth in Miami, writes that behavior like carrying a weapon or refusing to back down gives young people "the illusion of control," but what they desperately need is to learn real control—for example, when provoked, to walk away from a fight.

_____

* For a list of transitional expressions of cause and effect, see page 150.

(3) Next, conflict-resolution programs have been shown to reduce violent incidents and empower young people in a healthy way. Many programs and courses around the country are teaching teens and preteens to work through disagreements without violence. Tools include calmly telling one's own side of the story and listening to the other person without interrupting or blaming—skills that many adults don't have! Conflict Busters, a Los Angeles public school program, starts in the third grade; it trains students to be mediators, helping peers find their own solutions to conflicts ranging from "sandbox fights to interracial gang disputes," according to *Youthwatch: Statistics on Violence*, May 2012. Schools in Claremont, Connecticut, run a conflict-resolution course written by Dr. Luz Rivera, who said in a phone interview that fewer violent school incidents have been reported since the course began. Although conflict resolution is useful at any age, experts agree that students should first be exposed before they are hit by the double jolts of hormones and middle school.

(4) Finally, although opponents claim that this is a "Band-Aid" solution that does not address the root causes of teen violence—poverty, troubled families, bad schools, and drugs, to name a few—in fact, conflict-resolution training saves lives now. The larger social issues must be addressed, but they will take years to solve, whereas teaching students new attitudes and "people skills" will empower them immediately and serve them for a lifetime. For instance, fourteen-year-old Verna, who once called herself Vee Sinister, says that Ms. Rivera's course has changed her life: "I learned to stop and think before my big mouth gets me in trouble. I use the tools with my mother, and guess what? No more fights at school and screaming at home."

(5) The violence devastating Verna's generation threatens everyone's future. One proven way to help youngsters protect themselves from violence is conflict-resolution training that begins early. Although it is just one solution among many, this solution taps into great power: the hearts, minds, and characters of young people.

- The **thesis statement** in a persuasive essay clearly states the issue to be discussed and the writer's position on it. Underline or highlight the thesis statement.

- This introduction includes *facts*. What is the source of these facts and why does the writer include them here?

  _____

  _____

- Sometimes a writer needs to define terms he or she is using. What term does the writer define?

  _____

- How many reasons does this writer give to back up the thesis statement?

  _____

- Notice that the writer presents one reason per paragraph.

- Which reasons refer to an *authority*?

  _____

- Who are these authorities?

  _____

  _____

- How is the second reason supported?

  _____

- What is the source of information on Conflict Busters?

  _____

- Which reason is really an *answer to the opposition*?

  _____

- This reason also uses an *example*. What or who is the example?

  _____

- Underline or highlight the topic sentence of each body paragraph. Note that the thesis statement, topic sentences, and conclusion make up an **outline** or **plan** for the whole essay.

PRACTICE 13

This student's persuasive essay won a national essay contest sponsored by CCBA (Community College Baccalaureate). Read it and answer the questions.

IMAGINE A FOUR-YEAR COMMUNITY COLLEGE

(1) Imagine four-year institutions that allow for a pace and schedule that meet the needs of nontraditional students with non-academic obligations. Imagine institutions with an affordability that allows students to pay their own tuition as it comes due, in the absence of family wealth or large scholarships. Imagine colleges that take pride in their program and the philosophy of open admissions, rather than their ability to selectively admit few while turning down many. Imagine institutions like these all over the country, allowing continuity of family, work, and community between students and their hometowns. You have just imagined community colleges with four-year degree programs. Schedule, affordability, and open admissions policies make community colleges ideal to offer four-year degrees.

(2) A key concept of community colleges is to tailor offerings to students with small, sporadic amounts of time available for classes. I work, help run a non-profit

honor society on campus, attend full time classes, and am a cadet in the Corona de Tucson Firefighter Academy. Without the flexible schedule that Pima Community College affords me, I would be unable to complete all of these tasks simultaneously. Community colleges generally have very accommodating schedules, with courses available nights and weekends, self-paced on campus, and even online. Students who deserve and desire to complete a bachelor's degree may simply not have the availability to schedule classes between 7 A.M. and 5 P.M., but the community college would meet their needs.

(3) It is no coincidence that many students attending community colleges fall in the category of working poor. During freshman year, I struggled to pay tuition and book expenses; it was a year before I began receiving scholarships. Working in the food service industry, I had limited funds; luckily, I was able to utilize the library's books on reserve when I could not pay for my own. I saved thousands of dollars attending Pima Community College compared to what the University of Arizona would have charged me for the same number of credits. Yet my situation is not unique; millions of students would love to attend lavish universities, but incurring debts or failing to receive competitive scholarships deter worthy students from acquiring higher education. This is not to mention the fact that some full-capacity universities turn down valedictorians simply because they receive more perfect applications than they have seats available.

(4) Sometimes students need more than flexible hours or tuition to attend college; they need something nearby. Community colleges are exactly what the name entails, institutions of the community. Pima Community College has six campuses around town and online courses available. This has given me the ability to live with my sister and help her with mortgage payments while attending school. The community emphasis of these colleges allows students to stay in and help their community, family, and friends while pursuing higher education and personal enrichment. To imagine a solution to a problem and make it a reality is a staple of college education. Many have imagined a four-year community college—it must become a reality.

—John Windham, Student

1. What is this writer arguing *for*? Underline the thesis statement.

   _____

   _____

2. In the introduction, instead of a thesis statement, the writer asks readers three times to "Imagine . . . ." The last sentence of the introduction says, "You have just imagined community colleges with four-year degree programs." How effective is this introduction?

   _____

   _____

3. What three features of community colleges does the writer discuss in his argument?

   _____

4. This writer uses himself as an example throughout the essay. Is this persuasive? Would you say that his experience makes him an authority?

PRACTICE 14   **TEAMWORK: CRITICAL VIEWING AND WRITING**

In a group of four or five classmates, look closely at the public service advertisement below, which appeared on buses and billboards. Like many advertisements, this one is trying to *persuade* the viewer to adopt or agree with a certain view. Working together, write down the ad's "thesis statement" and argument. How persuasive is this ad?

Courtesy Friends of Animals

YOU LOOK JUST AS STUPID WEARING THEIRS.

Friends **o**f **A**nimals

www.friendsofanimals.org

Planning and Writing the Persuasive Essay

Before writing a persuasive essay, you should reread Chapter 13, "Persuasion." In particular, review the five methods of persuasion, all employed well in the first essay above:

1. Use facts
2. Cite authority
3. Give examples
4. Predict consequences
5. Answer the opposition

Keeping your readers in mind is key to persuading them, so craft your thesis statement carefully. Plan to devote one paragraph to each of your reasons, developing each paragraph with facts and discussion. Ample factual support is vital to successful persuasion. A good way to find interesting factual support is to do some basic **research**—for example, to find books or articles by or about experts on your subject or even to conduct your own interviews, as does the author of "Stopping Youth Violence."*

The rest of the section will guide you as you write a persuasive essay.

PRACTICE 15

1. Choose a topic from the list below or one your instructor has assigned. If possible, choose a subject you feel strongly about. Argue for or against, as you wish.

    1. I deserve a better grade on my _____ assignment (or in this course).

    2. America should control guns with stricter laws.

    3. All animal testing of medicines should be banned, even if such testing would save human lives.

    4. Every college student should be required to give three credit hours' worth of community service a year.

    5. The United States government should provide universal health care to all citizens.

    6. A college education is (not) worth the time and money.

    7. Gay couples should be allowed to adopt children in all states.

    8. I am a good fit for the position of _____.

    9. To better prepare students for the world of work, this college should do three things.

    10. The United States must find and deport all illegal aliens, including students with expired visas.

    11. Writer's choice: _____

2. Many students find using a graphic organizer helpful as they plan an essay. In your notebook, draw a blank 8-by-11-inch organizer like the one that follows or use the persuasive essay organizer on the *Evergreen* CourseMate; in it, create a plan for your essay. The information you write in each box will become a paragraph.

_____

* For information on summarizing and quoting outside sources and on using research in an essay, see Chapter 18, "Summarizing, Quoting, and Avoiding Plagiarism" and Chapter 19, "Strengthening an Essay with Research."

PERSUASIVE ESSAY ORGANIZER

Title — Write a title that forcefully or provocatively sets forth the issue.

Paragraph 1: Introduction & thesis statement — In box one, write a thesis statement that clearly states the issue and your position about it. Jot ideas for a strong and engaging introduction. Visualize your typical reader, and write with him or her in mind.

Paragraph 2: Reason 1 in the argument — In box two, write a topic sentence introducing the first reason (refer to the five methods of persuasion and try to use at least two in your essay). Prewrite ideas that clearly explain the first reason.

Paragraph 3: Reason 2 in the argument — In box three, write a topic sentence introducing the second reason. Especially if your topic is controversial, try to include an answer to the opposition. Brainstorm details and specifics that clearly and convincingly explain it.

Paragraph 4: Reason 3 in the argument — In box four, write a topic sentence introducing the third reason. Especially if your topic is controversial, try to include an answer to the opposition. Brainstorm details and specifics that clearly and convincingly explain it.

Paragraph 5, 6, and so on: Reason 4 in the argument — Write a topic sentence to introduce each remaining reason that will support and explain your thesis statement. For each, prewrite for facts and specifics to explain it fully. Continue until your last reason is presented. Double check the order in which you present the reasons; does it make logical sense?

Last paragraph: Conclusion — Jot ideas for your conclusion that bring home to the reader why he or she should agree with your position. Include a brief review of your argument and/or a final thought about the issue and its importance.

PRACTICE 16

Now referring to your plan, write the best first draft you can. Aim for clarity and persuasive power as you explain why your stand is the right one. Make sure your reasons follow the most effective order, and carefully choose *transitional expressions** to introduce each reason. Remember, factual support is key to a winning essay.

Let your draft cool for an hour or a day; then reread it as if you were a helpful, eagle-eyed stranger. Now revise and rewrite for clarity and ample support. Is each paragraph and reason developed fully? Do transitions make the flow of ideas clear? Does your conclusion bring the point home? Proofread for spelling, grammar, and sentence errors.

EXPLORING ONLINE

http://leo.stcloudstate.edu/acadwrite/comparcontrast.html
Helpful advice on writing a comparison or a contrast essay

http://grammar.ccc.commnet.edu/grammar/composition/argument.htm
Excellent tips on developing and supporting an argument

CourseMate for *Evergreen*
Visit *Evergreen* CourseMate for more practices and quizzes, videos to accompany the readings, career and job-search resources, ESL help, and live links to every Exploring Online in the book.

---

* For a list of transitional expressions for persuasion, see page 157.

CHAPTER 18

Summarizing, Quoting, and Avoiding Plagiarism

A: Avoiding Plagiarism

B: Writing a Summary

C: Using Direct and Indirect Quotation (Paraphrase)

Now more than ever before, it is important for you to know how to find, evaluate, and use information from **outside sources**—that is, sources outside yourself (for example, books, articles, Internet sites, or other people). In some college courses, you will write papers with no outside sources. However, many courses and jobs will require you to refer to outside sources as you write reports, essays, and research papers. Besides, information from outside sources can vastly enrich your writing with facts, statistics, experts' ideas, and more.

In this chapter, you will learn what **plagiarism** is and how to avoid it. You will also learn and practice three excellent ways to use outside sources in your writing: **summarizing**, **quoting directly**, and **quoting indirectly**.

A. Avoiding Plagiarism

Before we discuss how to summarize or quote from an outside source, it is all-important that you understand—so you can avoid—**plagiarism**. Plagiarism is failing to give proper credit to an author whose words or ideas you have used. That is, plagiarism means passing off someone else's words or ideas as your own. Whether intentional or careless, plagiarism is stealing. A college student who plagiarizes a paper may be expelled from the course or from college. In the business world, publishing material copied from someone else is a crime.

To avoid plagiarism, you must give proper credit to the original author, as this chapter and the next will explain. Meanwhile, keep this simple rule in mind: **Always tell your reader the source of any words and ideas not your own. Give enough information so that a reader who wants to find your original source can do so.**

PRACTICE 1

What is your college's policy on plagiarism? That is, what consequences or penalties follow if a student is found to have plagiarized a paper or other work? The reference librarian can help you find this information.

B. Writing a Summary

A **summary** presents the main idea and supporting points of a longer work *in much shorter form*. A summary might be one sentence, one paragraph, or several paragraphs long, depending on the length of the original and the nature of your assignment.

Summarizing is important both in college and at work. In a persuasive essay, you might summarize the ideas of an expert whose views support one of your points. A professor might ask you to summarize a book, a market survey, or even the plot of a film—that is, to condense it in your own words, presenting only the highlights. Of course, many essay exams also call for written summaries.

Compare this short newspaper article—the *source*—with the *summary* that follows:

Source

Fido may be cute, cuddly, and harmless. But in his genes, he's a wolf.

Researchers tracing the genetic family tree of man's best friend have confirmed that domestic dogs, from petite poodles to huge elkhounds, descended from wolves that were tamed 100,000 years ago.

"Our data show that the origin of dogs seems to be much more ancient than indicated in the archaeological record," said Robert K. Wayne of UCLA, the leader of a team that tested the genes from 67 dog breeds and 62 wolves on four continents.

Wayne said the study showed so many DNA changes that dogs had to have diverged genetically from wolves 60,000 to more than 100,000 years ago.

The study suggests that primitive humans living in a hunting and gathering culture tamed wolves and then bred the animals to create the many different types of dogs that now exist.

—Recer, Paul. "Dogs Tamed 100,000 Years Ago." *The Herald* 13 June 1997: 9A. Print.

Summary

> Dogs began evolving from wolves between 60,000 and 100,000 years ago, reports Paul Recer in *The Herald*. Apparently, humans tamed wolves far earlier than was previously thought. Researchers at UCLA, led by Robert K. Wayne, came to these conclusions after studying the genes of 67 breeds of dogs and 62 wolves on four continents (9A).

- Notice that sentence 1 states the author and source of the original article. Sentence 1 also states the main idea of the article. What is its main idea?

  _____

- What evidence supports this idea?

  _____

- The original is short, so the summary is very short—just three sentences long.

- The summary writer does not add his own opinions about dogs or evolution but simply states the main ideas of the source. Unlike many kinds of writing, a summary should not contain your personal opinions and feelings.

- Note that the page number of the original source appears in parentheses at the end of the summary.*

Preparing to Write a Summary

The secret of writing a good summary is clearly understanding the original. If you doubt this, try to summarize out loud Chapter 3 of your biology book. To summarize well, you have to know the subject matter.

Before you summarize a piece of writing, notice the title and subtitle (if there is one); these often state the main idea. Read quickly for meaning; then carefully read the work again, underlining or jotting down notes for yourself. What is the author's thesis or main point? What points does he or she offer in support? Be careful to distinguish between the most and least important points; your summary should include only the most important ones.

To help you understand *what the author thinks is important*, notice which ideas get the most coverage. Read with special care the topic sentence of each paragraph and the first and last paragraphs of the work. If you are summarizing a magazine article or a textbook chapter, the subheads (often in boldface type) point out important ideas.

> Your written summary should include the following:
> 1. The author, title, and source of the original
> 2. The main idea or thesis of the original, in your own words
> 3. The most important supporting ideas or points of the original, in your own words

---

* For more precise information on how to cite sources, see Chapter 19, "Strengthening an Essay with Research," Part C.

Try to present the ideas in your summary in proportion to those in the original. For instance, if the author devotes one paragraph to each of four ideas, you might give one sentence to each idea. To avoid plagiarism, when you finish, compare your summary with the original; that is, make sure you have not just copied the phrasing and sentences of the original.

A summary differs from much other writing in that it should *not* contain your feelings or opinions—just the facts. Your job is to capture the essence of the original, with nothing added.

Following are two summaries of a student essay in Chapter 17, "Types of Essays, Part 2," Part A, of this book. Which do you think is the better summary, A or B? Be prepared to say specifically why.

Summary A

(1) In the essay "E-Notes from an Online Learner," printed in Fawcett, *Evergreen*, Tenth Edition, student and mother Brenda Wilson contrasts her learning experiences in traditional and online classrooms. (2) Whereas Wilson's long commute to campus once made her late to class or anxious, she finds online classes more convenient because she can read lectures or submit coursework any time, from home. (3) Next, Ms. Wilson says that other students might prefer the energy of live class discussion, but she feels freer online, writing her thoughts with less self-consciousness. (4) Finally, she stresses that online students must be self-motivated, unlike regular students who can rely on professors to prod them or on the "group adrenaline rush [of] seeing other students hunched over their notebooks." (5) Less focused students might procrastinate and drop out. (6) Overall, Wilson prefers distance learning (238–239).

Summary B

(1) This excellent essay is by Brenda Wilson, student. (2) I enjoyed reading about online learning because I have never taken a course online. (3) This year Ms. Wilson attended her history class dressed in dancing cow pajamas and fluffy slippers. (4) This was not a bizarre college ritual but part of the University of Houston's Distance Education Program. (5) Virtual courses are very different. (6) She has a job and a son, so she is very busy, like many students today. (7) Online classes are great for this type of student, more convenient. (8) Students have to motivate themselves, and Ms. Wilson has only the soft bubbling noise of her aquarium screen saver to remind her to work. (9) She ends by saying it is 12:14 A.M. and her cat is nuzzling her fluffy pink slippers. (10) I also liked her cat's name.

● The test of a good summary is how well it captures the original. Which better summarizes Ms. Wilson's essay, A or B?

_____

● If you picked A, you are right. Sentence 1 states the author and title of the essay, as well as the name and edition of the book in which it appears. Sentence 1 also states the main idea of the original, which *contrasts* the author's experience of traditional classes and virtual classes. Does any sentence in B state the main idea of the original essay? _____

● Compare the original with the two summaries. How many points of contrast does A include? B? _____

● Does each writer summarize the essay *in his or her own words*? If not, which sentences might seem plagiarized? _____

● Writer A once quotes Ms. Wilson directly. How is this shown? Why do you think the summary writer chose this sentence to quote? _____

_____

● Do both summaries succeed in keeping personal opinion out? If not, which sentences contain the summary writer's opinion?_____

_____

● Note that summary writer A includes the source page number in parentheses at the end of the summarized material. On the other hand, writer B refers to Brenda Wilson but does not name her essay or the source in which it appears.

PRACTICE 2

In a group with three or four other classmates, choose just one of the following essays to summarize: "Girl Heroes in the House" (Chapter 16, Part A); "The Day of the Dead" (Chapter 16, Part C); "Stopping Youth Violence: An Inside Job" (Chapter 17, Part D); or "Skin Deep" (Chapter 14, Part E). Read your chosen essay in the group, aloud if possible. Then each person should write a one-paragraph summary of it, referring to the checklist below (15–20 minutes).

Now read your finished summaries aloud to your group. How well does each writer briefly capture the meaning of the original? Has he or she kept out personal opinion? What suggestions for improvement can you offer? Your instructor may wish to have the best summary in each group read aloud to the whole class.

PRACTICE 3

Flip through a copy of a current magazine: *Newsweek, People, Essence, Wired,* or another. Pick one article that interests you, read it carefully, and write a one- to three-paragraph summary of the article, depending on the length of the article. The points you include in your summary should reflect the emphasis of the original writer. Try to capture the essence of the article. Remember to give your source at the beginning, to keep out personal opinion, and to check your summary for plagiarism. Refer to the checklist.

Checklist

The Process of Writing a Summary

☐ 1. Notice the title and subtitle of the original; do these state its main idea?

☐ 2. Read the original quickly for meaning; then carefully read it again, underlining important ideas and jotting down notes for yourself.

☐ 3. Determine the author's thesis or main idea.

☐ 4. Now find the main supporting points. Subheads (if any), topic sentences, and the first and last paragraphs of the original may help you find key points.

☐ 5. Write your topic sentence or thesis statement, stating the author's thesis, title, source, and date of the original.

☐ 6. In your own words, give the author's most important supporting points, in the same order in which the author gives them. Keep the same proportion of coverage as the original.

☐ 7. Write your summary, skipping lines so you will have room to make corrections.

☐ 8. Now revise, asking yourself, "Will my summary convey to someone who has never read the original the author's main idea and key supporting points?"

☐ 9. Proofread, making neat corrections above the lines.

☐ 10. Compare your final draft with the original to avoid plagiarism.

C. Using Direct and Indirect Quotation (Paraphrase)

Sometimes you will want to quote an outside source directly. A quotation might be part of a summary or part of a longer paper or report. Quoting the words of others can add richness and authority to your writing; in fact, that is why I include a Quotation Bank at the end of this book—a kind of minireader of great thoughts. Use short quotations in these ways:

- Use a quotation to stress a key idea.
- Use a quotation to lend expert opinion to your argument.
- Use a quotation to provide a catchy introduction or conclusion.
- Use a quotation about your topic that is wonderfully written and "quotable" to add interest.

However, avoid using very long quotations or too many quotations. Both send the message that you are filling up space because you don't have enough to say. Of course, to avoid plagiarism, you always must credit the original author or speaker.

Here are some methods for introducing quotations:

Ways To Introduce Quotations

Mr. Taibi says, . . .   Ms. Luboff writes, . . .

One expert had this to say: . . . , one authority reported.

In a recent *Times* column,   According to Dr. Haynes, . . .
Maureen Dowd observes . . .

Following are a passage from a well-known book and two ways that students quoted the author:

Source

> On film or videotape, violence begins and ends in a moment. "Bang bang, you're dead." Then the death is over. This sense of action-without-consequences replicates and reinforces the dangerous "magical" way many children think. Do the twelve- and fourteen-year-olds who are shooting each other to death in Los Angeles, Chicago, or Washington, D.C., really understand that death is permanent, unalterable, final, tragic? Television certainly is not telling them so.
>
> —Prothrow-Stith, Deborah. *Deadly Consequences.* New York: Harper Perennial, 1991: 34. Print.

Two students who wrote about the effects of TV violence correctly quoted Dr. Prothrow-Stith as follows:

Direct Quotation

> "This sense of action-without-consequences replicates and reinforces the dangerous 'magical' way many children think," writes Dr. Deborah Prothrow-Stith in *Deadly Consequences* (34).

Indirect Quotation (Paraphrase)

> In *Deadly Consequences*, Prothrow-Stith points out that TV and movie violence, which has no realistic consequences, harms children by reinforcing the magical way in which they think (34).

- The first sentence gives Dr. Prothrow-Stith's exact words inside quotation marks. This is **direct quotation**. Note the punctuation.

- The second sentence uses the word *that* and gives the *meaning* of Prothrow-Stith's words without quotation marks. This is **indirect quotation**, or **paraphrase**. Note the punctuation.

- Both students correctly quote the writer and credit the source. Both include the page number in parentheses after the quoted material and before the period. (See Chapter 19, Part C, for more information on this style of citing sources.)

Now read this passage from a third student's paper:

Plagiarism

> On film and television, violence begins and ends in a minute, and then the death is over. Teenagers killing each other across the country don't realize that death is "unalterable, final, and tragic" because they do not see its consequences on TV.

- Can you see why this passage is plagiarized (and why the student received a failing grade)?

- Both the ideas and many of the words are clearly Prothrow-Stith's, yet the student never mentions her or her book. Four words from the original are placed in quotation marks, but the reader has no idea why. Instead, the student implies that all the ideas and words are his own. What exact words are plagiarized from the source? What ideas are plagiarized?

  _____

  _____

  _____

- Revise this passage as if it were your own, giving credit to the original author and avoiding plagiarism.

PRACTICE 4

Following are passages from two sources. Read each one, and then, as if you were writing a paper, quote two sentences from each, one directly quoting the author's words and one indirectly quoting the author's ideas. Review the boxed ways to introduce quotations and try several methods. Finally, write a brief summary of each passage. Check your work to avoid plagiarism.

Source 1

In most cultures throughout history, music, dance, rhythmic drumming, and chanting have been essential parts of healing rituals. Modern research bears out the connection between music and healing. In one study, the heart rate and blood pressure of patients went down when quiet music was piped into their hospital coronary care units. At the same time, the patients showed greater tolerance for pain and less anxiety and depression. Similarly, listening to music before, during, or after surgery has been shown to promote various beneficial effects—from alleviating anxiety to reducing the need for sedation by half. When researchers played Brahms' "Lullaby" to premature infants, these babies gained weight faster and went home from the hospital sooner than babies who did not hear the music. Music may also affect immunity by altering the level of stress chemicals in the blood. An experiment at Rainbow Babies and Children's Hospital found

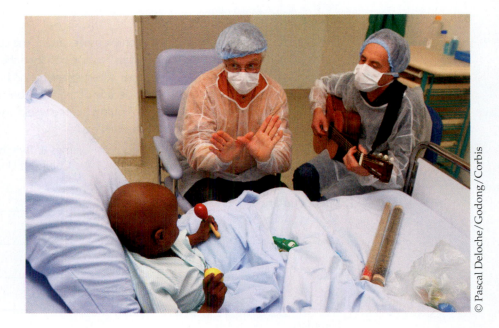

In the children's cancer ward in Villejuif, France, musicians play for a patient during music therapy.

© Pascal Deloche / Godong / Corbis

that a single thirty-minute music therapy session could increase the level of salivary IgA, an immunoglobulin that protects against respiratory infections.

Institute of Noetic Sciences with William Poole.
The Heart of Healing. Atlanta:
Turner Publishing, 1993: 134. Print.

Direct quotation: _____

_____

Indirect quotation: _____

_____

Summary:

_____

_____

_____

_____

_____

_____

Source 2

Assuming they reach maturity with consciousness intact, the current crop of teenagers will have spent years watching commercials. No one has done the numbers on what happens if you factor in radio, magazine, newspaper advertisements, and billboards, but today's teens probably have spent the equivalent of a decade of their lives being bombarded by bits of advertising information. In 1915, a person could go entire weeks without observing an ad. The average adult today sees three thousand every day.

James B. Twitchell, *Adcult USA*. New York:
Columbia University Press, 1996: 2. Print.

Direct quotation: _____

_____

Indirect quotation: _____

_____

Summary:

_____

_____

_____

_____

_____

_____

PRACTICE 5

Following are four sources and four quotations from student papers. If the student has summarized, directly quoted, or indirectly quoted the source correctly, write *C*. If you believe the source is plagiarized, write *P*; then revise the student's work as if it were your own to avoid plagiarism.

● Does each student clearly distinguish between his or her ideas and the source's?

● Does each student give enough information so that a reader could locate the original source?

Source 1

"Binge drinking, according to criteria used in periodic surveys by the Harvard researchers, is defined as five or more drinks on one occasion for a man or four or more drinks on one occasion for a woman. Students who reported one or two such episodes in the two weeks preceding the survey were classified as occasional binge drinkers; those reporting three or more were considered frequent binge drinkers."

Okie, Susan. "Survey: 44% of College Students Are Binge Drinkers."
Washington Post 25 Mar. 2002: A6. Print.

Student's Version

_____ Binge drinking is a dangerous problem on campuses, but college administrators are not doing enough to stop it. An amazing 44 percent of college students are binge drinkers. Let us define binge drinking as five or more drinks on one occasion for a man or four or more drinks on one occasion for a woman. College officials need to ask why so many students are drinking dangerously.

Source 2

"Researchers measuring brain and heart activity found that volunteers were as stimulated by imagining someone they loved smiling at them as they were by being told they'd won a cash prize. David Lewis, a psychologist and director of research at Mindlab International in Brighton, England, which conducted the study, says a warm smile can create a 'halo' effect, helping us 'feel more optimistic, more positive, and more motivated.'"

Rubin, Courtney. "Smile to Lift Your Mood."
U.S. News & World Report Dec 2010: 63. Print.

Student's Version

_____ Research is revealing that a smile can improve your mood. Psychologists in England have found that people who just think about being smiled at by a loved one feel as good as they do when they are told they have won money.

Source 3

"The risk of stroke increases with the number of fast-food restaurants in a neighborhood . . . . Researchers found [that] residents of neighborhoods with the highest number of fast-food restaurants had a 13 percent higher relative risk of suffering ischemic strokes than those living in areas with the lowest numbers of restaurants."

American Heart Association. "Number of Fast-Food Restaurants in
Neighborhood Associated with Stroke Risk." *ScienceDaily*. Science
Daily LLC 20 Feb. 2009. Web. 24 Feb. 2009.

Student's Version

_____ According to a news release by the American Heart Association, people who live near fast-food restaurants like McDonald's or Wendy's are at a higher risk for strokes than those who do not. As the number of restaurants rises, so does the risk.

Source 4

"The United States has less than 5 percent of the world's population. But it has almost a quarter of the world's prisoners. Indeed, the United States leads the world in producing prisoners, a reflection of a relatively recent and now entirely distinctive American approach to crime and punishment. Americans are locked up for crimes—from writing bad checks to using drugs—that would rarely produce prison sentences in other countries. And in particular they are kept incarcerated far longer than prisoners in other nations."

Liptak, Adam. "U.S. Prison Population Dwarfs That of Other Nations."
New York Times 23 Apr. 2008. Web. 16 Feb. 2012.

Student's Version

_____ It is time to rethink the way that America punishes people for crimes. We lock up people for crimes that don't carry prison sentences in other countries, and our prison sentences are longer. As a result, the United States has only 5% of the world population but 25% of the world's prisoners.

EXPLORING ONLINE

http://owl.english.purdue.edu/owl/resource/589/2/
Purdue OWL's site "Is It Plagiarism Yet?" gives helpful advice on what constitutes plagiarism

http://owl.english.purdue.edu/owl/resource/563/01/
Helpful review of direct and indirect quotation and summary

CourseMate for *Evergreen*
Visit *Evergreen* CourseMate for more practices and quizzes, videos to accompany the readings, career and job-search resources, ESL help, and live links to every Exploring Online in the book.

CHAPTER 19

Strengthening an Essay with Research

A: Improving an Essay with Research

B: Finding and Evaluating Outside Sources: Library and Internet

C: Adding Sources to Your Essay and Documenting Them Correctly

You will have opportunities in college to prepare formal research papers with many outside sources. However, you should not limit your definition of "research" to just such assignments. Whenever you have a question and seek an answer from a source outside yourself, you are doing **research**. Most of us research every day, whether or not we call it that—when we gather facts and opinions about the cheapest local restaurant, the college with the best fire science program, the safest new cars, or various medical conditions. In this chapter, you will learn skills valuable both in college and at work: how to improve your writing with interesting information from outside sources.

A. Improving an Essay with Research

Almost any essay, particularly one designed to *persuade* your reader, can benefit from the addition of outside material. In fact, even one outside source—a startling statistic or a memorable quote—can enrich your essay. Supporting your main points with outside sources can be an excellent way to establish your credibility, strengthen your argument, and add power to your words. Compare two versions of this student's paragraph:

> Inexperienced hikers often get in trouble because they worry about rare dangers like snakebites, but they minimize the very serious dangers of dehydration and exposure to cold. For example, my brother-in-law once hiked into the Grand Canyon with only a granola bar and a small bottle of water. He became severely dehydrated and was too weak to climb back up without help.

● This paragraph makes an important point about the dangers that inexperienced hikers can face. The example of the brother-in-law supports the main point, but the paragraph needs more complete support.

Now read the paragraph strengthened by some relevant facts from an outside source.

Inexperienced hikers often get in trouble because they worry about rare dangers like snakebites, but they minimize the very serious dangers of dehydration and exposure to cold. For example, my brother-in-law once hiked into the Grand Canyon with only a granola bar and a small bottle of water. He became severely dehydrated and was too weak to climb back up without help. He was lucky. According to the National Park Service website, over a hundred hikers die every year because they are not properly prepared for the environment. In addition, the NPS reports that over $5.6 million was spent in 2009 to perform 3,849 search-and-rescue operations, almost a third of them to save poorly prepared hikers like my brother-in-law ("Search and Rescue Report").

● What facts from the National Park Service website support the main point and add to the persuasive power of this paragraph?

_____

● What sentence of transition does the writer use to connect his example of the brother-in-law with facts from the outside source? What transitional words connect the fact about hikers' deaths each year?

_____

● Remember that just one well-chosen outside source can improve and enliven a paper.

Consider the facts in this chart from the U.S. Census:

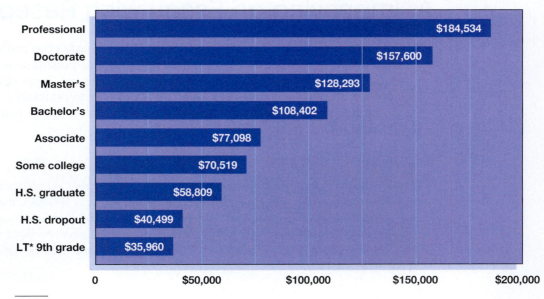

Average Family Income by Education of Householder, 2009

Professional	$184,534
Doctorate	$157,600
Master's	$128,293
Bachelor's	$108,402
Associate	$77,098
Some college	$70,519
H.S. graduate	$58,809
H.S. dropout	$40,499
LT* 9th grade	$35,960

0          $50,000 $100,000 $150,000 $200,000

_____
* LT: Less than

- What patterns do you see in this chart?

- How might you use this information in an essay?

Facts and statistics can make a strong statement, but there are many other ways to enhance your writing. Consider adding a good quotation to emphasize one of your key points. You can begin by looking through the Quotation Bank at the end of this book or an online version of *Bartlett's Quotations* at **http://www.bartleby .com/100/**. Or find and quote an expert on the subject you are writing about. For example, if your subject is the lack of recycling receptacles on your campus, an opinion from a Sierra Club official would give authority to your essay. And don't forget experts closer to home; details about a student you know who has begun a recycling campaign on campus would add life and emotion to your work. If your essay is about your family history or the school's registration system, you could interview a relative or a school administrator and use that material to add authority to your paper.

A good way to begin using research is to pick an essay you have recently written. Reread it, marking any places where outside sources might make it even better. Write down any questions you want answers to or information that you would like to find:

- What would I like to know more about?

- What outside source might make my essay more interesting?

- What information—fact, statistic, detail, or quotation—would make my essay more convincing?

- What people are experts on this topic? Where can I find them or their opinions?

CARMEN'S RESEARCH PROCESS

Student Carmen Gevana is learning to use outside sources. She plans to add research support to a favorite essay. She selects a cause and effect paper that examines the reasons her best friend went into credit-card debt and the devastating effects this debt had on her friend's life. In her paper, Carmen named two causes: credit-card companies using gifts to encourage students to apply for cards and students getting higher credit lines than they can realistically handle. The consequences Carmen discussed were unmanageable debt and ruined credit. Now Carmen wants to add two or three sources to support her own ideas. Her first question is whether heavy credit-card debt is a problem unique to her friend or more widespread among college students. She also wonders how much debt a typical college student carries. Finally, she hopes to find an expert opinion about the effects on college students.

Here is one way to visualize the research process presented in this chapter:

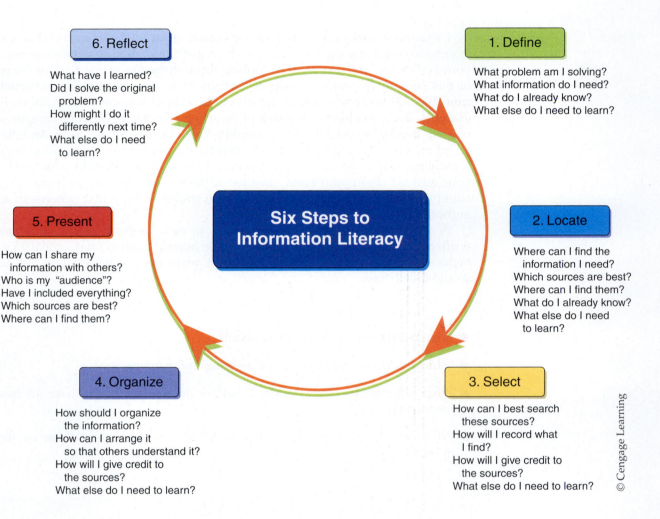

6. Reflect

What have I learned?
Did I solve the original
    problem?
How might I do it
    differently next time?
What else do I need
    to learn?

1. Define

What problem am I solving?
What information do I need?
What do I already know?
What else do I need to learn?

5. Present

How can I share my
    information with others?
Who is my "audience"?
Have I included everything?
Which sources are best?
Where can I find them?

**Six Steps to
Information Literacy**

2. Locate

Where can I find the
    information I need?
Which sources are best?
Where can I find them?
What do I already know?
What else do I need
    to learn?

4. Organize

How should I organize
    the information?
How can I arrange it
    so that others understand it?
How will I give credit to
    the sources?
What else do I need to learn?

3. Select

How can I best search
    these sources?
How will I record what
    I find?
How will I give credit to
    the sources?
What else do I need to learn?

PRACTICE 1

Choose one of the following: either your favorite paper written this term or a paper on a topic assigned by your instructor. Then read through your paper, marking any spots where an outside source—fact, statistic, expert opinion, or quotation—might strengthen your essay. Write down any questions that you want to answer.

B. Finding and Evaluating Outside Sources: Library and Internet

The next step is finding the information you seek—or something even better. This section will show you how to find sources in the library and on the Internet.

___

* From G. Wood, "Academic original sin: Plagiarism, the Internet, and librarians," The Journal of Academic Librarianship, 30(3), April 9, 2004, pp. 237–242. Used by permission.

Doing Research at the Library

Visit your college library, with your notes from Practice 1 in hand. Ask about any print guides, workshops, or websites that show you how to use the library facilities. Introduce yourself to the reference librarian, tell him or her what subject you are exploring, and ask for help finding and using any of these resources in your search:

1. **Online Catalog or Card Catalog**. This will show you what books are available on your topic. For every book that looks like it might be interesting, jot down its title, author, and call number (the number that lets you find the book in the library).

2. **Periodical Indexes**. The more current your topic, the more likely you are to find interesting information in periodicals—magazines, journals, and newspapers—rather than books. *The Readers' Guide to Periodical Literature* is a print resource, listing articles by subject. The library will also have computerized indexes like *InfoTrac*, *EBSCOhost*, and *Lexis Nexis*. Ask the librarian to help you explore these exciting resources.

3. **Statistical Sources**. If you are looking for statistics and facts, the library has volumes like *The Statistical Abstract of the United States* with fascinating information on population, education, immigration, crime, economic issues, and so on.

4. **Encyclopedias and Reference Books**. General books on subjects like geology or psychology can be helpful. Special reference books and encyclopedias exist for almost every area—for example, world soccer statistics, terrorism, or the birds of South America.

As you explore, you might see why experienced researchers often love what they do. They never know what they will find, and they learn the darnedest, most interesting things. However, they must **evaluate** each source. If you are writing about the space shuttle, a current article in the *Chicago Tribune* would more likely impress readers as a truthful source than, say, a story in the *National Enquirer* called "Space Aliens Ate My Laundry." Look at the date of a book or article; if your subject is current, your sources should be too. Is the author a respected expert on this subject? Is the information balanced and objective? The librarian can help you find strong sources.

Once you discover good information that will strengthen your essay, take clear and careful notes, using 4×6 note cards or your notebook. Use the techniques you learned in Chapter 18 to summarize and quote directly and indirectly; these will help you avoid accidental plagiarism. Write down everything you might need later. Print or buy copies of an article or book pages that are important. Don't leave the library without this information:

Book: Author name(s), title and subtitle, year of publication, publisher and location of publisher, exact pages of material quoted or summarized.

Magazine: Author name(s), title of article, title of magazine or journal, year, month, day of publication, volume and number, page numbers.

> ## CARMEN'S RESEARCH PROCESS
>
> Carmen visits her college library and gets help from the librarian using the computerized database *EBSCOhost*. Because Carmen's topic—student credit-card debt—is current, she assumes that newspapers and magazines will give her the most up-to-date information. Searching "credit-card debt," she finds a recent *Chicago Tribune* article called "Big Debt on Campus: Credit Offers Flood the Quad." She is surprised and excited to learn that credit problems like her friend's are a growing national problem. She copies the article and adds it to her source folder.

PRACTICE 2

In your college or local library, find the answers to the following questions; write the answers and the complete source for each piece of information. Your instructor might wish to have you work in competing teams.

1. List the full titles of five novels by Toni Morrison. What major prize did she win and in what year?

2. How many acres of rain forest are destroyed every day in Brazil?

3. What is the average hourly wage of men in the United States? Of women?

4. How many murders were committed in your town or city last year? Is the number up or down from ten years ago?

5. What was the newspaper headline in your hometown or city on the day and year of your birth? What stories dominated page 1?

PRACTICE 3

In your college or local library, find at least two excellent additions from outside sources that will improve your essay: a fact, statistic, example, quotation, or expert opinion. Write the information from each source precisely on 4 × 6 note cards, using quotation marks as you learned in Chapter 18, Part C, or make copies. Write down everything you will need later to cite the source: the book or magazine, article name, author name(s), and so on. Spell everything perfectly; copy exact punctuation of titles, and don't forget page numbers.

Doing Research on the Internet

The Internet is a wonderful source of information on just about everything—a great place to brainstorm, get ideas as you research, and find certain facts. However, it is harder to evaluate information on the Web than in print, as this section will explain, so be careful.

If you have Internet access at the library or at home, use one of the search engines below. Type in search words that narrow your subject the same way you narrow a topic in writing—for example, *credit-card debt, college students*. Spell correctly, and try different words if necessary. Chances are, you will have too many hits, rather than too few.

Google	www.google.com
Yahoo!	www.yahoo.com
Bing	www.bing.com

Evaluate each website carefully. Who sponsors the site? How balanced and unbiased is the information? Notice also the date of the site and article; many websites come and go in the night. With practice, Web researchers get better at spotting good and not-so-good sources of information. One tip is the Web address, or Uniform Resource Locator (URL) of each site. The last part of a URL indicates the type of organization that owns the site:

.com	=	company (aims to sell something and make a profit)
.org	=	nonprofit organization (aims to promote a cause)
.gov	=	government (provides many public information sites)
.edu	=	college or educational institution (aims to inform the public and promote itself)

For instance, if you are researching *asthma in children, treatments*, a government-sponsored health site might give more unbiased information than a company that sells asthma medications or a personal website called *Troy's Asthma Story*. For more help evaluating websites, search "evaluating Web sources" or visit **http://lib.nmsu.edu/instruction/evalcrit.html**.

As in the library—to avoid plagiarism later—take good notes, clearly marking words and ideas taken from your sources. Before you leave a website you wish to quote, cut and paste or print the material you want to refer to, and make sure you have full information to cite the source later in your paper:

Website: URL address, owner of site, author name(s), title of article, date written (if available), and date you accessed the website.

CARMEN'S RESEARCH PROCESS

Carmen chooses the Google search engine and types the search words, "college students, credit-card debt." The search engine returns several thousand sources! Carmen scrolls quickly through many different hits, until she finds one that looks promising. It's the website for Sallie Mae, a federal loan provider for college students. Carmen takes notes on a number of useful statistics and makes sure she has the URL address and other pertinent information before she logs off the computer.

PRACTICE 4

Go to **www.fedstats.gov** and learn how to find statistics quickly and easily. Answer these questions:

1. How many people live in the United States?

2. What is the leading cause of death in American men? Women?

3. What is the leading export from your state?

4. How many different ethnic groups live in your state?

5. How many new AIDS cases were reported in your state last year? What groups were hardest hit?

PRACTICE 5

Using one of the suggested search engines, find at least two good pieces of information to strengthen your essay—facts, statistics, expert opinions, and so on. Hone your search words and evaluate what you find. Take careful notes, and cut and paste or print the information you need. Did you find any good material that you were not expecting? (Did you find exciting information on another subject that you might use in another paper? Be sure to take down any information you might use in the future.)

This website, sponsored by the nation's largest company that helps people save, plan, and pay for college, is one of the sites Carmen visited.

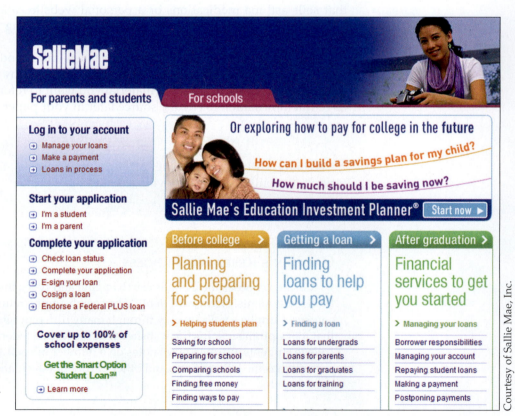

C. Adding Sources to Your Essay and Documenting Them Correctly

Now reread your original essay and the new material you found in your research process. Did you find other or better material than you looked for? Where in the paper will your outside sources be most effective? The next step is to use any of the three methods you learned in Chapter 18, Parts B and C—summary, direct quotation, or indirect quotation (paraphrase)—as you revise your essay and add your outside sources. This section will show you how.

The **MLA style** (named after the Modern Language Association) is a good method for documenting sources quickly and clearly. MLA style is also called *parenthetical* documentation because it puts source information in the body of the essay, in parentheses, rather than in cumbersome footnotes or endnotes.

A correct citation does two things:

- It tells your reader that the material is from an outside source.

- It gives your reader enough information to find the original source.

A correct citation appears in *two places* in your essay:

- **inside** the essay in parentheses

- **at the end** in a Works Cited list

Inside Your Essay: Summarize or Quote and Give Credit

When you quote an outside source in an essay, indicate that the material is not yours by introducing the quote with one of the phrases that you practiced in Part C of Chapter 18. If you use the author's name in this phrase, you will put only the page number in parentheses. If you leave the author unnamed, be sure to include both the author's last name and the page number in parentheses. If your source is a website, no page number is needed—just the author or first word of the title.

Here is the introductory paragraph from Carmen's original essay about credit-card debt.

> In her second year of college, when she was supposed to declare her major, my best friend Maya almost had to declare bankruptcy. In just two years, she had racked up $7,000 in credit-card debt. Starting with necessities such as textbooks and car repairs, Maya soon began charging everything from midnight pizza parties to shopping sprees at the mall. It didn't take long before she had accrued a debt far greater than her part-time campus job could cover. What caused this intelligent student and perhaps others like her to get into so much debt?

- This is a catchy introduction on a good topic. You can probably see why Carmen chose to do more with this paper.

Now read the same paragraph, strengthened and expanded by facts that Carmen found on the Internet:

> In her second year of college, when she was supposed to declare her major, my best friend Maya almost had to declare bankruptcy. In just two years, she had racked up $7,000 in credit-card debt. Starting with necessities such as textbooks and car repairs, Maya soon began charging everything from midnight pizza parties to shopping sprees at the mall. It didn't take long before she had accrued a debt far greater than her part-time campus job could cover. Yet Maya's is not an isolated case of bad financial management. According to a 2009 study conducted by Sallie Mae, the nation's largest college loan and savings company, 84 percent of undergraduates surveyed have at least one credit card. As they move through school, their debt grows, and the typical student graduates with a credit-card balance of $3,173 (Sallie Mae). At least two causes exist for the problem of increasing student credit-card debt, but steps can be taken to help.

● Through her research online, Carmen learned that students all over the country are carrying higher credit-card balances. This information adds power to Maya's story.

● What transitional sentence moves the paragraph from Maya's personal story to

   the bigger picture? _____

● What transitional expression introduces the Sallie Mae report? _____

   _____

● In this instance, the "author" of the article is a corporation, Sallie Mae. The full citation is found on the Works Cited pages at the end of the paper.

   Note: Electronic resources do not have set page numbers because everyone's printer is different, so no page number is shown in parentheses, as it would be with a book or article.

At the End of Your Essay: List Works Cited

The last page of your essay will be a list of all the sources you summarized, directly quoted, or indirectly quoted in your essay, in alphabetical order by the author's last name. If there is no named author, list the entry alphabetically by its title (in quotation marks). Title the page Works Cited, and center the title. Use the models below to format each source properly. (Don't worry about memorizing the forms; even experienced writers often have to check an MLA manual for the correct form.) If a citation goes beyond one line, indent any following lines five spaces to make it clear that the information belongs together.

Books

One author:

   Hijuelos, Oscar. *Thoughts Without Cigarettes: A Memoir*. New York: Gotham, 2011. Print.

More than one author:

Torre, Joe, and Tom Verducci. *The Yankee Years*. New York: Doubleday, 2009.
Print.

Encyclopedia:

"Panama Canal." *Encyclopedia Brittanica*. 2010 ed. Print.

Periodicals

Article in a newspaper:

Barron, James. "The Titanic Fascinated New York, the Port It Never Reached."
New York Times 9 Apr. 2012: 16. Print.

Article in a magazine:

Mueller, Tom. "Unearthing the Colosseum's Secrets." *Smithsonian* Jan. 2011:
26–35. Print.

Article in a journal:

Meehan, William, et al.* "Assessment and Management of Sports-Related
Concussions in United States High Schools." *American Journal of Sports
Medicine* 39.11 (2011): 2304–10. Print.

Electronic Sources

The rules for citing sources found on the World Wide Web have been simplified
(*MLA Handbook for Writers of Research Papers*, Seventh Edition, 2009). But because
websites can change (or disappear), you should include the owner of the site, the
date the site was created or updated, and the date on which you visited the site.
Don't provide the URL address unless the reader cannot locate the source without it.

Website:

"Global Warming." *National Geographic Society*. National Geographic Society,
2012. Web. 15 Feb. 2013.

Article in an online periodical:

Sanghavi, Darshak. "Are TV and Video Games Making Kids Fat?" *Slate.com*.
Slate Group, a Division of the Washington Post Company, 13 Apr. 2012.
Web. 4 Aug. 2012.

Work from a subscription service (give the name of the subscription service you used):

Blomberg, Lindsey. "The Great Pacific Garbage Patch." *E: The Environmental
Magazine* May/June 2011: 8. *MasterFILE Complete*. Web. 20 May 2012.

Multimedia

Film or video:

Bully. Dir. Lee Hirsch. Where We Live Films, 2011. DVD.

Radio or television program:

"Hooked." Narr. Morley Safer. *Sixty Minutes*. CBS. WCBS, New York, 29 Apr.
2012. Television.

Personal interview:

Santos, Mariela. Personal interview. 3 Jan. 2013.

---

* et al.: *and oth*ers; used to indicate multiple authors

These models cover the most common outside sources you will encounter in your research. If you need assistance with another source, you can find other models in one of the many websites that publish MLA guidelines. Try Purdue's Online Writing Lab at **https://owl.english.purdue.edu/owl/resource/747/01/**. (If your instructor requires APA style instead of MLA, click APA at the site above or try **http://writing.wisc.edu/Handbook/DocAPA.html**.)

CARMEN'S RESEARCH PROCESS

During her library and Internet research, Carmen had carefully copied the quotes and facts that she wanted to use in her essay onto index cards or photocopied relevant pages. Now, as she revises her essay to add these sources, she makes sure that she quotes her sources accurately and avoids unintentional plagiarism. As she rewrites her essay, she refers to Chapters 18 and 19. She uses transitional expressions to weave the outside sources smoothly into her essay. Then she prepares a Works Cited list, referring to the models above, as the last page of her paper.

Read Carmen's completed essay with research, "Drastic Plastic: Credit-Card Debt on Campus," at the end of this chapter.

PRACTICE 6

Below are five sources a student has compiled for a research essay on the history of the Olympics. Using the models above to guide you, prepare a Works Cited list for the paper that includes all five sources, properly formatted and in alphabetical order.

- A book by Nigel Spivey called *The Ancient Olympics: A History* that was published in New York, New York by Oxford University Press in 2006

- An article in the August 4, 2008, issue of *Newsweek* magazine called "The Road from Rome" written by David Maraniss and appearing on pages 50–54

- A website called *The Ancient Olympics* that was presented by Tufts University and last updated on August 13, 2004 (the student viewed it on March 18, 2013 at http://www .perseus.tufts.edu/Olympics/)

- A book by David Wallechinsky and Jaime Loucky titled *The Complete Book of the Olympics: 2012 Edition* published by Aurum Press in London in 2012, 1,300 pages long

- An article from the *Wall Street Journal* newspaper called "The Real History of the Olympics" that was written by Kyle Smith and appeared on page W11 on Feb. 10, 2006

Works Cited

_____

_____

_____

_____

_____

_____

_____

_____

_____

_____

PRACTICE 7

Now, using two of the three methods—summary, direct quotation, or indirect quotation—
add your research findings to your essay. Review Chapters 18 and 19 if you need to. Aim
to achieve two things: First, try to add the new material gracefully, using introductory
phrases so that it relates clearly to your ideas in the essay. Second, be careful to avoid
plagiarism by documenting your sources correctly, both inside the essay and in your
Works Cited list.

On the next page, you can read the final draft of Carmen's essay, which she has
strengthened with research.

Every research paper should begin on a new page.

Carmen Gevana
Professor Fawcett
English 100
22 May 2013

Drastic Plastic: Credit-Card Debt on Campus

Introduction

    In her second year of college, when she was supposed to declare her major, my best friend Maya almost had to declare bankruptcy. In just two years, she had racked up $7,000 in credit-card debt. Starting with necessities such as textbooks and car repairs, Maya soon began charging everything from midnight pizza parties to shopping sprees at the mall. It didn't take long before she had accrued a debt far greater than her part-time campus job could cover. Yet Maya's is not an isolated case of bad financial management. According to a 2009 study conducted by Sallie Mae, the nation's largest company that helps people save, plan, and pay for college, 84 percent of undergraduates surveyed have at least one credit card. As they move through school, their debt grows, and the typical student graduates with a credit-card balance of $3,173 (Sallie Mae). At least two causes exist for the problem of increasing student credit-card debt, but steps can be taken to help.

Indirectly quoted facts from Sallie Mae expand the topic; short title given, no page for website.

Thesis statement

Topic sentence: cause #1

    A major cause of growing student debt is that credit-card companies bombard college students the minute they step on campus. Targeting a profitable market of young consumers, these credit companies use many tactics to lure new college students into applying for their cards. Smiling salespeople stand behind tables offering free goodies like candy bars, school sweatshirts, and even airline tickets. They flood students' mailboxes with credit-card offers and pay the college bookstore to stuff applications into every plastic book bag. For my friend Maya, the temptation was too great. Before she had been in college a week, she had already applied for two cards, each with a large credit limit.

Developed by author's ideas, observations

Topic sentence: cause #2

    Maya's credit-card behavior illustrates the second cause for the widespread crisis in college debt—most college students spend more than they can repay. Companies that extend credit typically offer higher limits than their customers can handle. After all, the company makes its profit through charging interest, and interest only accrues if the customer cannot pay off the full balance every month. New credit-card users, especially college students who don't have a lot of extra cash and often lack training in how to handle money responsibly, may rapidly build a balance beyond their means. When this occurs, students may be able to cover little more than the minimum monthly payment of $15 to $25. With high average interest rates, the outstanding balance can grow quickly until the student ends up paying more interest than she originally charged.

Developed by author's ideas, observations

Gevana 2

Topic sentence: effects of heavy debt

The drastic effects of a reliance on plastic are clear. Some students end up with debts in the thousands that trail them for years. If they have to default on their cards or declare bankruptcy, a bad credit report can follow them into adulthood, hurting their chances to rent an apartment or purchase a home or car. Some students

Developed by author's ideas; suicide case source is author's cousin

have even fallen into depression and, in one or two extreme cases, suicide. At my cousin's college, the University of Oklahoma, a student committed suicide after being overwhelmed by a $3,000 credit-card debt. Thankfully, Maya avoided such serious consequences; however, her dependence on credit seriously affected her education. To avoid bankruptcy, she had to leave college for a semester to work full-time and pay off her debt.

Topic sentence: consequences gaining attention and actions taken

Indirect quote from Newsweek article and direct quote from Kobliner's book clearly cited

Fortunately, the consequences of students' ever-increasing credit-card debt are gaining more widespread attention. Lawmakers have been taking action. In May 2009, President Obama signed a federal law that prevents anyone under 21 years old from getting a credit card unless he or she can prove a stable source of income or get a parent to co-sign. The new law also bans credit card companies from baiting young college students with campus pizza parties and giveaways (Wu 16). Yet students should not wait for others to save them. Financial expert Beth Kobliner, in her book *Get a Financial Life*, advises, "Limiting your access to credit is a smart move whether you're a binge shopper or a model of self-control" (49). In short, any student can practice self-discipline

Advice to credit-card users forms conclusion

with credit by following three simple rules: 1) carry just one card, 2) use it only for emergencies, and 3) pay your entire balance every month.

Gevana 3

Works Cited

Works Cited should start a new page

Kobliner, Beth. *Get a Financial Life*. New York: Fireside/Simon, 2009. Print

Sallie Mae. "How Undergraduate Students Use Credit Cards: Sallie Mae's National Study of Usage Rates and Trends." *Salliemae.com*. Sallie Mae, Apr. 2009. Web. 11 May 2013.

Wu, Angela. "College Credit." *Newsweek* 27 Sept. 2010: 16. Print.

Topics for Research

1. Types of fat in foods
2. The effects of (or solutions for) illegal immigration
3. Zoos
4. Environmental topics, such as coral reef destruction or green burial (in ecopods)
5. Arguments for or against stem cell research
6. Prisons in America
7. Methods of persuasion in advertisements
8. Media violence
9. An idea to reform public schools
10. Gun control
11. Writer's choice

EXPLORING ONLINE

http://www.ccc.commnet.edu/mla/index.shtml
A thorough review of the research-paper process, including a section on how to outline your research paper

http://www.csuohio.edu/academic/writingcenter/mla.html
Clear, practical examples of how to insert material from outside sources in your papers

CourseMate for *Evergreen*
Visit *Evergreen* CourseMate for more practices and quizzes, videos to accompany the readings, career and job-search resources, ESL help, and live links to every Exploring Online in the book.

CHAPTER **20**

Writing Under Pressure: The Essay Examination

A: Budgeting Your Time

B: Reading and Understanding the Essay Question

C: Choosing the Correct Paragraph or Essay Pattern

D: Writing the Topic Sentence or the Thesis Statement

Being able to write under pressure is a key skill both in college and in the workplace. Throughout your college career, you will be asked to write **timed papers** in class and to take **essay examinations**. In fact, many English programs base placement and passing on timed essay exams. Clearly, the ability to write under pressure is crucial.

An **essay question** requires the same writing skills that a student uses in composing a paragraph or an essay. Even in history and biology, how well you do on an essay test depends partly on how well you write; yet many students, under the pressure of a test, forget or fail to apply what they know about good writing. This chapter will improve your ability to write under pressure. Many of the sample exam questions on the following pages were taken from real college examinations.

A. Budgeting Your Time

To do well on a timed essay or an essay test, it is not enough to know the material. You must also be able to call forth what you know, organize it, and present it in writing—all under pressure in a limited time.

Since most essay examinations are timed, it is important that you learn how to **budget** your time effectively so that you can devote adequate time to each question *and* finish the test. The following six tips will help you use your time well.

1. **Make sure you know exactly how long the examination lasts**. A one-hour examination may really be only fifty minutes; a two-hour examination may last only one hour and forty-five minutes.

2. **Note the point value of all questions and allot time accordingly to each question**. That is, allot the most time to questions that are worth the most points and less time to ones that are worth fewer.

3. **Decide on an order in which to answer the questions**. You do not have to begin with the first question on the examination and work, in order, to the last. Instead, you may start with the questions worth the most points. Some students prefer to begin with the questions they feel they can answer most easily, thereby guaranteeing points toward the final grade on the examination. Others combine the two methods. No matter which system you use, be sure to allot enough time to the questions that are worth the most points—whether you do them first or last.

4. **Make sure you understand exactly what each question asks you to do; then quickly prewrite and plan your answer**. It is all-important to take a breath, study the question, and make a quick scratch outline or plan of your answer *before you start to write*. Parts B through D of this chapter will guide you through these critical steps.

5. **Time yourself**. As you begin a particular question, calculate when you must be finished with that question in order to complete the examination, and note that time in the margin. As you write, check the clock every five minutes so that you remain on schedule.

6. **Finally, do not count on having enough time to recopy your work**. Skip lines and write carefully so that the instructor can easily read your writing as well as any neat corrections you might make.

PRACTICE 1

Imagine that you are about to take the two-hour history test shown below. Read the test carefully, noting the point value of each question, and then answer the questions that follow the examination.

Part I   Answer both questions. 15 points each.

1. Do you think that the Versailles Peace Treaty was a "harsh" one? Be specific.
2. List the basic principles of Karl Marx. Analyze them in terms of Marx's claim that they are scientific.

Part II   Answer two of the following questions. 25 points each.

3. Describe the origins of, the philosophies behind, and the chief policies of either Communist Russia or Fascist Italy. Be specific.

4. What were the causes of Nelson Mandela's presidential victory in South Africa in 1994?

5. European history of the nineteenth and twentieth centuries has been increasingly related to that of the rest of the world. Why? How? With what consequences for Europe?

Part III   Briefly identify ten of the following. 2 points each.

a. John Locke
b. Franco-Prussian War
c. Stalingrad
d. Cavour
e. Manchuria, 1931
f. Entente Cordiale
g. Existentialism
h. Jacobins
i. The Opium Wars
j. Social Darwinism
k. The Reform Bill of 1832
l. The most interesting reading you have done this term (from the course list)

1. Which part would you do first and why? _____

_____

How much time would you allot to the questions in this part and why? _____

_____

2. Which part would you do second and why? _____

_____

How much time would you allot to the questions in this part and why? _____

_____

3. Which part would you do last and why? _____

_____

How much time would you allot to the questions in this part and why? _____

_____

_____

B. Reading and Understanding the Essay Question

Before you begin writing, carefully examine each question to decide exactly what your purpose is: that is, what the instructor expects you to do.

● This question contains three sets of instructions.

> *Question:* Using <u>either</u> Communist China or Nazi Germany as a model,
> (a) <u>describe</u> the characteristics of a totalitarian <u>state</u>, and
> (b) <u>explain</u> how such a state was <u>created</u>.

- First, you must use "either Communist China or Nazi Germany as a model." That is, you must **choose** *one or the other* as a model.

- Second, you must **describe**, and third, you must **explain**.

- Your answer should consist of two written parts, a **description** and an **explanation**.

It is often helpful to underline the important words, as shown in the previous box, to make sure you understand the entire question and have noted all its parts.

> *The student must* (1) <u>choose</u> to write about <u>either</u> Communist China or Nazi Germany, not both; (2) <u>describe</u> the totalitarian state; (3) <u>explain</u> how such a state was created.

PRACTICE 2

Read each essay question and underline key words. Then, on the lines beneath the question, describe in your own words exactly what the question requires: (1) What directions does the student have to follow? (2) How many parts will the answer contain?

EXAMPLE What were the <u>causes</u> of the Cold War? What were its chief <u>episodes</u>? <u>Why</u> has there <u>not</u> been a "hot" war?

Student must *(1) tell what caused the Cold War (two or more causes), (2) mention main events of Cold War, (3) give reasons why we haven't had a full-scale war. The essay will have three parts: causes, main events, and reasons.*

1. State Newton's First Law and give examples from your own experience.

Student must _____

_____

_____

2. Choose one of the following terms. Define it, give an example of it, and then show how it affects *your* life: (a) freedom of speech, (b) justice for all, (c) equal opportunity.

   Student must _____

   _____

   _____

3. Shiism and Sunnism are the two great branches of Islam. Discuss the religious beliefs and the politics of each branch.

   Student must _____

   _____

4. Name and explain four types of savings institutions. What are three factors that influence one's choice of a savings institution?

   Student must _____

   _____

5. Steroids: the athlete's "unfair advantage." Discuss.

   Student must _____

   _____

   _____

6. Discuss the causes and consequences of the Broad Street cholera epidemic in mid-nineteenth-century London. What was the role of Dr. John Snow?

   Student must _____

   _____

7. Erik Erikson has theorized that adult actions toward children may produce either (a) trust or mistrust, (b) autonomy or self-doubt, (c) initiative or guilt. Choose one of the pairs above and give examples of the kinds of adult behavior that might create these responses in a child.

   Student must _____

   _____

   _____

   _____

8. The sixteenth century is known for the Renaissance, the Reformation, and the Commercial Revolution. Discuss each event, showing why it was important to the history of Western civilization.

   Student must _____

   _____

   _____

9. Define the Monroe Doctrine of the early nineteenth century and weigh the arguments for and against it.

   Student must _____

   _____

10. Simón Bolívar may not have been as great a hero as he was believed to be. Agree or disagree.

    Student must _____

    _____

    _____

    _____

C. Choosing the Correct Paragraph or Essay Pattern

Throughout this book, you have learned how to write various types of paragraphs and compositions. Many examinations will require you simply to **illustrate**, **define**, **compare**, and so forth. How well you answer questions may depend partly on how well you understand these terms.

1. *Illustrate* "behavior modification."
2. *Define* "greenhouse effect."
3. *Compare* Agee and Nin as diarists.

● The key words in these questions are *illustrate*, *define*, and *compare*—**instruction words** that tell you what you are supposed to do and what form your answer should take.

Here is a review list of some common instruction words used in college examinations.

1.	**Classify**:	Gather into categories, types, or kinds according to a single basis of division (see Chapter 11).
2.	**Compare**:	Point out similarities (see Chapter 10). Instructors often use *compare* to mean point out both *similarities* and *differences*.
3.	**Contrast**:	Point out differences (see Chapter 10).
4.	**Describe**:	Give an account of or capture pictorially (see Chapter 7).
5.	**Define**:	State clearly and exactly the meaning of a word or term (see Chapter 9). You may be required to write a single-sentence definition or a full paragraph. Instructors may use *identify* as a synonym for *define* when they want a short definition.
6.	**Discuss**: (analyze, describe, or explain)	Often an instructor uses these terms to mean "thoughtfully examine a subject, approaching it from different angles." These terms allow the writer more freedom of approach than many of the others.
7.	**Discuss causes**:	Analyze the reasons or causes for something; answer the question, Why? (see Chapter 12).
8.	**Discuss effects**:	Analyze the effects, consequences, or results of something (see Chapter 12).
9.	**Evaluate**:	Weigh the pros and cons, advantages and disadvantages (see Chapters 10 and 13).
10.	**Identify**:	Give a capsule who-what-when-where-why answer. Sometimes *identify* is a synonym for *define*.
11.	**Illustrate**:	Give one or more examples (see Chapter 5).
12.	**Narrate**: (trace)	Follow the development of something through time, event by event (see Chapters 6 and 8).
13.	**Summarize**:	Write the substance of a longer work in condensed form (see Chapter 18, Part B).
14.	**Take a stand**:	Persuade; argue for a particular position (see Chapter 13).

You should have no trouble deciding what kind of paragraph or composition to use if the question uses one of the terms just defined—*contrast, trace, classify,* and so on. However, questions are often worded in such a way that you have to discover what kind of paragraph or essay is required. What kind of paragraph or essay is required by each of the following questions?

EXAMPLE   What is *schizophrenia*?
(*Write a paragraph to. . . .*)   *define*

1. In one concise paragraph, give the main ideas of Simone de Beauvoir's famous book *The Second Sex*.   _____

2. What is the difference between veins and arteries?   _____

3. Follow the development of Wynton Marsalis's musical style.   _____

4. How do jet- and propeller-driven planes differ?   _____

5. Who or what is each of the following: the Gang of Four, Ho Chi Minh, Tiananmen Square?   _____

6. Explain the causes of the American Civil War.   _____

7. Explain what is meant by "magical realism."   _____

8. Take a stand for or against legalizing marijuana in this country. Give reasons to support your stand.   _____

9. Give two recent instances of military hazing that you consider "out of control."   _____

10. Divide into groups the different kinds of websites giving out medical information.   _____

D. Writing the Topic Sentence or the Thesis Statement

A good way to ensure that your answer truly addresses itself to the question is to compose a topic sentence or a thesis statement that contains the key words of the question.

Question: How do fixed-rate and adjustable-rate mortgages differ?

- The key words in this question are *fixed-rate* and *adjustable-rate mortgages*, and *differ*.

- What kind of paragraph or essay would be appropriate for this question? _____

_____

_____

Topic sentence or *thesis statement of answer*: Fixed-rate and adjustable-rate mortgages differ in three basic ways.

- The answer repeats the key words of the question: *fixed-rate, adjustable-rate, mortgages*, and *differ*.

PRACTICE 4

Here are eight examination questions. Write a topic sentence or thesis statement for each question by using the question as part of the answer. Pretend that you know all the material. Even though you may not know anything about the subjects, you should be able to formulate a topic sentence or thesis statement based on the question.

1. Contrast high school requirements in Jamaica with those in the United States.

   Topic sentence or thesis statement: _____

   _____

2. Do you think that the terrorist attacks of September 11, 2001, had any positive effects

   on Americans?

   Topic sentence or thesis statement: _____

   _____

   _____

3. What steps can a busy person take to reduce the destructive impact of stress in his or her life?

   Topic sentence or thesis statement: _____

   _____

   _____

4. Gay couples should be allowed to adopt children. Agree or disagree with this statement.

   Topic sentence or thesis statement: _____

   _____

   _____

5. Assume that you manage a small shop that sells men's apparel. What activities would

   you undertake to promote the sale of sportswear?

   Topic sentence or thesis statement: _____

   _____

   _____

6. The U.S. government should cover the medical costs of AIDS. Agree or disagree with

   this statement.

   Topic sentence or thesis statement: _____

   _____

   _____

7. The state should subsidize students in medical school because the country needs

   more doctors. Agree or disagree with this statement.

   Topic sentence or thesis statement: _____

   _____

   _____

8. Does religion play a more vital role in people's lives today than it did in your parents'

   generation?

   Topic sentence or thesis statement: _____

   _____

   _____

Checklist

The Process of Answering an Essay Question

☐ 1. Survey the test and note the point value for each question.

☐ 2. Calculate how much time you need for each question. Then check the clock as you write so that you complete all the questions.

☐ 3. Read each question carefully, underlining important words.

☐ 4. Determine how many parts the answer should contain.

☐ 5. Considering your audience (usually the teacher) and purpose, choose the paragraph or essay pattern that would best answer the question.

☐ 6. Write a topic sentence or a thesis statement that repeats the key words of the question.

☐ 7. Quickly freewrite or brainstorm ideas on scrap paper and arrange them in a logical order, making a scratch outline or plan.

☐ 8. Write your paragraph or essay neatly, skipping lines so you will have enough room to make corrections.

EXPLORING ONLINE

http://www.google.com

Don't get nervous; get an A. Search "taking essay exams" and find advice that truly helps you. You might wish to print it out.

http://www.counselingcenter.illinois.edu/?page_id=114

Do you get so anxious taking tests that you don't do your best? Explore this excellent site from the University of Illinois for tips, help, and a deeper understanding of the problem.

CourseMate for *Evergreen*

Visit *Evergreen* CourseMate for more practices and quizzes, videos to accompany the readings, career and job-search resources, ESL help, and live links to every Exploring Online in the book.

Writer's Workshop

Analyze a Social Problem

Because essays are longer and more complex than paragraphs, organizing an essay can be a challenge, even for experienced writers. Techniques like having a clear *controlling idea*, a good *thesis statement*, and a *plan or an outline* all help an essay writer manage the task. Another useful approach is dividing the subject into three parts, as one student does here. In your group or class, read the essay, aloud if possible, underlining the parts you find most powerful and paying special attention to organization.

It's Great to Get Old

(1) I knock at the door and patiently await an answer. I listen and hear the thump of a cane on the hard wood floor, edging slowly toward the door. "It's great to get old," my grandmother says facetiously[1] as she opens the door, apologizing for making me wait. Through her I learn firsthand the problems of the aged. Loneliness, lack of money, and ailing health are just some of the problems old people must deal with.

(2) For one thing, loneliness seems endemic[2] among old people in America. With difficulty getting around, many spend most of their time confined to their apartments, awaiting visits from family or friends. Through my grandmother, I realize that as much as old people's families may care about them, the family members obviously have lives of their own and cannot visit as much as old persons would like. And when people are very old, most of their friends have already died, so they spend most of their time alone.

(3) Poor health is also a major problem. Any number of physical ailments create a problem. Cataracts, for example, are a common eye problem among old people. Health problems can make life very difficult for an old person.

(4) Last but not least is the financial burden old people must cope with. The rising costs of basic necessities such as food, housing, and health care are especially difficult for old people to meet. Sadly, most are forced to compromise what they need for what they can afford. Take, for example, an old person who must choose between food and medications. This person might buy inexpensive pasta for dinner every night or sometimes not eat at all in order to pay for medications. Good nutrition must be forfeited for what he or she can afford. Financial problems also make life very difficult for an old person.

---

[1] facetiously: humorously

[2] endemic: typical in a certain place or population

(5) There is no easy way to ease the problems of the aged. Simply being aware of them is an important step in the right direction. If we turn our attention and compassion toward the elderly, we can begin to help them find solutions.

—Denise Nelley, Student

1. How effective is Ms. Nelley's essay?

    _____ Strong thesis statement?   _____ Good supporting details?

    _____ Logical organization?   _____ Effective conclusion?

2. Did the introductory paragraph catch your interest? Explain why or why not.

3. What is the controlling idea of the essay? What is the thesis statement?

4. This writer has skillfully organized her ideas. Her thesis names three problems facing the elderly. What are they? Does the body of the essay discuss these three problems in the same order that the thesis names them? If not, what changes would you suggest?

5. Are the three problems fully explained in paragraphs 2, 3, and 4? That is, does Ms. Nelley provide enough support for each problem? If not, what revision suggestions would you give the writer, especially for paragraph 3?

6. This student movingly presents some problems of the elderly. Do you think she should have included solutions? Why or why not?

7. Can you spot any error patterns (the same error two or more times) that this student should watch out for?

GROUP WORK

In your group or class, evaluate (or grade) Ms. Nelley's essay. Then, based on your evaluation, decide what changes or revisions would most improve the essay, and revise it accordingly, as if it were your own. If your group wishes to add any new ideas or support, brainstorm together and choose the strongest ideas. Rewrite as needed.

When you are done, evaluate the essay again, with your changes.

WRITING AND REVISING IDEAS

1. Discuss the ways in which a loved one's experience has taught you about a problem (addiction, AIDS, disability, and so on).

2. Analyze a social problem (racial profiling or shoplifting, for example).

Unit 5

Improving Your Writing

CHAPTER 21

Revising for Consistency and Parallelism

A: Consistent Tense

B: Consistent Number and Person

C: Parallelism

All good writing is **consistent**. That is, each sentence and paragraph in the final draft should move along smoothly without confusing shifts in **tense**, **number**, or **person**. In addition, good writing uses **parallel structure** to balance two or more similar words, phrases, or clauses.

Although you should be aware of consistency and parallelism as you write the first draft of your paragraph or essay, you might find it easier to **revise** for them—that is, to write your first draft and then, as you read it again later, check and rewrite for consistency and parallelism.

A. Consistent Tense

Consistency of tense means using the same verb tense whenever possible throughout a sentence or an entire paragraph. Do not shift from one verb tense to another—for example, from present to past or from past to present—unless you really mean to indicate different times.

1.	Inconsistent tense:	We *stroll* down Bourbon Street as the jazz bands *began* to play.
2.	Consistent tense:	We *strolled* down Bourbon Street as the jazz bands *began* to play.
3.	Consistent tense:	We *stroll* down Bourbon Street as the jazz bands *begin* to play.

- Sentence 1 begins in the present tense with the verb *stroll* but then slips into the past tense with the verb *began.* The tenses are inconsistent since both actions (strolling and beginning) occur at the same time.

- Sentence 2 is consistent. Both verbs, *strolled* and *began,* are now in the past tense.

- Sentence 3 is also consistent, using the present tense forms of both verbs, *stroll* and *begin.* The present tense here gives a feeling of immediacy, as if the action is happening now.*

Of course, you should use different verb tenses in a sentence or paragraph if they convey the meaning that you wish to convey:

> 4.   Last fall I *took* English 02; now I *am taking* English 13.

- The verbs in this sentence accurately show the time relationship between the two classroom experiences.†

PRACTICE 1

Read the following sentences carefully for meaning. Then correct any inconsistencies of tense by changing the verbs that do not accurately show the time of events.

EXAMPLE   I took a deep breath and opened the door; there stands a well-dressed man with a large box.

  Consistent: I took a deep breath and opened the door; there ~~stands~~ *stood* a well-dressed man with a large box.

  or

  Consistent: I ~~took~~ *take* a deep breath and ~~opened~~ *open* the door; there stands a well-dressed man with a large box.

1. Two seconds before the buzzer sounded, Lebron James sank a basket from midcourt, and the crowd goes wild.

2. Nestlé introduced instant coffee in 1938; it takes eight years to develop this product.

3. We expand our sales budget, doubled our research, and soon saw positive results.

---

* For more work on spotting verbs, see Chapter 26, "The Simple Sentence," Part C.

† For more work on particular verb tenses and forms, see Chapters 29, 30, and 31.

4. For 20 years, Dr. Dulfano observed animal behavior and seeks clues to explain the increasing violence among human beings.

5. I knew how the system works.

6. I was driving south on Interstate 90 when a truck approaches with its high beams on.

7. Two brown horses graze quietly in the field as the sun rose and the mist disappeared.

8. Lollie had a big grin on her face as she walks over and kicked the Coke machine.

9. Maynard stormed down the hallway, goes right into the boss's office, and shouts, "I want curtains in my office!"

10. The nurses quietly paced the halls, making sure their patients rest comfortably.

PRACTICE 2

Inconsistencies of tense are most likely to occur within paragraphs and longer pieces of writing. Therefore, it is important to revise your writing for tense consistency. Read this paragraph for meaning. Then revise, correcting inconsistencies of tense by changing incorrect verbs.

It was 1850. A poor German-born peddler named Levi Strauss came to San Francisco, trying to sell canvas cloth to tent makers. By chance he met a miner who complained that sturdy work pants are hard to find. Strauss had an idea, measures the man, and makes him a pair of canvas pants. The miner loved his new breeches, and Levi Strauss goes into business. Although he ordered more canvas, what he gets is a brown French cloth called *serge de Nîmes*, which Americans soon called "denim." Strauss liked the cloth but had the next batch dyed blue. He became successful selling work pants to such rugged men as cowboys and lumberjacks. In the 1870s, hearing about a tailor in Nevada adding copper rivets to a pair of the pants to make them stronger, Strauss patents the idea. When he died in 1902, Levi Strauss was famous in California, but the company keeps growing. In the 1930s, when Levi's jeans became popular in the East, both men and women wear them. By 2000, people all over the world had purchased 2.5 billion pairs of jeans.

U.S. soldiers trying to rest in "Ranger graves" like those the student describes in Practice 3

PRACTICE 3

The following paragraph is written in the past tense. Rewrite it in consistent present tense. Cross out each past tense verb and write the present tense form above it. Make sure all verbs agree with their subjects.*

The desert heat was vicious under the burlap that camouflaged me. I lay in my "Ranger grave," Army slang for the shallow holes soldiers dug into the sand, just big enough to conceal their bodies. A few thoughts worked their way through the haze of my brain, but mostly I dreamed about water—icy, sparkling water. I almost heard the clink of ice cubes in a Mason jar, dripping with condensation. I barely noticed the fine sand in my eyes. I didn't have enough fluid in my body to make tears. "Water truck!" The call floated down the nearly invisible line of graves that stretched across the sand. I peeked out as the water truck drove away through shimmering waves of heat. It left behind a water buffalo, a huge tank of water for the ground troops in our area. As the new guy in the squad, I had to fill our canteens. With my monkey suit for chemical attack, my machine gun, and extra ammo, I trudged out. The desert coated me with sand. My helmet felt huge on my head. Finally, I reached the tank and mentally pumped myself up. I was a paratrooper, a member of the 82nd Airborne, elite fighting force of the U.S. Army! My sense of duty and my mental ice pushed me onward. I sipped a little hot water, filled the canteens, and dragged them back to the men.

—Ray Christian, Student

———

* For more work on agreement, see Chapter 29, "Present Tense (Agreement)."

PRACTICE 4

The following paragraph is written in the present tense. Rewrite it in consistent past tense,* crossing out each present tense verb and writing the past tense form above it.

In the summer of 1816, four friends share a house in Switzerland. Days of rain force them to stay indoors. They begin telling ghost stories to ease the boredom. For awhile, they read aloud from *Tales of the Dead*, a collection of horror stories full of eerie graveyards, swirling fog, and restless spirits. Then one night, they decide to hold a contest to see who can write the most frightening ghost story. All four feel eager to compete. Two of the friends—Percy Bysshe Shelley and Lord Byron—are already famous poets. The other two—Dr. John Polidori and Mary Wollstonecraft Godwin, Shelley's wife-to-be—are also writers. Midnight passes, and they retire to their bedrooms. Mary closes her eyes, and imagination takes over. In her mind's eye, she sees a science student kneeling beside a creature he constructed. It is a hideous corpse of a man, but suddenly, it twitches with life. Horror-stricken, the young man runs away from his creation, hoping that the spark of life will sputter and die. Later, though, he wakes to find the monster standing over his bed. Following this nightmare, Mary writes her novel *Frankenstein* in a two-month rush. Published in 1818, *Frankenstein* becomes a classic, read by people around the world.

PRACTICE 5

Longer pieces of writing often use both the past tense and the present tense. However, switching correctly from one tense to the other requires care. Read the following essay carefully and note when a switch from one tense to another is logically necessary. Then revise verbs as needed.

A QUICK HISTORY OF CHOCOLATE

Most of us now take solid chocolate—especially candy bars—so much for granted that we find it hard to imagine a time when chocolate didn't exist. However, this delicious food becomes an eating favorite only about 150 years ago.

The ancient peoples of Central America began cultivating cacao beans almost 3,000 years ago. A cold drink made from the beans is served to Hernando Cortés, the Spanish conqueror, when he arrives at the Aztec court of Montezuma in 1519. The Spaniards took the beverage home to their king. He likes it so much that he kept the formula a secret. For the next 100 years, hot chocolate was the private drink of the Spanish nobility. Slowly,

---

* For more work on the past tense, see Chapter 30, "Past Tense."

it makes its way into the fashionable courts of France, England, and Austria. In 1657, a Frenchman living in London opened a shop where devices for making the beverage are sold at a high price. Soon chocolate houses appeared in cities throughout Europe. Wealthy clients met in them, sipped chocolate, conducted business, and gossip.

During the 1800s, chocolate became a chewable food. The breakthrough comes in 1828 when cocoa butter was extracted from the bean. Twenty years later, an English firm mixed the butter with chocolate liquor, which results in the first solid chocolate. Milton Hershey's first candy bar come on the scene in 1894, and Tootsie Rolls hit the market two years later. The popularity of chocolate bars soar during World War I when they are given to soldiers for fast energy. M&Ms gave the industry another boost during World War II; soldiers needed candy that wouldn't melt in their hands.

On the average, Americans today eat ten pounds of hard chocolate a year. Their number-one choice is Snickers, which sold more than a billion bars every year. However, Americans consume far less chocolate than many Western Europeans. The average Dutch person gobbled up more than 15 pounds a year while a Swiss packed away almost 20 pounds. Chocolate is obviously an international favorite.

B. Consistent Number and Person

Just as important as verb tense consistency is consistency of **number** and **person**.

Consistency of Number

Consistency of number means avoiding confusing shifts from singular to plural or from plural to singular within a sentence or paragraph. Choose *either* singular *or* plural; then be *consistent*.

1.	Inconsistent number:	*The wise jogger* chooses *their* running shoes with care.
2.	Consistent number:	*The wise jogger* chooses *his or her* running shoes with care.
3.	Consistent number:	*Wise joggers* choose *their* running shoes with care.

- Since the subject of sentence 1, *the wise jogger,* is singular, use of the plural pronoun *their* is *inconsistent.*

- Sentence 2 is *consistent*. The singular pronoun *his* (or *her*) now clearly refers to the singular *jogger.*

- In sentence 3, the plural number is used *consistently. Their* clearly refers to the plural *joggers.*

If you begin a paragraph by referring to a website designer as *she,* continue to refer to *her* in the **third person singular** throughout the paragraph:

> The new *website designer* created this streamlined website for our company. *She* explained that our old site was hard for customers to navigate. A slight increase in orders despite the difficult economy is probably the result of *her* work. Needless to say, we plan to use *her* again.

Do not confuse the reader by shifting unnecessarily to *they* or *you.*

PRACTICE 6

Correct any inconsistencies of **number** in the following sentences.* Also make necessary changes in verb agreement.

EXAMPLE   A singer must protect ~~their~~ *his or her* voice.

1. An individual's self-esteem can affect their performance.
2. Jorge started drinking diet sodas only last November, but already he hates the taste of it.
3. The headlines encouraged us, but we feared that it wasn't accurate.
4. The defendant has decided that he will represent oneself.
5. Dreams fascinate me; it is like another world.
6. If a person doesn't know how to write well, they will face limited job opportunities.
7. Oxford University boasts of the great number of ancient manuscripts they own.
8. Always buy corn and tomatoes when it is in season.
9. The average American takes their freedom for granted.
10. Women have more opportunities than ever before. She is freer to go to school, get a job, and choose the kind of life she wants.

---

* For more practice in agreement of pronouns and antecedents, see Chapter 33, "Pronouns," Part B.

Consistency of Person

Consistency of person—closely related to consistency of number—means using the same *person,* or indefinite pronoun form, throughout a sentence or paragraph whenever possible.

> *First person* is the most personal and informal in written work: (singular)
> *I,* (plural) *we*
>
> *Second person* speaks directly to the reader: (singular and plural) *you*
>
> *Third person* is the most formal and most frequently used in college writing:
> (singular) *he, she, it, one, a person, an individual, a student,* and so on; (plural)
> *they, people, individuals, students,* and so on

Avoid confusing shifts from one person to another. Choose one, and then be *consistent.* When using a noun in a general way—*a person, the individual, the parent*—be careful not to slip into the second person, *you,* but continue to use the third person, *he or she.*

> 4. Inconsistent person   A *player* collects $200 when *you* pass "Go."
>
> 5. Consistent person: A *player* collects $200 when *he or she* passes "Go."
>
> 6. Consistent person: *You* collect $200 when *you* pass "Go."

- In sentence 4, the person shifts unnecessarily from the third person, *a player,* to the second person, *you.* The result is confusing.

- Sentence 5 maintains consistent third person. *He or she* now clearly refers to the third person subject, *a player.*

- Sentence 6 is also consistent, using the second person, *you,* throughout.

Of course, inconsistencies of person and number often occur together, as shown in the next box.

> 7. Inconsistent person   Whether *one* enjoys or resents commercials,
>   and number: *we* are bombarded with them every hour of the day.
>
> 8. Consistent person   Whether *we* enjoy or resent commercials, *we*
>   and number: are bombarded with them every hour of the day.
>
> 9. Consistent person   Whether *one* enjoys or resents commercials,
>   and number: *he or she* (or *one*) is bombarded with them every
>   hour of the day.

- Sentence 7 shifts from the third person singular, *one,* to the first person plural, *we.*

- Sentence 8 uses the first person plural consistently.

- Sentence 9 uses the third person singular consistently.

PRACTICE 7

Correct the shifts in **person** in these sentences. If necessary, change the verbs to make them agree with any new subjects.

> **EXAMPLE** One should eliminate saturated fats from ~~your~~ *one's* diet.

1. Sooner or later, most addicts realize that you can't just quit when you want to.

2. One problem facing students on this campus is that a person doesn't know when the library will be open and when it will be closed.

3. One should rely on reason, not emotion, when they are forming opinions about such charged issues as abortion.

4. I have reached a time in my life when what others expect is less important than what one really wants to do.

5. Members of the orchestra should meet after the concert and bring your instruments and music.

6. The wise mother knows that she is asking for trouble if you let a small child watch violent television shows.

7. The student who participates in this program will spend six weeks in Spain and Morocco. You will study the art and architecture firsthand, working closely with an instructor.

8. You shouldn't judge a person by the way they dress.

9. If you have been working that hard, one needs a vacation.

10. People who visit the Caribbean for the first time are struck by the lushness of the landscape. The sheer size of the flowers and fruit amazes you.

PRACTICE 8

The following paragraph consistently uses third person singular—*the job applicant, the job seeker, he or she.* For practice in revising for consistency, rewrite the paragraph in **consistent third person plural**. Begin by changing *the job applicant* to *job applicants*. Then change verbs, nouns, and pronouns as necessary.

    In a job interview these days, the job applicant should stress his or her personal skills, rather than only technical skills. This strategy could increase his or her chances of getting hired. The job seeker should point out such skills as speaking and writing confidently, working well on a team, solving problems quickly, or managing people. These days, many employers assume that if an applicant has excellent "soft skills" like these, he or she can be trained in the technical fine points of the job.

_____

_____

_____

_____

_____

PRACTICE 9

Revise the following essay for inconsistencies of person and number. Correct any confusing shifts (changing words if necessary) to make the writing clear and *consistent* throughout.

IS OUR IDEA OF RACE CHANGING?

What is race, anyway? Is it skin color, country of origin, cultural traditions, biology? The students in Samuel Richards' sociology class at Pennsylvania State University are pondering these questions. Professor Richards encourages him or her to move beyond the black and white labels most people apply to themself and others.

To make his point that race and ethnicity are complex aspects of identity, Richards began offering a DNA test to any student who wanted to learn more about their racial heritage. Most students, naturally curious about his or her ancestors, rushed to sign up. The DNA tests were performed through a simple mouth swab by a professor of genetics, Mark Shriver. He tested for four DNA groups: Western European, West African, East Asian, and Native American.

The results received national attention. Many students discovered that he or she was mixed race, including some who believed they were 100 percent Caucasian or Asian. One white student, for example, learned that 14 percent of his DNA was African and 6 percent East Asian. "I was like, oh my God, that's me," he recalls. A.J. Dobbins knew he was black and perhaps had a white ancestor, but he was amazed to learn that one's DNA is 28 percent Caucasian, 70 percent sub-Saharan African, and 2 percent Native American.

Many hope that this experiment will chip away at prejudice, shaking people out of his rigid thinking. Critics, however, say the genetic tests are incomplete. They call DNA testing a fad and scoff at some of Richard's students who hoped to test multiracial in order to upset his or her parents. Yet more and more everyday people and celebrities are getting their DNA tested. Columnist Leonard Pitts, Jr., Oprah, and Brazilian soccer star Obina, to name just three, have used DNA results and historic records to trace one's heritage.

C. Parallelism

Parallelism, or **parallel structure**, is an effective way to add smoothness and power to your writing. **Parallelism** is a balance of two or more similar words, phrases, or clauses.

Compare the two versions of each of these sentences:

1. She likes dancing, swimming, and to box.
2. She likes *dancing, swimming,* and *boxing.*
3. The cable runs across the roof; the north wall is where it runs down.
4. The cable runs *across the roof* and *down the north wall.*
5. He admires people with strong convictions and who think for themselves.
6. He admires people *who have strong convictions* and *who think for themselves.*

● Sentences 2, 4, and 6 use **parallelism** to express parallel ideas.

● In sentence 2, *dancing, swimming,* and *boxing* are parallel; all three are the *-ing* forms of verbs, used here as nouns.

● In sentence 4, *across the roof* and *down the north wall* are parallel prepositional phrases, each consisting of a preposition and its object.

● In sentence 6, *who have strong convictions* and *who think for themselves* are parallel clauses beginning with the word *who.*

Sometimes two entire sentences can be parallel:

In a democracy we are all equal before the law. In a dictatorship we are all equal before the police.

—Millor Fernandes

● In what way are these two sentences parallel? _____

_____

Certain special constructions require parallel structure:

7. The fruit is *both* tasty *and* fresh.
8. He *either* loves you *or* hates you.
9. Yvette *not only* plays golf *but also* swims like a pro.
10. I would *rather* sing in the chorus *than* perform a solo.

● Each of these constructions has two parts:
   both . . . and
   (n)either . . . (n)or
   not only . . . but also
   rather . . . than

● The words, phrases, or clauses following each part must be parallel:
   tasty . . . fresh
   loves you . . . hates you
   plays golf . . . swims like a pro
   sing in the chorus . . . perform a solo

PRACTICE 10

Rewrite each of the following sentences, using parallel structure to accent parallel ideas.

EXAMPLE The summer in Louisiana is very hot and has high humidity. *The summer*

in Louisiana is very hot and humid.

1. Teresa is a gifted woman—a chemist, does the carpentry, and she can cook.

   _____

   _____

2. The shape of the rock, how big it was, and its color reminded me of a small turtle.

   _____

   _____

3. He is an affectionate husband, a thoughtful son, and kind to his kids.

   _____

   _____

4. Marvin was happy to win the chess tournament and he also felt surprised.

   _____

   _____

5. Dr. Tien is the kindest physician I know; she has the most concern of any physician I know.

   _____

   _____

6. Joe would rather work on a farm than spending time in an office.

   _____

   _____

7. Every afternoon in the mountains, it either rains or there is hail.

   _____

   _____

8. *Sesame Street* teaches children nursery rhymes, songs, how to be courteous, and being kind.

   _____

   _____

9. Alexis would rather give orders than taking them.

   _____

   _____

10. His writing reveals not only intelligence but also it is humorous.

    _____

    _____

PRACTICE 11

Write one sentence that is parallel to each sentence that follows, creating pairs of parallel sentences.

EXAMPLE On Friday night, she dressed in silk and sipped champagne.

On Monday morning, she put on her jeans and crammed for a history test.

1. When he was 20, he worked seven days a week in a fruit store.

   _____

   _____

2. The child in me wants to run away from problems.

   _____

   _____

3. The home team charged enthusiastically onto the field.

   _____

   _____

4. "Work hard and keep your mouth shut" is my mother's formula for success.

   _____

   _____

5. The men thought the movie was amusing.

   _____

   _____

PRACTICE 12

The following paragraph contains both correct and faulty parallel structures. Revise the faulty parallelism.

During World War II, United States Marines who fought in the Pacific possessed a powerful weapon that was also unbeatable: Navajo Code Talkers. Creating a secret code, Code Talkers sent and were translating vital military information. Four hundred twenty Navajos memorized the code, and it was used by them. It consisted of both common Navajo words and there were also about 400 invented words. For example, Code Talkers used the Navajo words for *owl*, *chicken hawk*, and *swallow* to describe different kinds of aircraft. Because Navajo is a complex language that is also uncommon, the Japanese military could not break the code. Although Code Talkers helped the Allied Forces win the war, their efforts were not publicly recognized until the code was declassified in 1968. On August 14, 1982, the first Navajo Code Talkers Day honored these heroes, who not only had risked their lives but also been developing one of the few unbroken codes in history.

PRACTICE 13

The following essay contains both correct and faulty parallel structures. Revise the faulty parallelism.

VINCENT VAN GOGH

Vincent Van Gogh sold only one painting in his lifetime, but his oil paintings later influenced modern art and establishing him as one of the greatest artists of all time. Born in Holland in 1853, Van Gogh struggled to find an inspiring career. After failing as a tutor and being a clergyman, he began to paint. Van Gogh's younger brother Theo supported him with money and also sending art supplies. Eventually, Van Gogh went to live with Theo in Paris, where the young artist was introduced to Impressionism, a style of painting that emphasizes light at different times of day. Using vivid colors and also with broad brush strokes, Van Gogh made powerful pictures full of feeling. His favorite subjects were landscapes, still lifes, sunflowers, and drawing everyday people. Perhaps his most famous picture, *Starry Night*, shows a wild night sky over a French village, with the moon and stars swirling in fiery circles.

Starry Night, Vincent Van Gogh

Starry Night was painted in southern France, a place of great beauty and the light was wonderful. There, in the last three years of his life, Van Gogh created 186 of his greatest works. Always shy and sometimes feeling depressed, he began to suffer from episodes of mental illness. Theo gentle but firmly urged him to keep painting. For years, Van Gogh's death in 1890 was considered a suicide by gunshot, but a recent book claims that the artist was bullied by local teenagers and they shot him. When Theo died soon after, his widow Joanna took the paintings back to Holland and was working hard to get recognition for her brother-in-law's genius. Today, the dynamic paintings of Vincent Van Gogh are admired, studied, and receive love all over the world.

EXPLORING ONLINE

http://www.vangoghmuseum.nl/vgm/index.jsp
Visit the Van Gogh Museum in the Netherlands and explore. Take notes on your experience.

http://www.vangoghgallery.com/
Find *Wheatfield with Crows*. Do you see any details in the painting that would suggest it was made just before the artist committed suicide?

EXPLORING ONLINE

http://grammar.ccc.commnet.edu/grammar/consistency.htm
Review consistency with examples, "repairs," and self tests.

http://grammar.ccc.commnet.edu/grammar/parallelism.htm
Write more stylishly with parallel words and phrases.

CourseMate for *Evergreen*
Visit *Evergreen* CourseMate for more practices and quizzes, videos to accompany the readings, career and job-search resources, ESL help, and live links to every Exploring Online in the book.

Revising for Sentence Variety

Good writers pay attention to **sentence variety**. They notice how sentences work together within a paragraph, and they seek a mix of different sentence lengths and types. Experienced writers have a variety of sentence patterns from which to choose. They try not to overuse one pattern.

This chapter will present several techniques for varying your sentences and paragraphs. Some of them you may already know and use, perhaps unconsciously. The purpose of this chapter is to make you more conscious of the **choices** available to you as a writer.

Remember, you achieve sentence variety by practicing, by systematically **revising** your papers, and by trying out new types of sentences or combinations of sentences.

A. Mix Long and Short Sentences

One of the basic ways to achieve sentence variety is to use both long and short sentences. Beginning writers tend to overuse short, simple sentences, which quickly become monotonous. Notice the length of the sentences in the following paragraph:

(1) There is one positive result of the rising crime rate. (2) This has been the growth of neighborhood crime prevention programs. (3) These programs really work. (4) They teach citizens to patrol their neighborhoods. (5) They teach citizens to work with the police. (6) They have dramatically reduced crime in cities and towns across the country. (7) The idea is catching on.

The sentences in the paragraph above are all nearly the same length, and the effect is choppy and almost childish. Now read this revised version, which contains a variety of sentence lengths:

(1) One cause of the falling crime rate in some cities is the growth of neighborhood crime prevention programs. (2) These programs really work. (3) By patrolling their neighborhoods and working with the police, citizens have shown that they can dramatically reduce crime. (4) The idea is catching on.

This paragraph is more effective because it mixes two short sentences, 2 and 4, and two longer sentences, 1 and 3. Although short sentences can be used effectively anywhere in a paragraph or an essay, they can be especially useful as introductions or conclusions, like sentence 4 above. Note the powerful effect of short sentences used between longer ones in the paragraph that follows. Underline the short sentences:

(1) Biting into a tabasco pepper is like aiming a flame-thrower at your parted lips. (2) There might be little reaction at first, but then the burn starts to grow. (3) A few seconds later the chili mush in your mouth reaches critical mass and your palate prepares for liftoff. (4) The message spreads. (5) The sweat glands open, your eyes stream, your nose runs, your stomach warms up, your heart accelerates, and your lungs breathe faster. (6) All this is normal. (7) But bite off more than your body can take, and you will be left coughing, sneezing, and spitting. (8) Tears stripe your cheeks, and your mouth belches like a dragon celebrating its return to life. (9) Eater beware!

—Jeremy MacClancy, *Consuming Culture: Why You Eat What You Eat*

PRACTICE 1

Revise and rewrite the following paragraph in a variety of sentence lengths. Recombine sentences in any way you wish. You may add connecting words or drop words, but do not alter the meaning of the paragraph. Compare your work with a fellow student's.

The park is alive with motion today. Joggers pound up and down the boardwalk. Old folks watch them from the benches. Couples row boats across the lake. The boats are green and wooden. Two teenagers hurl a Frisbee back and forth. They yell and leap. A shaggy white dog dashes in from nowhere. He snatches the red disk in his mouth. He bounds away. The teenagers run after him.

_____

_____

_____

_____

_____

B. Use a Question, a Command, or an Exclamation

The most commonly used sentence is the **declarative sentence**, which is a statement. However, an occasional carefully placed **question**, **command**, or **exclamation** is an effective way to achieve sentence variety.

The Question

> *Can exercise make us smarter?* Amazingly, the answer is yes, but only if we do certain kinds of exercise. After a decade of study, sports scientists report that students who ran or walked briskly for 30 minutes scored better on memory tests. Other studies confirm these results. Aerobic exercises like running, swimming, and brisk walking cause a dramatic increase in blood flow that stimulates the growth of new brain cells. Thus, a heart-pounding "cardio" workout three to five times a week actually boosts intelligence.

This paragraph begins with a question. The writer does not really expect the reader to answer it. Rather, it is a **rhetorical question**, one that will be answered by the writer in the course of the paragraph. A rhetorical question used as a topic sentence can provide a colorful change from the usual declarative sentences: *How healthy is the American diet? What is courage? Is cheating worth the risks?*

The Command and the Exclamation

> (1) Try to imagine using failure as a description of an animal's behavior. (2) Consider a dog barking for fifteen minutes, and someone saying, "He really isn't very good at barking, I'd give him a C." (3) How absurd! (4) It is impossible for an animal to fail because there is no provision for evaluating natural behavior. (5) Spiders construct webs, not successful or unsuccessful webs. (6) Cats hunt mice; if they aren't successful in one attempt, they simply go after another. (7) They don't lie there and whine, complaining about the one that got away, or have a nervous breakdown because they failed. (8) Natural behavior simply is! (9) So apply the same logic to your own behavior and rid yourself of the fear of failure.
>
> —Dr. Wayne W. Dyer, *Your Erroneous Zones*

The previous paragraph begins and ends with **commands**, or **imperative sentences**. Sentences 1, 2, and 9 address the reader directly and have as their implied subject *you*. They tell the reader to do something: *(You) try to imagine . . . , (you) consider . . . , (you) apply. . . .* Commands are most frequently used in giving directions,* but they can be used occasionally, as in the previous paragraph, for sentence variety.

Sentences 3 and 8 in the Dyer paragraph are **exclamations**, sentences that express strong emotion and end with an exclamation point. These should be used very sparingly. In fact, some writers avoid them altogether, striving for words that convey strong emotion instead.

Be careful with the question, the command, and the exclamation as options in your writing. Try them out, but use them—especially the exclamation—sparingly.

WRITING ASSIGNMENT

Write a paragraph that begins with a rhetorical question. Choose one of the questions below or compose your own. Be sure that the body of the paragraph really does answer the question.

1. How has college (or anything else) changed me?
2. Should people pamper their pets?
3. Is marriage worth the risks?

C. Vary the Beginnings of Sentences

Begin with an Adverb

Since the first word of many sentences is the subject, one way to achieve sentence variety is by occasionally starting a sentence with a word or words other than the subject.

For instance, you can begin with an **adverb**:†

1. He *laboriously* dragged the large crate up the stairs.
2. *Laboriously,* he dragged the large crate up the stairs.
3. The contents of the beaker *suddenly* began to foam.
4. *Suddenly,* the contents of the beaker began to foam.

● In sentences 2 and 4, the adverbs *laboriously* and *suddenly* are shifted to the first position. Notice the difference in rhythm that this creates, as well as the slight change in meaning: Sentence 2 emphasizes *how* he dragged the crate—*laboriously;* sentence 4 emphasizes the *suddenness* of what happened.

● A comma usually follows an adverb that introduces a sentence; however, adverbs of time—*often, now, always*—do not always require a comma. As a general rule, use a comma if you want the reader to pause briefly.

---

* For more work on giving directions, see Chapter 8, "Process."
† For more work on adverbs, see Chapter 35, "Adjectives and Adverbs."

PRACTICE 2

Rewrite the following sentences by shifting the adverbs to the beginning. Punctuate correctly.

EXAMPLE   He skillfully prepared the engine for the race.

Skillfully, he prepared the engine for the race.

1. Two deer moved silently across the clearing.

    _____

2. The chief of the research division occasionally visits the lab.

    _____

3. Proofread your writing always.

    _____

4. Children of alcoholics often marry alcoholics.

    _____

5. Jake foolishly lied to his supervisor.

    _____

PRACTICE 3

Begin each of the following sentences with an appropriate adverb. Punctuate correctly.

1. _____ the detective approached the ticking suitcase.

2. _____ Maria Sharapova powered a forehand past her opponent.

3. _____ she received her check for $25,000 from the state lottery.

4. _____ he left the beach.

5. _____ the submarine sank out of sight.

PRACTICE 4

Write three sentences of your own that begin with adverbs. Use different adverbs from those in Practices 2 and 3; if you wish, use *graciously, furiously, sometimes.* Punctuate correctly.

1. _____

2. _____

3. _____

Begin with a Prepositional Phrase

A **prepositional phrase** is a group of words containing a **preposition** and its **object** (a noun or pronoun). *To you, in the evening,* and *under the old bridge* are prepositional phrases.*

Preposition	Object
to	you
in	the evening
under	the old bridge

Here is a partial list of prepositions:

Common Prepositions

about	beneath	into	throughout
above	beside	near	to
across	between	of	toward
against	by	on	under
among	except	onto	up
at	for	out	upon
behind	from	over	with
below	in	through	without

For variety in your writing, begin an occasional sentence with a prepositional phrase:

5. Charles left the room *without a word.*
6. *Without a word,* Charles left the room.
7. A fat yellow cat lay sleeping *on the narrow sill.*
8. *On the narrow sill,* a fat yellow cat lay sleeping.

● In sentences 6 and 8, the prepositional phrases have been shifted to the beginning. Note the slight shift in emphasis that results. Sentence 6 stresses that Charles left the room *without a word,* and 8 stresses the location of the cat, *on the narrow sill.*

● Prepositional phrases that begin sentences are usually followed by commas. However, short prepositional phrases need not be.

___

* For work on spotting prepositional phrases, see Chapter 34, "Prepositions."

Prepositional phrases are not always movable; rely on the meaning of the sentence to determine whether they are movable:

> 9.   The dress *in the picture* is the one I want.
> 10.   Joelle bought a bottle *of white wine for dinner*.

- *In the picture* in sentence 9 is a part of the subject and cannot be moved. *In the picture the dress is the one I want* makes no sense.
- Sentence 10 has two prepositional phrases. Which one *cannot* be moved to the beginning of the sentence? Why?

_____

_____

PRACTICE 5

Underline the prepositional phrases in each sentence. Some sentences contain more than one prepositional phrase. Rewrite each sentence by shifting a prepositional phrase to the beginning. Punctuate correctly.

EXAMPLE   A large owl with gray feathers watched us from the oak tree.

From the oak tree, a large owl with gray feathers watched us.

1.   The coffee maker turned itself on at seven o'clock sharp.

_____

_____

2.   A growling Doberman paced behind the chainlink fence.

_____

_____

3.   A man and a woman held hands under the street lamp.

_____

_____

4.   They have sold nothing except athletic shoes for years.

_____

_____

5.   A group of men played checkers and drank iced tea beside the small shop.

_____

_____

PRACTICE 6

Begin each of the following sentences with a different prepositional phrase. Refer to the list and be creative. Punctuate correctly.

1. _____ we ordered potato skins, salad, and beer.

2. _____ a woman in horn-rimmed glasses balanced her checkbook.

3. _____ everyone congratulated Jim on his promotion.

4. _____ one can see huge sculptures in wood, metal, and stone.

5. _____ three large helium-filled balloons drifted.

PRACTICE 7

Write three sentences of your own that begin with prepositional phrases. Use these phrases if you wish: *in the dentist's office, under that stack of books, behind his friendly smile.* Punctuate correctly.

1. _____

2. _____

3. _____

D. Vary Methods of Joining Ideas*

Join Ideas with a Compound Predicate

A sentence with a **compound predicate** contains more than one verb, but the subject is *not* repeated before the second verb. Such a sentence is really composed of two simple sentences with the same subject:

1. The nurse entered.
2. The nurse quickly closed the door.
3. The nurse *entered* and quickly *closed* the door.

● *The nurse* is the subject of sentence 1, and *entered* is the verb; *the nurse* is also the subject of sentence 2, and *closed* is the verb.

_____

* For work on joining ideas with coordination and subordination, see Chapter 27, "Coordination and Subordination."

- When these sentences are combined with a compound predicate in sentence 3, *the nurse* is the subject of both *entered* and *closed* but is not repeated before the second verb.

- No comma is necessary when the conjunctions *and, but, or,* and *yet* join the verbs in a compound predicate.

A compound predicate is useful in combining short, choppy sentences:

4. He serves elaborate meals.
5. He never uses a recipe.
6. He *serves elaborate meals* yet *never uses a recipe.*
7. Aviators rarely get nosebleeds.
8. They often suffer from backaches.
9. *Aviators rarely get nosebleeds* but *often suffer from backaches.*

- Sentences 4 and 5 are joined by *yet*; no comma precedes *yet*.
- Sentences 7 and 8 are joined by *but*; no comma precedes *but*.

PRACTICE 8

Combine each pair of short sentences into one sentence with a compound predicate. Use *and, but, or,* and *yet*. Punctuate correctly.

EXAMPLE Toby smeared peanut butter on a thick slice of white bread.
He devoured the treat in 30 seconds.

Toby smeared peanut butter on a thick slice of white bread and devoured the

treat in 30 seconds.

1. Americans eat more than 800 million pounds of peanut butter.
   They spend more than $1 billion on the product each year.

   _____

   _____

2. Peanut butter was first concocted in the 1890s.
   It did not become the food we know for 30 years.

   _____

3. George Washington Carver did not discover peanut butter.
   He published many recipes for pastes much like it.

   _____

   _____

4. The average American becomes a peanut butter lover in childhood.
   He or she loses enthusiasm for it later on.

   _____

   _____

5. Older adults regain their passion for peanut butter.
   They consume great quantities of the delicious stuff.

   _____

   _____

PRACTICE 9

Complete the following compound predicates. Do *not* repeat the subjects.

1. Three Korean writers visited the campus and _____

   _____

2. The singer breathed heavily into the microphone but _____

   _____

3. Take these cans to the recycling center or _____

   _____

4. The newspaper printed the story yet _____

   _____

5. Three men burst into the back room and _____

   _____

PRACTICE 10

Write three sentences with compound predicates. Be careful to punctuate correctly.

1. _____

2. _____

3. _____

Join Ideas with an *-ing* Modifier

An excellent way to achieve sentence variety is by occasionally combining two sentences with an *-ing* **modifier**.

10. He peered through the microscope.
11. He discovered a squiggly creature.
12. *Peering through the microscope*, he discovered a squiggly creature.

- Sentence 10 has been converted to an *-ing* modifier by changing the verb *peered* to *peering* and dropping the subject *he*. *Peering through the microscope* now introduces the main clause, *he discovered a squiggly creature*.

- A comma sets off the *-ing* modifier from the word it refers to, *he*. To avoid confusion, the word referred to must appear in the immediately following clause.

An *-ing* modifier indicates that two actions are occurring at the same time. The main idea of the sentence should be contained in the main clause, not in the *-ing* modifier. In the preceding example, the discovery of the creature is the main idea, not the fact that someone peered through a microscope.

Be careful; misplaced *-ing* modifiers can result in confusing sentences: *He discovered a squiggly creature peering through the microscope.* (Was the creature looking through the microscope?)*

Convert sentence 13 into an *-ing* modifier and write it in the blank:

---

13. We drove down Tompkins Road.
14. We were surprised by the number of "for sale" signs.

15. _____ , we were
surprised by the number of "for sale" signs.

- The new *-ing* modifier is followed directly by the word to which it refers, *we*.

PRACTICE 11

Combine the following pairs of sentences by converting the first sentence into an *-ing* modifier. Make sure the subject of the main clause directly follows the *-ing* modifier. Punctuate correctly.

EXAMPLE   Jim searched for his needle-nose pliers.
He completely emptied the tool chest.

Searching for his needle-nose pliers, Jim completely emptied the tool chest.

1. She installed the air conditioner.
She saved herself $50 in labor.

_____

_____

2. The surgeons raced against time.
The surgeons performed a liver transplant on the child.

_____

_____

---

* For more work on avoiding confusing modifiers, see Part E of this chapter.

3. They conducted a survey of Jackson Heights residents.
   They found that most opposed construction of the airport.

   _____

   _____

4. Three flares spiraled upward from the little boat.
   They exploded against the night sky.

   _____

   _____

5. Virgil danced in the Pennsylvania Ballet.
   Virgil learned discipline and self-control.

   _____

   _____

6. The hen squawked loudly.
   The hen fluttered out of our path.

   _____

   _____

7. The engineer made a routine check of the blueprints.
   He discovered a flaw in the design.

   _____

   _____

8. Dr. Salazar opened commencement exercises with a humorous story.
   He put everyone at ease.

   _____

   _____

PRACTICE 12

Add either an introductory *-ing* modifier *or* a main clause to each sentence. Make sure that each *-ing* modifier refers clearly to the subject of the main clause.

> **EXAMPLE**   _Reading a book a week_____, Jeff increased his vocabulary.
>
> Exercising every day, _I lost five pounds_____.

1. _____, she felt a sense of accomplishment.

2. Growing up in Hollywood, _____

_____

3. _____, the father and son were reconciled.

4. Interviewing his relatives, _____

_____

5. _____, the wrecking ball swung through the air and smashed into the brick wall.

PRACTICE 13

Write three sentences of your own that begin with -*ing* modifiers. Make sure that the subject of the sentence follows the modifier and be careful of the punctuation.

1. _____

_____

2. _____

_____

3. _____

_____

Join Ideas with a Past Participial Modifier

Some sentences can be joined with a **past participial modifier**. A sentence that contains a *to be* verb and a **past participle*** can be changed into a past participial modifier:

16. Judith *is trapped* in a dead-end job.
17. Judith decided to enroll at the local community college.
18. *Trapped in a dead-end job*, Judith decided to enroll at the local community college.

● In sentence 18, sentence 16 has been made into a past participial modifier by dropping the helping verb *is* and the subject *Judith*. The past participle *trapped* now introduces the new sentence.

* For more work on past participles, see Chapter 31, "The Past Participle."

● A comma sets off the past participial modifier from the word it modifies, *Judith*. To avoid confusion, the word referred to must directly follow the modifier.

Be careful; misplaced past participial modifiers can result in confusing sentences: *Packed in dry ice, Steve brought us some ice cream.* (Was Steve packed in dry ice?)* Sometimes two or more past participles can be used to introduce a sentence:

> 19. The term paper *was revised* and *rewritten*.
> 20. It received an A.
> 21. *Revised and rewritten*, the term paper received an A.

● The past participles *revised* and *rewritten* become a modifier that introduces sentence 21. What word(s) do they refer to?

_____

PRACTICE 14

Combine each pair of sentences into one sentence that begins with a past participial modifier. Convert the sentence containing a form of *to be* plus a past participle into a past participial modifier that introduces the new sentence.

EXAMPLE Duffy was surprised by the interruption.
He lost his train of thought.

Surprised by the interruption, Duffy lost his train of thought.

1. My mother was married at the age of 16.
   My mother never finished high school.

   _____

   _____

2. The 2:30 flight was delayed by an electrical storm.
   It arrived in Lexington three hours late.

   _____

   _____

3. The old car was waxed and polished.
   It shone in the sun.

   _____

   _____

_____

* For more work on avoiding confusing modifiers, see Part E of this chapter.

4. The house was built by Frank Lloyd Wright.
   It has become famous.

   _____

   _____

5. The Nineteenth Amendment was ratified in 1920.
   It gave women the right to vote.

   _____

   _____

6. The manuscript seems impossible to decipher.
   It is written in code.

   _____

   _____

7. Dr. Bentley will address the pre-med students.
   He has been recognized for his contributions in the field of immunology.

   _____

   _____

8. Mrs. Witherspoon was exhausted by night classes.
   She declined the chance to work overtime.

   _____

   _____

PRACTICE 15

Complete each sentence by filling in *either* the past participial modifier *or* the main clause. Remember, the past participial modifier must clearly refer to the subject of the main clause.

EXAMPLE   Wrapped in blue paper and tied with string, *the gift arrived* _____.

Chosen to represent the team, Phil proudly accepted the trophy.

1. Made of gold and set with precious stones, _____

2. Overwhelmed by the response to her ad in *The Star*, _____

   _____

3. _____, Tom left no forwarding

address.

4. _____, we found a huge basket

   of fresh fruit on the steps.

5. Astonished by the scene before her, _____

PRACTICE 16

Write three sentences of your own that begin with past participial modifiers. If you wish, use participles from this list:

shocked	dressed	hidden	bent
awakened	lost	stuffed	rewired

Make sure that the subject of the sentence clearly follows the modifier.

1. _____

   _____

2. _____

   _____

3. _____

   _____

Join Ideas with an Appositive

A fine way to add variety to your writing is to combine two choppy sentences with an appositive. An **appositive** is a word or group of words that renames or describes a noun or pronoun:

> 22. Carlos is the new wrestling champion.
> 23. He is a native of Argentina.
> 24. Carlos, *a native of Argentina*, is the new wrestling champion.

- *A native of Argentina* in sentence 24 is an appositive. It renames the noun *Carlos*.
- An appositive must be placed either directly *after* the word it refers to, as in sentence 24, or directly *before* it, as follows:

> 25. *A native of Argentina*, Carlos is the new wrestling champion.

● Note that an appositive is set off by commas.

Appositives can add versatility to your writing because they can be placed at the beginning, in the middle, or at the end of a sentence. When you join two ideas with an appositive, place the idea you wish to stress in the main clause and make the less important idea the appositive:

26. Naomi wants to become a fashion model.
27. She is the daughter of an actress.
28. *The daughter of an actress,* Naomi wants to become a fashion model.

29. FACT made headlines for the first time only a few years ago.
30. FACT is now a powerful consumer group.
31. FACT, *now a powerful consumer group,* made headlines for the first time only a few years ago.

32. Watch out for Smithers.
33. He is a dangerous man.
34. Watch out for Smithers, *a dangerous man.*

Using an appositive to combine sentences eliminates unimportant words and creates longer, more fact-filled sentences.

PRACTICE 17

Combine the following pairs of sentences by making the *second sentence* an appositive. Punctuate correctly.

These appositives should occur at the *beginning* of the sentences.

EXAMPLE   My uncle taught me to use watercolors.
He is a well-known artist.

A well-known artist, my uncle taught me to use watercolors.

1. Dan has saved many lives.
He is a dedicated firefighter.

2. Acupuncture is becoming popular in the United States.
It is an ancient Chinese healing system.

3. The Cromwell Hotel was built in 1806.
   It is an elegant example of Mexican architecture.

   _____

   _____

These appositives should occur in the *middle* of the sentences. Punctuate correctly.

EXAMPLE His American history course is always popular with students.
It is an introductory survey.

His American history course, an introductory survey, is always popular with

students.

4. The Korean Ping-Pong champion won ten games in a row.
   She is a small and wiry athlete.

   _____

   _____

5. The pituitary is located below the brain.
   It is the body's master gland.

   _____

   _____

6. The elevator shudders violently and begins to rise.
   It is an ancient box of wood and hope.

   _____

   _____

These appositives should occur at the *end* of the sentences. Punctuate correctly.

EXAMPLE I hate fried asparagus.
It is a vile dish.

I hate fried asparagus, a vile dish.

© Africa Studio/Shutterstock.com

7. Jennifer flaunted her new camera.
   It was a Nikon with a telephoto lens.

   _____

   _____

8. At the intersection stood a hitchhiker.
    He was a young man dressed in a tuxedo.

    _____

    _____

9. We met for pancakes at the Cosmic Cafe.
    It was a greasy diner on the corner of 10th and Vine.

    _____

    _____

PRACTICE 18

Write three sentences using appositives. In one sentence, place the appositive at the *beginning*; in one sentence, place the appositive in the *middle*; and in one sentence, place it at the *end*.

1. _____

    _____

2. _____

    _____

3. _____

    _____

Join Ideas with a Relative Clause

Relative clauses can add sophistication to your writing. A **relative clause** begins with *who*, *which*, or *that* and describes a noun or pronoun. It can join two simple sentences in a longer, more complex sentence:

35. Jack just won a scholarship from the Arts Council.
36. He makes wire sculpture.
37. Jack, *who makes wire sculpture*, just won a scholarship from the Arts Council.

● In sentence 37, *who makes wire sculpture* is a relative clause, created by replacing the subject *he* of sentence 36 with the relative pronoun *who*.

● *Who* now introduces the subordinate relative clause and connects it to the rest of the sentence. Note that *who* directly follows the word it refers to, *Jack*.

The idea that the writer wishes to stress is placed in the main clause, and the subordinate idea is placed in the relative clause. Study the combinations in sentences 38 through 40 and 41 through 43.

> 38.   Carrots grow in cool climates.
> 39.   They are high in vitamin A.
> 40.   Carrots, *which* are high in vitamin A, grow in cool climates.
> 41.   He finally submitted the term paper.
> 42.   It was due six months ago.
> 43.   He finally submitted the term paper *that* was due six months ago.

● In sentence 40, *which are high in vitamin A* is a relative clause, created by replacing *they* with *which*. Which word in sentence 40 does *which* refer to?

_____

● What is the relative clause in sentence 43?

_____

● Which word does *that* refer to?

_____

Punctuating relative clauses can be tricky; therefore, you will have to be careful:*

> 44.   Claude, *who grew up in Haiti*, speaks fluent French.

● *Who grew up in Haiti* is set off by commas because it adds information about Claude that is not essential to the meaning of the sentence. In other words, the sentence would make sense without it: *Claude speaks fluent French.*

● *Who grew up in Haiti* is called a **nonrestrictive clause**. It does not restrict or provide vital information about the word it modifies.

> 45.   People *who crackle paper in theaters* annoy me.

● *Who crackle paper in theaters* is not set off by commas because it is vital to the meaning of the sentence. Without it, the sentence would read, *People annoy me;* yet the point of the sentence is that people *who crackle paper in theaters* annoy me, not all people.

● *Who crackle paper in theaters* is called a **restrictive clause** because it restricts the meaning of the word it refers to, *people*.

Note that *which* usually begins a nonrestrictive clause and *that* usually begins a restrictive clause.

———

* For more practice in punctuating relative clauses, see Chapter 37, "The Comma," Part D.

PRACTICE 19

Combine each pair of sentences by changing the second sentence into a relative clause introduced by *who, which,* or *that*. Remember, *who* refers to persons, *that* refers to persons or things, and *which* refers to things.

These sentences require **nonrestrictive relative clauses**. Punctuate correctly.

EXAMPLE   My cousin will spend the summer hiking in the Rockies.
She lives in Indiana.

My cousin, who lives in Indiana, will spend the summer hiking in the Rockies.

1. Scrabble has greatly increased my vocabulary.
   It is my favorite game.

   _____

   _____

2. Contestants on game shows often make fools of themselves.
   They may travel thousands of miles to play.

   _____

   _____

3. Arabic is a difficult language to learn.
   It has a complicated verb system.

   _____

   _____

The next sentences require **restrictive relative clauses**. Punctuate correctly.

EXAMPLE   He described a state of mind.
I have experienced it.

He described a state of mind that I have experienced.

4. The house is for sale.
   I was born in it.

   _____

   _____

5. My boss likes reports.
   They are clear and to the point.

   _____

   _____

6. People know how intelligent birds are.
   They have owned a bird.

   _____

   _____

PRACTICE 20

Combine each pair of sentences by changing one into a relative clause introduced by *who, which,* or *that.* Remember, *who* refers to persons, *that* refers to persons or things, and *which* refers to things.

Be careful of the punctuation. (Hint: *Which* clauses are usually set off by commas and *that* clauses are usually not.)

1. Her grandfather enjoys scuba diving.
   He is 77 years old.

   _____

   _____

2. You just dropped an antique pitcher.
   It was worth 2,000 dollars.

   _____

   _____

3. Parenthood has taught me acceptance, forgiveness, and love.
   It used to terrify me.

   _____

   _____

4. James Fenimore Cooper was expelled from college.
   He later became a famous American novelist.

   _____

   _____

5. The verb *to hector* means "to bully someone."
   It derives from a character in Greek literature.

   _____

   _____

E. Avoid Misplaced and Confusing Modifiers

As you practice varying your sentences, be sure that your modifiers say what you mean! Revise your work to avoid **misplaced**, **confusing**, or **dangling modifiers**.

> 1. Perching on a scarecrow in the cornfield, the farmer saw a large crow.

- Probably the writer did not mean that the farmer was perching on a scarecrow. Who or what, then, was *perching on a scarecrow in the cornfield*?

- *Perching* refers to the *crow*, of course, but the order of the sentence does not show this. This misplaced modifier can be corrected by turning the ideas around:

> The farmer saw a large crow perching on a scarecrow in the cornfield.

Do these sentences say what they mean? Are the modifiers misplaced or correct?

> 2. Covered with whipped cream, Tyrone carried a chocolate cake.
> 3. I sold the tin soldiers to an antique dealer that I found in the basement.
> 4. A homeless teenager, the nun helped the girl find a place to live.

- In sentence 2, does the past participial modifier *covered with whipped cream* refer to Tyrone or the cake? Rewrite the sentence so that the modifier is placed correctly:

_____

- In sentence 3, who or what does the relative clause *that I found in the basement* refer to? Rewrite the sentence so that the modifier is placed correctly:

_____

- In sentence 4, the misplaced appositive totally changes the meaning of the sentence. What did this writer mean to say?

_____

Sometimes a modifier is confusing because it does not refer to anything in the sentence. This is called a **dangling modifier** and must be corrected by rewriting.

5. Drilling for oil in Alaska, acres of wilderness were destroyed.

6. Tired and proud, the website was completed at midnight.

- In sentence 5, who or what was *drilling for oil*? The sentence doesn't tell us.

- *Drilling for oil* is a dangling modifier. It can be corrected only by rewording the sentence:

7. Drilling for oil in Alaska, the EndRun Company destroyed acres of wilderness.

- In sentence 6, *tired and proud* is a dangling modifier. Surely the website isn't tired and proud, so who is? Rewrite the sentence to say what the writer probably intended.

_____

PRACTICE 21

Correct any confusing, misplaced, or dangling modifiers. Rearrange words or rewrite as necessary.

1. Plump sausages, the dinner guests looked forward to the main course.

_____

_____

2. Soaring over the treetops in a hot air balloon, the view was spectacular.

_____

_____

3. Powered by hydrogen, the engineers designed a new kind of car.

_____

_____

4. I introduced my boyfriend to my father, who wanted to marry me.

_____

_____

5. Revised to highlight his computer expertise, Marcelo was proud of his new résumé.

_____

_____

6. Jim, who loved to lick car windows, drove his dog to the vet.

_____

_____

7. Banging inside the dryer, Carla heard the lost keys.

_____

_____

8. We complained about the proposed building to the mayor, which we found ugly and too large for the neighborhood.

_____

_____

F. Review and Practice

Before practicing some of the techniques of sentence variety discussed in this chapter, review them briefly:

1. Mix long and short sentences.
2. Add an occasional question, command, or exclamation.
3. Begin with an adverb: *Unfortunately,* the outfielder dropped the fly ball.
4. Begin with a prepositional phrase: *With great style,* the pitcher delivered a curve.
5. Join ideas with a compound predicate: The fans *roared and banged* their seats.
6. Join ideas with an *-ing* modifier: *Diving chin-first onto the grass,* Beltran caught the ball.
7. Join ideas with a past participial modifier: *Frustrated by the call,* the batter kicked dirt onto home plate.
8. Join ideas with an appositive: Beer, *the cause of much rowdiness,* should not be sold at games.
9. Join ideas with a relative clause: Box seats, *which are hard to get for important games,* are frequently bought up by corporations.

Of course, the secret of achieving sentence variety is practice. Choose one, two, or three of these techniques to focus on and try them out in your writing. Revise your paragraphs and essays with an eye to sentence variety.

PRACTICE 22

Revise and then rewrite this essay, aiming for sentence variety. Vary the length and pattern of the sentences. Vary the beginnings of some sentences. Join two sentences in any way you wish, adding appropriate connecting words or dropping unnecessary words. Punctuate correctly.

CLEAN AIR CRUSADER

At age 17, Erica Fernandez became an unlikely environmental hero. She had grown up in rural Mexico. In Mexico she took blue skies and clean water for granted. She was ten. The family emigrated to Oxnard, California. Erica was shocked by the terrible quality of her new environment. Thousands of cars, visible smog, and stifling air were daily realities. Worse, Erica's father suffered from respiratory problems. His respiratory problems grew dramatically worse. So did her own asthma.

Erica was a teenager. She heard about a proposed natural gas pipeline just off the coast. The pipeline would further pollute the air. It would release carbon dioxide. This was more carbon dioxide every year than 48,000 cars. Erica was angry. There was a large public hearing of the California State Lands Commission. Erica walked to the podium. She gave an electrifying speech. She expressed passionate concern for her father's lungs and the health of the community. The proposal failed. Erica Fernandez became a local hero. She was suddenly in demand as an environmental speaker.

The experience taught her that committed people can make a difference. She was accepted at Stanford University. At Stanford, she was named one of the ten outstanding college women in the U.S. She won a Jane Goodall Global Leadership Award. This allowed her to spend a summer in her native Mexico. There she fought the destruction of important forests. Erica Fernandez plans to become an environmental lawyer.

Erica Fernandez, who as a teenager became an environmental hero

CLEAN AIR CRUSADER

_____

_____

_____

_____

_____

_____

_____

_____

_____

_____

_____

_____

_____

_____

_____

_____

_____

EXPLORING ONLINE

http://grammar.ccc.commnet.edu/grammar/combining_skills.htm

Add sophistication to your writing. Review and scroll down for interactive, sentence-combining quizzes.

http://owl.english.purdue.edu/owl/resource/597/01

Are your modifiers dangling? Don't blush; revise.

CourseMate for _Evergreen_

Visit _Evergreen_ CourseMate for more practices and quizzes, videos to accompany the readings, career and job-search resources, ESL help, and live links to every Exploring Online in the book.

CHAPTER 23

Revising for Language Awareness

A: Exact Language: Avoiding Vagueness

B: Concise Language: Avoiding Wordiness

C: Fresh Language: Avoiding Triteness

D: Figurative Language: Similes and Metaphors

Although it is important to write grammatically correct English, good writing is more than just correct writing. Good writing has life, excitement, and power. It captures the attention of the reader and compels him or her to read further.

The purpose of this chapter is to increase your awareness of the power of words and your skill at making them work for you. The secret of effective writing is **revision**. Do *not* settle for the first words that come to you, but go back over what you have written, replacing dull or confusing language with exact, concise, fresh, and sometimes figurative language.

A. Exact Language: Avoiding Vagueness

Good writers express their ideas as *exactly* as possible, choosing *specific, concrete,* and *vivid* words and phrases. They do not settle for vague terms and confusing generalities.

Which sentence in each of the following pairs gives the more *exact* information? That is, which uses specific and precise language? Which words in these sentences make them sharper and more vivid?

1. A car went around the corner.
2. A battered blue Mustang careened around the corner.

3. Janet quickly ate the main course.
4. Janet devoured the plate of ribs in two and a half minutes.

5. The president did things that caused problems.
6. The president's military spending increased the budget deficit.

- Sentences 2, 4, and 6 contain language that is *exact*.
- Sentence 2 is more exact than sentence 1 because *battered blue Mustang* gives more specific information than the general term *car*. The verb *careened* describes precisely how the car went around the corner, fast and recklessly.
- What specific words does sentence 4 substitute for the more general words *ate, main course,* and *quickly* in sentence 3?

_____ , _____ , and

_____

Why are these terms more exact than those in sentence 3?

_____

_____

- What words in sentence 6 make it clearer and more exact than sentence 5?

_____

Concrete and detailed writing is usually exciting as well and makes us want to read on, as does this passage by N. Scott Momaday. Here this Native American writer describes his grandmother at prayer. Read it aloud if possible:

The last time I saw [my grandmother], she prayed standing by the side of her bed at night, naked to the waist, the light of a kerosene lamp moving upon her dark skin. Her long, black hair, always drawn and braided in the day, lay upon her shoulders and against her breasts like a shawl. I do not speak Kiowa, and I never understood her prayers, but there was something inherently sad in the sound, some merest hesitation upon the syllables of sorrow. She began in a high and descending pitch, exhausting her breath to silence; then again and again—and always the same intensity of effort, of something that is, and is not, like urgency in the human voice. Transported so in the dancing light among the shadows of her room, she seemed beyond the reach of time. But that was illusion; I think I knew then that I should not see her again.

—N. Scott Momaday, *The Way to Rainy Mountain*

Now compare a similar account written in general and inexact language:

> The last time I saw my grandmother, she was praying next to her bed. Her long hair was down, covering her. In the day, she always wore it up. I remember that her room had a kerosene lamp. I don't speak Kiowa, so I didn't understand what she was saying, but there was definitely something sad about it. I think I knew somehow that I was not going to see her again.

You do not need a large vocabulary to write exactly and well, but you do need to work at finding the right words to fit each sentence. As you revise, cross out vague or dull words and phrases and replace them with more exact terms. When you are tempted to write *I feel good*, ask yourself exactly what *good* means in that sentence: *relaxed? proud? thin? in love?* When people walk by, do they *flounce, stride, lurch, wiggle,* or *sneak?* When they speak to you, do people *stammer, announce, babble, murmur,* or *coo?* Question yourself as you revise; then choose the right words to fit that particular sentence.

PRACTICE 1

Lively verbs are a great asset to any writer. The following sentences contain four overused general verbs—*to walk, to see, to eat,* and *to be.* In each case, replace the general verb in parentheses with a more exact verb *chosen to fit the context of the sentence.* Use a different verb in every sentence. Consult a dictionary or thesaurus* if you wish.

EXAMPLES   In no particular hurry, we _____*strolled*_____ (walked) through the botanical gardens.

Jane _____*fidgets*_____ (is) at her desk and watches the clock.

1. With guns drawn, three police officers _____ (walked) toward the door of the warehouse.

2. As we stared in fascination, an orange lizard _____ (walked) up the wall.

3. The four-year-old _____ (walked) onto the patio in her mother's high-heeled shoes.

4. A furious customer _____ (walked) into the manager's office.

5. Two people who _____ (saw) the accident must testify in court.

6. We crouched for hours in the underbrush just to _____ (see) a rare white fox.

7. Three makeshift wooden rafts were _____ (seen) off the coast this morning.

8. For two years, the zoologist _____ (saw) the behavior of bears in the wild.

9. There was the cat, delicately _____ (eating) my fern!

10. Senator Gorman astounded the guests by loudly _____ (eating) his soup.

* A thesaurus is a book of *synonyms*—words that have the same or similar meanings.

11. All through the movie, she _____ (ate) hard candies in the back row.

12. Within seconds, Dan had bought two tacos from a street vendor and _____ (eaten) them both.

13. During rush hour, the temperature hit 98 degrees, and dozens of cars _____ (were) on the highway.

14. A young man _____ (is) on a stretcher in the emergency room.

15. Workers who _____ (are) at desks all day should make special efforts to exercise.

16. Professor Nuzzo _____ (was) in front of the blackboard, excited about this new solution to the math problem.

PRACTICE 2

The following sentences contain dull, vague language. Revise them using vivid verbs, specific nouns, and colorful adjectives. As the examples show, you may add and delete words.

EXAMPLES   A dog lies down in the shade.

A mangy collie flops down in the shade of a parked car

My head hurts

My head throbs

I have shooting pains in the left side of my head.

1. Everything about the man looked mean.

   _____

   _____

2. I feel good today for several reasons.

   _____

   _____

3. A woman in unusual clothes went down the street.

   _____

   _____

4. The sunlight made the yard look pretty.

   _____

   _____

5. What the company did bothered the townspeople.

_____

_____

6. The pediatrician's waiting room was crowded.

_____

_____

7. As soon as he gets home from work, he hears the voice of his pet asking for dinner.

_____

_____

8. The noises of construction filled the street.

_____

_____

9. When I was sick, you were helpful.

_____

_____

10. This college does things that make the students feel bad.

_____

_____

PRACTICE 3

A word that works effectively in one sentence might not work in another sentence. In searching for the right word, always consider the **context** of the sentence into which the word must fit. Read each of the following sentences for meaning. Then circle the word in parentheses that *most exactly fits* the context of the sentence.

EXAMPLE   Machu Picchu, which means "old peak" in the Quechua (words, language, lingo), is known as the "Lost City of the Incas."

1. Ever since the ruins of Machu Picchu were (buried, invented, discovered) in 1911 by Yale archaeologist Hiram Bingham, people all over the world have been fascinated by this mysterious site.

2. The ancient city (perches, hangs, wobbles) high atop a peak in the rugged Andes Mountains of Peru.

3. In the 1400s, using gray Andes granite, the Inca people (arranged, constructed, piled) the palace, temples, baths, and houses of Machu Picchu.

4. The carved stone blocks are so (strong, massive, humongous) that thousands of men would have been needed to move just one of them into place.

5. The (sophisticated, fluid, bubbly) plumbing and drainage system that brought running water to Machu Picchu still works today.

6. The city served not only as a (hideout, getaway, retreat) and fortress for the nobility but also as an observatory.

7. Many ceremonies took place around the Intihuatana stone, a kind of sundial that (casts, manufactures, emits) no shadow at noon on the two equinoxes, in March and in September.

8. According to legend, when spiritually sensitive people touch their foreheads to the Intihuatana stone, it (magically, accidentally, weirdly) opens their vision to the spirit world.

9. In 1533, Spanish conquistadors (ruthlessly, destructively, properly) destroyed the Inca civilization, but the invaders never found Machu Picchu.

10. Nevertheless, the cloud-capped city was (abandoned, missed, set aside) for 400 years.

11. Its rediscovery (torched, entered, ignited) the imaginations of scientists and adventurers, who still labor to unlock Machu Picchu's secrets.

12. Today many tourists (enjoy, battle, are awed by) altitude sickness just to trek up the mountain and gaze upon this beautiful, well-preserved sanctuary.

View of Machu Picchu, Peru

The following paragraph begins a mystery story. Using specific and vivid language, revise the paragraph to make it as exciting as possible. Then finish the story; be careful to avoid vague language.

The weather was bad. I was in the house alone, with a funny feeling that something was going to happen. Someone knocked at the door. I got up to answer it and found someone outside. She looked familiar, but I didn't know from where or when. Then I recognized her as a person from my past. I let her in although I was not sure I had done the right thing.

_____

_____

_____

_____

_____

_____

_____

_____

B. Concise Language: Avoiding Wordiness

Concise writing comes quickly to the point. It avoids **wordiness**—unnecessary and repetitious words that add nothing to the meaning.

Which sentence in each of the following pairs is more *concise*? That is, which does *not* contain unnecessary words?

1. Because of the fact that the watch was inexpensive in price, he bought it.
2. Because the watch was inexpensive, he bought it.

3. In my opinion I think that the financial aid system at Ellensville Junior College is in need of reform.
4. The financial aid system at Ellensville Junior College needs reform.

5. On October 10, in the fall of 2003, we learned the true facts about the Peruvian mummies.
6. On October 10, 2003, we learned the facts about the Peruvian mummies.

- Sentences 2, 4, and 6 are *concise*, whereas sentences 1, 3, and 5 are *wordy*.

- In sentence 1, *because of the fact that* is really a *wordy* way of saying *because*. *In price* simply repeats information already given by the word *inexpensive*.

- The writer of sentence 3 undercuts the point with the wordy apology of *in my opinion I think*. As a general rule, leave out such qualifiers and simply state the opinion; but if you do use them, use either *in my opinion* or *I think*, not both! Sentence 4 replaces *is in need of* with one direct verb, *needs*.

- *In the fall of* in sentence 5 is *redundant*; it repeats information already given by which word?

_____

- Why is the word *true* also eliminated in sentence 6?

_____

   Concise writing avoids wordiness, unnecessary repetition, and padding. Of course, conciseness does not mean writing short, bare sentences, but simply cutting out all deadwood and never using fifteen words when ten will do.

PRACTICE 5

The following sentences are *wordy*. Make them more *concise* by crossing out or replacing unnecessary words or by combining two sentences into one concise sentence. Rewrite each new sentence on the lines beneath, capitalizing and punctuating correctly.

EXAMPLES   The U.S. Census uncovers many interesting facts that have a lot of truth to them.

   The U.S. Census uncovers many interesting facts. _____

   In the year 1810, Philadelphia was called the cigar capital of the United States. The reason why was because the census reported that the city produced 16 million cigars each year.

   In 1810, Philadelphia was called the cigar capital of the United States _____

   because the census reported that the city produced 16 million each year. _____

1. The Constitution requires and says that the federal government of the United States must take a national census every ten years.

_____

_____

2. At first, the original function of the census was to ensure fair taxation and representation.

_____

_____

3. Since the first count in 1790, however, the census has been controversial. There are several reasons why the census has been controversial.

_____

_____

4. One reason why is because there are always some people who aren't included.

_____

_____

5. The 1990 census, for example, missed almost 5 million people, many of whom were homeless with no place to live.

_____

_____

6. For the 2000 census, the Census Bureau considered using statistical methods. The statistical methods would have been used instead of the traditional direct head count.

_____

_____

7. The Bureau would have directly counted about 90 percent of U.S. residents who live in the United States and then estimated the number and characteristics of the remainder of the rest of the people.

_____

_____

8. Those who opposed the idea believed that in their opinion statistical methods would have introduced new errors that were mistaken into the count.

_____

_____

9. The distribution of $100 billion in money, as well as the balance of power in the House of Representatives, depended on how and in which manner the census was conducted.

_____

_____

10. Despite controversy, the U.S. census still continues to serve a beneficial purpose that is for the good of the United States.

_____

_____

PRACTICE 6

Rewrite this essay *concisely,* cutting out all unnecessary words. Reword or combine sentences if you wish, but do not alter the meaning.

DR. ALICE HAMILTON, MEDICAL PIONEER

At the age of forty years old, Dr. Alice Hamilton became a pioneer in the field of industrial medicine. In 1910, the governor of Illinois appointed her to investigate rumors that people who were doing the work in Chicago's paint factories were dying from lead poisoning. The result of her investigation was the first state law that was passed to protect workers.

The following year, the U.S. Department of Labor hired this woman, Dr. Hamilton, to study industrial illness throughout the country of the United States. In the next decade, she researched and studied many occupational diseases, including tuberculosis among quarry workers and silicosis—clogged lungs—among sandblasters. To gather information, Dr. Hamilton went to the workplace—deep in mines, quarries, and underwater tunnels. She also spoke to the workers in their homes where they lived.

© Lisa F. Young/Shutterstock.com

With great zeal, Dr. Hamilton spread her message about poor health conditions on the job. What happened with her reports is that they led to new safety regulations, workers' compensation insurance, and improved working conditions in many industries. She wrote many popular articles and spoke to groups of interested citizens. In the year of 1919, she became the first woman to hold courses and teach at Harvard University. Her textbook which she wrote, *Industrial Poisons in the U.S.,* became the standard book on the subject. By the time she died in 1970—she was 101—she had done much to improve the plight of many working people. The reason why she is remembered today is because she cared at a time when many others seemed not to care at all.

C. Fresh Language: Avoiding Triteness

Fresh writing uses original and lively words. It avoids **clichés**, those tired and trite expressions that have lost their power from overuse.

Which sentence in each pair that follows contains fewer expressions that you have heard or read many times before?

1. Some people can relate to the hustle and bustle of city life.
2. Some people thrive on the energy and motion of city life.
3. This book is worth its weight in gold to the car owner.
4. This book can save the car owner hundreds of dollars a year in repairs.

● You probably found that sentences 2 and 4 contained fresher language. Which words and phrases in sentences 1 and 3 have you heard or seen before, in conversation, on TV, or in magazines and newspapers? List them:

_____

_____

Clichés and trite expressions like the following have become so familiar that they have almost no impact on the reader. Avoid them. Say what you mean in your own words:

Cliché: She is pretty as a picture.
Fresh: Her amber eyes and wild red hair mesmerize me.

Or occasionally, play with a cliché and turn it into fresh language:

Cliché: …as American as apple pie.
Fresh: …as American as a Big Mac.
Cliché: The grass is always greener on the other side of the fence.
Fresh: "The grass is always greener over the septic tank."—Erma Bombeck

The following is a partial list of trite expressions to avoid. Add to it any others that you overuse in your writing.

Trite Expressions and Clichés	
at this point in time	in this day and age
awesome	last but not least
better late than never	living hand to mouth
break the ice	one in a million
cold, cruel world	out of this world
cool, hot	sad but true
cry your eyes out	tried and true
easier said than done	under the weather
free as a bird	work like a dog
hustle and bustle	green with envy

PRACTICE 7

Cross out clichés and trite expressions in the following sentences and perhaps replace them with fresh and exact language of your own.

1. Getting a good job in this cold cruel economy can be easier said than done.

2. Many Americans are living hand to mouth, and even college graduates may be hitting a brick wall in the job market.

3. The keys are to keep your chin up and think outside the box, says career coach Bob Martinez.

4. He offers three useful tips for job seekers who are between a rock and a hard place.

5. First, don't cling like there's no tomorrow to one limited career goal.

6. If your dream is to become assistant marketing director for the Portland Trail Blazers, consider starting at any sports organization as low man on the totem pole by getting coffee and helping out.

7. Don't throw out the baby with the bathwater by ruling out an internship.

8. Next, don't rely only on tried and true websites like *monster.com.*

9. Reach out and touch someone by networking in person because having a contact inside the company is often the best way to get hired.

10. Last but not least, at job fairs or interviews, set yourself apart by bringing a writing sample or demonstrating your people skills.

D. Figurative Language: Similes and Metaphors

One way to add sparkle and exactness to your writing is to use an occasional simile or metaphor. A **simile** is a comparison of two things using the word *like* or *as*:

"He was *as ugly as* a wart." —Anne Sexton
"The frozen twigs of the huge tulip poplar next to the hill clack in the cold *like* tinsnips." —Annie Dillard

A **metaphor** is a similar comparison *without* the word *like* or *as*:

"My soul is a dark forest." —D. H. Lawrence
Love is a virus.

● The power of similes and metaphors comes partly from the surprise of comparing two apparently unlike things. A well-chosen simile or metaphor can convey a lot of information in very few words.

● Comparing a person to a wart, as Sexton does, lets us know quickly just how ugly that person is. And to say that *twigs clack like tinsnips* describes the sound so precisely that we can almost hear it.

● What do you think D. H. Lawrence means by his metaphor? In what ways is a person's soul like a *dark forest*?

_____

_____

_____

● The statement *love is a virus* tells us something about the writer's attitude toward love. What is it? In what ways is love like a virus?

_____

_____

_____

Similes and metaphors should not be overused; however, once in a while, they can be a delightful addition to a paper that is also exact, concise, and fresh.

PRACTICE 8

The author of the following paragraph describes a lake as winter turns to spring. She uses at least two similes and two metaphors. Underline the similes and circle the metaphors.

Mornings, a transparent pane of ice lies over the meltwater. I peer through and see some kind of water bug—perhaps a leech—paddling like a sea turtle between green ladders of lakeweed. Cattails and sweetgrass from the previous summer are bone dry, marked with black mold spots, and bend like elbows into the ice.

—Gretel Erlich, "Spring," *Antaeus*

PRACTICE 9

Think of several similes to complete each sentence that follows. Be creative! Then underline your favorite simile, the one that best completes each sentence.

EXAMPLE   My English class is like   *an orchestra.*
the Everglades.
an action movie.
a vegetable garden.

1. Job hunting is like _____

   _____

   _____

   _____

2. My room looks like _____

   _____

   _____

   _____

3. Writing well is like _____

   _____

   _____

   _____

4. Marriage is like _____

   _____

   _____

   _____

PRACTICE 10

Think of several metaphors to complete each sentence that follows. Jot down three or four ideas, and then underline the metaphor that best completes each sentence.

EXAMPLE   Love is   *a blood transfusion.*

                                         a sunrise.

                                         a magic mirror.

                                         a roller coaster ride.

1. The Internet is _____

   _____

   _____

   _____

2. Registration is _____

   _____

   _____

   _____

3. My car is _____

   _____

   _____

   _____

4. Courage is _____

   _____

   _____

   _____

WRITING ASSIGNMENTS

1. Good writing can be done on almost any subject if the writer approaches the subject with openness and with "new eyes." Take a piece of fruit or a vegetable—a lemon, a green pepper, a cherry tomato. Examine it as if for the first time. Feel its texture and parts, smell it, weigh it in your palm.

Now capture your experience of the fruit or vegetable in words. First jot down words and ideas, or freewrite, aiming for the most exact description possible. Don't settle for the first words you think of. Keep writing. Then go back over what you have written, underlining the most exact and powerful writing. Compose a topic sentence and draft a paragraph that conveys your unique experience of the fruit or vegetable.

2. In the paragraph that follows, Rick Bragg describes his home state in such rich, exact detail that it comes to life for the reader. Read his paragraph, underlining language that strikes you as *exact* and *fresh*. Can you spot the two similes? Can you find any especially vivid adjectives or unusual verbs?

My mother and father were born in the most beautiful place on earth, in the foothills of the Appalachians along the Alabama–Georgia line. It was a place where gray mists hid the tops of low, deep-green mountains, where redbone and bluetick hounds flashed through the pines as they chased possums into the sacks of old men in frayed overalls, where old women in bonnets dipped Bruton snuff and hummed "Faded Love and Winter Roses" as they shelled purple hulls, canned peaches and made biscuits too good for this world. It was a place where playing the church piano loud was near as important as playing it right, where fearless young men steered long, black Buicks loaded with yellow whiskey down roads the color of dried blood, where the first frost meant hog killin' time, and the mouthwatering smell of cracklin's would drift for acres from giant, bubbling pots. It was a place where the screams of panthers, like a woman's anguished cry, still haunted the most remote ridges and hollows in the dead of night, where children believed they could choke off the cries of night birds by circling one wrist with a thumb and forefinger and squeezing tight, and where the cotton blew off the wagons and hung like scraps of cloud in the branches of trees.

—Rick Bragg, *All Over But the Shoutin'*

Write a paragraph or essay in which you describe a place you know well and perhaps love. As you freewrite or brainstorm, try to capture the most precise and minute details of what you experienced or remember. Now revise your writing, making the language as *exact, concise,* and *fresh* as you can.

EXPLORING ONLINE

http://www.ccc.commnet.edu/sensen/part3/sixteen/techniques_using.html
Practice choosing exact language.

http://grammar.ccc.commnet.edu/grammar/concise.htm
Practice pruning excess words.

http://grammar.ccc.commnet.edu/grammar/vocabulary.htm
Build a powerful, college-level vocabulary: tips, quizzes, links.

CourseMate for *Evergreen*

Visit *Evergreen* CourseMate for more practices and quizzes, videos to accompany the readings, career and job-search resources, ESL help, and live links to every Exploring Online in the book.

CHAPTER **24**

Putting Your Revision Skills to Work

n Units 2 and 3, you learned to **revise** basic paragraphs, and in Unit 4, you learned to revise essays. All revising requires that you rethink and rewrite with such questions as these in mind:

> Can a reader understand and follow my ideas?
>
> Is my topic sentence or thesis statement clear?
>
> Does the body of my paragraph or essay fully support the topic or thesis statement?
>
> Does my paragraph or essay have unity? That is, does every sentence relate to the main idea?
>
> Does my paragraph or essay have coherence? That is, does it follow a logical order and guide the reader from point to point?
>
> Does my writing conclude, not just leave off?

Of course, the more writing techniques you learn, the more options you have as you revise. Unit 5 has moved beyond the basics to matters of style: consistency and parallelism, sentence variety, and clear, exact language. This chapter will guide you again through the revision process, adding questions like the following to your list:

> Are my verb tenses and pronouns consistent?
>
> Have I used parallel structure?
>
> Have I varied the length and type of my sentences?
>
> Is my language exact, concise, and fresh?

Many writers first revise and rewrite with questions like these in mind. They do *not* worry about grammar and minor errors at this stage. Then in a separate, final process, they **proofread**[*] for spelling and grammatical errors.

Here are two sample paragraphs by students, showing the first draft, the revisions made by the student, and the revised draft of each. Each revision has been numbered and explained to give you a clear idea of the thinking process involved.

Writing Sample 1

First Draft

I like to give my best performance. I must relax completely before a show. I often know ahead of time what choreography I will use and what I'll sing, so I can concentrate on relaxing completely. I usually do this by reading, etc. I always know my parts perfectly. Occasionally I look through the curtain to watch the people come in. This can make you feel faint, but I reassure myself and say I know everything will be okay.

Revisions

(1) *In order*
~~I like~~ to give my best performance, I must relax completely before a show.

(2) *and vocals*
I often know ahead of time what choreography I will use, and ~~what I'll sing,~~

(3) *during that long, last hour before curtain,*
(4)
so I can concentrate on relaxing, ~~completely.~~ I usually do this by reading,
(5) *an action-packed mystery, but sometimes I joke with the other performers or just walk around backstage.* (6)
(7) *peek*
~~etc.~~ I always know my parts perfectly. Occasionally I ~~look~~ through the curtain to

audience file (8) *me*
watch the ~~people come~~ in. This can make ~~you~~ feel faint, but I reassure myself,

(9) *"Vickie," I say, "the minute you're out there singing to the people, everything will be okay."*
~~and say I know everything will be okay.~~

Reasons for Revisions

1. Combine two short sentences. (sentence variety)

2. Make *choreography* and *vocals* parallel and omit unnecessary words. (parallelism)

3. Make time order clear: first discuss what I've done during the days before the performance, and then discuss the hour before performance. (time order)

4. Drop *completely*, which repeats the word used in the first sentence. (avoid wordiness)

5. This is important! Drop *etc.*, add more details, and give examples. (add examples)

---

[*] For practice in proofreading for particular errors, see individual chapters in Units 6 and 7. For practice in proofreading for mixed errors, see Chapter 39, "Putting Your Proofreading Skills to Work."

6. This idea belongs earlier in the paragraph—with what I've done during the days before the performance. (order)

7. Use more specific and interesting language in this sentence. (exact language)

8. Use the first person singular pronouns *I* and *me* consistently throughout the paragraph. (consistent person)

9. Dull—use a direct quotation, the actual words I say to myself. (exact language, sentence variety)

Revised Draft

In order to give my best performance, I must relax completely before a show. I often know ahead of time what choreography and vocals I will use, and I always know my parts perfectly, so during that long, last hour before curtain, I can concentrate on relaxing. I usually do this by reading an action-packed mystery, but sometimes I joke with the other performers or just walk around backstage. Occasionally I peek through the curtain to watch the audience file in. This can make me feel faint, but I reassure myself. "Vickie," I say, "the minute you're out there singing to the people, everything will be okay."

—Victoria DeWindt, Student

Writing Sample 2

First Draft

When I was little, I stuttered. I didn't even know it. Kids at school started teasing me, and I realized. Children can be very cruel. I became withdrawn and stopped talking at school. My grades were poor. My parents decided to put me in speech therapy, which really helped. I got faster and could often speak normally, without repeating any syllables. My speech therapists taught me lessons of compassion and patience. They totally put me on the path I am on today. They not only helped me in childhood, but in my career decision as well. I hope to help other young people.

Revisions

① When I was ~~little~~ *a child,* I stuttered. I didn't even know it. ② *until some children* ~~Kids~~ at school started

teasing me, ~~and I realized. Children can be very cruel.~~ ③ *yelling "Suh-Suh-Sarah."* I became withdrawn and

stopped talking at school. ~~My grades were poor.~~ ④ *When* *realized how poor my grades were, they* My parents decided to put me in

speech therapy, ~~which really helped.~~ ⑤ *Add new section below** I got faster and could often speak normally,

without repeating any syllables. *at all* ~~My speech therapists taught me~~ *Early* lessons

of compassion and patience. *from my speech therapists* ~~They totally~~ put me on the path I am on today.

* *Miss Lindsey and Mister Bob, my speech therapists, taught me to slow down and relax to pronounce words correctly. They taught me exercises and breathing techniques. Even when I struggled to get something right, they would praise and encourage me. Over time,*

⑥ *My speech therapists*   ⑦ *they inspired me to become a speech-language pathologist.*

~~They~~ not only helped me in childhood, but ~~in my career decision as well~~. I hope
                                                        ∧

to help other young people ⑧ *conquer their speaking obstacles because I know that*
                                    speaking easily will give them the confidence to succeed.

Reasons for Revisions

1. Add topic sentence that better fits the revised paragraph. (topic sentence)

2. Combine two short sentences. (sentence variety)

3. Add a good example of the children's cruelty. (exact language, avoid wordiness)

4. Combine two sentences and make order clear. (sentence variety, time order)

5. This is important! Tell in detail how these therapists helped me, and name them. (add examples, exact language)

6. *They* now seems to refer to *syllables*; change to *my speech therapists*. (pronoun substitution)

7. Oops. Tell what career I'm referring to. (exact language)

8. Be specific. Tell how I want to help young people, so the reader understands my passion. (add examples, exact language, sentence variety)

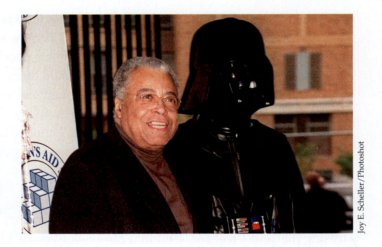

Although James Earl Jones stuttered so badly as a boy that he didn't speak for eight years, he became a great actor—and the voice of Darth Vader.

Joy E. Scheller/Photoshot

Revised Draft

    Early lessons of compassion and patience from my speech therapists put me on the path I am on today. When I was a child, I stuttered. I didn't even know it until some children at school started teasing me, yelling, "Suh-Suh-Sarah." I became withdrawn and stopped talking at school. When my parents realized how poor my grades were, they decided to put me in speech therapy. Miss Lindsey and Mister Bob, my speech therapists, taught me to slow down and relax to pronounce words correctly. They taught me exercises and breathing techniques. Even when I struggled to get something right, they would praise and encourage me. Over time, I got faster and could often speak normally, without repeating any syllables at all. My speech therapists not only helped me in childhood, but they inspired me to become a speech-language pathologist. I hope to help other young people conquer their speaking obstacles because I know that speaking easily will give them the confidence to succeed.

—Sarah Washington, Student

PRACTICE

Because revising, like writing, is a personal process, the best practice is to revise your own paragraphs and essays. Nevertheless, here is a first draft that needs revising.

Revise it *as if you had written it*. Mark your revisions on the first draft, using and building on the good parts, crossing out unnecessary words, rewriting unclear or awkward sentences, adding details, and perhaps reordering parts. Then, recopy your final draft on the lines. Especially, ask yourself these questions:

> Are my verb tenses and pronouns consistent?
> Have I used parallel structure to highlight parallel ideas?
> Have I varied the length and type of my sentences?
> Is my language exact, concise, and fresh?

First Draft

BREAKING THE YO-YO SYNDROME

For years, I was a yo-yo dieter. I bounced from fad diets to eating binges when I ate a lot. This leaves you tired and with depression. Along the way, though, I learned a few things. As a result, I personally will never go on a diet again for the rest of my life.

First of all, diets are unhealthy. Some of the low-carbohydrate diets are high in fat. Accumulating fat through meat, eggs, and the eating of cheese can raise blood levels of cholesterol and led to artery and heart disease. Other diets are too high in protein and can cause kidney ailments, and other things can go wrong with your body, too. Most diets also leave you deficient in essential vitamins and minerals that are necessary to health, such as calcium and iron.

In addition, diets are short-term. I lose about ten pounds. I wind up gaining more weight than I originally lost. I also get sick and tired of the restricted diet. On one diet, I ate cabbage soup for breakfast, lunch, and dinner. You are allowed to eat some fruit on day one, some vegetables on day two, and so on, but mostly you are supposed to eat cabbage soup. After a week, I never want to see a bowl of cabbage soup again. Because the diet was nutritionally unbalanced, I ended up craving bread, meat, and all the other foods I am not supposed to eat. Moreover, in the short-term, all one loses is water. You cannot lose body fat unless you reduce regularly and at a steady rate over a long period of time.

The last diet I tried was a fat-free diet. On this diet I actually gained weight while dieting. I am surprised to discover that you can gain weight on a fat-free diet snacking on fat-free cookies, ice cream, and cheese and crackers. I also learn that the body needs fat—in particular, the unsaturated fat in foods like olive oil, nuts, avocados, and salad dressings. If a dieter takes in too little fat, you are constantly hungry. Furthermore, the body thinks it is starving, so it makes every effort to try to conserve fat, which makes it much harder for one to lose weight.

In place of fad diets, I now follow a long-range plan. It is sensible and improved my health. I eat three well-balanced meals, exercise daily, and am meeting regularly with my support group for weight control. I am much happier and don't weigh as much than I used to be.

"And, on the lowest end of the caloric spectrum, we offer a leather chew toy."

Revised Draft

BREAKING THE YO-YO SYNDROME

_____

_____

_____

_____

_____

_____

_____

_____

_____

_____

_____

_____

_____

_____

_____

_____

_____

_____

_____

_____

_____

_____

_____

_____
_____
_____
_____
_____
_____
_____
_____
_____
_____
_____
_____
_____
_____

EXPLORING ONLINE

https://owl.english.purdue.edu/owl/resource/561/05/
Guidance for the writer who is about to revise.

http://owl.english.purdue.edu/owl/resource/561/01
Guidance for the writer who is about to revise and proofread

CourseMate for _Evergreen_

Visit _Evergreen_ CourseMate for more practices and quizzes, videos
to accompany the readings, career and job-search resources,
ESL help, and live links to every Exploring Online in the book.

Writer's Workshop

Examine Something That Isn't What It Appears to Be

Revising is the key to all good writing—taking the time to sit down, reread, and rethink what you have written. In this unit, you have practiced revising for consistent verb tense, consistent person, parallelism, sentence variety, and language awareness.

In your group or class, read this student's essay, aloud if possible. Underline the parts that strike you as especially effective, and put a checkmark by anything that might need revising.

Behind the Face of Beauty

(1) Beauty is her name. She walks with her head up high, five foot three in height, a hundred and ten pounds in weight, small waist and figure round in shape. Her hair is as long as a Native American's, with light brown eyes and a "killer smile." She has a caramel complexion that turns bronze in color during the summer.

(2) She has style and wore flashy jewelry that will make you stare in amazement. She has a ton of clothing that would make a movie star jealous. She was very sociable and did not have any trouble getting people to like her, mainly because of her sense of humor. Everyone enjoyed being around her, just as she enjoys having everyone around her. Men want to marry her, and women would just about do anything to have her confidence and strength.

(3) Heavenly is what she seems, but she is only disguised as an angel. She does not pay attention to men on foot, meaning, men without cars. Everything and everybody has to be within her control. If she can't dictate to you, she will try to destroy you and do it in a way you won't at first recognize. She'll criticize your brand new shoes so that you will return them. Once you have returned the shoes, you will see her wearing the same pair. Blasphemy is what she will accuse you of if you ever call her envious.

(4) Well into her thirties, the oldest of five, and raised in a broken home with her careless teenaged mother, she ran away and chose a life of so-called freedom. Self-hate is inside her soul, but she covers it up with a smile and a bag full of tricks and trades. Using manipulation and deceit is the only way she feels she can get her vengeance.

(5) When I was a girl, I used to watch different sweethearts shower her with gifts. The family adored her. She was my mother's firstborn. Her young friends catered to her. To them, she was a goddess. I cherished the ground she walked on. I had every intention of being just like her someday. She said she loved her "baby sis," but the minute you showed signs of confidence, she would make you cry by saying you were not strong.

(6) Now, tears are what I shed for her because she is lost. Until she finds the right path, she will continue to cover up with lavishness and luxury. She will hypnotize both men and women into being under her control. With time, others will learn that she is shallow and, to those who open their hearts to her, even dangerous.

—Tyesha Wiggins, Student

1. How effective is Ms. Wiggins's essay?

   _____ Strong thesis statement?   _____ Good supporting details?

   _____ Logical organization?   _____ Effective conclusion?

2. What do you like best about this essay? What details or sections most command your attention or make you think?

3. Although this student writes about someone she knows, she is also trying to make sense for herself and the reader of her sister's outward beauty and inner ugliness. Do you think she succeeds?

4. How do you think the author of this essay would define beauty? Do you think ideas of beauty are changing? You might want to read the results of a recent survey: http://www.racialicious.com/2011/03/23/allure-marks-shifting -beauty-standards-declares-the-all-american-beauty-ideal-dead/

5. Are all the verb tenses correct, or do you notice any inconsistent tense?

6. Are there any places where short, choppy sentences detract from the excellent content?

7. Can you spot any error patterns (the same error two or more times) that this student should watch out for?

GROUP WORK

In your group, revise Ms. Wiggins's essay as if it were your own. First, decide what problems need attention. Then rewrite those parts, sentence by sentence, aiming for a truly fine paper. Share your revision with the class, explaining why you made the changes you did.

WRITING AND REVISING IDEAS

1. Examine something that isn't what it appears to be or someone whose presentation contrasts with his or her character.

2. Write a definition of the word *beauty* or *ugliness*.

Unit 6

Reviewing the Basics

CHAPTER 25

Proofreading to Correct Your Personal Error Patterns

A: Identifying and Tracking Your Personal Error Patterns

B: Proofreading Strategies

The important last step in the writing process is proofreading: slowly reading your revised paragraph or essay in order to find and correct any errors in grammar, punctuation, and spelling.

Proofreading your own work before turning it in is vitally important because grammatical and other mistakes not only distract readers but give a negative impression of your skills and even intelligence. Many employers won't interview a candidate whose cover letter or résumé contains errors. Yet many new writers avoid proofreading or rush through it so quickly that they set themselves up for failure.

In fact, the more mistakes you tend to make, the more important proofreading is for you. This chapter will give you tools to build your skills as an error detective and writer. Then the rest of this unit and Unit 7 will further develop your proofreading skills, teaching you how to spot and correct many specific errors. In each chapter ahead, you'll get to practice a proofreading strategy that targets a particular mistake.

A: Identifying and Tracking Your Personal Error Patterns

Knowing what errors you tend to make and then proofreading for these errors will boost your success in college and at work.

Learn Your Error Patterns

An **error pattern** is any error you make two, three, or more times. For example, if a teacher has noted that one of your papers has several comma splices or numerous verb errors, those are *error patterns* that you need to work on. The first step in getting rid of these errors is becoming aware of them.

Here are four ways to discover your error patterns:

Papers. Study recently returned papers, making sure you understand the errors that have been marked. Check the inside back cover of this book for proofreading symbols your instructor might use, like *frag* for sentence fragment. Count the number of times each mistake appears.

Instructor. Ask your instructor to identify your error patterns. List them. Ask which three are the most serious.

Textbook. As you work through this book, notice chapters or practices where you keep making mistakes or writing incorrect answers. These are your error patterns.

Writing lab. Go to the writing lab with a paper you recently wrote. Ask a tutor to help identify the kinds of errors you make. Ask which three are the most serious.

PRACTICE 1   Consult your instructor, or bring a recent paper to the college writing lab. Get help in identifying your error patterns and start a written list. Ask which three error patterns most harm your written communication and your grade.

Create a Personal Error Patterns Chart

Let's say your instructor marks twelve errors on your English paper, and eight of them are verb agreement mistakes. This means that eight of your errors are really one error repeated eight times! Mastering this one error pattern would certainly improve your grade.

An excellent tool for tracking and beginning to master your errors is an **error chart** or **log**. This tool will show you what to study and what mistakes to watch for in your writing. Here is an example of one student's chart:

Personal Error Patterns Chart			
Error Type & Symbol	**Specific Error**	**Correction**	**Rule or Reminder**
Fragment *frag*	The house was saved. Because firefighters quickly doused the flames.	The house was saved because firefighters quickly doused the flames.	Don't punctuate a dependent clause as a complete sentence. (Ch. 28)
Sound-alikes *sp*	The scholarship committee has made it's decision.	The scholarship committee has made its decision.	*It's* = it is *Its* is possessive.
Pronoun agreement *agr*	Everyone brought their best dish to the feast.	Everyone brought his or her best dish to the feast.	*Everyone* is singular (indefinite pronoun) so pronoun must be singular. (Ch. 33, B)

- Each time you receive a marked paper, write every error name or type in column 1 (like *fragment* or *pronoun agreement*). Check the inside back cover to understand your instructor's proofreading symbols; for instance, *frag* for fragment.
- In column 2, copy the error as you wrote it.
- In column 3, correct the error. If you have trouble understanding what you did wrong, ask the instructor or search the index of this book for the pages you need.
- In column 4, jot the rule or ideas for fixing this type of mistake.
- When you have filled a page or more, look for *error patterns* that keep coming up. Keep a count of these in the left margin. Any error that appears in paper after paper will need a special plan of attack.

Continue to add errors from future papers, instructor conferences, and tests. As you work in this textbook, add to your chart any grammatical concepts that still confuse you. Whenever you master the correction of an error, cross it off the chart and celebrate your achievement.

PRACTICE 2

Using a recent paper of yours that was graded by an instructor, begin your Personal Error Patterns Chart. You can use the blank chart in this book or create your own chart as a Word file, adding rows as you need them. Some students design and draw their own charts. Follow this format:

Error Type & Symbol	Specific Error	Correction	Rule or Reminder

B. Proofreading Strategies

Whenever you write, honor your own writing process by setting aside enough time to perform each step, including proofreading. Just as it helps to take a break of hours or days between writing your first draft and revising, taking a break *before you proofread* is beneficial. Go for a walk. Call a friend. You cannot do a good job proofreading when you are tired. You will catch more errors with a rested mind and fresh outlook.

If possible, proofread in a quiet place where you won't be distracted—not at a dance club, not standing in the kitchen fixing dinner with the kids.

Many writers have found that the **proofreading strategies** described below help them see their own writing with a fresh eye. You will learn more strategies in subsequent chapters of this book. Try a number of methods and see which ones work best for you.

Proofreading Strategy 1:   *Allow enough time to proofread.*

Many students don't proofread at all, or they skim their paper for grammatical errors two minutes before class. This just doesn't work. Set aside enough time to proofread slowly and carefully, searching for errors and especially hunting for your personal error patterns.

Proofreading Strategy 2:   *Work from a paper copy.*

People who proofread on computers tend to miss more errors. If you write on a computer, do not proofread on the monitor. Instead, print a copy of your paper, perhaps enlarging the type to 14 point. Switching to a paper copy seems to help the brain see more clearly.

Proofreading Strategy 3:   *Read your words aloud.*

Reading silently makes it easier to skip over small errors or mentally fill in missing details whereas listening closely is a great way to hear mistakes. Listen and follow along on your printed copy, marking errors as you hear them.

a. Read your paper aloud to *yourself*. Be sure to read *exactly* what's on the page, and read with enthusiasm.

b. Ask a *friend* or *writing tutor* to read your paper out loud to you. Tell the reader you just want to hear your words and that you don't want any other suggestions right now.

Proofreading Strategy 4:   *Read "bottoms up," from the end to the beginning.*

One way to fool the brain into taking a fresh look at something you've written is to proofread the last sentence first. Read slowly, word by word. Then read the second-to-last sentence, and so on, all the way back to the first sentence.

Proofreading Strategy 5:   *Isolate your sentences.*

If you write on a computer, spotting errors is often easier if you reformat so that each sentence appears isolated, on its own line. Double space between sentences. This visual change can help the brain focus clearly on one sentence at a time.

Proofreading Strategy 6:   Check for one error at a time.

If you make many mistakes, proofread separately all the way through your paper for each error pattern. Although this process takes time, you will catch many more errors this way and make real progress. You will begin to eliminate some errors altogether as you learn about fixing each error and as you get better at spotting and correcting it. You will learn more recommended proofreading strategies in upcoming chapters.

PRACTICE 3

Janet Fekete/Getty Images

Grammar CSI. Help solve crimes against English! Working in teams, proofread your local newspapers, signs, ads, and other printed materials (like campus flyers and publications). When you locate an error in grammar, punctuation, capitalization, or spelling, collect the evidence: write down, photocopy, or use your cell phone to snap a picture of the offending mistake. Collect five to ten errors and create a presentation—a report, collage, or PowerPoint presentation displaying evidence from your crime scenes.

PRACTICE 4

Print out or make two photocopies of something you wrote recently for college or work. Ask someone to read the original out loud as you listen. On your copy, underline or highlight sentences or places that sound wrong. Also mark any places where the reader stumbles verbally. Rewrite the marked sentences.

PRACTICE 5

Choose a paper you wrote recently. Select one of the proofreading strategies and try it out on this paper. Read with full attention, keenly watching for your personal error patterns. Put a check in the margin beside each error. Then correct them neatly above the lines.

EXPLORING ONLINE

http://writing.wisc.edu/Handbook/Proofreading.html

Excellent proofreading advice from the University of Wisconsin OWL

http://owl.english.purdue.edu/owl/resource/561/01/

Proofreading tips from the Purdue University OWL, plus advice on correcting common errors made by college students

CourseMate for *Evergreen*

Visit *Evergreen* CourseMate for more practices and quizzes, videos to accompany the readings, career and job-search resources, ESL help, and live links to every Exploring Online in the book.

CHAPTER 26

The Simple Sentence

A: Defining and Spotting Subjects

B: Spotting Prepositional Phrases

C: Defining and Spotting Verbs

A. Defining and Spotting Subjects

To write well, you need to know how to write correct sentences. A sentence is a group of words that contains a **subject** and a **verb** and expresses a complete thought.

A subject is the *who* or *what* word that performs the action or the *who* or *what* word about which a statement is made:

> 1. Three *hunters* tramped through the woods.
> 2. The blue *truck* belongs to Ralph.

- In sentence 1, *hunters*, the *who* word, performs the action—"tramped through the woods."

- In sentence 2, *truck* is the *what* word about which a statement is made—"belongs to Ralph."

Some sentences have more than one subject, joined by *and*:

> 3. Her *aunt and uncle* love country music.

- In sentence 3, *aunt and uncle*, the *who* words, perform the action—they "love country music."

- *Aunt and uncle* is called a **compound subject**.

Sometimes an *-ing* word can be the subject of a sentence:

> 4. *Reading* strains my eyes.

● *Reading* is the *what* word that performs the action—"strains my eyes."

PRACTICE 1

Circle the subjects in these sentences.

1. Do you know the origin and customs of Kwanzaa?

2. This African American holiday celebrates black heritage and lasts for seven days—from December 26 through January 1.

3. Maulana Karenga introduced Kwanzaa to America in 1966.

4. In Swahili, Kwanzaa means "first fruits of the harvest."

5. During the holiday, families share simple meals of foods from the Caribbean, Africa, South America, and the American South.

6. Specific foods have special meanings.

7. For instance, certain fruits and vegetables represent the products of group effort.

8. Another important symbol is corn, which stands for children.

9. At each dinner, celebrants light a black, red, or green candle and discuss one of the seven principles of Kwanzaa.

10. These seven principles are unity, self-determination, collective work and responsibility, cooperative economics, purpose, creativity, and faith.

Lighting the candles at Kwanzaa

B. Spotting Prepositional Phrases

One group of words that may confuse you as you look for subjects is the prepositional phrase. A **prepositional phrase** contains a **preposition** (a word like *at, in, of, from,* and so forth) and its **object**.

Preposition	Object
at	the beach
on	time
of	the students

The object of a preposition *cannot* be the subject of a sentence. Therefore, spotting and crossing out the prepositional phrases will help you find the subject.

1. The sweaters in the window look handmade.
2. The sweaters ~~in the window~~ look handmade.
3. ~~On Tuesday,~~ a carton ~~of oranges~~ was left ~~on the porch~~.

● In sentence 1, you might have trouble finding the subject. But once the prepositional phrase is crossed out in sentence 2, the subject, *sweaters*, is easy to spot.

● In sentence 3, once the prepositional phrases are crossed out, the subject, *carton*, is easy to spot.

Here are some common prepositions that you should know:

Common Prepositions			
about	before	in	through
above	behind	into	to
across	between	like	toward
after	by	near	under
along	during	of	until
among	for	on	up
at	from	over	with

PRACTICE 2

Cross out the prepositional phrases in each sentence. Then circle the subject of the sentence.

1. From 6 A.M. until 10 A.M., Angel works out.

2. Local buses for Newark leave every hour.

3. Three of my friends take singing lessons.

4. That man between Ralph and Cynthia is the famous actor Hank the Hunk.

5. Near the door, a pile of laundry sits in a basket.

6. Toward evening, the houses across the river disappear in the thick fog.

7. Before class, Helena and I meet for coffee.

8. In one corner of the lab, beakers of colored liquid bubbled and boiled.

C. Defining and Spotting Verbs

Action Verbs

In order to be complete, every sentence must contain a **verb**. One kind of verb, called an **action verb**, expresses the action that the subject is performing:

1. The star quarterback *fumbled*.
2. The carpenters *worked* all day, but the bricklayers *went* home early.

● In sentence 1, the action verb is *fumbled*.

● In sentence 2, the action verbs are *worked* and *went*.*

Linking Verbs

Another kind of verb, called a **linking verb**, links the subject to words that describe or identify it:

3. Don *is* a fine mathematician.
4. This fabric *feels* rough and scratchy.

● In sentence 3, the verb *is* links the subject *Don* with the noun *mathematician*.

● In sentence 4, the verb *feels* links the subject *fabric* with the adjectives *rough* and *scratchy*.

---

* For work on compound predicates, see Chapter 22, "Revising for Sentence Variety," Part D.

Here are some common linking verbs:

Common Linking Verbs	
appear	feel
be (am, is, are, was, were, has been, have been, had been . . .)	look
become	seem

Verbs of More Than One Word—Helping Verbs

So far you have dealt with verbs of only one word—*fumbled, worked, is, feels*, and so on. But many verbs consist of more than one word:

> 5. He *should have taken* the train home.
> 6. *Are* Tanya and Joe *practicing* the piano?
> 7. The lounge *was painted* last week.

- In sentence 5, *taken* is the main verb; *should* and *have* are the **helping verbs**.
- In sentence 6, *practicing* is the main verb; *are* is the helping verb.
- In sentence 7, *painted* is the main verb; *was* is the helping verb.*

PRACTICE 3

RTimages/Shutterstock.com

Underline the verbs in these sentences.

1. By 2020, San Francisco will become the first zero-waste city in the world.

2. No city garbage will be sent to a landfill that year.

3. But first, 800,000 residents are learning new garbage habits.

4. Children in San Francisco now get recycling lessons in school.

5. They compost their lunch leftovers and use the fertilizer in school vegetable gardens.

6. In fact, all city dwellers must collect their food scraps and garden trimmings.

7. Recycling centers are accepting other waste, like plastic toys, old electronics, and styrofoam.

8. At malls and local Starbucks, videos remind shoppers to use the correct color-coded bins.

* For more work on verbs in the passive voice, see Chapter 31, "The Past Participle," Part E.

9. The city sponsors contests and gives prizes for empty black trash bins and full green or blue recycling bins in people's yards.

10. At 77 percent zero waste already, San Francisco has gained worldwide attention.

PROOFREADING STRATEGY

Being able to identify subjects and verbs will help you check your sentences for completeness and correct many serious writing errors (like fragments and run-on sentences in Chapter 28). To find subjects and verbs, **cross out** and **color code**:

1. Read each sentence slowly, crossing out any prepositional phrases.

2. Then either circle the subject and underline the verb or *color code your subjects and verbs*, using two different highlighters, like this:

   In the 1950s, a gallon of gas cost about 20 cents.

   Today, the fuel in our tanks is priced at nearly $4 for every gallon.

3. Finally, read each sentence slowly to make sure it expresses a complete thought and ends with a period.

PRACTICE 4   REVIEW

Cross out any prepositional phrases in each of the sentences below. Then either circle each subject and underline each verb or highlight the subject and verb in different colors.

1. Do you watch videos on YouTube?

2. This hugely popular website grew quickly out of an invention by three friends.

3. One night, Steve Chen shot a video of his pals Chad Hurley and Jawed Karim.

5. Surprisingly, the three buddies could find no easy way of sharing this video online.

6. Their solution was a video-sharing website.

7. Their friends loved it and inspired the young men to launch YouTube in 2005.

8. Within two years, YouTube had attracted millions of visitors and millions of dollars from investors.

9. Very easily, users can view or post videos on the site.

10. Today, YouTube's millions of videos inspire creativity, news reporting by everyday people, and some engaging craziness.

EXPLORING ONLINE

http://grammar.ccc.commnet.edu/grammar/quizzes/subjector.htm
Interactive subject quiz

http://www.dailygrammar.com/archive.html
Click "Lessons 6-10" (Verbs) and "Lessons 11-15" (Verbs) for a verb review.

http://a4esl.org/a/g3.html
Interactive preposition quizzes: scroll down to "Prepositions"

CourseMate for *Evergreen*
Visit *Evergreen* CourseMate for more practices and quizzes, videos
to accompany the readings, career and job-search resources,
ESL help, and live links to every Exploring Online in the book.

CHAPTER **27**

Coordination and Subordination

A: Coordination

B: Subordination

C: Semicolons

D: Conjunctive Adverbs

E: Review

A. Coordination

A **clause** is a group of words that includes a subject and a verb. If a clause can stand alone as a complete idea, it is an **independent clause** and can be written as a **simple sentence**.*

Here are two independent clauses written as simple sentences:

> 1. The dog barked all night.
> 2. The neighbors didn't complain.

You can join two clauses together by placing a comma and a **coordinating conjunction** between them:

> 3. The dog barked all night, *but* the neighbors didn't complain.
> 4. Let's go to the beach today, *for* it is too hot to do anything else.

---

* For more work on simple sentences, see Chapter 26, "The Simple Sentence."

- The coordinating conjunctions *but* and *for* join together two clauses.

- Note that the clause on each side of the coordinating conjunction can stand alone as a complete sentence.

- *A comma precedes each coordinating conjunction.*

  Here is a list of the most common coordinating conjunctions. To help you remember them, just think FANBOYS (the first letter of *for, and, nor, but, or, yet,* and *so*).

<table>
<tr><td colspan="4" align="center">**Coordinating Conjunctions**</td></tr>
<tr><td>and</td><td>for</td><td>or</td><td>yet</td></tr>
<tr><td>but</td><td>nor</td><td>so</td><td></td></tr>
</table>

  Be sure to choose the coordinating conjunction that best expresses the *relationship* between the two clauses in a sentence:

> 5. It was late, *so* I decided to take a bus home.
> 6. It was late, *yet* I decided to take a bus home.

- The *so* in sentence 5 means that the lateness of the hour caused me to take the bus. (The trains don't run after midnight.)

- The *yet* in sentence 6 means that despite the late hour I still decided to take a bus home. (I knew I might have to wait two hours at the bus stop.)

- Note that a comma precedes the coordinating conjunction.

PRACTICE 1

Read the following sentences for meaning. Then fill in the coordinating conjunction that *best* expresses the relationship between the two clauses. Don't forget to add the comma.

1. In 1853, a customer at Moon Lake Lodge in Saratoga, New York, thought his fried

   potatoes were too thick and soggy _____ he sent them back to the kitchen.

2. The Native American/African American chef, George Crum, took offense at this

   criticism of his cooking _____ he was a confident and cranky fellow.

3. Crum wanted to annoy his fussy customer_____ he angrily sliced some potatoes

   very thin, poured salt all over them, and fried them hard.

4. The chef expected the complaining patron to leave in a huff _____ he didn't.

5. Instead, the crispy potato thins pleased the customer immensely _____ he

   ordered more.

6. Crum, who soon opened his own restaurant, called his lucky invention "potato crunches" _____ he later renamed them "Saratoga Chips."

7. In the 1920s, traveling salesman Herman Lay began selling potato chips out of the trunk of his car _____ other companies began manufacturing them, too.

8. Now customers could order the tasty treat in restaurants _____ they could munch them at home.

9. However, chips at the bottom of the barrel or tin packaging would not stay fresh _____ would they stay crispy.

10. Entrepreneur Laura Scudder solved this problem by putting the chips between sheets of wax paper that she ironed together _____ the potato chip quickly became America's favorite snack.

PRACTICE 2

Combine these simple sentences with a coordinating conjunction. Punctuate correctly.

1. My daughter wants to be a mechanic. She spends every spare minute at the garage.

   _____

   _____

2. Ron dared not look over the edge. Heights made him dizzy.

   _____

   _____

3. Tasha's living room is cozy. Her guests always gather in the kitchen.

   _____

   _____

4. Meet me by the bicycle rack. Meet me at Lulu's Nut Shop.

   _____

   _____

5. In 1969, the first astronauts landed on the moon. Most Americans felt proud.

   _____

   _____

B. Subordination

Two clauses can also be joined with a **subordinating conjunction**. The clause following a subordinating conjunction is called a **subordinate** or **dependent clause** because it depends on an independent clause to complete its meaning:

> 1. We will light the candles *when Flora arrives*.

- *When Flora arrives* is a subordinate or dependent clause introduced by the subordinating conjunction *when*.
- By itself, *when Flora arrives* is incomplete; it depends on the independent clause to complete its meaning.*

Note that sentence 1 can also be written this way:

> 2. *When Flora arrives,* we will light the candles.

- The meaning of sentences 1 and 2 is the same, but the punctuation is different.
- In sentence 1, because the subordinate clause *follows* the independent clause, *no comma* is needed.
- In sentence 2, however, because the subordinate clause *begins* the sentence, it is followed by a *comma*.

Here is a partial list of subordinating conjunctions:

Subordinating Conjunctions		
after	if	unless
although	if only	until
as	in order that	when
as if	once	whenever
as though	provided that	where
because	rather than	whereas
before	since	wherever
even if	so that	whether
even though	though	while

---

* For more work on incomplete sentences, or fragments, see Chapter 28, "Avoiding Sentence Errors," Part B.

Be sure to choose the subordinating conjunction that *best expresses the relationship* between the two clauses in a sentence:

> 3. This course was excellent *because* Professor Green taught it.
> 4. This course was excellent *although* Professor Green taught it.

- Sentence 3 says that the course was excellent *because* Professor Green, a great teacher, taught it.
- Sentence 4 says that the course was excellent *despite the fact that* Professor Green, apparently a bad teacher, taught it.

PRACTICE 3

Read the following sentences for meaning. Then fill in the subordinating conjunction that *best* expresses the relationship between the two clauses.

1. We could see very clearly last night _____ the moon was so bright.

2. Violet read *Sports Illustrated* _____ Daisy walked in the woods.

3. _____ it is cold outside, our new wood-burning Franklin stove keeps us warm.

4. The students buzzed with excitement _____ Professor Hargrave announced that classes would be held at the zoo.

5. _____ his shoulder loosens up a bit, Ron will stay on the bench.

PRACTICE 4

Punctuate the following sentences by adding a comma where necessary. Put a C after any correct sentences.

1. Thousands of low-income children in Venezuela have been given a new life because Jose Antonio Abreu taught them to play classical music.

2. While some people only talked about the poverty and drugs destroying many young Venezuelans Abreu took action.

3. After he convinced government leaders that musical training builds self-worth, Abreu got funding to start children's orchestras.

4. The results have been amazing as communities proudly support their young musicians.

5. When the children practice their violins or oboes they are also learning discipline, valuable skills, and the joys of musical teamwork.

Brothers Wilfredo and
Onil Galarraga received
instruments and new
opportunities, thanks
to the Venezuelan
Children's Orchestra.

6. The program ignores pop and tropical musicians like Christina Aguilera and Oscar de Leon because Abreu wants his students to master classical artists like Mozart and Beethoven.

7. Since the program was launched a generation of talented Venezuelan musicians is already performing, composing, and teaching classical music.

8. Because the program has been so successful it is the model for new youth orchestras now being formed throughout the world.

PRACTICE 5

Combine each pair of the following ideas by using a subordinating conjunction. Write each combination twice, once with the subordinating conjunction at the beginning of the sentence and once with the subordinating conjunction in the middle of the sentence. Punctuate correctly.

EXAMPLE

We stayed on the beach.
The sun went down.

We stayed on the beach until the sun went down.

Until the sun went down, we stayed on the beach.

_____

_____

1. This cactus has flourished.

2. I talk to it every day.

_____

_____

_____

_____

3. Ralph takes the train to Philadelphia.

4. He likes to sit by the window.

_____

_____

_____

_____

5. I had known you were coming.

6. I would have vacuumed the guest room.

_____

_____

_____

_____

7. He was the first person to eat a slice of meat between two pieces of bread.

8. The sandwich was named after the Earl of Sandwich.

_____

_____

_____

_____

9. Akila was about to answer the final question.

10. The buzzer sounded.

_____

_____

_____

_____

11. Few soap operas remain on the radio.

12. Daytime television is filled with them.

_____

_____

_____

_____

13. She connected the speakers.

14. The room filled with glorious sound.

_____

_____

_____

_____

15. The chimney spewed black smoke and soot.

16. Nobody complained to the local environmental agency.

_____

_____

_____

_____

C. Semicolons

You can join two independent clauses by placing a **semicolon** between them. The semicolon takes the place of a conjunction:

1. She hopes to receive good grades this semester; her scholarship depends on her maintaining a 3.5 average.
2. Tony is a careless driver; he has had three minor accidents this year alone.

● Each of the sentences above could also be made into two *separate sentences* by replacing the semicolon with a period.

● Note that the first word after a semicolon is *not* capitalized (unless, of course, it is a word that is normally capitalized, like someone's name).

PRACTICE 6

Combine each pair of independent clauses by placing a semicolon between them.

1. The senator appeared ill at ease at the news conference he seemed afraid of saying the wrong thing.

2. The new seed catalogue, a 1,500-page volume, was misplaced the volume weighed 10 pounds.

3. On Thursday evening, Hector decided to go camping on Friday morning, he packed his bags and left.

4. This stream is full of trout every spring men and women with waders and fly rods arrive on its banks.

5. Not a single store was open at that hour not a soul walked the streets.

PRACTICE 7

Each independent clause that follows is the first half of a sentence. Add a semicolon and a second independent clause. Make sure your second thought is also independent and can stand alone.

1. At 2 A.M. I stumbled toward the ringing telephone _____

   _____

2. *People* magazine published my letter to the editor _____

   _____

3. The officer pulled over the speeding pickup truck _____

   _____

4. Cameras are not permitted in the museum _____

   _____

5. Computer skills are increasingly important in many careers _____

   _____

D. Conjunctive Adverbs

In earlier chapters on paragraph and essay writing, you practiced using **transitional expressions** like *however*, *for example*, and *therefore*. Most transitional expressions are **conjunctive adverbs**. A conjunctive adverb placed after a semicolon can help clarify the relationship between two clauses:

1. I like the sound of that stereo; *however*, the price is too high.
2. They have not seen that film; *moreover*, they have not been to a theater for three years.

● Note that a comma follows the conjunctive adverb.

Here is a partial list of conjunctive adverbs, or transitional expressions.*

Conjunctive Adverbs or Transitional Expressions	
Addition:	also, besides, furthermore, in addition, moreover
Comparison:	likewise, similarly
Contrast:	however, nevertheless, on the contrary, on the other hand
Example:	for example, for instance
Emphasis:	indeed, in fact, of course
Result:	consequently, therefore, thus

PRACTICE 8

Punctuate each sentence correctly by adding a semicolon, a comma, or both, where necessary. Put a *C* after any correct sentences.

1. I hate to wash my car windows nevertheless it's a job that must be done.

2. Sonia doesn't know how to play chess however she would like to learn.

3. Dean Fader is very funny in fact he could be a professional comedian.

4. Deep water makes Maurice nervous therefore he does not want to join the scuba dive team.

5. I like this painting; the soft colors remind me of tropical sunsets.

6. The faculty approved of the new trimester system; furthermore, the students liked it too.

7. Bill has an iPod plugged into his ear all day consequently he misses a lot of good conversations.

8. We toured the darkroom then we watched an actual photo shoot.

---

* For more transitional expressions, see page 63.

PRACTICE 9

Proofread this paragraph for coordination errors, missing punctuation, and one conjunctive adverb that does not express the right relationship between ideas. Add the correct punctuation or write your corrections above the lines, using a mix of semicolons and semicolons plus conjunctive adverbs.

(1) Successful college students learn how to take good notes in class. (2) One excellent note-taking method is the Cornell method experts say that it actually helps the brain learn. (3) A student using the Cornell method performs several steps. (4) Before class, he or she draws a line dividing notebook paper into two columns. (5) The narrower left-hand column will contain key words, and the wider right-hand column, notes. (6) During the lesson, the student records the professor's main ideas in the notes column, jotting important phrases, symbols, and abbreviations, but not complete sentences. (7) At the bottom of the page, the student leaves five or six lines blank. (8) As soon as possible after class, he or she rereads the notes and reduces them

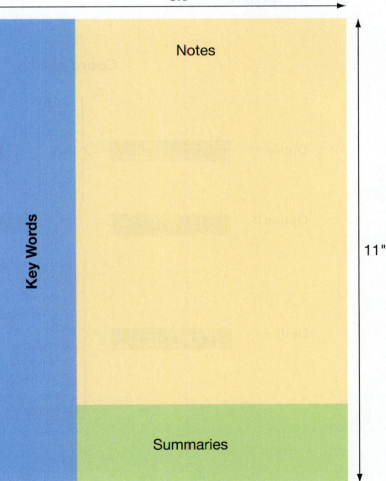

A sample page showing the Cornell note-taking method. Do you think this method would work better than the one you now use? Why or why not?

further by writing a few key words or questions in the left-hand column furthermore at the bottom of the page, the student writes a brief summary of the notes. (9) These "reducing" steps help the brain understand and remember the material, nevertheless, studying later for a test is easier. (10) To study, the student simply covers up the notes and recites the information aloud from memory, glancing at the key words and questions for hints. (11) Periodically reviewing like this helps the brain move course concepts gradually into long-term memory and improves recall on exams. (12) Finally, students should reflect on what they are learning, for example; they might ask how the ideas in their notes apply to real-life situations. Some people call the Cornell system the Five R's, for *record*, *reduce*, *recite*, *review*, and *reflect*.

E. Review

In this chapter, you have combined simple sentences by means of a **coordinating conjunction**, a **subordinating conjunction**, a **semicolon**, and a **semicolon** and **conjunctive adverb**. Here is a review chart of the sentence patterns discussed in this chapter.*

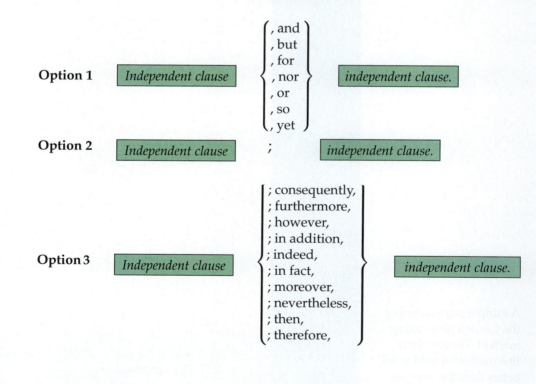

Coordination

Option 1 — Independent clause { , and / , but / , for / , nor / , or / , so / , yet } independent clause.

Option 2 — Independent clause ; independent clause.

Option 3 — Independent clause { ; consequently, / ; furthermore, / ; however, / ; in addition, / ; indeed, / ; in fact, / ; moreover, / ; nevertheless, / ; then, / ; therefore, } independent clause.

---

* For more ways to combine sentences, see Chapter 22, "Revising for Sentence Variety," Part D.

Subordination

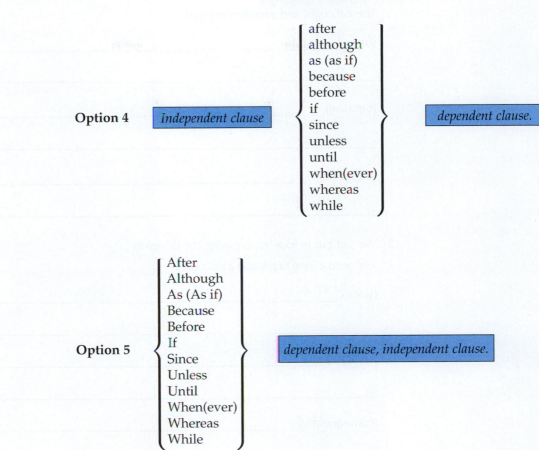

Option 4 Independent clause { after / although / as (as if) / because / before / if / since / unless / until / when(ever) / whereas / while } dependent clause.

Option 5 { After / Although / As (As if) / Because / Before / If / Since / Unless / Until / When(ever) / Whereas / While } dependent clause, independent clause.

PRACTICE 10

Read each pair of simple sentences to determine the relationship between them. Then join each pair in three different ways, using the conjunctions or conjunctive adverbs in parentheses at the left. Punctuate correctly.

EXAMPLE

The company picnic was canceled.
Rain started to fall in torrents.

(for) *The company picnic was canceled, for the rain started to fall in torrents.*

_____

(because) *Because the rain started to fall in torrents, the company picnic was canceled.*

_____

(therefore) *The rain started to fall in torrents; therefore, the company picnic was canceled.*

_____

1. My grandmother is in great shape.

   She eats right and exercises regularly.

   (for) _____

   _____

   (because) _____

   _____

   (therefore) _____

   _____

2. We just put in four hours paving the driveway.
   We need a long break and a cold drink.

   (since) _____

   _____

   (because) _____

   _____

   (consequently) _____

   _____

3. The bus schedule was difficult to read.
   Penny found the right bus.

   (but) _____

   _____

   (although) _____

   _____

   (however) _____

   _____

4. Don is an expert mechanic.

   He intends to open a service center.

   (and) _____

   _____

   (because) _____

   _____

(furthermore) _____

_____

5. We haven't heard from her.

We haven't given up hope.

(but) _____

_____

(although) _____

_____

(nevertheless) _____

_____

PROOFREADING STRATEGY

Using coordination and subordination will improve your writing, but you must proofread to make sure that you punctuate correctly.

1. First, **search for the seven coordinating conjunctions**, or FANBOYS, and highlight or underline each one. If the idea on each side of the comma can stand alone as a complete sentence, make sure that a comma comes before the coordinating conjunction.

   Correct   Correct
   Every day, she clocks out and leaves the pediatric ward tired but satisfied.

                     Incorrect   Correct
   Baby Chandra has improved, but the doctor and nurses continue to monitor her.

2. Next, **search your document for any subordinating conjunctions** (like *although*, *because*, *before*, *when*, etc.). Highlight or underline these words. If the dependent idea comes first in the sentence, make sure that a comma separates the dependent from the independent idea. Here are two examples:

   Independent idea   Dependent idea
   Schools are closed today because the city is buried under two feet of snow.

   Dependent idea   Incorrect   Independent idea
   Although the wedding was small and simple, the guests enjoyed the ceremony.

_____

* For more work on sentence variety, see Chapter 22, "Revising for Sentence Variety."

REVIEW

In your writing, aim for variety by mixing coordination, subordination, and simple sentences.* Revise the following paragraphs to eliminate monotonous simple sentences. First, read the paragraph to determine the relationships between ideas; then choose the conjunctions that best express these relationships, making your corrections above the lines. Proofread your work, using the strategy above to make sure you punctuate correctly.

Paragraph 1

Dating has always been a risky business. Television shows like *Blind Date* succeed. They let viewers leer at other people's embarrassing dates. Now the Internet is opening a whole new social frontier. It also is creating new dangers. Online, it is harder to spot nuts, flakes, and predators. We meet someone through e-mail. We lose our usual ways of judging people. According to Internet safety expert Parry Aftab, it is hard to gauge the truth of someone's statements. We cannot see, hear, and experience that person's eye contact, body language, dress, personal hygiene, and voice. Furthermore, most people lie. They begin to date online. Aftab says that men often fib about their income, fitness level, or amount of hair. Women shave pounds off their weight or years off their age. Cyber daters must remain skeptical, ask questions, and watch for red-flag comments. Your online love keeps calling herself Gilda or Bat Goddess of the Red Planet. It's probably time to log off.

Paragraph 2

Businessman Robert Johnson has blazed new trails throughout his career. No existing television network targeted African Americans. Johnson created the Black Entertainment

"On the Internet, nobody knows you're a dog."

Television network. The company started with a tiny budget and just two hours of daily programming. It became a huge success. BET grew to be the largest black-owned and -operated company in the country. Johnson created new jobs for hundreds of people. He himself became America's first African American billionaire. In 2005, he achieved yet another first. He became the first African American to gain controlling interest in an NBA team, the Charlotte Bobcats. One of his lifelong dreams had come true. He says that he is even prouder of another accomplishment. He wanted to create more economic opportunities for minorities. He has succeeded.

Paragraph 3

Cleopatra became Queen of Egypt at 17. She displayed a flair for ruling and was soon worshipped by her subjects. Julius Caesar, ruler of Rome, was sent to calm civil wars in Egypt in 51 B.C. Cleopatra was in hiding. She directed her servants to roll her up inside a large rug and smuggle her into the palace. Caesar was 52 and the most powerful man in the world. He was amazed to receive a gift-wrapped queen. Their relationship became one of history's greatest love stories. It lasted until Caesar's enemies murdered him. Later, Marc Antony came to Egypt to add African lands to the Roman Empire. He, too, fell in love with the spirited queen. He moved into her palace on the island of Antirhodos. This betrayal was too much for the Romans. Their navy attacked Cleopatra's fleet. Both Antony and Cleopatra killed themselves. They would not bow in defeat. The Romans smashed all statues of the queen. An earthquake sank her palace into the Mediterranean Sea. Fifteen hundred years passed. Undersea explorer Franck Goddio discovered Cleopatra's lost palace in 1996. Neither the Roman Empire nor the forces of nature could erase one of the most powerful and intriguing women who ever lived.

EXPLORING ONLINE

http://grammar.ccc.commnet.edu/grammar/quizzes/nova/nova1.htm
Interactive coordination quiz

http://depts.dyc.edu/learningcenter/owl/exercises/conjunctions_ex2.htm
Exercises in subordination, with answers

CourseMate for *Evergreen*
Visit *Evergreen* CourseMate for more practices and quizzes, videos
to accompany the readings, career and job-search resources,
ESL help, and live links to every Exploring Online in the book.

CHAPTER 28

Avoiding Sentence Errors

A: Avoiding Run-Ons and Comma Splices

B: Avoiding Fragments

A. Avoiding Run-Ons and Comma Splices

Be careful to avoid **run-ons** and **comma splices**.

A **run-on sentence** incorrectly runs together two independent clauses without a conjunction or punctuation. This error confuses the reader, who cannot tell where one thought stops and the next begins:

> 1. Run-on: My neighbor Mr. Hoffman is 75 years old he plays tennis every Saturday afternoon.

A **comma splice** incorrectly joins two independent clauses with a comma but no conjunction:

> 2. Comma splice: My neighbor Mr. Hoffman is 75 years old, he plays tennis every Saturday afternoon.

The run-on and the comma splice can be corrected in five ways:

> Use two separate sentences.   My neighbor Mr. Hoffman is 75 years old. He plays tennis every Saturday afternoon.

Use a coordinating conjunction. (See Chapter 27, Part A.)	My neighbor Mr. Hoffman is 75 years old, but he plays tennis every Saturday afternoon.
Use a subordinating conjunction. (See Chapter 27, Part B.)	Although my neighbor Mr. Hoffman is 75 years old, he plays tennis every Saturday afternoon.
Use a semicolon. (See Chapter 27, Part C.)	My neighbor Mr. Hoffman is 75 years old; he plays tennis every Saturday afternoon.
Use a semicolon and a conjunctive adverb. (See Chapter 27, Part D.)	My neighbor Mr. Hoffman is 75 years old; however, he plays tennis every Saturday afternoon.

PRACTICE 1

Some of these sentences contain run-ons or comma splices; others are correct. Put a C next to the correct sentences. Revise the run-ons and comma splices in any way you choose. Be careful of the punctuation.

1. Identity theft is the fastest-growing crime in the United States it costs society $49 to $50 billion a year.

   Revised: _____

   _____

2. The identity thief doesn't just steal someone's cash or jewelry, he or she poses as that person to open new accounts, take out loans, or even buy houses.

   Revised: _____

   _____

3. For the victim, identity theft can mean the shock of violation, large financial losses, and ruined credit.

   Revised: _____

   _____

4. Individuals today must protect themselves against identity theft the U.S. Department of Justice recommends the SCAM approach.

   Revised: _____

   _____

5. *S* is for *stingy* people should be stingy about giving their valuable social security, bank account, and credit-card numbers to others.

    Revised: _____

    _____

6. *C* stands for *check* all financial statements carefully for unauthorized withdrawals or purchases.

    Revised: _____

    _____

7. The *A* in SCAM reminds everyone to *ask* periodically for a copy of his or her credit report fraudulent accounts and activity will show up there.

    Revised: _____

    _____

8. The final step is *M*, *maintaining* careful records of bank and financial accounts, these records can help dispute any problems.

    Revised: _____

    _____

9. Trash cans and dumpsters still provide identity thieves with most of their valuable information, a final *S* might stand for *shred*.

    Revised: _____

    _____

10. Old checks, bank records, and credit-card offers from today's mail should never be tossed out they should be shredded or burned.

    Revised: _____

    _____

PRACTICE 2

Proofread the following paragraph for run-ons and comma splices. Correct them in any way you choose.

(1) College costs have risen dramatically in recent years, many students now have to tap multiple resources to cover their expenses. (2) These students are using their own savings and getting monetary help from parents and other relatives. (3) In addition, 78 percent of all college students now work at least part-time earning a paycheck helps them make ends meet. (4) Before they consider working even longer hours, these students should learn

to apply early and often for different kinds of financial aid. (5) Every year, they should fill out the Free Application for Federal Student Aid (FAFSA) form, ensuring consideration for grants that do not have to be repaid. (6) They should regularly check college newsletters or bulletin boards for scholarship announcements yet another option is applying for loans with reasonable repayment terms. (7) Financial survival is possible for college students experts say the secret is planning ahead, applying early, and combining different resources.

PROOFREADING STRATEGY

Proofread your work very carefully if comma splices are among your error patterns:

1. Go back through your draft and **circle every comma.**

2. For each comma, ask yourself, *"Would substituting a period for this comma create complete sentences that could stand alone on <u>both</u> sides of the comma?"*

No

When a strong hurricane is approaching, officials may order a mandatory

Yes

evacuation, residents must leave the area.

3. If the answer is yes, you have written a comma splice and will need to **replace the comma with a period or keep the comma and add a coordinating conjunction after it.**

When a strong hurricane is approaching, officials may order a mandatory evacuation, and residents must leave the area.

PRACTICE 3

Proofread the following essay for run-ons and comma splices. Correct them in any way you choose, writing your revised essay on a separate sheet of paper. Be careful of the punctuation.

HOW TO READ AN AD

(1) Most people insist that advertising does not affect them and that they tune out ads and commercials. (2) If these claims are true, however, why do companies spend billions a year on advertising? (3) For the Super Bowl alone, corporations rush to buy 30-second commercial spots at $3 million each, in fact, ads work very well, declares former advertising executive Stephen Garey, they bombard people with attractive pictures and the hidden message, "buy, buy, buy." (4) The best defense against this ad blitz is learning to read ads critically.

Study this ad for a famous cologne. Reread Practice 3, especially the list at the end of the second paragraph. How many advertisers' "techniques of persuasion" can you spot in the ad?

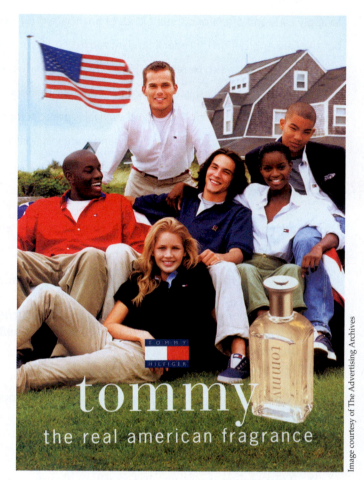

Image courtesy of The Advertising Archives

(5) Advertisers are master persuaders, their techniques are very different from those used in college and at work. (6) A student or worker often must take a stand, arguing for or against something he or she uses logical reasons and arguments to try and persuade others. (7) Advertisers, on the other hand, use illogical but powerful visual methods to persuade people to buy their products. (8) The Center for Media Literacy lists ten such "techniques of persuasion" in ads:

Humor	Friends	Fun	Sex appeal	Celebrity
Macho	Family	Nature	Cartoons	Wealth

(9) These techniques are emotional and indirect, often pictures are used to suggest pleasant associations with a product. (10) For instance, one ad might show happy people smoking, it links "friends" and "fun" with cigarettes. (11) Another ad shows a well-dressed man helping a beautiful woman into a car, associating "wealth," "macho," and perhaps "sex appeal" with that brand of automobile. (12) Flip through any popular magazine and see which techniques each ad uses look closely and ask yourself what *audience* is targeted by each ad. (13) What *methods* attract your attention and call to your dollars? (14) Are there *hidden messages*? (15) Looking critically at ads not only creates smarter consumers, it also trains the critical thinking skills that many professors and employers value.

B. Avoiding Fragments

Another error to avoid is the **sentence fragment**. A **sentence** must contain a subject and a verb and must be able to stand alone as a complete idea. A **sentence fragment** is incomplete. It lacks a subject, a verb, or both—or it does not stand alone as a complete idea.

Here are six common fragments and ways to correct them. The first three are among the most frequently made errors in college and business writing.

Dependent Clause Fragments

A dependent clause fragment often starts with a subordinating conjunction like *although, because, if, when*, and so on.*

Complete sentence: 1. Kirk decided to major in psychology.

Fragment: 2. After his sister was diagnosed with anorexia.

● Example 1 is a complete sentence.

● Example 2 is a fragment because it is a dependent clause beginning with the subordinating conjunction *after*. Furthermore, it is not a complete idea.

This fragment can be corrected in two ways:

Corrected: 3. Kirk decided to major in psychology after his sister was diagnosed with anorexia.

Corrected: 4. Kirk decided to major in psychology. His sister was diagnosed with anorexia.

● In sentence 3, the fragment is combined with the sentence before.

● In sentence 4, the fragment is changed into a complete sentence.

Relative Clause Fragments

A dependent clause fragment can also start with *who, whose, which*, or *that*.*

Complete sentence: 5. Mrs. Costa is a popular history professor.

Fragment: 6. Who never runs out of creative ideas.

● Example 5 is a complete sentence.

● Example 6 is a fragment because it is a relative clause beginning with *who*.† It is not a complete idea.

---

* For a longer list of subordinating conjunctions and more work on dependent clauses, see Chapter 27, "Coordination and Subordination," Part B.

† For more work on relative clauses, see Chapter 22, "Revising for Sentence Variety," Part D, and Chapter 29, "Present Tense (Agreement)," Part G.

This fragment can be corrected in two ways:

Corrected: 7. Mrs. Costa is a popular history professor who never runs out of creative ideas.

Corrected: 8. Mrs. Costa is a popular history professor. She never runs out of creative ideas.

- In sentence 7, it is combined with the sentence before.
- In sentence 8, the fragment is changed into a complete sentence.

-ing Fragments

An *-ing* fragment starts with an *-ing* verb form.

Complete sentence: 9. Joaquin can be seen on the track every morning.

Fragment: 10. Running a mile or two before breakfast.

- Example 9 is a complete sentence.
- Example 10 is a fragment because it lacks a subject and because an *-ing* verb form cannot stand alone without a helping verb.*

This fragment can be corrected in two ways:

Corrected: 11. Joaquin can be seen on the track every morning, running a mile or two before breakfast.

Corrected: 12. Joaquin can be seen on the track every morning. He runs a mile or two before breakfast.

- In sentence 11, the fragment is combined with the sentence before.
- In sentence 12, the fragment is changed into a complete sentence.

Watch out for fragments beginning with a subordinating conjunction; *who, which,* or *that*; or an *-ing* verb form. These groups of words cannot stand alone, but must be combined with another sentence or changed into a complete sentence.

---

* For more work on joining ideas with an *-ing* modifier, see Chapter 22, "Revising for Sentence Variety," Part D.

PRACTICE 4

Some of these examples are fragments; others are complete sentences. Put a C next to the complete sentences. Revise the fragments any way you choose.

1. When Sandra completes her commercial jet training.

    Revised: _____

    _____

2. Loudly talking on his cell phone, Ivan strolled through the mall.

    Revised: _____

    _____

3. A city that I have always wanted to visit.

    Revised: _____

    _____

4. If she speaks Portuguese fluently, she will probably get the job.

    Revised: _____

    _____

5. The comic strip *Peanuts*, which was created by Charles Schulz.

    Revised: _____

    _____

6. Interviewing divorced people for her research project.

    Revised: _____

    _____

7. Although some students bring laptop computers to class.

    Revised: _____

    _____

8. Frantically, the disc jockey flipping through stacks of CDs.

    Revised: _____

    _____

Prepositional Phrase Fragments

Complete sentence: 13. A huge telescope in Green Bank, West Virginia, scans for signs of life.

Fragment: 14. On stars 20 to 30 light years away.

- Sentence 13 is a complete sentence.
- Sentence 14 is a fragment because it is a prepositional phrase beginning with *on*. It lacks both a subject and a verb.

  This fragment can be corrected in two ways:

Corrected: 15. A huge telescope in Green Bank, West Virginia, scans for signs of life on stars 20 to 30 light years away.

Corrected: 16. A huge telescope in Green Bank, West Virginia, scans for signs of life. Its target is stars 20 to 30 light years away.

- Sentence 15 shows the easiest way to correct this fragment—by connecting it to the sentence before.
- In sentence 16, the fragment is changed into a complete sentence by adding a subject, *its target*, and a verb, *is*.

Appositive Phrase Fragments

Fragment: 17. A fine pianist.

Complete sentence: 18. Marsha won a scholarship to Juilliard.

- Example 17 is a fragment because it is an appositive—a noun phrase. It lacks a verb, and it is not a complete idea.*
- Example 18 is a complete sentence.

  This fragment can be corrected in two ways:

Corrected: 19. A fine pianist, Marsha won a scholarship to Juilliard.

Corrected: 20. Marsha is a fine pianist. She won a scholarship to Juilliard.

- In sentence 19, the fragment is combined with the sentence after it.
- In sentence 20, the fragment is changed into a complete sentence by adding a verb, *is*, and a subject, *she* (to avoid repeating *Marsha*).

———
* For more work on appositives, see Chapter 22, "Revising for Sentence Variety," Part D.

Infinitive Phrase Fragments

Complete sentence: 21. Lauri has always wanted to become a biologist.

Fragment: 22. To protect the environment.

- Example 21 is a complete sentence.
- Example 22 is a fragment because it lacks a subject and contains only the infinitive form of the verb—*to* plus the simple form of *protect*.

  This fragment can be corrected in two ways:

Corrected: 23. Lauri has always wanted to become a biologist and to protect the environment.

Corrected: 24. Lauri has always wanted to become a biologist. Her goal is to protect the environment.

- In sentence 23, the fragment is combined with the sentence before it.
- In sentence 24, the fragment is changed into a complete sentence.

  Watch out for phrase fragments. A prepositional phrase, appositive phrase, or infinitive cannot stand alone, but must be combined with another sentence or changed into a complete sentence.

PRACTICE 5

Now, proofread for fragments. Some of these examples are fragments; others are complete sentences. Put a *C* next to the complete sentences. Revise the fragments any way you choose.

1. To earn money for college.

   Revised: _____

   _____

2. Terrence, a graphic designer at *Sports Illustrated*.

   Revised: _____

   _____

3. Across the railroad tracks and down the riverbank.

   Revised: _____

   _____

4. A born comedian.

   Revised: _____

   _____

5. To answer phones for the AIDS Education Network.

   Revised: _____

   _____

6. On a coffee plantation in Jamaica.

   Revised: _____

   _____

7. That silver Razor scooter.

   Revised: _____

   _____

8. To find a job that you love.

   Revised: _____

   _____

Review Chart: Correcting Sentence Fragments

Type of Fragment	F *Fragment* / C *Corrected*
1. Dependent clause	F After Jake moved to Colorado.
	C After Jake moved to Colorado, he learned to ski.
2. Relative clause	F Who loves computer games.
	C My niece, who loves computer games, repairs my computer.
3. *-ing* modifier	F Surfing the Web.
	C Surfing the Web, we visited European art museum sites.
4. Prepositional phrase	F Inside the cave.
	C They found mastodon bones inside the cave.
5. Appositive	F A slow student.
	C Einstein, a slow student, proved to be a genius.
6. Infinitive	F To go dancing tonight.
	C She wants to go dancing tonight.

PROOFREADING STRATEGY

Sentence fragments are a serious error. To spot and correct them more easily in your writing, try the **bottom-up proofreading technique**. Start by reading the last sentence of your paper, carefully, word by word. Then read the second-to-last sentence, and so on, all the way from the "bottom to the top." For each sentence, ask:

1. Does this sentence have a *subject*, a *complete verb*, and express a *complete thought*?

2. Is this an incomplete thought that starts with a word like *because, although,* or *when*? If so, fragments like this often can be fixed by connecting them to the sentence before or after.

3. Is this an incomplete thought containing *who, which,* or *that*? If so, such fragments often can be fixed by connecting them to the sentence before or after.

If sentence fragments are one of your error patterns, log them in your Personal Error Patterns Chart and proofread every paper once through, just for fragments.

PRACTICE 6

Fragments are most likely to occur in paragraphs or longer pieces of writing. Proofread the paragraph below for fragments. Correct them in any way you choose, either adding the fragments to other sentences or making them into complete sentences.

(1) The sinking of the *Titanic* in 1912 has inspired 15 motion pictures over the years. (2) All of them requiring special effects. (3) What set James Cameron's *Titanic* apart, however, was his attention to detail. (4) Following the blueprints and plans for the original ship. (5) Cameron's team created scaled sets and models accurate down to the rivets. (6) Scenes of the ship in the water were made possible through the brilliant use of computer technology and a small model. (7) A larger model of the liner's huge cargo hold was needed. (8) To show the ocean rushing into the ship. (9) Although the model was only a quarter as large as the original. (10) It still had enough room for period luggage and a brand-new Renault. (11) The largest model was a 775-foot replica of the luxury ship. (12) Which reproduced every detail, from the ship's name lettered on the façade to the chairs on the deck. (13) That set took almost a year to build. (14) And a good chunk of the $287 million that Cameron spent on one of the most expensive movies ever made.

PRACTICE 7

Proofread this essay for fragments. Correct them in any way you choose, either adding the fragments to other sentences or making them into complete sentences. Be careful of the punctuation.

HER FOCUS IS SUCCESS

(1) If the way we react to adversity reveals our true character. (2) Maria Elena Ibanez is extraordinary. (3) This successful computer engineer and businesswoman is a master at refusing to let obstacles keep her from a goal.

(4) In 1973, 19-year-old Maria Elena left Colombia and arrived alone in Miami. (5) Speaking just a few words of English. (6) Her goal was to learn 50 new words a day. (7) By talking to people and reading children's books. (8) Soon she spoke well enough to enroll at Florida International University, earn a computer science degree, and so impressed college officials that they hired her as a programmer.

(9) In 1982, Maria Elena started her first company. (10) Because computers cost much more in South America than they did in the United States. (11) She decided to sell reasonably priced computers to South American dealers. (12) When some dealers hesitated to do business with such a young woman, she won their respect with her expertise and willingness to teach them about the new technology. (13) Soon she sold International Micro Systems. (14) The nation's 55th fastest growing private company, at a huge profit.

(15) In spite of this success, people laughed out loud when Maria Elena announced her new goal. (16) To sell computers throughout Africa. (17) She paid no attention and returned from her first selling trip with handfuls of orders. (18) Then in 1992, disaster struck.

(19) Hurricane Andrew plowed into Miami, exploding Maria Elena's house. (20) As she and her two small children hid in a closet. (21) In the morning, dazed, she walked to the offices and warehouse of her new company. (22) The building was a mangled mess of fallen walls, trees, wet paper, and smoking wires. (23) Sitting down on a curb, she cried, but as her employees began arriving. (24) She sprang into action.

(25) One worker said the company could set up in his home. (26) Which had electricity. (27) Working 24 hours a day and using cell phones, the employees called all their African customers. (28) To say everything was fine and their orders would be shipped on time. (29) International High Tech grew 700 percent that year. (30) Despite the most damaging hurricane in U.S. history.

(31) Maria Elena moved her company into its rebuilt offices. (32) Today she and the children live in an apartment. (33) Not a house. (34) Asked about losing every piece of clothing, every picture, every possession in her former home. (35) She laughs, says that most problems hide opportunities, and adds that now she has no lawn to mow.

PRACTICE 8   REVIEW

Proofread these paragraphs for run-ons, comma splices, and fragments. Correct the errors in any way you choose.

Paragraph 1

(1) Duct tape helped save the lives of the three astronauts aboard the damaged *Apollo 13* spacecraft in 1970, this strong, fabric-based adhesive tape is not just for fixing broken things anymore. (2) Now rolls of duct tape, creativity, and more than a dash of humor can bloom into a college scholarship. (3) In 2001, the Duck Tape Company sponsored the first national "Stuck at Prom" contest. (4) After managers learned that some high school students were sculpting colored rolls of duct tape into dresses and tuxedos for their senior proms. (5) The couple who designed the most imaginative and stylish formal wear from duct tape received a $5,000 scholarship to college. (6) The contest tapped into some goofy national yearning to design clothes with duct tape—or to laugh. (7) In 2011 alone, more than 330 couples from 44 states and four Canadian provinces competed two of the creative contestants were Katerina and Damian. (8) Who worked 350 hours and used 43 rolls of duct tape to complete their prom outfits and accessories. (9) Her dress was bright yellow, with a hem and spill of nearly 50 duct-tape flowers, because each flower had ten handmade petals, making these took the most time. (10) Damian's tux was trimmed in yellow, with individually cut blades of grass. (11) Although the clothes were heavy. (12) The college-bound couple says everyone loved their fashion statement. (13) In addition, the duct tape's insulating qualities made them the hottest couple on the dance floor.

Dressed head to toe in duct tape, the winners of the 2011 Stuck at Prom contest also scored college scholarships.

Paragraph 2

(1) Some teenagers seem to start the day tired, they are worn out even before they leave for school. (2) Once in class, they might doze off, even in the middle of an exciting lesson. (3) Are these students lazy, have they stayed out too late partying? (4) Medical research provides a different explanation for the exhaustion of these teens. (5) As children become adolescents, they develop an increased need for sleep, especially in the morning. (6) Unfortunately, most American high schools start around 7:30 A.M. many students have to get up as early as 5:00 A.M. (7) Scientists suggest that if students could start school later in the day. (8) They might get the extra sleep they need. (9) To test this theory, many schools have begun to experiment with later hours. (10) Congress is even paying the extra operating costs for schools that start after 9:00 A.M. (11) The hope is that teens will be less tired, furthermore, because schools that start later will end later, students will be off the streets and out of trouble during the late afternoon. (12) Which is prime mischief time.

PRACTICE 9 REVIEW

Proofread this essay for run-ons, comma splices, and fragments. Correct the errors in any way you choose, writing your revisions above the lines.

WORDS WITH FRIENDS—AND STRANGERS

(1) For years, America's favorite word game was Scrabble. (2) A game of skill and luck. (3) When people gather around a Scrabble board, they have fun, try to make words from randomly chosen letters, and often learn new words. (4) A nearby dictionary lets them challenge anyone. (5) Who guesses and invents a word. (6) Turns are time limited, searching the dictionary for words is not allowed.

(7) Now, Words with Friends, a mobile game app inspired by Scrabble. (8) Has exploded in popularity. (9) Actor Alec Baldwin refused to stop playing it before takeoff, he was kicked off a plane! (10) As in Scrabble, players score points by building words on a grid, but it's easier to get high scores, the letters have higher values. (11) Because guessing is allowed. (12) Some say this game is less challenging. (13) Players might be strangers. (14) Living miles apart. (15) Days might pass between moves, the phone pings when it's the next player's turn. (16) Therefore, some Words with Friends addicts play up to 20 games. (17) All at the same time.

(18) App players can chat with verbal rivals, so sometimes relationships form. (19) One Chicago woman clicked "random" and started playing against a Dutch firefighter. (20) Half way around the world. (21) They had more in common than a high skill level. (22) After chatting and Skyping. (23) They got engaged. (24) Words with Friends has even re-ignited sales of Scrabble sets. (25) Which are flying off the shelves as never before.

PRACTICE 10 REVIEW

Proofread this essay for run-ons, comma splices, and fragments. Correct the errors in any way you choose, writing your revisions above the lines.

YOU TUBE U

(1) Sometimes a casual experience can bloom into a calling, this happened to Salman Khan. (2) The young Bangladeshi American is now famous as the founder of Khan Academy, where anyone can study math, science, and other subjects for free on YouTube. (3) In 2004, Khan was working at a Boston investment fund. (4) When he learned that his cousin Nadia was struggling with sixth-grade math. (5) He offered to tutor her long distance. (6) Because she lived in New Orleans, they worked on the phone, using a shared Internet notepad, Khan's lessons were short, informal, and sometimes funny. (7) Soon Nadia was ahead of her class her brothers wanted tutoring as well.

(8) With a growing group of cousins and friends to tutor, all in different time zones. (9) Khan decided to post his lessons on YouTube. (10) Allowing each person to work at his or her own pace. (11) Strangers and adult learners started viewing the lessons, Khan knew he was onto something. (12) So far, he has recorded 2,700 tutorials, each one explaining a key concept in math, science, or philosophy. (13) Khan never appears in the videos, his handwriting fills the screen as he talks through a problem. (14) He doesn't try to cover everything, he offers material that fills important gaps and individualizes instruction.

(15) Although Kahn has received many offers to create a lucrative business. (16) He decided not to charge for his lessons. (17) In 2009 he quit his job to build Khan Academy full-time. (18) Since then, Khan Academy has received large donations from Bill Gates and from Google, which picked Khan's project as "an idea that can change the world." (19) Khan's goal is to offer help in more subjects, translate lessons into many languages, use rewards and paced problems. (20) To show children that learning is fun, and to provide free education for anyone who wants it.

The creator of Khan Academy online, Salman Khan, visits with students using his lessons.

© Joe Pugliese / AUGUST

EXPLORING ONLINE

www.khanacademy.org

Visit Khan Academy online and explore. Pick a video lesson on something you'd like to learn and watch it (each lesson is about 15 minutes long). Jot notes on your experience. What do you think of Khan's method? Could you follow easily? Would you return to this site or send your children or friends there?

EXPLORING ONLINE

http://grammar.ccc.commnet.edu/grammar/cgi-shl/quiz.pl/run-ons_add1.htm

Review and quizzes to help you root out run-ons

http://grammar.ccc.commnet.edu/grammar/quizzes/fragment_fixing.htm

Great tips and quizzes to help you find and fix sentence fragments

CourseMate for *Evergreen*

Visit the *Evergreen* CourseMate for more practices and quizzes, videos to accompany the readings, career and job-search resources, ESL help, and live links to every Exploring Online in this book.

CHAPTER 29

Present Tense (Agreement)

A: Defining Subject-Verb Agreement

B: Three Troublesome Verbs in the Present Tense: *To Be, To Have, To Do*

C: Special Singular Constructions

D: Separation of Subject and Verb

E: Sentences Beginning with *There* and *Here*

F: Agreement in Questions

G: Agreement in Relative Clauses

A. Defining Subject-Verb Agreement

Subjects and verbs in the present tense must **agree** in number; that is, singular subjects take verbs with singular endings, and plural subjects take verbs with plural endings.

Verbs in the Present Tense Sample Verb: *To Leap*			
Singular		**Plural**	
If the subject is	**the verb is**	**If the subject is**	**the verb is**
1st person: I	leap	we	leap
2nd person: you	leap	you	leap
3rd person: he she it	leaps	they	leap

● Use an -s or -es ending on the verb only when the subject is *he, she,* or *it* or the equivalent of *he, she,* or *it.*

The subjects and verbs in the following sentences agree:

> 1. He *bicycles* to the steel mills every morning.
> 2. They *bicycle* to the steel mills every morning.
> 3. This student *hopes* to go to social work school.
> 4. The planets *revolve* around the sun.

● In sentence 1, the singular subject, *he,* takes the singular form of the verb, *bicycles. Bicycles* agrees with *he.*

● In sentence 2, the plural subject, *they,* takes the plural form of the verb, *bicycle. Bicycle* agrees with *they.*

● In sentence 3, the subject, *student,* is equivalent to *he* or *she* and takes the singular form of the verb, *hopes.*

● In sentence 4, the subject, *planets,* is equivalent to *they* and takes the plural form of the verb, *revolve.*

Subjects joined by the conjunction *and* usually take a plural verb:

> 5. Kirk and Quincy *attend* a pottery class at the Y.

● The subject, *Kirk and Quincy,* is plural, the equivalent of *they.*

● *Attend* agrees with the plural subject.*

PRACTICE 1

Underline the subject and circle the correct present tense verb.

1. Many people (thinks, think) of scientific research as unrelated to everyday life.

2. Professor John Trinkaus (challenges, challenge) this idea.

3. He and his business students (investigates, investigate) such issues as supermarket manners, driving violations, and people's real feelings about Brussels sprouts.

4. They (observes, observe) and (records, record) data to shed light on human behavior.

_____

* For work on consistent verb tense, see Chapter 21, "Revising for Consistency and Parallelism," Part A.

5. For example, most shoppers (grabs, grab) pastries and rolls with their hands instead of tongs or tissues.

6. Of 100 supermarket shoppers, 85 (exceeds, exceed) the express line limit.

7. Thanks to Trinkaus, we (knows, know) more about rude and dangerous drivers.

8. Many drivers (parks, park) in fire zones or illegally (snatches, snatch) handicapped parking spots.

9. Only six people in ten (stops, stop) fully at stop signs.

10. In all these studies, observers (notes, note) the vehicle type and driver's sex.

11. Over and over again, women in vans (ranks, rank) as the worst offenders.

12. With a straight face, Trinkaus (investigates, investigate) baseball cap style and pedestrian shoe color.

13. His writings often (stimulates, stimulate) laughter first, then thinking.

14. The eccentric professor proudly (displays, display) his 2003 Ig Nobel Prize, a joke award for goofy research.

15. According to admirers, his work (sheds, shed) serious light on modern American culture.

B. Three Troublesome Verbs in the Present Tense: *To Be, To Have, To Do*

Choosing the correct verb form of *to be, to have,* and *to do* can be tricky. Study these charts:

	Reference Chart—*To Be* Present Tense			
	Singular		**Plural**	
	If the subject is	**the verb is**	**If the subject is**	**the verb is**
1st person:	I	am	we	are
2nd person:	you	are	you	are
3rd person:	he			
	she	is	they	are
	it			

Reference Chart—*To Have* Present Tense

	Singular		Plural	
	If the subject is	**the verb is**	**If the subject is**	**the verb is**
1st person:	I	have	we	have
2nd person:	you	have	you	have
3rd person:	he			
	she	has	they	have
	it			

Reference Chart—*To Do* Present Tense

	Singular		Plural	
	If the subject is	**the verb is**	**If the subject is**	**the verb is**
1st person:	I	do	we	do
2nd person:	you	do	you	do
3rd person:	he			
	she	does	they	do
	it			

PRACTICE 2

Write the correct present tense form of the verb in the space at the right of the pronoun.

To be	**To have**	**To do**
I _____	we _____	it _____
we _____	she _____	they _____
he _____	he _____	she _____
you _____	they _____	you _____
it _____	I _____	he _____
they _____	it _____	we _____
she _____	you _____	I _____

PRACTICE 3

Fill in the correct present tense form of the verb in parentheses.

1. Surfing _____ (to be) an extreme sport, and it _____ (to have) many fans.

2. Most beginners _____ (to do) basic moves on dry land—lying on the board, kneeling, and then rising to a hunched standing position.

3. An ocean beach with gentle, regular waves _____ (to be) the ideal place to start surfing.

4. Expert surfers _____ (to have) exceptional skills and _____ (to be) at home in the monster waves off Hawaii or Australia.

5. An expert _____ (to do) a "roller coaster" by soaring from the bottom to the top of a giant wave and down again.

6. "Riding a tube" _____ (to be) a thrilling trip through the transparent green tunnel of a giant wave.

7. Hawaiian coastlines _____ (to have) some of the world's best surfing.

8. Banzai Pipeline in Oahu _____ (to be) a famous surfing break; it

   _____ (to have) excellent tubes and waves three stories high.

9. Oahu's Sunset Rip, a notorious break, _____ (to have) several international surfing competitions.

10. For the surfer, wipeouts, flying boards, and sharks _____ (to be) constant dangers.

11. Yet the sport _____ (to have) new converts every year.

12. Many say that it _____ (to be) a spiritual experience.

C. Special Singular Constructions

Each of these constructions takes a **singular** verb:

Special Singular Constructions		
either (of) . . .	each (of) . . .	every one (of) . . .
neither (of) . . .	one (of) . . .	which one (of) . . .

1. *Neither* of the birds *has* feathers yet.
2. *Each* of the solutions *presents* difficulties.

● In sentence 1, *neither* means *neither one*. *Neither* is a singular subject and requires the singular verb *has*.

● In sentence 2, *each* means *each one*. *Each* is a singular subject and requires the singular verb *presents*.

However, an exception to this general rule is the case in which two subjects are joined by *(n)either . . . (n)or. . . .* Here, the verb agrees with the subject closer to it:

3. Neither the teacher nor the *pupils want* the semester shortened.
4. Either the graphs or the *map has* to be changed.

● In sentence 3, *pupils* is the subject closer to the verb. The plural subject *pupils* takes the verb *want*.

● In sentence 4, *map* is the subject closer to the verb. The singular subject *map* takes the verb *has*.

PRACTICE 4

Underline the subject and circle the correct verb in each sentence.

1. Each of these ferns (needs, need) special care.

2. One of the customers always (forget, forgets) his or her umbrella.

3. Which one of the flights (goes, go) nonstop to Dallas?

4. Every one of those cameras (costs, cost) more than I can afford.

5. Either you or Doris (is, are) correct.

6. Either of these flash drives (contain, contains) the information you need.

7. Do you really believe that one of these oysters (holds, hold) a pearl?

8. Neither of the twins (resembles, resemble) his parents.

9. One of the scientists (believes, believe) he can cure baldness.

10. Each of these inventions (has, have) an effect on how we spend our leisure time.

D. Separation of Subject and Verb

Sometimes a phrase or a clause separates the subject from the verb. First, look for the subject; then make sure that the verb agrees with the subject.

> 1. The economist's *ideas* on this matter *seem* well thought out.
> 2. *Radios* that were made in the 1930s *are* now collectors' items.

● In sentence 1, the *ideas* are well thought out. The prepositional phrase *on this matter* separates the subject *ideas* from the verb *seem.**

● In sentence 2, *radios* are now collectors' items. The relative clause *that were made in the 1930s* separates the subject *radios* from the verb *are.*

PRACTICE 5

Read each sentence carefully for meaning. Cross out any phrase or clause that separates the subject from the verb. Underline the subject and circle the correct verb.

1. The plums in that bowl (tastes, taste) sweet.

2. The instructions on the package (is, are) in French and Japanese.

3. Our new community center, which has a swimming pool and tennis courts, (keeps, keep) everyone happy.

4. The lampshades that are made of stained glass (looks, look) beautiful at night.

5. All the CD players on that shelf (comes, come) with a remote control.

6. A movie that lasts more than three hours usually (puts, put) me to sleep.

7. The man with the dark sunglasses (looks, look) like a typical movie villain.

8. The two nurses who check blood pressure (enjoys, enjoy) chatting with the patients.

9. The function of these metal racks (remains, remain) a mystery to me.

10. The lizard on the wall (has, have) only three legs.

E. Sentences Beginning with *There* and *Here*

In sentences that begin with ***there*** or ***here***, the subject usually follows the verb:

---

* For more work on prepositional phrases, see Chapter 26, "The Simple Sentence," Part B.

> 1. There *seem* to be two *flies* in my soup.
> 2. Here *is* my *prediction* for the coming year.

● In sentence 1, the plural subject *flies* takes the plural verb *seem*.

● In sentence 2, the singular subject *prediction* takes the singular verb *is*.

  You can often determine what the verb should be by reversing the word order: *two flies seem . . .* or *my prediction is. . . .*

PRACTICE 6

Underline the subject and circle the correct verb in each sentence.

1. There (goes, go) Tom Hanks.

2. There (is, are) only a few seconds left in the game.

3. Here (is, are) a terrific way to save money—make a budget and stick to it!

4. There (has, have) been robberies in the neighborhood lately.

5. Here (is, are) the plantains you ordered.

6. Here (comes, come) Jay, the television talk-show host.

7. There (is, are) no direct route to Black Creek from here.

8. There (seems, seem) to be something wrong with the doorbell.

9. Here (is, are) the teapot and sugar bowl I've been looking for.

10. There (is, are) six reporters in the hall waiting for an interview.

F. Agreement in Questions

In questions, the subject usually follows the verb:

> 1. What *is* the *secret* of your success?
> 2. Where *are* the *copies* of the review?

● In sentence 1, the subject *secret* takes the singular verb *is*.

● In sentence 2, the subject *copies* takes the plural verb *are*.

  You can often determine what the verb should be by reversing the word order: *the secret of your success is . . .* or *the copies are . . .*

PRACTICE 7

Underline the subject and circle the correct verb in each sentence.

1. How (does, do) the combustion engine actually work?

2. Why (is, are) Robert and Charity so suspicious?

3. Where (is, are) the new suitcases?

4. Which tour guide (have, has) a pair of binoculars?

5. (Are, Is) Dianne and Ramone starting a mail-order business?

6. What (seems, seem) to be the problem here?

7. Why (is, are) those boxes stacked in the corner?

8. (Is, Are) the mattress factory really going to close in June?

9. How (does, do) you explain that strange footprint?

10. Who (is, are) those people on the fire escape?

G. Agreement in Relative Clauses

A **relative clause** is a subordinate clause that begins with *who, which,* or *that.* The verb in the relative clause must agree with the antecedent of the *who, which,* or *that.**

1. People *who have a good sense of humor* make good neighbors.
2. Be careful of a scheme *that promises you a lot of money fast.*

● In sentence 1, the antecedent of *who* is *people. People* should take the plural verb *have.*

● In sentence 2, the antecedent of *that* is *scheme. Scheme* takes the singular verb *promises.*

PRACTICE 8

Underline the antecedent of the *who, which,* or *that.* Then circle the correct verb.

1. Most patients prefer doctors who (spends, spend) time talking with them.

2. The gnarled oak that (shades, shade) the garden is my favorite tree.

3. Laptop computers, which (has, have) some advantages over desktop computers, are becoming more popular.

---

* For more work on relative clauses, see Chapter 22, "Revising for Sentence Variety," Part D.

4. My neighbor, who (swims, swim) at least one hour a day, is 70 years old.

5. Planning ahead, which (saves, save) hours of wasted time, is a good way to manage time effectively.

6. Employers often appreciate employees who (asks, ask) intelligent questions.

7. This air conditioner, which now (costs, cost) $800, rarely breaks down.

8. Everyone admires her because she is someone who always (sees, see) the bright side of a bad situation.

9. He is the man who (creates, create) furniture from scraps of walnut, cherry, and birch.

10. Foods that (contains, contain) artificial sweeteners may be hazardous to your health.

PROOFREADING STRATEGY

If present tense verb agreement is one of your error patterns, you might **isolate** and **color code**. First, if you are writing on a computer, *isolate each sentence* on its own line. This will help your brain and eye focus on one sentence at a time. Next, find the subject and verb in each sentence; use highlighters to *color code* subjects yellow and verbs green. Cross out any confusing prepositional phrases.

Now check each color-coded pair for subject-verb agreement. 1. If you aren't sure, *change the subject to a pronoun*, and see if it agrees with the verb. 2. Do a final "audio check" and read the sentence aloud. Here are two examples:

they   are owned
The apartments on State Street is owned by the college.
he   wants
My friend want to rent one of them this fall.

PRACTICE 9   REVIEW

Proofread the following essay for verb agreement errors. You might try out the proofreading strategy to see if it works for you. Correct any errors by writing above the lines.

JOB HUNTING? THINK GREEN.

(1) These days, many job fairs and sites features green jobs, or green-collar jobs. (2) Just what is a green job? (3) A green job provide solid wages yet preserves rather than drains the earth's resources. (4) Workers who build hybrid cars have green jobs. (5) So do people who install "green roofs" on buildings—garden areas that purifies the air and prevent diseases like asthma. (6) Green-collar employees often take pride in their work because

Wind turbine workers in Ohio take down one of the giant turbines for repair.

they contribute to the health of the community. (7) Many colleges now offer courses that prepares students for a greener workforce. (8) Robert, Cheree, and Han illustrates this trend.

(9) Robert Gomez of Oakland, California, remembers his shock at losing a good job in commercial construction two years ago. (10) Today, at 52, thanks to a poster in the unemployment office, Robert have a certificate in solar panel installation from Merritt College and a new lease on life. (11) He installs solar energy panels on homes and buildings, a job he enjoys. (12) According to career counselors, people like Robert does well even during hard times because they stay flexible and get new training.

(13) Cheree Williams wants a green career. (14) She attends Evergreen State College in Eugene, Oregon, a school that wins awards for its environmental efforts. (15) Cheree study in the Food, Health, and Sustainability program; she learns earth-friendly farming methods in the school's organic garden. (16) With her degree, she hope to work in the public schools, building children's health and achievement through wise food choices.

(17) A third example is Han Bae, who loves chemistry and cars. (18) A career in the growing biofuels industry make sense for him, he believes. (19) At Central Carolina Community College, Han gets hands-on experience making and testing new fuels because a factory right on campus makes ethanol from different plant sources. (20) College vehicles actually runs on these fuels.

(21) Nationwide, enrollment in green courses increase every year, touching fields as diverse as prison administration and small business entrepreneurship.

EXPLORING ONLINE

http://grammar.ccc.commnet.edu/grammar/sv_agr.htm

Review the rules of subject-verb agreement; then scroll
to the bottom for three interactive quizzes.

http://a4esl.org/q/h/vm/svagr.html

Take this verb quiz and get instant feedback on your answers.

http://grammar.ccc.commnet.edu/grammar/cgi-shl/quiz.pl/agreement_add2.htm

Test your verb skills with this more difficult quiz.

CourseMate for *Evergreen*

Visit *Evergreen* CourseMate for more practices and quizzes, videos
to accompany the readings, career and job-search resources,
ESL help, and live links to every Exploring Online in the book.

CHAPTER 30

Past Tense

A: Regular Verbs in the Past Tense

B: Irregular Verbs in the Past Tense

C: A Troublesome Verb in the Past Tense: *To Be*

D: Troublesome Pairs in the Past Tense: *Can/Could, Will/Would*

A. Regular Verbs in the Past Tense

Regular verbs in the past tense take an *-ed* or *-d* ending:

1. The captain *hoisted* the flag.
2. They *purchased* a flat screen TV yesterday.
3. We *deposited* a quarter in the meter.

● *Hoisted, purchased*, and *deposited* are regular verbs in the past tense.

● Each verb ends in *-ed* or *-d*.

PRACTICE 1

Fill in the past tense of the regular verbs in parentheses.*

1. On July 8, 1947, the headline of the *Daily Record* in Roswell, New Mexico,

   _____ (announce) the U.S. military's capture of a "flying saucer."

———
* If you have questions about spelling, see Chapter 40, "Spelling," Parts D, E, and F.

2. Events surrounding this incident _____ (produce) one of the most famous
   and controversial UFO stories of all time.

3. A local sheep rancher first _____ (stumble) upon a large field of wreckage
   that _____ (resemble) sheets of tough, wafer-thin metal.

4. Several people who _____ (stop) at the crash site _____ (report)
   seeing bodies of space aliens.

5. Army officials _____ (gather) the fragments, _____ (transport) them to
   the Roswell Army Air Field, and _____ (issue) a press release about a mysterious
   disc.

6. Soon afterward, however, the military _____ (change) its story and
   _____ (identify) the object as a fallen weather balloon.

7. Reporters and the public _____ (ignore) the incident for 30 years, but in 1978, an
   Army major who _____ (search) the wreckage _____ (accuse) the military
   of lying.

8. Other eyewitnesses to the crash _____ (admit) seeing strange bodies, which
   they _____ (portray) as short, hairless beings with large heads.

9. Over 60 years later, scientists are debating whether the military actually _____
   (seize) and _____ (study) the remains of beings from outer space.

10. In 2008, astronaut and scientist Edgar Mitchell _____ (drop) a bombshell,
    stating that an alien craft indeed _____ (crash) at Roswell and the government
    _____ (cover) it up.

broukoid/Shutterstock.com

B. Irregular Verbs in the Past Tense

Irregular verbs do not take an *-ed* or *-d* ending in the past but change internally:

1. I *wrote* that letter in ten minutes.
2. Although the orange cat *fell* from a high branch, she escaped unharmed.
3. The play *began* on time but ended fairly late.

- *Wrote* is the past tense of *write*.
- *Fell* is the past tense of *fall*.
- *Began* is the past tense of *begin*.

Here is a partial list of irregular verbs:

Reference Chart
Irregular Verbs in the Past Tense

Simple Form	Past Tense	Simple Form	Past Tense
be	was, were	leave	left
become	became	let	let
begin	began	lie	lay
blow	blew	lose	lost
break	broke	make	made
bring	brought	mean	meant
build	built	meet	met
buy	bought	pay	paid
catch	caught	put	put
choose	chose	quit	quit
come	came	read	read
cut	cut	ride	rode
deal	dealt	rise	rose
dig	dug	run	ran
dive	dove (dived)	say	said
do	did	see	saw
draw	drew	seek	sought
drink	drank	sell	sold
drive	drove	send	sent
eat	ate	shake	shook
fall	fell	shine	shone (shined)
feed	fed	sing	sang
feel	felt	sit	sat
fight	fought	sleep	slept
find	found	speak	spoke
fly	flew	spend	spent
forbid	forbade	split	split
forget	forgot	spring	sprang
forgive	forgave	stand	stood
freeze	froze	steal	stole
get	got	stink	stank
give	gave	swim	swam
go	went	take	took
grow	grew	teach	taught
have	had	tear	tore

hear	heard	tell	told
hide	hid	think	thought
hold	held	throw	threw
hurt	hurt	understand	understood
keep	kept	wake	woke (waked)
know	knew	wear	wore
lay	laid	win	won
lead	led	write	wrote

PRACTICE 2

Fill in the past tense of the regular and irregular verbs in parentheses. If you are not sure of the past tense, use the chart on the previous page. Do not guess.

HISPANIC HEROES: SHAKING UP HOLLYWOOD

(1) For much of the last century, Hispanics in Hollywood _____ (remain) a small minority. (2) Many Latin actors either _____ (accept) such stereotyped roles as the gardener or _____ (change) their names, hoping to snag better roles. (3) Jo Raquel Tejada _____ (choose) the last name Welch, and Ramon Estevez _____ (become) Martin Sheen. (4) But a new century _____ (bring) deeper change—in the form of determined individuals who _____ (dream) of making or starring in movies and then _____ (fight) to open doors.

(5) Director Robert Rodriguez, for instance, _____ (succeed) after a rocky beginning. (6) As a young Texan, Rodriguez was rejected by the film school to which he _____ (apply). (7) Instead of getting discouraged, the 23-year-old _____ (take) off for Mexico with a movie camera, some friends, and $7,000. (8) The result was the film *El Mariachi*, a Spanish-language action comedy that Rodriguez later _____ (sell) to Columbia Pictures for worldwide distribution. (9) After that, he _____ (keep) entertaining moviegoers with low-budget, action-packed English-language films like *Desperado, Spy Kids*, and *From Dusk Till Dawn*. (10) He _____ (rake) in millions with his violent shoot-'em-up scenes and special effects. (11) Perhaps more important, Rodriguez _____ (put) Hispanics in top roles—for instance, casting Antonio Banderas as a dad, not a Hispanic dad, in *Spy Kids*. (12) "I find

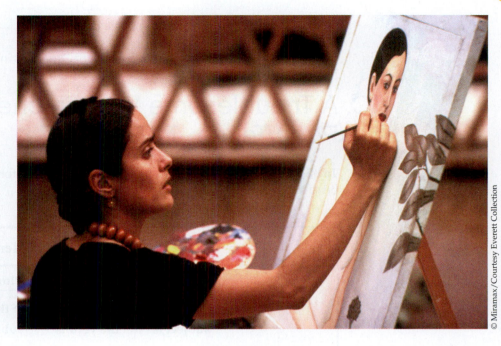

Salma Hayek as the Mexican painter Frida Kahlo, the dream role for which she fought.

that the best way through a closed door," Rodriguez once _____ (proclaim), "is

to kick it open."

(13) Another Hispanic who _____ (help) make her own

opportunities is Mexican-born actress and producer Salma Hayek. (14) Ironically, it was

Rodriguez who _____ (battle) Hollywood for approval to cast this unknown

actress in one of *Desperado*'s leading roles. (15) She _____ (do) not disappoint

him, and her performance _____ (catapult) her to fame. (16) From the time she

was 13, Hayek _____ (admire) Frida Kahlo and _____ (long) to play

the spirited Mexican painter in a film about her life. (17) Behind the scenes, Salma

_____ (strategize) brilliantly to get the movie made, secure rights, and beat out

Madonna for the part. (18) In the end, Hayek _____ (produce) and

_____ (star) in *Frida*, which _____ (open) in 2002. (19) Her

performance in that lead role _____ (earn) her an Academy Award nomination.

(20) This movie and Salma's depiction of the brainy scientist in *Spy Kids* _____

(expand) Hollywood's ideas about "suitable" Hispanic roles.

(21) Rodriguez and Hayek are just two examples of the new infusion of talent

in American movies. (22) In 2005, the mentor and his leading lady _____ (find) themselves together again—on a magazine cover. (23) Both —————— (win) spots

on *Time* magazine's list of the 25 Most Influential Hispanics in the United States.

C. A Troublesome Verb in the Past Tense: *To Be*

To be is the only verb that in the past tense has different forms for different persons. Be careful of subject-verb agreement:

Reference Chart—*To Be* Past Tense

	Singular		Plural	
	If the subject is	**the verb is**	**If the subject is**	**the verb is**
1st person:	I	was	we	were
2nd person:	you	were	you	were
3rd person:	he			
	she	was	they	were
	it			

- Note that the first person singular form and the third person singular form are the same—*was*.

Be especially careful of agreement when adding *not* to *was* or *were* to make a contraction:

> was + not = wasn't
> were + not = weren't

PRACTICE 3

Circle the correct form of the verb *to be* in the past tense. Do not guess. If you are not sure of the correct form, use the chart on pages 433–434.

1. Oprah Winfrey (was, were) always an avid reader.

2. In fact, books (was, were) sometimes her only comfort during her difficult childhood and painful adolescence.

3. When her producers (was, were) considering a TV book club, the world's most popular talk-show host (was, were) sure she could get the whole country reading.

4. Her first book club selection (was, were) *The Deep End of the Ocean* by Jacquelyn Mitchard, the story of a kidnapped child; the public's rush to buy books (wasn't, weren't) anticipated.

5. Mitchard's publishers (was, were) astonished to have to reprint the book nearly 20 times; all in all, 900,000 hardcovers and over 2 million paperbacks (was, were) sold.

6. Every book club pick (was, were) a huge success, and even people who didn't read found they (was, were) eagerly awaiting Winfrey's next selection.

7. Toni Morrison's *Sula* (was, were) suddenly a best seller, as (was, were) older classics by William Faulkner, John Steinbeck, and Carson McCullers.

8. Controversy (was, were) no stranger to the show; Oprah publically chided James Frey after *A Million Little Pieces*, his "true life story," (was, were) shown to be lies.

9. When the Book Club (was, were) closed in 2011 along with the Oprah Show, many readers (was, were) upset.

10. Just one year later, however, Oprah (was, were) so enthusiastic about Judith Stayed's book *Wild* that she launched a new Book Club with digital and social media features.

D. Troublesome Pairs in the Past Tense: Can/Could, Will/Would

Use *could* as the past tense of *can*.

1. Maria is extraordinary because she *can* remember what happened to her when she was three years old.
2. When I was in high school, I *could* do two sit-ups in an hour.

- In sentence 1, *can* shows the action is in the present.
- In sentence 2, *could* shows the action occurred in the past.

PRACTICE 4

Fill in either the present tense *can* or the past tense *could*.

1. Tom is so talented that he _____ play most music on the piano by ear.

2. He _____ leave the hospital as soon as he feels stronger.

3. Last week we _____ not find fresh strawberries.

4. When we were in Spain last summer, we _____ see all of Madrid from our hotel balcony.

5. As a child, I _____ perform easily in public, but I _____ no longer do it.

6. Anything you _____ do, he _____ do better.

7. Nobody _____ find the guard after the robbery yesterday.

8. These days, Fred _____ usually predict the weather from the condition of his bunions.

Use *would* as the past tense of *will*.

> 3. Roberta says that she *will* arrive with her camera in ten minutes.
> 4. Roberta said that she *would* arrive with her camera in ten minutes.

- In sentence 3, *will* points to the future from the present.
- In sentence 4, *would* points to the future from the past.

PRACTICE 5

Fill in either the present tense *will* or the past tense *would*.

1. Sean expected that he _____ arrive at midnight.

2. Sean expects that he _____ arrive at midnight.

3. I hope the sale at the used car lot _____ continue for another week.

4. I hoped the sale at the used car lot _____ continue for another week.

5. When Benny had time, he _____ color-code his computer disks.

6. When Benny has time, he _____ color-code his computer disks.

7. The chefs assure us that the wedding cake _____ be spectacular.

8. The chefs assured us that the wedding cake _____ be spectacular.

PROOFREADING STRATEGY

To proofread for past tense verb errors, especially if these are one of your error patterns, **highlight** and **read aloud**. First, read slowly through the text, underlining or highlighting the *main verb* or *verbs* in every sentence.

- Make sure that every *regular past tense verb* ends in *–d* or *–ed*.

- Carefully consider every *irregular past tense verb* to make sure it is in the correct form. If you aren't sure, check the past tense chart. Here are some examples:

> *learned*
> After homeless veteran Roy Foster got sober, he learn that many other
> *were*
> vets was homeless. Foster started Stand Down House to help them.
>
> CNN later named him Top Hero of 2009.

PRACTICE 6   REVIEW

Proofread the following essay for past tense errors. Using highlighters, try the proofreading strategy above to see if it works for you. Correct any errors by writing above the lines.

VIDEO GAME NATION

(1) In 1972, when Nolan Bushnell introduced the first video game to the mass market, few people imagined what the future hold. (2) Bushnell call his new company Atari; the game was Pong. (3) To play, two people simply bounced a digital ball back and forth on a black-and-white console, turning knobs to control their paddles. (4) Primitive by today's standards, Pong were a sensation in arcades and bars across the United States. (5) In 1975, Atari's home version of Pong outsolded all other items in the Sears Christmas catalog. (6) But that was just the beginning. (7) Over the next 35 years, electronic games becomed one of America's most popular pastimes, spawning a booming industry and new jobs.

(8) During the 1980s, the first generation of gamers flock to arcades to play Pac-Man, Donkey Kong, and Centipede. (9) Far-sighted tech companies like Sony, Nintendo, and Microsoft seen this growing market and gone to work. (10) They create home consoles, handheld systems, and of course, more and better games. (11) With the evolution of eye-popping 3-D graphics, realistic sound and action, and imaginative characters, video games begin to look more like television and movies than the electronic paddle-and-ball

game that started it all. (12) The public kept buying. (13) In 2004 alone, sales of game consoles and software total $6.2 billion.

(14) As the industry grew, so do controversy. (15) Critics warned that gamers just set on the couch instead of playing outside. (16) Many worryied about the violent content of some games. (17) Others argued that the puzzle-based adventure games of the 1990s and early 2000s teached useful skills. (18) Gamers has to reason, invent strategies, and foresee the consequences of their actions. (19) Despite the controversy, video games are now part of life for most American children, teens, and even adults. (20) In recent years, the average age of the video game player rise to 30.

(21) Some gamers longed to work in the field, but they needed training. (22) They knowed that companies, hoping to create the latest, greatest game, formed development teams composed of graphic designers, artists, musicians, computer and other technicians. (23) So it were students themselves who clamor for degree programs to teach them the necessary skills. (24) Some colleges—like New York's Rensselaer Polytechnic Institute and Pittsburgh's Carnegie Mellon University—responded quickly. (25) They establish interdisciplinary programs to prepare students for the fast-moving video game industry of the future.

EXPLORING ONLINE

http://grammar.ccc.commnet.edu/grammar/cgi-shl/par2_quiz.pl/ irregular_quiz.htm

Type in the irregular verbs; the computer checks you.

http://web2.uvcs.uvic.ca/elc/studyzone/330/grammar/pasted.htm

Review and quizzes: regular verbs

CourseMate for *Evergreen*

Visit *Evergreen* CourseMate for more practices and quizzes, videos to accompany the readings, career and job-search resources, ESL help, and live links to every Exploring Online in the book.

CHAPTER 31

The Past Participle

A. Past Participles of Regular Verbs

The **past participle** is the form of the verb that can be combined with the helping verb like *have* and *has* to make verbs of more than one word:

Present Tense	Past Tense	Helping Verb plus Past Participle
1. They *skate*.	1. They *skated*.	1. They *have skated*.
2. Beth *dances*.	2. Beth *danced*.	2. Beth *has danced*.
3. Frank *worries*.	3. Frank *worried*.	3. Frank *has worried*.

- *Skated, danced,* and *worried* are all past participles of regular verbs.

- Note that both the *past tense* and the *past participle* of regular verbs end in *-ed* or *-d*.

PRACTICE 1

The first sentence of each pair that follows contains a regular verb in the past tense. Fill in *have* or *has* plus the past participle of the same verb to complete the second sentence.

1. Arlen Ness earned his title, King of the Choppers.

   Arlen Ness _____ _____ his title, King of the Choppers.

2. Since 1967, Ness designed and manufactured one-of-a-kind motorcycles.

   Since 1967, Ness _____ _____ and _____ one-of-a-kind motorcycles.

3. The craftsmanship, performance, and eye-popping style of Ness bikes attracted worldwide attention.

   The craftsmanship, performance, and eye-popping style of Ness bikes

   _____ _____ worldwide attention.

4. Shaquille O'Neal and Aerosmith's Steven Tyler ordered custom Ness creations.

   Shaquille O'Neal and Aerosmith's Steven Tyler _____ _____ custom Ness creations.

5. A master builder and bike painter, Arlen Ness received many first-place trophies.

   A master builder and bike painter, Arlen Ness _____ _____ many first-place trophies.

6. Crowds lined up just to glimpse his elongated yellow chopper, "Top Banana."

   Crowds _____ _____ up just to glimpse his elongated yellow chopper, "Top Banana."

Arlen Ness rides "Top Banana," one of his eye-popping choppers.

From the book, *Arlen Ness, The King of Choppers,* by Michael Lichter. © Michael Lichter

7. Ness picked witty names like "Jelly Belly" for many bikes.

    Ness _____ _____ witty names like "Jelly Belly" for many bikes.

8. The curvy, green beauty, "Smooth-Ness," and the silver monster, "Mach Ness," both

    played on his famous name.

    The curvy, green beauty, "Smooth-Ness," and the silver monster, "Mach Ness," both

    _____ _____ on his famous name.

9. Corey Ness joined his father's multimillion-dollar company.

    Corey Ness _____ _____ his father's multimillion-dollar

    company.

10. Custom motorcycles turned into big business.

    Custom motorcycles _____ _____ into big business.

B. Past Participles of Irregular Verbs

Most verbs that are irregular in the past tense are also irregular in the past participle, as shown in the following chart.

Present Tense	Past Tense	Helping Verb plus Past Participle
1. We *sing*.	1. We *sang*.	1. We *have sung*.
2. Bill *writes*.	2. Bill *wrote*.	2. Bill *has written*.
3. I *think*.	3. I *thought*.	3. I *have thought*.

- Irregular verbs change from present to past to past participle in unusual ways.
- *Sung, written*, and *thought* are all past participles of irregular verbs.
- Note that the past tense and past participle of *think* are the same—*thought*.

Reference Chart Irregular Verbs, Past and Past Participle		
Simple Form	**Past Tense**	**Past Participle**
be	was, were	been
become	became	become
begin	began	begun
blow	blew	blown

break	broke	broken
bring	brought	brought
build	built	built
buy	bought	bought
catch	caught	caught
choose	chose	chosen
come	came	come
cut	cut	cut
deal	dealt	dealt
dig	dug	dug
dive	dove (dived)	dived
do	did	done
draw	drew	drawn
drink	drank	drunk
drive	drove	driven
eat	ate	eaten
fall	fell	fallen
feed	fed	fed
feel	felt	felt
fight	fought	fought
find	found	found
fly	flew	flown
forbid	forbade	forbidden
forget	forgot	forgotten
forgive	forgave	forgiven
freeze	froze	frozen
get	got	got (gotten)
give	gave	given
go	went	gone
grow	grew	grown
have	had	had
hear	heard	heard
hide	hid	hidden
hold	held	held
hurt	hurt	hurt
keep	kept	kept
know	knew	known
lay	laid	laid
lead	led	led
leave	left	left
let	let	let

lie	lay	lain
lose	lost	lost
make	made	made
mean	meant	meant
meet	met	met
pay	paid	paid
put	put	put
quit	quit	quit
read	read	read
ride	rode	ridden
rise	rose	risen
run	ran	run
say	said	said
see	saw	seen
seek	sought	sought
sell	sold	sold
send	sent	sent
shake	shook	shaken
shine	shone (shined)	shone (shined)
sing	sang	sung
sit	sat	sat
sleep	slept	slept
speak	spoke	spoken
spend	spent	spent
split	split	split
spring	sprang	sprung
stand	stood	stood
steal	stole	stolen
stink	stank	stunk
swim	swam	swum
take	took	taken
teach	taught	taught
tear	tore	torn
tell	told	told
think	thought	thought
throw	threw	thrown
understand	understood	understood
wake	woke (waked)	woken (waked)
wear	wore	worn
win	won	won
write	wrote	written

PRACTICE 2

The first sentence of each pair that follows contains an irregular verb in the past tense. Fill in *have* or *has* plus the past participle of the same verb to complete the second sentence.

1. Sean took plenty of time buying the groceries.

   Sean _____ _____ plenty of time buying the groceries.

2. We sent our latest budget to the mayor.

   We _____ _____ our latest budget to the mayor.

3. My daughter hid her diary.

   My daughter _____ _____ her diary.

4. The jockey rode all day in the hot sun.

   The jockey _____ _____ all day in the hot sun.

5. Hershey, Pennsylvania, became a great tourist attraction.

   Hershey, Pennsylvania, _____ _____ a great tourist attraction.

6. The company's managers knew about these hazards for two years.

   The company's managers _____ _____ about these hazards for two years.

7. Carrie floated down the river on an inner tube.

   Carrie _____ _____ down the river on an inner tube.

8. At last, our team won the bowling tournament.

   At last, our team _____ _____ the bowling tournament.

9. Larry and Marsha broke their long silence.

   Larry and Marsha _____ _____ their long silence.

10. Science fiction films were very popular this past year.

    Science fiction films _____ _____ very popular this past year.

PRACTICE 3

Complete each sentence by filling in *have* or *has* plus the past participle of the verb in parentheses. Some verbs are regular, some are irregular.

1. Soccer _____ _____ (gain) popularity in the United States ever since the 1994 World Cup was held in Pasadena, California.

2. Sports fans _____ _____ (see) the enthusiasm and passion that soccer arouses in such countries as Argentina, Brazil, Italy, and Portugal.

Alex Morgan of the USA scores during the 2011 Women's World Cup match against Japan.

Lars Baron–FIFA/Getty Images

3. The United States also _____ _____ (demonstrate) that it can win games in the biggest soccer competition in the world.

4. The U.S. women's soccer team _____ _____ (win) worldwide respect, earning Olympic gold medals in 2004, 2008, and again in 2012.

5. The names of female stars like Abby Wambach _____ _____ (become) household words, along with great male players like David Beckham.

6. Television coverage of matches _____ _____ (increase); in fact, 56 percent of U.S. adults watched the thrilling 2011 Women's World Cup final, in which Japan beat the United States in overtime.

7. Major League Soccer _____ _____ (add) new franchises and recently _____ _____ (begin) to attract stars from other countries.

8. Significantly, the game _____ _____ (grow) in popularity with suburban boys and girls.

9. The parents of these children _____ _____ (encourage) them to play a relatively safe but exciting sport.

10. Experts say that this generation, which _____ _____ (fall) in love with soccer, is changing the future of American athletics.

C. Using the Present Perfect Tense

The **present perfect tense** is composed of the present tense of *to have* plus the past participle. The present perfect tense shows that an action has begun in the past and is continuing into the present.

> 1. Past tense: Beatrice *taught* English for ten years.
> 2. Present perfect tense: Beatrice *has taught* English for ten years.

- In sentence 1, Beatrice *taught* English in the past, but she no longer teaches it. Note the use of the simple past tense, *taught*.
- In sentence 2, Beatrice *has taught* for ten years and is still teaching English *now*. *Has taught* implies that the action is continuing.

PRACTICE 4

Read these sentences carefully for meaning. Then circle the correct verb—either the **past tense** or the **present perfect tense**.

1. He (directed, has directed) the theater group for many years now.

2. Emilio lifted the rug and (has swept, swept) the dust under it.

3. She (went, has gone) to a poetry slam last night.

4. For the past four years, I (took, have taken) art classes in the summer.

5. We (talked, have talked) about the problem of your lateness for three days; it's time for you to do something about it.

6. While he was in Japan, he (took, have taken) many photographs of shrines.

7. She (won, has won) that contest ten years ago.

8. The boxers (fought, have fought) for an hour, and they look very tired.

9. He (applied, has applied) to three colleges and attended the one with the best sociology department.

10. The auto mechanics (had, have had) a radio show together for five years and are now extremely popular.

D. Using the Past Perfect Tense

The **past perfect tense** is composed of the past tense of *to have* plus the past participle. The past perfect tense shows that an action occurred further back in the past than other past action.

> 1. Past tense: Rhonda *left* for the movies.
> 2. Past perfect tense: Rhonda *had* already *left* for the movies by the time we *arrived*.

- In sentence 1, *left* is the simple past.
- In sentence 2, the past perfect *had left* shows that this action occurred even before another action in the past, *arrived*.

PRACTICE 5

Read these sentences carefully for meaning. Then circle the correct verb—either the *past tense* or the *past perfect tense*.

1. Tony came to the office with a cane last week because he (sprained, had sprained) his ankle a month ago.

2. As Janice (piled, had piled) the apples into a pyramid, she thought, "I should become an architect."

3. Juan (finished, had finished) his gardening by the time I (drove, had driven) up in my new convertible.

4. The man nervously (looked, had looked) at his watch and then walked a bit faster.

5. Roberto told us that he (decided, had decided) to enlist in the Marines.

6. The caller asked whether we (received, had received) our free toaster yet.

7. Last week he told me that he (forgot, had forgotten) to mail the rent check.

8. As the curtain came down, everyone (rose, had risen) and applauded the Brazilian dance troupe.

9. Scott (closed, had closed) his books and went to the movies.

10. The prosecutor proved that the defendant was lying; until then I (believed, had believed) he was innocent.

E. Using the Passive Voice (*To Be* and the Past Participle)

The **passive voice** is composed of the past participle with some form of *to be* (*am, is, are, was, were, has been, have been,* or *had been*). In the passive voice, the subject does not act but is *acted upon*.

Compare the passive voice with the active voice in the following pairs of sentences.

> 1. Passive voice: This newspaper *is written* by journalism students.
> 2. Active voice: Journalism students *write* this newspaper.
> 3. Passive voice: My garden *was devoured* by rabbits.
> 4. Active voice: Rabbits *devoured* my garden.

● In sentence 1, the subject, *this newspaper*, is passive; it is acted upon. In sentence 2, the subject, *students*, is active; it performs the action.

● Note the difference between the passive verb *is written* and the active verb *write*.

● However, both verbs (*is written* and *write*) are in the *present tense*.

● The verbs in sentences 3 and 4 are both in the *past tense: was devoured* (passive) and *devoured* (active).

  Use the passive voice sparingly. Write in the passive voice when you want to emphasize the receiver of the action rather than the doer.

PRACTICE 6

Fill in the correct *past participle* form of the verb in parentheses to form the passive voice. If you are not sure, check the chart on pages 443–445.

1. The barn was ——————— (build) by friends of the family.

2. These ruby slippers were ——————— (give) to me by my grandmother.

3. A faint inscription is ——————— (etch) on the back of the old gold watch.

4. At the garden party, Sheila and Una were ——————— (bite) by mosquitoes and gnats.

5. The getaway car is always ——————— (drive) by a man in a gray fedora.

6. Her articles have been ——————— (publish) in the *Texas Monthly*.

PRACTICE 7

Whenever possible, write in the *active*, not the *passive*, voice. Rewrite these sentences in the active voice, making all necessary verb and subject changes. Be sure to keep the sentence in the original tense.

EXAMPLE

Too many personal questions were asked by the interviewer.

The interviewer asked too many personal questions.

1.   The shot was blocked by the goalie.

   _____

2.   Her reputation was hurt by her rudeness.

   _____

3.   The law boards were passed by Eduardo and Noah.

   _____

4.   The noisy group was warned by the usher.

   _____

5.   We were shown how to create PowerPoint slides by the instructor.

   _____

F. Using the Past Participle as an Adjective

The **past participle** form of the verb can be used as an **adjective** after a linking verb:

> 1.   The window is *broken*.

● The adjective *broken* describes the subject *window*.

   The **past participle** form of the verb can sometimes be used as an adjective before a noun or a pronoun.

> 2.   This *fried* chicken tastes wonderful.

● The adjective *fried* describes the noun *chicken*.

PRACTICE 8

Use the past participle form of the verb in parentheses as an adjective in each sentence.

1.   My _____ (use) laptop was a great bargain at only $200.

2.   Bob is highly _____ (qualify) to install a water heater.

3. The _____ (air-condition) room was making everyone shiver.

4. The newly _____ (rise) cinnamon bread smelled wonderful.

5. Were you _____ (surprise) to hear about my raise?

6. He feels _____ (depress) on rainy days.

7. She knows the power of the _____ (write) word.

8. My gym teacher seems _____ (prejudice) against short people.

9. The _____ (embarrass) child pulled her jacket over her head.

10. We ordered _____ (toss) salad, _____ (broil) salmon,

_____ (mash) potatoes, and _____ (bake) apple rings.

PRACTICE 9

Proofread the following paragraph for errors in past participles used as adjectives. Correct the errors by writing above the lines.

(1) To experience the food of another culture is to appreciate that culture in new ways. (2) A fine example is the traditional Chinese wedding banquet, where each beautiful dish is chosen, prepare, and presented to carry a promise for the couple's future. (3) Carefully season shark's fin soup opens the feast; this rare and expensive treat signifies health and long life to both family lines. (4) Each table receives its own glazed Peking Duck to indicate the couple's fidelity. (5) In Chinese tradition, chicken represents the phoenix, a magic bird that rises from the ashes, and lobster represents the dragon. (6) Often combine and bake in a single dish, these two foods mark the peaceful union of two families. (7) Because the Chinese word for fish sounds like "abundance," a whole steamed fish is offered to the newly marry couple—a wish for prosperity. (8) At the end of the meal, satisfy guests enjoy dessert buns filled with lotus seeds, promising fertility and future children. (9) It should come as no surprise that an old-fashion Chinese banquet can last an entire day.

PROOFREADING STRATEGY

If past participle problems are among your error patterns, read your draft one word at a time and **search for the helping verbs** *has, have, had, is, am, are, was,* and *were*. Every time you find a helping verb, highlight or underline it. If you are using a computer, use the *"Find"* feature to locate these words in your draft. Whenever these helping verbs are part of a past participle verb, **check the past participle form**. If it's a regular verb, it should end in *–d* or *–ed*. If it's an irregular verb and you aren't sure, check the verb chart. How should the writer correct the incorrect past participles in these examples?

Correct   Incorrect
The manager has interviewed all the candidates, and she has chose

our new sales associate.

Incorrect Incorrect
My steak was grill and season to perfection.

PRACTICE 10   REVIEW

Proofread the following essay for past participle errors. Try the proofreading strategy above to see if it works for you. Correct any errors by writing above the lines.

LAUGHING AT THE NEWS

© Comedy Central/The Kobal Collection at Art Resource, NY

Comedian and fake news anchor Stephen Colbert

(1) In recent years, many people have stop reading newspapers and watching the nightly news. (2) Meanwhile, "fake news" comedy shows like *The Daily Show with Jon Stewart* and *The Colbert Report* have growed more popular. (3) Watch by many people, they are the only source of news for 40 percent of those 18 to 29.

(4) Since the mid-1970s, generations of television viewers have seen NBC's *Saturday Night Live* mock the news with its "Weekend Update," where comic actors posing as news anchors offer a few sentences about a current issue, follow by a punch line. (5) SNL's writers have took aim at everything from global warming and the budget crisis to world leaders. (6) Actress and writer Tiny Fey outdid herself in 2008 with her impressions of vice presidential candidate Sarah Palin, complete with winks, "beauty pageant walkin'," and a phony moose shoot dead on stage. (7) View millions of times on YouTube, Fey's skits are classics.

(8) Mixing a little news with a lot of laughs has rose to new heights on *The Daily Show* and *The Colbert Report* (pronounced "repore" with a silent *t* like the host's name). (9) These news parodies feature anchormen delivering updates, complete with video clips, reports from correspondents on location, and interviews with real politicians, authors, and celebrities. (10) The topics are all lift from current headlines, but the wise-cracking hosts, with their over-spray hair and intense facial expressions, have became masters at mining humor from their guests. (11) In one interview, Colbert revealed that a congressman who wanted the Ten Commandments display in every American courtroom could name only three commandments. (12) Adore by their fans, both hosts have won Emmys.

(13) As the line between news and comedy has blur, questions are being raise about the effects of "infotainment." (14) Worry about the trend, CNN reporter Christiane Amanpour fears viewers are becoming less educate. (15) Others insist that those who watch comedy news think more critically and that humor comes closer to the truth than wooden seriousness.

EXPLORING ONLINE

http://itech.pensacolastate.edu/writinglab/vbcross.htm

This crossword puzzle will test your past tense and past participles.

**http://grammar.ccc.commnet.edu/grammar/
quizzes/final-ed_option.htm**

To add or not to add -*ed*? This one is tricky; test yourself.

CourseMate for *Evergreen*

Visit *Evergreen* CourseMate for more practices and quizzes, videos
to accompany the readings, career and job-search resources,
ESL help, and live links to every Exploring Online in the book.

CHAPTER 32

Nouns

A: Defining Singular and Plural

B: Signal Words: Singular and Plural

C: Signal Words with *of*

A. Defining Singular and Plural

Nouns are words that refer to people, places, or things. They can be either singular or plural. **Singular** means one. **Plural** means more than one.

Singular	Plural
the glass	glasses
a lamp	lamps
a lesson	lessons

● As you can see, nouns usually add -*s* or -*es* to form the plural.

Some nouns form their plurals in other ways. Here are a few examples:

Singular	Plural	Singular	Plural
child	children	medium	media
crisis	crises	memorandum	memoranda (memorandums)
criterion	criteria	phenomenon	phenomena
foot	feet	syllabus	syllabi
goose	geese	tooth	teeth
man	men	woman	women

These nouns ending in -*f* or -*fe* change endings to -*ves* in the plural:

Singular	Plural
half	halves
knife	knives
life	lives
scarf	scarves
shelf	shelves
wife	wives
wolf	wolves

Hyphenated nouns form plurals by adding -*s* or -*es* to the main word:

Singular	Plural
brother-in-law	brothers-in-law
maid-of-honor	maids-of-honor
master-at-arms	masters-at-arms

Other nouns do not change at all to form the plural; here are a few examples:

Singular	Plural
deer	deer
equipment	equipment
fish	fish
merchandise	merchandise

If you are unsure about the plural of a noun, check a dictionary. For example, if you look up the noun *woman* in the dictionary, you may see an entry like this:

woman, women

The first word listed, *woman*, is the singular form of the noun; the second word, *women*, is the plural.

Some dictionaries list the plural form of a noun only if the plural is unusual. If no plural is listed, that noun probably adds -*s* or -*es*.* *Remember*: Do not add an -*s* to words that form plurals by changing an internal letter. For example, the plural of *man* is *men*, not *mens*; the plural of *woman* is *women*, not *womens*; the plural of *foot* is *feet*, not *feets*.

---

* For more work on spelling plurals, see Chapter 40, "Spelling," Part H.

PRACTICE 1

Make these singular nouns plural.

1. man _____

2. half _____

3. foot _____

4. son-in-law _____

5. moose _____

6. life _____

7. tooth _____

8. medium _____

9. woman _____

10. crisis _____

11. maid-of-honor _____

12. criterion _____

13. shelf _____

14. mouse _____

15. child _____

16. father-in-law _____

17. knife _____

18. deer _____

19. secretary _____

20. goose _____

B. Signal Words: Singular and Plural

A **signal word** tells you whether a singular or a plural noun usually follows. These signal words tell you that a singular noun usually follows:

Signal Words
a(n)   a single   another   each   every   one } house

These signal words tell you that a plural noun usually follows:

Signal Words
all   both   few   many   most   several   some   two (or more)   various } houses

PRACTICE 2

Some of the following sentences contain incorrect singulars and plurals. Correct the errors. Put a *C* after correct sentences.

1. By three years old, most children have firm ideas about how men and woman should behave.

2. Children develop their concepts about gender differences through *conditioning*, a process of learning that reinforces certain behaviors while discouraging other.

3. Conditioning occurs through the messages delivered by parents, peer, and the media.

4. Research shows that parents begin to treat their childrens differently as early as 24 hour after birth.

5. Fathers hold their infant girls gently and speak softly to them, but they bounce baby boys, playing "airplane" and tickling their feets.

6. Mothers, too, condition gender roles; they reward little girls who play quietly and help with chores, while excusing the loud play of boys as natural.

7. Once in school, children quickly learn that certain kinds of make-believe—such as playing house or having tea parties—are girls' games; boys are encouraged by their friend to crash cars and shoot toy guns.

8. While the boundaries are less rigid for girls at this stage, most boys who show any interest in feminine clothes or activity will be mocked by their peers.

Myrleen Pearson/PhotoEdit, Inc.

© Ellen B. Senisi/The Image Works

Gender conditioning starts early. Is it okay for boys to play with dolls and girls with trucks?

9. Many TV ad play a key conditioning role by showing boys involved in sports or jobs and girls playing indoors with toy ovens or dolls.

10. By limiting choices for most child, perhaps we ignore many talents and interest that might greatly enhance their lifes and society as a whole.

C. Signal Words with *of*

Many signal words are followed by *of . . .* or *of the. . . .* Usually, these signal words are followed by a **plural** noun (or a collective noun) because they really refer to one or more from a larger group.

one of the
each of the } pictures is . . .
many of the
a few of the } pictures are . . .
lots of the

● *Be careful*: The signal words *one of the* and *each of the* are followed by a **plural** noun, but the verb is **singular** because only the signal word (*one* or *each*) is the real subject.*

One of the coats *is* on sale.
Each of the flowers *smells* sweet.

PRACTICE 3

Fill in your own nouns in the following sentences. Use a different noun in each sentence.

1. Since Jacob wrote each of his _____ with care, the As came as no surprise.

2. You are one of the few _____ I know who can listen to the radio and play video games at the same time.

3. Naomi liked several of the new _____ but remained faithful to her long-time favorites.

_____

* For more work on this type of construction, see Chapter 29, "Present Tense (Agreement)," Part C.

4. Many of the _____ carried laptops.

5. Determined to win the Salesperson of the Year award, Clyde called on all of his

_____ two or three times a month.

6. One of the _____ makes no sense.

PROOFREADING STRATEGY

Incorrect singular and plural nouns are considered serious errors, so proofread with care if these are among your error patterns.

First, **search each sentence for signal words and phrases** (such as *an, each, one, many, several, a few*) that "announce" the need for either a singular or a plural noun. Underline or color code these signal words. Code in a different color all phrases like *one of the…* and *a few of the…* that are always followed by a plural. **Locate the noun** following each signal word and check for correctness.

Notice how the color-coded signal words in this example make it easier to see if the nouns are correct.

c
Many architects submitted designs for the new monument, but only one of

drawings   judges
the drawing impressed both judge.

PRACTICE 4   REVIEW

Proofread the following essay for errors in singular and plural nouns. Try out the proofreading strategy above to see if it works for you. Correct any errors by writing above the lines.

HAPPINESS 101

(1) At Harvard University, up to 900 student per semester pack a lecture hall for Professor Tal Ben-Shahar's course on happiness. (2) Called "Positive Psychology," the class explores current research on what makes peoples truly happy. (3) It is one of the most popular course on campus. (4) Students learn that they are more likely to experience joy if they participate in activitys that they find meaningful as well as pleasurable. (5) For example, a person who enjoys playing the piano might perform once a month for the residents of a nursing homes, thus adding meaning to pleasure. (6) Students also discover that more happiness comes to people who accept every one of their feeling—even fear, sadness, and anger—without self-judgment.

(7) Professor Ben-Shahar's students learn a few more criterion for a cheerful life. (8) They find out that rushing to do too much in a short time increases anxiety and depression, while simplifying life increases enjoyment. (9) Furthermore, several study prove that expressing gratitudes can lift a person's spirits, so it seems the many woman and man who keep a daily gratitude journals are on to something.

(10) One of the most important lesson, though, is that contentment depends on a person's state of mind, not his or her status or bank account. (11) Happy people see the glasses as half full rather than half empty. (12) They also view all of their failure not as disasters or crisis but learning opportunities. (13) Fortunately, research indicates that this kind of optimisms can be learned. (14) Those who are able to shift their thoughts to focus on the positive can change their lifes for the better.

PRACTICE 5   TEAMWORK: CRITICAL THINKING AND WRITING

In a group with classmates, reach agreement about which one of Professor Ben-Shahar's principles for happiness in Practice 4 is the most important. What three reasons best explain why your group reached this conclusion? Pick one person to jot down the group's ideas. Be prepared to share your reasoning with the class.

EXPLORING ONLINE

http://grammar.ccc.commnet.edu/grammar/quizzes/cross/plurals_gap.htm
Interactive noun plurals quiz: test yourself!

http://grammar.ccc.commnet.edu/grammar/quizzes/final-s_option.htm
Do you know when to add -s to nouns and verbs? Test yourself.

http://www.grammar-quizzes.com/agr_countnounprac2.html
ESL writers, try this interactive noun exercise.

CourseMate for *Evergreen*
Visit *Evergreen* CourseMate for more practices and quizzes, videos to accompany the readings, career and job-search resources, ESL help, and live links to every Exploring Online in the book.

CHAPTER 33

Pronouns

A. Defining Pronouns and Antecedents

Pronouns take the place of or refer to nouns, other pronouns, or phrases. The word that the pronoun refers to is called the **antecedent** of the pronoun.

> 1. *Eric* ordered *baked chicken* because *it* is *his* favorite dish.
> 2. *Simone and Lee* painted *their* room.
> 3. *I* like *camping in the woods* because *it* gives *me* a chance to be alone with *my* thoughts.

- In sentence 1, *it* refers to the antecedent *baked chicken*, and *his* refers to the antecedent *Eric*.

- In sentence 2, *their* refers to the plural antecedent *Simone and Lee*.

- In sentence 3, *it* refers to the antecedent *camping in the woods*. This antecedent is a whole phrase. *Me* and *my* refer to the pronoun antecedent *I*.

PRACTICE 1

In each sentence, a pronoun is circled. Write the pronoun first and then its antecedent, as shown in the example.

EXAMPLE

Have you ever wondered why we exchange rings in (our) wedding ceremonies?

our ___ *we* ___

1. Today when people buy wedding rings, they follow an age-old tradition.

   _____

2. Rich Egyptian grooms gave their brides gold rings 5,000 years ago.

   _____

3. To Egyptian couples, the ring represented eternal love; it was a circle without beginning or end.

   _____

4. By Roman times, gold rings had become more affordable, so ordinary people could also buy them.

   _____

5. Still, many a Roman youth had to scrimp to buy his beloved a ring.

   _____

6. The first bride to slip a diamond ring on her finger lived in Venice about 500 years ago.

   _____

7. The Venetians knew that setting a diamond in a ring was an excellent way of displaying its beauty.

   _____

8. Nowadays, two partners exchange rings to symbolize the equality of their relationship.

   _____

Jaroslaw Grudzinski/Shutterstock.com

B. Making Pronouns and Antecedents Agree

A pronoun must *agree* with its antecedent in number and person.*

1. When *Tom* couldn't find *his* pen, *he* asked to borrow mine.
2. The three *sisters* wanted to start *their* own business.

● In sentence 1, *Tom* is the antecedent of *his* and *he*. Since *Tom* is singular and masculine, the pronouns referring to *Tom* are also singular and masculine.

_____

* For more work on pronoun agreement, see Chapter 21, "Revising for Consistency and Parallelism," Part B.

● In sentence 2, *sisters* is the antecedent of *their*. Since *sisters* is plural, the pronoun referring to *sisters* must also be plural.

As you can see from these examples, making pronouns agree with their antecedents is usually easy. However, three special cases can be tricky.

1. Indefinite Pronouns

anybody
anyone
everybody
everyone
nobody
no one
one
somebody
someone

} Each of these words is **singular**. Any pronoun that refers to one of them must also be singular: *he, him, his, she,* or *her*.

3. *Anyone* can quit smoking if *he* or *she* wants to.
4. *Everybody* should do *his* or *her* best to keep the reception area uncluttered.

● *Anyone* and *everybody* require the singular pronouns *he, she, his,* and *her*.

In the past, writers used *he* or *him* to refer to both men and women. Now, however, many writers use *he or she, his or her,* or *him or her*. Of course, if *everyone* or *someone* is a woman, use *she* or *her*; if *everyone* or *someone* is a man, use *he* or *him*. For example:

5. *Someone* left *her* new dress in a bag on the sofa.
6. *Everyone* is wearing *his* new tie.

PRACTICE 2

Fill in the correct pronoun and circle its antecedent. Make sure each pronoun agrees in number and person with its antecedent.

1. Anyone can become a good cook if _____ tries.

2. Someone dropped _____ lipstick behind the bookcase.

3. No one in the mixed doubles let _____ guard down for a minute.

4. Everybody wants _____ career to be rewarding.

5. Everyone is entitled to _____ full pension.

6. Mr. Hernow will soon be here, so please get _____ contract ready.

7. One should wear a necktie that doesn't clash with _____ suit.

8. The movie theater was so cold that nobody took off _____ coat.

2. Special Singular Antecedents

each (of) . . .
either (of) . . .
neither (of) . . .
every one (of) . . .
one (of) . . .

Each of these constructions is **singular**. Any pronoun that refers to one of them must also be singular.*

7. *Neither* of the two men paid for *his* ticket to the wrestling match.
8. *Each* of the houses has *its* own special charm.

● The subject of sentence 7 is the singular *neither*, not *men*; therefore, the singular masculine pronoun *his* is required.

● The subject of sentence 8 is the singular *each*, not the plural *houses*; therefore, the singular pronoun *its* is required.

PRACTICE 3

Fill in the correct pronoun and circle its antecedent. Make sure each pronoun agrees in number and person with its antecedent.

1. Each of the men wanted to be _____ own boss.

2. One of the saleswomen left _____ sample case on the counter.

3. Every one of the colts has a white star on _____ forehead.

4. Neither of the actors knew _____ lines by heart.

5. Neither of the dentists had _____ office remodeled.

6. Each of these arguments has _____ flaws and _____ strengths.

7. Every one of the jazz bands had _____ own distinctive style.

8. Either of these smartphones will work very well if _____ is properly cared for.

3. Collective Nouns

Collective nouns represent a group of people but are usually considered **singular**. They usually take singular pronouns.

_____

* For more work on prepositional phrases, see Chapter 26, "The Simple Sentence," Part B.

9. The *jury* reached *its* decision in three hours.

10. The debating *team* is well known for *its* fighting spirit.

● In sentence 9, *jury* is a collective noun. Although it has several members, the jury acts as a unit—as one. Therefore, the antecedent *jury* takes the singular pronoun *its*.

● In sentence 10, why does the collective noun *team* take the singular pronoun *its*?

Here is a partial list of collective nouns:

Common Collective Nouns		
class	family	panel
college	flock	school
committee	government	society
company	group	team
faculty	jury	tribe

PRACTICE 4

Read each sentence carefully for meaning. Circle the antecedent and then fill in the correct pronoun.

1. My family gave me all _____ support when I went back to school.

2. The government should reexamine _____ domestic policy.

3. The college honored _____ oldest graduate with a reception.

4. Eco-Wise has just begun to market a new pollution-free detergent that _____ is proud of.

5. The panel will soon announce _____ recommendations to the hospital.

6. The two teams gave _____ fans a real show.

7. The jury deliberated for six days before _____ reached a verdict.

8. After touring the Great Pyramid, the class headed back to Cairo in _____ air-conditioned bus.

C. Referring to Antecedents Clearly

A pronoun must refer *clearly* to its antecedent. Avoid vague, repetitious, or ambiguous pronoun references.

1. Vague pronoun: At the box office, they said that tickets were no longer available.

2. Revised: { The cashier at the box office said . . .

       or

3. Revised: At the box office, I was told . . . }

- In sentence 1, who is *they? They* does not clearly refer to an antecedent.
- In sentence 2, *the cashier* replaces *they.*
- In sentence 3, the problem is avoided by a change of language.*

4. Repetitious pronoun: In the article, *it* says that Tyrone was a boxer.

5. Revised: { The article says that . . .

       or

6. Revised: It says that . . . }

- In sentence 4, *it* merely repeats *article*, the antecedent preceding it.
- Use either the pronoun or its antecedent, but not both.

7. Ambiguous pronoun: Mr. Tedesco told his son that *his* car had a flat tire.

8. Revised: Mr. Tedesco told his son that the younger man's car had a flat tire.

9. Revised: Mr. Tedesco told his son Paul that Paul's car had a flat tire.

- In sentence 7, *his* could refer either to Mr. Tedesco or to his son.

PRACTICE 5

Revise the following sentences, removing vague, repetitious, or ambiguous pronoun references. Make the pronoun references clear and specific.

1. In this book it says that hundreds of boys are injured each year copying wrestling stunts they see on TV.

   Revised: _____

   _____

   _____

   * For more work on using exact language, see Chapter 23, "Revising for Language Awareness," Part A.

2. On the radio they warned drivers that the Interstate Bridge was closed.

   Revised: _____

   _____

3. Sandra told her friend that she shouldn't have turned down the promotion.

   Revised: _____

   _____

4. In North Carolina they raise tobacco.

   Revised: _____

   _____

5. The moving van struck a lamppost; luckily, no one was injured, but it was badly damaged.

   Revised: _____

   _____

6. Professor Grazel told his parrot that he had to stop chewing telephone cords.

   Revised: _____

   _____

7. On the news, it said that more Americans than ever are turning to nontraditional medicine.

   Revised: _____

   _____

8. Keiko is an excellent singer, yet she has never taken a lesson in it.

   Revised: _____

   _____

9. Vandalism was once so out of control at the local high school that they stole sinks and lighting fixtures.

   Revised: _____

   _____

10. Rosalie's mother said she was glad she had decided to become a paralegal.

    Revised: _____

    _____

D. Special Problems of Case

Personal pronouns take different forms depending on how they are used in a sentence. Pronouns can be **subjects**, **objects**, or **possessives**.

Pronouns used as **subjects** are in the **subjective case**:

1. *He* and *I* go snowboarding together.
2. The peaches were so ripe that *they* fell from the trees.

● *He, I*, and *they* are in the subjective case.

Pronouns that are **objects of verbs** or **prepositions** are in the **objective case**. Pronouns that are **subjects of infinitives** are also in the **objective case**:

3. A sudden downpour soaked *her*. (object of verb)
4. Please give this card to *him*. (object of preposition)
5. We want *them* to leave right now. (subject of infinitive)*

● *Her, him*, and *them* are in the objective case.

Pronouns that **show ownership** are in the **possessive case**:

6. The carpenters left *their* tools on the windowsill.
7. This flower has lost *its* brilliant color.

● *Their* and *its* are in the possessive case.

Pronoun Case Chart

Singular	Subjective	Objective	Possessive
1st person	I	me	my (mine)
2nd person	you	you	your (yours)
3rd person	he	him	his (his)
	she	her	her (hers)
	it	it	its (its)
	who	whom	whose
	whoever	whomever	
Plural	**Subjective**	**Objective**	**Possessive**
1st person	we	us	our (ours)
2nd person	you	you	your (yours)
3rd person	they	them	their (theirs)

* An infinitive is *to* + *the simple form of a verb* (to purchase, to study).

Using the correct case is usually fairly simple, but three problems require special care.

1. Case in Compound Constructions

A **compound construction** consists of two nouns, two pronouns, or a noun and a pronoun joined by *and*. Make sure that the pronouns in a compound construction are in the correct case.

> 8. *Serge* and *I* went to the pool together.
> 9. Between *you* and *me*, this party is a bore.

- In sentence 8, *Serge* and *I* are subjects.
- In sentence 9, *you* and *me* are objects of the preposition *between*.

Never use *myself* as a substitute for either *I* or *me* in compound constructions.

PRACTICE 6

Determine the case required by each sentence, and circle the correct pronoun.

1. Harriet and (he, him) plan to enroll in the police academy.
2. A snowdrift stood between the subway entrance and (I, me).
3. Tony used the software and then returned it to Barbara and (I, me, myself).
4. The reporter's questions caught June and (we, us) off guard.
5. By noon, Julio and (he, him) had already cleaned the garage and mowed the lawn.
6. These charts helped (she, her) and (I, me) with our statistics homework.
7. Professor Woo gave Diane and (she, her) extra time to finish the geology final.
8. Between you and (I, me), I have always preferred country music.

2. Case in Comparisons

Pronouns that complete **comparisons** may be in the **subjective, objective**, or **possessive** case:

> 10. His son is as stubborn as *he*. (subjective)
> 11. The cutbacks will affect you more than *me*. (objective)
> 12. This essay is better organized than *mine*. (possessive)

To decide on the correct pronoun, simply complete the comparison mentally and then choose the pronoun that naturally follows:

13. She trusts him more than I . . . (trust him).
14. She trusts him more than . . . (she trusts) . . . me.
15. Orlo's dog is as energetic as theirs . . . (is).

● Note that in sentences 13 and 14, the case of the pronoun in the comparison can change the meaning of the entire sentence.

PRACTICE 7

Circle the correct pronoun.

1. Your hair is much shorter than (she, her, hers).
2. We tend to assume that others are more self-confident than (we, us).
3. She is just as funny as (he, him).
4. Is Hanna as trustworthy as (he, him)?
5. Although they were both research scientists, he received a higher salary than (she, her).
6. I am not as involved in this project as (they, them).
7. Sometimes we become impatient with people who are not as quick to learn as (we, us).
8. Michael's route involved more overnight stops than (us, our, ours).

3. Use of *Who* (or *Whoever*) and *Whom* (or *Whomever*)

Who and **whoever** are in the **subjective** case. **Whom** and **whomever** are in the **objective** case.

16. *Who* is at the door?
17. For *whom* is that gift?
18. *Whom* is that gift for?

● In sentence 16, *who* is the subject.
● The same question is written two ways in sentences 17 and 18. In both, *whom* is the object of the preposition *for*.

Sometimes, deciding on who or whom can be tricky:

19. I will give the raise to *whoever* deserves it.
20. Give it to *whomever* you like.

- In sentence 19, *whoever* is the subject in the clause *whoever deserves it*.

- In sentence 20, *whomever* is the object in the clause *whomever you like*.

If you have trouble deciding on who or whom, change the sentence to eliminate the problem.

> 21. I prefer working with people *whom* I don't know as friends.
>   *or*
>   I prefer working with people I don't know as friends.

PRACTICE 8

Circle the correct pronoun.

1. (Who, Whom) will deliver the layouts to the ad agency?

2. To (who, whom) are you speaking?

3. (Who, Whom) prefers hiking to skiing?

4. For (who, whom) are those boxes piled in the corner?

5. The committee will award the scholarship to (whoever, whomever) it chooses.

6. (Who, Whom) do you wish to invite to the open house?

7. At (who, whom) did the governor fling the cream pie?

8. I will hire (whoever, whomever) can use a computer and speak Korean.

E. Using Pronouns with *-self* and *-selves*

Pronouns with *-self* or *-selves* can be used in two ways—as reflexives or as intensives.

A reflexive pronoun indicates that someone did something to himself or herself:

> 1. My daughter Miriam felt very grown up when she learned to dress *herself*.

- In sentence 1, Miriam did something to *herself*; she *dressed herself*.

An intensive pronoun emphasizes the noun or pronoun it refers to:

> 2. Anthony *himself* was surprised at how relaxed he felt during the interview.

● In sentence 2, *himself* emphasizes that Anthony—much to his surprise—was not nervous at the interview.

The following chart will help you choose the correct reflexive or intensive pronoun.

Antecedent	Reflexive or Intensive Pronoun	
Singular	I	myself
	you	yourself
	he	himself
	she	herself
	it	itself
Plural	we	ourselves
	you	yourselves
	they	themselves

Note that in the plural *-self* is changed to *-selves*.

● **Be careful**: Do not use reflexives or intensives as substitutes for the subject of a sentence.

Incorrect: Harry and *myself* will be there on time.

Correct: Harry and *I* will be there on time.

PRACTICE 9

Fill in the correct reflexive or intensive pronoun. Be careful to make pronouns and antecedents agree.

1. Though he hates to cook, André _____ sautéed the mushrooms.

2. Rhoda found _____ in a strange city with only the phone number of a cousin whom she had not seen for years.

3. Her coffee machine automatically turns _____ on in the morning and off in the evening.

4. The librarian and I rearranged the children's section _____.

5. When it comes to horror films, I know that you consider _____ an expert.

6. They _____ didn't care if they arrived on time or not.

7. After completing a term paper, I always buy _____ a little gift to celebrate.

8. Larry _____ was surprised at how quickly he grew to like ancient history.

PROOFREADING STRATEGY

One of the most common pronoun errors is using the plural pronouns *they, them,* or *their* incorrectly to refer to a singular antecedent. If this one of your error patterns, **search your draft for *they, them,* and *their*** and **highlight or underline them**. If you are using a computer, use the *"Find"* feature to locate these words.

Take a moment to **identify the antecedent** for each of these highlighted words by drawing an arrow from the highlighted word to its antecedent. Do the two words agree?

his or her

Because **anyone** can create a website and post <mark>their</mark> opinions,

researchers must use <mark>their</mark> critical thinking skills to make sure that

online information is correct.

PRACTICE 10   REVIEW

Proofread the following essay for pronoun errors. You might wish to try the proofreading strategy above. Then correct each pronoun error in any way you choose.

THE MANY LIVES OF JACKIE CHAN

(1) Few movie stars can claim a career as unusual as him. (2) For one thing, Jackie Chan performs his death-defying stunts hisself. (3) Although he was a huge star in Asia for more than 20 years, fame eluded him in the United States until recently.

(4) Chan was born in Hong Kong in 1954. (5) Because him and his parents were so poor, he was sent to live and study at the Peking Opera School. (6) There, they trained him in acting, dancing, singing, sword fighting, and kung fu. (7) When the school closed in 1971, their lessons paid off for Chan in an unexpected way.

(8) Chan worked as a stuntman and fight choreographer and landed acting roles in several films, including Bruce Lee's *Enter the Dragon*. (9) Lee, he died in 1973, and Chan was the natural choice to fill Lee's shoes. (10) In several films, Chan tried to imitate Lee, but the films were unsuccessful. (11) In 1978, however, Chan came up with the idea of turning Lee's tough style into comedy. (12) *Snake in the Eagle's Shadow* and *Drunken Master* were hilarious hits; it established "kung fu comedy." (13) Jackie Chan became one of Hong Kong's most popular stars.

(14) However, Hollywood directors did not appreciate Chan as a stuntman, actor, comedian, director, and scriptwriter all in one, and its early American films flopped. (15) Chan understood his own strengths better than them. (16) He returned to Hong Kong, but him and his fans always believed he could make a U.S. comeback. (17) This happened

Jackie Chan and Jaden
Smith in *The Karate Kid*.

when *Rumble in the Bronx*, China's most popular film ever, was dubbed in English.
(18) Finally, they began to appreciate this manic, bruised, and battered action hero who
films were refreshingly nonviolent. (19) Since then, Chan's U.S. films, like *Rush Hour* (and
Rush Hour 2, 3, and *4*), and *The Karate Kid* films are being received as well as its Hong Kong
counterparts.

EXPLORING ONLINE

http://grammar.ccc.commnet.edu/grammar/cgi-shl/quiz.pl/pronouns_add1.htm
Interactive pronoun quiz; click for pronoun review.

http://a4esl.org/q/h/vm/pronouns.html
Pronoun quiz: especially helpful for ESL writers

CourseMate for *Evergreen*
Visit *Evergreen* CourseMate for more practices and quizzes, videos
to accompany the readings, career and job-search resources,
ESL help, and live links to every Exploring Online in the book.

CHAPTER **34**

Prepositions

A: Working with Prepositional Phrases

B: Prepositions in Common Expressions

A. Working with Prepositional Phrases

Prepositions are words like *about, at, behind, into, of, on*, and *with*.* They are followed by a noun or a pronoun, which is called the **object** of the preposition. The preposition and its object are called a **prepositional phrase**.

1. Ms. Fairworth hurried *to the computer lab*.
2. Students *with a 3.5 grade average* will receive a special award.
3. Traffic *at this corner* is dangerously heavy.

● In sentence 1, the prepositional phrase *to the computer lab* explains where Ms. Fairworth hurried.

● In sentence 2, the prepositional phrase *with a 3.5 grade average* describes which students will receive a special award.

● Which is the prepositional phrase in sentence 3 and what word does it describe?

_____

_____

* For more work on prepositions, see Chapter 26, "The Simple Sentence," Part B.

In/On for Time

Two prepositions often confused are *in* and *on*. Use *in* before months not followed by a specific date, before seasons, and before years that do not include specific dates.

1. *In March*, the skating rink will finally open for business.
2. Rona expects to pay off her car *in 2015*.

Use *on* before days of the week, before holidays, and before months if a date follows.

3. *On Sunday*, the Kingston family spent the day at the beach.
4. *On January 6*, Bernard left for a month of mountain climbing.

In/On for Place

In means *inside* a place.

1. Tonia put her DVD player *in the bedroom*.
2. Many country groups got their start *in Nashville*.

On means *on top of* or *at a particular place*.

3. That mess *on your desk* needs to be cleared off.
4. Pizza Palace will be opening a new parlor *on Highland Avenue*.

PRACTICE 1

Fill in the correct prepositions in the following sentences. Be especially careful of *in* and *on*.

1. _____ a little town _____ the coast of the Dominican Republic, baseball

   is a way of life.

2. Once known for cattle and sugar, San Pedro de Macoris has been exporting world-

   class baseball players _____ the major leagues _____ over 50 years.

3. Hall-of-Famer Juan Marichal and versatile shortshop José Reyes are just two Dominicans who have made names _____ themselves _____ the majors.

4. Other stars born in or _____ San Pedro de Macoris are Pedro Martinez, Alfonso Soriano, and David Ortiz.

5. Baseball was first introduced _____ the island _____ American mill and plantation owners, who encouraged their workers to learn the game.

6. Because equipment was expensive, boys from poor families often batted _____ a tree branch, using a rolled-up sock _____ place _____ a ball.

7. Each young man dreamed that he would be discovered _____ the baseball scouts and sent to play _____ *las ligas mayores*.

8. Amazing numbers _____ these players succeeded, and many Dominican athletes later returned to invest _____ the local economy.

9. For example, Robinson Cano bought 6,000 baseball uniforms _____ youngsters and donated four ambulances and four school buses _____ his hometown.

10. Major league teams, including the Dodgers, Giants, and Expos, now operate year-round training camps _____ the island, hoping to cultivate the athletes _____ tomorrow.

B. Prepositions in Common Expressions

Prepositions are often combined with other words to form fixed expressions. Determining the correct preposition in these expressions can sometimes be confusing. Following is a list of some troublesome expressions with prepositions. Consult a dictionary if you need help with others.

Expressions with Prepositions	
Expression	**Example**
according to	*According to* the directions, this flap fits here.
acquainted with	Tom became *acquainted with* his classmates.
addicted to	He is *addicted to* soap operas.
afraid of	Tanya is *afraid of* flying.
agree on (a plan)	Can we *agree on* our next step?

agree to (something or another's proposal)	Roberta *agreed to* her secretary's request for a raise.
angry about or at (a thing)	Jake seemed *angry about* his meager bonus.
angry with (a person)	Sonia couldn't stay *angry with* Felipe.
apply for (a position)	By accident, the twins *applied for* the same job.
approve of	Do you *approve of* bilingual education?
argue about (an issue)	I hate *arguing about* money.
argue with (a person)	Edna *argues with* everyone about everything.
capable of	Mario is *capable of* accomplishing anything he attempts.
complain about (a situation)	Patients *complained about* the long wait to see the dentist.
complain to (a person)	Knee-deep in snow, Jed vowed to *complain to* a maintenance person.
comply with	Each contestant must *comply with* contest regulations.
consist of	This article *consists of* nothing but false accusations and half-truths.
contrast with	The light blue shirt *contrasts* sharply *with* the dark brown tie.
correspond with (write)	We *corresponded with* her for two months before we met.
deal with	Ron *deals* well *with* temporary setbacks.
depend on	Miriam can be *depended on* to say embarrassing things.
different from	Children are often *different from* their parents.
differ from (something)	A DVD player *differs from* a VCR in many ways.
differ with (a person)	Kathleen *differs with* you on the gun control issue.
displeased with	Ms. Withers was *displeased with* her doctor's advice to eat less fat.
fond of	Ed is *fond of* his pet tarantula.
grateful for	Be *grateful for* having so many good friends.
grateful to (someone)	The team was *grateful to* the coach for his inspiration and confidence.
identical to	Scott's ideas are often *identical to* mine.
inferior to	Saturday's performance was *inferior to* the one I saw last week.
in search of	I hate to go *in search of* change at the last moment before the toll.
interested in	Willa is *interested in* results, not excuses.
interfere with	That dripping faucet *interferes with* my concentration.
object to	Martin *objected to* the judge's comment.
protect against	This heavy wool scarf will *protect* your throat *against* the cold.
reason with	It's hard to *reason with* an angry person.
rely on	If Toni made that promise, you can *rely on* it.

reply to	He wrote twice, but the president did not *reply to* his letters.
responsible for	Kit is *responsible for* making two copies of each document.
sensitive to	Professor Godfried is *sensitive to* his students' concerns.
shocked at	We were *shocked at* the graphic violence in that PG-rated film.
similar to	Some poisonous mushrooms appear quite *similar to* the harmless kind.
speak with (someone)	Geraldine will *speak with* her supervisor about a raise.
specialize in	This disc jockey *specializes in* jazz of the 1920s and the 1930s.
struck by	We were *struck by* the brilliant colors of fish and coral on the reef.
succeed in	Oscar *succeeded in* painting the roof in less than five hours.
superior to	It's clear that the remake is *superior to* the original.
take advantage of	Celia *took advantage of* the snow day to visit the science museum.
worry about	Never *worry about* more than one problem at a time.

PRACTICE 2

Fill in the preposition that correctly completes each of the following expressions.

1. Today's students feel more financial and emotional stress than past generations, according _____ the annual American Freshman Survey.

2. Every year since 1966, the Higher Education Research Institute has been responsible _____ this survey of hundreds of thousands of college students.

3. The fascinating results show what students each year hope _____, worry _____, complain _____, depend _____, and hold dear.

4. Because of the poor economy and uncertain career prospects, students surveyed in 2010 were afraid _____ not being as successful as their parents.

5. Adding to their anxiety, many college students must work, apply _____ financial aid, and rely _____ loans, so they are in debt even before they earn a degree.

6. Researchers were struck _____ a gender gap in stress levels; 39 percent of young

   women often feel overwhelmed, more than twice the number of men.

7. One theory is that, outside of school, men relieve stress with video games and sports

   while women often feel more responsible _____ chores at home.

8. On the positive side, the students' reported anxieties contrast _____ their

   strong determination to succeed _____ college and help their communities.

9. Today's students are comfortable with diversity and concerned _____ equality,

   with a majority supporting the rights of gay couples to adopt.

10. Most freshmen believe that they are capable _____ achieving their goals and

    that obstacles will not interfere _____ their high hopes for the future.

PROOFREADING STRATEGY

If preposition mistakes are one of your error patterns, try this strategy. Using the feedback you've received from instructors and tutors who know your writing, **record the five prepositions that give you the most trouble** on your Personal Error Patterns Chart.

   Carefully scan your writing for each of these five prepositions. If you are using a computer, use the *"Find"* feature to locate these words in your draft or color code them as in the example below. Then **make sure that you have used each of the prepositions correctly.**

On   in
In May 5, many people on the United States celebrate the holiday

Cinco de Mayo with Mexican food, music, and dancing.

PRACTICE 3   REVIEW

Proofread this essay for preposition errors, using the proofreading strategy described above. Cross out the errors and write your corrections above the lines.

DR. BEN CARSON, PIONEER BRAIN SURGEON

(1) Today, Dr. Benjamin Carson of Johns Hopkins Hospital is internationally known as the

man to call from tricky brain surgeries in children. (2) He routinely takes out challenging

cases such as removing parts of the brain to stop seizures or repairing deformities of the

skull and face. (3) On 1987, he made medical history over successfully separating a pair of

conjoined (or Siamese) twins in a 22-hour operation.

(4) This gifted physician was not always a high achiever, however. (5) As a child, he grew up fatherless on Detroit. (6) He now says that, like many off the people he knew, he had a low opinion at himself. (7) Consequently, his grades were poor, and he was prone with violent outbursts and disruptive behavior. (8) Nevertheless, his mother, a high-school dropout who worked two or three jobs at a time to support her two sons, believed he was capable to doing better and refused to give out on him. (9) Convinced that education provided the only escape against poverty, she insisted that Ben and his brother read and complete their homework. (10) Thanks on her encouragement, Ben experienced a turning point one day when a teacher brought rock samples at school. (11) Because of a book he had read, Ben was able to identify all off them. (12) Suddenly, he knew that he wasn't the slow learner he had always thought himself to be. (13) Today Dr. Carson declares, "When I thought I was stupid, I acted like a stupid person. (14) When I thought I was smart, I acted like a smart person and achieved like a smart person." (15) His hunger of knowledge grew, and he rose on the top of his class, going on to attend Yale University.

(16) Nonetheless, Carson would have to overcome another obstacle. (17) Even as late as his first year of medical school, a faculty adviser counseled him to drop off because he wasn't "medical school material." (18) Fortunately, he ignored this advice, by then having discovered his strengths. (19) He knew that he was a careful person with excellent hand-eye coordination. (20) He enjoyed dissecting things, and he could think three-dimensionally. (21) With these skills, he decided, he could specialize on brain surgery.

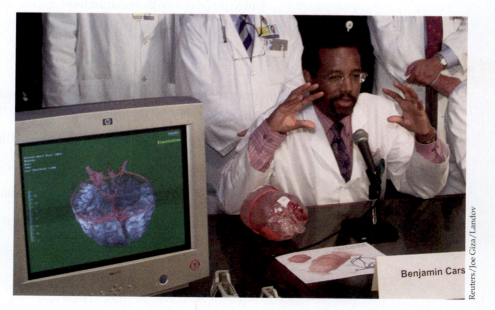

Dr. Ben Carson holds a press conference about a difficult brain surgery.

(22) Today Dr. Carson performs three to five life-saving operations a day. (23) On addition, he and his wife have founded the Carson Scholars, a scholarship program for students who succeed on academic subjects. (24) He said he got the idea when he visited schools to speak and saw huge trophies honoring athletic achievements but none for academic achievers. (25) He invested $500,000 of his own money to start rewarding children like he once was about trophies, publicity, and money for college. (26) These scholars are the ones, Carson believes, "who will keep us Number 1, not the guy with the 25-foot jump shot."

EXPLORING ONLINE

http://grammar.ccc.commnet.edu/grammar/quizzes/preposition_quiz1.htm
Graded preposition quiz

http://a4esl.org/q/f/z/zz36mas.htm
Interactive quiz: swim with the manatees as you practice prepositions!

CourseMate for *Evergreen*

Visit *Evergreen* CourseMate for more practices and quizzes, videos to accompany the readings, career and job-search resources, ESL help, and live links to every Exploring Online in the book.

CHAPTER **35**

Adjectives and Adverbs

A: Defining and Using Adjectives and Adverbs

B: The Comparative and the Superlative

C: A Troublesome Pair: *Good/Well*

A. Defining and Using Adjectives and Adverbs

Adjectives and **adverbs** are two kinds of descriptive words. **Adjectives** describe or modify nouns or pronouns. They explain what kind, which one, or how many.

> 1. A *black* cat slept on the piano.
>
> 2. We felt *cheerful*.
>
> 3. *Three* windows in the basement need to be replaced.

- The adjective *black* describes the noun *cat*. It tells what kind of cat, a *black* one.

- The adjective *cheerful* describes the pronoun *we*. It tells what kind of mood we were in, *cheerful*.

- The adjective *three* describes the noun *windows*. It tells how many windows, *three*.

    Adverbs describe or modify verbs, adjectives, and other adverbs. They tell how, in what manner, when, where, and to what extent.

484

4. Joe dances *gracefully*.

5. *Yesterday* Robert left for a weekend of sky diving.

6. Brigit is *extremely* tall.

7. He travels *very* rapidly on that skateboard.

● The adverb *gracefully* describes the verb *dances*. It tells how Joe dances, *gracefully*.

● The adverb *yesterday* describes the verb *left*. It tells when Robert left, *yesterday*.

● The adverb *extremely* describes the adjective *tall*. It tells how tall (to what extent), *extremely* tall.

● The adverb *very* describes the adverb *rapidly*, which describes the verb *travels*. It tells how rapidly he travels, *very* rapidly.

Many adjectives can be changed into adverbs by adding an *-ly* ending. For example, *glad* becomes *gladly*, *hopeful* becomes *hopefully*, *awkward* becomes *awkwardly*.

Note the pairs on this list; they are easily confused:

Adjectives	Adverbs
awful	awfully
bad	badly
poor	poorly
quick	quickly
quiet	quietly
real	really
sure	surely

8. The fish tastes *bad*.
9. It was *badly* prepared.

● In sentence 8, the adjective *bad* describes the noun *fish*.

● In sentence 9, the adverb *badly* describes the verb *was prepared*.

PRACTICE 1

Circle the correct adjective or adverb in parentheses. Remember that adjectives modify nouns or pronouns; adverbs modify verbs, adjectives, or adverbs.

1. Have you ever seen (real, really) emeralds?

2. Try to do your work in the library (quiet, quietly).

3. We will (glad, gladly) take you on a tour of the Crunchier Cracker factory.

4. Lee, a (high, highly) skilled electrician, rewired his entire house last year.

5. She made a (quick, quickly) stop at the scanner.

6. It was (awful, awfully) wet today; the sleet filled our shoes.

7. The fans from Cleveland (enthusiastic, enthusiastically) clapped for the Browns.

8. Are you (sure, surely) this bus stops in Dusty Gulch?

9. He (hasty, hastily) wrote the essay, leaving out several important ideas.

10. It was a funny joke, but the comedian told it (bad, badly).

11. Tina walked (careful, carefully) down the icy road.

12. Sam swims (poor, poorly) even though he spends hours posing on the beach.

13. Sasha the crow is an (unusual, unusually) pet and a (humorous, humorously) companion.

14. The painting is not (actual, actually) a Picasso; in fact, it is a (real, really) bad imitation.

15. It is an (extreme, extremely) hot day, and I (sure, surely) could go for some (real, really) orange juice.

B. The Comparative and the Superlative

The **comparative** of an adjective or adverb compares two persons or things:

> 1. Ben is *more creative* than Robert.
> 2. Marcia runs *faster* than the coach.

- In sentence 1, Ben is being compared with Robert.

- In sentence 2, Marcia is being compared with the coach.

The **superlative** of an adjective or adverb compares three or more persons or things:

> 3. Sancho is the *tallest* of the three brothers.
> 4. Marion is the *most intelligent* student in the class.

- In sentence 3, Sancho is being compared with the other two brothers.

- In sentence 4, Marion is being compared with all the other students in the class.

Adjectives and adverbs of one syllable usually form the **comparative** by adding -*er*. They form the **superlative** by adding -*est*.

Adjective	Comparative	Superlative
fast	fast*er*	fast*est*
smart	smart*er*	smart*est*
tall	tall*er*	tall*est*

Adjectives and adverbs of more than one syllable usually form the **comparative** by using *more*. They form the **superlative** by using *most*.

Adjective	Comparative	Superlative
beautiful	*more* beautiful	*most* beautiful
brittle	*more* brittle	*most* brittle
serious	*more* serious	*most* serious

Note, however, that adjectives that end in -*y* (like *happy, lazy,* and *sunny*) change the -*y* to -*i* and add -*er* and -*est*.

Adjective	Comparative	Superlative
happy	happ*ier*	happ*iest*
lazy	laz*ier*	laz*iest*
sunny	sunn*ier*	sunn*iest*

PRACTICE 2

Write the comparative or the superlative of the words in parentheses. Remember: use the comparative to compare two items; use the superlative to compare more than two. Use -*er* or -*est* for one-syllable words; use *more* or *most* for words of more than one syllable.*

1. The ocean is _____ (cold) than we thought it would be.

2. Please read your lines again, _____ (slowly) this time.

3. Which of these two roads is the _____ (short) route?

4. Which of these three highways is the _____ (short) route?

_____

* If you have questions about spelling, see Chapter 40, "Spelling," Part G.

5. Leola is the _____ (busy) person I know.

6. That red felt hat with feathers is the _____ (outlandish) one I've

seen.

7. Today is _____ (warm) than yesterday, but Thursday was the

_____ (warm) day of the month.

8. The down coat you have selected is the _____ (expensive) one in

the store.

9. Each one of Woody's stories is _____ (funny) than the last.

10. As a rule, mornings in Los Angeles are _____ (hazy) than

afternoons.

11. Is Paolo _____ (tall) than Louie? Is Paolo the _____

(tall) player on the team?

12. If you don't do these experiments _____ (carefully), you will blow

up the chemistry lab.

13. This farmland is much _____ (rocky) than the farmland in Iowa.

14. Therese says that Physics 201 is the _____ (challenging) course she

has ever taken.

15. Mr. Wells is the _____ (wise) and _____

(experienced) leader in the community.

PRACTICE 3

Proofread the following paragraph for comparative and superlative errors. Cross out
unnecessary words and write your corrections above the lines.

(1) Wikipedia is a free online encyclopedia that offers information about thousands
of topics. (2) Created in 2001, it has become one of the most popularest sites on
the Internet—and one of the most controversial. (3) Unlike *Britannica* and other
encyclopedias of a more early time, Wikipedia is not an expensive set of books; it exists
only online at *www.wikipedia.org*. (4) Its most great innovation is also its most biggest
problem: readers can also help write content. (5) The "wiki" software allows anyone
who visits the site to add or edit an entry. (6) Supporters believe that thousands of

minds produce entries that are often completer and accurater than those in traditional encyclopedias. (7) Yet mistakes and sabotage have occurred. (8) A U.S. Congressperson changed his Wikipedia profile to make it positiver. (9) The entry on Harriet Tubman, rescuer of southern slaves, gave the wrong birthplace and stated as fact several disproved stories. (10) Jokers, vandals, and even racists have planted lies in some entries. (11) Wikipedia's 800 volunteer administrators labor to approve each change, making sure that a revised entry is more effectiver than the previous one. (12) While correcting such errors is more easier and fast than in print encyclopedias, some teachers and professors caution students not to cite Wikipedia as an information source.

EXPLORING ONLINE

http://www.wikipedia.org

Choose a subject that you know something about and evaluate the Wikipedia entry. First, read the Wikipedia article; take notes or print it. Now visit the library and check the facts. Ask the librarian if you need help. Did you find any false information, or is the entry reliable? How would you rate Wikipedia, based on this one entry?

C. A Troublesome Pair: *Good/Well*

Adjective	Comparative	Superlative
good	better	best
bad	worse	worst
Adverb	**Comparative**	**Superlative**
well	better	best
badly	worse	worst

Be especially careful not to confuse the adjective **good** with the adverb **well**:

1. Jessie is a *good* writer.
2. She writes *well*.

- *Good* is an **adjective** modifying *writer*.
- *Well* is an **adverb** modifying *writes*.

PRACTICE 4

Fill in either the adjective *good* or the adverb *well* in each blank.

1. Corned beef definitely goes _____ with cabbage.

2. How _____ do you understand Spanish?

3. He may not take phone messages very _____, but he is _____ at handling computer problems.

4. Exercise is a _____ way to stay in shape; eating _____ will help you maintain _____ health.

5. Tony looks _____ in his new goatee.

6. This is a _____ arrangement: I wash, you dry.

7. On rainy nights, Sheila loves to curl up with a _____ book.

8. The old Persian carpet and oak desk are a _____ match; they go _____ together.

9. Both teams played _____; it was a _____ game.

10. They are _____ neighbors and are _____ liked in the community.

PRACTICE 5

Fill in the correct comparative or superlative of the word in parentheses.

1. Lucinda is a _____ (good) chemist than she is a mathematician.

2. Bascomb was the _____ (bad) governor this state has ever had.

3. When it comes to staying in shape, you are _____ (bad) than I.

4. Of the two sisters, Leah is the _____ (good) markswoman.

5. You can carry cash when you travel, but using a credit card is _____ (good).

6. Our goalie is the _____ (good) in the league; yours is the _____ (bad).

7. When it comes to bad taste, movies are _____ (bad) than television.

8. Your sore throat seems _____ (bad) than it was yesterday.

9. Gina likes snorkeling _____ (good) than fishing; she loves scuba diving

   _____ (good) of all.

10. A parka is the _____ (good) protection against a cold wind; it is certainly

   _____ (good) than a scarf.

PROOFREADING STRATEGY

To help you proofread for *adjective* and *adverb* errors, use two highlighters to code the text. Read slowly, and **mark every adjective purple and every adverb gray** (or colors of your choice) like the sentences below from one student's paper.

Next check every purple and gray word, one by one. **Ask yourself what word each one describes.** For example, *What word does* <u>talented</u> *describe?* (*Talented* describes *Jada*, a noun; thus, the adjective *talented* is correct.) *What does the word* <u>real</u> *describe?* (*Real* describes *talented*, an *adjective*, so *real* is incorrect.) *What word does* <u>beautiful</u> *describe?* (*Beautiful* describes *plays*, a verb; so, the adjective *beautiful* is incorrect.)

really

My friend Jada is ~~real~~ talented. She writes songs and plays the guitar

beautifully   amazing

~~beautiful.~~ She has the ~~most~~ ~~amazingest~~ voice in our group.

PRACTICE 6   REVIEW

Proofread the following essay for adjective and adverb errors, using the proofreading strategy described above. Correct the errors by writing above the lines.

JULIA MORGAN, ARCHITECT

(1) Julia Morgan was one of San Francisco's most finest architects, as well as the first woman licensed as an architect in California. (2) In 1902, Morgan became the first woman to finish successful the program in architecture at the School of Fine Arts in Paris. (3) Returning to San Francisco, she opened her own office and hired and trained a very talented staff that eventual grew to 35 full-time architects. (4) Her first major commission was to reconstruct the Fairmont Hotel, one of the city's bestest-known sites, which had been damaged bad in the 1906 earthquake. (5) Morgan earned her reputation by designing elegant homes and public buildings out of inexpensively and available materials and by treating her clients real good. (6) She went on to design more than 800 residences, stores, churches, offices, and educational buildings, most of them in California.

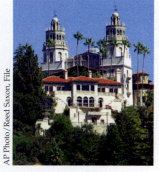

San Simeon, Julia
Morgan's masterpiece

(7) Her bestest customer was William Randolph Hearst, one of the country's most rich newspaper publishers. (8) Morgan designed newspaper buildings and more than 20 pleasure palaces for Hearst in California and Mexico. (9) She maintained a private plane and pilot to keep her moving from project to project. (10) The most big and famousest of her undertakings was sure San Simeon. (11) Morgan worked on it steady for 20 years. (12) She converted a large ranch overlooking the Pacific into a hilltop Mediterranean village composed of three of the beautifullest guest houses in the world. (13) The larger of the three was designed to look like a cathedral and incorporated Hearst's fabulous art treasures from around the world. (14) The finished masterpiece had 144 rooms and was larger than a football field. (15) San Simeon is now one of the most visited tourist attractions in California and seems to grow popullarer each year.

EXPLORING ONLINE

http://a4esl.org/q/f/z/zz60fck.htm
Choose the correct adjective or adverb, and check your answers.

http://a4esl.org/q/h/9901/gc-advadj.html
Interactive practice: comparative and superlative forms

http://grammar.ccc.commnet.edu/grammar/adjectives.htm
Everything you wanted to know about adjectives

CourseMate for *Evergreen*

Visit *Evergreen* CourseMate for more practices and quizzes, videos to accompany the readings, career and job-search resources, ESL help, and live links to every Exploring Online in the book.

CHAPTER 36

The Apostrophe

A: The Apostrophe for Contractions

B: The Apostrophe for Ownership

C: Special Uses of the Apostrophe

A. The Apostrophe for Contractions

Use the **apostrophe** in a **contraction** to show that letters have been omitted.

1. *I'll* buy that coat if it goes on sale.
2. At nine *o'clock* sharp, the store opens.

- *I'll*, a contraction, is a combination of *I* and *will. Wi* is omitted.
- The contraction *o'clock* is the shortened form of *of the clock*.

Be especially careful in writing contractions that contain pronouns:

<table>
<tr><td colspan="2" align="center">**Common Contractions**</td></tr>
<tr><td>I + am = I'm</td><td>it + is or has = it's</td></tr>
<tr><td>I + have = I've</td><td>we + are = we're</td></tr>
<tr><td>I + will or shall = I'll</td><td>let + us = let's</td></tr>
<tr><td>you + have = you've</td><td>you + are = you're</td></tr>
<tr><td>you + will or shall = you'll</td><td>they + are = they're</td></tr>
<tr><td>he + will or shall = he'll</td><td>they + have = they've</td></tr>
<tr><td>she + is or has = she's</td><td>who + is or has = who's</td></tr>
</table>

The Scream by Edvard Munch

PRACTICE 1

Proofread these sentences and, above the lines, supply any apostrophes missing from the contractions.

1. When Edvard Munch painted *The Scream* in his native Norway in 1893, he couldnt have known that it would become world-famous—and the center of an unsolved mystery.

2. The painting shows an anguished person whos either screaming or covering his ears to muffle a scream.

3. Its become such a powerful symbol of modern stress and anxiety that its sometimes printed on office mugs as a joke.

4. But art lovers and stressed-out jokers arent the only ones whove admired *The Scream*.

5. Incredibly, the pictures been stolen twice, and the second time, it wasnt recovered.

6. In 1994, thieves snatched one of four versions of the painting from a gallery in Oslo, Norway, yet theyve since been convicted, and the painting was found unharmed.

7. But in August 2004, shocked visitors at Norways Munch Museum couldnt believe it when two armed bandits ripped another version of the painting out of the wall and escaped.

8. Experts dont agree on an exact figure, but theyve guessed that *The Scream* is worth between $50 and $70 million.

9. Thieves usually demand a ransom for such a famous artwork because they cant sell it openly.

10. However, those whove stolen *The Scream* didnt ask for money, and the crime remains one of the great unsolved art heists of all time.

B. The Apostrophe for Ownership

Use the apostrophe to show ownership: Add an *'s* if a noun or an indefinite pronoun (like *someone, anybody,* and so on) does not already end in *-s:*

---

1. I cannot find my *friend's* book bag.
2. *Everyone's* right to privacy should be respected.
3. *John and Julio's* apartment has striped wallpaper.
4. The *children's* clothes are covered with mud.

- The *friend* owns the book bag.
- *Everyone* owns the right to privacy.
- Both John and Julio own one apartment. The apostrophe follows the compound subject *John and Julio.*
- The *children* own the clothes.

    Add only an apostrophe to show ownership if the word already ends in *-s:**

---

5. My *aunts'* houses are filled with antiques.
6. The *knights'* table was round.
7. *Mr. Jonas'* company manufactures sporting goods and uniforms.

- My *aunts* (at least two of them) own the houses.
- The *knights* (at least two) own the table.
- *Aunts* and *knights* already end in *-s,* so only an apostrophe is added.
- *Mr. Jonas* owns the company. *Mr. Jonas* already ends in *-s,* so only an apostrophe is added.

---

* Some writers add an *-'s* to one-syllable proper names that end in *-s:* James's bike.

Note that *possessive pronouns never take an apostrophe: his, hers, theirs, ours, yours, its*:

> 8. *His* car gets twenty miles to the gallon, but *hers* gets only ten.
> 9. That computer is *theirs; ours* is coming soon.

PRACTICE 2

Proofread the following sentences and add apostrophes where necessary to show ownership. In each case, ask yourself if the word already ends in -*s*. Put a C after any correct sentences.

1. Bills bed is a four-poster.

2. Martha and Davids house is a log cabin made entirely by hand.

3. Somebodys cell phone was left on the sink.

4. During the eighteenth century, ladies dresses were heavy and uncomfortable.

5. Have you seen the childrens watercolor set?

6. Mr. James fried chicken and rice dish was crispy and delicious.

7. The class loved reading about Ulysses travels.

8. The Surgeon Generals latest report was just released.

9. Our citys water supply must be protected.

10. He found his ticket, but she cannot find hers.

11. Every spring, my grandmothers porch is completely covered with old furniture for sale.

12. Jacks car is the same color as ours.

13. Celias final, a brilliant study of pest control on tobacco farms, received a high grade.

14. The mens locker room is on the right; the womens is on the left.

15. The program is entering its final year.

C. Special Uses of the Apostrophe

Use an apostrophe in certain expressions of time:

> 1. I desperately need a *week's* vacation.

- Although the week does not own a vacation, it is a vacation of a week—*a week's vacation*.

Use an apostrophe to pluralize lowercase letters, words, and numbers that normally do not have plurals:

> 2. Be careful to cross your *t*'s.
> 3. Your *8*'s look like *f*'s.
> 4. Don't use so many *but*'s in your writing.

Use an apostrophe to show omitted numbers:

> 5. The class of '72 held its annual reunion last week.

PRACTICE 3

Proofread these sentences and add an apostrophe wherever necessary.

1. Cross your *t*s and dot your *i*s.

2. I would love a months vacation on a dude ranch.

3. Too many *and*s make this paragraph dull.

4. Those *9*s look crooked.

5. You certainly put in a hard days work!

PROOFREADING STRATEGY

Knowing the two main uses of apostrophes—contractions and possessives—will help you avoid the mistake of sticking apostrophes where they don't belong, for instance, into plural nouns or possessive pronouns like hers or its.

Go through your draft and highlight every word that contains an apostrophe. If you are using a computer, use the "Find" feature to locate all apostrophes in your draft.

For every apostrophe, you should be able to answer YES to one of two questions:

Is this apostrophe used to form a contraction?

Is this apostrophe used to indicate possession?

Yes   No—encounters   Yes

Example: Lee's dive trip didn't include any shark encounter's, but he wasn't sorry.

To find missing apostrophes, highlight all words ending in –s. If the word is a plural, leave it alone. If the word is a possessive noun, add an apostrophe.

Sandel's   OK—plural

Example: In Professor Sandels course on justice, students debate important ethical

OK—plural   other's

issues yet respect each others opinions.

PRACTICE 4   REVIEW

Proofread the following essay for apostrophe errors, using the proofreading strategy above if you wish. Correct the errors by adding apostrophes above the lines where needed and crossing out those that do not belong.

THE TRUE STORY OF SUPERMAN

rook76/Shutterstock.com

(1) Sometimes, things just dont work out right. (2) That's how the creators of Superman felt for a long time.

(3) Supermans first home wasnt the planet Krypton, but Cleveland. (4) There, in 1933, Superman was born. (5) Jerry Siegels story, "Reign of Superman," accompanied by Joe Shuster's illustrations, appeared in the boys own magazine, *Science Fiction*. (6) Later, the teenagers continued to develop their idea. (7) Superman would come to Earth from a distant planet to defend freedom and justice for ordinary people. (8) He would conceal his identity by living as an ordinary person himself. (9) Siegel and Shuster hoped their characters strength and morality would boost peoples spirits' during the Great Depression.

(10) At first, the creators werent able to sell their concept; then, Action Comics' Henry Donnenfield bought it. (11) In June of 1938, the first *Superman* comic hit the stands. (12) Superman's success was immediate and overwhelming. (13) Finally, Americans had a

hero who wouldnt let them down! (14) Radio and TV shows, movie serials, feature films, and generations of superheroes' followed.

(15) While others made millions from their idea, Siegel and Shuster didnt profit from its' success. (16) They produced Superman for Action Comics for a mere 15 dollars a page until they were fired a few years later when Joe Shusters eyes began to fail. (17) They sued, but they lost the case. (18) For a long time, both lived in poverty, but they continued to fight. (19) In 1975, Siegel and Shuster finally took their story to the press; the publicity won them lifelong pensions. (20) The two mens long struggle had ended with success.

EXPLORING ONLINE

http://grammar.ccc.commnet.edu/grammar/quizzes/apostrophe_quiz2.htm
Graded practice: Apostrophe or no apostrophe? This is the question.

http://www.towson.edu/ows/exerciseapos.htm
Apostrophe practice makes perfect.

CourseMate for *Evergreen*
Visit *Evergreen* CourseMate for more practices and quizzes, videos
to accompany the readings, career and job-search resources,
ESL help, and live links to every Exploring Online in the book.

CHAPTER 37

The Comma

A. Commas for Items in a Series

Use commas to separate the items in a series:*

> 1. You need *bolts, nuts,* and *screws.*
> 2. I will be happy to *read your poem, comment on it,* and *return it to you.*
> 3. *Mary paints pictures, Robert plays the trumpet,* but *Sam just sits and dreams.*

Do not use commas when all three items are joined by *and* or *or*:

> 4. I enjoy *biking* and *skating* and *swimming.*

———

* For work on parallelism, see Chapter 21, "Revising for Consistency and Parallelism," Part C.

PRACTICE 1

Punctuate the following sentences:

1. At the banquet, Ed served a salad of juicy red tomatoes crunchy green lettuce and stringless snap beans.

2. As a nursing assistant, Reva dispensed medication disinfected wounds and took blood samples.

3. Ali visited Santa Barbara Concord and Berkeley.

4. Hiking rafting, and snowboarding are her favorite sports.

5. The police found TV sets blenders and blow dryers stacked to the ceiling in the abandoned house.

6. I forgot to pack some important items for the trip to the tropics: insect repellent sunscreen and antihistamine tablets.

7. Don't eat strange mushrooms walk near the water or feed the squirrels.

8. Everyone in class had to present an oral report write a term paper and take a final.

9. We brought a Ouija board a Scrabble set and a Boggle game to the party.

10. To earn a decent wage make a comfortable home and educate my children—those are my hopes.

B. Commas with Introductory Phrases, Transitional Expressions, and Parentheticals

Use a comma after most introductory phrases of more than two words:*

1. *By four in the afternoon,* everybody wanted to go home.
2. *After the game on Saturday,* we all went dancing.

Use commas to set off transitional expressions:

3. Ferns, *for example,* need less sunlight than flowering plants.
4. Instructors, *on the other hand,* receive a lower salary than assistant professors.

---

* For more work on introductory phrases, see Chapter 22, "Revising for Sentence Variety," Part C.

Use commas to set off parenthetical elements:

> 5. *By the way*, where is the judge's umbrella?
> 6. Nobody, *it seems*, wants to eat the nut burgers.

● *By the way* and *it seems* are called parenthetical expressions because they appear to be asides, words not really crucial to the meaning of the sentence. They could almost appear in parentheses: *(By the way) where is the judge's umbrella?*

Other common parenthetical expressions are *after all, actually, as a matter of fact,* and *to tell the truth.*

PRACTICE 2

Punctuate the following sentences:

1. Frankly I always suspected that you were a born saleswoman.

2. All 12 jurors by the way felt that the defendant was innocent.

3. On every April Fools' Day he tries out a new, dumb practical joke.

4. In fact Lucinda should never have written that poison-pen letter.

5. Close to the top of Mount Washington the climbers paused for a tea break.

6. To tell the truth that usher needs a lesson in courtesy.

7. Near the end of the driveway a large lilac bush bloomed and brightened the yard.

8. He prefers as a rule serious news programs to the lighter sitcoms.

9. To sum up Mr. Choi will handle all the details.

10. During my three years in Minnesota I learned how to deal with snow.

C. Commas for Appositives

Use commas to set off appositives:*

> 1. Yoko, *our new classmate*, is our best fielder.
> 2. *A humorous and charming man*, he was a great hit with my parents.
> 3. This is her favorite food, *ketchup sandwiches*.

● Appositive phrases like *our new classmate, a humorous and charming man*, and *ketchup sandwiches* rename or describe nouns and pronouns—*Yoko, he, food*.

―――――
* For more work on appositives, see Chapter 22, "Revising for Sentence Variety," Part D.

4. Hip hop mogul Simmons launched Def Jam Recordings.
5. His ex-wife, Kimora, succeeded with her company Baby Phat.

● A one-word appositive is not set off by commas when it is essential to the meaning of the sentence. Without the appositive *Simmons*, we do not know who launched Def Jam Recordings.

● A one-word appositive is set off by commas when it is not essential to the meaning of the sentence. The name *Kimora* does not affect the meaning of the sentence.

PRACTICE 3

Punctuate the following sentences.

1. The Rock the popular wrestler and actor starred in movies and made a video with musician Wyclef Jean.

2. Long novels especially ones with complicated plots force me to read slowly.

3. Rolando a resident nurse hopes to become a pediatrician.

4. I don't trust that tire the one with the yellow patch on the side.

5. Tanzania a small African nation exports cashew nuts.

6. Watch out for Phil a man whose ambition rules him.

7. Ms. Liu a well-known nutritionist lectures at public schools.

8. A real flying ace Helen will teach a course in sky diving.

9. We support the Center for Science in the Public Interest a consumer education and protection group.

10. My husband Bill owns two stereos.

D. Commas with Nonrestrictive and Restrictive Clauses

A **relative clause** is a clause that begins with *who*, *which*, or *that* and modifies a noun or pronoun. There are two kinds of relative clauses: **nonrestrictive** and **restrictive**.*
A **nonrestrictive relative clause** is not essential to the meaning of the sentence:

1. Raj, *who is a part-time aviator*, loves to tinker with machines of all kinds.

---

* For more work on nonrestrictive and restrictive clauses, see Chapter 22, "Revising for Sentence Variety," Part D.

- *Who is a part-time aviator* is a relative clause describing *Raj*. It is a nonrestrictive relative clause because it is not essential to the meaning of the sentence. The point is that *Raj loves to tinker with machines of all kinds*.

- **Commas** set off the nonrestrictive relative clause.

A **restrictive relative clause** is essential to the meaning of the sentence:

> 2. People *who do their work efficiently* make good students.

- *Who do their work efficiently* is a relative clause describing *people*. It is a restrictive relative clause because it is *essential* to the meaning of the sentence. Without it, sentence 2 would read, *People make good students*. But the point is that certain people make good students—*those who do their work efficiently*.

- Restrictive relative clauses do *not* require commas.

PRACTICE 4

Set off the nonrestrictive relative clauses in the following sentences with commas. Note that *which* usually begins a nonrestrictive relative clause and *that* usually begins a restrictive clause. Remember: Restrictive relative clauses are *not* set off by commas. Write a *C* after each correct sentence.

1. Olive who always wanted to go into law enforcement is a detective in the Eighth Precinct.

2. Employees who learn to use the new computers may soon qualify for a merit raise.

3. Polo which is not played much in the United States is very popular in England.

4. A person who always insists upon telling you the truth is sometimes a pain in the neck.

5. Statistics 101 which is required for the business curriculum demands concentration and perseverance.

6. Robin who is usually shy at large parties spent the evening dancing with Arsenio who is everybody's favorite dance partner.

7. This small shop sells furniture that is locally handcrafted.

8. His uncle who rarely eats meat consumes enormous quantities of vegetables, fruits, and grains.

9. Pens that slowly leak ink can be very messy.

10. Valley Forge which was the site of Washington's winter quarters draws many tourists every spring and summer.

E. Commas for Dates and Addresses

Use commas to separate the elements of an address. Note, however, that no punctuation is required between the state and ZIP code if the ZIP code is included.

> 1. Please send the books to *300 West Road, Stamford, CT 06860.*
> 2. We moved from *1015 Allen Circle, Morristown, New Jersey,* to *Farland Lane, Dubuque, Iowa.*

Use commas to separate the elements of a date:

> 3. The sociologists arrived in Tibet on *Monday, January 18, 2009,* and planned to stay for two years.
> 4. John DeLeon arrived *from Baltimore in January* and will be our new shortstop this season.

Do not use a comma with a single-word address or date preceded by a preposition:

> 5. I expect to have completed my B.A. in physical education by June 2010.

PRACTICE 5

Punctuate the following sentences. Write a *C* after each correct sentence.

1. The unusual names of many American towns reflect our history and sense of humor.

2. In February 1878, Ed Schieffelin told friends that he was joining the California Gold Rush, and they warned, "The only thing you'll find out there will be your own tombstone."

3. But Schieffelin found silver in Arizona and named his settlement Tombstone, now famous for the shootout at the O.K. Corral on October 26 1881.

4. The residents of another mining town wanted to honor the chicken-like ptarmigan bird, but an argument about the word's spelling led them to select Chicken Alaska instead.

5. It was Christmas Eve, December 24 1849 when residents of a small rural community chose to name their town Santa Claus.

6. Every Christmas since the 1920s, volunteers have replied to the thousands of children's letters that pour into the town's post office, located at 45 N. Kringle Place Santa Claus Indiana 47579.

7. Hell, Michigan, got its name when crusty resident George Reeves was asked his opinion and replied, "I don't care. You can name it Hell if you want to."

8. At a 10K race there on August 13 2005 runners went home with T-shirts announcing, "I Ran Thru Hell."

9. On January 20 2000 the town of Halfway Oregon became the "World's First Dot Com City" when it officially changed its name to Half.com.

10. Choosing the right name can be difficult, as the folks who founded Nameless Tennessee can attest.

F. Minor Uses of the Comma

Use a comma after answering a question with *yes* or *no*:

> 1. *No*, I'm not sure about that answer.

Use a comma when addressing someone directly and specifically naming the person spoken to:

> 2. *Alicia*, where did you put my law books?

Use a comma after interjections like *ah, oh,* and so on:

> 3. *Ah*, these coconuts are delicious.

Use a comma to contrast:

> 4. Harold, *not Roy*, is my scuba-diving partner.*

PRACTICE 6

Punctuate the following sentences.

1. Yes I do think you will be famous one day.

2. Well did you call a taxi?

3. The defendant ladies and gentlemen of the jury does not even own a red plaid jacket.

4. Cynthia have you ever camped in the Pacific Northwest?

5. No I most certainly will not marry you.

6. Oh I love the way they play everything to a salsa beat.

7. The class feels Professor Molinor that your grades are unrealistically high.

8. He said march not swagger.

9. Perhaps but I still don't think that the carburetor fits there.

10. We all agree Ms. Crawford that you are the best jazz bassist around.

PROOFREADING STRATEGY

Armed with the eight comma rules, you can proofread effectively for comma errors.

1. **Circle or highlight every comma in your draft.** This forces your eye and brain to focus on each one of them. If you are writing on a computer, use the "*Find*" feature to locate all your commas.

2. For every comma, ask, *Does one of the eight comma rules explain why this comma needs to be here?* If you aren't sure, review the rules in the chapter. Make any needed corrections, like this:

---

* For help using commas with coordinating and subordinating conjunctions—and help avoiding run-ons, commas splices, and fragments—see Chapters 27 and 28.

C (introductory phrase)
For centuries, vampire stories have been told around the world.

X (appositive—add second comma)
Stephenie Meyer, author of the four *Twilight* books weaves vampires

into a teenage love triangle.

C (items in a series)
Twilight, New Moon, Eclipse, and *Breaking Dawn* have sold 100 million

X (not coordination—remove comma)
copies, and have been translated into 37 languages.

PRACTICE 7 REVIEW

Using the proofreading strategy explained on the previous page, proofread the following essay for comma errors—either missing commas or commas used incorrectly. Correct the errors above the lines.

PIXAR PERFECT

(1) A company called Pixar has transformed animated films. (2) It was started in 1986 by Steven Jobs the head of Apple Computer and creator of the iPod and iPhone. (3) Applying technical imagination to story-telling Pixar has produced some of the most successful and beloved movies ever made. (4) *Toy Story, A Bug's Life Finding Nemo, Monsters, Inc., Wall-E, Up,* and *Cars* appealed to both children and adults by combining engaging stories memorable characters, and cutting-edge computer animation.

(5) Pixar's action-packed plots carry emotional punch. (6) In *Finding Nemo* for instance, Nemo's father searches for his missing son in the vast ocean and learns about the bonds of family love. (7) *Monsters, Inc.* explores the theme of facing fears as it follows two monsters attempting to return a wayward toddler to her room. (8) In *Wall-E,* an outdated robot on the abandoned planet Earth meets a sleek robot from space falls in love and helps save the planet.

(9) Pixar populates these plots with lovable heroes and diabolical villains. (10) Although none of them is technically a human characters like Woody, Buzz Lightyear, Sully, Nemo, and Wall-E win moviegoers' hearts with their "humanity." (11) Woody is upset when a new toy replaces him as the favorite. (12) Lonely Wall-E longs to win the the heart of shiny Eve. (13) The characters seem even more real because stars like Ellen Degeneres, Tom Hanks, Tim Allen, John Goodman, and Billy Crystal bring their voices to life.

(14) Finally Pixar animators use the latest computer-animation technology and meticulous detail to create realistic 3-D images. (15) Monster Sully's shaggy blue coat ripples in the wind for example because animators created a separate computer model

Lightning McQueen and tow truck Mater tangle with spies in *Cars 2*.

for each of its 2.3 million individual hairs. (16) To convey strong emotion with almost no words *Wall-E*'s animators studied the movements of machines like NASA's Mars Rover and watched silent films and those with little dialogue such as *2001: A Space Odyssey*.

(17) Pixar's films have impressed critics as well as audiences. (18) In fact its movies have won 205 Academy Awards Golden Globes and other top film prizes.

EXPLORING ONLINE

http://www.pixar.com/behind_the_scenes/
The site, "Behind the Scenes," offers a quick tour of the Pixar process through the experience of the director, artists, and technicians who work on a film and bring it to life.

EXPLORING ONLINE

http://owl.english.purdue.edu/owl/resource/607/01/
Quick rules for commas and review.

http://grammar.ccc.commnet.edu/grammar/quizzes/commas_fillin.htm
Interactive quiz: Where have all the commas gone?

CourseMate for *Evergreen*
Visit *Evergreen* CourseMate for more practices and quizzes, videos to accompany the readings, career and job-search resources, ESL help, and live links to every Exploring Online in this book.

CHAPTER 38

Mechanics

A: Capitalization

B: Titles

C: Direct Quotations

D: Minor Marks of Punctuation

A. Capitalization

Always capitalize the following: *names, nationalities, religions, races, languages, countries, cities, months, days of the week, documents, organizations,* and *holidays.*

> 1. The *Protestant* church on the corner will offer *Spanish* and *English* courses starting *Thursday, June* 3.

Capitalize the following *only* when they are used as part of a proper noun: *streets, buildings, historical events, titles,* and *family relationships.*

> 2. We saw *Professor Rodriguez* at *Silver Hall,* where he was delivering a talk on the *Spanish Civil War.*

Do not capitalize these same words when they are used as common nouns:

> 3. We saw the professor at the lecture hall, where he was delivering a talk on a civil war.

Capitalize geographic locations but not directions:

4. The tourists went to the *South* for their winter vacation.
5. Go south on this boulevard for three miles.

Capitalize academic subjects only if they refer to a specific named and numbered course:

6. Have you ever studied psychology?
7. Last semester, I took *Psychology* 101.

PROOFREADING STRATEGY

Incorrect capitalization is a red-flag error in college writing. If capitalization is one of your error patterns, try this:

1. Circle or color code every **proper noun** (nouns of specific people, places, and things) and **capitalized word**.

2. Now check one by one to **make sure that you have correctly capitalized**. This student coded her proper nouns yellow:

> **Example:** In February, 2012, lady gaga [Lady Gaga] launched her new Born This way Foundation [Born This Way] at Harvard university [University]. The foundation uses digital tools to promote Kindness, Bravery [kindness bravery], acceptance, and empowerment.

PRACTICE 1

Capitalize wherever necessary in the following sentences. Put a C after each correct sentence.

1. Barbara Kingsolver, a well-known novelist, nonfiction writer, and poet, was born on april 8, 1955, in annapolis, maryland.

2. She grew up in rural kentucky and then went to college in indiana; after graduating, she worked in europe and since then has lived in and around tucson, arizona.

3. In college, Kingsolver majored first in music and then in biology; she later withdrew from a graduate program in biology and ecology at the university of arizona to work in its office of arid land studies.

4. Kingsolver's first novel, *The Bean Trees*, has become a classic; it is taught in english classes and has been translated into more than 65 languages.

5. The main character, named taylor greer, is considered one of the most memorable women in modern american literature.

6. In a later novel, *The Poisonwood Bible*, Kingsolver follows the family of a baptist minister in its move to the congo.

7. The fanaticism of reverend price brings misery to his family and destruction to the villagers he tries to convert to christianity.

8. Kingsolver's writing always deals with powerful political and social issues, but her novels don't sound preachy because she is a wonderful storyteller.

9. She has won awards and prizes from the american library association and many other organizations; she also has earned special recognition from the united nations national council of women.

10. This gifted writer, who plays drums and piano, performs with a band called rock bottom remainders; other band members are also notable writers—stephen king, amy tan, and dave barry.

B. Titles

Capitalize words of a title except short prepositions, short conjunctions, and the articles *the, an,* and *a*. Always capitalize the first and last words of the title, no matter what they are:

> 1. I liked *The Invisible Man* but found *The House on the River* slow reading.

Italicize or underline the titles of long works: *books,* newspapers and magazines, television shows, plays, record albums, operas,* and *films*.

Put quotation marks around shorter works or parts of longer ones: *articles, short stories, poems, songs, scenes from plays,* and *chapters from full-length books*.

---

* The titles and parts of sacred books are not italicized or underlined and are not set off by quotation marks: Job 5:6, Koran 1:14, and so on.

2. Have you read Hemingway's "The Killers" yet?

3. We are assigned "The Money Market" in *Essentials of Economics* for homework in my marketing course.

● "The Killers" is a short story.

● "The Money Market" is a chapter in the full-length book *Essentials of Economics*.

Do not underline or use quotation marks around the titles of your own papers.

PRACTICE 2

Capitalize these titles correctly. Do not underline or use quotation marks in this practice.

1. inside women's college basketball

2. the genius of frank lloyd wright

3. breath, eyes, memory

4. an insider's guide to the music industry

5. the orchid thief

6. dave barry's guide to marriage and/or sex

7. how to build a website

8. a history of violence in american movies

9. harry potter and the goblet of fire

10. currents from the dancing river

PRACTICE 3

Wherever necessary, underline or place quotation marks around each title in the sentences below so that the reader will know at a glance what type of work the title refers to. Put a C after any correct sentence.

EXAMPLE   Two of the best short stories in that volume are "Rope" and "The New Dress."

1. African American writer Langston Hughes produced his first novel, Not Without Laughter, when he was a student at Lincoln University in Pennsylvania.

The writer Langston Hughes

2. By that time, he had already been a farmer, a cook, a waiter, and a doorman at a Paris nightclub; he had also won a prize for his poem The Weary Blues, which was published in 1925 in the magazine Opportunity.

3. In 1926 Hughes wrote his famous essay The Negro Artist and the Racial Mountain, which appeared in the Nation magazine; he wanted young black writers to write without shame or fear about the subject of race.

4. Because he spoke Spanish, Hughes was asked in 1937 by the newspaper the Baltimore Afro-American to cover the activities of blacks in the International Brigades in Spain during the Spanish Civil War.

5. For the rest of his life, he wrote articles in newspapers such as the San Francisco Chronicle, the New York Times, and the Chicago Defender.

6. In fact, for more than 20 years he wrote a weekly column for the Chicago Defender in which he introduced a character named Simple, who became popular because of his witty observations on life.

7. The stories about Simple were eventually collected and published in five books; two of those books are Simple Speaks His Mind and Simple Takes a Wife.

8. In 1938, Hughes established the Harlem Suitcase Theater in Manhattan, where his play Don't You Want to Be Free? was performed.

9. Because Hughes's poetry was based on the rhythms of African American speech and music, many of his poems have been set to music, including Love Can Hurt You, Dorothy's Name Is Mud, and Five O'Clock Blues.

10. Few modern writers can rival Hughes's enormous output of fine poems, newspaper articles, columns, and novels.

C. Direct Quotations

1. He said, "These are the best seats in the house."

- The direct quotation is preceded by a comma or a colon.
- The first letter of the direct quotation is capitalized.
- Periods always go *inside* the quotation marks.

2. He asked, "Where is my laptop?"
3. Stewart yelled, "I don't like beans!"

● Question marks and exclamation points go inside the quotation marks if they are part of the direct words of the speaker.

4. "That was meant for the company," he said, "but if you wish, you may have it."
5. "The trees look magnificent!" she exclaimed. "It would be fun to climb them all."

● In sentence 4, the quotation is one single sentence interrupted by *he said*. Therefore, a comma is used after *he said*, and *but* is not capitalized.
● In sentence 5, the quotation consists of two different sentences. Thus a period follows *exclaimed*, and the second sentence of the quotation begins with a capital letter.

PROOFREADING STRATEGY

If quotation marks are one of your personal error patterns, try this strategy.

1. **Scan your draft** for sentences in which you give **someone's exact words**.

2. **Check these sentences** for correct use of commas, quotation marks, and capitalization.

3. Make sure that you have provided both **beginning and end quotation marks**.

The police officer asked "do you know how fast you were going?" [Do]

Mike answered "I was texting so I couldn't see the speedometer."

---

* For more work on the distinction between direct quotation and paraphrase, see Chapter 18, Part C, "Using Direct and Indirect Quotation (Paraphrase)."

PRACTICE 4

Insert quotation marks where necessary in each sentence. Use the proofreading strategy to make sure you have capitalized and punctuated correctly.

1. The sign reads don't even think about parking here.

2. Alexander Pope wrote to err is human, to forgive divine.

3. Well, it takes all kinds she sighed.

4. He exclaimed you look terrific in those jeweled sandals

5. The article said Most American children do poorly in geography.

6. These books on ancient Egypt look interesting he replied but I don't have time to read them now.

7. Although the rain is heavy she said we will continue harvesting the corn.

8. Give up caffeine and get lots of rest the doctor advised.

9. The label warns this product should not be taken by those allergic to aspirin.

10. Red, white, and blue Hillary said are my favorite colors.

D. Minor Marks of Punctuation

1. The Colon

Use a colon to show that a direct quotation will follow or to introduce a list:*

1. This is the opening line of his essay: "The airplane is humanity's greatest invention."
2. There are four things I can't resist in warm weather: fresh mangoes, a sandy beach, cold drinks, and a hammock.

Use a colon to separate the chapter and verse in a reference to the Bible or to separate the hour and minute:

3. This quotation comes from Genesis 1:1.
4. It is now exactly 4:15 P.M.

---

* Avoid using a colon after any form of the verb *to be* or after a preposition.

2. Parentheses

Use parentheses to enclose a phrase or word that is not essential to the meaning of the sentence:

> 5. Herpetology (the study of snakes) is a fascinating area of zoology.
> 6. She left her hometown (Plunkville) to go to the big city (Fairmount) in search of success.

3. The Dash

Use a dash to emphasize a portion of a sentence or to interrupt the sentence with an added element:

> 7. This is the right method—the only one—so we are stuck with it.

The colon, parentheses, and the dash should be used sparingly.

PRACTICE 5

Punctuate these sentences with colons, dashes, or parentheses.

1. Calvin asked for the following two light bulbs, a pack of matches, a lead pencil, and a pound of grapes.

2. They should leave by 11 30 P.M.

3. The designer's newest fashions magnificent leather creations were generally too expensive for the small chain of clothing stores.

4. Harvey the only Missourian in the group remains unconvinced.

5. She replied, "This rock group The Woogies sounds like all the others I've heard this year."

6. If you eat a heavy lunch as you always do remember not to go swimming immediately afterward.

7. By 9:30 P.M., the zoo veterinarian a Dr. Smittens had operated on the elephant.

8. Note these three tips for hammering in a nail hold the hammer at the end of the handle, position the nail carefully, and watch your thumb.

9. Whenever Harold Garvey does his birdcalls at parties as he is sure to do everyone begins to yawn.

10. Please purchase these things at the hardware store masking tape, thumbtacks, apple-green paint, and some sandpaper.

PRACTICE 6   REVIEW

Proofread the following essay for errors in capitalization, quotation marks, colons, parentheses, and dashes. Correct the errors by writing above the lines.

THE PASSION OF THOMAS GILCREASE

(1) Thomas Gilcrease, a descendent of creek indians, became an instant Millionaire when oil was discovered on his homestead in 1907. (2) He spent most of his fortune collecting objects that tell the story of the american frontier, particularly of the Native American experience. (3) The Thomas Gilcrease institute of american history and arts in Tulsa, oklahoma, is the result of his lifelong passion.

© Gilcrease Museum, Tulsa, OK

Mourning Her Brave by George de Forest Brush, a painting in the Gilcrease Collection. Name five details in the painting that create its somber mood.

(4) This huge collection more than 10,000 works of art, 90,000 historical documents, and 250,000 native american artifacts, spans the centuries from 10,000 B.C. to the 1950s. (5) Awed visitors can view nearly 200 George Catlin paintings of Native American life. (6) They can walk among paintings and bronze sculptures by Frederic Remington with names like *The Coming And Going Of The Pony Express* that call up images of the West. (7) Museumgoers can admire Thomas Moran's watercolors that helped persuade Congress to create yellowstone, the first national park. (8) In addition, visitors are treated to works by modern Native Americans, such as the display of wood sculptures by the cherokee Willard Stone.

(9) The museum also houses many priceless documents an original copy of the declaration of independence, the oldest known letter written from the new world, and the papers of Hernando Cortés. (10) A new glass storage area even allows visitors to view the 80 percent of the holdings that are not on display. (11) Thousands of beaded moccasins and buckskin dresses line the shelves, and a collection of magnificent war bonnets hangs from brackets.

(12) When the Gilcrease Institute opened its doors on May 2, 1949, *Life* magazine declared it is the best collection of art and literature ever assembled on the American frontier and the Indian. (13) Thousands of visitors agree.

EXPLORING ONLINE

http://grammar.ccc.commnet.edu/grammar/cgi-shl/par_numberless_quiz.pl/caps_quiz.htm

Graded capitalization practice

http://grammar.ccc.commnet.edu/grammar/quizzes/punct_fillin.htm

Mixed practice: test your skill with many marks of punctuation.

CourseMate for *Evergreen*

Visit *Evergreen* CourseMate for more practices and quizzes, videos to accompany the readings, career and job-search resources, ESL help, and live links to every Exploring Online in the book.

CHAPTER 39

Putting Your Proofreading Skills to Work

Throughout this unit, you have tried out proofreading strategies for different kinds of errors. This chapter gives you the opportunity to put your proofreading skills to work in even more challenging situations. As you proofread the paragraphs and essays that follow, you must look for any—and every—kind of error, just as you would in the real world of college and work. The first four practices tell you what kinds of errors to look for; if you have trouble, go back to those chapters and review. The other practices, however, contain a random mix of errors with no clues at all.

- Before you start, review your **Personal Error Patterns Chart** that you learned to keep in Chapter 25. Watch out for the errors you tend to make.

- Use the **proofreading strategies** that work best for you, like color highlighting, reading out loud, and reading from the bottom up. Apply your favorite strategies here.

- Refer to the proofreading checklist at the end of this chapter for a quick reminder of what to look for.

- Keep a **dictionary** handy. If you are not sure of the spelling of a word, look it up.

PROOFREADING

Proofread this paragraph, correcting any errors above the lines. To review, see these chapters:

Chapter 28	run-ons, comma splices, fragments
Chapter 29	present tense problems, subject-verb agreement
Chapter 31	past participle problems
Chapter 32	noun errors
Chapter 36	apostrophe errors

(1) What do dancing cockatoos, reporters bloopers, and a child leaving the dentist have in common? (2) They are all subject of videos that went "viral" on the Internet. (3) Most of these videos were film by ordinary people. (4) And then posted online. (5) From the tsunami of videos uploaded to YouTube every year, a few seems to touch something universal that translates across cultures, they can rack up millions of hits. (6) Its rare to make millions of people laugh, viral videos share certain themes. (7) Many features babys doing cute things, animals doing cute things, or people of all age doing idiotic things. (8) A video in which twin toddlers have an animate conversation in gibberish charmed viewers on five continents. (9) A short clip called Sneezing Panda was watched almost 6 million times. (10) The most popular videos can make money for their creators'. (11) David DeVore Sr. filmed his son, still woozy after a dental procedure. (12) When his video, "David After Dentist," went viral. (13) YouTube offered to partner with him. (14) He now collect revenues from ads running with his video. (15) One cant plan to make a viral video, experts warn, so they advise dreamers to stay in college.

PRACTICE 2   **PROOFREADING**

Proofread this paragraph, correcting any errors above the lines. To review, see these chapters:

Chapter 28	run-ons, comma splices, fragments
Chapter 29	present tense problems, subject-verb agreement
Chapter 30	past tense problems
Chapter 31	past participle problems

(1) Mount Everest is the tallest mountain in the world. (2) The highest point on Earth, and the dangerous dream of every mountain climber. (3) Everest set in the Himalaya Mountains of central Asia and rise 29,028 feet. (4) The deadliest threat to climbers are not the steep, icy slopes or even the bitter cold and ferocious winds it is the lack of air. (5) Air at the top of Everest has only one-third the oxygen of air below, so without preparation, the average person would live less than an hour at the summit. (6) In fact, altitude sickness begin at 8,000 feet, with headache, nausea, and confusion. (7) At 12,000

feet, the brain and lungs starts filling with fluid, which can lead to death. (8) How, then, has anyone ever climbed Everest, the answer is acclimatization. (9) Mountaineers climb slowly, about 2,000 feet a day, and they drink huge amounts of water. (10) They also carry oxygen. (11) Amazingly, in 1980, the first person to climb Everest solo was also the first to climb it without oxygen. (12) That was Reinhold Messner from Italy. (13) Who later wrote in *Climbing* magazine that the lack of air "saps your judgment and strength, even your ability to feel anything at all. I don't know how I made it." (14) Over 219 climbers have died scaling Mount Everest, nonetheless, this danger keeps tempting others to try their skills and their luck.

PRACTICE 3   PROOFREADING

Proofread this paragraph, correcting any errors above the lines. To review, see these chapters:

Chapter 28   run-ons, comma splices, and fragments
Chapter 30   past tense errors
Chapter 31   past participle problems
Chapter 35   adjective and adverb errors

(1) Lisa Ling's love of adventure and desire to shed light on serious social issues propelled her into the ranks of respected television reporters at a very young age. (2) At 16, encourage by her speech teacher, she auditioned and was chose to be a host of *Scratch*, a television magazine for teens. (3) By the time she was 18, Ling had became one of the most youngest reporters for Channel One News, a network that broadcasts daily to 8 million middle and high school students around the United States her high-energy personality, curiosity, daring, and compassion holded viewers' attention. (4) In her early twenties, she was pick as Channel One's senior war correspondent. (5) Reporting on difficult and dangerous issues in war-torn Afghanistan, Iran, and Iraq. (6) The intrepid Ling tracked down cocaine labs in the Colombian jungle, interviewing guerrillas fighting civil wars, investigated a Russian company accused of smuggling nuclear weapons, and sipped

Reporter Lisa Ling chats with Barbara Walters on *The View*.

Donna Svennevik/Getty Images

tea with the Dalai Lama. (7) Oprah Winfrey tapped her as a special correspondent, the young reporter's passionate stories about illegal immigrants, AIDS orphans in Uganda, and bride-burning in India moved audiences to tears and action. (8) After a brief role on *The View*, Ling return to her first love, international reporting. (9) As the first woman to host National Geographic's *Explorer* series, she fearless traveled the globe, interviewing female suicide bombers or convicts in U.S. prisons. (10) Now the host of her own show, *Our America with Lisa Ling*, she continues to tackle our society's most challenging problems, including heroin addiction and teenaged prostitution. (11) This student of the world urges young people to travel and learn about other cultures. (12) Because knowledge and compassion empower us all.

PRACTICE 4   PROOFREADING

Proofread this paragraph, correcting any errors above the lines. To review, see these chapters:

Chapter 21   parallelism errors

Chapter 28   run-ons, comma splices, fragments

Chapter 29   present tense problems, subject-verb agreement

Chapter 32   noun errors

Chapter 35   adjective and adverb errors

(1) Do you know your learning style? (2) Finding out might help you succeed in college. (3) A learning style is a preferred way of taking in new information. (4) The four major learning styles is *visual, auditory, reading/writing*, and *hands-on*. (5) Most people use all of these method, however, one method might work more better than others. (6) For example, Lupe discovered in college that she has a dominant *visual* learning style. (7) New facts or concepts are most clearest to her if they are presented in diagrams, charts, photographs, or videos. (8) Lupe realized that she can deepen her understanding by drawing pictures to depict the information she hears and reads. (9) Nathan, on the other hand, has a dominant *auditory* style he needs to hear spoken explanations and also talk about what he is learning. (10) He absorbs course work best by reading aloud, participation in class discussions, and tape-recording and then listening to his notes. (11) Terrell has a *reading/writing* style. (12) Because his mind soaks up information best in the form of written words. (13) Terrell enjoys learning through books, handouts, PowerPoint presentations, and notes, he benefits from writing summaries and journal entries to process what he sees and hears. (14) The fourth learning style—*hands-on*—describe the preference of Emilio, who learns most efficient by moving, doing, and using all his sense. (15) Whenever possible, he tries to handle objects, participate in performances, conduct hands-on experiments, and use trial-and-error. (16) An understanding of learning styles give each of these students new skills to help master any academic subject.

PRACTICE 5   PROOFREADING

This passage contains many of the errors you have learned to avoid in Unit 6. Proofread each sentence carefully, and then correct each error above the line.

(1) If you want to eat well and do our planet a favor become a Vegetarian. (2) Most vegetarian's eat eggs, milk, dairy products and fish. (3) All youre giving up are leathery steak's and overcooked chicken. (4) A vegetarian dinner might begin with a greek salad of,

crisp cucumbers, sweet red onion black olives, and a sprinkling of feta cheese.

(5) Youll think you're sitting in a little café overlooking the mediterranean sea. (6) For

the main course, head to mexico for tamale pie. (7) A rich, flavorful dish made of pinto

beans's, brown rice, green peppers and tomatoes. (8) On the table of course is a loaf

of warm bread.

(9) Do you have room for dessert? how about some ben and jerrys ice cream, made in

vermont? (10) As you linger over a cup of french espresso coffee think how your vegetarian

meal was delicious, nutritious, and a help to our planet. (11) If more people ate vegetarian

the land given to raising cattle and crops to feed cattle could be used for raising grain,

many of the worlds hungry people could be fed. (12) To read about vegetarianism, get the

best-known guide *laurels kitchen: a handbook for vegetarian cookery and nutrition.*

PRACTICE 6   PROOFREADING

This essay contains many of the errors you have learned to avoid in Unit 6. Proofread each
sentence carefully, and then correct each error above the line.

(1) Some of the most popularest programs on television today are the *CSI* dramas,

which depict crime scene investigators using state-of-the-art equipment and old-

fashioned detective work to solve crimes. (2) These shows not only entertain 60 million

viewers a week but have also stimulate great interest in forensics as a career, in fact,

demand for training has reached record levels. (3) According to the American academy of

forensic sciences, the many jobs in forensics allows people to apply their love of science

to the pursuit of justice and public safety.

(4) Forensic scientists are curious, detail-oriented people whom like to think and puts

puzzles together. (5) They also need to work good in groups. (6) Unlike *CSI* characters

on TV, who perform many varied tasks, real forensic scientists usually specialize on one

area and then pool their expertise to help police nab criminals. (7) For example, crime

scene examiners go to the places where crimes have occurred to locate, photograph, collect, and transportation of physical evidence like fingerprints and blood samples. (8) On the other hand, crime laboratory analysts stay in the lab. (9) Using microscopes, DNA tests, firearms tests, and other techniques and equipments to make sense of crime scene evidence.

(10) Each of these jobs require a bachelor's degree. (11) Two specialtys requiring a master's degree are forensic anthropology; which involves identifying people from skeletal remains. And psychological profiling. (12) Using behavioral clues to "read" the mind of a killer or other criminal. (13) One specialty, medical examiner, requires a medical degree. (14) Although this is the highest-paid forensics career. (15) It requires a tough personality able to perform autopsies on crime victims to determine exact cause of death. (16) Real-world forensic scientists admit that their jobs are not quite as glamorous as those of their television counterparts however, they describe their work as challenging, interesting, and with rewards.

PRACTICE 7 **PROOFREADING**

This essay contains many of the errors you learned to avoid in Unit 6. Proofread each sentence carefully, and then correct each error above the line.

IN THE MARKET FOR A USED CAR?

(1) For several year's now, used car sales have exceeded new car sales. (2) Good used cars can be founded at dealers, (3) And through newspaper ads. (4) You might also let your friends know your in the market for a used car, they might know of someone who wants to sell their car. (5) Wherever you look for a used car keep the following tips in mind.

(6) First shop before you need the car. (7) This way you can decide exactly what type of car suit you most best. (8) Do you want a compact. (9) Or a midsize car? (10) What features are important to you? (11) Should you get an american-made car or a japanese, german, or other import? (12) If you shop when you are'nt desperate, you are more likely to make a good choice and negotiate good.

(13) Second narrow your choices to three or four cars, and do some research. (14) Start with the *kelley blue book used car price manual*, online at **http://www.kbb.com**. (15) The blue book as its called for short gives the current value by model year and features. (16) Its also a good idea to check *consumer reports* magazine. (17) Every april issue lists good used car buys and cars to avoid. (18) Based on what you learn go back and test-drive the cars that interest you the mostest. (19) Drive each for at least an hour, drive in stop-and-go traffic in the highway, in winding roads, and in hills.

(20) When you do decide on a car ask your mechanic to look at it. (21) Be sure to get a written report that include an estimate of what repair's will cost. (22) Money spent at this point is money spent wise, if the seller wont allow an inspection, take your business elsewhere.

(23) When you buy a used car you want dependability and value. (24) Follow these tip's, youll be able to tell a good buy when you see it.

PRACTICE 8

PROOFREADING

This essay contains many of the errors you learned to avoid in Unit 6. Proofread each sentence carefully, and then correct each error above the line.

GATORS AND CROCS

(1) With their scaly bodies slit eyes and long tails, alligators and crocodiles look a lot like dinosaurs. (2) In fact alligators and crocodiles descended from the same family as dinosaurs. (3) While its true that alligators and crocodiles look a lot alike, they differ in three ways.

(4) First alligators and crocodiles are found in different parts of the world. (5) Alligators be found in china, central america, and south america. (6) On the other hand, crocodiles are found in africa (especially around the nile river), australia, southeast asia, india, cuba, and the west indies. (7) Only in the southern united states is both alligators and crocodiles found. (8) In all cases however alligator's and crocodile's live in hot, tropical

regions. (9) Reptiles are cold-blooded, so at temperatures below 65 degrees, alligators and crocodiles gets sluggish and cannot hunt.

(10) Alligators and crocodiles also differ in appearance. (11) Alligators has broader flatter snouts that are rounded at the end. (12) Crocodiles has narrower almost triangular snouts. (13) The best way to tell the difference is to view both from the side when they have their mouths closed, you can see only upper teeth on an alligator, but you can also see four lower teeth on a croc. (14) If you get really close you can see that alligators have a space between they're nostrils whereas the nostrils of crocs are very close together.

(15) Finally alligators and crocodiles are temperamentally different. (16) Alligators are not aggressive they are even a bit shy. (17) They will lie in wait along a riverbank for prey when on land, they move slow and uneven. (18) Crocodiles, however, are much more aggressive. (19) They are fast and mean, they often stalk they're prey. (20) The australian freshwater crocodile and the nile crocodile can even run on land, with their front and back legs working together like a dog. (21) Nile crocodiles kill hundred's of people every year.

(22) Alligators and crocodiles have outlived the dinosaurs, but they might not survive hunters who want to turn them into shoes wallets briefcases and belts. (23) In 1967, the u.s. government declared alligators an endangered species. (24) Fortunately american alligators have repopulated and are now reclassified as threatened. (25) Importing crocodile and alligator skins are banned worldwide, but some species is still threatened. (26) These frightening and fascinating ancient creatures need help worldwide if they are to survive.

PROOFREADING STRATEGY

A proofreading checklist like the one below can be an effective tool for remembering what to look for when reviewing your own writing.

Proofreading Checklist

- Check for sentence fragments, comma splices, and run-on sentences.

- Check for verb errors: present tense *–s* endings (verb agreement), past tense *–ed* endings, past participles, and tense consistency.

- Check for incorrect singular and plural nouns, incorrect pronouns, confused adjectives and adverbs, and incorrect prepositions.

- Check all punctuation: commas, apostrophes, semicolons, quotation marks.

- Check all capitalization.

- Check spelling and look-alikes/sound-alikes.

- Check for omitted words and typos.

- Check layout, format, titles, dates, and spacing.

- Check for all personal error patterns.

EXPLORING ONLINE

http://writingcenter.unc.edu/handouts/proofreading/

How to proofread: a brief audiovisual demonstration

http://grammar.ccc.commnet.edu/grammar/

Interactive grammar and writing help. Explore, learn, review!

http://owl.english.purdue.edu/owl/resource/561/01

Overview of proofreading, with useful tips

CourseMate for *Evergreen*

Visit *Evergreen* CourseMate for more practices and quizzes, videos to accompany the readings, career and job-search resources, ESL help, and live links to every Exploring Online in the book.

Writers' Workshop

Adopt a New Point of View

No matter how excellent the content of an essay, report, or business letter, grammatical errors will diminish its impact. Ironically, errors call attention to themselves. Learning to proofread your writing may not seem terribly exciting, but it is an all-important skill.

When this student received the interesting assignment to *write as if you are someone or something else*, he decided to see what it was like to be a roach. His audience: humans. His tone: wacky. In your group or class, read his essay, aloud if possible. Underline details or sentences that are especially effective or humorous, and **proofread** as you go. If you spot any errors, correct them.

It's Not Easy Being a Roach

(1) It's not easy being a roach. My life consist of the constant struggle to survive. We have existed for millions of years, yet we still do not get the respect that we deserve. We have witnessed the dawn of the dinosaur and the building of Rome. We have experienced two world wars, enjoyed the benefits of cable television, and feasted our eyes on many women taking showers. Being small has its advantages, and it doesn't hurt to be quick either. Because we have live so long. You would think that respect would be ours, but that is not the case.

(2) We are looked upon as pests rather than pets, we are quieter than household pets. We don't eat much, and contrary to popular belief, we are very clean. Sure, some of us prefers the wild life of booze, drugs, and unprotected sex with other insects, but that doesn't mean that most of us are not seeking a happy life that includes love and affection from you humans. I think it's high time that you appreciated our value as insects, pets, and potential lifelong companions.

(3) I might have six legs, but that doesn't mean I can handle all the burdens that come with being a roach. My wife is pregnant again, which means 10,000 more mouths to feed. It's bad enough that I have to find a meal fit for thousands I also live in fear of becoming a Roach McNugget. For some strange reason, rodents consider us food. Do I look scrumptious to you? Does my body ignite wild fantasies of sinful feasting? I think not. Mice and rats refuse to respect us because they see us as midnight munchies.

(4) I don't ask for much—a home, some food, and maybe an occasional pat on the head. If I can't have these simple things, I would prefer somebody simply step on me. A fast, hard crunch would do— no spraying me with roach spray, no Roach Motel. I may be on the lower end of the species chain, but that doesn't mean I'm not entitled to live out my dreams. I am roach and hear me roar!

(5) When you humans kill each other off with nuclear bombs, we will still be around. With luck on our side, we will grow into big monsters because of exposure to radiation. Then I don't think those of you who remains will enjoy being chased around by giant, glowing roaches—all because you humans didn't want to hug a roach when you had the chance.

(6) One more thing: stop trying to kill us with that pine-scented roach spray. It doesn't kill us it just makes us smell bad. If I want to smell like pine trees, I will go and frolic in some wood, naked and free. You people really tick me off.

—Israel Vasquez, Student

1. How effective is Mr. Vasquez's essay?

   _____ Strong thesis statement?   _____ Good supporting details?

   _____ Logical organization?   _____ Effective conclusion?

2. Discuss your underlinings. What details or lines in the essay did you like the most? Explain as exactly as possible why you like something or why it made you laugh.

3. Mr. Vasquez's sense of humor comes through to readers. Does he also achieve his goal of presenting a roach's point of view?

4. Would you suggest any revisions? Is this essay effective or offensive? Why? Does the final paragraph provide a strong and humorous conclusion, or does it seem like an afterthought?

5. This essay contains several serious grammar errors. Can you find and correct them? What two error patterns does this fine writer need to watch out for?

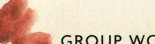 ## GROUP WORK

In writing as in life, it is often easier to spot other people's errors than our own. In your group or class, discuss *your* particular error patterns and how you have learned to catch them. Do you have problems with comma splices, *-ed* verb endings, or prepositional phrases? Discuss any proofreading tricks and techniques you have learned to spot and correct those errors successfully in your own papers. Have someone jot down the best techniques that your group mates have used, and be prepared to share these with the class.

WRITING AND REVISING IDEAS

1. Adopt a new point of view; discuss your life as a bird, animal, insect, or object.

2. Write as a person of another gender, ethnic group, or period in history.

Unit 7

Strengthening Your Spelling

532

CHAPTER 40

Spelling

A. Suggestions for Improving Your Spelling

Accurate spelling is an important ingredient of good writing. No matter how interesting your ideas are, if your spelling is poor, your writing will not be effective.

Some Tips for Improving Your Spelling

- **Look closely at the words on the page**. Use any tricks you can to remember the right spelling. For example, "The *a*'s in *separate* are separated by an *r*," or "*Dessert* has two *s*'s because you want two desserts."

- **Use a dictionary**. Even professional writers frequently check spelling in a dictionary. As you write, underline the words you are not sure of and look them up when you write your final draft. If locating words in the dictionary is a real problem for you, consider a "poor speller's dictionary."

● **Use a spell checker**. If you write on a computer, make a habit of using the spell-check software. See Part B for tips and cautions about spell checkers.

● **Keep a list of the words you misspell**. Look over your list whenever you can and keep it handy as you write.

● **Look over corrected papers for misspelled words (often marked *sp*.)**. Add these words to your list. Practice writing each word three or four times.

● **Test yourself**. Use flash cards or have a friend dictate words from your list or from this chapter.

● **Review the basic spelling rules explained in this chapter**. Take time to learn the material; don't rush through the entire chapter all at once.

● **Study the spelling list on page 543, and test yourself on these words**.

● **Read through Chapter 41, "Look-Alikes/Sound-Alikes," for commonly confused words (*their*, *there*, and *they're*, for instance)**. The practices in that chapter will help you eliminate some common spelling errors from your writing.

B. Computer Spell Checkers

Almost all computer programs are equipped with a spell checker. A spell checker picks up spelling errors and gives you alternatives for correcting them. Get in the habit of using this feature as your first and last proofreading task.

What a spell checker cannot do is think. If you've mistyped one word for another—*if* for *it*, for example—the spell checker cannot bring it to your attention. If you've written *then* for *than*, the spell checker cannot help. Proofread your paper *after* using the spell checker. For questions about words that sound the same but are spelled differently, check Chapter 41, "Look-Alikes/Sound-Alikes." Run spell check again after you've made all your corrections. If you've introduced a new error, the spell checker will let you know.

PRACTICE 1

With a group of four or five classmates, read this poem, which "passed" spell check. Can your group find and correct all the errors that the spell checker missed?

Eye halve a spelling check her,

It came with my pea see.

It clearly marques four my revue,

Miss steaks eye can knot sea.

I've run this poem threw it.

Your Shirley please too no

Its letter perfect in it's weigh.

My checker tolled me sew.

C. Spotting Vowels and Consonants

To learn some basic spelling rules, you must know the difference between vowels and consonants.

> The **vowels** are *a, e, i, o,* and *u.*
> The **consonants** are *b, c, d, f, g, h, j, k, l, m, n, p, q, r, s, t, v, w, x,* and *z.*
> The letter *y* can be either a vowel or a consonant, depending on its sound:
>
> | | |
> |---|---|
> | **daisy** | **sky** |
> | **yellow** | **your** |

- In both *daisy* and *sky, y* is a vowel because it has a vowel sound: an *ee* sound in *daisy* and an *i* sound in *sky.*

- In both *yellow* and *your, y* is a consonant because it has the consonant sound of *y.*

PRACTICE 2

Write *v* for vowel and *c* for consonant in the space on top of each word. Be careful of the *y*.

EXAMPLE

```
 c   v   c   v   c
 h   o   p   e   d
```

1.
```
 _   _   _   _
 r   e   l   y
```

2.
```
 _   _   _   _   _   _   _
 p   e   r   h   a   p   s
```

3.
```
 _   _   _   _   _   _   _
 i   n   s   t   e   a   d
```

4.
```
 _   _   _   _
 y   a   w   n
```

5.
```
 _   _   _   _   _
 f   o   r   g   e
```

6.
```
 _   _   _   _   _   _   _   _   _
 b   y   s   t   a   n   d   e   r
```

D. Doubling the Final Consonant (in Words of One Syllable)

When you add a suffix or an ending that begins with a vowel (like *-ed, -ing, -er, -est*) to a word of one syllable, double the final consonant *if* the last three letters of the word are *consonant-vowel-consonant* or *c-v-c.*

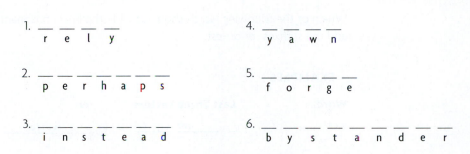

> | | |
> |---|---|
> | **plan + ed = planned** | **swim + ing = swimming** |
> | **thin + est = thinnest** | **light + er = lighter** |

● *Plan, swim,* and *thin* all end in *cvc*; therefore, the final consonants are doubled.

● *Light* does not end in *cvc*; therefore, the final consonant is not doubled.

PRACTICE 3

Which of the following words should double the final consonant? Check to see whether the word ends in *cvc*. Then add the suffixes *-ed* and *-ing*.

EXAMPLES

Word	Last Three Letters	-*ed*	-*ing*
drop	cvc	dropped	dropping
boil	vvc	boiled	boiling
1. tan			
2. brag			
3. mail			
4. peel			
5. wrap			

PRACTICE 4

Which of the following words should double the final consonant? Check for *cvc*. Then add the suffixes *-er* or *-est*.

EXAMPLES

Word	Last Three Letters	-*er*	-*est*
wet	cvc	wetter	wettest
cool	vvc	cooler	coolest
1. deep			
2. short			
3. red			
4. dim			
5. bright			

E. Doubling the Final Consonant (in Words of More Than One Syllable)

When you add a suffix that begins with a vowel to a word of more than one syllable, double the final consonant *if*:

(1) the last three letters of the word are *cvc*, and

(2) the accent or stress is on the *last* syllable.

> **begin + ing = beginning**   **control + ed = controlled**

- *Begin* and *control* both end in *cvc.*
- In both words, the stress is on the last syllable: *be-gin', con-trol'.* (Pronounce the words aloud and listen for the correct stress.)
- Therefore, *beginning* and *controlled* double the final consonant.

> **listen + ing = listening**   **visit + ed = visited**

- *Listen* and *visit* both end in *cvc.*
- However, the stress is *not* on the last syllable: *lis'-ten, vis'-it.*
- Therefore, *listening* and *visited* **do not** double the final consonant.

PRACTICE 5

Which of the following words should double the final consonant? First, check for *cvc*; then check final stress. Then add the suffixes *-ed* and *-ing*.

EXAMPLES

Word	Last Three Letters	-ed	-ing
repel	cvc	repelled	repelling
enlist	vcc	enlisted	enlisting
1. happen			
2. admit			
3. offer			
4. prefer			
5. compel			

F. Dropping or Keeping the Final *E*

When you add a suffix that begins with a vowel (like *-able, -ence, -ing*), drop the final *e*.

move + ing = moving   **pure + ity = purity**

● *Moving* and *purity* both drop the final *e* because the suffixes *-ing* and *-ity* begin with vowels.

When you add a suffix that begins with a consonant (like *-less, -ment, -ly*), keep the final *e*.

home + less = homeless   **advertise + ment = advertisement**

● *Homeless* and *advertisement* keep the final *e* because the suffixes *-less* and *-ment* begin with consonants.

Here are some exceptions to memorize:

argument	courageous	knowledgeable	truly
awful	judgment	simply	manageable

PRACTICE 6

Add the suffix indicated for each word.

EXAMPLES

hope + ing = _____*hoping*_____

hope + ful = _____*hopeful*_____

1. love + able = _____

2. love + ly = _____

3. pure + ly = _____

4. pure + er = _____

5. complete + ing = _____

6. complete + ness = _____

7. enforce + ment = _____

8. enforce + ed = _____

9. arrange + ing = _____

10. arrange + ment = _____

PRACTICE 7

Add the suffix indicated for each word.

EXAMPLES

come + ing = _____coming_____

rude + ness = _____rudeness_____

1. guide + ance = _____   6. sincere + ly = _____

2. manage + ment = _____   7. like + able = _____

3. dense + ity = _____   8. response + ible = _____

4. polite + ly = _____   9. judge + ment = _____

5. motive + ation = _____   10. fame + ous = _____

G. Changing or Keeping the Final Y

When you add a suffix to a word that ends in -*y*, change the *y* to *i* if the letter before the *y* is a consonant.
Keep the final *y* if the letter before the *y* is a vowel.

happy + ness = happiness   portray + ed = portrayed

● The *y* in *happiness* is changed to *i* because the letter before the *y* is a consonant, *p*.

● The *y* in *portrayed* is not changed because the letter before it is a vowel, *a*.

However, when you add -*ing* to words ending in *y*, always keep the *y*:

copy + ing = copying   delay + ing = delaying

Here are some exceptions to memorize:

day + ly = daily   pay + ed = paid
lay + ed = laid   say + ed = said

PRACTICE 8

Add the suffix indicated to each of the following words.

EXAMPLES

marry + ed = _____married_____

buy + er = _____buyer_____

1. try + ed = _____
2. vary + able = _____
3. worry + ing = _____
4. pay + ed = _____
5. enjoy + able = _____

6. wealthy + est = _____
7. day + ly = _____
8. duty + ful = _____
9. display + s = _____
10. occupy + ed = _____

PRACTICE 9

Add the suffix in parentheses to each word.

1. beauty (fy) _____
   (ful) _____
   (es) _____
2. lonely (er) _____
   (est) _____
   (ness) _____

3. betray (ed) _____
   (ing) _____
   (al) _____
4. study (es) _____
   (ous) _____
   (ing) _____

H. Adding -S or -ES

Nouns usually take an -s or an -es ending to form the plural. Verbs take an -s or -es in the third person singular (he, she, or it).

Add -es instead of -s if a word ends in ch, sh, ss, x, or z (the -es adds an extra syllable to the word):

> **box + es = boxes**   **crutch + es = crutches**   **miss + es = misses**

Add -es instead of -s for most words that end in o:

> **do + es = does**   **hero + es = heroes**
> **echo + es = echoes**   **tomato + es = tomatoes**
> **go + es = goes**   **potato + es = potatoes**

Here are some exceptions to memorize:

pianos   sopranos

radios   solos

When you change the final *y* to *i* in a word,* add *-es* instead of *-s*:

fry + es = fries   **marry + es = marries**   **candy + es = candies**

PRACTICE 10

Add *-s* or *-es* to the following nouns and verbs, changing the final *y* to *i* when necessary.

EXAMPLES

sketch _____*sketches*_____

echo _____*echoes*_____

1. watch _____

2. tomato _____

3. reply _____

4. company _____

5. bicycle _____

6. piano _____

7. donkey _____

8. dictionary _____

9. boss _____

10. hero _____

I. Choosing *IE* or *EI*

Write *i* before *e*, except after *c* or in an *ay* sound like *neighbor* or *weigh*.

achieve, niece   **deceive**   **vein**

● *Achieve* and *niece* are spelled *ie*.

● *Deceive* is spelled *ei* because of the preceding *c*.

● *Vein* is spelled *ei* because of its *ay* sound.

However, words with a *shen* sound are spelled with an *ie* after the *c*: *ancient, conscience, efficient, sufficient*.

Here are some exceptions to memorize:

either   seize

neither   society

foreign   their

height   weird

_____

* See Part G of this chapter for more on changing or keeping the final *y*.

PRACTICE 11

Pronounce each word out loud. Then fill in either *ie* or *ei*.

1. bel __ __ ve
2. __ __ ght
3. effic __ __ nt
4. n __ __ ther
5. cash __ __ r

6. ch __ __ f
7. soc __ __ ty
8. rec __ __ ve
9. fr __ __ nd
10. consc __ __ nce

11. h __ __ ght
12. ach __ __ ve
13. v __ __ n
14. for __ __ gn
15. perc __ __ ve

PRACTICE 12   REVIEW

Test your knowledge of the spelling rules in this chapter by adding suffixes to the following words. If you have trouble, the part in which the rule appears is shown in parentheses.

	Part		Part
1. nerve + ous _____	(F)	6. occur + ed _____	(E)
2. drop + ed _____	(D)	7. carry + ing _____	(G)
3. hope + ing _____	(F)	8. tomato + s/es _____	(H)
4. busy + ness _____	(G)	9. believe + able _____	(F)
5. radio + s/es _____	(H)	10. day + ly _____	(G)

PRACTICE 13   REVIEW

Circle the correctly spelled word in each pair.

1. writting, writing
2. receive, recieve
3. begining, beginning
4. greif, grief
5. relaid, relayed

6. piece, peice
7. resourceful, resourcful
8. argument, arguement
9. marries, marrys
10. thier, their

J. Spelling Lists

Commonly Misspelled Words

Following is a list of words that are often misspelled. As you can see, they are words that you might use daily in speaking and writing. The trouble spot, the part of each word that is usually spelled incorrectly, has been put in bold type.

To help yourself learn these words, you might copy each one twice, making sure to underline the trouble spot, or copy the words on flash cards and have someone test you.

Commonly Misspelled Words

1. absen**ce**	26. ei**ghth**	51. maint**enance**	76. re**cog**nize
2. a**c**quaint**ance**	27. emba**rrass**	52. math**e**matics	77. refe**re**nce
3. a**cross**	28. envir**on**ment	53. mean**t**	78. **rhy**thm
4. a**dd**ress	29. espe**cially**	54. mor**t**gage	79. ridi**cu**lous
5. **a lot**	30. ex**agge**rate	55. ne**cess**ary	80. **schedule**
6. ans**wer**	31. exer**cise**	56. ner**vous**	81. **sci**entific
7. a**pp**ointment	32. famil**iar**	57. notic**eable**	82. separate
8. a**pp**roxima**te**	33. fina**lly**	58. o**cc**asion	83. sim**ilar**
9. arg**u**ment	34. for**eign**	59. o**ccurr**ence	84. sin**ce**
10. a**thle**te	35. gove**rn**ment	60. opin**ion**	85. spe**ech**
11. begi**nn**ing	36. gramma**r**	61. optimist	86. stren**gth**
12. beha**vi**or	37. guid**ance**	62. particular	87. su**cc**ess
13. busi**ness**	38. hei**ght**	63. **per**form	88. **sur**prise
14. cal**en**dar	39. i**ll**egal	64. **per**haps	89. **tau**ght
15. ca**reer**	40. immed**iately**	65. perso**nn**el	90. tempe**ra**ture
16. cons**ci**ence	41. import**ant**	66. **phy**si**cally**	91. tho**rough**
17. cons**cious**	42. in**teg**ration	67. po**ssess**	92. though**t**
18. crow**ded**	43. in**telli**gent	68. po**ssible**	93. thr**ough**
19. defin**ite**	44. inte**re**st	69. practi**cal**	94. tire**d**
20. de**scribe**	45. inte**rf**ere	70. **pre**fer	95. **tru**ly
21. desp**erate**	46. jew**el**ry	71. pre**ju**dice	96. until
22. di**ff**erent	47. ju**dgm**ent	72. privil**ege**	97. us**ually**
23. dis**app**oint	48. knowle**dge**	73. prob**ably**	98. vacuum
24. dis**app**rove	49. laboratory	74. **psy**cholo**gy**	99. w**eight**
25. doesn't	50. mai**ntain**	75. pu**rsue**	100. wri**tt**en

"First off, there's no 'y' in résumé . . . "

www.Cartoon Stock.com

Personal Spelling List

In your notebook, keep a list of words that *you* misspell. Add words to your list from corrected papers and from the exercises in this chapter. First, copy each word as you misspelled it, underlining the trouble spot; then write the word correctly. Study your list often. Use this form:

As I Wrote It	Correct Spelling
1. *probly*	*probably*
2.	
3.	

PROOFREADING STRATEGY

If poor spelling is one of your personal error patterns, keep your Personal Spelling List of errors and a dictionary beside you as you write, and try these strategies:

1. Use the **bottom-up proofreading technique**. Read your draft sentence by sentence from the last sentence to the first. This will help you spot possible misspellings and typos more easily.

2. Ask **someone who is a good speller** to read your draft and help you spot any misspellings and typos. Then correct these yourself; this will help you learn correct spellings. Tutors in your college's writing lab or classmates who have a good eye for errors can be excellent sources of help.

PRACTICE 14   REVIEW

Using the bottom-up technique described above, proofread the following essay for spelling errors. (Be careful: There are misspelled words from both the exercises in this chapter and the spelling list.) Correct any errors by writing above the lines.

SNIFFING FOR A CURE

(1) In addition to the joy and love they bring to humans, some dogs peform practicle tasks as well, from guiding the blind to detecting bombs. (2) But a recently proven canine skill may be the most surpriseing and usefull of all: dogs can smell cancer. (3) In 1989, a medical journal reported that a woman's dog kept niping at a mole on her leg. (4) The pooch's wierd behavior sent her to the doctor, who diagnosed cancer and saved her life. (5) Similer stories of dogs sniffing cancers had been told for years, but this one dropped a small bomb.

(6) It grabbed the intrest of Dr. Michael McCullough, a sientist in California. (7) He knew that dogs pick up scents 10,000 times better than humans. (8) McCullough also knew that tumors release diffrent chemicals from healthy cells; these chemicals must have odors. (9) He and his team trained five dogs to reconize breath samples from early-stage breast and lung cancer patients. (10) Incredably, in 2006, their results showed that the dogs' succes at sniffing out breast cancer was 88 percent and lung cancer, 99 percent!

(11) Research in Germany confirms that traned dogs could save thousands of lives by catching cancer early. (12) The goal is to get a breathalyzer-like sample from every pateint during routine medical exams. (13) Our best friends might be our best disease detectors, too.

EXPLORING ONLINE

http://grammar.ccc.commnet.edu/grammar/cgi-shl/quiz20.pl/spelling_quiz3.htm
Interactive spelling test: three endings

http://www.esldesk.com/esl-quizzes/misspelled-words/index.htm
Challenge yourself: 500 commonly misspelled words in English. Learn new words and quiz yourself.

CourseMate for *Evergreen*

Visit *Evergreen* CourseMate for more practices and quizzes, videos to accompany the readings, career and job-search resources, ESL help, and live links to every Exploring Online in the book.

CHAPTER 41

Look-Alikes/ Sound-Alikes

The pairs or sets of words in this chapter might look or sound alike, but they have different meanings. Review this chart, studying any words that confuse you (for instance, *it's* and *its* or *affect* and *effect*). Add these to your Personal Error Patterns Chart and be sure to do the practice exercises in this chapter.

Word	Meaning	Examples
a	Used before a word beginning with a consonant or a consonant sound	*a* man *a* house *a* union (here *u* sounds like the consonant *y*)
an	Used before a word beginning with a vowel (a, e, i, o, u) or silent h	*an* igloo *an* apple *an* hour (*h* in *hour* is silent)
and	Joins words or ideas together	Emma *and* Daisuke are taking the same biology class.
accept	To receive	I *accepted* his offer of help.
except	Other than; excluding	Everyone *except* Marcelo thinks it's a good idea.
affect	To have an influence on; to change	Her father's career as a chef *affected* her decision to attend culinary school.
effect	(noun) The result of a cause or an influence (verb) To cause	Careful proofreading had a positive *effect* on Carl's grades. Will the U.S. Senate be able to *effect* changes in the tax law?
been	Past participle form of *to be*; usually used after the helping verb *have, has,* or *had*	She has *been* a poet for ten years.
being	The *–ing* form of *to be*; usually used after the helping verb *is, are, am, was,* or *were*	They are *being* helped by the salesperson.

546

buy	To purchase	My aunt *buys* antique furniture at garage sales.
by	Near; by means of; before	They walked *by* and didn't say hello.
it's	Contraction of *it is* or *it has*	*It's* time to go fishing.
its	A possessive that shows ownership	Industry must do *its* share to curb pollution.
know	To have knowledge or understanding	Carlos *knows* he has to finish by 6 P.M.
knew	Past tense of the verb *know*	I *knew* it.
no	A negative	He is *no* longer dean of academic affairs.
new	Recent, fresh, unused	I love your *new* hat.
lose	To misplace; not to win	Be careful not to *lose* your way on those back roads.
loose	Too large; not tightly fitting	This shirt is not my size; it's *loose*.
past	That which has already occurred; it is over with	Never let the *past* interfere with your hopes for the future.
passed	The past tense of the verb *to pass*	The wild geese *passed* overhead.
quiet	Silent, still	The woods are *quiet* tonight.
quit	To give up; to stop doing something	Last year I *quit* drinking.
quite	Very; exactly	He was *quite* tired after skateboarding for two hours.
rise	To get up by one's own power	The moon *rises* at 9 P.M.
raise	To lift an object; to grow or increase	*Raise* your right hand.
sit	To seat oneself	*Sit* up straight.
set	To place or put something down	Don't *set* your workout clothes on the dining room table.
suppose	To assume or guess	Nhean *supposes* that geology will be interesting.
supposed	Ought to or should (it is followed by *to*)	You were *supposed* to wash and wax the car.
their	A possessive that shows ownership	The singers couldn't find *their* wigs.
there	Indicates a direction; also a way of introducing a thought	I wouldn't go *there* again. *There* is a fly in my soup.
they're	A contraction: *they + are = they're*	If *they're* coming, count me in.
then	Afterward; at that time	First we went to the concert, and *then* we had pizza and champagne.
than	Used in a comparison	She is a better student *than* I.
through	In one side and out the other; finished; by means of	The rain came *through* the open window. *Through* practice, I can do anything.
though	Although (used with *as, though* means *as if*)	*Though* he rarely speaks, he has a huge vocabulary. It was *as though* I had never ridden a bicycle.

to	Toward	We are going *to* the computer lab.
	To can also be combined with a verb to form an infinitive	Where do you want *to* go for lunch?
too	Also; very	Eugene is going skydiving, *too*.
two	The number 2	There are *two* new nursing courses this term.
use	To make use of	Why do you *use* green ink?
used	In the habit of; accustomed to (it is followed by *to*)	I am not *used* to getting up at 4 A.M.
weather	Refers to atmospheric conditions	In June, the *weather* in Spain is lovely.
whether	Implies a question	*Whether* or not you succeed depends on you.
where	Implies place or location	*Where* have you been all day?
were	The past tense of *are*	We *were* driving south when the hurricane hit.
we're	A contraction: *we + are = we're*	Since *we're* in the city, let's go to the zoo.
whose	Implies ownership and possession	*Whose* Kindle is that?
who's	A contraction of *who is* or *who has*	*Who's* knocking at the window?
your	A possessive that shows ownership	*Your* knowledge astonishes me!
you're	A contraction: *you + are = you're*	*You're* the nicest person I know.

Personal Look-Alikes/Sound-Alikes List

In your Personal Error Patterns Chart or your notebook, keep a list of look-alikes and sound-alikes that you have trouble with. Add words to your list from corrected papers and from the exercises in this chapter; consider such pairs as *adapt/adopt, addition/edition, device/devise, stationery/stationary,* and so forth.

First, write the word you used incorrectly; then write its meaning or use it correctly in a sentence, whichever best helps you remember. Now do the same with the word you meant to use.

Word **Meaning**

1. *though* *means although*

    through *We hiked through the woods.*

2. _____ _____

    _____ _____

3. _____ _____

    _____ _____

4. _____ _____

    _____ _____

PRACTICE 1

Write a paragraph using as many of the look-alikes and sound-alikes as possible. Exchange paragraphs with a classmate and check each other's work.

PRACTICE 2

Read each sentence carefully and then circle the correct word or words. If you aren't sure, refer to the chart.

1. The Trail of Tears has long (been, being) one of the United States' most shameful memorials.

2. This historic trail traces the path traveled by 16,000 Cherokee forced (buy, by) the U.S. government to leave (their, there) homelands.

3. Like their Seminole, Chickasaw, Choctaw, and Creek neighbors (whose, who's) lands the white settlers wanted, the Cherokee marched westward at gunpoint (threw, through) five states.

4. From Tennessee through Arkansas, they walked in snow and bitter winter (weather, whether), many without warm clothing or even shoes.

5. Weakened by starvation, disease, and cold, they pushed (too, to) Indian Territory in what is now eastern Oklahoma.

6. In March 1839, about 12,000 reached (their, they're) final destination, a thousand miles from home.

7. Behind them (where, were) the graves of 4,000 grandparents, parents, (an, and) children who were unable to complete the punishing journey.

8. In the Cherokee language, this relocation is called *Nu na da ul tsun yi,* which means "The Place (Where, Were) They Cried."

9. Today, the Trail of Tears cuts the American landscape like (a, an) scar.

10. (Its, It's) a (quiet, quite) but powerful reminder of (passed, past) mistakes that most Americans hope will not be made again.

"The Trail of Tears,"
painted by American
artist Robert Lindneux
in 1942

© The Granger Collection, New York

PRACTICE 3

The following paragraphs contain 19 look-alike/sound-alike errors. Proofread for these errors, writing the correct word choice above the line.

(1) If your fighting a cold, feeling blue, or just wanting to live a long, healthy life, you should no about a force more potent then pills: your friends. (2) Researchers are discovering that friendship is quiet important to both physical and psychological well-being. (3) People with strong friendships are less likely then others to get colds, perhaps because there less stressed. (4) Friends help us fight serious diseases, to. (5) A 2006 study of 3,000 nurses with breast cancer found that women with good friends were for times more likely to live than women with no close friends. (6) Interestingly, there survival rates were not effected by weather or not they had husbands. (7) Both sexes live longer if they have close friends, through.

(8) Friendship even rises our confidence level as we face challenges. (9) University of Virginia researchers use a fascinating model to study this. (10) They took students to the base of a steep hill, put weighted backpacks on them, an asked them to estimate the steepness of the hill they we're about to climb. (11) The students who stood next to there friends gave lower estimates of the hill's steepness than those who stood alone. (10) The longer the friends had known each other, the less steep the hill looked two them! (11) Our friends not only help us cut lose and have fun but also make tough times a bit easier.

Friendships promote both physical and mental health, according to researchers.

iStockphoto.com/Jacob Wackerhausen

PRACTICE 4 TEAMWORK: CRITICAL THINKING AND WRITING

In a group with several classmates, go over your answers to Practice 3. Did you find and correct all 19 errors? Now discuss the experiment conducted by the University of Virginia (paragraph 2). Do you agree that this experiment shows that friends make us more confident in facing challenges? If so, can your group think of two reasons why this might be true?

PROOFREADING STRATEGY

If you tend to confuse the look-alikes/sound-alikes, **keep your Personal Error Patterns Chart updated** with the specific words you misuse, such as *their* and *there*, *affect* and *effect*, and *your* and *you're*.

Every time you proofread, **search your draft for every one of the words you confuse.** If you are using a computer, use the *"Find"* feature to locate them. Then double-check the meaning of the sentence to make sure that you've used and spelled the word correctly.

PRACTICE 5 REVIEW

The following essay contains a number of look-alike/sound-alike errors. Proofread for these errors, paying special attention to the words on your Personal Error Patterns Chart. Write each correct word above the line.

ISABEL ALLENDE

(1) Possibly the best-known female writer of Latin-American literature, Isabel Allende has survived many political and personal tragedies. (2) Most of those events have found there way into her books. (3) Born in 1942, Allende was raise by her mother in Chile after her parents' divorce. (4) When her uncle, President Salvador Allende, was killed during a military coup in 1973, she fled. (5) For the next 17 years, she lived in Venezuela, were she was unable to find work and felt trapped in a unhappy marriage.

(6) One day, learning that her grandfather was dying in Chile, Allende began to write him a long letter; that letter grew until it became her first novel. (7) Still her most famous book, *The House of the Spirits* established Allende's style of writing, which combines political realism

and autobiography with dreams, spirits, an magic. (8) The novel, which was banned in Chile, was translated into more then 25 languages and in 1994 was made into a movie.

(9) Buy 1988, Allende had divorced, moved to northern California, remarried, and written her fourth novel, *The Infinite Plan*, which is her second husband's story. (10) Her next book traced the profound affect on Allende of the death of her daughter, Paula. (11) The book *Paula*, like *The House of the Spirits*, was suppose to be a letter, this time too her daughter, who lay in a coma in a Madrid hospital.

(12) After *Paula* was published, Allende stopped writing for several years. (13) She started again in 1996, on January 8, the same day of the year that she had begun every one of her books. (14) The result was *Aphrodite*, a nonfiction book about food and sensuality that was quiet different from Allende's passed work. (15) With renewed energy to right again, Allende spun the tale of an independent woman who leaves her home in Chile to move to San Francisco during the Gold Rush. (16) Two novels, *Daughter of Fortune* and *Portrait in Sepia*, complete her story.

(17) Isabel Allende is famous for been a passionate storyteller who's writing captures both the Latin-American and the universal human experience. (18) As the first Latina to write a major novel in the mystical tradition, she not only created a sensation, but she paved the way for other female Hispanic writers, including Julia Alvarez and Sandra Cisneros.

EXPLORING ONLINE

http://grammar.ccc.commnet.edu/grammar/notorious2.htm#quizzes

Excellent look-alikes/sound-alikes quizzes

http://a4esl.org/q/h/homonyms.html

Confused by English words that sound alike? Practice and learn
with these excellent quizzes.

CourseMate for _Evergreen_

Visit _Evergreen_ CourseMate for more practices and quizzes, videos
to accompany the readings, career and job-search resources,
ESL help, and live links to every Exploring Online in the book.

Writers' Workshop

Discuss a Time When You Felt Blessed

Some writers are naturally good spellers, and others are not. If you belong to the latter group, this unit has given you some techniques and tools for overcoming your spelling problems.

In your group or class, read this student's essay, aloud if possible. Underline the ideas and sentences you find especially effective. If you spot any spelling errors, correct them.

Rain

(1) It is interesting to watch the way people act when rain starts falling. Most run for cover, especialy the women who just got there hair done. The guy with the brand new shoes also trys to find a dry spot. Many people think, "They're goes the day." That's what I thought before I went to the big sand box.

(2) It happened last year around March. President Bush decided Iraq was a threat to the United States, and of course being a Marine meant I was one of the first to go. Our first weeks were the hardest because we had to get aclimated to the whether. Iraq has got to be one of the hotest places on Earth, and I swear that you can be motionless and still be soaked with sweat. The glare almost hurts, even in sunglasses. Those days I prayed for rain as I never thought I would.

(3) It finely happened in the middle of June; I was outside my tent doing pushups with a fellow Marine. The sky did not darken or cloud up. Instead, the rain came down in one great splash as if the sky had held on for awhile and just could not hold on any longer. We all smiled at the sky and then noded at each other. At that moment, we felt we were been blessed. Some guys took there shirts off, and some started jumping around like little kids. Not one of us ran for cover, and those who were inside there tents came out to join in the celebration. For a few minutes, we all forgot that we were at war.

(4) That rain gave us new energy and hope. We knew from that day on that everything was going to be all right. Even those who disliked each other shook hands in the name of rain. We felt more then special because God had shown us his blessings.

(5) When I got back home last August, I took my girlfriend to the movies. As we left the theater, it started to rain. Everybody started runing into the subway station, and most looked fustrated because the rain had ruined their night. My girlfriend started pulling my arm, but

I slowed my pace. She asked if I was crazy because I was not rushing like everyone else. I smiled at her and told her that I wanted to walk in Central Park. She laughed at me; however, she agreed because, as she said, I had just come back from war, and she wanted to please me. During our walk, I felt the same joy I had felt that day in June. I told her how that moment blessed us in the hell of war, and how special rain can be.

—Gayber E. Guzman, Student

1. How effective is Mr. Guzman's essay?

   _____ Strong thesis statement?   _____ Good supporting details?

   _____ Logical organization?   _____ Effective conclusion?

2. Discuss your underlinings. What details or lines in the essay did you like the most? Explain as exactly as possible why something struck you as interesting or moving.

3. Every narrative should have a clear point. What point does Mr. Guzman make by telling this story?

4. Have you had an experience of sudden appreciation for small things or of knowing clearly what really matters? What prompted this insight?

5. This student's spelling errors are distracting in an otherwise thoughtful and well-written essay. What suggestions would you make to him for improving his spelling?

6. Do you see any error patterns (one error made two or more times) that this student needs to watch out for?

 GROUP WORK

In your group, find and correct the spelling errors in this essay. See if your group can find every error. Hint: There are 15 misspelled or confused words.

WRITING AND REVISING IDEAS

1. Discuss a time when you felt blessed.

2. Discuss something you took for granted and fully appreciated only after it was gone.

Unit 8

Reading Selections*

*For a list of the readings organized according to theme, see page TI-1

Reading Strategies for Writers

The 19 enjoyable and thought-provoking reading selections that follow deal with many of the concerns you have as a student, as a worker, and as a member of a family. Your instructor may ask you to read and think about a selection for class discussion or for a composition either at home or in class.

The more carefully you read these selections, the better you will be able to discuss and write about them. Below are ten strategies that can help you become a more effective reader and writer:

1. **Note the title**. A title, of course, is your first clue as to what the selection is about. For example, the title "The Addiction Solution We Never Use" lets you know that the selection will discuss a solution for addiction and probably the reasons it isn't used or should be used.

   A title may also tell you which method of development the author is using. For instance, a selection entitled "Gaga or Madonna?" might be a comparison/contrast essay, perhaps contrasting the two performers' creativity, outrageousness, or lasting impact; one entitled "Stages of a Child's Moral Development" might be a process piece explaining how a child learns to make moral choices.

2. **Underline main ideas**. If you read a long or difficult selection, you may forget some of the important ideas soon after you have finished the essay. However, underlining or highlighting these key ideas as you read will later help you review more easily. You may wish to number main ideas to help you follow the development of the author's thesis.

3. **Write your reactions in the margins**. Feel free to express your agreement or disagreement with the ideas in a selection by commenting "yes," "no," "Important—compare with Jessica Bennett's essay," or "Is he kidding?" in the margins.

   You will often be asked to write a "reaction paper," a composition explaining your thoughts about or reaction to the author's ideas. The comments that you have recorded in the margins will help you formulate a response.

4. **Prepare questions**. As you tackle more difficult reading selections, you may come across material that is hard to follow. Of course, reread the passage to see if a second reading helps. If it does not, put a question mark in the margin.

   Ask a friend or the instructor to help answer your questions. Do not be embarrassed to ask for explanations in class. Instructors appreciate careful readers who want to be sure that they completely understand what they have read.

557

5. **Note possible composition topics.** As you read, you may think of topics for compositions related to the ideas in the selection. Jot these topics in the margins or write about them in your journal. They may become useful if your instructor asks you for an essay based on the selection.

6. **Note effective writing.** If you are particularly moved by a portion of the selection—a phrase, a sentence, or an entire paragraph—underline or highlight it. You may wish to quote it later in class or use it in your composition.

7. **Circle unfamiliar words.** As you read, you will occasionally come across unfamiliar words. If you can guess what the word means from its context—from how it is used in the sentence or in the passage—do not interrupt your reading to look it up. Interruptions can cause you to lose the flow of ideas in the selection. Instead, circle the word and check it in a dictionary later.

8. **Vary your pace.** Some essays can be read quickly and easily. Others may require more time if the material is difficult or if much of the subject matter is unfamiliar to you. Be careful not to become discouraged, skimming a particularly difficult section just to get through with it. Extra effort will pay off.

9. **Reread.** If possible, budget your time so you can read the selection a second or even a third time. One advantage of rereading is that you will be able to discuss or write about the essay with more understanding. Ideas that were unclear may become obvious; you may even see new ideas that you failed to note the first time around.

   Another advantage is that by the second or third reading, your responses may have changed. You may agree with ideas you rejected the first time; you may disagree with ones you originally agreed with. Rereading gives you a whole new perspective!

10. **Do not overdo it.** Marking the selection as you read can help you become a better reader and writer. However, too many comments may defeat your purpose. You may not be able to decipher the mass—or mess—of underlinings, circles, and notes that you have made. Be selective.

The following essay has been marked, or annotated, by a student. Your responses might be different. Use this essay as a model to help you annotate other selections in this book—and reading material for your other courses as well.

MARTIN LINDSTROM

What Your Supermarket Knows About You

"What Your Supermarket Knows About You" by Martin Lindstrom from TIME. Used by permission of Martin Lindstrom.

affluent = wealthy people

The global financial crisis of 2008 hit consumers hard. Two years later, and they're still reeling. Spending is down across the board, and even the more affluent are watching their pennies. In this fearful climate, retailers are applying ever more scientific and psychological tactics to lure them back. This was made clear to me on a memorable day in 2010 when I visited the laboratory outside of Chicago of one of the world's largest consumer goods manufacturers. 1

Main idea: retailers use special tactics to get us to buy things

After driving for nearly two hours, I reached my destination: a huge, imposing warehouse, with no outward signage, and a vast parking lot full of cars. A friendly receptionist checked my identity, had me sign all sorts of paperwork, and directed me through a door labeled Control Room. It was massive, and resembled images I've seen of NASA's operations 2

Is this an illustration essay?

area—row upon row of people staring intently at hundreds of screens, only they were monitoring shoppers pushing carts around the aisles of a supermarket that had been designed to test their responses to different marketing strategies. "Take a careful look at this lady," said one of the monitors, pointing to a middle-aged woman on the screen. "She's about to enter our latest speed-bump area. It's designed to have her spend 45 seconds longer in this section, which can increase her average spend by as much as 73%. I call it the zone of seduction."

This particular section of the market was different from the usual 3 aisle. For a start, it had different floor tiles—a type of parquetry imparting a sense of quality. And instead of the cart gliding imperceptibly across nondescript linoleum, it made a clickety-clack sound, causing the shopper to instinctively slow down. The shopper's speed was displayed at the top of the screen, and as soon as she entered the zone, her pace noticeably slowed. She began looking at a tall tower of Campbell's soup, and then plucked a can off the top. Bingo! The sign in front of the display read: "1.95. Maximum three cans per customer." Before the shopper slowly sauntered off, she had carefully selected three cans for her cart.

Sophisticated as we may be, there's no getting away from our more 4 primitive survival technique of hoarding food to see us through lean times. So when we come across a deal that appeals to this ancient instinct, dopamine is released in our brain, giving us an instant rush of pleasure. My guide explained the exercise: "Yesterday we ran exactly the same offer, with two distinct differences. There was a dollar sign in front of the price, and no 'Maximum 3 cans per customer' line. We also gave the shoppers smaller-sized carts and changed the floor tiles." These seemingly small changes translated into big differences. On the first day of the experiment, only 1 in 103 purchased Campbell's soup. Today, however, it seemed that 1 in every 14 succumbed—a sevenfold increase.

Over several months of experimenting with signage, the team noticed 5 that using a dollar sign in front of the price decreases our likelihood of making the purchase. The dollar sign is a symbol of cost, rather than gain. Removing the sign helps the consumer sidestep the harsh reality of outstanding bills and longer-term financial concerns. No doubt the larger cart and the changed floor tiles also played their part, but what was most surprising was our need to hoard. The dictum allowing only three cans per customer sealed the deal.

The next time you go grocery shopping, take a look at the signs, the 6 type of floor, and even the carts. Everything has been designed with an eye towards getting you to grab those three cans of something that was not on your list. The more attention you pay to the details, the more aware you'll become of how you're being manipulated. One thing is for certain; whoever made those three cans will be watching you just as closely.

Writing ideas—
- *Visit Wal-Mart and identify tactics and their effects.*
- *Think more about how all stores convince us to buy. What other ways do they manipulate customers? Clothing stores—lively music, flattering light, "skinny mirrors"?*
- *Observe shoppers and their behavior in the store.*
- *Ways to be a wiser, savvier consumer*

ELLEN GOODMAN

Multitasking or Mass ADD?[1]

"In Multitasking Olympics, We all lose" by Ellen Goodman. Reprinted by permission of International Creative Management, Inc. Copyright by Ellen Goodman.

Many busy people believe that multitasking—doing two or more things at once—makes them more efficient and successful. The more e-mails, text messages, phone calls, and Internet downloads they can juggle, the more productive they feel. But recent studies turn this idea upside down. In this article from the Record Searchlight, *Pulitzer Prize-winning columnist Ellen Goodman argues that our misguided passion for multitasking comes at a high price.*

Once I considered myself a champion multitasker. This was in the days when the Olympic event of technological multitasking was unloading the dishwasher while talking on the phone. Fast forward: I am at a computer with a land phone to my left and an iPhone to my right. As I type into my Word program, Google is alerting me to the latest news in the health care debate, e-mails are coming in on two of my three accounts, and I have a text message from my daughter. Even this, however, puts me at the low end of the multitask scale since I am not Facebooking while surfing the Net, downloading iTunes, and driving. 1

The truth is that I am terrible at multitasking. Worse yet, I have believed that my inability to simultaneously YouTube and IM makes me a technological dinosaur. Surely, the younger generation look down at my inability to text and talk the way I look down on someone's inability to walk and chew gum at the same time. More to the point, I have lived with the conviction that the people watching TV while Twittering and surfing the Web have a secret skill, like polyphonics who can sing two notes at the same time. 2

Now I find out from Stanford's Clifford Nass that there is no secret. High multitaskers are not better at anything, even multitasking. They are worse. Nass, who teaches human–computer interactions, led a research team that studied 100 students, high and low multitaskers. The high ones focused poorly, remembered less, and were more easily distracted. They couldn't shift well from one task to another and they couldn't organize well. They couldn't figure out what was important and what wasn't. 3

"We didn't enter this research trying to beat on multitaskers but to find out their talent," says Nass. "And we found out they had none." 4

Nass has yet to study whether they were bad at paying attention to begin with or were driven to distraction. But there's a suspicion, he says, that "we may be breeding a generation of kids whose ability to pay attention may be destroyed." Before I exhale in relief and bond with others waving this research in front of their children's (distracted) faces, a couple of things have to be noted. First of all, as Nass ruefully says, many multitaskers believe they are the efficient exception. They can talk and chew e-mails at the same time. Second and related, simultaneous media immersion[2] has become the new norm. 5

....

1. ADD: (Attention Deficit Disorder) inability to focus one's attention and concentrate on a task
2. immersion: deep involvement

This is what normal looks like. It's the norm in offices where people are often required to keep chat rooms open and respond to e-mail within 30 minutes. It's in sports arenas where fans in mega-buck seats actually watch the game on big-screen TVs and text friends. It's in college classrooms where the professor's lecture competes with the social networking site on a laptop. It's also the new social norm. It's part of a world in which people walk together side by side talking separately on cell phones. Where you hear the click of a friend's keyboard while you're talking on the phone. And where Nass recently watched two students holding a serious conversation while one was surfing the Internet.

If the ratcheting up of media multitasking is teaching us not to pay attention, is it also training us not to expect attention? Nass, who is turning his research to everything from airline pilots to fourth-graders, has begun to wonder about students. "I don't know that this generation values focused attention. The notion that attention is at the core of a relationship is declining," he suspects. "Is saying to someone 'I am going to give you my undivided attention' still one of the greatest gifts I can give?" Or has multitasking led us to a kind of attention infidelity?

What we are learning is our limits. Not just on the highway where texting-while-driving is as common as it is terrifying, but at the dinner table where kids insist (wrongly) that they can text and talk, at the office where multitasking is multidistracting, and in relationships where face-to-face competes with Facebook. It turns out that we have only so many coins to pay attention. How do we hold their value in a media world?

I'll explain just as soon as I answer this e-mail. . . . Now then, where was I?

DISCUSSION AND WRITING QUESTIONS

1. Does Goodman's first paragraph effectively introduce her essay? Does it make you want to keep reading? Be specific.

2. Do you multitask? What tasks do you often perform simultaneously? After reading this article, do you still believe that you are good at shifting your attention among several things at once?

3. What, according to the author, are some negative effects of multitasking? Would you add any other drawbacks to her list? Are we really "breeding a generation of kids whose ability to pay attention may be destroyed" (paragraph 5)? If so, what effects would that have on their lives?

4. The researcher, Clifford Nass, says that "undivided attention" (paragraph 7) is the greatest gift that we can give others. Do you agree? Give a specific example to support your opinion.

WRITING ASSIGNMENTS

1. For one week, conduct an experiment: refuse to multitask. When you talk on the phone, don't surf the Internet or send text messages. When you eat dinner or do homework, do only that. After a week, write a frank essay about the benefits and drawbacks you experienced when you focused on one thing at a time.

2. Contrast a "champion multitasker" you know with someone who *never* multitasks. Consider such points of contrast as their productivity, their personalities, their stress levels, their success at the tasks they attempt.

3. Harvard Medical School now sends young doctors to art classes. Apparently, doctors who learn to pay close attention to works of visual art become much better at studying and diagnosing their patients during visits. Why do you think this might be true? Should everyone go to art class?

SANDRA CISNEROS

Only Daughter

"Only Daughter" by Sandra Cisneros. Copyright by Sandra Cisneros. First published in *Glamour*, November 1990. By permission of Susan Bergholz Literary Services, New York, NY and Lamy, NM. All rights reserved.

Sandra Cisneros is the author of The House on Mango Street *and other books. She often writes about the experience of being bicultural, bilingual, and female. Here, she explores the ways in which her birth family helped define who she is—and is not.*

1 Once, several years ago, when I was just starting out my writing career, I was asked to write my own contributor's note for an anthology I was part of. I wrote: "I am the only daughter in a family of six sons. *That* explains everything."

2 Well, I've thought about that ever since, and yes, it explains a lot to me, but for the reader's sake I should have written: "I am the only daughter in a *Mexican* family of six sons." Or even: "I am the only daughter of a Mexican father and a Mexican-American mother." Or: "I am the only daughter of a working-class family of nine." All of these had everything to do with who I am today.

3 I was/am the only daughter and *only* a daughter. Being an only daughter in a family of six sons forced me by circumstance to spend a lot of time by myself because my brothers felt it beneath them to play with a *girl* in public. But that aloneness, that loneliness, was good for a would-be writer—it allowed me time to think and think, to imagine, to read, and prepare myself.

4 Being only a daughter for my father meant my destiny would lead me to become someone's wife. That's what he believed. But when I was in the fifth grade and shared my plans for college with him, I was sure he understood. I remember my father saying, "*Qué bueno, mi'ja,* that's good." That meant a lot to me, especially since my brothers thought the idea hilarious. What I didn't realize was that my father thought college was good for girls—good for finding a husband. After four years in college and two more in graduate school, and still no husband, my father shakes his head even now and says I wasted all that education.

5 In retrospect, I'm lucky my father believed daughters were meant for husbands. It meant it didn't matter if I majored in something silly like English. After all, I'd find a nice professional eventually, right? This allowed me the liberty to putter about embroidering my little poems and stories without my father interrupting with so much as a "What's that you're writing?"

6 But the truth is, I wanted him to interrupt. I wanted my father to understand what it was I was scribbling, to introduce me as "My only daughter, the

Sandra Cisneros placed this photo of herself at an old town in Mexico on her website. What do the clothing, jewelry, and location say about this woman?

writer." Not as "This is only my daughter. She teaches." *Es maestra*—teacher. Not even *profesora*.

In a sense, everything I have ever written has been for him, to win his 7
approval even though I know my father can't read English words, even though my father's only reading includes the brown-ink *Esto* sports magazines from Mexico City and the bloody *¡Alarma!* magazines that feature yet another sighting of *La Virgen de Guadalupe* on a tortilla or a wife's revenge on her philandering[1] husband by bashing his skull in with a *molcajete* (a kitchen mortar made of volcanic rock). Or the *fotonovelas*, the little picture paperbacks with tragedy and trauma erupting from the characters' mouths in bubbles.

My father represents, then, the public majority. A public who is uninterested 8
in reading, and yet one whom I am writing about and for, and privately trying to woo.

When we were growing up in Chicago, we moved a lot because of my 9
father. He suffered bouts of nostalgia. Then we'd have to let go our flat, store the furniture with mother's relatives, load the station wagon with baggage and bologna sandwiches and head south. To Mexico City.

We came back, of course. To yet another Chicago flat, another Chicago 10
neighborhood, another Catholic school. Each time, my father would seek out the parish priest in order to get a tuition break, and complain or boast: "I have seven sons."

He meant *siete hijos*, seven children, but he translated it as "sons." "I have 11
seven sons." To anyone who would listen. The Sears Roebuck employee who sold us the washing machine. The short-order cook where my father ate his ham-and-eggs breakfasts. "I have seven sons." As if he deserved a medal from the state.

My papa. He didn't mean anything by that mistranslation, I'm sure. But 12
somehow I could feel myself being erased. I'd tug my father's sleeve and whisper: "Not seven sons. Six! And *one daughter*."

1. philandering: unfaithful

When my oldest brother graduated from medical school, he fulfilled my 13
father's dream that we study hard and use this—our heads, instead of this—
our hands. Even now my father's hands are thick and yellow, stubbed by a
history of hammer and nails and twine and coils and springs. "Use this," my
father said, tapping his head, "and not this," showing us those hands. He
always looked tired when he said it.

Wasn't college an investment? And hadn't I spent all those years in college? 14
And if I didn't marry, what was it all for? Why would anyone go to college and
then choose to be poor? Especially someone who had always been poor.

Last year, after ten years of writing professionally, the financial rewards 15
started to trickle in. My second National Endowment for the Arts Fellowship.
A guest professorship at the University of California, Berkeley. My book,
which sold to a major New York publishing house.

At Christmas, I flew home to Chicago. The house was throbbing, same as 16
always; hot *tamales* and sweet *tamales* hissing in my mother's pressure cooker, and
everybody—my mother, six brothers, wives, babies, aunts, cousins—talking too
loud and at the same time, like in a Fellini² film, because that's just how we are.

I went upstairs to my father's room. One of my stories had just been 17
translated into Spanish and published in an anthology of Chicano writing, and
I wanted to show it to him. Ever since he recovered from a stroke two years
ago, my father likes to spend his leisure hours horizontally. And that's how
I found him, watching a Pedro Infante movie on Galavisión and eating rice
pudding.

There was a glass filmed with milk on the bedside table. There were several 18
vials of pills and balled Kleenex. And on the floor, one black sock and a plastic
urinal that I didn't want to look at but looked at anyway. Pedro Infante was
about to burst into song, and my father was laughing.

I'm not sure if it was because my story was translated into Spanish, or 19
because it was published in Mexico, or perhaps because the story dealt with
Tepeyac, the *colonia* my father was raised in and the house he grew up in, but
at any rate, my father punched the mute button on his remote control and read
my story.

I sat on the bed next to my father and waited. He read it very slowly. As 20
if he were reading each line over and over. He laughed at all the right places
and read lines he liked out loud. He pointed and asked questions: "Is this
So-and-so?" "Yes," I said. He kept reading.

When he was finally finished, after what seemed like hours, my father 21
looked up and asked: "Where can we get more copies of this for the relatives?"

Of all the wonderful things that happened to me last year, that was the 22
most wonderful.

DISCUSSION AND WRITING QUESTIONS

1. In what two ways can the title of this essay, "Only Daughter," be
   interpreted?

2. What expectations did the author's father have for his daughter? Did his
   limited expectations create any advantages for her? Why did the father's
   comment "I have seven sons" bother her so much?

----

2. Fellini: an Italian movie director whose films were full of strange, unforgettable characters

3. In paragraphs 16 through 18, Cisneros describes one of her trips home. She includes vivid details that help the reader "see" and "feel" life inside her parents' house. Which details do you find especially effective? Although the home is in Chicago, which details capture the family's Mexican heritage?

4. For years, the author wanted her father's attention and approval. Why do you think he finally appreciated her achievement as a writer?

WRITING ASSIGNMENTS

1. In a group with three or four classmates, share statements about your personal history like those in Cisneros's opening paragraphs. First, take five minutes working on your own, and then define yourself, using a

   two- or three-sentence pattern: "I am _____

   _____. That explains everything."

   Revise your sentences until you feel they capture a truth about you. Now share and discuss these statements with your group. What is most and least effective or intriguing about each? Use your definition as the main idea for a paper to be written at home.

2. Have you (or has someone you know) wanted another person's approval so badly that it influenced how you conducted your life? Who was the person whose approval you sought, and why was that approval so important? What did you do to please him or her and what happened? Was it worth it?

3. What were your family's expectations for you as you grew up, and how did those expectations affect your life choices? Were the expectations high or low? Did your gender or place in the family (oldest, middle, youngest) affect them? Did you accept or reject the family's vision for you?

BRENT STAPLES

A Brother's Murder

"About Men: A Brother's Murder" by Brent Staples from THE NEW YORK TIMES. Copyright The New York Times. All rights reserved. Used by permission.

Brent Staples grew up in a rough, industrial city. He left to become a successful journalist, but his younger brother remained. Staples's story of his brother is a reminder of the grim circumstances in which so many young men of the inner city find themselves today.

It has been more than two years since my telephone rang with the news that my younger brother Blake—just twenty-two years old—had been murdered. The young man who killed him was only twenty-four. Wearing a ski mask, he emerged from a car, fired six times at close range with a massive .44 Magnum, then fled. The two had once been inseparable friends. A senseless rivalry— 1 beginning, I think, with an argument over a girlfriend—escalated[1] from posturing,[2] to threats, to violence, to murder. The way the two were living, death could have come to either of them from anywhere. In fact, the assailant had already survived multiple gunshot wounds from an accident much like the one in which my brother lost his life.

As I wept for Blake I felt wrenched backward into events and circumstances   2 that had seemed light-years gone. Though a decade apart, we both were raised in Chester, Pennsylvania, an angry, heavily black, heavily poor, industrial city southwest of Philadelphia. There, in the 1960s, I was introduced to mortality, not by the old and failing, but by beautiful young men who lay wrecked after sudden explosions of violence. The first, I remembered from my fourteenth year—Johnny, brash lover of fast cars, stabbed to death two doors from my house in a fight over a pool game. The next year, my teenage cousin, Wesley, whom I loved very much, was shot dead. The summers blur. Milton, an angry young neighbor, shot a crosstown rival, wounding him badly. William, another teenage neighbor, took a shotgun blast to the shoulder in some urban drama and displayed his bandages proudly. His brother, Leonard, severely beaten, lost an eye and donned a black patch. It went on.

I recall not long before I left for college, two local Vietnam veterans—one   3 from the Marines, one from the Army—arguing fiercely, nearly at blows about which outfit had done the most in the war. The most killing, they meant. Not much later, I read a magazine article that set that dispute in a context. In the story, a noncommissioned officer—a sergeant, I believe—said he would pass up any number of affluent, suburban-born recruits to get hard-core soldiers from the inner city. They jumped into the rice paddies with "their manhood on their sleeves," I believe he said. These two items—the veterans arguing and the sergeant's words—still characterize for me the circumstances under which black men in their teens and twenties kill one another with such frequency. With a touchy paranoia born of living battered lives, they are desperate to be *real* men. Killing is only machismo taken to the extreme. Incursions[3] to be punished by death were many and minor, and they remain so: they include stepping on the wrong toe, literally; cheating in a drug deal; simply saying "I dare you" to someone holding a gun; crossing territorial lines in a gang dispute. My brother grew up to wear his manhood on his sleeve. And when he died, he was in that group—black, male and in its teens and early twenties— that is far and away the most likely to murder or be murdered.

I left the East Coast after college, spent the mid- and late 1970s in Chicago   4 as a graduate student, taught for a time, then became a journalist. Within ten years of leaving my hometown, I was overeducated and "upwardly mobile," ensconced[4] on a quiet, tree-lined street where voices raised in anger were scarcely ever heard. The telephone, like some grim umbilical, kept me connected to the old world with news of deaths, imprisonings and misfortune. I felt emotionally beaten up. Perhaps to protect myself, I added a psychological dimension to the physical distance I had already achieved. I rarely visited my hometown. I shut it out.

As I fled the past, so Blake embraced it. On Christmas of 1983, I traveled   5 from Chicago to a black section of Roanoke, Virginia, where he then lived.

1. escalated: increased
2. posturing: trying to appear tough
3. incursions: attacks, violations
4. ensconced: settled comfortably

The desolate public housing projects, the hopeless, idle young men crashing against one another—these reminded me of the embittered town we'd grown up in. It was a place where once I would have been comfortable, or at least sure of myself. Now, hearing of my brother's forays[5] into crime, his scrapes with police and street thugs, I was scared, unsteady on foreign terrain.[6]

I saw that Blake's romance with the street life and the hustler image had flowered dangerously. One evening that late December, standing in some Roanoke dive among drug dealers and grim, hair-trigger losers, I told him I feared for his life. He had affected the image of the tough he wanted to be. But behind the dark glasses and the swagger, I glimpsed the baby-faced toddler I'd once watched over. I nearly wept. I wanted desperately for him to live. The young think themselves immortal, and a dangerous light shone in his eyes as he spoke laughingly of making fools of the policemen who had raided his apartment looking for drugs. He cried out as I took his right hand. A line of stitches lay between the thumb and index finger. Kickback from a shotgun, he explained, nothing serious. Gunplay had become part of his life.

I lacked the language simply to say: Thousands have lived this for you and died. I fought the urge to lift him bodily and shake him. This place and the way you are living smells of death to me, I said. Take some time away, I said. Let's go downtown tomorrow and buy a plane ticket anywhere, take a bus trip, anything to get away and cool things off. He took my alarm casually. We arranged to meet the following night—an appointment he would not keep. We embraced as though through glass. I drove away.

As I stood in my apartment in Chicago holding the receiver that evening in February 1984, I felt as though part of my soul had been cut away. I questioned myself then, and I still do. Did I not reach back soon enough or earnestly enough for him? For weeks I awoke crying from a recurrent dream in which I chased him, urgently trying to get him to read a document I had, as though reading it would protect him from what had happened in waking life. His eyes shining like black diamonds, he smiled and danced just beyond my grasp. When I reached for him, I caught only the space where he had been.

DISCUSSION AND WRITING QUESTIONS

1. Staples says that he was "introduced to mortality" in Chester, Pennsylvania, in the 1960s (paragraph 2). What does he mean?

2. What does the author mean when he says his brother grew up to "wear his manhood on his sleeve" (paragraph 3)? Does he imply that there are other ways of expressing masculinity?

3. Staples speaks of a dream in which he holds a document for his brother to read (paragraph 8). What do you suppose that document might say? What does this dream seem to say about communication between the two brothers?

4. Staples begins his narrative by describing the moment at which he hears of Blake's death. Why does he *start* with this event, instead of moving toward it?

---

5. forays: undertakings, trips
6. terrain: ground

WRITING ASSIGNMENTS

1. Write a narrative about a shocking incident that took place in your neighborhood. Like Staples, you may want to start with the incident, and then narrate the smaller events in the story that led up to it. Or you can follow time order and end with the incident.

2. Do you think Brent Staples could have done more to change his brother? Can we really influence others to change their lives?

3. In a group with three or four classmates, discuss the most significant problem facing young people in the inner city today. Is it crime? Drugs? Lack of educational or employment opportunities? Choose one problem and decide how it can be solved. Your instructor may ask you to share your solution with the class. Then write your own paper, discussing the problem you think is most significant and proposing a solution.

JHUMPA LAHIRI

My Two Lives

"My Two Lives" by Jhumpa Lahiri from NEWSWEEK, MSNBC.com. Copyright. Used by permission of the author via William Morris Entertainment.

Jhumpa Lahiri is an Indian American who writes about immigrants to the United States—their struggles to make a home for themselves and conflicts between first- and second-generation immigrants. Lahiri's first book of short stories, Interpreter of Maladies, *won the coveted Pulitzer Prize. In this* Newsweek *essay, she discusses her own slow process of merging her lives "on either side of the hyphen."*

1

I have lived in the United States for almost 37 years and anticipate growing old in this country. Therefore, with the exception of my first two years in London, "Indian-American" has been a constant way to describe me. Less constant is my relationship to the term. When I was growing up in Rhode Island in the 1970s, I felt neither Indian nor American. Like many immigrant offspring, I felt intense pressure to be two things, loyal to the old world and fluent in the new, approved of on either side of the hyphen. Looking back, I see that this was generally the case. But my perception as a young girl was that I fell short at both ends, shuttling between two dimensions that had nothing to do with one another.

2

At home I followed the customs of my parents, speaking Bengali[1] and eating rice and dal[2] with my fingers. These ordinary facts seemed part of a secret, utterly alien way of life, and I took pains to hide them from my American friends. For my parents, home was not our house in Rhode Island but Calcutta, where they were raised. I was aware that the things they lived for—the Nazrul[3] songs they listened to on the reel-to-reel,[4] the family they

---

1. Bengali: the language spoken in eastern India and Bangladesh
2. dal: a simmered, spicy lentil dish
3. Nazrul: Bangladeshi poet who supported India's independence
4. reel-to-reel: an early magnetic tape recorder

missed, the clothes my mother wore that were not available in any store in any mall—were at once as precious and as worthless as an outmoded[5] currency.

I also entered a world my parents had little knowledge or control of: school, books, music, television, things that seeped in and became a fundamental aspect of who I am. I spoke English without an accent, comprehending the language in a way my parents still do not. And yet there was evidence that I was not entirely American. In addition to my distinguishing name and looks, I did not attend Sunday school, did not know how to ice-skate, and disappeared to India for months at a time. Many of these friends proudly called themselves Irish-American or Italian-American. But they were several generations removed from the frequently humiliating process of immigration, so that the ethnic roots they claimed had descended underground whereas mine were still tangled and green. According to my parents, I was not American, nor would I ever be no matter how hard I tried. I felt doomed by their pronouncement, misunderstood and gradually defiant. In spite of the first lessons of arithmetic, one plus one did not equal two but zero, my conflicting selves always canceling each other out.

When I first started writing, I was not conscious that my subject was the Indian-American experience. What drew me to my craft was the desire to force the two worlds I occupied to mingle on the page as I was not brave enough, or mature enough, to allow in life. My first book was published in 1999, and around then, on the cusp[6] of a new century, the term "Indian-American" has become part of this country's vocabulary. I've heard it so often that these days, if asked about my background, I use the term myself, pleasantly surprised that I do not have to explain further. What a difference from my early life, when there was no such way to describe me, when the most I could do was to clumsily and ineffectually explain.

As I approach middle age, one plus one equals two, both in my work and in my daily existence. The traditions on either side of the hyphen dwell in me like siblings, still occasionally sparring, one outshining the other depending on the day. But like siblings they are intimately familiar with one another, forgiving and intertwined. When my husband and I were married five years ago in Calcutta, we invited friends who had never been to India, and they came full of enthusiasm for a place I avoided talking about in my childhood, fearful of what people might say. Around non-Indian friends, I no longer feel compelled to hide the fact that I speak another language. I speak Bengali to my children, even though I lack the proficiency to teach them to read or write the language. As a child I sought perfection and so denied myself the claim to any identity. As an adult I accept that a bicultural upbringing is a rich but imperfect thing.

While I am American by virtue of the fact that I was raised in this country, I am Indian thanks to the efforts of two individuals. I feel Indian not because of the time I've spent in India or because of my genetic composition but rather because of my parents' steadfast presence in my life. They live three hours from my home; I speak to them daily and see them about once a month. Everything will change once they die. They will take certain things with

The Indian god Ganesha, lord of success, remover of obstacles

3

4

5

6

---

5. outmoded: dated
6. cusp: edge or turning point

them—conversations in another tongue, and perceptions about the difficulties of being foreign. Without them, the back-and-forth life my family leads, both literally and figuratively, will at last approach stillness. An anchor will drop, and a line of connection will be severed.

I have always believed that I lack the authority my parents bring to being Indian. But as long as they live, they protect me from feeling like an imposter. Their passing will mark not only the loss of the people who created me but the loss of a singular way of life, a singular struggle. The immigrant's journey, no matter how ultimately rewarding, is founded on departure and deprivation, but it secures for the subsequent generation a sense of arrival and advantage. I can see a day coming when my American side, lacking the counterpoint India has until now maintained, begins to gain ascendancy[7] and weight. It is in fiction that I will continue to interpret the term "Indian-American," calculating that shifting equation, whatever answers it may yield.

DISCUSSION AND WRITING QUESTIONS

1. As a child, Lahiri felt "intense pressure to be two things, loyal to the old world and fluent in the new." Do you think this pressure to choose between two identities is common, especially in children from immigrant families? What other contrasts does the author mention?

2. Lahiri calls the process of immigrating and adjusting to a new culture *humiliating* (paragraph 3). Do you think this is true for all immigrants? Why or why not? Has the immigration experience changed since Lahiri arrived in the 1970s at age three?

3. Do you ever feel that you too must manage two (or more) different lives even though you are not an immigrant? Be specific. If yes, do you feel torn between these lives or do you feel whole?

4. In the last paragraph, Lahiri seems to say that her parents are "real" Indians and she is an imposter; that "everything will change once they die." Do you find anything troubling about this perspective on the origins of cultural identity? Are our connections with the past this fragile?

WRITING ASSIGNMENTS

1. Most people juggle multiple identities—as students, workers, friends, spouses, parents. Write an essay titled "My Two Lives." Choose two of your identities and then either contrast the two or show how they share important similarities.

2. Is it necessary to spend most of one's life in one's native country to be an authority on that culture? Is it possible to be born in the U.S. and still represent one's cultural heritage to others? How?

3. Websites and blogs are becoming valuable tools for preserving cultures and traditions around the world. Describe how you would design a website, blog, or YouTube video to share or preserve an important element of your background. Take a look at the Cultural Awareness Project at **www.unitedplanet.org** to get ideas.

....
7. ascendancy: superiority, advantage

DAVE BARRY

Driving While Stupid

Dave Barry, "Driving While Stupid," MIAMI HERALD. Used by permission of Tribune Media Services.

Humorist Dave Barry loves to poke fun at Miami, his hometown ("Motto: an automatic-fire weapon in every home"). Barry has written over 30 books, none of which, he claims, contains useful information; he won a Pulitzer Prize for his humor columns that until 2005 ran in over 500 newspapers. Currently, Barry aspires to "continued immaturity followed by death." In this Miami Herald *column, he takes on bad drivers.*

So I have to tell you what I saw on the interstate the other night. First, though, you must understand that this was not just any old interstate. This was I-95 in downtown Miami, proud home of the worst darned drivers in the world.   1

I realize some of you are saying: "Oh yeah? If you want to see REALLY bad drivers, you should come to MY city!" Listen, I understand that this is a point of civic honor, and I am sure that the drivers in your city are all homicidal[1] morons. But trust me when I tell you that there is no way they can compete with the team that Miami puts on the road.   2

I know what I'm talking about. I have driven in every major U.S. city, including Boston, where the motorists all drive as though there is an open drawbridge just ahead, and they need to gain speed so they can jump across it.   3

www.CartoonStock.com

---

1. homicidal: murderous; intending to kill someone

I have also driven in Italy, where there is only one traffic law, which is
that no driver may ever be behind any other driver, the result being that at all
times, all the motorists in the nation, including those in funeral processions,
are simultaneously trying to pass. 4

I have ridden in a taxi in the Argentinean city of Mar del Plata (literally,
"Cover your eyes"), where (a.) nobody ever drives slower than 65 miles per
hour, even inside parking garages, and (b.) at night, many motorists drive with
their headlights off, because—a taxi driver told me this, and he was absolutely
serious—this extends the life of your bulbs. When he said this, we were in a
major traffic jam caused by an accident involving a truck and a horse. 5

I have also ridden on a bus in China, plowing through humongous[2]
traffic snarls involving trucks, cars, bicycles, ox-drawn carts and pedestrians,
all aggressively vying[3] for the same space, and where the bus driver would
sometimes physically push pedestrians out of the way. I don't mean with his
hands. I mean with the BUS. 6

My point is that I have seen plenty of insane driving techniques, and I am
telling you for a fact that no place brings so many of these techniques together
as Miami, where a stop sign has no more legal significance to most motorists
than a mailbox. The police down here have given up on enforcing the traffic
laws. If they stop you and find a human corpse in your trunk, they'll let you
off with a warning if it's your first one. 7

So I've seen pretty much everything on the roads here. Nevertheless, I
was surprised by the driver on the interstate the other night. I heard him
before I saw him, because his car had one of those extremely powerful
sound systems, in which the bass notes sound like nuclear devices being
detonated[4] in rhythm. So I looked in the mirror and saw a large convertible
with the top down overtaking me at maybe 600 miles per hour. I would
have tried to get out of his path, but there was no way to know what his
path was, since he was weaving back and forth across five lanes (out of a
possible three). 8

Fortunately, he missed me, and as he went past, I got a clear view of why he
was driving so erratically:[5] He was watching a music video. He was watching
it on a video screen that had been installed where the sun visor usually goes,
RIGHT IN FRONT OF HIS FACE, blocking his view of the road. I don't want to
sound like an old fud, but this seems to me to be just a tad hazardous. I distinctly
recall learning in driver's education class that, to operate a car, you need to be able
to see where the car is going, in case the need arises (you never know!) to steer. 9

Of course, more and more, drivers do not have time for steering, as they are
busy making phone calls, eating, reading, changing CDs, putting on makeup,
brushing their teeth, etc. I recently received mail from an alert reader named
Kate Chadwick who reports that she drove behind a man who was SHAVING
HIS HEAD, with his "visor mirror positioned just so, windows wide open for
hair disposal, and for a significant portion of the ride, no hands on the wheel." 10

But at least these drivers are able, from time to time, to glance at the road
whereas the guy I saw on I-95 basically could see only his video. I hope you agree
with me that this is insane. I also hope you are not reading this in your car. 11

....

2. humongous: huge, enormous

3. vying: competing

4. detonated: exploded

5. erratically: without a fixed or regular path

DISCUSSION AND WRITING QUESTIONS

1. Barry's essay is funny but focuses on a serious subject. What point does he make about some drivers?

2. How does Barry develop his persuasive thesis that Miami drivers are the worst in the world? How does he answer the opposition who might claim that other towns have the worst drivers?

3. Have you witnessed people "driving while stupid"? Give examples of roadway behaviors you have witnessed. In your view, how common is it to see people engaging in activities other than driving while they are driving?

4. Why in your view do some people engage in dangerous behaviors—like drug use, unprotected sex, or "sexting"—without seeming to notice the danger?

WRITING ASSIGNMENTS

1. Review Chapter 16, Part A, and then write a humorous illustration essay about self-defeating ways that people behave at work, study (or don't), or try to impress others. You might title your essay "Working (Attending College, or Dating) While Stupid."

2. Write a serious essay of persuasion on the subject of dangerous drivers. You might wish to argue for a forceful penalty for drivers caught "multitasking" while driving, or convince readers of the need for more driver training, or try to persuade drivers that driving without full concentration is taking their own lives and others' lives too lightly.

3. Discuss a time when you engaged in or witnessed dangerous behaviors. What happened? Did you learn anything from the experience?

ANA VECIANA-SUAREZ

When Greed Gives Way to Giving

Ana Veciana Suarez, "When Greed Gives Way to Giving," THE RECORD, p. L5 (MIAMI HERALD). Used by permission of Tribune Media Services.

If you suddenly made millions of dollars, what would you do with the money? Here Miami Herald columnist Ana Veciana-Suarez reports one man's surprising response to that situation. Like many newspaper writers, she employs a casual tone and style, but the questions she raises are profound.

In the flurry of life, you probably missed this story. I almost did, and that would have been too bad. Over in Belleville, Minnesota, a 67-year-old man named Bob Thompson sold his road-building company for $422 million back in July. He did not, as we would expect, buy himself a jet or an island, not even a new home. Instead, Thompson decided to share the wealth.   1

He divided $128 million among his 550 workers. Some checks exceeded annual salaries. And for more than 80 people, the bonus went beyond their wildest expectations: They became millionaires. Thompson even included some retirees and widows in his plan. What's more, he paid the taxes on those proceeds—about $25 million.

Employees were so flabbergasted[1] that the wife of an area manager tearfully said: "I think the commas are in the wrong place." The commas were right where they belonged. Thompson had made sure of that, had made sure, too, that not one of the workers would lose his or her job in the buyout.

I sat at the breakfast table stunned. I just don't know too many people or companies that would do something like that. Sure, many employers offer profit-sharing and stock-option plans. But outright giving? Nah. Employees rarely share in the bounty when the big payoff comes. In fact, many end up losing their jobs, being demoted,[2] seeking transfers, or taking early retirement. Insecurity—or better yet, the concept of every man for himself—is a verity[3] of work life in America.

Yet here is one man defying all of the stereotypes. I search for clues in his life, but find nothing out of the ordinary, nothing that stands out. He started the business in his basement with $3,500, supported by his schoolteacher wife. He has owned the same modest house for 37 years. His wood-paneled office has no Persian rugs or oil paintings, only photos of three children and five grandchildren. He admits to an indulgence or two: a Lincoln and an occasional Broadway show.

Yet he possesses something as priceless as it is rare: generosity. And he seems to be sheepishly modest even about that. "It's sharing good times, that's really all it is," he told a reporter. "I don't think you can read more into it. I'm a proud person. I wanted to go out a winner, and I wanted to go out doing the right thing." We all want to do the right thing, but blessed by a windfall,[4] would we have done as Thompson did? Maybe. I don't know. Honestly, I'm embarrassed to say I'm not sure I would have.

Perhaps, however, the more appropriate question is this: In our own more limited circumstances, do we share with others in the same spirit Thompson showed? Do we give beyond expectations? For most of us, generosity comes with limits. It is, by and large, a sum without sacrifice, a respectable token.

Some might say that Thompson's munificence[5] was token-like. After all, the $153 million is less than a third of his $422 million payoff. That kind of reasoning, however, misses the mark. Few of us give away even 10 percent, and if our income increases, the tendency is not to share more but to buy more, to hoard[6] more. Not Thompson. After finishing with his employees, he plans to continue giving away much of what's left of the $422 million.

---

1. flabbergasted: astonished; shocked
2. demoted: reduced in status or rank
3. verity: truth or reality
4. windfall: sudden, unexpected good fortune or personal gain
5. munificence: great generosity
6. hoard: accumulate in a private supply, usually more than needed

I suspect he is on to something. In a society where success tends to 9
be measured in what we can acquire, this guy instead is preaching and
practicing the opposite. Success, he is telling us, is in the giving back.
He seems to have mastered what many of us have yet to understand: the
difference between need and want, between the basic essentials and our
inchoate[7] desires. He has, by golly, defined *enough*. Maybe that's all the
wealth he needs.

DISCUSSION AND WRITING QUESTIONS

1. The author first tells the factual story of Bob Thompson's "windfall"
   and then discusses its meaning. What does she believe is the point, or
   importance, of his story?

2. Do you agree with the author that generosity is a rare quality in today's
   society? If so, why do you think this is true? If you know a truly generous
   person, describe his or her generosity to the class.

3. Buddhism, one of the world's major religions, teaches that the
   causes of human suffering are greed and selfish desire. Would you
   agree, or is this overstated? What is wrong with greed and selfish
   desire?

4. What point does the author make in the last sentence about the
   concept of "enough"? What is your own personal definition of
   "enough"?

WRITING ASSIGNMENTS

1. Do you know a person who "gives beyond expectations" or even makes
   personal sacrifices to help others? Write an essay illustrating that person's
   generosity with specific examples.

2. Veciana-Suarez discusses two definitions of success: the idea that success
   is acquiring as much as we can and Bob Thompson's idea that success is
   "giving back" (paragraph 9). Which of these is closer to the truth for you?
   Write an essay honestly exploring your personal definition of the word
   success.

3. What career path have you chosen to pursue or are considering
   now? Will that career lead you to your idea of success? Write about
   the top three rewards of that career for you (for example, salary,
   mental stimulation, security, fun, the chance to give back, to travel,
   and so on).

....
7. inchoate: only partially formed or developed

MALCOLM GLADWELL

10,000 Hours

Does success depend more on inborn talent or on hard work and practice? In this excerpt from his best-selling book Outliers: The Story of Success, *author Malcolm Gladwell discusses fascinating recent studies about what makes a winner in any field—be it business, music, basketball, or computer science.*

For almost a generation, psychologists around the world have been engaged in a spirited debate over a question that most of us would consider to have been settled years ago. The question is this: Is there such a thing as innate[1] talent? The obvious answer is yes. Not every hockey player born in January ends up playing at the professional level.[2] Only some do—the innately talented ones. Achievement is talent plus preparation. The problem with this view is that the closer psychologists look at the careers of the gifted, the smaller the role innate talent seems to play and the bigger the role preparation seems to play. 1

Exhibit A in the talent argument is a study done in the early 1990s by the psychologist K. Anders Ericsson and two colleagues at Berlin's elite Academy of Music. With the help of the Academy's professors, they divided the school's violinists into three groups. In the first group were the stars, the students with the potential to become world-class soloists. In the second were those judged to be merely "good." In the third were students who were unlikely to ever play professionally and who intended to be music teachers in the public school system. All of the violinists were then asked the same question: Over the course of your entire career, ever since you first picked up the violin, how many hours have you practiced? 2

Everyone from all three groups started playing at roughly the same age, around five years old. In those first few years, everyone practiced roughly the same amount, about two or three hours a week. But when the students were around the age of eight, real differences started to emerge. The students who would end up the best in their class began to practice more than everyone else: six hours a week by age nine, eight hours a week by age twelve, sixteen hours a week by age fourteen, and up and up, until by the age of twenty they were practicing—that is, purposefully and single-mindedly playing their instruments with the intent to get better—well over thirty hours a week. In fact, by the age of twenty, the elite performers had each totaled ten thousand hours of practice. By contrast, the merely good students had totaled eight thousand hours, and the future music teachers had totaled just over four thousand hours. 3

Ericsson and his colleagues then compared amateur pianists with professional pianists. The same pattern emerged. The amateurs never practiced more than about three hours a week over the course of their childhood, and 4

---

1. innate: possessed at birth; inborn
2. Studies have found that most professional Canadian hockey players were born between January and March.

by the age of twenty they had totaled two thousand hours of practice. The professionals, on the other hand, steadily increased their practice time every year, until by the age of twenty they, like the violinists, had reached ten thousand hours.

The striking thing about Ericsson's study is that he and his colleagues couldn't find any "naturals," musicians who floated effortlessly to the top while practicing a fraction of the time their peers did. Nor could they find any "grinds," people who worked harder than everyone else, yet just didn't have what it takes to break the top ranks. Their research suggests that once a musician has enough ability to get into a top music school, the thing that distinguishes one performer from another is how hard he or she works. That's it. And what's more, the people at the very top don't work just harder or even much harder than everyone else. They work much, *much* harder. 5

The idea that excellence at performing a complex task requires a critical minimum level of practice surfaces again and again in studies of expertise. In fact, researchers have settled on what they believe is the magic number for true expertise: ten thousand hours. 6

"The emerging picture from such studies is that ten thousand hours of practice is required to achieve the level of mastery associated with being a world-class expert—in anything," writes the neurologist Daniel Levitin. "In study after study, of composers, basketball players, fiction writers, ice skaters, concert pianists, chess players, master criminals, and what have you, this number comes up again and again. Of course, this doesn't address why some people get more out of their practice sessions than others do. But no one has yet found a case in which true world-class expertise was accomplished in less time. It seems that it takes the brain this long to assimilate[3] all that it needs to know to achieve true mastery." 7

This is true even of people we think of as prodigies.[4] Mozart, for example, famously started writing music at six. But, writes the psychologist Michael Howe in his book *Genius Explained*, 8

> by the standards of mature composers, Mozart's early works are not outstanding. The earliest pieces were all probably written down by his father, and perhaps improved in the process. Many of Wolfgang's childhood compositions, such as the first seven of his concertos for piano and orchestra, are largely arrangements of works by other composers. Of those concertos that only contain music original to Mozart, the earliest that is now regarded as a masterwork (No. 9, K. 271) was not composed until he was twenty-one: by that time Mozart had already been composing concertos for ten years. 9

The music critic Harold Schonberg goes further: Mozart, he argues, actually "developed late," since he didn't produce his greatest work until he had been composing for more than twenty years. 10

To become a chess grandmaster also seems to take about ten years. (Only the legendary Bobby Fischer got to that elite level in less than that amount of time: it took him nine years.) And what's ten years? Well, it's roughly how long it takes to put in ten thousand hours of hard practice. Ten thousand hours is the magic number of greatness. 11

---

3. assimilate: absorb and understand
4. prodigies: children who display exceptional talent

Here is the explanation for what was so puzzling about the rosters of the [12] Czech and Canadian national sports teams. There was practically no one on those teams born after September 1, which doesn't seem to make any sense. You'd think that there should be a fair number of Czech hockey or soccer prodigies born late in the year who are so talented that they eventually make their way into the top tier as young adults, despite their birth dates.

But to Ericsson and those who argue against the primacy[5] of talent, that [13] isn't surprising at all. That late-born prodigy doesn't get chosen for the all-star team as an eight-year-old because he's too small. So he doesn't get the extra practice. And without that extra practice, he has no chance at hitting ten thousand hours by the time the professional hockey teams start looking for players. And without ten thousand hours under his belt, there is no way he can ever master the skills necessary to play at the top level. Even Mozart—the greatest musical prodigy of all time—couldn't hit his stride until he had his ten thousand hours in. Practice isn't the thing you do once you're good. It's the thing you do that makes you good.

DISCUSSION AND WRITING QUESTIONS

1. Underline the author's thesis (paragraph 1). What examples in the body of the essay illustrate his point that preparation, not talent, builds expertise? Are you surprised by these findings? Why or why not?

2. The author cites research studies that support his argument. Pick one study and tell what makes it a credible, trustworthy source of information.

3. Do you think that practice improves our performance in everyday life? For instance, do most drivers drive more safely after a decade behind the wheel? Are parents better at parenting when they've put in ten years? Do college students have better study skills than high school students because they've passed the magic ten-year mark (from age 8, just beginning homework, to age 18, mastering how to study)? Explain.

4. Describe someone you know or admire who has developed a special talent through sheer hard work and practice. Is there a talent that *you* would be willing to cultivate with ten years (10,000 hours) of practice? Does this essay make you want to change anything about your work habits or goals?

WRITING ASSIGNMENTS

1. Many parents, hoping to discover and cultivate their children's innate talent, enroll their kids in sports, dance, music, or art lessons, or in child beauty pageants at a young age. Select one of these activities and argue for or against encouraging children's participation in it.

2. According to Gladwell, "Achievement is talent plus preparation" (paragraph 1). Others argue that people who excel (such as great leaders

---

5. primacy: the state of being first

or math geniuses) are "born, not made." Select one of these two ideas and write an illustration essay to develop your main point.

3. Write a process essay, explaining how to improve a specific skill (such as shooting foul shots, proofreading your writing, or saving money at the supermarket). In your explanation of the steps, make recommendations about the length and frequency of practice times.

JESSICA BENNETT

The Flip Side of Internet Fame

In this era of "viral videos" that race from one computer user to thousands or even millions of others with a few clicks of a mouse, almost anyone can quickly become an international celebrity—or a laughingstock. Newsweek writer Jessica Bennett explores the dark side of this Internet phenomenon and asks what privacy means when cameras and high speed are everywhere.

In 2002, Ghyslain Raza, a chubby Canadian teen, filmed himself acting out 1 a fight scene from "Star Wars" using a makeshift light saber. His awkward performance was funny, in part because it wasn't meant to be. And it certainly was never meant to be public: for nearly a year the video remained on a shelf in Raza's school's TV studio, where he'd filmed it. Sometime in 2003, though, another student discovered the video, digitized it and posted it online—and Raza's nightmare began. Within days, "Star Wars Kid" had become a viral frenzy. It was posted on hundreds of blogs, enhanced by music and special effects, and watched by millions. Entire websites were dedicated to the subject; one was even named one of *Time's* 50 best sites of 2003. Had that teenager wanted to be famous, he couldn't have asked for anything better. But in Raza's case it became a source of public humiliation, precisely what every kid fears the most.

Razas of the world take note: among the generation that's been reared 2 online, stories like this are becoming more and more common. They serve as important reminders of a dark side of instant Internet fame: humiliation. Already dozens of websites exist solely to help those who would shame others. There are sites for posting hateful rants about ex-lovers (DontDateHimGirl.com) and bad tippers (www.lousytippers.com), and for posting cell-phone images of public bad behavior (http://www.ihollaback.org/) and lousy drivers. As a new book makes clear in powerful terms, such sites can make or break a person, in a matter of seconds.

"Anybody can become a celebrity or a worldwide villain in an instant," 3 says Daniel Solove, a law professor at George Washington University and author of *The Future of Reputation: Gossip, Rumor and Privacy on the Internet* (Yale). "Some people may revel in that. But others might say that's not the role they wanted to play in life."

"Dog poop girl" wasn't the public role a South Korean student had in mind 4 when, in 2005, she refused to clean up after her dog in the subway in Seoul.

A minor infraction, perhaps, but another passenger captured the act on a cell-phone camera, posted it online and created a viral frenzy. The woman was harassed into dropping out of college. More recently a student at Lewis & Clark University in Portland, Ore., was publicly accused—on Facebook, the social-networking site—of sexually assaulting another student. Normally, such allegations[1] on campus are kept confidential. But in this case a Facebook group revealed his name, with the word "rapist" for the world to see, before the incident was ever even reported to the authorities. The accused teen was never arrested or charged, but he might as well have been: bloggers picked up the story, and a local alt-weekly put it on its cover, revealing graphic details of the encounter as described by the alleged[2] victim, without including the supposed perpetrator's version of events.

Public shaming, of course, is nothing new. Ancient Romans punished wrongdoers by branding them on the forehead—slaves caught stealing got *fur* (Latin for thief) and runaways got *fug* (fugitive). In Colonial America, heretics[3] were clamped into stocks in the public square, thieves had their hands or fingers cut off, and adulterers were forced to wear a scarlet A. More recently a U.S. judge forced a mail thief to wear a sign announcing his crime outside a San Francisco post office; in other places sex offenders have to post warning signs on their front lawns. 5

Although social stigma[4] can be a useful deterrent,[5] "the Internet is a loose cannon," says ethicist[6] Jim Cohen of Fordham University School of Law in New York. Online there are few checks and balances and no due process[7]—and validating the credibility of a claim is difficult, to say the least. Moreover, studies show that the anonymity of the Net encourages people to say things they normally wouldn't. *JuicyCampus*, a gossip website for U.S. college students, has made headlines by tapping into this urge. The site solicits juicy rumors under the protection of anonymity for sources. But what may have begun as fun and games has turned into a venue[8] for bigoted[9] rants and stories about drug use and sex that identify students by name. "Anyone with a grudge can maliciously[10] and sometimes libelously[11] attack defenseless students," Daniel Belzer, a Duke senior, told *Newsweek* in December. 6

Regulators find sites like JuicyCampus[12] hard to control. Laws on free speech and defamation[13] vary widely between countries. In the United States, proving libel requires the victim to show that his or her persecutor[14] intended malice, while the British system puts the burden on the defense to show that a statement is not libelous (making it much easier to prosecute). A 1996 U.S. law—Section 230 of the Communications Decency Act—specifically protects 7

1. allegations: claims or accusations as yet unproven
2. alleged: claimed but not proven
3. heretics: people who hold controversial opinions
4. stigma: a mark of disgrace
5. deterrent: that which prevents or discourages an action
6. ethicist: one who studies ethics and morality
7. due process: the following of rules to protect individual rights
8. venue: location
9. bigoted: prejudiced
10. maliciously: spitefully
11. libelously: with the intention of damaging someone's reputation
12. Juicy Campus: a website promoting campus gossip, shut down in 2009
13. defamation: damage to a person's reputation through written material
14. persecutor: tormentor

the operators of websites from liability[15] for the speech of their users. As long as the host of a site doesn't post or edit content, it has no liability. (If AOL, say, were held responsible for every poster, it would quickly go out of business.)

So, then, what's to stop a person from posting whatever he wants about you, if he can do so anonymously and suffer no repercussions?[16] For people who use blogs and social-networking sites like diaries, putting their personal information out there for the world to see, this presents a serious risk. "I think young people are seduced by the citizen-media notion of the Internet: that everyone can have their minutes of fame," says Barry Schuler, the former CEO of AOL who is now the coproducer of a new movie, *Look*, about public video surveillance. "But they're also putting themselves out there—forever."

Shaming victims, meanwhile, have little legal recourse.[17] Identifying posters often means having to subpoena[18] an anonymous IP address.[19] But that could lead nowhere. Many people share IP addresses on college networks or Wi-Fi hotspots, and many websites hide individual addresses. Even if a victim identifies the defamer, bloggers aren't usually rich enough to pay big damage awards. Legal action may only increase publicity—the last thing a shaming victim wants. "The law can only do so much," warns Solove.

Once unsavory[20] information is posted, it's almost impossible to retrieve. The family of the "Star Wars Kid," who spent time in therapy as a result of his ordeal, filed suit against the students who uploaded his video, and settled out of court. But dozens of versions of his video are still widely available, all over the Net. One of the bad boyfriends featured on DontDateHimGirl .com also sued, but his case was dismissed due to lack of jurisdiction.[21] The accused rapist at Lewis & Clark has also hired lawyers. But Google his name today, and the first entry has the word "rapist" in its title. If the "Star Wars Kid" has anything to teach us, it's that shame, like the force, will always be with you.

DISCUSSION AND WRITING QUESTIONS

1. This author uses examples to develop her point that viral videos can humiliate people and cause real harm. What examples does she give?

2. What kind of order does the author use to present examples in the first four paragraphs? All had their privacy violated for different reasons. Do you have more sympathy for some of these people than others? Why?

3. Have you or anyone you know ever posted videos, photographs, or personal information on the Internet? What are the potential consequences should that information fall into the hands of someone who bears a grudge?

15. liability: legal responsibility
16. repercussions: consequences
17. legal recourse: right to seek a legal remedy
18. subpoena: to order someone to appear in court
19. IP address: Internet Protocol number that identifies an individual computer in a network
20. unsavory: unpleasant or offensive
21. jurisdiction: power to apply the law

4. In paragraph 5, the author provides examples of public shaming used as punishment throughout history. Choose one of these public punishments and give the reasons why it was (or is) a fair or unfair punishment.

WRITING ASSIGNMENTS

1. According to the author, studies show that "the anonymity of the Net encourages people to say things they normally wouldn't" (paragraph 6). In your experience, is it true that anonymity makes it easier for people to say things that they would not say to someone's face? Give examples that support your view.

2. Psychologists claim that gossiping has some useful benefits, such as networking with others or forming social alliances. Do you agree? What do you think motivates people to gossip, in person or online? What functions does gossip serve?

3. The rapid growth of the Internet has taken violations of privacy to new levels; adequate laws to protect people do not yet exist. Does everyone deserve privacy protections, even for potentially harmful online activities? For instance, some gossip sites let individuals post information about others anonymously. Do you think this is right? Why or why not?

MAIA SZALAVITZ

How *Not* to Raise a Bully: The Early Roots of Empathy

With disturbing regularity, we hear news stories about bullied children and wonder why their suffering wasn't prevented. In this Time *magazine article, neuroscience[1] journalist Maia Szalavitz argues that parents and teachers can prevent bullying by teaching children empathy, a key human ability that experts claim is disappearing. Szalavitz is co-author of the book* Born for Love: Why Empathy is Essential—and Endangered.

Since the Jan. 14 death of Phoebe Prince, the 15-year-old in South Hadley, Mass., who committed suicide after being bullied by fellow students, many onlookers have meditated on whether the circumstances that led to her after-school hanging might have been avoided. Could teachers have stepped in and stopped the bullying? Could parents have done more to curtail[2] bad behavior? Or could preventive measures have been started years ago, in early childhood, long before bullies emerged and started heaping abuse on their peers? 1

Increasingly, neuroscientists, psychologists, and educators believe that bullying and other kinds of violence can indeed be reduced by encouraging empathy at an early age. Over the past decade, research in empathy—the ability to put ourselves in another person's shoes—has suggested that it is key, if not *the* key, to all human social interaction and morality. Without empathy, we would have no cohesive[3] society, no trust and no reason not to murder, cheat, steal, or lie. At best, we would act only out of self-interest; at worst, we would be a collection of sociopaths[4]. 2

---

1. neuroscience: branch of science that studies the brain
2. curtail: cut short
3. cohesive: holding together tightly
4. sociopaths: mentally ill people who lack any concern for others

Although human nature has historically been seen as essentially selfish, recent science suggests that it is not. The capacity for empathy is believed to be innate in most humans, as well as some other species—chimps, for instance, will protest the unfair treatment of others, refusing to accept a treat they have rightfully earned if another chimp doing the same work fails to get the same reward.   3

The first stirrings of human empathy typically appear in babyhood: newborns cry when hearing another infant's cry, and studies have shown that children as young as 14 months offer unsolicited[5] help to adults who appear to be struggling to reach something. Babies have also shown a distinct preference for adults who help rather than hinder others.   4

Canadian school children relate to a visiting baby through the Roots of Empathy program.

But like language, the development of this inherent tendency may be affected by early experience. As evidence, look no further than ancient Greece and the millennia-old child-rearing practices of Sparta and Athens. Spartans, who were celebrated almost exclusively as warriors, raised their ruling-class boys in an environment of uncompromising brutality—enlisting them in boot camp at age 7 and starving them to encourage enough deviousness[6] and cunning to steal food, which skillfully bred yet more generations of ruthless killers.   5

In Athens, future leaders were brought up in a more nurturing and peaceful way, at home with their mothers and nurses, starting education in music and poetry at age 6. They became pioneers of democracy, art, theater, and culture. "Just like we can train people to kill, the same is true with empathy. You can be taught to be a Spartan or an Athenian—and you can be taught to be both," says Teny Gross, executive director of the outreach group Institute for the Study and Practice of Nonviolence in Providence, R.I., and a former sergeant in the Israeli army.   6

What the ancient Greeks intuited is supported by research today. Childhood—as early as infancy—is now known to be a critical time for the development of empathy. And although children can be astonishingly resilient[7], surviving and sometimes thriving despite abuse and neglect, studies show that those who experience such early trauma are at much greater risk of becoming aggressive or even psychopathic later on, bullying other children or being victimized by bullies themselves.   7

....
5. unsolicited: not requested
6. deviousness: deceit, indirection
7. resilient: able to bounce back or recover after trauma

© Melanie Gordon

Simple neglect can be surprisingly damaging. In 2007, researchers published the first randomized, controlled study of the effect of being raised in an orphanage; that study, and subsequent research on the same sample of Romanian orphans, found that compared with babies placed with a foster family, those who were sent to institutions had lower IQs, slower physical growth, problems with human attachment, and differences in functioning in brain areas related to emotional development. 8

Institutionalized infants do not experience being the center of a loving family's attention; instead, they are cared for by a rotating staff of workers, which is inherently neglectful. The infants miss out on intensive, one-on-one affection and attachment with a parental figure, which babies need at that vulnerable age. Without that experience, they learn early on that the world is a cold, insecure and untrustworthy place. Their emotional needs having gone unmet, they frequently have trouble understanding or appreciating the feelings of others. 9

Nearly 90% of brain growth takes place in the first five years of life, and the minds of young children who have been neglected or traumatized often fail to make the connection between people and pleasure. That deficit can make it difficult for them to feel or demonstrate love later on. "You can enhance empathy by the way you treat children," says Martin Hoffman, an emeritus professor of psychology at New York University and a pioneer of empathy research, "or you can kill it by providing a harsh punitive[8] environment." 10

DISCUSSION AND WRITING QUESTIONS

1. How does the author define *empathy*? Why is empathy so important (paragraph 2)? Why would feeling empathy make someone less likely to bully or less likely to watch in silence?

2. Why does the author contrast child-rearing practices in two ancient Greek cities—Athens and Sparta (paragraphs 5 and 6)? Do these two examples relate to her main point? How?

3. What causes someone to bully another person? What "payoff" does the bully get? What is the payoff for those who join with or ignore the bully?

4. A recent study shows that today's college students are 40 percent less empathic than students in 30 years ago. Do you believe this disturbing finding is true? If yes, what could have caused this change?

WRITING ASSIGNMENTS

1. Narrate an incident in which you witnessed bullying, participated in it, or were victimized by it. What happened? Why? What might have prevented it?

2. You are in charge of creating an anti-bullying program for six- to eight-year-olds. What will your central message be? What approach would best engage your young audience? Should you put on a play or act out scenes? Have the children make paintings? Describe your program and explain the reasoning behind it.

3. The five high school students who bullied Phoebe Prince were charged and prosecuted. Pleading guilty to criminal harassment to avoid more serious charges, they were sentenced to probation and/or community service. Do you think criminal punishments for bullying would help prevent it? Argue for or against these penalties.

8. punitive: punishing

ELISSA ENGLUND

Good Grammar Gets the Girl

Elissa Englund, "Good Grammar Gets the Girl" from www.statenews.com/index.php/article/2005/09/good_grammar_gets_the_girl. Reprinted by permission of the author and State News.

Can excellent grammar help you find romance? Elissa Englund thinks it can. A senior at Michigan State University in 2005, she had just joined an online dating service and was struck by the importance of grammatical first impressions. She wrote this humorous article, with tips for improving "grammatical hotness," for the college newspaper. Today Ms. Englund works as a copy editor for Time Magazine *in New York City. You can check out her blog and photographs at TooManyCommas.com.*

1   In the few weeks that I've been a member of an online dating service, I've had an interesting range of people contact me. Meet Craig (not his real name). He's a 28-year-old Virgo seeking a lady who is "fun to be around." He says he finished college and is employed full-time. All in all, he seems like a pretty together guy—until you read his message.

2   "Hi! I love to have fun weather it at work or hang out with friends," wrote Craig in his introductory conversation, which I've left with the original grammar. "I'm an optimistic because like is to short too be a pessimistic."

3   In our second conversation, he informed me, "I don't like it when people play games and our dishonest. I have been burned to many times."

4   Sorry, Craig. You seem a little "to dumb" to date.

5   I'm sure Craig is actually very smart. I'm sure he's very sweet. But in the online dating world, that just won't cut it, babe. Our society has reverted to the written word as one of the initial means of conversation. Although these love letters generally aren't written on parchment with quill pens, many first impressions are based solely on how you express yourself through the English language.

6   With the explosion of the Internet, many couples have exchanged their first flirting words through instant messages, e-mail, and online dating services. Grammar isn't just a subject taught in seventh grade or a thing you worry about when writing a cover letter any longer. If you can't spell, use grammar, or express yourself through writing, you're going to be in trouble with the ladies.

7   But have no fear! There are options, one of them being a nifty thing called spell check. But spell check, as I'm sure you know, can fail you. Poor Craig, for example, had no misspellings but a slew[1] of incorrect usages. "Our" should have been "are." He mixed up "too" and "to" and "weather" and "whether." And this girl deleted him from her contact list forever.

8   Sure, maybe I'm shallow. But it makes as bad of an impression as a guy wearing a muscle shirt and daisy dukes to a swank[2] club. It makes you seem trashy, not sweet.

9   But I'm not totally heartless, so for all of you who are lacking in grammar hotness, I'm here. Clip out these rules. Tape them to your computer. And most importantly, reread something before sending it on. A lot of times, you'll catch the errors yourself. Be the Internet Romeo we all know you can be. Nobody ever rejected a guy because his grammar was too good. I promise.

---

1. slew: large number
2. swank: elegant and expensive

How to use stellar[3] grammar to get a hot date: 10

1. With plurals, never use an apostrophe.

   Hotter than Zack Morris:[4] "I'm looking for girls who love to laugh."

   Fewer dates than Screech Powers:[5] "All my past girlfriend's dumped me when I cheated."

2. Possessives almost always use an apostrophe.

   Singular:

   Zack: "I always treat my girlfriend's mother with respect."

   Screech: "I still steal my sisters diary and read it."

   Plural:

   Zack: "My friends' favorite thing about me is my sense of humor."

   Screech: "My last three girlfriend's parents hated me."

3. Know the difference between "it's" and "its." "It's" is a contraction of "it is"; "its" is possessive.

   Zack: "It's sexy when a girl is successful and intelligent."

   Zack: "Here's a rose; I had the florist trim its thorns."

   Screech: "I like when its raining because I can see through your shirt."

4. "They're" is a contraction of "they are." "There" refers to direction or location. "Their" is ownership. Likewise, "you're" is a contraction of "you are," and "your" is ownership.

   Zack: "There is something about your personality that is so magnetic."

   Screech: "You're dress looks great, but it would look better on my floor."

5. Have you ever read Tupac Shakur's[6] poetry? Yeah, it's awful. Apparently, it's thug not to capitalize and to nix[7] spelling whole words to abbreviate "you" to "u," "are" to "r," and "for" to "4." But it makes you look like an eighth grader passing notes.

   Zack: "I have a surprise for you when we go out tomorrow."

   Screech: "i can't wait 4 us 2 get 2gethr so u can c my bed."

Being a communication Casanova is really quite simple; it just requires 11 that you take the effort to memorize a few quick rules and reread your writing before hitting "send." Consider it the online dating equivalent of running a comb through your hair and flossing your teeth. The extra effort shows, and the ladies will notice. And if you think you're already a syntax Superman, look me up. I'll be waiting, red pen in hand.

....

3. stellar: excellent

4. Zack Morris: handsome character on the 1990s high school sitcom *Saved by the Bell*

5. Screech Powers: nerdy character on *Saved by the Bell*

6. Tupac Shakur: Widely admired American rap singer who was murdered at age 25

7. nix: to reject or eliminate

DISCUSSION AND WRITING QUESTIONS

1. Have you ever passed judgment on someone because of his or her writing or speaking skills? What specific conclusions do people tend to draw about a person whose writing or speech is filled with grammatical errors?

2. In your opinion, how important is a first impression in personal life? At work? Can a bad first impression always be overcome? When are first impressions the most important?

3. Englund develops her essay with grammatically correct and incorrect examples. How effective are these examples? Why does she pretend they are written by sitcom characters Zack and Screech? Working with a partner, find and edit all of the errors in the incorrect examples.

4. This essay is humorous, but it aims to persuade. How effective is the writer's argument? Would this essay inspire someone who doesn't care about his or her writing skills to improve? Does it make you want to improve?

WRITING ASSIGNMENTS

1. In a workplace or personal situation, have you ever been surprised by the importance of writing or writing skills? Describe such a time.

2. Many people have become concerned about the erosion of good writing skills caused by widespread use of texting lingo, with its abbreviations (RU for "are you" and IC for "I see"), shortcuts (IDR for "I don't remember") and misspellings (thru for "through"), and dropped capitalization and punctuation. Is this concern a valid one? What are other positive and negative consequences of heavy use of texting lingo among young people?

3. If you were writing an article for the college newspaper with the purpose of waking students up about the importance of excellent writing skills, how would you do it? Plan a strategy, brainstorm, and write your article. Once it is revised and snappy, submit it to the newspaper for publication.

IAN FRAZIER

On the Rez

"On the Rez" excerpt from ON THE REZ by Ian Frazier. Copyright © by Ian Frazier. Reprinted by permission of Farrar, Straus and Giroux, LLC. and The Wylie Agency LLC.

Do you think a single act of courage or heroism can reverse decades of misunderstanding? In his book On the Rez, *Ian Frazier tells the true story of SuAnne Marie Big Crow, who faced a taunting crowd and decided to answer its jeers with a surprising gift.*

Some people who live in the cities and towns near reservations treat their Indian neighbors decently; some don't. In Denver and Minneapolis and Rapid City police have been known to harass Indian teenagers and rough up

Indian drunks and needlessly stop and search Indian cars. Local banks whose deposits include millions in tribal funds sometimes charge Indians higher interest rates than they charge whites. Gift shops near reservations sell junky caricature[1] Indian pictures and dolls, and until not long ago beer coolers had signs on them that said INDIAN POWER. In a big discount store in a reservation-border town a white clerk observes a lot of Indians waiting at the checkout and remarks, "Oh, they're Indians—they're used to standing in line." Some people in South Dakota hate Indians, unapologetically, and will tell you why; in their voices you can hear a particular American meanness that is centuries old.

When teams from Pine Ridge play non-Indian teams, the question of race is always there. When Pine Ridge is the visiting team, usually the hosts are courteous and the players and fans have a good time. But Pine Ridge coaches know that occasionally at away games their kids will be insulted, their fans will feel unwelcome, the host gym will be dense with hostility, and the referees will call fouls on Indian players every chance they get. Sometimes in a game between Indian and non-Indian teams the difference in race becomes an important and distracting part of the event.

One place where Pine Ridge teams used to get harassed regularly was the high school gymnasium in Lead, South Dakota. Lead is a town of about 3,200 northwest of the reservation, in the Black Hills. It is laid out among the mines that are its main industry, and low, wooded mountains hedge it around. The brick high school building is set into a hillside. The school's only gym in those days was small, with tiers of gray-painted concrete on which the spectator benches descended from just below the steel-beamed roof to the very edge of the basketball court—an arrangement that greatly magnified the interior noise.

In the fall of 1988 the Pine Ridge Lady Thorpes[2] went to Lead to play a basketball game. SuAnne was a full member of the team by then. She was a freshman, fourteen years old. Getting ready in the locker room, the Pine Ridge girls could hear the din from the Lead fans. They were yelling fake Indian war cries, a "*woo-woo-woo*" sound. The usual plan for the pre-game warm-up was for the visiting team to run onto the court in a line, take a lap or two around the floor, shoot some baskets, and then go to their bench at courtside. After that the home team would come out and do the same, and then the game would begin. Usually the Thorpes lined up for their entry more or less according to height, which meant that senior Doni De Cory, one of the tallest, went first. As the team waited in the hallway leading from the locker room, the heckling got louder. Some fans were waving food stamps, a reference to the reservation's receiving federal aid. Others yelled, "Where's the cheese?"—the joke being that if Indians were lining up, it must be to get commodity cheese. The Lead high school band had joined in, with fake Indian drumming and a fake Indian tune. Doni De Cory looked out the door and told her teammates, "I can't handle this." SuAnne quickly offered to go first in her place. She was so eager that Doni became suspicious. "Don't embarrass us," Doni told her. SuAnne said, "I won't. I won't embarrass you." Doni gave her the ball, and SuAnne stood first in line.

2

3

4

1. caricature: cartoon
2. Lady Thorpes: named for Native American Jim Thorpe, one of the greatest athletes of all time

She came running onto the court dribbling the basketball, with her 5
teammates running behind. On the court the noise was deafening. SuAnne
went right down the middle and suddenly stopped when she got to center
court. Her teammates were taken by surprise, and some bumped into each
other. Coach Zimiga, at the rear of the line, did not know why they had
stopped. SuAnne turned to Doni De Cory and tossed her the ball. Then she
stepped into the jump-ball circle at center court, facing the Lead fans. She
unbuttoned her warm-up jacket, took it off, draped it over her shoulders,
and began to do the Lakota shawl dance. SuAnne knew all the traditional
dances (she had competed in many powwows as a little girl), and the dance
she chose is a young woman's dance, graceful and modest and show-offy all at
the same time. "I couldn't believe it—she was powwowin', like, 'Get down!'"
Doni De Cory recalls. "And then she started to sing." SuAnne began to sing in
Lakota, swaying back and forth in the jump-ball circle, doing the shawl dance,
using her warm-up jacket for a shawl. The crowd went completely silent. "All
that stuff the Lead fans were yelling—it was like she *reversed* it somehow," a
teammate says. In the sudden quiet all they could hear was her Lakota song.
SuAnne dropped her jacket, took the ball from Doni De Cory, and ran a lap
around the court dribbling expertly and fast. The audience began to cheer
and applaud. She sprinted to the basket, went up in the air, and laid the ball
through the hoop, with the fans cheering loudly now. Of course, Pine Ridge
went on to win the game.

For the Oglala, what SuAnne did that day almost immediately took on the 6
status of myth. People from Pine Ridge who witnessed it still describe it in
terms of awe and disbelief. Amazement swept through the younger kids when
they heard. "I was, like, '*What* did she just do?'" recalls her cousin Angie Big
Crow, an eighth grader at the time. All over the reservation people told and
retold the story of SuAnne at Lead. Anytime the subject of SuAnne came up
when I was talking to people on Pine Ridge, I would always ask if they had
heard about what she did at Lead, and always the answer was a smile and a
nod—"Yeah, I was there," or "Yeah, I heard about that." To the unnumbered
big and small slights of local racism that the Oglala have known all their lives
SuAnne's exploit made an emphatic reply.

Back in the days when Lakota war parties still fought battles against other 7
tribes and the Army, no deed of war was more honored than the act of counting
coup. To "count coup" means to touch an armed enemy in full possession of
his powers with a special stick called a coup stick, or with the hand. The touch
is not a blow, and serves only to indicate how close to the enemy you came. As
an act of bravery, counting coup was regarded as greater than killing an enemy
in single combat, greater than taking a scalp or horses or any prize. Counting
coup was an act of almost abstract courage, of pure playfulness taken to the
most daring extreme. Very likely, to do it and survive brought an exhilaration
to which nothing else could compare. In an ancient sense that her Oglala kin
could recognize, SuAnne counted coup on the fans of Lead.

And yet this coup was an act not of war but of peace. SuAnne's coup strike 8
was an offering, an invitation. It gave the hecklers the best interpretation, as
if their silly, mocking chants were meant only in good will. It showed that
their fake Indian songs were just that—fake—and that the real thing was
better, as real things usually are. We Lakota have been dancing like this for

centuries, the dance said; we've been doing the shawl dance since long before you came, before you got on the boat in Glasgow or Bremerhaven, before you stole this land, and we're still doing it today. And isn't it pretty, when you see how it's supposed to be done? Because finally, what SuAnne proposed was to invite us—us onlookers in the stands, namely, the non-Lakota rest of this country—to dance too. She was in the Lead gym to play, and she invited us all to play. The symbol she used to include us was the warm-up jacket. Everyone in America has a warm-up jacket. I've got one, probably so do you, so did (no doubt) many of the fans at Lead. By using the warm-up jacket as a shawl in her impromptu shawl dance she made Lakota relatives of us all.

"It was funny," Doni De Cory says, "but after that game the relationship between Lead and us was tremendous. When we played Lead again, the games were really good, and we got to know some of the girls on the team. Later, when we went to a tournament and Lead was there, we were hanging out with the Lead girls and eating pizza with them. We got to know some of their parents, too. What SuAnne did made a lasting impression and changed the whole situation with us and Lead. We found out there are some really good people in Lead." 9

America is a leap of the imagination. From its beginning people have had only a persistent idea of what a good country should be. The idea involves freedom, equality, justice, and the pursuit of happiness; nowadays most of us probably could not describe it much more clearly than that. The truth is, it always has been a bit of a guess. No one has ever known for sure whether a country based on such an idea is really possible, but again and again we have leaped toward the idea and hoped. What SuAnne Big Crow demonstrated in the Lead high school gym is that making the leap is the whole point. The idea does not truly live unless it is expressed by an act; the country does not live unless we make the leap from our tribe or focus group or gated community or demographic[3] and land on the shaky platform of that idea of a good country which all kinds of different people share. 10

DISCUSSION AND WRITING QUESTIONS

1. How was the Pine Ridge girls' basketball team usually treated when they played games at Lead? What larger problem between Indians and non-Indians in South Dakota was reflected in this behavior?

2. SuAnne's performance of the Lakota shawl dance to a silent gymnasium full of people is described in powerful detail. What descriptive details does the author include to make that scene come alive for the reader?

3. What did the students at Lead discover during SuAnne's dance that caused them to change their opinions about Lakota Indians? What made the Pine Ridge players decide that "there are some really good people in Lead" (paragraph 9)?

4. The author calls SuAnne's dance an act of courage. What was courageous about her dance that day? Consider in your answer her age, the history between Pine Ridge and Lead, and the behavior of the audience before the game.

....

3. demographic: group of similar people

WRITING ASSIGNMENTS

1. SuAnne Marie Big Crow's actions that day made her a hero for the people of the Pine Ridge reservation. With a group of classmates, brainstorm the qualities that make someone a hero. Then, select two or three of these qualities and write an essay defining heroism. You may wish to illustrate with an anecdote of your own about someone who performed like a hero in a difficult situation.

2. How can we promote tolerance in the world? Think of a conflict that you have experienced or heard about—perhaps between two ethnic groups, gangs, families, or individuals. What specific actions would you recommend to help promote understanding and tolerance between the two sides?

3. Frazier says that equality and justice do not live until they are expressed in action—until "we make the leap from our tribe or group" into a larger community that "different people share" (paragraph 10). Write an essay in which you describe someone who has made such a leap, such as reaching out to an outsider, standing up against a stereotype, or moving to a new country or community.

KAREN CASTELLUCCI COX

Four Types of Courage

"In these times when many students wonder anxiously what the future will bring, courage may be more important than ever," claims Karen Castellucci Cox, a professor of English at City College of San Francisco. In this inspiring essay, she examines four different kinds of courage first set forth by psychologist Rollo May, applying his categories to contemporary challenges.

Most people think they know what courage is. When asked to name a   1
courageous person, many pick a Hollywood hero like Jack Bauer, the impossibly capable action star of television's *24*. Others choose real-life heroes, often those who confront great physical danger like firefighters or soldiers. Indeed, our culture teaches us to view courage as a kind of Rambo-style bravado. Consider these cases, however: Chardee, a battered wife who finally leaves her husband; Luis, who goes against his family's wishes to pursue his dream of becoming an actor; Ann, who cares for a father with Alzheimer's disease, patiently having the same conversations day after day yet infusing their small apartment with good cheer and kindness. Do any of these people exhibit courage? In his classic book *The Courage to Create*, American psychologist Rollo May invites us to examine more deeply the quality he believes is essential to a meaningful life. Courage, he insists, is not just one emotion among others, but the foundation on which all other virtues and values rest. May divides courage into four distinct types—physical, social, moral, and creative.

Physical courage is familiar to most people: the ability to confront bodily pain or danger with self-possession, usually for a greater goal or good. For example, when Hurricane Katrina hit the Gulf Coast in August 2005, causing devastating floods in New Orleans, local police raced to curb looting and rescue the stranded. These officers had no experience facing such a catastrophic emergency and little training in search-and-rescue. Yet they risked their lives to save desperate and angry citizens amid surging water, threat of disease, and even sniper fire. The pressure proved too much for some; several dozen deserted. But the truly remarkable fact was that 1,700 men and women continued to report to work each day, exhibiting the brand of physical courage that May believes capable of transforming society.

Physical courage has lost much of its usefulness in contemporary life, May cautions. Whereas our society once applauded the self-reliant pioneer, now we egg on the Tony Sopranos,[1] who justify their violence with talk of disrespect or frontier justice. What masquerades as physical courage in television, films, music videos, and games is often little better than the bully's swagger on the playground. A more productive physical courage, like that of the New Orleans officers, puts the body on the line, not to overpower or harm others, but to serve and protect them.

The second category, social courage, is the type demanded of us in daily life. This is the courage to have meaningful relationships, to dare to reveal who we really are, to tell the truth in public forums despite the risks. The child who faces peer disapproval to befriend an unpopular classmate demonstrates social courage. The 55-year-old woman who goes back for her college degree though she fears she will feel out of place demonstrates social courage. The employee who volunteers to give a business presentation despite a lifelong terror of public speaking demonstrates social courage. Marriage, parenthood, any relationship that calls for an engagement of the heart and mind invites this brand of courage. May writes, "It is easier in our society to be naked physically than to be naked psychologically or spiritually." But when one chooses to open oneself, despite real risks of embarrassment, rejection, or worse, the reward is the chance of making a profound connection in a world of superficial ones.

Moral courage may exact an even heavier toll. The one who exhibits moral courage usually recognizes the suffering of others and decides to help despite the consequences. Aung San Suu Kyi is such a figure. The daughter of a diplomat and a general who was assassinated after negotiating Burma's independence from Great Britain in 1947, Suu Kyi was inspired by her parents to spend her life promoting democracy and human rights in Burma. When an oppressive military gained control of the government in 1988, Suu Kyi stepped into a leadership position, helping to found a democratic party and speaking publicly throughout Burma. Her inspiring vision drew huge crowds, and when her popularity became a threat, she was followed, harassed, and arrested. Suu Kyi spent a total of fifteen years under house arrest, a sacrifice that meant living apart from her grown sons and not being able to visit her dying husband in England. Her moral courage was recognized when she won the Nobel Peace Prize in 1991. Beloved by Burmese citizens and admired worldwide as a democratic leader, she was re-arrested and held under house arrest until 2010.

Moral courage is found as well in ordinary people who take a stand. Between April and July 1994, nearly one million people were killed in a

---

1. Tony Soprano: lead character in *The Sopranos*, a dramatic HBO series about a Mafia family

Military firefighters in Alaska risk their lives to put out a blaze in a lodging facility.

mass genocide[2] in Rwanda; Hutu[3] extremists murdered their Tutsi[3] neighbors while the international community looked the other way. But one man, Paul Rusesabagina, did not look the other way. The son of farmers and a modest hotel manager, Rusesabagina at first wanted to protect only his wife and children. Gradually, however, he began to comprehend the scope of the brutality. He devised a way to hide Tutsi refugees in his hotel until they could be carried to safety. In all, Rusesabagina is responsible for single-handedly saving the lives of 1,268 people. His story, told in the film *Hotel Rwanda*, is reminder that moral courage can be found wherever a person chooses action over apathy.[4]

The final category is creative courage, "discovering new forms, patterns" and solutions that no one has yet imagined and that might even promote a better future. A writer, musician, or inventor shows creative courage when he or she rejects the status quo,[5] seeing beyond what *is* to create something new. President Lincoln called Harriet Beecher Stowe, the "little woman who wrote the book that started this great war." Her 1851 novel *Uncle Tom's Cabin*, while it didn't actually provoke the Civil War, created a groundswell[6] of public outrage against slavery through its detailed and moving descriptions. Another example is *Rent*, one of the longest-running shows on Broadway. *Rent* was the first musical to address the HIV health crisis through life-affirming personal stories aimed at the general public. An uplifting musical form helped the public face difficult issues.

7

Not just the arts, but all professions, require creative courage. Tim Berners-Lee, for instance, is credited with inventing the World Wide Web, maybe the most important innovation of our time. In 1991, he set up the first website and began networking his computer with others around the country. Concerned that patenting his discovery would make the growing Web too expensive for general use, Berners-Lee chose to keep the technology public. In doing so, he

8

....

2. genocide: the systematic and planned execution of an entire national, racial, or ethnic group

3. Hutu . . . Tutsi: two of the three ethnic groups that occupy Rwanda and Burundi

4. apathy: lack of interest or concern

5. status quo: existing condition or state of affairs

6. groundswell: a sudden gathering of force

passed up a personal fortune and risked mockery for his "foolish" insistence that the World Wide Web should belong to everyone.

Of course, the four types of courage sometimes overlap. Tobacco executive Jeffrey Wigand was motivated by moral courage when he revealed in the 1990s that Big Tobacco[7] was hiding the truth about nicotine causing cancer. This whistle blower[8] demonstrated physical courage as well, refusing to be silenced by veiled threats of violence. Wigand's social courage was tested as the case hit the media, the business community shunned[9] him, and his own family deserted him. And when his old life was shattered, this man somehow found the creative courage to build a new one. 9

"Courage has many faces," writes Katherine Martin, the author of *Women of Courage*. "We lose much when we dismiss it in ourselves, thinking we don't measure up." The classification that May sets forth invites us to find and cultivate courage in our own lives, to ask what blocks our daring, and then to stand and try. 10

DISCUSSION AND WRITING QUESTIONS

1. How does the author classify courage in this essay? That is, what four categories of courage does she identify? What is the source of these categories?

2. Provide one additional example of each type of courage. Draw your illustrations from your own or loved ones' experiences, the news, history, or this textbook.

3. What are the most common obstacles to behaving courageously? Fear? Apathy? Selfishness? What, in your opinion, most often "blocks our daring" (paragraph 10)?

4. A street campaign called "Stop Snitchin'," begun in 2004, urges people in urban neighborhoods not to speak to police investigating local crimes— not to share tips and information that might solve those crimes. T-shirts, hip hop albums, and other marketing devices tell people to keep silent and sometimes threaten them. Does it take courage to stop snitching or to keep talking? Why?

WRITING ASSIGNMENTS

1. Discuss a time when you or someone close to you displayed one or more of the four types of courage described in this essay.

2. Write a classification essay about another concept, emotion, or term— such as success, friends, mistakes, or lies—and break it into different types or "faces."

3. Are you facing right now a situation or problem that will require courage to confront and correct? First, state the problem. Has a lack of courage in the past made it worse? If you applied true courage to the situation, what might be the outcome?

---

7. Big Tobacco: nickname for the three most powerful tobacco companies in the United States
8. whistle blower: an employee or member of an organization who exposes misconduct or corruption
9. shunned: rejected, ignored

WANG PING

Book War

"Book War" by Wang Ping. Commissioned by The Friends of the Minneapolis Public Library for The New Minneapolis Central Library Groundbreaking, May 20, 2003. Reprinted with the permission of Wang Ping. All rights reserved. No part of this text excerpt may be used or reproduced in any manner whatsoever without the prior written permission of Wang Ping.

Have you ever lived in a country whose government tried to control what you read, said, wore, or even believed? Author Wang Ping grew up in China during the violent "Cultural Revolution" of the late 1960s when Communist Chairman Mao Zedong closed schools, banned books, and imprisoned or killed thousands of citizens. In this true story, a curious child tries to learn in a place where reading the wrong book could bring a death sentence.

1   I discovered "The Little Mermaid," my first fairy tale, in 1968. That morning, when I opened the door to light my stove, I found my new neighbor, a girl a few years older, sitting under the streetlight, a book in her lap. The red plastic wrap indicated it was Mao's collected work. She must have been there all night long, for her hair and shoulders were covered with frost, and her body shivered violently from cold. Another loyal Maoist, I thought to myself. Then I heard her sobbing. I got curious. What kind of person would weep from reading Mao's words: I walked over and peeked over her shoulders. What I saw made me freeze in fear and excitement. The book in her hands had nothing to do with Mao; it was Hans Christian Andersen's fairy tales, the story of "The Little Mermaid." Since I had heard the story in my kindergarten, I was determined to read it myself someday. Just when I was ready, the Cultural Revolution began. Schools were closed, books, condemned as "poisonous weeds," were burnt on streets, and the rest were confiscated.[1]

2   My clever neighbor had disguised the "poisonous weed" with the scarlet cover of Mao's work. Engrossed[2] in the story, she didn't realize my presence behind her until I started weeping. She jumped up, fairy tales clutched to her budding chest. Her panic-stricken face said she was ready to fight me to death if I dared to report her. We stared at each other for an eternity. Suddenly she started laughing, pointing at my tear-stained face. She knew then that her secret was safe with me.

3   She gave me twenty-four hours to read the fairy tales, and I loaned her *The Arabian Nights,* which was missing the first fifteen pages and the last story, but no matter. The girl squealed and danced in the dawn light. When we finished each other's books, we decided to start an underground book exchange network. With strict rules and determination, we had books to read almost every day, all "poisonous" classics.

4   Soon I excavated[3] a box of books my mother had buried beneath the chicken coop. I pried it open with a screwdriver, and pulled out one treasure after another: *The Dream of the Red Chamber, The Book of Songs, Grimms' Fairy Tales, Romeo and Juliet, Huckleberry Finn, American Dream,* each wrapped with waxed paper.

5   I devoured them all, in rice paddies[4] and wheat fields, on my way home from school and errands. I tried to be careful. The consequences could have

---

1. confiscated: seized
2. engrossed: completely absorbed
3. excavated: dug up
4. rice paddies: flooded land used for growing rice

been catastrophic,[5] not only for myself but also for my entire family, had these books fallen into wrong hands. But my "enemy" was my own mother. Once she discovered I had unearthed her treasure box, she set out to destroy these "time bombs," combing every possible place in the house. It was a hopeless battle. My mother knew my habits, my little tricks. I couldn't outsmart her. Whenever she caught me red-handed, she'd order me to tear the pages and place them in the stove, and she'd sit nearby, tears in her eyes, muttering: "This is for your safety, everyone's safety." And my heart, our hearts, turned into ashes.

When the last book was gone, I went to sit in the chicken coop. Hens surrounded me, pecking at my closed fists for food. As tears flowed, the stories became alive from inside. They flapped their wings and flew out of my mouth like mourning doves. I started telling them to my siblings, friends, and neighbors; stories I'd read from those forbidden treasures, stories I made up for myself and my audience. We gathered on summer nights, during winter darkness. When I saw stars rising in their dimmed eyes, I knew I had won the war. 6

DISCUSSION AND WRITING QUESTIONS

1. In a repressive regime, why would the government ban books or reading? How could books, including fairy tales or stories from other countries, be considered "poisonous weeds," dangerous to those in power?

2. Why does the author's mother destroy her own books once she finds out that her daughter loves them too? Would you, as a parent, have done the same thing?

3. Wang Ping uses many *metaphors* (poetic comparisons, see Chapter 23, Part D) in telling her story. For example, to the mother, the books her daughter is reading are "time bombs" (paragraph 5). Why does she say this? Find the two metaphors in the last sentence and explain what this sentence means.

4. What is the value of stories? Are stories sometimes just as important as books that contain factual information?

WRITING ASSIGNMENTS

1. What activity or right, if any, would you risk your life to fight for if the government suddenly forbade you from engaging in that activity? Explain your answer.

2. Do Americans devalue literacy? Why don't many Americans read regularly? If books were banned in this country, do you think more people might want to read? Explain.

3. Should any book ever be censored for any reason? Argue for or against censorship of books. To support your argument, use examples from such websites as **http://www.ala.org/advocacy/banned/ frequentlychallenged/challengedclassics**.

....
5. catastrophic: disastrous

LEONARD PITTS

A Risk-Free Life

Leonard Pitts, "Life Makes You and Me Risk-Takers," THE MIAMI HERALD © THE MIAMI HERALD. Reprinted by permission.

If you could tinker with the genes of your unborn children to protect them from a disease—or even to select their gender or physical traits—would you do it? How far would you go to take control of nature and of chance? Pulitzer-Prize-winning columnist Leonard Pitts argues that people who seek this level of control are denying one of life's most basic truths.

I don't have the heart—or, perhaps more accurately, the heartlessness—to beat up on a lady whose only sin was the desire to have a healthy baby. So don't read any of what follows as a criticism of the woman—her name has not been released—who went to a geneticist[1] to have her eggs screened for the gene that causes Alzheimer's.[2]   **1**

That disease is a clear and present danger in the life of this woman. Her family is reportedly one of about a dozen in the world carrying a genetic flaw that virtually assures them of developing Alzheimer's—and doing so while tragically young. A sister started showing symptoms at the age of 38, a brother at 35. Experts say it's a virtual certainty that this woman, who is 30, will develop the mind-destroying affliction[3] by the time she's 40.   **2**

Her problem was that she desperately wanted a child. Now, as just reported in the *Journal of the American Medical Association*, she and her husband have one. And another is on the way. It's likely that when the woman's daughter, who was born a year ago, turns 10, her mom will no longer recognize her. Had she been conceived by normal means, the daughter would have faced a 50–50 chance of suffering a similar fate. Instead, she and her sibling have been freed from what amounts to a family curse.   **3**

If I were in this woman's place, I can't tell you that I wouldn't have done the same thing she did. At the same time, I'd be lying if I didn't admit to being troubled by some of the moral and ethical doors that are swinging open here.   **4**

It is not, it seems to me, that big a leap from screening for fatal disease to screening for hair color, height, weight or susceptibility[4] to allergies. Given that many cultures value females less than they do males, will we see fewer girls being born? Will self-hating blacks sign up to give their children light skin and so-called "good" hair? Will self-hating Asians want to do away with almond eyes? Will there come a day when the fertility doctor hands you a checklist and you choose characteristics—one from Column A, two from Column B—putting a human being together like you would a meal in a take-out restaurant?   **5**

----

1. geneticist: a scientist who studies genes, which pass traits from parents to children
2. Alzheimer's: an incurable brain disorder characterized by memory loss, confusion, loss of language, and finally, death
3. affliction: a state of suffering or pain
4. susceptibility: the state of being easily affected

iStockphoto.com/Cindy Singleton

I fear—and believe—the inevitable answer to all of the above is yes. It's in our nature. We seek to remove from the equation that gremlin,[5] chance.

That's an old impulse that you and I have raised to a whole new level. The world has never seen control freaks like us. We make bestsellers out of self-help books that purport[6] to help us put our emotional and financial houses in order. We line up to buy the latest gadget that promises to save time and simplify chores. We put the whole world in an electronic box that sits on a desk. We seek uniformity, predictability, security.

But guess what? Stuff still happens. As they did when the cliché[7] was fresh, the best laid plans of mice and men still manage to go astray. You wonder when or whether human beings will ever concede that their ability to guarantee their own destinies is finite[8] at best. We do what we can, but we can never do enough. So the two children who are now freed from the threat of Alzheimer's still face the risk that they will suffer cancer, heart disease, stroke, or someday step off the curb in front of a city bus. In the words of Gilda Radner,[9] "It's always something."

Indeed. For her, it was ovarian cancer. And I guess it would be easy to look at a thing like that and regard it as an intrusion upon your life. But life IS ovarian cancer. It's Alzheimer's, it's heart attack, it's mental illness, it's uncertainty, and it is suffering. Yet it is also, in the very same instant, laughter that makes your head swim, faith that makes your heart soar. It is triumph, hope, pleasure and, with apologies to Al Green,[10] love and happiness as well.

To live is to be surprised, I think. And shocked. You wake up in the morning to find out what happens next.

I have no condemnation[11] for a mother who only wanted the best for her children. But at the same time, I think there's something foolish and self-defeating in this impulse we have to make life risk-free. That's a contradiction in terms.

DISCUSSION AND WRITING QUESTIONS

1. Do you agree or disagree with the actions of the woman who had her eggs screened for the gene that causes Alzheimer's disease? Would you have done the same thing? Should a person even have a child when he or she knows that early disease will deprive that child of a parent?

2. Do you think that Pitts's fear about a future when we'll probably be "putting a human being together like you would a meal in a take-out restaurant" (paragraph 5) is valid? Why or why not?

3. Pitts writes, "To live is to be surprised. And shocked" (paragraph 10). Do you agree? Have you ever had an unpleasant or even tragic experience that brought surprising growth or blessings?

....

5. gremlin: a trouble-making elf
6. purport: to claim
7. cliché: overused, worn-out expression
8. finite: having a limited existence
9. Gilda Radner: American comedienne and actress who died from ovarian cancer in 1989
10. Al Green: American soul singer, one of whose hits was "Love and Happiness"
11. condemnation: strong disapproval

4. How well do you prepare for or handle life's unpredictable twists and turns? Would you say that you're able to strike a healthy balance between "uniformity, predictability, and security" (paragraph 7) on the one hand and exciting or scary new challenges on the other?

WRITING ASSIGNMENTS

1. Narrate a time when you tried hard to control a situation, but hurt, shock, or the unexpected occurred anyway. What happened? Did you learn any lessons from this experience?

2. Contrast someone you know who often takes risks with someone you know who avoids risks. Think of attitudes and behaviors that reveal the differences between them, and select three points of contrast to structure your writing.

3. The Serenity Prayer asks for three things: "God grant me the serenity to accept the things I cannot change, courage to change the things I can, and the wisdom to know the difference." If you were to apply this prayer to a problem in your life now, would acceptance, courage, or wisdom help you the most? Be specific.

CHRISTOPHER N. BACORN

Dear Dads: Save Your Sons

According to the National Fatherhood Initiative, an estimated 24.7 million children (36.3 percent) do not live with their biological fathers. About 40 percent of these children have not seen their fathers during the past year. Psychologist Christopher N. Bacorn puts human faces on these statistics in this provocative Newsweek essay. These kids don't need a shrink, he argues; they need a dad.

1 I had seen a hundred like him. He sat back on the couch, silently staring out the window, an unmistakable air of sullen[1] anger about him. He was 15 and big for his age. His mother, a woman in her mid-30s, sat forward on the couch and, on the edge of tears, described the boy's heartbreaking descent into alcohol, gang membership, failing grades and violence. She was small, thin, worn out from frantic nights of worry and lost sleep waiting for him to come home. She had lost control of him, she admitted freely. Ever since his father had left, four years ago, she had had trouble with him. He had become more and more unmanageable and then, recently, he had hurt someone in a fight. Charges had been filed, counseling recommended.

2 I listened to the mother's anguished[2] story. "Are there any men in his life?" I asked. There was no one. She had no brothers, her father was dead and her

---
1. sullen: resentful, sulking
2. anguished: feeling terrible physical or mental pain

who are you spending
your quality time with?

have you been a dad today?

for more ideas call 800-790-DADS or visit www.fatherhood.org

ex-husband's father lived in another state. She looked up at me, her eyes hopeful. "Will you talk with him?" she asked. "Just speak with him about what he's doing. Maybe if it came from a professional…" she added, her voice trailing off. "It couldn't hurt."

I did speak with him. Maybe it didn't hurt, but like most counseling with 15-year-old boys, it didn't seem to help either. He denied having any problems. Everyone else had them, but he didn't. After half an hour of futility,[3] I gave up.

I have come to believe that most adolescent boys can't make use of professional counseling. What a boy can use, and all too often doesn't have, is the fellowship of men—at least one man who pays attention to him, who spends time with him, who admires him. A boy needs a man he can look up to. What he doesn't need is a shrink.

That episode, and others like it, set me thinking about children and their fathers. As a nation, we are racked[4] by youth violence, overrun by gangs, guns and drugs. The great majority of youthful offenders are male, most without fathers involved in their lives in any useful way. Many have never even met their fathers.

....

3. futility: uselessness
4. racked: tortured or suffering from

What's become of the fathers of these boys? Where are they? Well, I can tell you where they're not. They're not at PTA meetings or piano recitals. They're not teaching Sunday school. You won't find them in the pediatrician's office, holding a sick child. You won't even see them in juvenile court, standing next to Junior as he awaits sentencing for burglary or assault. You might see a few of them in the supermarket, but not many. You will see a lot of women in these places—mothers and grandmothers—but you won't see many fathers.   6

So, if they're not in these places, where are the fathers? They are in diners and taverns, drinking, conversing, playing pool with other men. They are on golf courses, tennis courts, in bowling alleys, fishing on lakes and rivers. They are working in their jobs, many from early morning to late at night. Some are home watching television, out mowing the lawn or tuning up the car. In short, they are everywhere, except in the company of their children.   7

Of course there are men who do spend time with children, men who are covering for all those absentee fathers. The Little League coaches, Boy Scout leaders, Big Brothers and schoolteachers who value contact with children, who are investing in the next generation, sharing time and teaching skills. And there are many fathers who are less visible but no less valuable, those who quietly help with homework, baths, laundry, and grocery shopping. Fathers who read to their children, drive them to ballet lessons, who cheer at soccer games. Fathers who are on the job. These are the real men of America, the ones holding society together. Every one of them is worth a dozen investment bankers, a boardroom full of corporate executives and all of the lawmakers west of the Mississippi.   8

Poverty prevention: What would happen if the truant[5] fathers of America began spending time with their children? It wouldn't eliminate world hunger, but it might save some families from sinking below the poverty line. It wouldn't bring peace to the Middle East, but it just might keep a few kids from trying to find a sense of belonging with their local street-corner gang. It might not defuse[6] the population bomb, but it just might prevent a few teenage pregnancies.   9

If these fathers were to spend more time with their children, it just might have an effect on the future of marriage and divorce. Not only do many boys lack a sense of how a man should behave; many girls don't know either, having little exposure themselves to healthy male-female relationships. With their fathers around, many young women might come to expect more than the myth that a man's chief purpose on earth is to impregnate them and then disappear. If that would happen, the next generation of absentee fathers might never come to pass.   10

Before her session ended, I tried to give this mother some hope. Maybe she could interest her son in a sport: how about basketball or soccer? Any positive experience involving men or other boys would expose her son to teamwork, cooperation and friendly competition. But the boy was contemptuous[7] of my suggestions. "Those things are for dorks," he sneered. He couldn't wait to leave. I looked at his mother. I could see the   11

....

5. truant: absent without permission

6. defuse: to make less dangerous

7. contemptuous: feeling scorn or disdain

embarrassment and hopelessness in her face. "Let's go, Ma," he said, more as a command than a request. I walked her out through the waiting room, full of women and children, mostly boys, of all ages. Her son was already in the parking lot. I shook her hand. "Good luck," I said, "Thank you," she replied, without conviction. As I watched her go, my heart, too was filled with a measure of hopelessness. But anger was there too, anger at the fathers of these boys. Anger at fathers who walk away from their children, leaving them feeling confused, rejected and full of suffering. What's to become of boys like this? What man will take an interest in them? I can think of only one kind—a judge.

DISCUSSION AND WRITING QUESTIONS

1. At both the beginning and end of this persuasive essay, Bacorn describes a mother and her 15-year-old son. Why does he focus on their story? Would the argument be as effective if he had begun with paragraph 4 and ended with paragraph 10?

2. Do you agree with the author that a boy needs "the fellowship of men" and "a man he can look up to" (paragraph 4)? Does this essay underestimate—or even insult—the millions of single mothers raising healthy sons?

3. In paragraphs 9 and 10, what positive consequences for boys and girls does Bacorn predict if truant fathers spent time with their children? Do you agree with his predictions, or is he exaggerating?

4. The author does not press to see the angry 15-year-old boy again, claiming that professional counseling for adolescent boys is a waste of time. What is your opinion about his decision?

WRITING ASSIGNMENTS

1. Playing sports can save some young men, writes Bacorn. What else could be done? Write an essay discussing other ways to help boys stay out of trouble and succeed. Visit **www.supportingoursons.org** or **www.fatherhood.org** for ideas.

2. Write about your own father's (or mother's) involvement in your upbringing. Was he (or she) an involved parent, an absentee parent, or somewhere in between? Based on your experience, what factors help a child become a healthy man or woman?

3. In a group of four or five classmates, study the public service advertisement (PSA) on page 600, recently released by the National Fatherhood Initiative. Can you identify its subject, audience, and purpose? Could this ad persuade some men to change their behavior? Why or why not? Use your notes from the group to plan and write an essay on fathers or mothers who can live at home but still be absentee.

ANDREW SULLIVAN

Why the M Word Matters to Me

Andrew Sullivan, "Why the 'M' Word Matters to Me," TIME MAGAZINE. Copyright © Used by permission.

In recent years, debate has flared between advocates of traditional marriage and those who support a same-sex couple's right to marry. Some states have granted gay couples this right while others remain adamantly opposed. In this Time *magazine article, blogger and author Andrew Sullivan takes a stand on the issue.*

As a child, I had no idea what homosexuality was. I grew up in a traditional home—Catholic, conservative, middle class. Life was relatively simple: education, work, family. I was raised to aim high in life, even though my parents hadn't gone to college. But one thing was instilled[1] in me. What mattered was not how far you went in life, how much money you earned, how big a name you made for yourself. What really mattered was family and the love you had for one another. The most important day of your life was not graduation from college or your first day at work or a raise or even your first house. The most important day of your life was when you got married. It was on that day that all your friends and all your family got together to celebrate the most important thing in life: your happiness—your ability to make a new home, to form a new but connected family, to find love that put everything else into perspective.

But as I grew older, I found that this was somehow not available to me. I didn't feel the things for girls that my peers did. All the emotions and social rituals and bonding of teenage heterosexual life eluded[2] me. I didn't know why. No one explained it. My emotional bonds to other boys were one-sided; each time I felt myself falling in love, they sensed it, pushed it away. I didn't and couldn't blame them. I got along fine with my buds in a nonemotional context, but something was awry,[3] something not right. I came to know almost instinctively that I would never be a part of my family the way my siblings might one day be. The love I had inside me was unmentionable, anathema.[4] I remember writing in my teenage journal one day, "I'm a professional human being. But what do I do in my private life?"

I never discussed my real life. I couldn't date girls and so immersed myself in schoolwork, the debate team, school plays, anything to give me an excuse not to confront reality. When I looked toward the years ahead, I couldn't see a future. There was just a void. Was I going to be alone my whole life? Would I ever have a most important day in my life? It seemed impossible, a negation,[5] an undoing. To be a full part of my family, I had to somehow not be me. So, like many other gay teens, I withdrew, became neurotic, depressed, at times close to suicidal. I shut myself in my room with my books night after night while my peers developed the skills needed to form real relationships and loves. In wounded pride, I even voiced a rejection of family and marriage. It was the only way I could explain my isolation.

....

1. instilled: implanted
2. eluded: escaped or avoided
3. awry: wrong
4. anathema: someone or something that is loathed, damned, or cursed
5. negation: denial

It took years for me to realize that I was gay, years more to tell others and more time yet to form any kind of stable emotional bond with another man. Because my sexuality had emerged in solitude—and without any link to the idea of an actual relationship—it was hard later to reconnect sex to love and self-esteem. It still is. But I persevered,[6] each relationship slowly growing longer than the last, learning in my 20s and 30s what my straight friends had found out in their teens. But even then my parents and friends never asked the question they would have asked automatically if I were straight: *So, when are you going to get married*? *When will we be able to celebrate it and affirm it and support it?* In fact, no one—no one—has yet asked me that question.

When people talk about gay marriage, they miss the point. This isn't about gay marriage. It's about marriage. It's about family. It's about love. It isn't about religion. It's about civil[7] marriage licenses. Churches can and should have the right to say no to marriage for gays in their congregations, just as Catholics say no to divorce, but divorce is still a civil option. These family values are not options for a happy and stable life. They are necessities. Putting gay relationships in some other category—civil unions, domestic partnerships, whatever— may alleviate[8] real human needs, but by their very euphemism,[9] by their very separateness, they actually build a wall between gay people and their families. They put back the barrier many of us have spent a lifetime trying to erase.

It's too late for me to undo my past. But I want above everything else to remember a young kid out there who may even be reading this now. I want to let him know that he doesn't have to choose between himself and his family anymore. I want him to know that his love has dignity, that he does indeed have a future as a full and equal part of the human race. Only marriage will do that. Only marriage can bring him home.

DISCUSSION AND WRITING QUESTIONS

1. Have you, like Sullivan, ever had to choose between yourself and your family (paragraph 6)? Did you ever disappoint one or more family members because they had expectations for you that you could not fulfill for some reason?

2. Do you agree with Sullivan that there should be just one civil marriage license for all citizens, not separate categories for heterosexual and for same-sex couples? Why or why not?

3. In Chapter 13, you learned five methods of persuasion: facts, referring to an authority, examples, predicting consequences, and answering the opposition. In the first four paragraphs, the author uses his own life as an example. How many other methods does he use to develop his argument for same-sex marriage?

4. Sullivan argues that marriage is a vital institution. In your opinion, what are the benefits of getting and staying married? What are the possible problems or traps? Are you married, or do you want to marry some day? Why or why not?

---

6. persevered: kept going despite difficulties
7. civil: relating to the state or citizens
8. alleviate: to make more bearable
9. euphemism: an indirect and more pleasant expression substituted for a harsh, honest statement

WRITING ASSIGNMENTS

1. Write a rebuttal to Sullivan's essay, arguing against same-sex marriage. Develop your argument with two or three well-developed reasons.

2. In paragraph 5, the author says that love, marriage, and family are necessary for "a happy and stable life." Do you agree? In your opinion, what are the essential ingredients for a happy, stable life?

3. The meaning of "family" has changed in recent years. Now, many households include a single parent or grandparent, step-relations, gay parents, and so forth. Write an extended definition of the word "family" that takes into account modern realities. Use examples to support your definition.

MICHAEL LEVIN

The Case for Torture

"The Case for Torture" by Michael E. Levin, NEWSWEEK. Reprinted by permission of the author.

Leaders like Martin Luther King Jr. and Mahatma Ghandi have preached nonviolence no matter what, and many people agree that deliberately injuring another person is wrong. However, philosophy professor Michael Levin argues in this startling essay that torture is sometimes necessary.

It is generally assumed that torture is impermissible,[1] a throwback to a more brutal age. Enlightened societies reject it outright, and regimes suspected of using it risk the wrath of the United States. 1

I believe this attitude is unwise. There are situations in which torture is not merely permissible but morally mandatory. Moreover, these situations are moving from the realm of imagination to fact. 2

Suppose a terrorist has hidden an atomic bomb on Manhattan Island which will detonate at noon on July 4 unless... (here follow the usual demands for money and release of his friends from jail). Suppose, further, that he is caught at 10 A.M. of the fateful day, but—preferring death to failure—won't disclose where the bomb is. What do we do? If we follow due process—wait for his lawyer, arraign him—millions of people will die. If the only way to save those lives is to subject the terrorist to the most excruciating possible pain, what grounds can there be for not doing so? I suggest there are none. In any case, I ask you to face the question with an open mind. 3

Torturing the terrorist is unconstitutional? Probably. But millions of lives surely outweigh constitutionality. Torture is barbaric? Mass murder is far more barbaric. Indeed, letting millions of innocents die in deference[2] to one who 4

....

1. impermissible: not allowed

2. deference: respectful submission

flaunts his guilt is moral cowardice, an unwillingness to dirty one's hands. If *you* caught the terrorist, could you sleep nights knowing that millions died because you couldn't bring yourself to apply the electrodes?

Once you concede that torture is justified in extreme cases, you have admitted that the decision to use torture is a matter of balancing innocent lives against the means needed to save them. You must now face more realistic cases involving more modest numbers. Someone plants a bomb on a jumbo jet. He alone can disarm it, and his demands cannot be met (or if they can, we refuse to set a precedent³ by yielding to his threats). Surely we can, we must, do anything to the extortionist⁴ to save the passengers. How can we tell 300, or 100, or 10 people who never asked to be put in danger, "I'm sorry, you'll have to die in agony, we just couldn't bring ourselves to..."

Here are the results of an informal poll about a third, hypothetical,⁵ case. Suppose a terrorist group kidnapped a newborn baby from a hospital. I asked four mothers if they would approve of torturing kidnappers if that were necessary to get their own newborns back. All said yes, the most "liberal" adding that she would administer it herself.

I am not advocating torture as punishment. Punishment is addressed to deeds irrevocably⁶ past. Rather, I am advocating torture as an acceptable measure for preventing future evils. So understood, it is far less objectionable than many extant⁷ punishments. Opponents of the death penalty, for example, are forever insisting that executing a murderer will not bring back his victim (as if the purpose of capital punishment were supposed to be resurrection, not deterrence⁸ or retribution).⁹ But torture, in the cases described, is intended not to bring anyone back but to keep innocents from being dispatched.¹⁰ The most powerful argument against using torture as a punishment or to secure confessions is that such practices disregard the rights of the individual. Well, if the individual is all that important—and he is—it is correspondingly important to protect the rights of individuals threatened by terrorists. If life is so valuable that it must never be taken, the lives of the innocents must be saved even at the price of hurting the one who endangers them.

Better precedents for torture are assassination and preemptive¹¹ attack. No Allied¹² leader would have flinched at assassinating Hitler¹³ had that been possible. (The Allies did assassinate Heydrich.¹⁴) Americans would be angered to learn that Roosevelt could have had Hitler killed in 1943—thereby shortening the war and saving millions of lives—but refused on moral grounds. Similarly, if nation A learns that nation B is about to launch an unprovoked attack, A has a right to save itself by destroying B's military capability first. In the same way,

3. precedent: a possible example in similar situations
4. extortionist: one who gets something by force or threat
5. hypothetical: assumed to be true for the purposes of argument
6. irrevocably: impossible to change
7. extant: existing
8. deterrence: preventing similar acts
9. retribution: punishment
10. dispatched: killed
11. preemptive attack: striking first, before the enemy does
12. Allied: in World War II, the Allied powers included the United States, Britain, France, the Soviet Union, and China
13. Hitler: dictator of Nazi Germany who ordered the murder of millions of Jews and others
14. Heydrich: a Nazi organizer of mass executions

if the police can by torture save those who would otherwise die at the hands of kidnappers or terrorists, they must.

There is an important difference between terrorists and their victims that should mute talk of the terrorists' "rights." The terrorist's victims are at risk unintentionally, not having asked to be endangered. But the terrorist knowingly initiated his actions. Unlike his victims, he volunteered for the risks of his deed. By threatening to kill for profit or idealism, he renounces civilized standards, and he can have no complaint if civilization tries to thwart him by whatever means necessary.

Just as torture is justified only to save lives (not extort confessions or recantations),[15] it is justifiably administered only to those *known* to hold innocent lives in their hands. Ah, but how can the authorities ever be sure they have the right malefactor?[16] Isn't there a danger of error and abuse? Won't We turn into Them?

Questions like these are disingenuous[17] in a world in which terrorists proclaim themselves and perform for television. The name of their game is public recognition. After all, you can't very well intimidate a government into releasing your freedom fighters unless you announce that it is your group that has seized its embassy. "Clear guilt" is difficult to define, but when 40 million people see a group of masked gunmen seize an airplane on the evening news, there is not much question about who the perpetrators are. There will be hard cases where the situation is murkier. Nonetheless, a line demarcating[18] the legitimate use of torture can be drawn. Torture only the obviously guilty, and only for the sake of saving innocents, and the line between Us and Them will remain clear.

There is little danger that the Western democracies will lose their way if they choose to inflict pain as one way of preserving order. Paralysis in the face of evil is the greater danger. Some day soon a terrorist will threaten tens of thousands of lives, and torture will be the only way to save them. We had better start thinking about this.

DISCUSSION AND WRITING QUESTIONS

1. What is the author's main point—his thesis? According to Levin, in what specific circumstances should torture be used? Do you agree that someone who refuses to torture a terrorist is guilty of moral cowardice?

2. What arguments *against* torture does the author answer in paragraph 4? Are his answers convincing? His introduction also answers the opposition (paragraphs 1 and 2). Why do you think Levin spends so much time answering the opposition in this essay?

3. Levin first argues that torturing one person to save millions of lives would be acceptable; then he works down from millions to 300, 100, 10, and finally, a single infant (paragraphs 3–6). Would you, like the four mothers, approve of torturing someone who kidnapped your newborn if this would get your infant back?

4. Why does Levin argue that torture should never be used as punishment (paragraph 7)?

....

15. recantations: taking back of previous statements
16. malefactor: evildoer
17. disingenuous: falsely innocent-seeming
18. demarcating: setting boundaries

WRITING ASSIGNMENTS

1. Conduct an informal poll of mothers based on a hypothetical kidnap case, as Levin does in paragraph 6. Ask at least five mothers whether they would support torture of the kidnapper and why. Organize your findings and write a paper presenting them.

2. Write an essay called "A Case for (or Against) Racial Profiling." Consider whether authorities should use racial or ethnic profiling to identify possible terrorists at airports and elsewhere. What about profiling on highways (where African Americans are sometimes stopped for DWB, "driving while black")? Carefully plan your argument before you write.

3. Write a reply to Michael Levin's essay. Develop an argument against torture under any circumstances. For ideas search "Amnesty International, torture test" or "United Nations, torture."

ALICE WALKER

Beauty: When the Other Dancer Is the Self

Being physically injured can be terrifying; coming to terms with a permanent disability can be a painful, difficult process. Alice Walker, a noted fiction writer, poet, and author of The Color Purple, *tells of her feelings and experiences before, during, and after an injury that changed her life.*

It is a bright summer day in 1947. My father, a fat, funny man with beautiful eyes and a subversive wit,[1] is trying to decide which of his eight children he will take with him to the county fair. My mother, of course, will not go. She is knocked out from getting most of us ready: I hold my neck stiff against the pressure of her knuckles as she hastily completes the braiding and then beribboning of my hair. 1

My father is the driver for the rich old white lady up the road. Her name is Miss Mey. She owns all the land for miles around, as well as the house in which we live. All I remember about her is that she once offered to pay my mother thirty-five cents for cleaning her house, raking up piles of her magnolia leaves, and washing her family's clothes, and that my mother—she of no money, eight children, and a chronic earache—refused it. But I do not think of this in 1947. I am two and a half years old. I want to go everywhere my daddy goes. I am excited at the prospect of riding in a car. Someone has told me fairs are fun. That there is room in the car for only three of us doesn't faze[2] me at all. Whirling happily in my starchy frock, showing off my biscuit-polished patent-leather shoes and lavender socks, tossing my head in a way that makes my ribbons bounce, I stand, hands on hips, before my father. "Take me, Daddy," I say with assurance; "I'm the prettiest!" 2

---

1. subversive wit: sarcastic, sharp sense of humor
2. faze: discourage

Later, it does not surprise me to find myself in Miss Mey's shiny black car, sharing the back seat with the other lucky ones. Does not surprise me that I thoroughly enjoy the fair. At home that night I tell the unlucky ones all I can remember about the merry-go-round, the man who eats live chickens, and the teddy bears, until they say: that's enough, baby Alice. Shut up now, and go to sleep.

It is Easter Sunday, 1950. I am dressed in a green, flocked, scalloped-hem dress (handmade by my adoring sister, Ruth) that has its own smooth satin petticoat and tiny hot-pink roses tucked into each scallop. My shoes, new T-strap patent leather, again highly biscuit-polished. I am six years old and have learned one of the longest Easter speeches to be heard that day, totally unlike the speech I said when I was two: "Easter lilies / pure and white / blossom in / the morning light." When I rise to give my speech I do so on a great wave of love and pride and expectation. People in the church stop rustling their new crinolines. They seem to hold their breath. I can tell they admire my dress, but it is my spirit, bordering on sassiness (womanishness), they secretly applaud.

"That girl's a little *mess*," they whisper to each other, pleased.

Naturally I say my speech without stammer or pause, unlike those who stutter, stammer, or, worst of all, forget. This is before the word "beautiful" exists in people's vocabulary, but "Oh, isn't she the cutest thing!" frequently floats my way. "And got so much sense!" they gratefully add... for which thoughtful addition I thank them to this day.

It was great fun being cute. But then, one day, it ended.

I am eight years old and a tomboy. I have a cowboy hat, cowboy boots, checkered shirt and pants, all red. My playmates are my brothers, two and four years older than I. Their colors are black and green, the only difference in the way we are dressed. On Saturday nights we all go to the picture show, even my mother; Westerns are her favorite kind of movie. Back home, "on the ranch," we pretend we are Tom Mix, Hopalong Cassidy, Lash LaRue (we've even named one of our dogs Lash LaRue); we chase each other for hours rustling cattle, being outlaws, delivering damsels from distress. Then my parents decide to buy my brothers guns. These are not "real" guns. They shoot "BBs," copper pellets my brothers say will kill birds. Because I am a girl, I do not get a gun. Instantly I am relegated to[3] the position of Indian. Now there appears a great distance between us. They shoot and shoot at everything with their new guns. I try to keep up with my bow and arrows.

One day while I am standing on top of our makeshift "garage"—pieces of tin nailed across some poles—holding my bow and arrow and looking out toward the fields, I feel an incredible blow in my right eye. I look down just in time to see my brother lower his gun.

Both brothers rush to my side. My eye stings, and I cover it with my hand. "If you tell," they say, "we will get a whipping. You don't want that to happen, do you?" I do not. "Here is a piece of wire," says the older brother, picking it up from the roof; "say you stepped on one end of it and the other flew up and hit you." The pain is beginning to start. "Yes," I say. "Yes, I will say that is what happened." If I do not say this is what happened, I know my brothers will find ways to make me wish I had. But now I will say anything that gets me to my mother.

....

3. relegated to: assigned

The writer Alice Walker

Confronted by our parents we stick to the lie agreed upon. They place   11
me on a bench on the porch and I close my left eye while they examine the
right. There is a tree growing from underneath the porch that climbs past the
railing to the roof. It is the last thing my right eye sees. I watch as its trunk, its
branches, and then its leaves are blotted out by the rising blood.

I am in shock. First there is intense fever, which my father tries to break   12
using lily leaves bound around my head. Then there are chills: my mother tries
to get me to eat soup. Eventually, I do not know how, my parents learn what
has happened. A week after the "accident" they take me to see a doctor. "Why
did you wait so long to come?" he asks, looking into my eye and shaking his
head. "Eyes are sympathetic,"[4] he says. "If one is blind, the other will likely
become blind too."

This comment of the doctor's terrifies me. But it is really how I look that   13
bothers me most. Where the BB pellet struck there is a glob of whitish scar
tissue, a hideous cataract, on my eye. Now when I stare at people—a favorite
pastime, up to now—they will stare back. Not at the "cute" little girl, but at
her scar. For six years I do not stare at anyone, because I do not raise my head.

Years later, in the throes[5] of a mid-life crisis, I ask my mother and sister whether   14
I changed after the "accident." "No," they say, puzzled. "What do you mean?"

What do I mean?   15

I am eight, and, for the first time, doing poorly in school, where I have been   16
something of a whiz since I was four. We have just moved to the place where

....

4. sympathetic: closely connected

5. throes: a condition of struggle

the "accident" occurred. We do not know any of the people around us because this is a different county. The only time I see the friends I knew is when we go back to our old church. The new school is the former state penitentiary. It is a large stone building, cold and drafty, crammed to overflowing with boisterous,[6] ill-disciplined children. On the third floor there is a huge circular imprint of some partition that has been torn out.

"What used to be there?" I ask a sullen girl next to me on our way past it to lunch.   17

"The electric chair," says she.   18

At night I have nightmares about the electric chair, and about all the people reputedly[7] "fried" in it. I am afraid of the school, where all the students seem to be budding criminals.   19

"What's the matter with your eye?" they ask, critically.   20

When I don't answer (I cannot decide whether it was an "accident" or not), they shove me, insist on a fight.   21

My brother, the one who created the story about the wire, comes to my rescue. But then brags so much about "protecting" me, I become sick.   22

After months of torture at the school, my parents decide to send me back to our old community, to my old school. I live with my grandparents and the teacher they board. But there is no room for Phoebe, my cat. By the time my grandparents decide there is room, and I ask for my cat, she cannot be found. Miss Yarborough, the boarding teacher, takes me under her wing, and begins to teach me to play the piano. But soon she marries an African—a "prince," she says—and is whisked away to his continent.   23

At my old school there is at least one teacher who loves me. She is the teacher who "knew me before I was born" and bought my first baby clothes. It is she who makes life bearable. It is her presence that finally helps me turn on the one child at the school who continually calls me "one-eyed bitch." One day I simply grab him by his coat and beat him until I am satisfied. It is my teacher who tells me my mother is ill.   24

My mother is lying in bed in the middle of the day, something I have never seen. She is in too much pain to speak. She has an abscess in her ear. I stand looking down on her, knowing that if she dies, I cannot live. She is being treated with warm oils and hot bricks held against her cheek. Finally a doctor comes. But I must go back to my grandparents' house. The weeks pass but I am hardly aware of it. All I know is that my mother might die, my father is not so jolly, my brothers still have their guns, and I am the one sent away from home.   25

"You did not change," they say.   26

Did I imagine the anguish of never looking up?   27

I am twelve. When relatives come to visit I hide in my room. My cousin Brenda, just my age, whose father works in the post office and whose mother is a nurse, comes to find me. "Hello," she says. And then she asks, looking at my recent school picture, which I did not want taken, and on which the "glob," as I think of it, is clearly visible, "You still can't see out of that eye?"   28

"No," I say, and flop back on the bed over my book.   29

---

6. boisterous: rowdy and noisy
7. reputedly: supposedly

That night, as I do almost every night, I abuse my eye. I rant and rave at it, in front of the mirror. I plead with it to clear up before morning. I tell it I hate and despise it. I do not pray for sight. I pray for beauty. 30

"You did not change," they say. 31

I am fourteen and baby-sitting for my brother Bill, who lives in Boston. He is my favorite brother and there is a strong bond between us. Understanding my feelings of shame and ugliness he and his wife take me to a local hospital, where the "glob" is removed by a doctor named O. Henry. There is still a small bluish crater where the scar tissue was, but the ugly white stuff is gone. Almost immediately I become a different person from the girl who does not raise her head. Or so I think. Now that I've raised my head I win the boyfriend of my dreams. Now that I've raised my head I have plenty of friends. Now that I've raised my head classwork comes from my lips as faultlessly as Easter speeches did, and I leave high school as valedictorian, most popular student, and queen, hardly believing my luck. Ironically, the girl who was voted most beautiful in our class (and was) was later shot twice through the chest by a male companion, using a "real" gun, while she was pregnant. But that's another story in itself. Or is it? 32

"You did not change," they say. 33

It is now thirty years since the "accident." A beautiful journalist comes to visit and to interview me. She is going to write a cover story for her magazine that focuses on my latest book. "Decide how you want to look on the cover," she says. "Glamorous, or whatever." 34

Never mind "glamorous," it is the "whatever" that I hear. Suddenly all I can think of is whether I will get enough sleep the night before the photography session: if I don't, my eye will be tired and wander, as blind eyes will. 35

At night in bed with my lover I think up reasons why I should not appear on the cover of a magazine. "My meanest critics will say I've sold out," I say. "My family will now realize I write scandalous books." 36

"But what's the real reason you don't want to do this?" he asks. 37

"Because in all probability," I say in a rush, "my eye won't be straight." 38

"It will be straight enough," he says. Then, "Besides, I thought you'd made your peace with that." 39

And I suddenly remember that I have. 40

I remember: 41

I am talking to my brother Jimmy, asking if he remembers anything unusual about the day I was shot. He does not know I consider that day the last time my father, with his sweet home remedy of cool lily leaves, chose me, and that I suffered and raged inside because of this. "Well," he says, "all I remember is standing by the side of the highway with Daddy, trying to flag down a car. A white man stopped, but when Daddy said he needed somebody to take his little girl to the doctor, he drove off." 42

I remember: 43

I am in the desert for the first time. I fall totally in love with it. I am so overwhelmed by its beauty, I confront for the first time, consciously, the meaning of the doctor's words years ago: "Eyes are sympathetic. If one is blind, the other will likely become blind too." I realize I have dashed about the world madly, looking at this, looking at that, storing up images against the fading of the light. But I might have missed seeing the desert! The shock of that possibility—and 44 gratitude for over twenty-five years of sight—sends me literally to my knees. Poem after poem comes—which is perhaps how poets pray.

On Sight

I am so thankful I have seen
The Desert
And the creatures in the desert
And the desert Itself.

The desert has its own moon
Which I have seen
With my own eye.
There is no flag on it.

Trees of the desert have arms
All of which are always up
That is because the moon is up
The sun is up
Also the sky
The stars
Clouds
None with flags.
If there *were* flags, I doubt
the trees would point.
Would you?

But mostly, I remember this: 45

I am twenty-seven, and my baby daughter is almost three. Since her birth 46
I have worried about her discovery that her mother's eyes are different from other people's. Will she be embarrassed? I think. What will she say? Every day she watches a television program called "Big Blue Marble." It begins with a picture of the earth as it appears from the moon. It is bluish, a little battered-looking, but full of light, with whitish clouds swirling around it. Every time I see it I weep with love, as if it is a picture of Grandma's house. One day when I am putting Rebecca down for her nap, she suddenly focuses on my eye. Something inside me cringes, gets ready to try to protect myself. All children are cruel about physical differences, I know from experience, and that they don't always mean to be is another matter. I assume Rebecca will be the same.

But no-o-o-o. She studies my face intently as we stand, her inside and me 47
outside her crib. She even holds my face maternally between her dimpled little hands. Then, looking every bit as serious and lawyerlike as her father, she says, as if it may just possibly have slipped my attention: "Mommy, there's a world in your eye." (As in, "Don't be alarmed, or do anything crazy.") And then, gently, but with great interest: "Mommy, where did you get that world in your eye?"

For the most part, the pain left then. (So what, if my brothers grew up 48
to buy even more powerful pellet guns for their sons and to carry real guns themselves. So what, if a young "Morehouse man" once nearly fell off the steps of Trevor Arnett Library because he thought my eyes were blue.) Crying and laughing I ran to the bathroom, while Rebecca mumbled and sang herself to sleep. Yes indeed, I realized, looking into the mirror. There

was a world in my eye. And I saw that it was possible to love it: that in fact, for all it had taught me of shame and anger and inner vision, I did love it. Even to see it drifting out of orbit in boredom, or rolling up out of fatigue, not to mention floating back at attention in excitement (bearing witness, a friend has called it), deeply suitable to my personality, and even characteristic of me.

That night I dream I am dancing to Stevie Wonder's song "Always" (the name of the song is really "As," but I hear it as "Always"). As I dance, whirling and joyous, happier than I've ever been in my life, another bright-faced dancer joins me. We dance and kiss each other and hold each other through the night. The other dancer has obviously come through all right, as I have done. She is beautiful, whole and free. And she is also me.   49

DISCUSSION AND WRITING QUESTIONS

1. When did the author stop being "cute"? Is she happy about this change?

2. Why do you think her family insists that she did not change after the shooting?

3. Until her operation at age 14, Walker speaks of hating her injured eye. By the end of the essay, she dances with another "dancer," who is "beautiful, whole and free. And she is also me." What makes the author change her mind about her "deformity"?

4. The author uses particular words and phrases to indicate time or chronological order in her narrative. Find the words that indicate time order. At one point in her narrative, she breaks this time order to skip back into the past. In which paragraph does this flashback occur?

WRITING ASSIGNMENTS

1. Write about an unpleasant event or experience that resulted in personal growth for you. Your writing need not focus on something as painful as Alice Walker's injury. What is important is how you came to terms with the experience and what you ultimately learned from it.

2. Tell a story about being thrust into a completely unfamiliar situation. You might describe your reaction to attending a new school, starting a new job, or moving to a new city. Present concrete details of your experience. Organize the story around your most vivid memories, like meeting new classmates for the first time, or your first few days on the new job.

3. In a group with three or four classmates, discuss the accident that injured Walker's eye and the children's cover-up (paragraphs 8–11). Her brothers, ten and twelve, were given BB guns. How did these guns change the relationships among siblings even before the accident? Why did this happen? Are BB guns "real guns"? Have you known someone injured by "gun play"? How can such accidents be prevented? Write a paper on your own in which you present one to three ways in which Walker's injury—or one that you know about—could have been prevented.

Quotation Bank

This collection of wise and humorous statements has been assembled for you to read, enjoy, and use in a variety of ways as you write. You might choose quotations that you particularly agree or disagree with and use them as the basis of journal entries and writing assignments. Sometimes when writing a paragraph or an essay, you may find it useful to include a quotation to support a point you are making. Alternatively, you may simply want to read through these quotations for ideas and for fun. As you come across other intriguing statements by writers, add them to the list—or write some of your own.

Education

Knowledge is power.   1
—*Francis Bacon*

Everyone is ignorant, only on different subjects.   2
—*Will Rogers*

Never be afraid to sit awhile and think.   3
—*Lorraine Hansberry*

A mind stretched by a new idea can never go back to its original dimensions.   4
—*Oliver Wendell Holmes, Jr.*

The contest between education and TV . . . has been won by television.   5
—*Robert Hughes*

This thing called "failure" is not the falling down, but the staying down.   6
—*Mary Pickford*

Tell me what you pay attention to, and I will tell you who you are.   7
—*José Ortega y Gasset*

We learn something by doing it. There is no other way.   8
—*John Holt*

Work and Success

We are what we repeatedly do. Excellence, then, is not an act, but a habit.   9
—*Aristotle*

He who does not hope to win has already lost.   10
—*José Joaquín de Olmedo*

The harder you work, the luckier you get.   11
—*Gary Player*

Float like a butterfly, sting like a bee.   12
—*Muhammad Ali*

All glory comes from daring to begin.   13
—*Anonymous*

Show me a person who has never made a mistake,
and I'll show you a person who has never achieved much.
—*Joan Collins*   14

Nice guys finish last.   15
—*Leo Durocher*

Do as the bull in the face of adversity: charge.   16
—*José de Diego*

Should you not find the pearl after one or two divings, don't
blame the ocean! Blame your diving! You are not going deep enough.   17
—*P. Yogananda*

I merely took the energy it takes to pout and wrote some blues.   18
—*Duke Ellington*

I write when I'm inspired, and I see to it that I'm inspired
at nine o'clock every morning.   19
—*Peter De Vries*

Love
If you want to be loved, be lovable.   20
—*Ovid*

After ecstasy, the laundry.   21
—*Zen saying*

The first duty of love is to listen.   22
—*Paul Tillich*

A successful marriage requires falling in love many
times, always with the same person.   23
—*Mignon McLaughlin*

Love is a fire, but whether it's going to warm your hearth
or burn down your house, you can never tell.   24
—*Dorothy Parker*

The way to love anything is to realize that it might be lost.   25
—*G. K. Chesterton*

It's like magic. When you live by yourself, all your
annoying habits are gone!   26
—*Merrill Marko*

Friends and Family
Love is blind; friendship closes its eyes.   27
—*Anonymous*

Friendship with oneself is all important because without it
one cannot be friends with anyone else in the world.   28
—*Eleanor Roosevelt*

You do not know who is your friend and who is your
enemy until the ice breaks.   29
—*Eskimo proverb*

Your children need your presence more than your presents. 30
—*Jesse Jackson*

Children need love, especially when they do not deserve it. 31
—*Harold S. Hulbert*

Ourselves in Society

America is not a melting pot. It is a sizzling cauldron. 32
—*Barbara Ann Mikulski*

When spider webs unite, they can tie up a lion. 33
—*Ethiopian proverb*

A smile is the shortest distance between two people. 34
—*Victor Borge*

Freedom does not always win. This is one of the
bitterest lessons of history. 35
—*A. J. P. Taylor*

If you think you're too small to have an impact, try
going to bed with a mosquito. 36
—*Anita Koddick*

Courage isn't the absence of fear; it is action in the face of fear. 37
—*S. Kennedy*

Racism is still a major issue because it is a habit. 38
—*Maya Angelou*

What women want is what men want: they want respect. 39
—*Marilyn vos Savant*

Basically people are people . . . but it is our differences
which charm, delight, and frighten us. 40
—*Agnes Newton Keith*

Wisdom for Living

Look within! The secret is inside you! 41
—*Hui Neng*

One who wants a rose must respect the thorn. 42
—*Persian proverb*

To live a creative life, we must lose our fear of being wrong. 43
—*Joseph Chilton Pearce*

People who keep stiff upper lips find that it's damn
hard to smile. 44
—*Judith Guest*

Self-pity in its early stages is as snug as a feather mattress.
Only when it hardens does it become uncomfortable. 45
—*Maya Angelou*

When three people call you a donkey, put on a saddle. 46
—*Spanish proverb*

Self-examination—if it is thorough enough—is always the
first step towards change.
—*Thomas Mann*

47

If you can't change your fate, change your attitude.
—*Amy Tan*

48

Time is a dressmaker specializing in alterations.
—*Faith Baldwin*

49

Living in the lap of luxury isn't bad, except you never know
when luxury is going to stand up.
—*Orson Welles*

50

Egoist. A person of low taste, more interested in himself than me.
—*Ambrose Bierce*

51

Envy is a kind of praise.
—*John Gay*

52

What doesn't destroy me strengthens me.
—*Friedrich Nietzsche*

53

Life shrinks and expands in proportion to one's courage.
—*Anaïs Nin*

54

I'm not afraid to die. I just don't want to be there when it happens.
—*Woody Allen*

55

Additional Help and Practice for ESL/ELL Students

Count and Noncount Nouns

Count nouns* refer to people, places, or things that are separate units. You can always count them and often physically point to them. Note that, in English, the following nouns are used as plural count nouns: *police, jeans, pajamas, Middle Ages, scissors, shorts.*

Count Noun	Sample Sentence (Note the underlined words used with count nouns)
television	The marketing department purchased <u>ten</u> large-screen **televisions**.
drive	John had to buy <u>a</u> new flash **drive** to hold the graphics he completed for art class.
assignment	How <u>many</u> **assignments** did you complete last night?
police	The **police** <u>are</u> stationed around the perimeter of the house.

Noncount nouns refer to things that you cannot count separately. Some noncount nouns refer to ideas, feelings, and other things that you cannot see or touch; other noncount nouns refer to food or beverages.

---

* For more on nouns, see Chapters 32 and 26, Part A.

Noncount Noun	Sample Sentence (Note the underlined words used with noncount nouns)
integrity	A politician's **integrity** <u>is</u> frequently tested.
information	We have been waiting for <u>some</u> **information** about the exam.
homework	How <u>much</u> **homework** do you have to finish tonight?
milk	**Milk** <u>is</u> available with 2 percent fat, 1 percent fat, and no fat.

Three signs can help you identify noncount nouns: (1) nouns that have the same verb form (for example, *help, to help; cash, to cash*), (2) words that occur only in noun form (e.g., *equipment, vocabulary*), and (3) nouns with certain endings.

Following is a list of common endings on noncount nouns. This is not complete but meant as a guide.

Endings on Many Noncount Nouns

-ance/ence: insurance, patience, persistence
-ness: frankness, nervousness
-age: courage, postage, luggage, leverage
-sure or *-ture*: pressure, furniture
-fare: welfare, warfare
-th: health, warmth, wealth, strength, truth
-ice: advice, juice, practice
-tion: information, inspiration, respiration, transportation
-esty/ity: honesty, continuity, integrity
-ware/wear: software, sportswear, silverware
-ment: development, equipment
-work: homework, metalwork (exception: network)

PRACTICE 1

Choose the correct word in each pair in the following sentences. Be prepared to explain your choice.

1. After moving to the condominium, they decided to buy new (furniture, furnitures).

2. An important key to learning a second language is memorizing (vocabulary, vocabularies).

3. The crew took a lot of video (equipment, equipments) to the film shoot.

4. This class was difficult because of all the (homework, homeworks) we had to complete.

5. This class was difficult because of all the (exercise, exercises) we had to complete.

6. The (scissor, scissors) lay on the color copier.

7. Waldo set up some computer (network, networks) for the company.

8. The patient's (respiration, respirations) seemed normal.

Some nouns have both count and noncount meanings. Usually, the count meaning is concrete while the noncount meaning is abstract. Note that the count and noncount meanings of some nouns (for example, *corn, iron*) differ significantly.

Count Meaning	Noncount Meaning
Almost all of the **lights** in the office went out. Only the exit **light** is still burning.	Technicians can now send messages as pulses of **light** through optic wires.
Some loud **sounds** are coming from the street. The last **sound** was a shout of victory from a sports fan.	The speed of **sound** is slower than the speed of light.
I found a great store with **teas** and **cakes** from different countries. I bought a loose green **tea** and a chocolate **cake** there.	Do you like **tea** with **cake**? Would you prefer green or black **tea**?
Two broken **irons** lay on the washer in the laundry room. One working **iron** sat in the cabinet.	**Iron** is a strong metal used to make heavy machinery.

PRACTICE 2

Circle the correct word in each pair in the following sentences. Be prepared to explain your choice.

1. I always have (coffee, coffees) with dessert. Please give us two Persian (coffee, coffees) and two orders of baklava.

2. You have work (experience, experiences) in this field, I see. Tell me about your various (experience, experiences) at the ABC Company, where you held several positions.

3. Ship builders use a lot of (iron, irons) to build cruise and war ships.

4. Most modern (iron, irons) are made of plastic and steel, so they are light and easy to use.

5. To make Maria's wonderful salsa, you need to grill some fresh (corn, corns).

6. He had several (corn, corns) from years of wearing tight leather shoes.

7. If all cars had both front and side air bags, more (life, lives) would be saved.

8. How (time, times) passes! We have met several (time, times) by chance since we became engineers.

Articles with Count and Noncount Nouns

Indefinite Articles

The words *a* and *an* are **indefinite articles**. They refer to one *nonspecific* (indefinite) thing. For example, "a woman" refers to *any* woman, not a particular woman. **The article *a* or *an* is used before a singular count noun.***

Singular Count Noun	With Indefinite Article
music video	a music video
question	a question
umbrella	an umbrella

The indefinite article *a* or *an* is never used before a noncount noun:

Noncount Noun	Sample Sentence
music	*Correct:* I enjoy music. *Incorrect:* I enjoy a music.
courage	*Correct:* She displayed courage. *Incorrect:* She displayed a courage.

Be careful: An indefinite article *can* be used with a quantifier (a word that specifies the noun's quantity) and a noncount noun:

Noncount Noun	Noncount Noun with Quantifier
information	The hackers were looking for *a piece of* information that was classified.
news	Let me give you *a bit of* news.

PRACTICE 3

Cross out *a* or *an* if it is used incorrectly in the sentences below. Be ready to explain your answers.

1. We need *a* special luggage for the camping trip.
2. She gave us *an* advice that helped our project succeed.
3. She gave us *a* piece of advice that helped our project succeed.

---

* For information about when to use *an* instead of *a*, see Chapter 41.

4. They are transferring to *a* university located somewhere in Los Angeles.

5. To drive on California freeways, one needs *a* patience.

6. I am in the mood for *a* fish, perhaps *a* piece of salmon and *a* green vegetable.

7. Mr. Lee will offer *a* help if you give him *a* call.

8. We heard *a* laughter coming from the other room.

Definite Article

The word *the* is the only **definite article** in English. It usually refers to one or more specific (definite) things. For example, "the doctor" refers not to *any doctor* but to a specific doctor. "The doctors" refers to two or more specific doctors. **The article the can be used before any singular or plural count noun:** *the moon, the soccer players, the Chinese ambassador.**

The can be used before a noncount noun *only* if that noun is specifically identified, usually by a prepositional phrase† or relative clause.‡

Noncount Noun	Sample Sentence
food	*Correct: The* food <u>at the party</u> was delicious. (specific food) *Incorrect:* All living things must have *the* food to survive. (nonspecific food)
poetry	*Correct: The* poetry <u>that she writes</u> is richly detailed. (specific poetry) *Incorrect:* He enjoys reading *the* poetry. (nonspecific poetry)

Review of Article Usage

	Count Nouns		Noncount Nouns
	Singular	**Plural**	
Indefinite	Use *a/an*. *A chair would be useful. Let's buy one.* (refers to a nonspecified chair)	No article *Chairs come in many different styles.* (refers to nonspecified chairs)	No article *Furniture comes in many different styles.* (refers to nonspecified furniture)
Definite	Use *the*. *The chair we bought is comfortable.* (refers to a specific chair)	Use *the*. *The chairs we bought are comfortable.* (refers to specific chairs)	Use *the*. *The furniture we bought is comfortable.* (refers to specific furniture)

---

* In fact, every singular count noun must be preceded by a "determiner": that is, by a definite or indefinite article; by a pronoun such as *his, her, their, our,* and *my*; by *this, that, these, those*; or by a word such as *many, most, all, both, every,* or *some*, or by a number.

† For more on prepositional phrases, see Chapter 34.

‡ For more on relative clauses, see Chapter 22, Part D.

PRACTICE 4

Write the article *the* where needed in each blank. Write X where no article is needed. Be prepared to explain your answers. (More than one answer is correct in some cases.)

Who said that _____ life never changes? Recent research has shown that _____ human body has changed significantly, especially during _____ past 200 years. Dr. Robert Fogel at _____ University of Chicago and other scientists around world have concluded that a significant change in _____ peoples' physical size has taken place. They note that _____ modern humans are much taller and heavier than _____ people were only a couple of centuries ago. _____ same scientists also found that humans today are much healthier than their ancestors. _____ Chronic diseases occur 10 to 25 years later than they used to, and older people today experience fewer disabilities. _____ same trend was also found for _____ mental health. _____ average IQ, for example, has increased for decades, and mental illnesses are diagnosed and treated much more effectively today. Because of these changes, we now enjoy _____ happier, healthier, longer, and more productive lives.

Verbs Followed by a Gerund or an Infinitive

A **gerund** is the *–ing* form of the verb used as a noun.

> *Watching* my weight is harder during the cold months.
> They enjoy *hiking* in the Rocky Mountains.

In the first sentence, *watching* is the simple subject of the sentence.* In sentence two, *hiking* is the object of the verb *enjoy*.† Some common English verbs can be followed by a gerund. Example: Joaquin quit *smoking*.

Verbs That Can Be Followed by a Gerund

appreciate	consider	enjoy	mention	quit	risk
avoid	discuss	finish	mind	recommend	suggest
complete	dislike	keep	postpone	remember	understand

———

* For more on simple subjects, see Chapter 26, Part A.
† For more on objects of verbs, see Chapter 33, Part D.

The verbs in the previous box are never followed by an infinitive (*to* + the simple form of the verb):

Verb	Sample Sentence
dislike	*Correct:* I *dislike* **cooking** on weeknights. *Incorrect:* I *dislike* **to cook** on weeknights.
discuss	*Correct:* Let's *discuss* **taking** a trip to Asia. *Incorrect:* Let's *discuss* **to take** a trip to Asia.

Other English verbs can be followed by an **infinitive** (but never by a gerund). Example: He expects *to graduate* in June.

Verbs That Can Be Followed by an Infinitive

afford	attempt	demand	hope	mean	offer
agree	choose	expect	intend	need	refuse
appear	dare	fail	learn	plan	wish
ask	decide	forget	like	promise	

Some verbs can be followed by a **noun or pronoun and** an **infinitive** (but never by a gerund). Example: She asked *him to dance.*

Verbs That Can Be Followed by Noun or Pronoun + Infinitive

advise	caution	expect	invite	persuade	teach
allow	convince	hire	order	remind	tell
ask	encourage	instruct	permit	require	want

The verbs listed above are never followed by a gerund:

Verb	Sample Sentence
afford	*Correct:* They can *afford* **to buy** the tickets. *Incorrect:* They can *afford* **buying** the tickets.
agree	*Correct:* I *agree* **to lend** you $100 this week. *Incorrect:* I *agree* **lending** you $100 this week.
plan	*Correct:* He *plans* **to move** to Ohio this summer. *Incorrect:* He *plans* **moving** to Ohio this summer.

A few verbs can be followed by *either* **a gerund or an infinitive** without a change in meaning. Example: They *began* to **write.** They *began* **writing.**

Verbs That Can Be Followed by a Gerund or an Infinitive

begin	hate	prefer
continue	like	start
dislike	love	try

Some verbs can be followed by *either* **a gerund** *or* **an infinitive,** but the meaning of the verb differs depending on the form (gerund or infinitive) used:

He stopped *seeing* her. (**Meaning:** He is not seeing/dating her anymore.)

He stopped *to see* her. (**Meaning:** He made a stop to see/visit her.)

PRACTICE 5

Circle the correct form (gerund or infinitive) to follow the verb in each sentence.

1. Many Americans enjoy (to watch, watching) television.

2. Because this is the store's busy season, we will postpone (to visit, visiting) our friends until spring.

3. Yuri asked Mia (to repair, repairing) the DVD player.

4. Mae Lee regretted (to miss, missing) the auto show.

5. Barring any unforeseen problems, the family expects me (to complete, completing) my degree by this summer.

6. Bae will persuade Edgar (to join, joining) us at the library.

7. Please keep (to sing, singing). We both want (to hear, hearing) another song.

8. Remember that Bruno's party is a surprise, so please do not mention our (to go, going) to the bakery and (to buy, buying) this huge cake.

PRACTICE 6

Circle the correct verb in each sentence. If you need help, review the verb lists.

1. I (prefer, want) listening to NPR during breakfast.

2. Ichiro (suggests, hopes) to finish his coursework this semester so that he can graduate in May.

3. Given the high cost of housing, he (plans, recommends) sharing an apartment with another serious student.

4. The mayor (hoped, advised) the city council not to pass legislation that would hurt local retailers.

5. Now that she has a good job, she can (afford, consider) to buy a new car.

6. I enjoyed the evening very much. I (appreciate, thank) your inviting me.

7. Several students (decided, kept) working after the chemistry lab closed.

8. He (loves, anticipates) to get up early and go running along the river.

For more practice and assessment in ESL-related issues in English, visit CourseMate for *Evergreen*.

Credits

This page constitutes an extension of the copyright page. We have made every effort to trace the ownership of all copyrighted material and to secure permission from copyright holders. In the event of any question arising as to the use of any material, we will be pleased to make the necessary corrections in future printings. Thanks are due to the following authors, publishers, and agents for permission to use the material indicated.

Page 558: "What Your Supermarket Knows About You" by Martin Lindstrom from TIME, October 21, 2011. Used by permission of Martin Lindstrom.

Page 560: "In Multitasking Olympics, We All Lose" by Ellen Goodman. Reprinted by permission of International Creative Management, Inc. Copyright © 2009 by Ellen Goodman.

Page 562: "Only Daughter" by Sandra Cisneros. Copyright © 1990 by Sandra Cisneros. First published in GLAMOUR, November 1990. By permission of Susan Bergholz Literary Services, New York, NY and Lamy, NM. All rights reserved.

Page 565: "About Men: A Brother's Murder" by Brent Staples from THE NEW YORK TIMES, March 30, 1986. Copyright © 1986 The New York Times. All rights reserved. Used by permission.

Page 568: "My Two Lives" by Jhumpa Lahiri from NEWSWEEK, MSNBC.com, March 5, 2006. Copyright © 2006. Used by permission of the author via William Morris Entertainment.

Page 571: Dave Barry, "Driving While Stupid," MIAMI HERALD, September 22, 2002. Used by permission of Tribune Media Services

Page 573: Ana Veciana-Suarez, "When Greed Gives Way to Giving," THE RECORD, October 10, 1999, p. L5 (MIAMI HERALD). Used by permission of Tribune Media Services.

Page 576: "The 10,000-Hour Rule" from OUTLIERS by Malcolm Gladwell. Copyright © 2008 by Malcolm Gladwell. By permission of Little, Brown and Company. All rights reserved.

Page 579: "The Flip Side of Internet Fame" by Jessica Bennett from NEWSWEEK, February 21, 2008. Copyright © 2008. The Newsweek/Daily Beast Company LLC. All rights reserved. Used by permission.

Page 582: "How Not to Raise a Bully: The Early Roots of Empathy" by Maia Szalavitz from TIME Magazine, April 17, 2010. Copyright © 2010 Time Inc. Reprinted by permission.

Page 585: Elissa Englund, "Good Grammar Gets the Girl" from www.statenews .com/index.php/article/2005/09/good_grammar_gets_the_girl. Reprinted by permission of the author and State News.

628

Index

Thematic Index of the Reading Selections

These thematic clusters suggest some ways to group and discuss the reading selections in Unit 8.

Rhetorical Index

The following index first classifies the paragraphs and essays in this text according to rhetorical mode and then according to rhetorical mode by chapter. (Those paragraphs with added errors for students to correct are not included.)

Rhetorical Modes

Rhetorical Modes by Chapter

 **2** Prewriting to Generate Ideas

Description

Mr. Martin, the reason, 9
Writers' Workshop: "Sounds and Smells of Home," 18

Mixed Modes

Two weeks ago, 15

14 The Process of Writing an Essay

15 The Introduction, the Conclusion, and the Title

16 Types of Essays, Part 1

17 Types of Essays, Part 2

18 Summarizing, Quoting, and Avoiding Plagiarism

19 Strengthening an Essay with Research

Rhetorical Modes in the Reading Selections

Revising and Proofreading Symbols

The following chart lists common writing errors and the symbols that instructors often use to mark them. For some errors, your instructor may wish to use symbols other than the ones shown. You may wish to write these alternate symbols in the blank column.

Standard Symbol	Instructor's Alternate Symbol	Error	For help, see Chapter
adj		Incorrect adjective form	35
adv		Incorrect adverb form	35
agr		Incorrect subject-verb agreement	26; 29
		Incorrect pronoun-antecedent agreement	33, Parts A and B
apos		Missing or incorrect apostrophe	36
awk		Awkward expression	23
cap		Missing or incorrect capital letter	38, Part A
case		Incorrect pronoun case	33, Part D
⊙		Missing or incorrect comma	27, Parts A and B; 36
coh		Lack of coherence	4
⊙		Missing or incorrect colon	38, Part D
con d		Inconsistent discourse	20, Part C
con p		Inconsistent person	21, Part B
con t		Inconsistent verb tense	21, Part A
coord		Incorrect coordination	27, Part A
cs		Comma splice	28, Part A
⊖		Missing or incorrect dash	38, Part D
dev		Incomplete paragraph or essay development	3, Parts C, D, and E; 14, Parts D, E, and F
dm		Dangling or confusing modifier	22, Part E
ed		Missing -ed, past tense or past participle	30, Part A; 31, Part A
frag		Sentence fragment	22, Part D; 27, Part B; 28, Part B
¶		Missing indentation for new paragraph	3, Part A
⓪		Missing or incorrect parenthesis	38, Part D
‖		Faulty parallelism	21, Part C
pl		Missing or incorrect plural form	32
pp		Incorrect past participle form	31
⊙⊙⊘		Missing or incorrect end punctuation	22, Part B
quot		Missing or incorrect quotation marks	38, Part C
rep		Unnecessary repetition	3, Parts D and F
ro		Run-on sentence	28, Part A
⊙		Missing or incorrect semicolon	27, Part C
sub		Incorrect subordination	27, Part B
sp		Spelling error	40
		Look-alike, sound-alike error	41
sup		Inadequate support	3, Part F
title		Title needed	15, Part C
trans		Transition needed	4, Part B; 14, Part E
trite		Trite expression	23, Part C
ts		Poor or missing topic sentence or thesis statement	3, Parts A and B; 14, Part B
u		Lack of paragraph or essay unity	3, Part F; 14, Parts D, E, and F
w		Unnecessary words	24, Part B
○		Too much space	39
℘		Words or letters to be deleted	39
?		Unclear meaning	23, Part A
^		Omitted words	39
~		Words or letters in reverse order	39